The Top UK Pharmaceutical Manufacturers

Profiles of the leading 1750 companies

John D Blackburn

Editor

dp

First Edition

Summer 2019

ISBN-13: 978-1-912736-26-3

ISBN-10: 1-912736-26-8

All rights reserved. No part of this publication may be reproduced, distributed, or transmitted in any form or by any means, including photocopying, recording, or other electronic or mechanical methods, without our prior written permission, except in the case of brief quotations embodied in critical reviews and certain other non-commercial uses permitted by copyright law. For permission requests, please write to us.

Copyright © 2019 Dellam Publishing Limited

Printed in 8pt Nimbus Sans L

Designed by URW++ Design and Development GmbH

Dellam Publishing Limited

2 Heath Drive, Sutton, Surrey, SM2 5RP

Fax: 020 8770 7478   email: enquiries@dellam.com

SAN: 0177881   EAN/GLN: 5030670177882

Table of Contents

1 Acknowledgements iv

2 Introduction v

3 Total Assets League Table 1

- As a measure of size, total assets is preferable to turnover which is influenced by profit margins and whether companies are capital or labour intensive.

4 Age of Companies 11

- Each company is ranked by its date of incorporation. Newcomers are defined as those registered since 2017.

5 Geographic Distribution 23

- Each company is classed by county.

6 Company Profiles 35

- Full company name, date incorporated, net worth, total assets, registered office, activities, shareholders and parent company, directors (with date of birth, nationality and occupation) and number of employees (if available).

7 Index of Directorships 149

- Alphabetical list of directors showing their directorships. If several directors have identical names then their date of birth is shown.

8 Standard Industrial Classification 193

- These codes are used to classify businesses by the type of economic activity in which they are engaged.

9 *finis* 201

Acknowledgements

This is a long and detailed publication containing thousands of facts and figures. It is only to be expected, despite continuous and repeated editing and checking, that errors may occur. In such cases, once we are aware of any, we publish a correction on our website.

Readers are encouraged to check regularly at www.dellam.com/books for any corrections and updates.

Although we take extreme care to ensure accuracy and being up-to-date, we cannot accept responsibility for any errors or omissions.

Contains public sector information licensed under Open Government Licence v3.0. from The Charity Commission (England and Wales) and The Charity Commission for Northern Ireland. © Crown Copyright and database right (2018).

Contains information from the Scottish Charity Register supplied by the Office of the Scottish Charity Regulator and licensed under the Open Government Licence v.2.0. © Crown Copyright and database right (2018).

Contains OS data © Crown copyright and database right (2018)

Contains Royal Mail data © Royal Mail copyright and database right (2018)

Contains National Statistics data © Crown copyright and database right (2018)

Contains Office for National Statistics © Crown copyright and database right (2018)

Maps based on those produced by the Office for National Statistics Geography GIS & Mapping Unit (2012 and 2018).

Contains HM Land Registry data © Crown copyright and database right (2018).

Contains Parliamentary information licensed under the Open Parliament Licence v3.0.

House of Commons Library Briefing Papers licensed under the Open Parliament Licence v3.0.

Contains Food Standards Agency data © Crown copyright and database right (2018).

Contains Eurostat data, 1995-2018, copyright European Commission by the Decision of 12 December 2011.

Maps based on produced by ONS Geography GIS & Mapping Unit.

Contains Companies House data supplied under section 47 and 50 of the Copyright, Designs and Patents Act 1988 and Schedule 1 of the Database Regulations (SI 1997/3032).

We appreciate your interest in our publications, and your comments and suggestions are always welcome. Please contact us at enquiries@dellam.com.

Introduction

This study looks at all companies registered in the United Kingdom where they identify themselves as manufacturers of basic pharmaceutical products or preparations.

This study includes companies that are dormant or non-trading some of which might be latent while others may operate under their owners' names but incorporate to protect the business name. In addition, all newly incorporated companies are included. The study will exclude those companies that do not specifically identify themselves as manufacturers of basic pharmaceutical products or preparations.

The aim of this study is to provide an overview of the key movers and shakers in the UK manufacture of pharmaceuticals sector. Only key data has been isolated, particularly the company's net worth and total assets, but also its full name, date incorporated, registered office, other activities, shareholders, directors (with date of birth, occupation and nationality) and number of employees.

Two indicators of size are used: net worth and total assets. These are preferable to turnover which is influenced by profit margins and whether the companies are capital or labour intensive.

In the years 2016, 2017 and 2018, new company incorporations in the manufacture of pharmaceuticals sector were 128, 161 and 254 respectively.

Pharmaceuticals was the only sector to show reduced sales between 2016 and 2017, decreasing by just under £1.4 billion (11%) to £11.4 billion.

Price inflation in this sector for the years 2010 to 2018 was 100.0, 100.9, 102.3, 103.4, 104.1, 103.7, 106.7, 108.3 and 112.4 respectively.

The Association of the British Pharmaceutical Industry (ABPI) is the UK trade body that represents the research-based bio-pharmaceutical industry in the UK and their members supply 80% of all branded medicines used by the NHS.

Estimated total NHS spending on medicines in England grew from £13 billion in 2010-2011 to £17.4 billion in 2016-2017, an average growth of around 5 per cent a year. Hospitals account for nearly half of total NHS spending on medicines.

The sector is a mixture of large UK-headquartered companies such as AstraZeneca and GSK, manufacturing and research sites for other global companies, and a significant proportion of SMEs and micro businesses, researching and manufacturing branded, generic and over-the-counter medicines.

The pharmaceutical sector is one of the UK's most productive industries, generating £41.8 billion turnover and contributing around one per cent of the UK's output and 7.7% of manufacturing GVA. The sector employs 62,600 people across 543 companies, supported by 1,314 service and supply companies comprising a further 51,000 people.

In 2016, the UK exported £24.9 billion of pharmaceutical products, of which £11.9 billion (48%) went to the EU. At the same time, the UK imported £24.8 billion of pharmaceutical products, of which £18.2 billion (73%) were from the EU, giving a trade deficit of £6.3 billion.

Standard cataloguing guidelines for company names in the profile section have been used, but there will be occurrences when the name may not be strictly alphabetical. A certain licence was adopted where it was felt that strictly alphabetical could lead to improper cataloguing. Some company names have been shortened in the league tables for aesthetic reasons.

John D Blackburn
Editor

This page is intentionally left blank

The Top UK Pharmaceutical Manufacturers   dellam

Total Assets League Table

The Top UK Pharmaceutical Manufacturers

Company	Revenue	Company	Revenue
Astrazeneca PLC	£63,353,999,360	Knoll UK Investments Unlimited	£146,950,176
Smith & Nephew PLC	£5,709,930,496	UCB Pharma Limited	£141,030,000
SmithKline Beecham Limited	£2,496,000,000	Macarthys Laboratories Limited	£137,148,992
Hikma Pharmaceuticals Public Limited Company	£2,459,349,504	Patheon UK Limited	£130,475,168
Thermo Fisher Scientific Life Holdings Limited	£1,730,963,968	Porvair PLC	£127,947,000
Hikma UK Limited	£1,696,593,792	Aesica BC Limited	£121,700,000
Norton Healthcare Limited	£1,498,274,944	Quantum Pharma Holdings Limited	£121,374,000
Glaxo Operations UK Limited	£1,324,759,040	Vitabiotics Limited	£119,392,768
Eli Lilly and Company Limited	£1,206,620,032	Thornton & Ross Limited	£119,136,000
Indivior PLC	£1,087,758,976	Intervet UK Production Limited	£118,581,000
Hikma Pharmaceuticals International Limited	£1,053,292,032	Oxford Immunotec Limited	£115,932,000
AAH Pharmaceuticals Limited	£999,052,032	Laxmi BNS Holdings Limited	£109,609,696
GE Healthcare Limited	£932,070,016	Oxford Immunotec Global PLC	£108,605,648
Pioneer UK Midco 1 Limited	£893,723,520	Eli Lilly Group Limited	£108,451,000
Accord Healthcare Limited	£891,985,984	Porton Biopharma Limited	£102,041,000
LEH Pharma Ltd	£850,437,888	Wave Life Sciences UK Limited	£101,130,000
Indivior UK Limited	£848,174,016	Bard Pharmaceuticals Limited	£100,001,000
LRC Products Limited	£776,812,032	Life Technologies BPD UK Limited	£99,384,000
Fisons Limited	£771,542,016	Teva NI Limited	£97,861,032
GE Healthcare UK Limited	£748,172,032	Lofthouse of Fleetwood Limited	£97,787,144
GlaxoSmithKline Consumer Healthcare UK Trading	£685,875,968	BCM Limited	£90,600,000
Merck Sharp & Dohme Limited	£607,619,008	Penn Pharma Group Limited	£89,409,000
Actavis Holdings UK II Limited	£603,851,008	Napp Pharmaceutical Group Limited	£87,942,000
Clinigen Group PLC	£594,351,360	Generics (U.K.) Limited	£85,286,000
Teva UK Limited	£561,601,984	GW Pharma Limited	£84,644,096
Ipsen Biopharm Limited	£561,416,000	Dr. Reddy's Laboratories (EU) Limited	£84,630,296
Roche Products Limited	£474,462,016	Eco Animal Health Ltd.	£84,152,288
Smith Kline & French Laboratories Limited	£464,873,984	Prometic Pharma SMT Limited	£82,372,512
Eisai Manufacturing Limited	£454,234,976	Colorcon Limited	£81,699,008
Janssen-Cilag Limited	£415,416,992	Cell Medica Limited	£80,010,000
Circassia Pharmaceuticals PLC	£402,400,000	Catalent CTS (Edinburgh) Limited	£79,866,568
John Wyeth & Brother Limited	£393,776,992	Church & Dwight UK Limited	£77,353,000
Albany Molecular Research Limited	£371,956,992	Shire Pharmaceuticals Limited	£75,774,000
Dechra Limited	£355,960,992	Baxalta UK Limited	£74,718,000
Novartis Grimsby Limited	£348,511,008	Norton Healthcare (1998) Limited	£73,701,000
Pioneer UK Midco 2 Limited	£340,309,856	Almac Pharma Services Limited	£71,079,248
Alliance Pharmaceuticals Limited	£305,403,008	Omega Pharma Limited	£67,744,000
Napp Pharmaceutical Holdings Limited	£304,665,984	Diomed Developments Limited	£66,227,728
Novartis Pharmaceuticals UK Limited	£303,975,008	Wockhardt UK Limited	£65,638,000
Baxter Healthcare Limited	£296,004,992	Boehringer Ingelheim Animal Health UK Limited	£62,210,000
Protherics UK Limited	£283,756,000	Elemis Limited	£61,136,348
Bristol-Myers Squibb Pharmaceuticals Limited	£276,734,016	Envigo RMS (UK) Limited	£60,876,000
Piramal Critical Care Limited	£276,387,680	Fresenius Kabi Limited	£60,723,000
Merial Limited	£272,727,264	Genus Pharmaceuticals Limited	£58,685,000
Catalent U.K. Swindon Zydis Limited	£266,815,008	OBG Holding Limited	£58,080,152
Seqirus Vaccines Limited	£263,800,000	Aesica Queenborough Limited	£56,800,000
Ortho-Clinical Diagnostics	£253,118,000	Norgine Limited	£56,208,000
Aesica Pharmaceuticals Limited	£246,000,000	Quantum Pharmaceutical Limited	£55,414,000
MacFarlan Smith Limited	£219,838,000	C P Pharmaceuticals Limited	£54,467,000
Accord-UK Ltd	£206,463,008	Hologic Ltd.	£52,481,000
Genzyme Limited	£205,024,992	Breath Limited	£52,331,824
Mercury Pharma Group Limited	£202,432,240	Allergy Therapeutics PLC	£51,016,000
Fujifilm Diosynth Biotechnologies UK Limited	£198,200,000	Penn Pharmaceutical Services Limited	£50,982,000
PCI Penn UK Holdco Limited	£177,702,000	Bob Martin (UK) Limited	£50,035,164
Norbrook Laboratories Limited	£171,416,992	Quantum Pharma 2014 Limited	£49,960,000
Auden McKenzie (Pharma Division) Limited	£166,636,032	Sterling Pharma Solutions Limited	£49,927,000
Boehringer Ingelheim Limited	£157,427,008	Air Liquide Limited	£49,642,000
May & Baker Limited	£157,120,992	Chemidex Pharma Limited	£48,929,356
Bespak Europe Limited	£155,496,992	Fine Organics Limited	£47,671,000

The Top UK Pharmaceutical Manufacturers

Company	Value
Sandoz Limited	£47,303,000
Crescent Pharma Limited	£47,265,104
Qiagen Manchester Limited	£47,177,324
Rosemont Pharmaceuticals Limited	£46,942,000
Thompson and Capper Limited	£46,262,000
Qualasept Holdings Limited	£45,933,204
Indivior EU Limited	£45,776,016
Wrafton Laboratories Limited	£45,168,000
Mercury Pharmaceuticals Limited	£44,843,036
Sinclair Pharmaceuticals Limited	£43,112,000
BBI Solutions OEM Limited	£41,639,000
Alba Bioscience Limited	£41,367,804
Aesica M2 Limited	£41,200,000
Aesica M1 Limited	£41,200,000
Dermal Laboratories Limited	£40,770,980
Dr Reddy's Laboratories (UK) Limited	£36,693,180
G.R. Lane Health Products Limited	£35,044,788
Qualasept Limited	£34,878,516
Zeltiq Limited	£34,529,580
Emerald Kalama Chemical Limited	£34,191,000
Brunel Healthcare Manufacturing Limited	£33,375,000
A Nelson & Co Limited	£33,033,000
Advanced Medical Solutions Limited	£32,903,000
Teva Laboratories UK Limited	£32,736,420
T.G. Eakin Limited	£32,058,536
Nelson & Russell Holdings Limited	£31,932,000
Allergan Biologics Limited	£30,806,000
Essential Pharma Limited	£30,423,222
Terumo BCT Ltd.	£30,228,952
Hospira UK Limited	£30,085,000
Calea UK Limited	£30,017,000
Allergy Therapeutics (UK) Limited	£29,611,000
Ennogen Healthcare Ltd	£29,465,110
Ranir Limited	£28,971,104
Zogenix Europe Limited	£28,842,276
G. & M. Procter Limited	£28,281,000
Nicobrand Limited	£28,111,060
Getinge UK Limited	£27,519,000
West Pharmaceutical Services Cornwall Limited	£27,493,000
D.D.D. Limited	£27,138,234
Taisho Pharmaceutical (Europe) Limited	£26,349,054
Nova Laboratories Limited	£26,162,616
Mentholatum Company Limited (The)	£25,760,000
Fresenius Kabi Oncology PLC	£25,414,000
Alliance Medical Radiopharmacy Limited	£25,311,000
Bio-Rad AbD Serotec Ltd	£23,531,758
Molnlycke Health Care Limited	£23,249,000
Kowa Pharmaceutical Europe Co. Ltd.	£22,979,906
BCM Specials Limited	£22,076,000
Aptuit (Oxford) Limited	£21,646,620
M & A Pharmachem Limited	£21,316,352
Celgene UK Manufacturing Limited	£20,968,104
Oxford Biodynamics PLC	£20,941,000
Remedi Medical Holdings Limited	£20,844,708
Morningside Pharmaceuticals Limited	£20,841,896
Amneal Pharma UK Holdings Limited	£20,340,656
A1 Pharmaceuticals Holdings Limited	£20,243,268
RSR Limited	£19,709,656
Medlock Medical Limited	£18,744,000
Focus Pharmaceuticals Limited	£18,041,368
Emergent Countermeasures International Ltd	£18,005,000
Advanz Pharma Generics (UK) Limited	£16,854,356
Badgequo Limited	£16,825,688
Seven Seas Limited	£16,648,000
Swedish Orphan Biovitrum Ltd	£16,528,444
Albumedix Ltd	£16,125,000
Maelor Laboratories Limited	£16,086,000
Ranir (Holdings) Limited	£15,928,748
Equalbrief Limited	£15,318,588
AbbVie Australasia Holdings Limited	£15,283,000
Catalent UK Supply Chain Limited	£15,276,553
Hichrom Limited	£15,070,568
Kent Pharmaceuticals Limited	£14,979,000
Microskin PLC	£14,849,522
Bach Flower Remedies Limited	£14,821,000
Aspar Pharmaceuticals Limited	£14,759,634
Schering-Plough Limited	£14,245,000
Milton Lloyd Limited	£14,223,723
Octapharma Limited	£14,170,924
Contura Holdings Limited	£14,137,711
Vernalis (R & D) Limited	£14,107,000
AMO United Kingdom Limited	£14,102,000
Vivimed Labs Europe Ltd	£13,855,000
Bell,Sons & Co.(Druggists) Limited	£13,834,928
PCCA (UK) Holdings Limited	£13,744,165
MW Encap (Holdings) Limited	£13,716,701
Pharmaserve (North West) Limited	£13,113,160
Celgene UK Manufacturing (II) Limited	£12,935,121
TCS Biosciences Limited	£12,692,194
Aesica Holdco Limited	£12,500,000
Morningside Healthcare Limited	£12,387,210
Brown & Burk UK Limited	£12,304,449
Nutrition Group PLC	£11,890,243
MW Encap Limited	£11,825,646
Ernest Jackson & Co. Limited	£11,159,000
Intrapharm Laboratories Limited	£11,116,160
Aspen Medical Europe Limited	£11,015,000
Parkacre Enterprises Limited	£10,942,910
Surepharm Services Limited	£10,754,378
Marlborough Pharmaceuticals Limited	£10,607,300
Catalent Micron Technologies Limited	£10,539,052
P.I.E. Pharma Limited	£10,276,358
Candles UK Ltd	£10,000,000
Aura-Soma Products Limited	£9,999,667
Cod Beck Blenders Limited	£9,919,414
Masters Pharmaceuticals Limited	£9,841,748
Wasdell Manufacturing Limited	£9,811,889
Principle Healthcare International Limited	£9,670,585
Weleda (U.K.) Limited	£9,472,708
Manx Healthcare Limited	£9,309,355
Geotek Coring Limited	£9,263,396
A. Menarini Diagnostics Limited	£9,254,251
Herrco Cosmetics Limited	£9,066,244
Custom Pharmaceuticals Limited	£8,963,656
Rapid Nutrition PLC	£8,777,363
Combe International Limited	£8,769,294
Quay Pharmaceuticals Limited	£8,695,925
Ono Pharma UK Ltd.	£8,618,626

Company	Revenue	Company	Revenue
Typharm Limited	£8,434,921	Miltenyi Biotec Limited	£3,925,877
Nextpharma Technologies Holding Limited	£8,285,816	DX Products Limited	£3,858,872
Sharp Clinical Services (UK) Limited	£8,185,346	Epax Pharma UK Ltd	£3,847,000
Pharmapac (U.K.) Limited	£8,128,585	Diba Industries Limited	£3,840,090
Algal Omega 3 Ltd	£8,034,759	Sinclair Animal and Household Care Limited	£3,824,774
Life Molecular Imaging Limited	£7,825,845	Hexpress Healthcare Limited	£3,810,796
Centaur Healthcare Limited	£7,735,275	The Organic Pharmacy Limited	£3,790,621
Infirst Healthcare Limited	£7,689,849	Bio Pure Technology Ltd	£3,785,923
Recipharm Limited	£7,638,000	Cambridge Healthcare Supplies Limited	£3,763,750
Auralis Limited	£7,632,000	Star Pharmaceuticals Limited	£3,741,231
Cycle Pharmaceuticals Ltd	£7,528,174	Quest HC Limited	£3,707,726
Pierre Fabre Limited	£7,420,965	Quest Ingredients Limited	£3,689,597
Custom Powders Limited	£7,411,054	Skinnytan UK Limited	£3,681,050
Pharmaxo Pharmacy Services Limited	£7,044,014	Wychem Limited	£3,637,020
Micropharm Limited	£6,670,762	Ascot Laboratories Limited	£3,542,153
Aesica Formulation Development Limited	£6,617,000	Aguettant Limited	£3,517,982
Ayrton Saunders Limited	£6,504,914	Novo Nordisk Holding Limited	£3,432,000
Solent Oral Care Ltd	£6,321,358	The Bio-Medical Engineering Ltd	£3,426,955
Rapidscan Pharma Solutions EU Limited	£6,254,000	Hikmacure Limited	£3,402,692
Castex Products Limited	£6,165,279	Symbiosis Pharmaceutical Services Limited	£3,259,841
Contura Limited	£6,162,399	Atnahs Pharma US Limited	£3,258,626
Amphastar UK Ltd	£6,161,978	Paxvax Ltd	£3,241,071
Focus Pharma Holdings Limited	£6,046,418	MC2 Therapeutics Limited	£3,161,694
BVM Medical Limited	£6,019,489	Cartell UK Limited	£3,109,127
Hyperbiotics PLC	£5,944,005	Key Organics Limited	£3,107,000
Millpledge Limited	£5,821,375	AB Biotechnology Limited	£3,102,728
Lifeplan Products Limited	£5,748,236	Lincoln Medical Limited	£3,048,369
Niche Generics Limited	£5,714,967	Delta Diagnostics (UK) Ltd	£3,006,092
Klinge Chemicals Limited	£5,697,768	Advent Bioservices Ltd	£2,983,529
Fontus Health Ltd	£5,603,802	Ferndale Pharmaceuticals Limited	£2,920,641
Fulhold Pharma Limited	£5,499,010	Wallis Licensing Limited	£2,893,737
Reig Jofre UK Limited	£5,463,440	Dalkeith Laboratories Limited	£2,869,766
Ipca Laboratories UK Limited	£5,369,833	Seacross Pharmaceuticals Ltd	£2,809,240
Cross Healthcare Limited	£5,331,699	World Medicine Limited	£2,779,074
Cambridge Sensors Ltd	£5,299,370	Charnwood Molecular Limited	£2,761,419
Resolution Chemicals Limited	£5,262,351	Wallace Manufacturing Chemists Limited	£2,760,487
Macopharma (UK) Limited	£5,246,038	Iroko Products Limited	£2,743,691
Reelvision Print Limited	£5,243,202	New Nordic Limited	£2,740,352
Technical Textile Services Limited	£5,219,491	Innova Biosciences Ltd	£2,699,841
Pharmvit Limited	£5,199,113	Bioneb PVT Limited	£2,661,241
Pharmasol Limited	£5,107,678	Vita (Europe) Limited	£2,655,111
Cellon UK Limited	£4,957,396	Uni Health Distribution Ltd	£2,576,881
Strides Pharma UK Ltd	£4,940,967	Therakind Limited	£2,573,014
Synergy Biologics Limited	£4,931,767	Summit Veterinary Pharmaceuticals Limited	£2,558,834
Egalet Limited	£4,843,679	Milton Pharmaceutical Company UK Limited	£2,509,607
Aimmune Therapeutics UK Limited	£4,700,801	Medicareplus International Ltd	£2,495,702
Ipsco Limited	£4,689,000	Ennogen Pharma Ltd	£2,487,233
Vertical Pharma Resources Limited	£4,686,000	Polychem Limited	£2,453,003
Catalent MTI Pharma Solutions Limited	£4,602,633	Proveca Limited	£2,439,543
PCCA Limited	£4,557,221	Sogeval UK Limited	£2,425,692
Guerbet Argentina Limited	£4,426,000	Syner-Med Pharmaceuticals (Kenya) Limited	£2,405,535
Health Innovations (UK) Limited	£4,387,863	Geistlich Sons Limited	£2,377,402
South Wales Specials Limited	£4,370,433	Integrated Pharmaceutical Services (IPS) Limited	£2,359,000
Principle Healthcare Limited	£4,341,947	Typharm Developments Limited	£2,354,344
Onyx Scientific Limited	£4,226,662	Provita Eurotech Ltd	£2,331,792
NZP UK Limited	£4,205,742	Essential Nutrition Limited	£2,308,159
Pari Medical Limited	£4,119,982	Percuro Medica Ltd	£2,295,998
Peckforton Pharmaceuticals Limited	£4,014,318	International Scientific Supplies Limited	£2,276,886
Ransom Naturals Limited	£3,996,917	Phico Therapeutics Limited	£2,222,978

The Top UK Pharmaceutical Manufacturers

Company	Value	Company	Value
MacLeods Pharma UK Limited	£2,208,099	Exonate Limited	£1,076,488
ADS Biotec Limited	£2,154,967	Protak Scientific Limited	£1,069,487
Pharma Pack Limited	£2,143,835	Phytovation Limited	£1,059,008
Essential Pharmaceuticals Limited	£2,120,814	Derms Development Limited	£1,058,250
Vernalis Development Limited	£2,042,000	The London Specialist Pharmacy Limited	£1,050,060
Oriel Therapeutics Limited	£2,029,000	As-Tec Chemicals Limited	£1,049,730
Ideal Manufacturing Limited	£2,007,665	Sarissa Biomedical Limited	£1,048,218
Dermato Logical Limited	£1,963,435	M D M Healthcare Ltd	£1,039,737
Carefusion U.K. 244 Limited	£1,902,221	Vitrition UK Ltd.	£1,020,005
Sterling Pharmaceuticals Limited	£1,900,247	Alinter Limited	£1,018,269
New Cheshire Salt Works Limited	£1,870,000	Abbott Vascular Devices (2) Limited	£1,014,000
Eaststone Limited	£1,853,162	Regent Pharmaceuticals Limited	£976,710
Hipra UK and Ireland Limited	£1,828,547	Arcadia Pharma Limited	£975,709
Dextra Laboratories Limited	£1,801,955	Birchwood Pharma Ltd	£950,473
McAleer & Donnelly Pharmacy Limited	£1,793,918	Instavit Limited	£936,964
Satelec (UK) Limited	£1,788,970	Crawford Manufacturing Limited	£936,289
Bray Group Limited	£1,772,642	Taylor of London Limited	£902,441
Technical & General Limited	£1,756,937	Asterisk LifeSciences Ltd	£870,254
CTI Life Sciences Limited	£1,717,657	Byrom (South Wales) Limited	£865,794
Nanopharm Limited	£1,692,641	ZVF Pharma Ltd	£856,515
Biocolor Limited	£1,631,405	Donglun Limited	£827,787
Hyperbiotics Corp Ltd	£1,631,282	Biostatus Ltd	£827,393
DTR Medical Limited	£1,624,281	Teisen Products Limited	£823,749
Blistex Limited	£1,612,094	Pharmaspec Limited	£820,418
Calla Lily Personal Care Ltd	£1,601,679	Maxearn Limited	£819,693
Hyperdrug Pharmaceuticals Ltd	£1,587,031	Arch Chemicals Products Limited	£816,199
Crescent Manufacturing Limited	£1,560,729	Welby Healthcare Limited	£806,679
Cambridge Healthcare Supplies 2012 Limited	£1,546,776	Paradox Omega Oils Ltd	£804,343
Redrose Manufacturing Limited	£1,546,502	Hope Pharmaceuticals, Ltd.	£800,029
Primius Lab Limited	£1,539,422	IGMA Limited	£797,653
Penlan Healthcare Limited	£1,539,291	Celgene UK Manufacturing (III) Limited	£792,012
Longshawe Packaging Limited	£1,512,588	Panpharma UK Limited	£786,139
Cosmarida 2010 Limited	£1,509,333	Diagnostic Reagents Limited	£766,052
Selborne Biological Services Limited	£1,493,572	Oat Services Limited	£747,780
PTC Therapeutics, Limited	£1,489,343	Bio-Tech Solutions Limited	£719,453
Reaxa Limited	£1,474,072	Cross Chemicals UK Limited	£718,412
LDN Pharma Limited	£1,454,918	Craintern (UK) Limited	£715,867
Matthews & Wilson Limited	£1,439,577	Health + Plus Limited	£711,817
Corpus Nostrum Limited	£1,417,190	N.T. Laboratories Limited	£696,199
Bodywise Limited	£1,395,130	Northumbria Pharma Ltd	£685,320
Nikkiso UK Co., Ltd.	£1,366,738	Neoceuticals Limited	£683,471
Medley Pharma Limited	£1,342,462	Isola Manufacturing Co.(Wythenshawe) Limited	£677,537
Merck Serono Europe Limited	£1,333,400	Vit Supermarket Ltd	£660,654
BHR Pharmaceuticals Limited	£1,293,107	Ayrton Saunders and Company Ltd	£658,492
Neomedic Limited	£1,256,184	Prozomix Limited	£648,337
Lab 21 Healthcare Limited	£1,248,000	Leeds Industries (UK) Ltd	£644,510
Rotapharm Limited	£1,222,298	G.H. Zeal Limited	£642,830
HFA Healthcare Products Limited	£1,214,447	Ace Direct Ltd	£641,579
Biofortuna Ltd	£1,202,620	S M Consultancy (MK) Limited	£640,010
Infohealth Limited	£1,198,344	Veterinary Immunogenics Limited	£634,395
MDX Healthcare Ltd	£1,193,625	Talley Environmental Care Limited	£634,092
Nunataq Limited	£1,180,021	Phyto Products Limited	£630,571
Bioavexia Ltd	£1,170,247	DHTD Limited	£628,795
HAV Vaccines Limited	£1,161,696	Phamar Limited	£620,002
LPC Medical (UK) Limited	£1,115,289	Essential Health Products Limited	£594,911
Medical Export Company Limited	£1,108,841	Stockcare Limited	£590,150
Abryl Formulations Ltd	£1,106,677	Batchable Enterprises Limited	£584,016
Proteintech Europe Limited	£1,105,635	Pharmacy Advisory Services Limited	£582,602
Kew Health and Beauty Limited	£1,097,569	Cool Herbals Limited	£567,579

Chatfield Pharmaceuticals Limited	£563,914	Insmed Limited	£315,312
Vitame Ltd	£556,800	MDI Medical (N.I.) Limited	£313,460
Pharmacell Medication Systems Limited	£537,741	Unicomm Pro Limited	£312,089
D.D.S.A.Pharmaceuticals Limited	£533,468	Syri Limited	£311,732
Temag Pharma Ltd	£533,385	Clean Beauty Co Limited	£310,663
J.L.Bragg (Ipswich) Limited	£532,982	Severn Biotech Limited	£308,940
Halewood Chemicals Ltd	£530,408	Wallace Pharma Limited	£308,656
Nova Bio-Pharma Technologies Limited	£526,751	Lisoma International Limited	£305,915
Cox Pharmaceutical Ltd	£522,514	Blackburn Distributions Ltd	£302,300
Nuvision Biotherapies Limited	£517,857	Saifee Healthcare Limited	£295,977
Rutland Biodynamics Limited	£507,999	Geryon Pharma Limited	£285,358
Trecona Limited	£502,029	Synergy Specials Limited	£284,068
Microspec Ltd	£488,539	Torbet Laboratories Limited	£283,956
Cardiome UK Limited	£488,073	Medisante Limited	£273,248
Tantillus Synergy Limited	£485,357	Abtek (Biologicals) Limited	£273,075
Sher Limited	£477,405	Ambe Limited	£272,796
Roma Pharmaceuticals Limited	£473,433	Bio-Life International Limited	£271,949
Teva Pharma Holdings Limited	£471,293	Goat Nutrition Limited	£271,710
Apollo Pharma Ltd	£451,909	Amarevida Limited	£268,698
E J Templeton Limited	£445,595	Vivalabs Europe Limited	£265,142
Sussex Biologicals Ltd	£441,739	London Pharma Capital Limited	£264,052
Avicenna Herbal Products Limited	£441,551	Dr. Max Pharma Limited	£262,845
Rimmerdax Limited	£440,670	Scottish Bioenergy Cooperative Ventures Limited	£248,793
Biologix Laboratories Limited	£432,251	Aromesse Limited	£248,377
Supamed Limited	£432,000	OTC Concepts Limited	£245,821
Medicol Limited	£428,545	Duffy Assets Ltd	£243,977
JIT Laboratories Limited	£426,538	Maxwellia Ltd	£243,922
Courtin and Warner Limited	£421,968	Acime UK Limited	£237,739
Salcura Limited	£417,175	Biopharma Laboratories (UK) Limited	£236,877
Ria Generics Limited	£415,742	Opiant Pharmaceuticals UK Limited	£230,235
Capa Vision Limited	£400,007	Ecohydra Technologies Limited	£230,094
Harlequin BPI Ltd	£389,701	Bioplus Tech Ltd	£229,940
Linosa Limited	£383,493	World Medicine Ophthalmics Limited	£229,597
Webottle Ltd	£382,893	Cho Consulting Ltd.	£227,176
Hartington Pharma Limited	£382,010	Suzie Who Limited	£226,033
Bio-Health Limited	£381,357	Westech Scientific Instruments Limited	£225,055
Pharmaserve Limited	£379,783	Cuttlefish Limited	£223,861
Herbal Concepts Limited	£377,384	Europa-Technia Limited	£219,080
Stegram Pharmaceuticals Limited	£375,203	Pioneer UK Holdings Limited	£219,060
Osteoporosis Research Ltd	£372,162	International Technidyne Corporation Limited	£217,826
Juice Sauz Ltd	£366,669	Koolpak Limited	£216,661
Four Pharmaceuticals Limited	£365,517	Kensington Pharma Ltd	£213,240
Microsens Biophage Limited	£362,622	Swann-Morton (Europe) Limited	£213,062
Insense Limited	£362,373	Avanor Healthcare Ltd	£206,200
Koasta Limited	£359,501	Kaizen Ceramics Ltd	£202,921
Incline Therapeutics Europe Ltd.	£347,378	Commercial and Academic Services Limited	£202,415
Savoy Laboratories (International) Limited	£347,033	Sestri (Sales) Limited	£200,052
Blackrock Pharmaceuticals Limited	£345,957	North Star Healthcare Limited	£198,019
Zerenex Molecular Limited	£344,318	Manx Pharma Ltd	£195,131
Thorpe Laboratories Limited	£342,466	Ampha Limited	£189,953
Sutherland Health Limited	£340,311	Stablepharma Limited	£185,308
Cutera Limited	£339,636	Pharmaclarity Limited	£177,162
Bioextractions Wales Limited	£339,104	Biopharm (U.K.) Limited	£176,362
RP & MP Investments Limited	£337,054	TLD Sachets Limited	£174,314
Hunger Control Limited	£335,209	International Medication Systems (U.K.) Limited	£174,000
Hygieia Medical Ltd	£327,866	Georganics Ltd	£170,919
Life on Healthcare Ltd	£324,916	Hygitech Limited	£170,398
SNS Limited	£322,517	Skindoc Formula Limited	£169,000
Coating Systems (International) Limited	£318,268	Agroceutical Products Ltd	£166,026

The Top UK Pharmaceutical Manufacturers

Encapsula Limited	£165,949	Personal Care Packs Limited	£84,528
EVL Biologicals Ltd	£164,105	Shirley Price Aromatherapy Limited	£83,766
Tell Products,Limited	£163,440	Merad Pharmaceuticals Limited	£83,608
Lifeshield Limited	£161,652	Hewlett Healthcare Limited	£83,590
Fernhurst Pharmacy Limited	£161,133	Therapi Natural Products Ltd	£82,019
Aclaris Therapeutics International Limited	£160,258	Infinitus Enterprise Limited	£81,859
Drugsdirect Global Ltd	£157,215	AXG Ltd	£81,133
Phytacol Limited	£152,552	Anna-Med (UK) Ltd	£79,376
Woundil Limited	£150,002	Prime Test Limited	£78,696
Farmigea UK Ltd	£147,677	Ariera Pharma Limited	£77,058
Biotechflow Ltd	£146,561	Cast Healthcare Ltd	£76,034
Euro OTC Pharma UK Limited	£144,420	Rhino Education Ltd	£73,432
Sage Therapeutics Limited	£143,230	Flavour-Tech UK Limited	£73,287
R D T Technology Limited	£142,795	Trintech Services Limited	£72,968
Quotient Diagnostics Limited	£141,604	Diep Tran Consultancy Ltd	£72,794
Aim-Straight Limited	£141,499	Clarke Pharma Consulting Limited	£72,489
Chamcotec Ltd	£139,000	Vivonics Preclinical Limited	£71,510
Jai Pharma Limited	£136,047	Green House Monitoring Limited	£71,318
Limehurst Limited	£135,317	Vitaxis International Limited	£71,117
Cool Gell Limited	£134,916	Surrey Pharma Ltd	£70,912
Ayush Ayurveda Care Limited	£134,613	Venture Healthcare Ltd	£70,522
Fernsoft Limited	£132,753	GB QP Services Limited	£68,794
Univit Ltd	£132,244	Biopharma Stability Testing Laboratory Limited	£68,707
Cytetech Limited	£131,187	Teklab (ML) Ltd	£68,548
New Directions Europe Ltd	£129,612	Leptrex Ltd.	£68,222
Extruded Pharmaceuticals Ltd	£127,200	Woundcare Limited	£66,644
Flavour Maker Limited	£126,700	Avacare Limited	£66,536
Swift Dent Engineering Services Limited	£126,067	PLS Microbiology Limited	£66,029
Xeal Pharma Ltd	£125,211	Pfylori Limited	£65,814
Lochview Pharm Ltd.	£122,362	Ecobrands Limited	£65,191
Yorkshire Hygiene Solutions Limited	£120,088	Skyrocket Phytopharma (UK) Limited	£64,862
Abatron Limited	£118,186	Eulysis UK Limited	£64,661
Nutripharm Limited	£114,209	Adpharm Limited	£64,542
Maltron International Limited	£111,471	Universal Business Services UK Limited	£64,494
Indigo Diagnostics Limited	£110,380	PSR Analytical Services Ltd	£64,056
The Herbal Factory Ltd	£109,210	Chiropody Express Limited	£63,081
Winross Limited	£109,198	Edwards' Analytical Limited	£62,842
Allmarks Products Limited	£108,808	Better Call Paul Limited	£62,794
Mediskills Limited	£108,034	Aeropax International Limited	£62,530
Botanica International Limited	£107,313	IOLAMD Ltd	£62,207
Pharmacy Medicines Ltd	£106,463	Medical Technologies Limited	£61,228
Lewtress Natural Health Limited	£106,276	Osgen Pharmaceuticals Limited	£61,191
Beegood Enterprises Limited	£105,829	Lucy Annabella Ltd	£60,257
Dreamskin Health Limited	£104,260	Soleaero Limited	£60,100
Lipidev Ltd	£103,073	Boley Nutraceuticals Ltd.	£60,100
Recentia Limited	£102,382	Cupid Peptide Company Limited	£59,798
Morar Design Limited	£102,328	Raught Limited	£59,352
RLC Technology Limited	£102,216	PG Pharma Ltd	£59,250
GFC Diagnostics Limited	£99,620	P2 Healthcare Limited	£57,760
Pharmadynamics UK Limited	£98,490	Kee Logic Limited	£57,104
Starkwell Validation Limited	£97,934	Norma Chemicals Limited	£56,908
Transdermal Technology & Systems (TTS) Limited	£96,169	A Q V S Limited	£56,170
Cotswold Health Limited	£95,060	Pharm-Assist (Regulatory Services) Limited	£55,844
RG and Co Limited	£93,822	GB Quality Consulting Services Limited	£54,730
UK Animal Products Limited	£93,649	Cellpath USA Limited	£54,666
Renascience Pharma Limited	£91,135	PVR Works Ltd	£53,789
Dermaco Limited	£90,017	Vitra Pharmaceuticals Ltd	£53,661
Jac+Q Limited	£86,631	Ectomedica Limited	£53,545
Neo Laboratories Limited	£84,823	Bamford & Wolfe Ltd	£52,830

Company	Value	Company	Value
IM Herd Ltd	£52,790	Cognitive Bioscience Limited	£28,572
Bio Farma Ltd	£52,539	VBD Drug Safety Ltd	£28,466
Positive Diagnostics Ltd	£52,275	Prep Skincare Products Limited	£28,371
Ana Maria Serban Ltd	£51,044	Cost Saving Solutions Limited	£28,252
Opal IP Limited	£50,100	Bioceuticals Limited	£27,895
KMX Healthcare Ltd	£49,946	Automation Control Expertise Limited	£27,787
Ortholese Limited	£49,272	Brainpower Group Ltd.	£27,691
Summer Healthcare Limited	£48,537	Medpro Health Limited	£27,356
Celtic Wellbeing Ltd	£48,432	Active Medical Technology Limited	£27,302
Varydose Limited	£48,393	Onipede Clinical Research Ltd	£27,292
Thornit Canker Ltd.	£47,880	Ardilla Technologies UK Ltd	£27,161
Wildrush Limited	£47,486	Vaxaid Ltd.	£27,052
KMCI Services Ltd	£46,954	Emerge Biotech Ltd	£26,826
Phytoceutical Limited	£46,953	CPT Science Ltd	£26,793
EV Pharma Solutions Ltd	£46,631	Muhammad 786 Limited	£26,723
Captium Limited	£46,282	Inflazome UK Limited	£26,600
Renew Medical UK Limited	£45,921	Lamicare Health Ltd	£26,550
Silver Shell Limited	£45,310	Workstead Limited	£26,168
KKG Consulting Limited	£45,003	Mayfair & Hayes Pharmaceuticals Ltd	£26,024
HMS Vilgo UK Ltd	£44,929	AKD Pharma Limited	£25,691
KR Regulatory Limited	£44,792	Shanmonrie Services Limited	£25,236
Bateman Quality Associates Limited	£43,144	Biteback Products Ltd	£25,060
NHC Limited	£43,007	RM Medical Care Ltd	£25,053
SKN-RG Ltd	£42,945	Aura Fragrances Limited	£25,023
Oxbridge Pharma Limited	£42,607	Pharmacenna Ltd	£25,004
Carmel Herbals Limited	£42,416	Ochil Skincare Company Ltd	£24,315
Instrument Research Company Limited	£42,069	Diana Drummond Limited	£24,241
Fermenta Biotech (UK) Limited	£41,772	Dolphins Limited	£24,101
Compliance & Validation Solutions Ltd	£40,092	Slo Drinks Limited	£23,685
Pete Randle Grinding & Son Limited	£39,994	Root2tip Haircare Solutions Ltd	£23,551
Roonivoolin Naturals Ltd	£38,923	Tregenna Technical Services Limited	£23,428
Ladysystems International Limited	£38,481	Chimerix UK Limited	£23,305
Aroma World Limited	£38,114	Itreatskin Limited	£23,200
Trauma Trays Limited	£38,051	Medison Pharma Limited	£23,045
Uvamed Ltd	£37,878	Insuphar Laboratories Limited	£22,952
Prulab Pharma Ltd	£37,810	Wellness Lab Ltd	£22,325
Casra Consultancy (UK) Limited	£37,674	First Impressions Denture Centre Ltd	£21,746
Trogon Regulatory Ltd	£37,666	Dodi Enterprise Ltd	£21,651
Premax Europe Limited	£37,085	Euratlantic-Cosmepharm Limited	£21,288
PT Direct Limited	£36,633	Handiskin Limited	£21,074
Active Cosmetic Ingredients Ltd	£35,900	Hollins Denture Clinic Limited	£21,065
Avanzcare Limited	£35,101	Aesica Trustee Company Limited	£21,000
Phetalz Ltd	£34,752	Green Groot Limited	£20,680
GBBC Ltd	£34,677	Breckland International Ltd.	£20,597
Approved Pharma Solutions Ltd	£34,111	Avisius Research Limited	£20,198
Druglab118 Ltd	£33,827	Bio-Sync International Limited	£20,188
EVC Compounding Ltd	£33,294	Chafred Consultancy Limited	£20,122
Apollo Prosthetics Limited	£32,536	European First Aid Limited	£20,000
Isca Biochemicals Limited	£31,746	Infection Monitoring and Control Ltd	£19,789
Go-Kyo Science Limited	£31,287	My Shea Limited	£19,600
Engelpharma UK Limited	£31,183	Emergencypharm Ltd.	£19,456
Skin Cell Labs Limited	£31,060	Smart Instruments UK Limited	£19,360
Active Cosmethics International Limited	£31,055	Arrow Generics Limited	£18,901
Pharma QP Solutions Ltd	£30,932	Langdales Limited	£18,646
NSK Locums Limited	£30,439	Cambcol Ltd	£18,640
BtechLaboratories (UK) Ltd.	£30,015	Daz Solutions Ltd.	£17,945
Max Medical Products Ltd	£29,718	EVL Biologicals 23 Ltd	£17,747
Health Plus Limited	£29,166	R Judge Consultancy Ltd	£17,639
Chalpharm Consultancy Limited	£28,995	Isovitality Nutriceuticals Limited	£17,114

Moroccan Natural Resources Limited	£17,071	Medical Regulatory Consulting Ltd	£6,468		
Hyperion Biotechnology Limited	£16,339	Claris LifeSciences (UK) Limited	£6,283		
Nektar Therapeutics UK Limited	£16,113	Flourish Ventures Ltd	£6,256		
Pinewood Healthcare Limited	£16,000	Herbal Right UK Limited	£6,215		
Make Skincare Ltd.	£15,551	Ilody Skincare Ltd	£6,061		
Y4U Limited	£15,409	Natural Way Limited	£6,023		
Reem Tanning Company Limited	£15,039	Clickhealth Limited	£5,987		
Testfield UK Ltd	£14,943	E-Breathe Ltd.	£5,838		
Ayurmedics Clinic Limited	£14,785	Zindaclin Limited	£5,725		
Henri L.Jaccaz & Co. Limited	£14,763	Total Pharma Ltd	£5,718		
Blackley 2010 Limited	£14,734	Nutrasulin Ltd.	£5,687		
Pegasus Equine Diagnostics Limited	£14,508	AS Pharma Consultancy Limited	£5,665		
Durja Pharma Limited	£14,452	Innov8tor Limited	£5,368		
S.L.Cassidy Limited	£14,183	Bio Provide 18 Ltd	£5,329		
Pfertec Limited	£14,096	Derma Solutions Ltd	£5,300		
PAB Apothecary Ltd	£13,902	Falls Care Limited	£5,065		
Acle Urban Gardens Limited	£13,611	Pure Peace Ltd	£5,036		
21CEC PX Pharm Ltd	£13,583	ADC Healthcare Limited	£5,019		
Shiraz Pharm Limited	£13,554	Immbio Therapeutics Limited	£5,010		
Ezoogle UK Limited	£13,243	Vitane Pharma Limited	£4,817		
Nacur Healthcare Ltd	£13,162	Onsite Diagnostics Limited	£4,694		
Apotek Services Ltd	£12,703	Everything for Eczema Limited	£4,590		
Salutem Supplements Ltd	£12,615	Sultan & Sons Enterprises Limited	£4,505		
Newmed Consultancy Limited	£12,170	Edward Daniel Limited	£4,432		
Idrolabs Limited	£12,088	Hashmats Health Ltd	£4,303		
Caithness Biotechnologies Limited	£12,018	RPL (UK) Limited	£4,100		
Biomedical Nutrition Ltd	£11,704	Unconventional E & P Services Limited	£3,932		
Jela Pharm Limited	£11,601	Antibody Store Limited	£3,855		
Afzal Pharma Ltd	£11,556	Charis Consult Limited	£3,740		
RRA Green Cross Limited	£11,326	Atlantia UK Ltd	£3,651		
JGPSK Limited	£11,153	P & S Nano Limited	£3,628		
Total Pharmacare Ltd	£11,140	Sandine Zartaux Holding Ltd	£3,544		
KVK Limited	£10,571	Biosynth Europe Limited	£3,511		
3rd Hour Limited	£10,457	Lumibio Ltd	£3,465		
UK Biopharma Ltd	£10,316	Vita Sun Ltd	£3,441		
Herbapharmedica Limited	£10,192	Myoproducts Limited	£3,400		
Mark Aziz Limited	£9,938	Maycross Sports Limited	£3,316		
EHB Limited	£9,719	Pharmacy Warehouse Limited	£3,217		
MK Ventures Limited	£9,638	One Stop 15 Limited	£3,004		
FR Products Limited	£9,540	CKC Aromatherapy Beauty Products Limited	£2,890		
Theramit Limited	£9,503	Euro Diagnostics Limited	£2,800		
Forensic Rescue Limited	£9,442	MyHairDoctor Ltd	£2,778		
CT-You Ltd	£9,361	Winchpharma (Consumer Healthcare) Ltd	£2,538		
Hydranure Ltd	£9,243	Nimasol Limited	£2,537		
Tickletec Limited	£9,105	Pacific Height Limited	£2,468		
St. George Technology Limited	£9,101	Kalfar Health Ltd	£2,458		
The Mammoet Cannabis Limited	£8,850	Blends for Massage Limited	£2,346		
Nicofix (Europe) Limited	£8,757	QOL Therapeutics UK Limited	£2,336		
Gimews Welding Limited	£8,631	M Jallow Ltd	£2,328		
Comfort Ventures Limited	£8,500	MacFarlane Martin Ltd	£2,308		
Nagashree Ltd	£8,495	Pharma XP Consulting Ltd	£2,184		
Ethno Botanical Resources Limited	£7,642	Natural Dermatology Ltd	£2,008		
Enchanted Brave Limited	£7,582	Interaction Chempharm Ltd	£2,000		
Greeco Arab Products Ltd.	£7,510	Y Consultancy Ltd	£1,975		
Jenarron Therapeutics Limited	£7,441	Mudd By Alix Ltd.	£1,900		
Fine Treatment Limited	£7,022	Akvion Limited	£1,872		
Elena's Nature Collection Limited	£7,021	Kamada Biopharma Limited	£1,684		
Leap Pharma Ltd	£6,841	Vitalogic Limited	£1,632		
Jim & Sheila Ltd.	£6,626	Sizwe Limited	£1,626		

Company	Amount	Company	Amount
Stuckola-Pharma Limited	£1,474	More Poland Limited	£169
Dynamic Development Laboratories Co Ltd	£1,454	Chemagain Limited	£153
Frontline Trading Limited	£1,401	J J Design and Engineering Limited	£118
Crescent API Limited	£1,376	Tal Pharma and Chemicals Limited	£103
Skin Naturale Ltd	£1,312	Sauflon (Manufacturing) Limited	£100
Corcept Therapeutics UK Limited	£1,290	Quicksilver Scientific Europe Limited	£100
Hairblends Limited	£1,179	Curx Pharma (UK) Limited	£100
Biosuspensions Limited	£1,124	Placebex Ltd	£100
Viridian Pharma Limited	£1,000	Microvisk Technologies International Limited	£100
Medina Corp. Ltd	£1,000	Medlabs Europe Ltd	£100
Evorin Pharma Limited	£1,000	Plackett Limited	£100
Clarornell Consulting and Trading Ltd	£982	Universal Cell Therapeutics Ltd.	£100
Atlantis Skincare Ltd	£939	Zota Healthcare Limited	£100
Biotherics Limited	£923	Invictus R & D Ltd	£82
Rena Specials Limited	£899	Herman Claude Ltd	£72
Allfresh Products Limited	£889	Qures Healthcare Limited	£66
Hutrade Ltd.	£871	ZO-X Ltd	£51
Fontridge Pharmaceutical Research and Development Ltd	£836	Protiaso Ltd	£42
The Bolton Pharmaceutical Company 100 Ltd	£823	Traditional Pure Potions Ltd	£37
LMP (UK) Limited	£788	Organic Lifecare Ltd.	£26
Ward Surgical & Supplies Ltd	£771	Lawrance Pharma Limited	£12
Beautanix Limited	£756	The Heavenly Herb Company Ltd.	£12
Brassard Limited	£657	Naia (London) Limited	£10
Dr. Tuhin Dev Skin Care Limited	£621	4soap Limited	£10
Mumma Love Organics Limited	£546	Bio Provide Ltd	£7
Petbiocell UK Ltd	£500	The Natural Cornish Company Ltd	£6
RPH Innovations Limited	£499	Bio Provide 19 Ltd	£2
The Beautiful Splint Company CIC	£477	Bescot Healthcare UK Limited	£2
N9NE Cosmetics Ltd	£445	Bena Cosmetics (UK) Limited	£1
M V Locums Limited	£412	Designerx Europe Limited	£1
AWA Export Limited	£403	Xanadu Valley Limited	£1
AA Zentivus Ltd	£400	Unigreg Worldwide Limited	£1
Braun International Limited	£399	Bioreactor Corporation Limited	£1
Joyce Pharmac Services Ltd	£265	Bio Provide 20 Ltd	£1
Inskin Skincare Ltd	£241	Biokemix Worldwide Ltd	£1
Well & Well Pharma UK Ltd	£200		

Age of Companies

The Top UK Pharmaceutical Manufacturers

1800s
Dendron Limited
Fisons Limited
Schering-Plough Limited
Smith Kline & French Laboratories

1900-1909
Accord-UK Ltd
Roche Products Limited
Vivimed Labs Europe Ltd

1910-1919 [5]
AAH Pharmaceuticals Limited
D.D.D. Limited
Ernest Jackson & Co. Limited
Novartis Pharmaceuticals UK Ltd
John Wyeth & Brother Limited

1920-1929 [9]
Guerbet Argentina Limited
Mentholatum Co Ltd
New Cheshire Salt Works Ltd
Norgine Limited
Novartis Grimsby Limited
Thompson and Capper Limited
Thornton & Ross Limited
UCB Pharma Limited
Weleda (U.K.) Limited

1930-1939 [11]
Bell,Sons & Co.(Druggists) Ltd
Catalent U.K. Swindon Encaps Ltd
Infohealth Laboratories Ltd
Isola Manufacturing Co.(Wythenshawe)
Kerbina,Limited
Eli Lilly and Co Ltd
A Nelson & Co Limited
Seven Seas Limited
Smith & Nephew PLC
South Wales Specials Limited
Teva UK Limited

1940-1949 [10]
Aspen Medical Europe Limited
Baxter Healthcare Limited
Church & Dwight UK Limited
Fleet Laboratories Limited
F.Maltby & Sons Limited
Matthews & Wilson Limited
Norma Chemicals Limited
E.R.Squibb & Sons Limited
Tell Products,Limited
Wallace Manufacturing Chemists Ltd

1950-1959 [11]
C P Pharmaceuticals Limited
Concorde Perfumery and Cosmetics Ltd
Courtin and Warner Limited
Halewood Chemicals Ltd
Macarthys Laboratories Limited
Neo Laboratories Limited
Rusco Limited
G.D.Searle & Co.Limited
Supersun Nutrition Limited
Teva Laboratories UK Limited
Wallis Laboratory Limited

1960-1969 [35]
Blistex Limited
Boehringer Ingelheim Limited
Chelsea Drug & Chemical Co Ltd
Chempro Limited
D.D.S.A.Pharmaceuticals Ltd
Diagnostic Reagents Limited
Diomed Developments Limited
Dista Products Limited
Elanco Europe Ltd.
Geistlich Sons Limited
Glaxo Operations UK Limited
LRC Products Limited
G.R. Lane Health Products Ltd
Lilly Industries Limited
Lilly Research Centre Limited
Lofthouse of Fleetwood Limited
MacFarlan Smith Limited
Medical Supply Co Ltd
Merck Sharp & Dohme Limited
Napp Pharmaceutical Group Ltd
Norbrook Laboratories Limited
Norton Healthcare Limited
Omega Pharma Limited
Pharmax Limited
Rhodia Pharma Solutions Ltd
Rosemont Pharmaceuticals Ltd
Savoy Laboratories (International)
H.E. Stringer (Perfurmery) Ltd
Teklab (ML) Ltd
Torbet Laboratories Limited
Typharm Limited
Van Vleck and Olivers Limited
Wallis Laboratory (Sales) Ltd
West Pharmaceutical Services Cornwall
Wychem Limited

1970-1979 [43]
Abatron Limited
Albumedix Ltd
Alinter Limited
Arch Chemicals Products Ltd
Bard Pharmaceuticals Limited
J.L.Bragg (Ipswich) Limited
Bray Group Limited
Chatfield Pharmaceuticals Ltd
Colorcon Limited
Combe International Limited
Cottage Garden Cosmetics and Gifts
Cross Chemicals UK Limited
Custom Pharmaceuticals Limited
Custom Powders Limited
Diba Industries Limited
T.G. Eakin Limited
Elanco Animal Vaccines Limited
Envigo RMS (UK) Limited
Pierre Fabre Limited
GE Healthcare Limited
Greenfield Pharmaceuticals Ltd
International Medication Systems (U.K.)
Janssen-Cilag Limited
Klinge Chemicals Limited
Eli Lilly Group Limited
Linosa Limited
Milton Lloyd Limited
M & A Pharmachem Limited
Millpledge Limited
Novo Nordisk Holding Limited
Penn Pharmaceutical Services Ltd
Pharmvit Limited
Purce Associates Limited

Ranir Limited
Raught Limited
Rimmerdax Limited
Sarakan Limited
Selborne Biological Services Ltd
Sestri (Sales) Limited
Sinclair Pharmaceuticals Ltd
Teva Pharmaceuticals Limited
Teva Research Laboratories (NI) Ltd
Vitabiotics Limited

1980-1989 [88]
Abtek (Biologicals) Limited
Aeropax International Limited
Air Liquide Limited
Allfresh Products Limited
Aura-Soma Products Limited
B.C. Medical Limited
BVM Medical Limited
Badgequo Limited
Bio-Health Limited
Bio-Medical Services Limited
Bio-Rad AbD Serotec Ltd
Bionet Research Limited
Biopharm (U.K.) Limited
Bodywise Limited
Boehringer Ingelheim Animal Health UK
Castex Products Limited
Catalent Micron Technologies Ltd
Catalent U.K. Swindon Zydis Ltd
Catalent UK Supply Chain Ltd
Chemidex Pharma Limited
Cod Beck Blenders Limited
Corpus Nostrum Limited
Cosmana Limited
Dermal Laboratories Limited
Diana Drummond Limited
Donglun Limited
Dr Reddy's Laboratories (UK) Ltd
Dr. Reddy's Laboratories (EU) Ltd
Elemis Limited
Equalbrief Limited
Essential Nutrition Limited
Fine Organics Limited
Fresenius Kabi Limited
Generics (U.K.) Limited
Genus Pharmaceuticals Limited
Genzyme Limited
Getinge UK Limited
Goat Nutrition Limited
Health + Plus Limited
Hichrom Limited
Hickson W.A. Chemicals Limited
Hospira UK Limited
Hyperdrug Pharmaceuticals Ltd
Ideal Manufacturing Limited
International Technidyne Corporation
Ipsen Biopharm Limited
Kalms Limited
Key Organics Limited
Lifeplan Products Limited
Eli Lilly (Basingstoke) Ltd
Eli Lilly Holdings Limited
Longshawe Packaging Limited
MDI Medical (N.I.) Limited
Macopharma (UK) Limited
Masters Pharmaceuticals Ltd
May & Baker Limited
Medical Export Co Ltd
Medicol Limited
A. Menarini Diagnostics Ltd
Mercury Pharma Group Limited

Millbrook (NI) Limited
N.T. Laboratories Limited
NZP UK Limited
Octapharma Limited
Pharmaserve Limited
Phyto Products Limited
Pliva Pharma Limited
Point International Limited
Polychem Limited
Porvair PLC
G. & M. Procter Limited
Resolution Chemicals Limited
Sandoz Limited
Sauflon (Manufacturing) Ltd
Scipac Limited
Severn Biotech Limited
Sharp Clinical Services (UK) Ltd
Shire Pharmaceuticals Limited
SmithKline Beecham Limited
Stegram Pharmaceuticals Ltd
Stockcare Limited
Surepharm Services Limited
TCS Biosciences Limited
Technical & General Limited
Teisen Products Limited
Teva NI Limited
Trintech Services Limited
Vernalis (R & D) Limited

1990-1994 [57]
Advanced Medical Solutions Ltd
Advanz Pharma Generics (UK) Ltd
Age Reversal Europe Ltd.
Aspar Pharmaceuticals Limited
Astrazeneca PLC
Aurum Pharmaceuticals Limited
BCM Limited
BHR Pharmaceuticals Limited
Bach Flower Remedies Limited
Batchable Enterprises Limited
Biocolor Limited
Bristol-Myers Squibb Pharmaceuticals
Calea UK Limited
Cambridge Sensors Ltd
Carmel Herbals Limited
Chirotech Technology Limited
Coating Systems (International) Ltd
Commercial and Academic Services Ltd
Eco Animal Health Ltd.
Ecobrands Limited
Ethno Botanical Resources Ltd
Euro Medical Equipment Limited
Europa-Technia Limited
Fernsoft Limited
Geotek Coring Limited
Health Plus Limited
Hermes Pharmaceutical Limited
Hologic Ltd.
IS Pharmaceuticals Limited
Koolpak Limited
Lab 21 Healthcare Limited
Eli Lilly Leasing Limited
Limehurst Limited
MW Encap Limited
Manx Healthcare Limited
Mercury Pharmaceuticals Ltd
Morningside Pharmaceuticals Ltd
Nektar Therapeutics UK Limited
Nova Laboratories Limited
Ortho-Clinical Diagnostics
Pari Medical Limited
Plus Orthopedics (UK) Limited

Provita Eurotech Ltd
Sanofi-Synthelabo Limited
Sogeval UK Limited
Strides Pharma UK Ltd
Sutherland Health Limited
Suzie Who Limited
Swann-Morton (Europe) Limited
Technical Textile Services Ltd
Tyne Care Limited
Vernalis Development Limited
Veterinary Immunogenics Ltd
Vitra Pharmaceuticals Ltd
Wallis Licensing Limited
Wrafton Laboratories Limited
G.H. Zeal Limited

1995 [19]
Amarevida Limited
Aura Fragrances Limited
Biostatus Ltd
Biotech Design and Validation Ltd.
Braun International Limited
Breckland International Ltd.
European First Aid Limited
Hewlett Healthcare Limited
IGMA Limited
Merck Serono Europe Limited
Miltenyi Biotec Limited
New Nordic Limited
Olbas Limited
Peckforton Pharmaceuticals Ltd
Redrose Manufacturing Limited
Shah-British Enterprises Ltd
St. George Technology Limited
Syner-Med Pharmaceuticals (Kenya)
Welby Healthcare Limited

1996 [18]
ADS Biotec Limited
APS/Berk Limited
Active Medical Technology Ltd
Alliance Pharmaceuticals Ltd
Contura Limited
Dermaco Limited
Dolphins Limited
Euratlantic-Cosmepharm Limited
Intervet UK Production Limited
Isopath Limited
Langdales Limited
MW Encap (Holdings) Limited
Maltron International Limited
Manx Pharma Ltd
P.I.E. Pharma Limited
Pfertec Limited
Pharmapac (U.K.) Limited
Summan International Limited

1997 [19]
Ayrton Saunders Limited
Byrom (South Wales) Limited
Cambridge Healthcare Supplies Ltd
Fermenta Biotech (UK) Limited
Four Pharmaceuticals Limited
GE Healthcare UK Limited
Hospira Aseptic Services Ltd
Intrapharm Laboratories Ltd
Kent Pharmaceuticals Limited
Maelor Laboratories Limited
Merial Limited
Napp Pharmaceutical Holdings Ltd
Natural Way Limited

Neomedic Limited
Nicobrand Limited
Protherics UK Limited
SNS Limited
Tersan Pharmaceuticals Ltd.
Vita (Europe) Limited

1998 [23]
Actavis Holdings UK II Limited
Active Cosmethics International Ltd
Advanced Healthcare Systems Ltd
Allergy Therapeutics (UK) Ltd
Bespak Europe Limited
Bio Pure Technology Ltd
Calla Lily Personal Care Ltd
Charnwood Molecular Limited
Europharma Limited
Fresenius Kabi Oncology PLC
HK Pharma Limited
Herbal Concepts Limited
Lifeshield Limited
Lisoma International Limited
Mediskills Limited
Micropharm Limited
Molnlycke Health Care Limited
Norton Healthcare (1998) Ltd
Ono Pharma UK Ltd.
Phytoceutical Limited
Taisho Pharmaceutical (Europe) Ltd
Vericore Limited
Vitrition UK Ltd.

1999 [21]
Ambe Limited
Auden McKenzie (Pharma Division) Ltd
Cool Gell Limited
DHTD Limited
Dalkeith Laboratories Limited
GW Pharma Limited
Life Technologies BPD UK Ltd
Makjay Pharmaceutical Limited
Medicam Limited
Microsens Biophage Limited
Nelson & Russell Holdings Ltd
Nelsons Aura Limited
PCCA Limited
Patheon UK Limited
Pfylori Limited
RSR Limited
Ria Generics Limited
Satelec (UK) Limited
UK Animal Products Limited
Ward Surgical & Supplies Ltd
Y4U Limited

2000 [25]
Arrow Generics Limited
As-Tec Chemicals Limited
Beacon Pharmaceuticals Limited
Breath Limited
Brown & Burk UK Limited
Chiropody Express Limited
Essential Health Products Ltd
Fontridge Pharmaceutical Research and Development
Hunger Control Limited
Infohealth Limited
Ingel Technologies Limited
Insense Limited
Kowa Pharmaceutical Europe Co Ltd
Lincoln Medical Limited

McAleer & Donnelly Pharmacy Ltd
Merad Pharmaceuticals Limited
NHC Limited
Onyx Scientific Limited
Organic Pharmacy Limited
Phico Therapeutics Limited
Quest Ingredients Limited
Seqirus Vaccines Limited
Star Pharmaceuticals Limited
Ventarc Limited
Wallace Pharma Limited

2001 [21]
AbbVie Australasia Holdings Ltd
Abbott Vascular Devices (2) Ltd
Celgene UK Manufacturing (II) Ltd
Elena's Nature Collection Ltd
Emerald Kalama Chemical Ltd
Forensic Rescue Limited
LPC Medical (UK) Limited
Eli Lilly Holding Co Ltd
Mandeville Medicines Limited
Maxearn Limited
Milton Pharmaceutical Company UK Ltd
Morningside Healthcare Limited
Nia Nova Ltd
Oat Services Limited
Organic Herbs for Health Ltd
Organic Herbs for Life Limited
Principle Healthcare Limited
Qiagen Manchester Limited
Quay Pharmaceuticals Limited
Vitalogic Limited
Y Consultancy Ltd

2002 [42]
AMO United Kingdom Limited
Accord Healthcare Limited
Allergan Biologics Limited
Alliance Medical Radiopharmacy Ltd
Apex Pharmaceuticals Ltd.
Aromesse Limited
Bio-Tech Solutions Limited
Biologix Laboratories Limited
Brunel Healthcare Manufacturing Ltd
Cellon UK Limited
Cutera Limited
DTR Medical Limited
Dechra Limited
Focus Pharmaceuticals Limited
Innova Biosciences Ltd
International Scientific Supplies
Henri L.Jaccaz & Co. Limited
Joribunda Limited
Lilly Property Limited
Eli Lilly Property Limited
Lilly Resources Limited
Eli Lilly Resources Limited
Bob Martin (UK) Limited
Nanopharm Limited
Niche Generics Limited
OTC Concepts Limited
Oxbridge Pharma Limited
Oxford Immunotec Limited
PSR Analytical Services Ltd
Penlan Healthcare Limited
Pharmasol Limited
Quotient Diagnostics Limited
Regent Generics Limited
Rutland Biodynamics Limited
Salcura Limited

Sarissa Biomedical Limited
Sinclair Animal and Household Care
Soleaero Limited
Spear Therapeutics Limited
Supamed Limited
Swedish Orphan Biovitrum Ltd
Viridian Pharma Limited

2003 [26]
21CEC PX Pharm Ltd
Aguettant Limited
Akvion Limited
Almac Pharma Services Limited
Avisius Research Limited
Bolton Pharmaceutical Company 100 Ltd
Candles UK Ltd
Claris LifeSciences (UK) Ltd
Craintern (UK) Limited
Crescent Pharma Limited
Cross Healthcare Limited
Dermapharm Skincare Limited
Essential Generics Limited
Ferndale Pharmaceuticals Ltd
Ipca Laboratories UK Limited
JIT Laboratories Limited
Life Molecular Imaging Limited
Medical Technologies Limited
Medlock Medical Limited
Nextpharma Technologies Holding Ltd
Pharma Pack Limited
Pharmacy Advisory Services Ltd
Positive Diagnostics Ltd
Pete Randle Grinding & Son Ltd
Reaxa Limited
Thorpe Laboratories Limited

2004 [34]
Aesica Pharmaceuticals Limited
Albany Molecular Research Ltd
Allergy Therapeutics PLC
Aquabalm Limited
Bena Cosmetics (UK) Limited
Bio-Sync International Limited
Biomed Supplies Limited
Bowmed Limited
CPT Science Ltd
Catalent CTS (Edinburgh) Ltd
Celgene UK Manufacturing Ltd
Derms Development Limited
Dreamskin Health Limited
Ecohydra Technologies Limited
Jim & Sheila Ltd.
KVK Limited
Kew Health and Beauty Limited
Knoll UK Investments Unlimited
Lewtress Natural Health Ltd
MK Ventures Limited
Occidem Biotech Limited
Pharmaspec Limited
Phytovation Limited
Piramal Critical Care Limited
Principle Healthcare International
Quantum Pharmaceutical Limited
RPL (UK) Limited
SS Products International Ltd
Shanmonrie Services Limited
Terumo BCT Ltd.
United Colors of London (UK) Ltd
Univit Ltd
Winston Laboratories Limited
World Medicine Limited

2005 [35]
Aesica Formulation Development Ltd
Aesica Trustee Co Ltd
Anna-Med (UK) Ltd
Auralis Limited
Biomimetic Therapeutics Ltd
Biosynth Europe Limited
Botanica International Limited
Cell Medica Limited
Cuttlefish Limited
Fluidx Limited
Frontline Trading Limited
GB QP Services Limited
Hikma Pharmaceuticals PLC
Hikma UK Limited
J J Design and Engineering Ltd
Jasan Technical Services Ltd
Koasta Limited
MC2 Therapeutics Limited
Marlborough Pharmaceuticals Ltd
Maycross Sports Limited
Microspec Ltd
NSK Locums Limited
Nacur Healthcare Ltd
Nejati Dental Instruments and Supplies (UK)
Neoceuticals Limited
Parkacre Enterprises Limited
Pharm-Assist (Regulatory Services)
Mimi Pisano Limited
Qualasept Limited
R D T Technology Limited
Rotapharm Limited
Sepal Pharma PLC
Sher Limited
Slo Drinks Limited
Smart Formula Limited

2006 [34]
Alba Bioscience Limited
Avanor Healthcare Ltd
BCM Specials Limited
Baby Face Cosmetics Limited
Bio-Life International Limited
Carefusion U.K. 244 Limited
Celgene UK Manufacturing (III) Ltd
Circassia Pharmaceuticals PLC
Cool Herbals Limited
Engelpharma UK Limited
Fujifilm Diosynth Biotechnologies UK
G.A.S. Vets (UK) Limited
Great Northern Apothecary Co. Ltd
Herbal Right UK Limited
Immbio Therapeutics Limited
Karnot Limited
Kee Logic Limited
Ladysystems International Ltd
Pegasus Equine Diagnostics Ltd
Pharmaceutical Equipment Ltd
Shirley Price Aromatherapy Ltd
Proteintech Europe Limited
RLC Technology Limited
RRA Green Cross Limited
Reelvision Print Limited
S.C.A.C. Limited
Snor-Ring Limited
Sterling Pharma Solutions Ltd
Therakind Limited
Therapi Natural Products Ltd
Transdermal Technology & Systems (TTS)
Wockhardt UK Limited
Woundcare Limited
Zerenex Molecular Limited

2007 [52]

AKD Pharma Limited
AVI BioPharma International Ltd
Aesica Queenborough Limited
Aim-Straight Limited
Alpex Pharma (UK) Limited
American Distilling & Mfg Ltd
Apollo Prosthetics Limited
Mark Aziz Limited
Biocryst UK Limited
Biopharma Laboratories (UK) Ltd
Blackburn Distributions Ltd
Blackrock Pharmaceuticals Ltd
Cardiome UK Limited
Casra Consultancy (UK) Limited
Comfort Ventures Limited
Edward Daniel Limited
Dermato Logical Limited
Doctor Pharma Manufacturing UK Ltd
Dr. Tuhin Dev Skin Care Ltd
Eaststone Limited
Eisai Manufacturing Limited
Eleosinc Limited
Fernhurst Pharmacy Limited
Focus Pharma Holdings Limited
GFC Diagnostics Limited
Hartington Pharma Limited
Health Innovations (UK) Ltd
Herman Claude Ltd
Insmed Limited
Iroko Products Limited
MacLeods Pharma UK Limited
Magna Pharmaceuticals Ltd
Medicareplus International Ltd
Nicofix (Europe) Limited
Nutrition Group PLC
Oxford Biodynamics PLC
Pacific Height Limited
Paradox Omega Oils Ltd
Penn Pharma Group Limited
Pharmaserve (North West) Ltd
S M Consultancy (MK) Limited
Scottish Bioenergy Cooperative Ventures
Sterling Pharmaceuticals Ltd
TLD Sachets Limited
Talley Environmental Care Ltd
Tantillus Synergy Limited
Tawil Co Limited
Unicomm Pro Limited
Vertical Pharma Resources Ltd
Viropharma Limited
Workstead Limited
Woundil Limited

2008 [26]

Ayush Ayurveda Care Limited
Bateman Quality Associates Ltd
Beautylab UK Limited
Biofortuna Ltd
Biosuspensions Limited
Brassard Limited
CM & D Pharma Limited
CTI Life Sciences Limited
Cartell UK Limited
Clinigen Group PLC
Clyde Chemist Limited
Encapsula Limited
Healing Fusions Ltd
Hyperion Catalysis EU Limited
M D M Healthcare Ltd
Oriel Therapeutics Limited

PTGO Sever UK Limited
Percuro Medica Ltd
Pharmadynamics UK Limited
Prozomix Limited
Russell and Denver Ltd
Siga Pharmaceuticals (Europe) Ltd
Sultan & Sons Enterprises Ltd
Summer Healthcare Limited
Temag Pharma Ltd
World Max Power Enterprise Ltd

2009 [33]

Abbott Iberian Investments Ltd
Acorda Therapeutics Limited
Algae Biotechnology Products Ltd
Aroma World Limited
Automation Control Expertise Ltd
Beautiful Splint Company CIC
Biotherics Limited
Chamcotec Ltd
Cho Consulting Ltd.
Crawford Healthcare (R & D) Ltd
Dermatologix Ltd
Geoprep Limited
Go-Kyo Science Limited
Grip Enterprises Limited
HAV Vaccines Limited
Hannah V Limited
Herrco Cosmetics Limited
Hyperion Biotechnology Limited
Integrated Pharmaceutical Services (IPS)
Life on Healthcare Ltd
London Specialist Pharmacy Ltd
London Surgical Limited
Nillergen Limited
Nova Bio-Pharma Technologies Ltd
Onipede Clinical Research Ltd
Peakdale Chemistry Services Ltd
Pharmaxo Pharmacy Services Ltd
Phytacol Limited
Pneumoflex E.U. Limited
Shiraz Pharm Limited
Summit Veterinary Pharmaceuticals
Total Pharma Ltd
Vit Supermarket Ltd

January-June 2010 [31]

100% Organics Limited
Ayrton Saunders and Co Ltd
Penny Badger Limited
Bio Farma Ltd
Clothopharma Limited
Cognitive Bioscience Limited
Cost Saving Solutions Limited
Cox Pharmaceutical Ltd
DX Products Limited
Finer Feet Ltd
Green House Monitoring Limited
Hashmats Health Ltd
Indivior UK Limited
Laxmi BNS Holdings Limited
Lochview Pharm Ltd.
Medisante Limited
Merrimack Pharmaceuticals U.K. Ltd
Moroccan Natural Resources Ltd
Nutripharm Limited
PLS Microbiology Limited
Pharma QP Solutions Ltd
Rainbow Engineering Services Ltd
Ranir (Holdings) Limited
Symbiosis Pharmaceutical Services

Taylor of London Limited
Theramit Limited
Vaxaid Ltd.
Well & Well Pharma UK Ltd
World Medicine Ophthalmics Ltd
Zindaclin Limited
Zogenix Europe Limited

July-December 2010 [22]

Biotechflow Ltd
Blackley 2010 Limited
Cast Healthcare Ltd
Cosmarida 2010 Limited
Dr. Max Pharma Limited
Egalet Limited
Essential Pharmaceuticals Ltd
Everything for Eczema Limited
Fine Contract Research Limited
Green Manufacturing Partners Ltd
Hipra UK and Ireland Limited
JGPSK Limited
Laboratoire Mergens (UK) Ltd
Lumibio Ltd
Max Medical Products Ltd
Proveca Limited
Rapidscan Pharma Solutions EU Ltd
Root2tip Haircare Solutions Ltd
Stuckola-Pharma Limited
Synergy Biologics Limited
Syri Limited
UK Healthcare Pharma Limited

January-June 2011 [37]

& Stuff Naturally Ltd
AWA Export Limited
Active Cosmetic Ingredients Ltd
Ascot Laboratories Limited
Birchwood Pharma Ltd
Cambridge Collagen Company (UK) Ltd
Cellpath USA Limited
Designerx Europe Limited
Duffy Assets Ltd
Epax Pharma UK Ltd
Essential Pharma Limited
Flourish Ventures Ltd
Fourrts (UK) Pharmacare Ltd
Hexpress Healthcare Limited
Hikma Pharmaceuticals International
Infinitus Enterprise Limited
Insuphar Laboratories Limited
LEH Pharma Ltd
LMP (UK) Limited
Lucy Annabella Ltd
Medical Regulatory Consulting Ltd
Noorik Biopharmaceuticals Ltd
Parakill Limited
Pharma Future Ltd
Qures Healthcare Limited
RGCC Pharma Limited
Ransom Naturals Limited
Rotapharm Pharmaceutical Ltd
Seacross Pharmaceuticals Ltd
Sentinel Health Limited
Smart Instruments UK Limited
Tal Pharma and Chemicals Ltd
Unigreg Worldwide Limited
Varydose Limited
Vitaxis International Limited
World Medicine Pharmaceutical Ltd
Xanadu Valley Limited

July-December 2011 [33]
Aesica BC Limited
Aesica Holdco Limited
Aesica M1 Limited
Aesica M2 Limited
Aptuit (Oxford) Limited
Ardilla Technologies UK Ltd
Celtic Wellbeing Ltd
Clarornell Consulting and Trading Ltd
Clickhealth Limited
Cotswold Health Limited
Ennogen Healthcare Ltd
Ennogen Pharma Ltd
Eulysis UK Limited
HOCL Limited
Inskin Skincare Ltd
Isca Biochemicals Limited
Key Empire Resources (UK) Ltd
Leptrex Ltd.
M V Locums Limited
MDX Healthcare Ltd
My Shea Limited
Nagashree Ltd
Natural Cornish Co Ltd
Natural Dermatology Ltd
Pharmacy Medicines Ltd
Primius Lab Limited
Resolution Generics Limited
Roonivoolin Naturals Ltd
SKN-RG Ltd
Synergy Specials Limited
Vitane Pharma Limited
Winross Limited
Zeltiq Limited

January-March 2012 [19]
Agroceutical Products Ltd
Cycle Pharmaceuticals Ltd
Dana's Creations Ltd
Ectomedica Limited
Herbapharmedica Limited
Humn Pharmaceuticals (UK) Ltd
Jai Pharma Limited
Jenarron Therapeutics Limited
Make Skincare Ltd.
Mento-Neem International Ltd
New Directions Europe Ltd
Osteoporosis Research Ltd
PTC Therapeutics, Limited
Rapid Nutrition PLC
Rhino Education Ltd
Skin Naturale Ltd
Stablepharma Limited
E J Templeton Limited
Thornit Canker Ltd.

April-June 2012 [18]
Ace Direct Ltd
Biopharma Stability Testing Laboratory
Capa Vision Limited
Chitomerics Limited
Cupid Peptide Co Ltd
Fontus Health Ltd
Indivior EU Limited
Infirst Healthcare Limited
Lamicare Health Ltd
Leap Pharma Ltd
Myoproducts Limited
P & S Nano Limited
Pharmacenna Ltd
Protiaso Ltd

RG and Co Limited
Reem Tanning Co Ltd
Sizwe Limited
Westech Scientific Instruments Ltd

July-September 2012 [22]
A & E Plasters and Dressings Ltd
AAA Pharmaceuticals Limited
Ardent Pharma Limited
Biocentra Limited
Bioceuticals Limited
Centaur Healthcare Limited
Crawford Manufacturing Limited
Diep Tran Consultancy Ltd
Edwards' Analytical Limited
Falls Care Limited
First Impressions Denture Centre Ltd
Greenova Healthcare UK Ltd.
Harlequin BPI Ltd
Herbal Factory Ltd
Medicareplus Limited
Prep Skincare Products Limited
Recipharm Limited
Sedigel Limited
Toothsmith Limited
UK Biopharma Ltd
Winchpharma (Consumer Healthcare) Ltd
Yorkshire Hygiene Solutions Ltd

October-December 2012 [26]
AB Biotechnology Limited
Acime UK Limited
Atlantia UK Ltd
Cambridge Healthcare Supplies 2012
Catalent MTI Pharma Solutions Ltd
Crescent API Limited
Daz Solutions Ltd.
Dodi Enterprise Ltd
Hannah and Hugh Ltd
Incline Therapeutics Europe Ltd.
Infection Monitoring and Control Ltd
Joyce Pharmac Services Ltd
Lawrance Pharma Limited
M3 Cosmetics Limited
MB UN Ltd
Microskin PLC
ND Pharma & Biotech Ltd
Nimasol Limited
Orb Global Ltd
Pharmacy Warehouse Limited
Pinewood Healthcare Limited
Shea By Day Ltd
Skyrocket Phytopharma (UK) Ltd
Surrey Pharma Ltd
Typharm Developments Limited
Virodefense Limited

January-March 2013 [17]
Adpharm Limited
BBI Solutions OEM Limited
Beegood Enterprises Limited
Beneficial Oils Ltd
Brainstorm Cell Therapeutics UK Ltd
Derma Solutions Ltd
Druglab118 Ltd
EHB Limited
Emerge Biotech Ltd
Kaizen Ceramics Ltd
Orbus Therapeutics Ltd
Personal Care Packs Limited
Phetalz Ltd

Prime Test Limited
QOL Therapeutics UK Limited
Quicksilver Scientific Europe Ltd
Thistle Soaps Ltd

April-June 2013 [18]
A1 Pharmaceuticals Holdings Ltd
Alliance Medical Molecular Imaging
Amneal Pharma UK Holdings Ltd
Ana Maria Serban Ltd
Arc Devices (NI) Limited
Arcadia Pharma Limited
Chalpharm Consultancy Limited
GBBC Ltd
Hahydra Technologies Ltd
Hikmacure Limited
Hollins Denture Clinic Limited
Hope Pharmaceuticals, Ltd.
Hutrade Ltd.
Jela Pharm Limited
Maxwellia Ltd
Phamar Limited
Quest Healthcare Solutions Ltd
Starkwell Validation Limited

July-September 2013 [17]
Albert Pharma Chemicals Ltd
Ayurmedics Clinic Limited
Delta Diagnostics (UK) Ltd
Geryon Pharma Limited
Hygieia Medical Ltd
Instavit Limited
Lifetime Products Limited
Medpro Health Limited
New Eleusis Limited
Nunataq Limited
Ortholese Limited
Oxford Immunotec Global PLC
Pharm E-Cig Ltd
Quest Healthcare Aseptics Ltd
Quest Healthcare Injectables Ltd
Quest Healthcare Non-Injectables Ltd
Veradis Specials Limited

October-December 2013 [18]
Advent Bioservices Ltd
Bioextractions Wales Limited
Bioplus Tech Ltd
Enchanted Brave Limited
Exonate Limited
Gley Skincare Limited
Medina Corp. Ltd
Medison Pharma Limited
Morar Design Limited
Nikkiso UK Co., Ltd.
Paxvax Ltd
Regent Pharmaceuticals Limited
Remedi Medical Holdings Ltd
Samritz Healthcare Ltd
Swift Dent Engineering Services Ltd
That Cream Ltd
Thermo Fisher Scientific Life Holdings
Twisbee (UK) Limited

The Top UK Pharmaceutical Manufacturers

January-March 2014 [18]
AA Zentivus Ltd
AXG Ltd
Aramiss Technology Limited
Beacon Green Limited
CT-You Ltd
Euro OTC Pharma UK Limited
Evorin Pharma Limited
Fulhold Pharma Limited
Handiskin Limited
Kamada Biopharma Limited
Mexichem Medical HFA Trading Ltd
PCCA (UK) Holdings Limited
Pharma XP Consulting Ltd
Pulmeze Limited
Shanghai Neopharm Co., Ltd
Sussex Biologicals Ltd
Unconventional E & P Services Ltd
Vitame Ltd

April-June 2014 [14]
Afzal Pharma Ltd
Bescot Healthcare UK Limited
Bioreactor Corporation Limited
Chemagain Limited
Chemvet UK Limited
Fine Treatment Limited
Instrument Research Co Ltd
Lipidev Ltd
MacFarlane Martin Ltd
PAB Apothecary Ltd
Universal Business Services UK Ltd
Uvamed Ltd
ZO-X Ltd
ZVF Pharma Ltd

July-September 2014 [25]
AS Pharma Consultancy Limited
Approved Pharma Solutions Ltd
Bio-Medical Engineering Ltd
Bioceutics UK Ltd
Biomedical Nutrition Ltd
Chela Animal Health Limited
Etmo UK Limited
Farmigea UK Ltd
GlaxoSmithKline Consumer Healthcare (UK) Trading
HFA Healthcare Products Ltd
IM Herd Ltd
Indivior PLC
Maklary Ltd
Medley Pharma Limited
Optronica Limited
PCI Penn UK Holdco Limited
Pentonova Limited
Pharma Syntech Ltd
RP & MP Investments Limited
RPH Innovations Limited
Renew Medical UK Limited
Skindoc Formula Limited
Vivonics Preclinical Limited
Wasdell Manufacturing Limited
Xcelonce Limited

October-December 2014 [25]
Asterisk LifeSciences Ltd
Baxalta UK Limited
Cambcol Ltd
Charis Consult Limited
Chimerix UK Limited
Durja Pharma Limited
EVL Biologicals Ltd
Emergencypharm Ltd.
Georganics Ltd
Ipsco Limited
Medicus Integrated Medicine Ltd
Microgenetics Limited
P2 Healthcare Limited
Pollenase Limited
Porton Biopharma Limited
Protak Scientific Limited
Quantum Pharma 2014 Limited
Quantum Pharma Holdings Ltd
Reig Jofre UK Limited
Rena Specials Limited
Salenco Limited
Sandine Zartaux Holding Ltd
Skin Defence Limited
Skinnytan UK Limited
Wren Hygiene Limited

January 2015 [15]
Abryl Formulations Ltd
Caithness Biotechnologies Ltd
Columbia Laboratories (UK) Ltd
Curx Pharma (UK) Limited
HMS Vilgo UK Ltd
Home Health Limited
LDN Pharma Limited
Liquid Comb Limited
Molecular Profiles Ltd
Mumma Love Organics Limited
MyHairDoctor Ltd
Ochil Skincare Co Ltd
Recentia Limited
Total Pharmacare Ltd
Trogon Regulatory Ltd

February 2015 [11]
3rd Hour Limited
Anatics Life Sciences Limited
Bio Provide 18 Ltd
Bio Provide 19 Ltd
Bio Provide 20 Ltd
Bio Provide Ltd
EVL Biologicals 23 Ltd
Mayfair & Hayes Pharmaceuticals Ltd
Pharmacell Medication Systems Ltd
Renascience Pharma Limited
Tregenna Technical Services Ltd

March 2015 [10]
Beautanix Limited
Chrome Surgical Ltd.
Crichton Consultancy Services Ltd
Drugsdirect Global Ltd
Greeco Arab Products Ltd.
Healthcare Consortium Ltd
London Pharma Capital Limited
Panpharma UK Limited
Pegasus Pharma Limited
Testfield UK Ltd

April 2015 [10]
Aimmune Therapeutics UK Ltd
Algal Omega 3 Ltd
Biokemix Worldwide Ltd
Euro Diagnostics Limited
Kensington Pharma Ltd
Nuvision Biotherapies Limited
Pharmaclarity Limited
Placebex Ltd
Portola Pharma UK Limited
Sands Fulton Limited

May 2015 [8]
Captium Limited
S.L.Cassidy Limited
Compliance & Validation Solutions Ltd
Ezoogle UK Limited
Living Skin Care Limited
Uni Health Distribution Ltd
Vapour Chef Ltd
Venture Healthcare Ltd

June 2015
Flavour-Tech UK Limited
Naia (London) Limited
PT Direct Limited
Traditional Pure Potions Ltd

July 2015 [6]
ADC Healthcare Limited
Aclaris Therapeutics International
Emergent Countermeasures International
Incepta Pharma UK Limited
Mendelikabs Europe Limited
SKN-RG Research & Development Ltd

August 2015
2020 Organics Limited
Bioneb PVT Limited
RM Medical Care Ltd

September 2015 [5]
Clean Beauty Co Limited
Hygitech Limited
Idrolabs Limited
Mirror 5 Ltd
Stride-Davies Pharma Limited

October 2015 [9]
Apollo Pharma Ltd
Atlantis Skincare Ltd
R Judge Consultancy Ltd
Miss Derriere Ltd
Nnadi's Healthcare and Pharmaceuticals
Nutra Aid Ltd.
Osgen Ltd.
Oxford Pharmaceuticals Limited
Vivalabs Europe Limited

November 2015 [7]
Astagen Therapeutics Limited
Chafred Consultancy Limited
Ilody Skincare Ltd
Juice Sauz Ltd
Mr Derriere Ltd
PharmaYouth Ltd.
Quest HC Limited

December 2015 [7]
Crescent Manufacturing Limited
Jac+Q Limited
Kalfar Health Ltd
Muhammad 786 Limited
Prometic Pharma SMT Limited
Tips & Tricks Ltd
Trecona Limited

January 2016 [10]
Atnahs Pharma US Limited
Hairblends Limited
Indigo Diagnostics Limited
Intelligent Fabric Technologies Holdings
Leeds Industries (UK) Ltd
Mak Health Limited
OBG Holding Limited
Saifee Healthcare Limited
Tate Pharma Ltd
Vita Sun Ltd

February 2016 [8]
Brainpower Group Ltd.
Dynamik Products Ltd
EV Pharma Solutions Ltd
Innov8tor Limited
North Star Healthcare Limited
Opal IP Limited
Swiss Pharma Dynamic Ltd
Wope - Migraine Ltd

March 2016 [12]
Apotek Services Ltd
EVC Compounding Ltd
Extruded Pharmaceuticals Ltd
FR Products Limited
Incepta Blackrock Limited
Longwood Medevice Ltd
Luoda UK Limited
Microvisk Technologies International
Onsite Diagnostics Limited
P2-Molteni Pharma Limited
Skincare Innovation Ltd
Wildrush Limited

April 2016 [17]
Amphastar UK Ltd
Avacare Limited
Avicenna Herbal Products Ltd
Cytetech Limited
IQ Pharmatech Limited
Iceni Pharmaceuticals Limited
Invictus R & D Ltd
M Jallow Ltd
Maculeh Ltd
Made in Nature Ltd
Medlabs Europe Ltd
Osgen Pharmaceuticals Limited
Qualasept Holdings Limited
Silver Shell Limited
Teva Pharma Holdings Limited
Trauma Trays Limited
Xeal Pharma Ltd

May 2016 [12]
4soap Limited
Acle Urban Gardens Limited
Antibody Store Limited
Better Call Paul Limited
Boley Nutraceuticals Ltd.
Chaos Businezz Solutions Ltd
Contura Holdings Limited
Hemp Broker Ltd
Musclemantra Ltd
Nonivlok Limited
Pharmagen Direct Limited
Virgo Trade UK Limited

June 2016 [16]
Atlantis Research Limited
Bioavexia Ltd
Care and Wear Collection Ltd
Detraxi Ltd
Dextra Laboratories Limited
HBNatura Ltd
IOLAMD Ltd
PG Pharma Ltd
Petbiocell UK Ltd
Pioneer UK Holdings Limited
Pioneer UK Midco 1 Limited
Pioneer UK Midco 2 Limited
Roma Pharmaceuticals Limited
Salutem Supplements Ltd
Tickletec Limited
Xylomed Pharmaceuticals Ltd

July 2016 [5]
Almisbar Limited
Derma Bathe Limited
Hydranure Ltd
Vision Laboratories Limited
Xersizer Limited

August 2016 [8]
Ardiou Healthcare Ltd
Britanica Medicines & Medical Equipment
Cambridge Innovation Group Ltd
Nelovy Healthcare Ltd
Premax Europe Limited
Resok Healthcare Ltd
Revive Herbal UK Ltd
Salicin Healthcare Limited

September 2016 [8]
Ampha Limited
KKG Consulting Limited
KMX Healthcare Ltd
Medi-Cure Bio Ergonomics Ltd
N9NE Cosmetics Ltd
Rojal Pharm USA Limited
Wellington Unit Limited
Zink Tattoo Care Limited

October 2016 [11]
Blend & Glow Limited
E-Breathe Ltd.
Eezilean International Limited
Heavenly Herb Co Ltd.
Hyperbiotics Corp Ltd
Hyperbiotics PLC
Inspire Flavours Ltd
Miracol Ltd
Nutrasulin Ltd.
Seven Seas Healthcare Limited
VBD Drug Safety Ltd

November 2016 [11]
Beckley Labs Limited
Beckley Research and Innovations Ltd
Dynamic Development Laboratories Co Ltd
Isovitality Nutriceuticals Ltd
More Poland Limited
Nanotherapeutics UK Limited
One Stop 15 Limited
Opiant Pharmaceuticals UK Ltd
PVR Works Ltd
Quality Products 360 Ltd
Sparsanctuary Limited

December 2016 [10]
Adam Project Ltd
Bohemia Pharmaceuticals Ltd.
Curis Life Ltd
Inflazome UK Limited
KR Regulatory Limited
Northumbria Pharma Ltd
Organic Lifecare Ltd.
Plackett Limited
Skinlikes Limited
Vita Animal Health Ltd

January 2017 [12]
Ariera Pharma Limited
Gesco Cosmetics Limited
IQ5 Consultancy Limited
Mirroman Ltd
Nanomed Ltd
Parbold Therapeutics Limited
Re-Vire Limited
Seven Days Vitamin Co Ltd
Tetraphase UK Limited
Urban Homestead London Ltd
Vitabonna Development Limited
Webottle Ltd

February 2017 [20]
Advanced Retention Therapeutics & Research
Alisha GXP QP Consultancy Ltd
Allmarks Products Limited
Animal Herbals Ltd
Blends for Massage Limited
Cherwell Therapeutics Ltd.
Concentrates Warehouse Limited
Global Herbs Holdings Ltd
Great British Bee Co Ltd
Itreatskin Limited
KMCI Services Ltd
Man Oil Co Ltd
Prulab Pharma Ltd
Pure Peace Ltd
Redrose Nutraceuticals Limited
Skin Cell Labs Limited
Spey Limited
Spey Pharma Limited
UK Seven Seas Pharma Limited
Vita Bee Health Ltd

March 2017 [16]
Bamford & Wolfe Ltd
Biteback Products Ltd
CKC Aromatherapy Beauty Products Ltd
Cambridge Advanced Technologies Ltd
Chapar 2016 Ltd
Chapar 2017 Ltd
Corcept Therapeutics UK Ltd
GB Quality Consulting Services Ltd
Gynopharma Ltd
Keybiotech Ltd
Medicleanse Limited
Sage Therapeutics Limited
T-In Medical Limited
Universal Cell Therapeutics Ltd.
Wellness Lab Ltd
Zota Healthcare Limited

The Top UK Pharmaceutical Manufacturers

April 2017 [5]
BtechLaboratories (UK) Ltd.
Green Groot Limited
JSN Chemicals Limited
Mudd By Alix Ltd.
Wave Life Sciences UK Limited

May 2017 [9]
Algipharma UK Limited
Alps Biosciences Limited
Flavour Maker Limited
Gelu Life Limited
Interaction Chempharm Ltd
Mammoet Cannabis Limited
Nutrapharm Ltd
Think Noo Limited
Your Noo Edge Ltd.

June 2017 [7]
Avanzcare Limited
Connoisseur Clouds Ltd
Elixir Pure UK Limited
Ibeautify Ltd
Intapharm Laboratories Limited
Ithonpharma Ltd
Solent Oral Care Ltd

July 2017 [17]
Alcott Healthcare Limited
Allen & Jain Industries Ltd
Apisera Ltd
Avista Holding Co., Ltd.
Cancer Genetics Ltd
Castpol Ltd
DSP Beauty Development Ltd
Gimews Welding Limited
Integrated Pharma Services (UK) Ltd
Microbiome Technologies Ltd
Nature + Nurture Limited
Nutridote Ltd
Pharmacy Business Consultancy Ltd
Selepharm Ltd
Shellmarks Limited
Viatem Limited
Yic Bio Ltd.

August 2017 [17]
1nhaler Ltd
Ace Interventional Medical Ltd
Clarke Pharma Consulting Ltd
Coast Science UK Limited
Enn-Muk Limited
Glycanova UK Limited
Lift Health Limited
Maco Edge Limited
Marigold Projects Jamaica Ltd
Medical Ethics UK Limited
N2SA Limited
Oncoparp Ltd
Q Health Direct Ltd
Revive Us Limited
Shekinah Health Consultancy Ltd
Speakers at The Limits Ltd.
Telix Life Sciences (UK) Ltd

September 2017 [11]
Dach Cosmeceutics Limited
Edinburgh Nano Limited
Edinburgh Nanotechnology Ltd
Fendall's Ltd.
Materia Prima Ltd
Muamko Uzuri Limited
Royce Health Sciences Ltd
SAS Pharma Limited
Sarepta International UK Ltd.
TTS Manufacturing Limited
Tithonus Ltd

October 2017 [14]
Amarox Limited
Herbal Food Life Limited
Jai Clinical Services Limited
Linnaeus Herbals Limited
Lothian Laboratories Ltd
Newmed Consultancy Limited
Norma Chemicals (U K) Ltd
Panaomics Limited
Pellis Care Limited
Pharmakrysto Ltd
Recassa Limited
Rucals Ltd
United Pharma Group Limited
Wilsons Pharma Limited

November 2017 [23]
11084049 Ltd
A Q V S Limited
A Shroom with a View Ltd
Berhael Trading Limited
Bio & Pharma Ltd.
Bodeli Consultants Limited
Gary Boon Ltd
Boost Hair Limited
Celex Oncology Innovations Ltd
Cornish Lavender Limited
Dil More Remedies UK Ltd
Ether Cosmetics Ltd
Evida Ltd
Florence Health & Beauty Ltd
GM Biopharma Ltd
Higgs Pharma Private Limited
Langeland Ltd
Lipcote & Co Limited
Lux Viridis Services Ltd
Mayuveda R & D Limited
Rosalique Skincare Limited
Sonifar Pharma Expert Limited
Thexo Pharmacial Limited

December 2017 [10]
Abaxon Biologics Ltd
Accliff Ltd
Aptitud Pharma Ltd
Exactmer Limited
Ganges Thames Pharmaceuticals & Chemicals
Kohilam Limited
Nano and Nature Pharma Ltd
RSH QP Services Limited
Simcere UK Limited
Vaccine Manufacturing and Innovation Centre UK

January 2018 [15]
Apotheke San Biagio SRL Ltd
Brown Exclusive (Worldwide) Ltd
CBD Pharma Ltd
Huayawei Biomedical Co Ltd
Invizius Limited
Lea Pharma Limited
Lukas Lab Limited
Man Pharma Limited
Marine Labs Limited
Mayfair Ventures Management Ltd
SH Snakes UK Ltd.
Solarius UK & Overseas Limited
Universal Generics Limited
Vitactive Limited
Vivi Yeah Limited

February 2018 [21]
Acme UK Inc Limited
Canna Care Limited
Evopharm Limited
FV Supplement Ltd
Festus Olatoye & Onyekachi Uka London
Gitflex Ltd
Glacier Nutrition Ltd
Global Healthcare Innovations Ltd
Health Marque Ltd
Hedgarth Ltd
Hermes Pharma Limited
Homicon Prime International Ltd
Jasmine.Touch Ltd
Kinerva Ltd
Mineral Pharma Limited
Ohemaa's Skincare Ltd.
Pine Technologies Limited
Protezione Herbals PVT Ltd
Rescued By Nature Limited
Retrogrow Limited
Thread and Co UK Limited

March 2018 [21]
Abfero Limited
Bioactive Health Ltd
Biolyse Pharma Europe Limited
Crane Bag Limited
Euroclinical Ltd
FPL - Formulating Partnership Ltd
Fresenius Kabi DG Limited
Healthbiotics Ltd
Hexa-Halers Ltd
Horizon Medical Supplies UK Ltd
Kentish Soap Co Ltd
Maia Pharma Ltd
Nocov Ltd
Pharmazy Limited
Quest Pharm Limited
Sinduram Healthcare International Ltd
Synergy Pharma Consultancy Ltd
Uro Innovations Limited
Virtual Reaction Limited
Wark Services Limited
Xinax Ltd

April 2018 [31]
S Adu Ltd
Afro Hair and Beauty International
Aid Pharma Limited
Amroz Pharm Limited
Ark Technologies Ltd
Avix Pharmaceuticals Limited
Boothmasked Ltd
CBDHealthcare Ltd
Cannacureyou Ltd
Chembinoid Pharma Limited
Cocodentax Ltd
EN RUS Group Limited
Ekom Pharma Ltd
Fortingall Advanced Therapeutics Ltd.
Fortingall Therapeutics International
Hydro Fresh Ltd
Kew Organic Limited
Keziah Ltd
Little Green Beehive Ltd
Noohra Limited
Peptone Ltd
Pharmaco Group Limited
Primetonic Ltd
Quality Skincare Ltd
RMW Laboratories Limited
Retrobot Ltd
Rowblast Ltd
Sic Services Ltd
UK Steriles Ltd
Ultrasound Enterprises Limited
World Technologies for Long Life CN.

May 2018 [22]
Alta Flora Ltd
Aucure Medical Technologies Ltd
Balmy Fox Ltd
Blackpool Medicines Limited
Booteatox Limited
Brewtaal Ltd
Elanco UK AH Limited
Fluss Limited
Hadley Rose Limited
Health Remit Limited
Heavenly Group of Co Ltd
Hemma Healthcare Teronta Ltd
Herbal Republic Ltd
Jini Ltd
Letdrop Ltd
Pharma Device Delivery Limited
Private Trichology Clinic Ltd
Recipharm HC Limited
Shabelle Ltd
Skin Euphoria Limited
Softgel Solutions Ltd
Unit 6 Gateway Limited

June 2018 [16]
Bioceuticals Group Ltd
Cannabidiol UK Ltd
Fairywire Ltd
Farasha-Cosmetics Ltd
Invos Ltd
Jellyhills Ltd
Millicent Pharma (NI) Limited
One Second Supplements Limited
Pharma Maiden Ltd
Prime Medical Equipment Ltd
Promtain Ltd
Redlight Exchange Ltd
Simkar Healthcare Ltd

Soft Coughs Ltd
Stem Cell Technology Ltd
Synnlon Limited

July 2018 [33]
2tonk Limited
Alvinsons Medical (PVT) Ltd
Bacvacc Ltd
Bandfiled Ltd
Biodan Ltd.
Biotanical Ltd
Bisurall Ltd
Bulgarian Healthy Products Ltd
Cingem Ltd
Forbleries Ltd
Genotact Ltd
Glasport Bio UK Limited
Glasstomato Ltd
Limitless Med Ltd
Livbio Limited
Mantiza Ltd
Milepitch Ltd
Milewackers Ltd
Nuradec Ltd
Offit Nootropics Limited
Pentail Enzymes Limited
Pharmacann Ltd
Pharmcom Trading Limited
Pharmlife Industry Ltd
N Popov Ltd
Prothea-X Limited
Purple Healthcare Limited
Tribe Therapeutics UK Limited
Unir Unlimited
Vedabio Health Ltd
Vitaact Ltd
Westway Health UK Limited
Zomi Ltd

August 2018 [17]
Al Razi Pharma UK Ltd
Auramedicann Ltd
Bam Balm Ltd
Britpharma UK Limited
Dermaperfetca Ltd
Finca Skin Organics Limited
JNRMCL Ltd
Luxury CBD Oils Ltd
Manta - Cognitive Fuels Ltd
Medicann Pharma (UK) Ltd
Miongam Ltd
Naturafam Limited
Primal Core UK Ltd
Rubyquartz Ltd
Seadbincold Ltd
Spectrum Biomedical UK Limited
Triumph Pharma Ltd

September 2018 [15]
A-Rich Nutrition Ltd
Ad Hoque Ltd
Celadon Pharma Ltd
Dr Pradeep Reddy's Laboratories (UK & EU)
E.P.G Pharma Ltd
GMP Manufacturing Ltd
Imphatec Ltd
Jones Balm Limited
MHR Pharmacy Ltd
Madhusudhana Solutions Limited
NKK Investments Limited
PW Green UK II Limited

Pharmach Ltd
RLS Pharma Ltd
St Andrews Botanics Limited

October 2018 [24]
Acarrier Limited
Advanz Pharma (UK) Limited
Alhaddag Phrma Ltd
Aspensnetas Biopharma Ltd
R & R Black Brilliant Ventures PLC
Brosis Ltd
C 3 Innovations Limited
CB Doctor UK Ltd
CBD Biotech Limited
CBPlus Ltd
Dr Russo Cosmetics Limited
Graviti Healthcare Limited
Halligarth Bioadvisors Ltd
JPI Care Limited
Khattak Resolution Ltd
Martini International Ltd
Microfluidx Ltd
Nabros Pharma (UK) Ltd
Pharmau Healthcare Ltd
Rejuvenile Ltd
Savoo Care Limited
St Labs Limited
Tuscania Consulting Limited
Wogue One Limited

November 2018 [22]
Acme Pharmatek Ltd
Alexi Laboratories Ltd
Apobec Discovery Ltd
Aventa International Corporation Ltd
Brazilian Kimberlite Clay Ltd
Covestus Limited
Cutman Ltd
Derma Hair and Body Shop Ltd
Dong Hwa UK Ltd
ESW Healthcare Limited
Erimol Ltd
Kenmare Medical Limited
NKCell Plus PLC
Organic CBD Products Limited
Organic Hemp Oils Limited
Plantgenic Ltd
Reld Tech Ltd
Sanhak Ltd
This Product Ltd
Tomorrow Biotech Ltd
Ukann Limited
iCell Therapeutics Ltd

December 2018 [17]
Appex Ltd
Biocon Pharma UK Limited
CBD Grow Tech Ltd
Cannerald Group Ltd
East West Naturals Limited
Genetis PLC
Geoorganics Limited
IPS International Corporation Ltd
Kiniksa Pharmaceuticals (UK), Ltd.
Lipsy Couture Limited
Noble Green (Essex) Limited
Pharmacare International Ltd
Pro Bono Bio Limited
SK Network Ltd
Sahara Biomedix Ltd
Skinska Pharmaceutica Limited
Unyte Pharma Ltd

The Top UK Pharmaceutical Manufacturers

January 2019 [21]
Celadon Pharmaceuticals Ltd
Clyde Valley Cannaceuticals Ltd
DCMP 8E Cepac Limited
Dark Knight Holdings Limited
Dushey Limited
Farm Bionics Ltd
Hexagon Therapeutics Limited
Hlinka Pharma Ltd
Inkhancement Limited
Kalula Cosmetics Ltd
Maxvac Ltd
Medics Kingdom Limited
Nutramax Ltd
Opix Ltd
Oxford Supramolecular Biotechnology
Pharma Zad Ltd
Purely Health Ltd
Reddy Quality Services Ltd
Seborgo Limited
Sina Pharm Limited
Vitaminiv Franchising Limited

February 2019 [30]
Alphacells Biotechnologies Ltd
Asaya Cosmeceuticals Limited
Batel Limited
CKS Scientific Limited
Comed Healthcare UK Ltd
Confidence Plus Ltd
Dermatek Limited
Dushey Med Limited
Eclipse Pharma Ltd
Essenfuture Ltd
Flourish Products Ltd
Follifix Ltd
Furoid Ltd
GM Globalhealth Ltd
Genomix Ltd
HARC Therapeutics Limited
Impact Pharma Solutions Ltd
Infirst Limited
Invitrohair Ltd
Juno Britain Ltd
Medicaleaf Limited
Medtrack Ltd
Natural Miracles Limited
Pharm Recon Ltd
Quantum Biomed Farms PLC
RSI Chemrep Limited
Ripple MC Pharma Ltd
Sequana LifeSciences Ltd
Synergetic Global Limited
Wenimed Ltd

This page is intentionally left blank

Geographic Distribution by County

Co Antrim [23]
Algal Omega 3 Ltd
Arc Devices (NI) Limited
Beneficial Oils Ltd
Biocolor Limited
Botanica International Limited
E-Breathe Ltd.
Erimol Ltd
Hygieia Medical Ltd
Idrolabs Limited
Inspire Flavours Ltd
Isopath Limited
Jasmine.Touch Ltd
Jenarron Therapeutics Limited
MDI Medical (N.I.) Limited
Millbrook (NI) Limited
Millicent Pharma (NI) Limited
Paradox Omega Oils Ltd
Purce Associates Limited
Roonivoolin Naturals Ltd
Terumo BCT Ltd.
Teva NI Limited
Teva Research Laboratories (NI) Ltd
Webottle Ltd

Co Armagh
Almac Pharma Services Limited
JNRMCL Ltd
This Product Ltd

Co Down
T.G. Eakin Limited
Finca Skin Organics Limited
Hyperion Biotechnology Limited
Norbrook Laboratories Limited

Co Fermanagh
Berhael Trading Limited
Organic CBD Products Limited
Organic Hemp Oils Limited

Co Londonderry
Cast Healthcare Ltd
Hydro Fresh Ltd
Nicobrand Limited

Co Tyrone [5]
CKC Aromatherapy Beauty Products Ltd
Lucy Annabella Ltd
McAleer & Donnelly Pharmacy Ltd
Provita Eurotech Ltd
Univit Ltd

Argyll
Diana Drummond Limited

Argyll & Bute
Lochview Pharm Ltd.

Ayrshire
Jim & Sheila Ltd.
Mammoet Cannabis Limited
Skinlikes Limited
E J Templeton Limited

Clackmannanshire
Ochil Skincare Co Ltd

Dumfries-shire
A & E Plasters and Dressings Ltd
Morar Design Limited

Fife
GB Quality Consulting Services Ltd
Karnot Limited

Lanarkshire [19]
Abaxon Biologics Ltd
Algae Biotechnology Products Ltd
Avista Holding Co., Ltd.
Bescot Healthcare UK Limited
Catalent U.K. Swindon Zydis Ltd
Clyde Valley Cannaceuticals Ltd
Confidence Plus Ltd
Crichton Consultancy Services Ltd
Hydranure Ltd
Opal IP Limited
P2 Healthcare Limited
P2-Molteni Pharma Limited
Scottish Bioenergy Cooperative Ventures
Seadbincold Ltd
Torbet Laboratories Limited
Tuscania Consulting Limited
Welby Healthcare Limited
Winross Limited
Zink Tattoo Care Limited

Peebles-shire
1nhaler Ltd

Perth & Kinross
St Andrews Botanics Limited

Renfrewshire
Kee Logic Limited
G. & M. Procter Limited

Stirlingshire
S.C.A.C. Limited
Symbiosis Pharmaceutical Services

Sutherland
Carmel Herbals Limited

Anglesey
MB UN Ltd

Bedfordshire [15]
Alpex Pharma (UK) Limited
Bam Balm Ltd
Clickhealth Limited
Dermaco Limited
Dermatologix Ltd
East West Naturals Limited
HK Pharma Limited
Insense Limited
Ortholese Limited
Oxford Supramolecular Biotechnology
Regent Pharmaceuticals Limited
Renascience Pharma Limited
Sarissa Biomedical Limited
Seacross Pharmaceuticals Ltd
Sultan & Sons Enterprises Ltd

Berkshire [35]
AMO United Kingdom Limited
AbbVie Australasia Holdings Ltd
Abbott Iberian Investments Ltd
Abbott Vascular Devices (2) Ltd
Alhaddag Phrma Ltd
Boehringer Ingelheim Animal Health UK
Boehringer Ingelheim Limited
CT-You Ltd
CTI Life Sciences Limited
Covestus Limited
Doctor Pharma Manufacturing UK Ltd
Greenova Healthcare UK Ltd.
Health Remit Limited
Hospira Aseptic Services Ltd
Hospira UK Limited
Indivior PLC
Interaction Chempharm Ltd
Intrapharm Laboratories Ltd
Jai Clinical Services Limited
Knoll UK Investments Unlimited
Kowa Pharmaceutical Europe Co Ltd
LRC Products Limited
Langdales Limited
Lipidev Ltd
Man Oil Co Ltd
A. Menarini Diagnostics Ltd
Merial Limited
Nikkiso UK Co., Ltd.
Peckforton Pharmaceuticals Ltd
Mimi Pisano Limited
Pulmeze Limited
Renew Medical UK Limited
Seqirus Vaccines Limited
Sutherland Health Limited
UCB Pharma Limited

Buckinghamshire [34]
Apex Pharmaceuticals Ltd.
Aspar Pharmaceuticals Limited
Badgequo Limited
Blackrock Pharmaceuticals Ltd
Blend & Glow Limited
BtechLaboratories (UK) Ltd.
Chalpharm Consultancy Limited
FPL - Formulating Partnership Ltd
Furoid Ltd
GE Healthcare Limited
GE Healthcare UK Limited
Gelu Life Limited
Hairblends Limited
Heavenly Group of Co Ltd
Herman Claude Ltd
Incepta Blackrock Limited
Intervet UK Production Limited
Invitrohair Ltd
Janssen-Cilag Limited
Mandeville Medicines Limited
Nonivlok Limited
Pharmagen Direct Limited
Prothea-X Limited
RP & MP Investments Limited
Rapidscan Pharma Solutions EU Ltd
S M Consultancy (MK) Limited
Schering-Plough Limited
Sestri (Sales) Limited
Sogeval UK Limited
Sparsanctuary Limited
Spectrum Biomedical UK Limited
TCS Biosciences Limited
Tersan Pharmaceuticals Ltd.
Zeltiq Limited

Cambridgeshire [38]
ADS Biotec Limited
Astrazeneca PLC
Bard Pharmaceuticals Limited
Bateman Quality Associates Ltd
Biocentra Limited
Biologix Laboratories Limited
Cambcol Ltd
Cambridge Advanced Technologies Ltd
Cambridge Collagen Company (UK) Ltd
Cambridge Sensors Ltd
Chirotech Technology Limited
Corpus Nostrum Limited
Cycle Pharmaceuticals Ltd
Daz Solutions Ltd.
Dermatek Limited
Diba Industries Limited
Diep Tran Consultancy Ltd
Ectomedica Limited
Exonate Limited
GW Pharma Limited
Immbio Therapeutics Limited
Inflazome UK Limited
Innova Biosciences Ltd
Ladysystems International Ltd
Napp Pharmaceutical Group Ltd
Napp Pharmaceutical Holdings Ltd
Nia Nova Ltd
Nuradec Ltd
Pellis Care Limited
Pentail Enzymes Limited
Pharmacy Medicines Ltd
Phico Therapeutics Limited
Prometic Pharma SMT Limited
Sahara Biomedix Ltd
Satelec (UK) Limited
Swedish Orphan Biovitrum Ltd
Vernalis (R & D) Limited
Vernalis Development Limited

Cardiganshire
Lewtress Natural Health Ltd
Protherics UK Limited

Carmarthenshire
Biopharm (U.K.) Limited
Micropharm Limited

Cheshire [47]
Aclaris Therapeutics International
Advanced Healthcare Systems Ltd
Advanced Medical Solutions Ltd
Ariera Pharma Limited
Bodeli Consultants Limited
Calea UK Limited
Claris LifeSciences (UK) Ltd
Coast Science UK Limited
Concentrates Warehouse Limited
Crawford Healthcare (R & D) Ltd
Crawford Manufacturing Limited
Custom Powders Limited
Derms Development Limited
Elixir Pure UK Limited
Emerald Kalama Chemical Ltd
Euro Diagnostics Limited
Fresenius Kabi Limited
Fulhold Pharma Limited
IM Herd Ltd
Hexa-Halers Ltd
Hyperion Catalysis EU Limited
IS Pharmaceuticals Limited
Integrated Pharma Services (UK) Ltd
Isola Manufacturing Co.(Wythenshawe)
Kalfar Health Ltd
Life Technologies BPD UK Ltd
Made in Nature Ltd
Maxwellia Ltd
Mexichem Medical HFA Trading Ltd
Natural Miracles Limited
New Cheshire Salt Works Ltd
Petbiocell UK Ltd
Proteintech Europe Limited
Reaxa Limited
Recipharm HC Limited
Selepharm Ltd
Sinclair Pharmaceuticals Ltd
Skin Naturale Ltd
Slo Drinks Limited
Starkwell Validation Limited
Thermo Fisher Scientific Life Holdings
Thompson and Capper Limited
Universal Cell Therapeutics Ltd.
Unyte Pharma Ltd
Vivonics Preclinical Limited
Winchpharma (Consumer Healthcare) Ltd
Zindaclin Limited

Cleveland [8]
3rd Hour Limited
Fernsoft Limited
Fine Contract Research Limited
Fine Organics Limited
Fujifilm Diosynth Biotechnologies UK
Jac+Q Limited
MacLeods Pharma UK Limited
Nicofix (Europe) Limited

Clwyd [8]
C P Pharmaceuticals Limited
Celtic Wellbeing Ltd
Ipsen Biopharm Limited
Pharma Pack Limited
Pinewood Healthcare Limited
Wallis Laboratory Limited
Wallis Licensing Limited
Wockhardt UK Limited

Co Durham [18]
Allfresh Products Limited
Antibody Store Limited
Clarke Pharma Consulting Ltd
Druglab118 Ltd
Edwards' Analytical Limited
Getinge UK Limited
Healing Fusions Ltd
Hyperdrug Pharmaceuticals Ltd
Northumbria Pharma Ltd
Quantum Pharma 2014 Limited
Quantum Pharma Holdings Ltd
Quantum Pharmaceutical Limited
Redrose Manufacturing Limited
Redrose Nutraceuticals Limited
Salicin Healthcare Limited
Skincare Innovation Ltd
Teklab (ML) Ltd
Tregenna Technical Services Ltd

Cornwall [7]
100% Organics Limited
Bio Pure Technology Ltd
Cornish Lavender Limited
Natural Cornish Co Ltd
Organic Herbs for Health Ltd
Organic Herbs for Life Limited
West Pharmaceutical Services Cornwall

Cumbria
Lumibio Ltd
Nutripharm Limited
Veterinary Immunogenics Ltd

Denbighshire
Microvisk Technologies International

Derbyshire [12]
Beacon Pharmaceuticals Limited
Beautanix Limited
Bio-Sync International Limited
Brunel Healthcare Manufacturing Ltd
Castex Products Limited
Cottage Garden Cosmetics and Gifts
Cutman Ltd
Harlequin BPI Ltd
KKG Consulting Limited
Kent Pharmaceuticals Limited
Silver Shell Limited
Weleda (U.K.) Limited

Devon [14]
Accord-UK Ltd
Arrow Generics Limited
Auden McKenzie (Pharma Division) Ltd
Balmy Fox Ltd
Biotanical Ltd
Breath Limited
CBPlus Ltd
Dodi Enterprise Ltd
Isca Biochemicals Limited
Reig Jofre UK Limited
Rosemont Pharmaceuticals Ltd
Trogon Regulatory Ltd
Uro Innovations Limited
Wrafton Laboratories Limited

Dorset [9]
Curis Life Ltd
Derma Bathe Limited
HOCL Limited
Hadley Rose Limited
Kenmare Medical Limited
Pharmaceutical Equipment Ltd
Protiaso Ltd
Salutem Supplements Ltd
Trintech Services Limited

Dyfed
Avicenna Herbal Products Ltd

Essex [46]
A1 Pharmaceuticals Holdings Ltd
Albert Pharma Chemicals Ltd
Alinter Limited
Amneal Pharma UK Holdings Ltd
Aurum Pharmaceuticals Limited
Blends for Massage Limited
CBD Biotech Limited
Cool Herbals Limited
Craintern (UK) Limited
Dermal Laboratories Limited
Diomed Developments Limited
Encapsula Limited
Green House Monitoring Limited
IPS International Corporation Ltd
Kew Health and Beauty Limited
Lukas Lab Limited
M3 Cosmetics Limited
Macarthys Laboratories Limited
Maltron International Limited
Manta - Cognitive Fuels Ltd
Materia Prima Ltd
Medi-Cure Bio Ergonomics Ltd
Merad Pharmaceuticals Limited
My Shea Limited
Neo Laboratories Limited
Noble Green (Essex) Limited
Norma Chemicals (U K) Ltd
Norma Chemicals Limited
Oncoparp Ltd
Pharmacell Medication Systems Ltd
RM Medical Care Ltd
SKN-RG Research & Development Ltd
Savoy Laboratories (International)
Soleaero Limited
Stem Cell Technology Ltd
Swift Dent Engineering Services Ltd
UK Animal Products Limited
UK Healthcare Pharma Limited
Viridian Pharma Limited
Vision Laboratories Limited
Vitaminiv Franchising Limited
Wallace Manufacturing Chemists Ltd
Wallace Pharma Limited
Ward Surgical & Supplies Ltd
Wenimed Ltd
Westech Scientific Instruments Ltd

Flintshire
Chamcotec Ltd
Quay Pharmaceuticals Limited
Xcelonce Limited

Glamorgan [28]
Aeropax International Limited
Algipharma UK Limited
Arcadia Pharma Limited
BBI Solutions OEM Limited
Byrom (South Wales) Limited
Chrome Surgical Ltd.
Cupid Peptide Co Ltd
DTR Medical Limited
Dark Knight Holdings Limited
Dr. Tuhin Dev Skin Care Ltd
KMCI Services Ltd
Medical Ethics UK Limited
Norgine Limited
Ortho-Clinical Diagnostics
PCI Penn UK Holdco Limited
Penn Pharma Group Limited
Penn Pharmaceutical Services Ltd

Pioneer UK Holdings Limited
Pioneer UK Midco 1 Limited
Pioneer UK Midco 2 Limited
Q Health Direct Ltd
Quotient Diagnostics Limited
SAS Pharma Limited
Scipac Limited
Softgel Solutions Ltd
Solarius UK & Overseas Limited
South Wales Specials Limited
Stride-Davies Pharma Limited

Gloucestershire [14]
Aimmune Therapeutics UK Ltd
Biotechflow Ltd
Clothopharma Limited
Cotswold Health Limited
Fendall's Ltd.
Kalms Limited
G.R. Lane Health Products Ltd
Medical Supply Co Ltd
Milton Pharmaceutical Company UK Ltd
Olbas Limited
Sarakan Limited
Supersun Nutrition Limited
Unigreg Worldwide Limited
Xylomed Pharmaceuticals Ltd

Gwent
Bioextractions Wales Limited
Chemvet UK Limited

Gwynedd
Compliance & Validation Solutions Ltd

Hampshire [52]
American Distilling & Mfg Ltd
Aura Fragrances Limited
CKS Scientific Limited
Carefusion U.K. 244 Limited
Crescent API Limited
Crescent Manufacturing Limited
Crescent Pharma Limited
Dach Cosmeceutics Limited
Dista Products Limited
Elanco Animal Vaccines Limited
Elanco Europe Ltd.
Elanco UK AH Limited
Engelpharma UK Limited
Equalbrief Limited
Evida Ltd
First Impressions Denture Centre Ltd
Fresenius Kabi Oncology PLC
GBBC Ltd
Greenfield Pharmaceuticals Ltd
Imphatec Ltd
Ingel Technologies Limited
Jai Pharma Limited
M Jallow Ltd
Eli Lilly (Basingstoke) Ltd
Eli Lilly Group Limited
Eli Lilly Holding Co Ltd
Eli Lilly Holdings Limited
Lilly Industries Limited
Eli Lilly Leasing Limited
Lilly Property Limited
Eli Lilly Property Limited
Lilly Research Centre Limited
Lilly Resources Limited
Eli Lilly Resources Limited

Eli Lilly and Co Ltd
Living Skin Care Limited
New Directions Europe Ltd
Oat Services Limited
Penlan Healthcare Limited
Pharmlife Industry Ltd
Qures Healthcare Limited
Revive Us Limited
SH Snakes UK Ltd.
Sauflon (Manufacturing) Ltd
Selborne Biological Services Ltd
Talley Environmental Care Ltd
Theramit Limited
Vericore Limited
Vita (Europe) Limited
Vita Animal Health Ltd
Vita Bee Health Ltd
Workstead Limited

Herefordshire
Agroceutical Products Ltd
Quest Ingredients Limited
Wren Hygiene Limited

Hertfordshire [66]
Acme UK Inc Limited
Aesica BC Limited
Aesica Formulation Development Ltd
Aesica Holdco Limited
Aesica M1 Limited
Aesica M2 Limited
Aesica Pharmaceuticals Limited
Aesica Queenborough Limited
Aesica Trustee Co Ltd
Ascot Laboratories Limited
Avacare Limited
Mark Aziz Limited
Bespak Europe Limited
Biopharma Laboratories (UK) Ltd
Blistex Limited
Chempro Limited
Chitomerics Limited
Concorde Perfumery and Cosmetics Ltd
Cosmana Limited
Cutera Limited
D.D.D. Limited
Dendron Limited
Dreamskin Health Limited
Eisai Manufacturing Limited
Emerge Biotech Ltd
Fleet Laboratories Limited
Four Pharmaceuticals Limited
Fourrts (UK) Pharmacare Ltd
Generics (U.K.) Limited
Glasstomato Ltd
Hannah V Limited
Hermes Pharma Limited
Intelligent Fabric Technologies Holdings
Joyce Pharmac Services Ltd
KR Regulatory Limited
Lift Health Limited
Linnaeus Herbals Limited
Linosa Limited
Marigold Projects Jamaica Ltd
Masters Pharmaceuticals Ltd
Merck Sharp & Dohme Limited
Nanopharm Limited
Neomedic Limited
Niche Generics Limited
Pfertec Limited
Pfylori Limited

Pharma XP Consulting Ltd
Prulab Pharma Ltd
Rainbow Engineering Services Ltd
Reddy Quality Services Ltd
Retrogrow Limited
Rhodia Pharma Solutions Ltd
Roche Products Limited
Samritz Healthcare Ltd
Simcere UK Limited
Skyrocket Phytopharma (UK) Ltd
Smart Formula Limited
Strides Pharma UK Ltd
H.E. Stringer (Perfurmery) Ltd
Synnlon Limited
Temag Pharma Ltd
Tips & Tricks Ltd
VBD Drug Safety Ltd
Van Vleck and Olivers Limited
Vitane Pharma Limited
Vitra Pharmaceuticals Ltd

Humberside
Epax Pharma UK Ltd

Isle of Wight
Bodywise Limited
Vapour Chef Ltd

Kent [59]
2tonk Limited
Advanced Retention Therapeutics & Research
Ambe Limited
Anatics Life Sciences Limited
Ardilla Technologies UK Ltd
Astagen Therapeutics Limited
Automation Control Expertise Ltd
Bio Provide 18 Ltd
Bio Provide 19 Ltd
Bio Provide 20 Ltd
Bio Provide Ltd
Bio-Health Limited
Birchwood Pharma Ltd
Charis Consult Limited
Church & Dwight UK Limited
Colorcon Limited
Comfort Ventures Limited
EVL Biologicals 23 Ltd
EVL Biologicals Ltd
Ennogen Healthcare Ltd
Ennogen Pharma Ltd
Falls Care Limited
Fine Treatment Limited
Fontridge Pharmaceutical Research and Development
Georganics Ltd
Goat Nutrition Limited
Instrument Research Co Ltd
Intapharm Laboratories Limited
J J Design and Engineering Ltd
Joribunda Limited
Kentish Soap Co Ltd
Kerbina,Limited
Leptrex Ltd.
Mak Health Limited
Maxvac Ltd
Medicaleaf Limited
Medicam Limited
Medicol Limited
Miracol Ltd
N.T. Laboratories Limited

Nagashree Ltd
New Nordic Limited
Noohra Limited
Nutrasulin Ltd.
Opiant Pharmaceuticals UK Ltd
PG Pharma Ltd
Pharm-Assist (Regulatory Services)
Pharmadynamics UK Limited
Positive Diagnostics Ltd
Pure Peace Ltd
Revive Herbal UK Ltd
Salenco Limited
G.D.Searle & Co.Limited
Shekinah Health Consultancy Ltd
Twisbee (UK) Limited
Uni Health Distribution Ltd
Vitame Ltd
Vitaxis International Limited
John Wyeth & Brother Limited

Lancashire [83]
Ace Direct Ltd
Acime UK Limited
Acme Pharmatek Ltd
Active Medical Technology Ltd
Aid Pharma Limited
Apollo Pharma Ltd
As-Tec Chemicals Limited
Atlantis Research Limited
Baby Face Cosmetics Limited
Batchable Enterprises Limited
Bena Cosmetics (UK) Limited
Bio Farma Ltd
Bioceutics UK Ltd
Biofortuna Ltd
Blackburn Distributions Ltd
Blackley 2010 Limited
Blackpool Medicines Limited
Bolton Pharmaceutical Company 100 Ltd
Boothmasked Ltd
CBD Grow Tech Ltd
Casra Consultancy (UK) Limited
Chembinoid Pharma Limited
Delta Diagnostics (UK) Ltd
Dushey Limited
Dushey Med Limited
Eaststone Limited
Enchanted Brave Limited
Ezoogle UK Limited
Pierre Fabre Limited
Fluidx Limited
Geistlich Sons Limited
Genotact Ltd
Gitflex Ltd
Herbal Right UK Limited
Hexagon Therapeutics Limited
Hollins Denture Clinic Limited
Hologic Ltd.
Isovitality Nutriceuticals Ltd
Itreatskin Limited
Jellyhills Ltd
Kaizen Ceramics Ltd
Kensington Pharma Ltd
Lipsy Couture Limited
Lofthouse of Fleetwood Limited
M & A Pharmachem Limited
MHR Pharmacy Ltd
Maxearn Limited
Medical Regulatory Consulting Ltd
Medlock Medical Limited
Miss Derriere Ltd
Molnlycke Health Care Limited

Mr Derriere Ltd
Nutrition Group PLC
Octapharma Limited
PVR Works Ltd
Parbold Therapeutics Limited
Peakdale Chemistry Services Ltd
PharmaYouth Ltd.
Pharmacy Business Consultancy Ltd
Primetonic Ltd
Promtain Ltd
Proveca Limited
Purely Health Ltd
Qiagen Manchester Limited
RPL (UK) Limited
RSR Limited
Recipharm Limited
Reelvision Print Limited
Reem Tanning Co Ltd
Rejuvenile Ltd
Retrobot Ltd
Rowblast Ltd
Rubyquartz Ltd
Seborgo Limited
Shiraz Pharm Limited
Sonifar Pharma Expert Limited
Spear Therapeutics Limited
Summer Healthcare Limited
Suzie Who Limited
Technical Textile Services Ltd
Unit 6 Gateway Limited
Virtual Reaction Limited
Zerenex Molecular Limited

Leicestershire [34]
Ace Interventional Medical Ltd
Almisbar Limited
Aramiss Technology Limited
Aspen Medical Europe Limited
BVM Medical Limited
Biostatus Ltd
Biosuspensions Limited
Biotherics Limited
Caithness Biotechnologies Ltd
Cannabidiol UK Ltd
Charnwood Molecular Limited
EHB Limited
Handiskin Limited
Hewlett Healthcare Limited
Hichrom Limited
Jasan Technical Services Ltd
Jela Pharm Limited
LPC Medical (UK) Limited
Lifeplan Products Limited
Marine Labs Limited
Medical Technologies Limited
Morningside Healthcare Limited
Nova Bio-Pharma Technologies Ltd
Nova Laboratories Limited
Personal Care Packs Limited
Pollenase Limited
Shirley Price Aromatherapy Ltd
RLC Technology Limited
Royce Health Sciences Ltd
Rusco Limited
Sharp Clinical Services (UK) Ltd
Simkar Healthcare Ltd
Trauma Trays Limited
Uvamed Ltd

Lincolnshire [12]
Aromesse Limited
Aura-Soma Products Limited
Boost Hair Limited
Braun International Limited
Green Manufacturing Partners Ltd
Juice Sauz Ltd
F.Maltby & Sons Limited
Parkacre Enterprises Limited
Ripple MC Pharma Ltd
Rosalique Skincare Limited
Salcura Limited
Sinclair Animal and Household Care

London [412]
11084049 Ltd
AB Biotechnology Limited
AVI BioPharma International Ltd
Accliff Ltd
Acorda Therapeutics Limited
Active Cosmethics International Ltd
Adam Project Ltd
Adpharm Limited
S Adu Ltd
Advanz Pharma (UK) Limited
Advanz Pharma Generics (UK) Ltd
Advent Bioservices Ltd
Afro Hair and Beauty International
Akvion Limited
Al Razi Pharma UK Ltd
Alexi Laboratories Ltd
Allen & Jain Industries Ltd
Alta Flora Ltd
Amroz Pharm Limited
Anna-Med (UK) Ltd
Apisera Ltd
Apotek Services Ltd
Apotheke San Biagio SRL Ltd
Appex Ltd
Aptitud Pharma Ltd
Aquabalm Limited
Ardiou Healthcare Ltd
Ark Technologies Ltd
Asaya Cosmeceuticals Limited
Asterisk LifeSciences Ltd
Atlantia UK Ltd
Atnahs Pharma US Limited
Aucure Medical Technologies Ltd
Auralis Limited
Auramedicann Ltd
Avanzcare Limited
Aventa International Corporation Ltd
B.C. Medical Limited
Bach Flower Remedies Limited
Bacvacc Ltd
Penny Badger Limited
Bamford & Wolfe Ltd
Baxalta UK Limited
Beautylab UK Limited
Beckley Labs Limited
Beckley Research and Innovations Ltd
Bio & Pharma Ltd.
Bioceuticals Group Ltd
Biocon Pharma UK Limited
Biocryst UK Limited
Biokemix Worldwide Ltd
Biomimetic Therapeutics Ltd
Bioneb PVT Limited
Bionet Research Limited
Biosynth Europe Limited
R & R Black Brilliant Ventures PLC

Bohemia Pharmaceuticals Ltd.
Booteatox Limited
Brainstorm Cell Therapeutics UK Ltd
Brassard Limited
Brazilian Kimberlite Clay Ltd
Brewtaal Ltd
Britanica Medicines & Medical Equipment
Britpharma UK Limited
Brosis Ltd
CBD Pharma Ltd
Calla Lily Personal Care Ltd
Cambridge Innovation Group Ltd
Cancer Genetics Ltd
Candles UK Ltd
Cannerald Group Ltd
Capa Vision Limited
Captium Limited
Care and Wear Collection Ltd
Celadon Pharma Ltd
Celgene UK Manufacturing (II) Ltd
Celgene UK Manufacturing (III) Ltd
Celgene UK Manufacturing Ltd
Cell Medica Limited
Chaos Businezz Solutions Ltd
Chatfield Pharmaceuticals Ltd
Chela Animal Health Limited
Chelsea Drug & Chemical Co Ltd
Chimerix UK Limited
Cingem Ltd
Clarornell Consulting and Trading Ltd
Clean Beauty Co Limited
Cocodentax Ltd
Comed Healthcare UK Ltd
Contura Holdings Limited
Contura Limited
Corcept Therapeutics UK Ltd
Cox Pharmaceutical Ltd
Cross Chemicals UK Limited
Cross Healthcare Limited
Curx Pharma (UK) Limited
D.D.S.A.Pharmaceuticals Ltd
DCMP 8E Cepac Limited
DSP Beauty Development Ltd
Edward Daniel Limited
Derma Hair and Body Shop Ltd
Dermaperfetca Ltd
Designerx Europe Limited
Detraxi Ltd
Dolphins Limited
Dong Hwa UK Ltd
Donglun Limited
Dr Pradeep Reddy's Laboratories (UK & EU)
Dr Russo Cosmetics Limited
Dr. Max Pharma Limited
Dynamic Development Laboratories Co Ltd
EN RUS Group Limited
Eclipse Pharma Ltd
Ecobrands Limited
Edinburgh Nano Limited
Edinburgh Nanotechnology Ltd
Eezilean International Limited
Egalet Limited
Eleosinc Limited
Essenfuture Ltd
Ether Cosmetics Ltd
Etmo UK Limited
Europharma Limited
Evorin Pharma Limited
Exactmer Limited
FR Products Limited
FV Supplement Ltd
Farasha-Cosmetics Ltd

Farm Bionics Ltd
Farmigea UK Ltd
Fermenta Biotech (UK) Limited
Festus Olatoye & Onyekachi Uka London
Flourish Products Ltd
Fluss Limited
Focus Pharma Holdings Limited
Focus Pharmaceuticals Limited
Follifix Ltd
Fresenius Kabi DG Limited
GM Biopharma Ltd
GM Globalhealth Ltd
Ganges Thames Pharmaceuticals & Chemicals
Genetis PLC
Genomix Ltd
Geoorganics Limited
Geoprep Limited
Geotek Coring Limited
Glasport Bio UK Limited
Gynopharma Ltd
HARC Therapeutics Limited
HAV Vaccines Limited
HBNatura Ltd
HMS Vilgo UK Ltd
Halligarth Bioadvisors Ltd
Hartington Pharma Limited
Hedgarth Ltd
Hemma Healthcare Teronta Ltd
Herbapharmedica Limited
Hermes Pharmaceutical Limited
Hexpress Healthcare Limited
Hikma Pharmaceuticals International
Hikma Pharmaceuticals PLC
Hikma UK Limited
Hikmacure Limited
Hlinka Pharma Ltd
Home Health Limited
Homicon Prime International Ltd
Hope Pharmaceuticals, Ltd.
Hunger Control Limited
Hygitech Limited
IGMA Limited
IOLAMD Ltd
IQ Pharmatech Limited
IQ5 Consultancy Limited
Ibeautify Ltd
Ilody Skincare Ltd
Impact Pharma Solutions Ltd
Incepta Pharma UK Limited
Infirst Healthcare Limited
Infirst Limited
Insmed Limited
Instavit Limited
Insuphar Laboratories Limited
International Technidyne Corporation
Invictus R & D Ltd
Invos Ltd
Iroko Products Limited
Jini Ltd
Jones Balm Limited
Juno Britain Ltd
KMX Healthcare Ltd
Kamada Biopharma Limited
Key Organics Limited
Keybiotech Ltd
Klinge Chemicals Limited
Kohilam Limited
LDN Pharma Limited
LEH Pharma Ltd
Lamicare Health Ltd
Langeland Ltd

The Top UK Pharmaceutical Manufacturers

Lawrance Pharma Limited
Letdrop Ltd
Life on Healthcare Ltd
Liquid Comb Limited
Livbio Limited
Milton Lloyd Limited
London Pharma Capital Limited
London Specialist Pharmacy Ltd
London Surgical Limited
Lux Viridis Services Ltd
MK Ventures Limited
MW Encap (Holdings) Limited
MW Encap Limited
Maco Edge Limited
Macopharma (UK) Limited
Maculeh Ltd
Madhusudhana Solutions Limited
Maia Pharma Ltd
Maklary Ltd
Marlborough Pharmaceuticals Ltd
Max Medical Products Ltd
Mayfair Ventures Management Ltd
Medicann Pharma (UK) Ltd
Medics Kingdom Limited
Medina Corp. Ltd
Medison Pharma Limited
Medlabs Europe Ltd
Medpro Health Limited
Medtrack Ltd
Mendelikabs Europe Limited
Mentholatum Co Ltd
Merck Serono Europe Limited
Mercury Pharma Group Limited
Mercury Pharmaceuticals Ltd
Merrimack Pharmaceuticals U.K. Ltd
Microfluidx Ltd
Microsens Biophage Limited
Microskin PLC
Mirroman Ltd
Moroccan Natural Resources Ltd
Muamko Uzuri Limited
Musclemantra Ltd
MyHairDoctor Ltd
Myoproducts Limited
N2SA Limited
ND Pharma & Biotech Ltd
NKCell Plus PLC
NKK Investments Limited
Nacur Healthcare Ltd
Naia (London) Limited
Nano and Nature Pharma Ltd
Nanomed Ltd
Nanotherapeutics UK Limited
Naturafam Limited
Nelovy Healthcare Ltd
A Nelson & Co Limited
Nelson & Russell Holdings Ltd
Nelsons Aura Limited
New Eleusis Limited
Nnadi's Healthcare and Pharmaceuticals
Nocov Ltd
Noorik Biopharmaceuticals Ltd
Nunataq Limited
Nutra Aid Ltd.
Offit Nootropics Limited
Ohemaa's Skincare Ltd.
Omega Pharma Limited
One Second Supplements Limited
Onipede Clinical Research Ltd
Ono Pharma UK Ltd.
Opix Ltd
Orb Global Ltd

Orbus Therapeutics Ltd
Organic Pharmacy Limited
Osgen Ltd.
Osgen Pharmaceuticals Limited
Osteoporosis Research Ltd
Oxbridge Pharma Limited
PTC Therapeutics, Limited
PTGO Sever UK Limited
PW Green UK II Limited
Pacific Height Limited
Panaomics Limited
Pari Medical Limited
Peptone Ltd
Percuro Medica Ltd
Pharm Recon Ltd
Pharma Future Ltd
Pharma Maiden Ltd
Pharma Zad Ltd
Pharmacare International Ltd
Pharmacenna Ltd
Pharmach Ltd
Pharmaco Group Limited
Pharmacy Warehouse Limited
Pharmazy Limited
Pharmcom Trading Limited
Pine Technologies Limited
Placebex Ltd
Plus Orthopedics (UK) Limited
Point International Limited
N Popov Ltd
Portola Pharma UK Limited
Premax Europe Limited
Primal Core UK Ltd
Prime Medical Equipment Ltd
Primius Lab Limited
Pro Bono Bio Limited
Protezione Herbals PVT Ltd
Quality Products 360 Ltd
Quantum Biomed Farms PLC
Quicksilver Scientific Europe Ltd
RGCC Pharma Limited
RLS Pharma Ltd
RPH Innovations Limited
RSI Chemrep Limited
Ranir (Holdings) Limited
Ranir Limited
Rapid Nutrition PLC
Recassa Limited
Recentia Limited
Redlight Exchange Ltd
Regent Generics Limited
Rescued By Nature Limited
Resok Healthcare Ltd
Resolution Chemicals Limited
Resolution Generics Limited
Rhino Education Ltd
Rojal Pharm USA Limited
Rotapharm Limited
Rotapharm Pharmaceutical Ltd
Russell and Denver Ltd
SK Network Ltd
SKN-RG Ltd
SS Products International Ltd
Sage Therapeutics Limited
Sandine Zartaux Holding Ltd
Sarepta International UK Ltd.
Sentinel Health Limited
Sepal Pharma PLC
Sequana LifeSciences Ltd
Shanghai Neopharm Co., Ltd
Shanmonrie Services Limited
Shellmarks Limited

Shire Pharmaceuticals Limited
Siga Pharmaceuticals (Europe) Ltd
Sina Pharm Limited
Sizwe Limited
Skin Euphoria Limited
Skindoc Formula Limited
Skinnytan UK Limited
Smith & Nephew PLC
Solent Oral Care Ltd
Spey Limited
Spey Pharma Limited
St Labs Limited
Stuckola-Pharma Limited
Summit Veterinary Pharmaceuticals
Surrey Pharma Ltd
Swiss Pharma Dynamic Ltd
Taisho Pharmaceutical (Europe) Ltd
Taylor of London Limited
Technical & General Limited
Telix Life Sciences (UK) Ltd
Tell Products, Limited
Testfield UK Ltd
Tetraphase UK Limited
That Cream Ltd
Therakind Limited
Thexo Pharmacial Limited
Think Noo Limited
Thread and Co UK Limited
Tithonus Ltd
Tomorrow Biotech Ltd
Total Pharmacare Ltd
Tribe Therapeutics UK Limited
Triumph Pharma Ltd
UK Steriles Ltd
Ukann Limited
Unconventional E & P Services Ltd
Unicomm Pro Limited
United Colors of London (UK) Ltd
United Pharma Group Limited
Urban Homestead London Ltd
Vaccine Manufacturing and Innovation Centre UK
Varydose Limited
Virgo Trade UK Limited
Viropharma Limited
Vita Sun Ltd
Vitabiotics Limited
Vitalogic Limited
Vivi Yeah Limited
Wallis Laboratory (Sales) Ltd
Wark Services Limited
Wave Life Sciences UK Limited
Well & Well Pharma UK Ltd
Westway Health UK Limited
Wilsons Pharma Limited
Wogue One Limited
Wope - Migraine Ltd
World Medicine Limited
World Medicine Ophthalmics Ltd
World Medicine Pharmaceutical Ltd
World Technologies for Long Life CN.
Xanadu Valley Limited
Y Consultancy Ltd
Y4U Limited
Yic Bio Ltd.
Your Noo Edge Ltd.
G.H. Zeal Limited
Zomi Ltd
Zota Healthcare Limited
iCell Therapeutics Ltd

Lothian [5]
Age Reversal Europe Ltd.
Connoisseur Clouds Ltd
Lothian Laboratories Ltd
Trecona Limited
Ultrasound Enterprises Limited

Merseyside [24]
AKD Pharma Limited
Abtek (Biologicals) Limited
Allergan Biologics Limited
Ayrton Saunders Limited
Ayrton Saunders and Co Ltd
Bell,Sons & Co.(Druggists) Ltd
Celex Oncology Innovations Ltd
European First Aid Limited
Geryon Pharma Limited
Longwood Medevice Ltd
M D M Healthcare Ltd
Medley Pharma Limited
Microspec Ltd
Miongam Ltd
Mirror 5 Ltd
OBG Holding Limited
Panpharma UK Limited
Pharm E-Cig Ltd
Pharmapac (U.K.) Limited
Pharmaserve (North West) Ltd
Pharmaserve Limited
Pharmasol Limited
Ransom Naturals Limited
Transdermal Technology & Systems (TTS)

Middlesex [74]
AA Zentivus Ltd
AS Pharma Consultancy Limited
Abryl Formulations Ltd
Accord Healthcare Limited
Aim-Straight Limited
Alcott Healthcare Limited
Alps Biosciences Limited
Amarox Limited
Bio-Medical Engineering Ltd
Bristol-Myers Squibb Pharmaceuticals
Brown & Burk UK Limited
Cardiome UK Limited
Chemagain Limited
Cognitive Bioscience Limited
DHTD Limited
Dil More Remedies UK Ltd
EV Pharma Solutions Ltd
Ecohydra Technologies Limited
Ekom Pharma Ltd
Euro Medical Equipment Limited
Europa-Technia Limited
Fernhurst Pharmacy Limited
Finer Feet Ltd
Glaxo Operations UK Limited
GlaxoSmithKline Consumer Healthcare (UK) Trading
Graviti Healthcare Limited
Green Groot Limited
Halewood Chemicals Ltd
Hannah and Hugh Ltd
Hashmats Health Ltd
Huayawei Biomedical Co Ltd
Infinitus Enterprise Limited
Infohealth Laboratories Ltd
Infohealth Limited
Inkhancement Limited
Innov8tor Limited

JPI Care Limited
JSN Chemicals Limited
Ernest Jackson & Co. Limited
Keziah Ltd
Koasta Limited
Laxmi BNS Holdings Limited
Leap Pharma Ltd
MDX Healthcare Ltd
Man Pharma Limited
Medicareplus International Ltd
Medicareplus Limited
Mineral Pharma Limited
Nabros Pharma (UK) Ltd
Nejati Dental Instruments and Supplies (UK)
Nutramax Ltd
Occidem Biotech Limited
Organic Lifecare Ltd.
P.I.E. Pharma Limited
Pharmvit Limited
Piramal Critical Care Limited
RRA Green Cross Limited
Raught Limited
Root2tip Haircare Solutions Ltd
SNS Limited
Savoo Care Limited
Seven Seas Limited
Shabelle Ltd
Shah-British Enterprises Ltd
Sinduram Healthcare International Ltd
Smith Kline & French Laboratories
SmithKline Beecham Limited
E.R.Squibb & Sons Limited
Star Pharmaceuticals Limited
Synergy Pharma Consultancy Ltd
Syri Limited
Universal Business Services UK Ltd
Vedabio Health Ltd
ZVF Pharma Ltd

Midlothian [15]
Abatron Limited
Alba Bioscience Limited
Castpol Ltd
Cellon UK Limited
Cho Consulting Ltd.
Eulysis UK Limited
Fortingall Advanced Therapeutics Ltd.
Fortingall Therapeutics International
Humn Pharmaceuticals (UK) Ltd
Iceni Pharmaceuticals Limited
Invizius Limited
MacFarlan Smith Limited
MacFarlane Martin Ltd
Mediskills Limited
Synergetic Global Limited

Monmouthshire
Luxury CBD Oils Ltd
Natural Dermatology Ltd

Norfolk [14]
Acle Urban Gardens Limited
Avanor Healthcare Ltd
Baxter Healthcare Limited
Breckland International Ltd.
Cambridge Healthcare Supplies 2012
Cambridge Healthcare Supplies Ltd
Chapar 2016 Ltd
Chapar 2017 Ltd
Duffy Assets Ltd
Phetalz Ltd

Porvair PLC
Typharm Developments Limited
Typharm Limited
Veradis Specials Limited

Northamptonshire [15]
Bandfiled Ltd
Bisurall Ltd
Cartell UK Limited
Durja Pharma Limited
Forbleries Ltd
Frontline Trading Limited
Ideal Manufacturing Limited
Mantiza Ltd
Medicus Integrated Medicine Ltd
Milepitch Ltd
Milewackers Ltd
Morningside Pharmaceuticals Ltd
Remedi Medical Holdings Ltd
TLD Sachets Limited
Vitactive Limited

Northumberland [8]
Great Northern Apothecary Co. Ltd
Heavenly Herb Co Ltd.
Nimasol Limited
PCCA (UK) Holdings Limited
PCCA Limited
Prozomix Limited
Sterling Pharma Solutions Ltd
Thistle Soaps Ltd

Nottinghamshire [24]
Albumedix Ltd
BCM Limited
BCM Specials Limited
Biolyse Pharma Europe Limited
Biopharma Stability Testing Laboratory
Brown Exclusive (Worldwide) Ltd
CBDHealthcare Ltd
Catalent UK Supply Chain Ltd
Columbia Laboratories (UK) Ltd
E.P.G Pharma Ltd
Hipra UK and Ireland Limited
M V Locums Limited
Martini International Ltd
Molecular Profiles Ltd
Nutrapharm Ltd
Nuvision Biotherapies Limited
Pharmacann Ltd
Phyto Products Limited
Plackett Limited
Sher Limited
Unir Unlimited
Wellness Lab Ltd
World Max Power Enterprise Ltd
ZO-X Ltd

Oxfordshire [31]
Abfero Limited
Ampha Limited
Apobec Discovery Ltd
Aptuit (Oxford) Limited
Bio-Life International Limited
Bio-Rad AbD Serotec Ltd
Bray Group Limited
C 3 Innovations Limited
Cherwell Therapeutics Ltd.
Circassia Pharmaceuticals PLC
Diagnostic Reagents Limited
Envigo RMS (UK) Limited
GFC Diagnostics Limited
Glacier Nutrition Ltd
Higgs Pharma Private Limited
Koolpak Limited
Lipcote & Co Limited
Matthews & Wilson Limited
Medicleanse Limited
Mento-Neem International Ltd
Nillergen Limited
Optronica Limited
Oxford Biodynamics PLC
Oxford Immunotec Global PLC
Oxford Immunotec Limited
Pharma Device Delivery Limited
Phytacol Limited
Phytovation Limited
Speakers at The Limits Ltd.
Therapi Natural Products Ltd
Virodefense Limited

Pembrokeshire
P & S Nano Limited

Powys
Cellpath USA Limited
Ithonpharma Ltd

Rutland
Rutland Biodynamics Limited

Shropshire
Essential Health Products Ltd

Somerset [29]
Aguettant Limited
Albany Molecular Research Ltd
Amphastar UK Ltd
Ana Maria Serban Ltd
Biomed Supplies Limited
Commercial and Academic Services Ltd
Crane Bag Limited
Dextra Laboratories Limited
Drugsdirect Global Ltd
Elemis Limited
Hyperbiotics Corp Ltd
Hyperbiotics PLC
Incline Therapeutics Europe Ltd.
International Medication Systems (U.K.)
Kiniksa Pharmaceuticals (UK), Ltd.
Lifeshield Limited
Make Skincare Ltd.
Bob Martin (UK) Limited
Medisante Limited
More Poland Limited
N9NE Cosmetics Ltd
NZP UK Limited

PT Direct Limited
Plantgenic Ltd
Pneumoflex E.U. Limited
RMW Laboratories Limited
Roma Pharmaceuticals Limited
Stablepharma Limited
Zogenix Europe Limited

Staffordshire [10]
Aspensnetas Biopharma Ltd
Batel Limited
Centaur Healthcare Limited
Clinigen Group PLC
Cost Saving Solutions Limited
Dynamik Products Ltd
LMP (UK) Limited
Longshawe Packaging Limited
PSR Analytical Services Ltd
Surepharm Services Limited

Suffolk [12]
J.L.Bragg (Ipswich) Limited
Coating Systems (International) Ltd
Genzyme Limited
Grip Enterprises Limited
Herrco Cosmetics Limited
Kalula Cosmetics Ltd
Newmed Consultancy Limited
Pharma QP Solutions Ltd
Prime Test Limited
Thornit Canker Ltd.
Total Pharma Ltd
Wychem Limited

Surrey [72]
A-Rich Nutrition Ltd
ADC Healthcare Limited
AXG Ltd
Alphacells Biotechnologies Ltd
Ardent Pharma Limited
Ayurmedics Clinic Limited
Beegood Enterprises Limited
Bioactive Health Ltd
Bioceuticals Limited
Bioplus Tech Ltd
Boley Nutraceuticals Ltd.
Bulgarian Healthy Products Ltd
CM & D Pharma Limited
Chemidex Pharma Limited
Combe International Limited
Dana's Creations Ltd
Derma Solutions Ltd
Dermapharm Skincare Limited
Dermato Logical Limited
Eco Animal Health Ltd.
Emergent Countermeasures International
Essential Generics Limited
Essential Pharma Limited
Essential Pharmaceuticals Ltd
Fisons Limited
GB QP Services Limited
Healthbiotics Ltd
Hemp Broker Ltd
Herbal Factory Ltd
Integrated Pharmaceutical Services (IPS)
Ipsco Limited
Henri L.Jaccaz & Co. Limited
R Judge Consultancy Ltd
KVK Limited
Kew Organic Limited
Key Empire Resources (UK) Ltd

Lab 21 Healthcare Limited
Lea Pharma Limited
Leeds Industries (UK) Ltd
MC2 Therapeutics Limited
Makjay Pharmaceutical Limited
May & Baker Limited
Maycross Sports Limited
Miltenyi Biotec Limited
NHC Limited
Natural Way Limited
Nextpharma Technologies Holding Ltd
North Star Healthcare Limited
Novartis Grimsby Limited
Novartis Pharmaceuticals UK Ltd
Oriel Therapeutics Limited
Phamar Limited
Pharmaclarity Limited
Polychem Limited
Prep Skincare Products Limited
Protak Scientific Limited
QOL Therapeutics UK Limited
Reld Tech Ltd
Ria Generics Limited
Rimmerdax Limited
Sandoz Limited
Sanofi-Synthelabo Limited
Sic Services Ltd
Snor-Ring Limited
Stegram Pharmaceuticals Ltd
Syner-Med Pharmaceuticals (Kenya)
Toothsmith Limited
UK Seven Seas Pharma Limited
Venture Healthcare Ltd
Vertical Pharma Resources Ltd
Vivalabs Europe Limited
Winston Laboratories Limited

Sussex [50]
21CEC PX Pharm Ltd
A Shroom with a View Ltd
Alisha GXP QP Consultancy Ltd
Allergy Therapeutics (UK) Ltd
Allergy Therapeutics PLC
Animal Herbals Ltd
Avix Pharmaceuticals Limited
Beacon Green Limited
Courtin and Warner Limited
Custom Pharmaceuticals Limited
Cuttlefish Limited
Cytetech Limited
Elena's Nature Collection Ltd
Ethno Botanical Resources Ltd
Euratlantic-Cosmepharm Limited
Euro OTC Pharma UK Limited
Everything for Eczema Limited
Flavour Maker Limited
Global Healthcare Innovations Ltd
Global Herbs Holdings Ltd
Glycanova UK Limited
Hahydra Technologies Ltd
Health + Plus Limited
Health Plus Limited
Horizon Medical Supplies UK Ltd
Indigo Diagnostics Limited
Laboratoire Mergens (UK) Ltd
Limehurst Limited
Lisoma International Limited
Luoda UK Limited
Microbiome Technologies Ltd
Mumma Love Organics Limited
Novo Nordisk Holding Limited
One Stop 15 Limited

Onsite Diagnostics Limited
PLS Microbiology Limited
Pharma Syntech Ltd
Phytoceutical Limited
R D T Technology Limited
RSH QP Services Limited
Skin Defence Limited
Soft Coughs Ltd
St. George Technology Limited
Sussex Biologicals Ltd
T-In Medical Limited
Tickletec Limited
Traditional Pure Potions Ltd
Universal Generics Limited
Wildrush Limited
Woundil Limited

Tyne & Wear [12]
A Q V S Limited
CPT Science Ltd
Clyde Chemist Limited
Gimews Welding Limited
Ipca Laboratories UK Limited
Onyx Scientific Limited
Pegasus Equine Diagnostics Ltd
Pharmakrysto Ltd
Sanhak Ltd
Smart Instruments UK Limited
Tate Pharma Ltd
Tyne Care Limited

Warwickshire [21]
AAH Pharmaceuticals Limited
Afzal Pharma Ltd
Air Liquide Limited
Alliance Medical Molecular Imaging
Alliance Medical Radiopharmacy Ltd
Avisius Research Limited
BHR Pharmaceuticals Limited
Bioreactor Corporation Limited
Biotech Design and Validation Ltd.
Chafred Consultancy Limited
Evopharm Limited
Herbal Food Life Limited
JGPSK Limited
Life Molecular Imaging Limited
Little Green Beehive Ltd
Manx Healthcare Limited
Manx Pharma Ltd
Medical Export Co Ltd
Nutridote Ltd
TTS Manufacturing Limited
Tantillus Synergy Limited

West Midlands [56]
AAA Pharmaceuticals Limited
Ad Hoque Ltd
Allmarks Products Limited
Alvinsons Medical (PVT) Ltd
Amarevida Limited
Ayush Ayurveda Care Limited
Better Call Paul Limited
Bioavexia Ltd
Biodan Ltd.
CB Doctor UK Ltd
Cannacureyou Ltd
S.L.Cassidy Limited
Celadon Pharmaceuticals Ltd
Extruded Pharmaceuticals Ltd
Fontus Health Ltd
Go-Kyo Science Limited

Guerbet Argentina Limited
HFA Healthcare Products Ltd
Health Marque Ltd
Healthcare Consortium Ltd
Hutrade Ltd.
JIT Laboratories Limited
Khattak Resolution Ltd
Kinerva Ltd
Lifetime Products Limited
Limitless Med Ltd
Magna Pharmaceuticals Ltd
Mayfair & Hayes Pharmaceuticals Ltd
Mudd By Alix Ltd.
NSK Locums Limited
PAB Apothecary Ltd
Paxvax Ltd
Pegasus Pharma Limited
Pentonova Limited
Pharmaspec Limited
Purple Healthcare Limited
Quality Skincare Ltd
Quest HC Limited
Quest Healthcare Aseptics Ltd
Quest Healthcare Injectables Ltd
Quest Healthcare Non-Injectables Ltd
Quest Healthcare Solutions Ltd
Quest Pharm Limited
Saifee Healthcare Limited
Shea By Day Ltd
Sterling Pharmaceuticals Ltd
Summan International Limited
Supamed Limited
Synergy Biologics Limited
Synergy Specials Limited
Tawil Co Limited
UK Biopharma Ltd
Vitaact Ltd
Vitabonna Development Limited
Xeal Pharma Ltd
Xinax Ltd

Wiltshire [18]
Alliance Pharmaceuticals Ltd
Biteback Products Ltd
Catalent CTS (Edinburgh) Ltd
Catalent MTI Pharma Solutions Ltd
Catalent Micron Technologies Ltd
Catalent U.K. Swindon Encaps Ltd
Forensic Rescue Limited
Great British Bee Co Ltd
Lincoln Medical Limited
Maelor Laboratories Limited
Microgenetics Limited
Patheon UK Limited
Pharmaxo Pharmacy Services Ltd
Porton Biopharma Limited
Qualasept Holdings Limited
Qualasept Limited
Ventarc Limited
Wasdell Manufacturing Limited

Worcestershire [7]
Apollo Prosthetics Limited
Nature + Nurture Limited
Pete Randle Grinding & Son Ltd
Severn Biotech Limited
Teisen Products Limited
Viatem Limited
Woundcare Limited

Yorkshire [98]
& Stuff Naturally Ltd
2020 Organics Limited
4soap Limited
APS/Berk Limited
AWA Export Limited
Acarrier Limited
Actavis Holdings UK II Limited
Active Cosmetic Ingredients Ltd
Approved Pharma Solutions Ltd
Arch Chemicals Products Ltd
Aroma World Limited
Atlantis Skincare Ltd
Beautiful Splint Company CIC
Bio-Medical Services Limited
Bio-Tech Solutions Limited
Biomedical Nutrition Ltd
Gary Boon Ltd
Bowmed Limited
Brainpower Group Ltd.
Canna Care Limited
Chiropody Express Limited
Cod Beck Blenders Limited
Cool Gell Limited
Cosmarida 2010 Limited
DX Products Limited
Dalkeith Laboratories Limited
Dechra Limited
Dr Reddy's Laboratories (UK) Ltd
Dr. Reddy's Laboratories (EU) Ltd
ESW Healthcare Limited
EVC Compounding Ltd
Emergencypharm Ltd.
Enn-Muk Limited
Essential Nutrition Limited
Euroclinical Ltd
Fairywire Ltd
Ferndale Pharmaceuticals Ltd
Flavour-Tech UK Limited
Florence Health & Beauty Ltd
Flourish Ventures Ltd
G.A.S. Vets (UK) Limited
GMP Manufacturing Ltd
Genus Pharmaceuticals Limited
Gesco Cosmetics Limited
Gley Skincare Limited
Greeco Arab Products Ltd.
Health Innovations (UK) Ltd
Herbal Concepts Limited
Herbal Republic Ltd
Hickson W.A. Chemicals Limited
Indivior EU Limited
Indivior UK Limited
Infection Monitoring and Control Ltd
Inskin Skincare Ltd
International Scientific Supplies
Mayuveda R & D Limited
Millpledge Limited
Muhammad 786 Limited
Nektar Therapeutics UK Limited
Neoceuticals Limited
Norton Healthcare (1998) Ltd
Norton Healthcare Limited
OTC Concepts Limited
Oxford Pharmaceuticals Limited
Parakill Limited
Pharmacy Advisory Services Ltd
Pharmau Healthcare Ltd
Pharmax Limited
Pliva Pharma Limited
Principle Healthcare International
Principle Healthcare Limited

The Top UK Pharmaceutical Manufacturers

Private Trichology Clinic Ltd
RG and Co Limited
Re-Vire Limited
Rena Specials Limited
Rucals Ltd
Sands Fulton Limited
Sedigel Limited
Seven Days Vitamin Co Ltd
Seven Seas Healthcare Limited

Skin Cell Labs Limited
Skinska Pharmaceutica Limited
Stockcare Limited
Swann-Morton (Europe) Limited
Tal Pharma and Chemicals Ltd
Teva Laboratories UK Limited
Teva Pharma Holdings Limited
Teva Pharmaceuticals Limited
Teva UK Limited

Thornton & Ross Limited
Thorpe Laboratories Limited
Vaxaid Ltd.
Vit Supermarket Ltd
Vitrition UK Ltd.
Vivimed Labs Europe Ltd
Wellington Unit Limited
Xersizer Limited
Yorkshire Hygiene Solutions Ltd

This page is intentionally left blank

Company Profiles

& Stuff Naturally Ltd
Incorporated: 13 May 2011
Registered Office: 6 Scarcroft Road, York, YO23 1NB
Major Shareholder: Margaret Ann Hodge
Officers: Margaret Ann Hodge [1952] Director/Therapist

100% Organics Limited
Incorporated: 10 February 2010
Registered Office: Suite 6, Crestregarne, Mawnan Smith, Falmouth, Cornwall, TR11 5JP
Officers: George Patrick Allnutt, Secretary; Marianne Jane Tregoning [1949] Director/Cosmetic Formulator

11084049 Ltd
Incorporated: 27 November 2017
Registered Office: International House, 12 Constance Street, London, E16 2DQ

1nhaler Ltd
Incorporated: 11 August 2017
Registered Office: Upper Whitfield, West Linton, Peebles-shire, EH46 7AY
Shareholders: Lisa Charleston McMyn; Donald Smith
Officers: Lisa Charleston McMyn [1971] Director; Donald Smith [1972] Director/Inventor

2020 Organics Limited
Incorporated: 21 August 2015
Registered Office: 1021f Harrogate Road, Bradford, BD10 0LT
Major Shareholder: Nigel Patrick Silcox
Officers: Nigel Patrick Silcox [1955] Director

21CEC PX Pharm Ltd
Incorporated: 2 June 2003
Net Worth: £12,834 *Total Assets:* £13,583
Registered Office: 45 Oaklands, Westham, Pevensey, E Sussex, BN24 5AW
Major Shareholder: Claire Chan Bleasdale
Officers: Dr Claire Chan Bleasdale [1957] Director

2tonk Limited
Incorporated: 27 July 2018
Registered Office: 95 Silverhurst Drive, Tonbridge, Kent, TN10 3QJ
Shareholders: Ben William Holden; Benjamin Charles Beatty
Officers: Ben William Holden, Secretary; Benjamin Charles Beatty [1995] Director/Chef; Ben William Holden [1991] Director/Chef

3rd Hour Limited
Incorporated: 21 February 2015 *Employees:* 2
Net Worth: £184 *Total Assets:* £10,457
Registered Office: 18 Scarborough Street, Hartlepool, Cleveland, TS24 7DA
Shareholders: Adrian Douglas-Bell; Stephanie Douglas-Bell
Officers: Adrian Douglas-Bell [1959] Director; Stephanie Douglas-Bell [1953] Director

4soap Limited
Incorporated: 16 May 2016
Net Worth: £10 *Total Assets:* £10
Registered Office: 100-102 Beverley Road, Hull, HU3 1YA
Major Shareholder: Stephen Lewis Jones
Officers: Steven Lewis Jones [1967] Director

A & E Plasters and Dressings Ltd
Incorporated: 17 August 2012
Registered Office: 166 Irish Street, Dumfries, DG1 2NJ
Major Shareholder: John David Murray
Officers: John David Murray [1954] Director/Salesman

A Q V S Limited
Incorporated: 27 November 2017
Net Worth: £42,030 *Total Assets:* £56,170
Registered Office: Town Hall Chambers, High Street East, Wallsend, Tyne & Wear, NE28 7AT
Major Shareholder: Ian Malcolm Rawlinson
Officers: Ian Malcolm Rawlinson [1951] Director/Qualification Engineer

A Shroom with a View Ltd
Incorporated: 29 November 2017
Registered Office: 13 Stanford Avenue, Brighton, BN1 6AD
Major Shareholder: Thomas Crane
Officers: Thomas Crane [1991] Director/Researcher

A-Rich Nutrition Ltd
Incorporated: 26 September 2018
Registered Office: Suite 307, 226 High Street, Croydon, Surrey, CR9 1DF
Major Shareholder: Alicia Tomora Amylinda Richmond
Officers: Alicia Tomora Amylinda Richmond [1989] Director

A1 Pharmaceuticals Holdings Limited
Incorporated: 30 April 2013 *Employees:* 37
Net Worth: £14,493,644 *Total Assets:* £20,243,268
Registered Office: Unit 20 & 21 Easter Industrial Park, Ferry Lane South, Rainham, Essex, RM13 9BP
Officers: Carmen Lewis [1965] Director/Secretary Administrator; Gary Stephen Lewis [1960] Director/Pharmacist

AA Zentivus Ltd
Incorporated: 28 January 2014 *Employees:* 1
Net Worth Deficit: £21,589 *Total Assets:* £400
Registered Office: 327 Rayners Lane, Pinner, Middlesex, HA5 5EH
Shareholders: Munish Gadhri; Ajay Sharma
Officers: Dr Munish Gadhri [1978] Director/Dentist; Ajay Sharma [1978] Director

AAA Pharmaceuticals Limited
Incorporated: 1 August 2012
Registered Office: 113-115 Anderton Park Road, Birmingham, B13 9DQ
Officers: Ravinder Singh Phull [1962] Director

AAH Pharmaceuticals Limited
Incorporated: 27 July 1912 *Employees:* 2,989
Net Worth: £203,798,000 *Total Assets:* £999,052,032
Registered Office: Sapphire Court, Walsgrave Triangle, Coventry, Warwicks, CV2 2TX
Parent: Admenta Holdings Limited
Officers: Nichola Louise Legg, Secretary; Toby Matthew Anderson [1973] Director; Marcus Hilger [1977] Finance Director [German]; Catherine McDermott [1968] Operations Director; Nigel Swift [1966] Marketing & Sales Director

AB Biotechnology Limited
Incorporated: 20 December 2012 *Employees:* 26
Net Worth: £1,569,920 *Total Assets:* £3,102,728
Registered Office: c/o Brown Rudnick, 8 Clifford Street, London, W1S 2LQ
Major Shareholder: Irina Epshteyn
Officers: Illia Pavlovskyi [1971] Director [Ukrainian]; Serge Scotto [1954] Director [French]

The Top UK Pharmaceutical Manufacturers

Abatron Limited
Incorporated: 15 May 1979
Net Worth: £79,463 *Total Assets:* £118,186
Registered Office: 4th Floor, 115 George Street, Edinburgh, EH2 4JN
Officers: John Graham Goldsworth, Secretary; John Graham Goldsworth [1929] Director/Lawyer; Richard John McMorran [1949] Director/Accountant

Abaxon Biologics Ltd
Incorporated: 11 December 2017
Registered Office: 8 Hillfield Drive, Glasgow, G77 6GD
Parent: Axon Healthcare Investments
Officers: Dr Govindsinh Chavada [1978] Director/Doctor

Abbott Iberian Investments Limited
Incorporated: 10 November 2009
Registered Office: Vanwall Business Park, Vanwall Road, Maidenhead, Berks, SL6 4XE
Shareholders: Abbott Laboratories Inc.; Abbott Laboratories Inc.
Officers: Kevan Gogay, Secretary; Neil Harris [1974] Director/General Manager; Georgios Mountrichas [1977] Director/General Manager [Greek]; Brian Yoor [1969] Director/Business Executive [American]

Abbott Vascular Devices (2) Limited
Incorporated: 16 October 2001
Net Worth Deficit: £740,000 *Total Assets:* £1,014,000
Registered Office: Abbott House, Vanwall Business Park, Vanwall Road, Maidenhead, Berks, SL6 4XE
Parent: Abbott Vascular Devices Ltd
Officers: Kevan Gogay, Secretary; Neil Harris [1974] Director/General Manager; Brian Yoor [1969] Director/Business Executive [American]

AbbVie Australasia Holdings Limited
Incorporated: 19 November 2001
Net Worth: £15,267,000 *Total Assets:* £15,283,000
Registered Office: AbbVie House, Vanwall Business Park, Vanwall Road, Maidenhead, Berks, SL6 4UB
Parent: AbbVie Ltd
Officers: Kyle Poots, Secretary; Jerome Stephane Bouyer [1969] Director/Business Executive [French]; William Joseph Chase [1967] Director/Chief Financial Officer [American]; Gwenan Mair White [1969] UK Director of Communications

Abfero Limited
Incorporated: 14 March 2018
Registered Office: Longwall Venture Partners, Quad One, Becquerel Avenue, Harwell, Didcot, Oxon, OX11 0RA
Parent: Abfero Pharmaceuticals, Inc
Officers: Steven Keith Burke [1960] Director/Physician [American/Irish]; Thomas Xavier Neenan [1958] Director/Chemist [American/Irish]

Abryl Formulations Ltd
Incorporated: 27 January 2015
Net Worth: £155,140 *Total Assets:* £1,106,677
Registered Office: Waters Meet, Willow Avenue, Denham, Uxbridge, Middlesex, UB9 4AF
Shareholder: Vijay Kumar
Officers: Vijay Kumar [1972] Director [Indian]

Abtek (Biologicals) Limited
Incorporated: 2 September 1981 *Employees:* 9
Net Worth: £123,227 *Total Assets:* £273,075
Registered Office: 145 Edge Lane, Edge Hill, Liverpool, L7 2PG
Shareholders: Robert Turner; Stuart Charles Turner
Officers: Jean Margaret Turner, Secretary; Robert Turner [1940] Director/Chemist; Stuart Charles Turner [1972] Technical Director

Acarrier Limited
Incorporated: 22 October 2018
Registered Office: 57 Market Street, Thornton, Bradford, BD13 3EN
Major Shareholder: Almas Khawar Ahmed
Officers: Dr Almas Khawar Ahmed [1986] Director/Pharmaceuticals

Accliff Ltd
Incorporated: 12 December 2017
Registered Office: Suite 29, 334 Kennington Lane, Vauxhall, London, SE11 5HY
Officers: Gareth Nailor [1985] Director

Accord Healthcare Limited
Incorporated: 21 November 2002 *Employees:* 1,197
Net Worth: £7,378,000 *Total Assets:* £891,985,984
Registered Office: Sage House, 319 Pinner Road, North Harrow, Middlesex, HA1 4HF
Officers: Pradeep Bhagia, Secretary; Dr James Burt [1974] Director/Chemical Engineer; Binish Hasmukhbhai Chudgar [1963] Director/Businessman [Indian]; Anthony Leonard Cordrey [1961] Senior Director - EU Strategic Operations; Lord Jitesh Kishorekumar Gadhia [1970] Director; John Geoffrey Goddard [1951] Director; Roger Marquilles Escola [1975] Director/Head of Legal Affairs - Europe [Spanish]; Nilesh Parmar [1968] Director; Phillip Semmens [1971] Director/Vice President Hospitals - Europe

Accord-UK Ltd
Incorporated: 30 December 1903 *Employees:* 658
Previous: Actavis UK Limited
Net Worth: £99,572,000 *Total Assets:* £206,463,008
Registered Office: Whiddon Valley, Barnstaple, Devon, EX32 8NS
Parent: Accord Healthcare Limited
Officers: Nadine Jakes, Finance Director [German]; Dr James Burt [1974] Director/Chemical Engineer; Nadine Jakes [1975] Executive Director Finance & IT [German]; Sandra Lee [1963] Managing Director Operations; Priscilla Anne Lethbridge [1969] HR Director; Jonathan Wilson [1972] Managing Director UK

Ace Direct Ltd
Incorporated: 2 April 2012 *Employees:* 7
Net Worth: £21,808 *Total Assets:* £641,579
Registered Office: 245 Entwisle Road, Rochdale, Lancs, OL16 2LJ
Shareholders: Mazahar Hussain; Rakhmat Jan
Officers: Mazahar Hussain [1972] Director/Pharmacist

Ace Interventional Medical Ltd
Incorporated: 17 August 2017
Registered Office: Bvm House, Trinity Lane, Hinckley, Leics, LE10 0BL
Officers: Chetna Harsad Chikhlia [1985] Director; Emily Catherine White [1990] Director

Acime UK Limited
Incorporated: 3 December 2012
Net Worth Deficit: £65,738 *Total Assets:* £237,739
Registered Office: 3rd Floor, 82 King Street, Manchester, M2 4WQ
Major Shareholder: Herve Dubly
Officers: Herve Dubly [1964] Director [French]; Matthew John Duncan [1972] Director/UK Sales Manager

Aclaris Therapeutics International Limited
Incorporated: 17 July 2015
Net Worth Deficit: £742,998 *Total Assets:* £160,258
Registered Office: 3rd Floor, 1 Ashley Road, Altrincham, Cheshire, WA14 2DT
Parent: Aclaris Therapeutics, Inc.
Officers: Kamil Ali-Jackson, Secretary; Frank Ruffo [1965] Director [American]; Neal Walker [1970] Director/President & CEO [American]

Acle Urban Gardens Limited
Incorporated: 12 May 2016
Net Worth: £4,047 *Total Assets:* £13,611
Registered Office: Unit 6 Damgate Lane, Acle, Norwich, NR13 3DJ
Major Shareholder: Nicholas Curtis
Officers: Susan Allison, Secretary; Nicholas Curtis [1984] Director/Electrician; Aaron Junior Pack [1992] Director

Acme Pharmatek Ltd
Incorporated: 21 November 2018
Registered Office: 6 Greenfield Gardens, Fulwood, Preston, Lancs, PR2 8BL
Major Shareholder: Asim Ismail Bawa
Officers: Ahsan Bawa [1985] Director; Asim Ismail Bawa [1957] Director [Pakistani]

Acme UK Inc Limited
Incorporated: 23 February 2018
Registered Office: Churchill House, 136-137 Stirling Way, Borehamwood, Herts, WD6 2HP
Major Shareholder: Rohit Nitin Sharma
Officers: Rohit Nitin Sharma [1982] Director [Indian]

Acorda Therapeutics Limited
Incorporated: 3 March 2009
Registered Office: Lower Ground Floor, One George Yard, London, EC3V 9DF
Parent: Acorda Therapeutics Inc
Officers: Ron Cohen [1956] Director/President & CEO [American]; Jane Wasman [1956] Director/Lawyer [American]

Actavis Holdings UK II Limited
Incorporated: 28 April 1998
Net Worth: £316,351,008 *Total Assets:* £603,851,008
Registered Office: Ridings Point, Whistler Drive, Castleford, W Yorks, WF10 5HX
Parent: Actavis Holdings UK Ltd
Officers: Dean Michael Cooper [1972] Director/Chartered Accountant; Kim Innes [1968] Director/General Manager

Active Cosmethics International Limited
Incorporated: 3 November 1998
Net Worth: £11,672 *Total Assets:* £31,055
Registered Office: 64 Baker Street, London, W1U 7GB
Officers: Jean Louis Michel Bisson [1950] Director [French]

Active Cosmetic Ingredients Ltd
Incorporated: 15 March 2011
Net Worth: £11,763 *Total Assets:* £35,900
Registered Office: 7 Fox Close, Emley, Huddersfield, W Yorks, HD8 9SH
Officers: Jacqueline Nichols, Secretary; Christopher James Nichols [1952] Director; Jacqueline Nichols [1956] Director/Housewife

Active Medical Technology Limited
Incorporated: 26 July 1996
Previous: Active Media Technology Limited
Net Worth Deficit: £7,343 *Total Assets:* £27,302
Registered Office: 365 Atherton Road, Hindley Green, Wigan, Lancs, WN2 3XD
Major Shareholder: Paul Boulton
Officers: Paul Boulton, Secretary/Director; Paul Boulton [1959] Director

Ad Hoque Ltd
Incorporated: 5 September 2018
Registered Office: 316 Farm Street, Birmingham, B19 2UF
Major Shareholder: Radhwan Hoque
Officers: Radhwan Hoque [1993] Sales Director

Adam Project Ltd
Incorporated: 15 December 2016
Registered Office: 20-22 Wenlock Road, London, N1 7GU
Officers: Mario Fontana [1988] Director [Italian]

ADC Healthcare Limited
Incorporated: 10 July 2015
Net Worth: £1,532 *Total Assets:* £5,019
Registered Office: 20 Hamilton Way, Wallington, Surrey, SM6 9NJ
Major Shareholder: Kazi Sharmin Nahar
Officers: Kazi Sharmin Nahar [1979] Director/Manager [Bangladeshi]; Dr Khondaker Mirazur Rahman [1977] Director/Teaching

Adpharm Limited
Incorporated: 1 March 2013
Net Worth: £3,860 *Total Assets:* £64,542
Registered Office: First Floor, Roxburghe House, 273-287 Regent Street, London, W1B 2HA
Shareholders: Ivan Berkes; Jacqueline Berkes
Officers: Ivan Berkes [1968] Director/Strategy Consultant [Slovak]

ADS Biotec Limited
Incorporated: 1 October 1996 *Employees:* 15
Previous: Transgenomic Limited
Net Worth: £904,091 *Total Assets:* £2,154,967
Registered Office: 22 Station Road, Cambridge, CB1 2JD
Officers: Susan Elizabeth Bowie, Secretary; Susan Elizabeth Bowie [1971] Director/Financial Controller; Vijay Dube [1958] Director/Engineer [Canadian]; Tsutomu Kojima [1955] Director/Management [Japanese]

S Adu Ltd
Incorporated: 4 April 2018
Registered Office: 38 Crestway, London, SW15 5BY
Major Shareholder: Stephanie Adu
Officers: Stephanie Adu [1992] Director/Pharmacist

Advanced Healthcare Systems Limited
Incorporated: 15 May 1998
Registered Office: Premier Park, 33 Road One, Winsford Industrial Estate, Winsford, Cheshire, CW7 3RT
Parent: Advanced Medical Solutions Limited
Officers: Edward Johnson, Secretary; Edward Johnson [1972] Director/Chief Financial Officer; Christopher Meredith [1966] Director/Chief Executive Officer

Advanced Medical Solutions Limited
Incorporated: 29 November 1991 *Employees:* 257
Net Worth: £28,861,000 *Total Assets:* £32,903,000
Registered Office: Premier Park, 33 Road One, Winsford Industrial Estate, Winsford, Cheshire, CW7 3RT
Parent: Advanced Medical Solutions Group PLC
Officers: Edward Johnson, Secretary; Edward Johnson [1972] Director/Chief Financial Officer; Christopher Meredith [1966] Chief Executive Director

Advanced Retention Therapeutics & Research Ltd
Incorporated: 23 February 2017
Registered Office: 23 Empire Walk, Greenhithe, Kent, DA9 9FU
Major Shareholder: Marpin
Officers: Marpin [1988] Director [Indonesian]

Advanz Pharma (UK) Limited
Incorporated: 11 October 2018
Registered Office: Capital House, 85 King William Street, London, EC4N 7BL
Major Shareholder: Robert James Sully
Officers: Robert James Sully [1972] Director/Lawyer

Advanz Pharma Generics (UK) Limited
Incorporated: 30 October 1992
Previous: Mercury Pharma (Generics) Limited
Net Worth: £1,524,555 *Total Assets:* £16,854,356
Registered Office: Capital House, 85 King William Street, London, EC4N 7BL
Parent: Mercury Pharma Group Limited
Officers: Robert Sully, Secretary; Adeel Ahmad [1973] Director/Chief Financial Officer [Canadian]; Graeme Neville Duncan [1973] Director/Chief Executive Officer; Vikram Laxman Kamath [1977] Director/Vice President Finance and Group Controller [Indian]

Advent Bioservices Ltd
Incorporated: 3 October 2013 *Employees:* 5
Previous: Cognate Bioservices Limited
Net Worth: £719,742 *Total Assets:* £2,983,529
Registered Office: The Atrium, North Stables Market, Camden, London, NW1 8AH
Officers: Linda Fairing Powers [1955] Director/Chairman [American]

Aeropax International Limited
Incorporated: 11 March 1980
Net Worth: £11,006 *Total Assets:* £62,530
Registered Office: Unit 4 Castell Close, Llansamlet, Swansea, SA7 9FH
Major Shareholder: Christopher Stephen Racey
Officers: Christopher Stephen Racey, Secretary; Christopher Stephen Racey [1958] Director; Jacqueline Mary Racey [1954] Director

Aesica BC Limited
Incorporated: 15 July 2011
Net Worth Deficit: £8,300,000 *Total Assets:* £121,700,000
Registered Office: Suite B Breakspear Park, Breakspear Way, Hemel Hempstead, Herts, HP2 4TZ
Parent: Aesica M2 Limited
Officers: Andrew Leonard Jackson, Secretary; Jonathan Martin Glenn [1968] Director; Paul Andrew Hayes [1966] Director

Aesica Formulation Development Limited
Incorporated: 22 December 2005
Net Worth Deficit: £1,614,000 *Total Assets:* £6,617,000
Registered Office: Suite B Breakspear Park, Breakspear Way, Hemel Hempstead, Herts, HP2 4TZ
Parent: Aesica Queenborough Limited
Officers: Andrew Leonard Jackson, Secretary; Dr Manja Hermina Elisabeth Maria Boerman [1966] Director [Dutch]; Jonathan Martin Glenn [1968] Director; Paul Andrew Hayes [1966] Director

Aesica Holdco Limited
Incorporated: 23 August 2011
Net Worth: £9,200,000 *Total Assets:* £12,500,000
Registered Office: Suite B Breakspear Park, Breakspear Way, Hemel Hempstead, Herts, HP2 4TZ
Parent: Consort Medical PLC
Officers: Andrew Leonard Jackson, Secretary; Dr Manja Hermina Elisabeth Maria Boerman [1966] Director [Dutch]; Jonathan Martin Glenn [1968] Director; Paul Andrew Hayes [1966] Director

Aesica M1 Limited
Incorporated: 10 August 2011
Net Worth: £2,300,000 *Total Assets:* £41,200,000
Registered Office: Suite B Breakspear Park, Breakspear Way, Hemel Hempstead, Herts, HP2 4TZ
Parent: Aesica Holdco Limited
Officers: Andrew Leonard Jackson, Secretary; Jonathan Martin Glenn [1968] Director; Paul Andrew Hayes [1966] Director

Aesica M2 Limited
Incorporated: 10 August 2011
Net Worth: £10,400,000 *Total Assets:* £41,200,000
Registered Office: Suite B Breakspear Park, Breakspear Way, Hemel Hempstead, Herts, HP2 4TZ
Parent: Aesica M1 Limited
Officers: Andrew Leonard Jackson, Secretary; Jonathan Martin Glenn [1968] Director; Paul Andrew Hayes [1966] Director

Aesica Pharmaceuticals Limited
Incorporated: 23 July 2004 *Employees:* 191
Net Worth: £133,800,000 *Total Assets:* £246,000,000
Registered Office: Suite B Breakspear Park, Breakspear Way, Hemel Hempstead, Herts, HP2 4TZ
Parent: Aesica BC Limited
Officers: Andrew Leonard Jackson, Secretary; Dr Manja Hermina Elisabeth Maria Boerman [1966] Director [Dutch]; Jonathan Martin Glenn [1968] Director; Paul Andrew Hayes [1966] Director

Aesica Queenborough Limited
Incorporated: 22 August 2007 *Employees:* 457
Net Worth: £9,200,000 *Total Assets:* £56,800,000
Registered Office: Suite B Breakspear Park, Breakspear Way, Hemel Hempstead, Herts, HP2 4TZ
Parent: Aesica Pharmaceuticals Limited
Officers: Andrew Leonard Jackson, Secretary; Dr Manja Hermina Elisabeth Maria Boerman [1966] Director [Dutch]; Jonathan Martin Glenn [1968] Director; Paul Andrew Hayes [1966] Director

Aesica Trustee Company Limited
Incorporated: 8 December 2005
Net Worth Deficit: £37,000 *Total Assets:* £21,000
Registered Office: Suite B Breakspear Park, Breakspear Way, Hemel Hempstead, Herts, HP2 4TZ
Parent: Aesica Pharmaceuticals Limited
Officers: Andrew Leonard Jackson, Secretary; Jonathan Martin Glenn [1968] Director; Paul Andrew Hayes [1966] Director

Afro Hair and Beauty International Limited
Incorporated: 12 April 2018
Registered Office: 3 Greenwich High Road, London, SE10 8JL
Officers: Verna Angela McKenzie, Secretary; Verna Angela McKenzie [1961] Director/Event Organiser; Renford Smith [1952] Director/Electrician

Afzal Pharma Ltd
Incorporated: 17 June 2014
Net Worth: £244 *Total Assets:* £11,556
Registered Office: 19 Loudon Avenue, Coundon, Coventry, Warwicks, CV6 1JJ
Officers: Zahara Afzal [1988] Director/Pharmacist

Age Reversal Europe Ltd.
Incorporated: 10 June 1994
Registered Office: 6a The Glebe, East Saltoun, E Lothian, EH34 5HG
Shareholder: Charles Murdoch Davidson
Officers: Charles Murdoch Davidson, Secretary/Director; Jack McLaughlin [1943] Director/Retired

Agroceutical Products Ltd
Incorporated: 8 February 2012
Net Worth: £159,983 *Total Assets:* £166,026
Registered Office: The Old Stables, Fedwlydan, Glasbury on Wye, Hereford, HR3 5ND
Officers: Stephen Christopher Head, Secretary; Jonathan Denis Beatson-Hird [1960] Director; Stephen Christopher Head [1971] Director/General Manager [Australian]; Sir Roger Spencer Jones [1943] Director; David John Palmer [1942] Director; Kevin Marc Stephens [1966] Director/Manager

Aguettant Limited
Incorporated: 17 November 2003 *Employees:* 10
Net Worth: £2,452,954 *Total Assets:* £3,517,982
Registered Office: No 1 Farleigh House, Old Weston Road, Flax Bourton, Bristol, BS48 1UR
Officers: Eric Rougemond [1969] Director [French]

Aid Pharma Limited
Incorporated: 18 April 2018
Registered Office: Woodlands, Leigh Meadows, Walton-le-Dale, Preston, Lancs, PR5 4DG
Parent: ABC Pharma Limited
Officers: Alan Barnard, Secretary; Alan Barnard [1968] Director; Dhirendra Somaiya [1953] Director

Aim-Straight Limited
Incorporated: 16 October 2007
Net Worth Deficit: £28,853 *Total Assets:* £141,499
Registered Office: The Debt, South Hill Avenue, Harrow, Middlesex, HA1 3PA
Shareholder: Michael Henry Shelton
Officers: Michael Henry Shelton, Secretary; Peter Colin Eglington Maxwell [1953] Director; Michael Henry Shelton [1951] Director/Solicitor

Aimmune Therapeutics UK Limited
Incorporated: 24 April 2015 *Employees:* 17
Net Worth: £2,325,209 *Total Assets:* £4,700,801
Registered Office: Carrick House, Lypiatt Road, Cheltenham, Glos, GL50 2QJ
Parent: Aimmune Therapeutics Inc.
Officers: Susan Elizabeth Barrowcliffe [1958] Director; Eric Hands Claude Bjerkholt [1959] Director [American]; Douglas Thomas Sheehy [1966] Director/Lawyer [American]

Air Liquide Limited
Incorporated: 25 February 1987 *Employees:* 9
Net Worth: £33,468,000 *Total Assets:* £49,642,000
Registered Office: Station Road, Coleshill, Warwicks, B46 1JY
Parent: Air Liquide UK Limited
Officers: Russell Bateman, Secretary; Remi Characon [1962] Director/Business Executive [French]; John Joseph Condes [1960] Director/General Manager; Philippe Marcel Georges Escudie [1963] Director/Chief Operating Officer [French]; Matthew John Hasnip [1971] Director; Lucia Sainz de Mier [1975] Director [Spanish]

AKD Pharma Limited
Incorporated: 19 April 2007
Net Worth Deficit: £661 *Total Assets:* £25,691
Registered Office: Penny Lane Business Centre, 374 Smithdown Road, Liverpool, L15 5AN
Major Shareholder: Anthony Coyle
Officers: Karen Coyle, Secretary; Anthony Coyle [1960] Director/Pharmaceutical Engineer

Akvion Limited
Incorporated: 9 April 2003
Net Worth Deficit: £198,655 *Total Assets:* £1,872
Registered Office: Floor 6, Quadrant House, 4 Thomas More Square, London, E1W 1YW
Shareholders: Mikhail Lazarev; Dmitry Lazarev
Officers: Dmitry Lazarev [1974] Director [Russian]

Al Razi Pharma UK Ltd
Incorporated: 9 August 2018
Registered Office: 41 Brent House, 50 Wandsworth Road, London, SW8 2FL
Major Shareholder: Talal Almeshal
Officers: Dr Talal Almeshal [1977] Director; Saeed Radad Alzahrani [1959] Director/Chairman [Saudi Arabian]

Alba Bioscience Limited
Incorporated: 18 October 2006 *Employees:* 258
Net Worth: £18,286,036 *Total Assets:* £41,367,804
Registered Office: 5 James Hamilton Way, Milton Bridge, Penicuik, Midlothian, EH26 0BF
Shareholders: U.S. Bank National Association; Quotient Limited
Officers: Roland Wheatley Boyd, Secretary; Roland Wheatley Boyd [1956] Director/Chartered Accountant; Jeremy Alexander Stackawitz [1975] Director/President [American]

Albany Molecular Research Limited
Incorporated: 16 February 2004
Net Worth: £192,670,896 *Total Assets:* £371,956,992
Registered Office: First Floor, 10 Temple Back, Bristol, BS1 6FL
Officers: Christopher Mark Davidson Froggatt [1975] Director/Chartered Accountant; Stacie Phillips [1974] Director/Attorney [American]

Albert Pharma Chemicals Limited
Incorporated: 14 August 2013
Registered Office: 106a Albert Road, Ilford, Essex, IG1 1HT
Shareholder: Omer Habib
Officers: Khadija Habib, Secretary; Fatima Habib [1989] Director [Pakistani]; Khadija Habib [1986] Director; Lubna Habib [1962] Director; Omer Habib [1985] Director

Albumedix Ltd
Incorporated: 29 October 1973 Employees: 96
Previous: Novozymes Biopharma UK Limited
Net Worth: £10,747,000 Total Assets: £16,125,000
Registered Office: Castle Court, 59 Castle Boulevard, Nottingham, NG7 1FD
Major Shareholder: Peter Rosholm
Officers: Andrew Julian Thorpe, Secretary; Joseph Donald Debethizy [1950] Director/Biotechnology Manager [American]; Jonas Skjodt Moller [1986] Director/Chief Operating Officer [Danish]; Peter Rosholm [1965] Director/Chief Executive [Danish]; Andrew Julian Thorpe [1967] Director/Accountant

Alcott Healthcare Limited
Incorporated: 21 July 2017
Registered Office: 34 The Chase, Pinner, Middlesex, HA5 1SN
Shareholders: Gurpreet Singh Arneja; Pavneet Kaur Arneja
Officers: Gurpreet Singh Arneja [1975] Director [Indian]; Pavneet Kaur Arneja [1976] Director [Indian]

Alexi Laboratories Ltd
Incorporated: 27 November 2018
Registered Office: Office 4, 219 Kensington High Street, Kensington, London, W8 6BD
Officers: Charles Borodiansky [1955] Director [French]; Jean Yves Pastinelli [1957] Director [French]

Algae Biotechnology Products Limited
Incorporated: 7 April 2009
Registered Office: 9 Kings Drive, Dullatur, Glasgow, G68 0HS
Major Shareholder: Iain Stewart Anderson Young
Officers: Iain Stewart Anderson Young [1959] Director/Consulting Engineer

Algal Omega 3 Ltd
Incorporated: 21 April 2015 Employees: 23
Net Worth Deficit: £2,540,541 Total Assets: £8,034,759
Registered Office: 2nd Floor, Murray's Exchange, 1 Linfield Road, Belfast, BT12 5DR
Officers: Stephen William Chesnutt [1961] Director; David Winston Chick [1941] Director; Robert James Davis [1948] Director; Timothy Robert Haig [1962] Director [Canadian]; John Carter Risley [1948] Director [Canadian]; Stanley William Leo Spavold [1959] Director [Canadian]

Algipharma UK Limited
Incorporated: 30 May 2017
Registered Office: The Maltings, East Tyndall Street, Cardiff Bay, CF24 5EA
Parent: Algipharma AS
Officers: Arne Dessen [1959] Director/Executive Chairman [Norwegian]; Dr. Philip Desmond Rye [1962] R&D Director

Alhaddag Phrma Ltd
Incorporated: 2 October 2018
Registered Office: Aramex House, Old Bath Road, Colnbrook, Slough, SL3 0NS
Shareholders: Abdullah Wahebi Alwahebi; Naif Wahebi Alwahebi
Officers: Abdullah Wahebi Alwahebi [1985] Director/President [Saudi Arabian]

Alinter Limited
Incorporated: 25 February 1977 Employees: 2
Net Worth: £1,017,028 Total Assets: £1,018,269
Registered Office: Jubilee House, 3 The Drive, Great Warley, Brentwood, Essex, CM13 3FR
Major Shareholder: Mary Joan Tate
Officers: Mary Joan Tate, Secretary/Director; Mary Joan Tate [1945] Director; Simon Robert Geoffrey Tate [1977] Director

Alisha GXP QP Consultancy Ltd
Incorporated: 10 February 2017
Registered Office: 196 Northbourne Road, Eastbourne, E Sussex, BN22 8RU
Officers: Shalini Lakshmidevi Lalta [1985] Director [Dutch]

Allen & Jain Industries Limited
Incorporated: 31 July 2017
Registered Office: 1 Berkeley Square, London, W1J 6EA
Parent: Allen & Jain Consulting
Officers: Benjamin Frederick Allen [1993] Director/Entrepreneur

Allergan Biologics Limited
Incorporated: 24 September 2002 Employees: 130
Previous: Actavis Biologics Limited
Net Worth Deficit: £72,347,000 Total Assets: £30,806,000
Registered Office: 12 Estuary Banks, Speke, Liverpool, L24 8RB
Parent: Eden Biopharma Group Limited
Officers: Patricia Maria Haran, Secretary; Judith Tomkins, Secretary; Crawford David Brown [1962] Director/Scientist

Allergy Therapeutics (UK) Limited
Incorporated: 7 January 1998 Employees: 250
Net Worth Deficit: £87,187,000 Total Assets: £29,611,000
Registered Office: Dominion Way, Worthing, W Sussex, BN14 8SA
Parent: Allergy Therapeuatics Holdings Limited
Officers: Sara Louise Goldsbrough, Secretary; Manuel Llobet [1964] Director [Spanish]; Nicolas Alexander Ulrich Wykeman [1964] Director

Allergy Therapeutics PLC
Incorporated: 1 June 2004 Employees: 499
Net Worth: £23,034,000 Total Assets: £51,016,000
Registered Office: Dominion Way, Worthing, W Sussex, BN14 8SA
Shareholder: Abbott Laboratories
Officers: Sara Louise Goldsbrough, Secretary; Peter Sinclair Jensen [1950] Director; Scott Michael Leinenweber [1971] Director [American]; Manuel Llobet [1965] Director/Chief Executive Officer; Dr Babatunde Adekunle Otulana [1956] Director/Physician [American/Nigerian]; Stephen Rushworth Smith [1953] Director; Nicolas Alexander Ulrich Wykeman [1964] Director

Allfresh Products Limited
Incorporated: 5 December 1986
Net Worth Deficit: £1,822 Total Assets: £889
Registered Office: 2 Carisbrooke Walk, Darlington, Co Durham, DL3 9XW
Shareholder: Cliford Joseph Field
Officers: Clifford Joseph Field [1933] Director/Consultant Engineer

Alliance Medical Molecular Imaging Limited
Incorporated: 22 May 2013
Registered Office: ICENI Centre, Warwick Technology Park, Gallows Hill, Warwick, CV34 6DA
Parent: Alliance Medical Limited
Officers: Howard Alexander David Marsh [1974] Director/Accountant; Petrus Phillippus Van Der Westhuizen [1971] Director/Chief Financial Officer [South African]; Peter John Winchester [1971] Director

Alliance Medical Radiopharmacy Limited
Incorporated: 7 October 2002 Employees: 50
Net Worth: £18,145,000 Total Assets: £25,311,000
Registered Office: ICENI Centre, Warwick Technology Park, Gallows Hill, Warwick, CV34 6DA
Parent: Alliance Medical Limited
Officers: Nicholas James Burley [1968] Director/Chairman; Howard Alexander David Marsh [1974] Director; Petrus Phillippus Van Der Westhuizen [1971] Director/Chief Financial Officer [South African]

Alliance Pharmaceuticals Limited
Incorporated: 16 September 1996 *Employees:* 123
Net Worth: £43,179,000 *Total Assets:* £305,403,008
Registered Office: Avonbridge House, Bath Road, Chippenham, Wilts, SN15 2BB
Parent: Alliance Pharma PLC
Officers: Chrysanthos Theoclis Chrysanthou, Secretary; Peter Jonathan Butterfield [1975] Director; Alexander James Hanbury Duggan [1970] Director/Chief Commercial Officer; Andrew Timothy Franklin [1966] Director; Stephen Martin Kidner [1968] Chief Scientific & Operations Director

Allmarks Products Limited
Incorporated: 3 February 2017
Net Worth: £79,711 *Total Assets:* £108,808
Registered Office: Office 1, Izabella House, 24-26 Regent Place, Birmingham, B1 3NJ
Officers: Raja Rizwan [1977] Director/Sales

Almac Pharma Services Limited
Incorporated: 7 January 2003 *Employees:* 639
Net Worth: £35,823,712 *Total Assets:* £71,079,248
Registered Office: Almac House, 20 Seagoe Industrial Estate, Craigavon, Co Armagh, BT63 5QD
Shareholders: Almac Group (UK) Limited; Almac Group (UK) Limited
Officers: Colin Hayburn, Secretary; Alan David Armstrong [1958] Director; Stephen Campbell [1961] Director; Colin Hayburn [1969] Director; Graeme McBurney [1969] Managing Director; Kevin Stephens [1960] Director

Almisbar Limited
Incorporated: 15 July 2016
Registered Office: 31 High View Close, Leicester, LE4 9LJ
Major Shareholder: Noon Elhag
Officers: Dr Noon Abdelgaffar Hussein Elhag [1977] Director/Doctor [Sudanese]

Alpex Pharma (UK) Limited
Incorporated: 15 February 2007
Registered Office: 25a Becher Close, Renhold, Bedford, MK41 0LP
Officers: Shahbaz Shoja Ardalan [1957] Director [Swiss]; Sara Jane Kettleborough [1989] Director

Alphacells Biotechnologies Limited
Incorporated: 19 February 2019
Registered Office: 6 Kings Road, Sutton, Surrey, SM2 6DG
Shareholders: Rongjun Chen; Meimei Zou
Officers: Dr Rongjun Chen [1976] Director/Senior Lecturer [Chinese]; Meimei Zou [1975] Director of Operations

Alps Biosciences Limited
Incorporated: 4 May 2017
Registered Office: c/o Kaman and Co, 50 Salisbury Road, Hounslow, Middlesex, TW4 6JQ
Major Shareholder: Umang Rajendrakumar Patel
Officers: Umang Rajendrakumar Patel [1991] Director [Indian]

Alta Flora Ltd
Incorporated: 30 May 2018
Registered Office: First Floor, Moray House, 23-31 Great Titchfield Street, London, W1W 7PA
Major Shareholder: Gavin Hilary Sathianathan
Officers: Gavin Hilary Sathianathan [1978] Director

Alvinsons Medical (PVT) Ltd
Incorporated: 17 July 2018
Registered Office: 506 Moseley Road, Birmingham, B12 9AH
Shareholder: Saadia Ashraf
Officers: Saadia Ashraf [1974] Director/Law Student

Amarevida Limited
Incorporated: 31 July 1995 *Employees:* 2
Previous: Stockbridge International Limited
Net Worth: £17 *Total Assets:* £268,698
Registered Office: Kings Chambers, Queens Cross, High Street, Dudley, W Midlands, DY1 1QT
Shareholders: Roger Errol Clive Hawkins; Sally-Anne Hawkins
Officers: Sally-Anne Hawkins, Secretary; Dr Roger Hawkins [1948] Director/Manager Operations

Amarox Limited
Incorporated: 5 October 2017
Registered Office: Congress House, 14 Lyon Road, Harrow, Middlesex, HA1 2EN
Officers: Venkata Narasa Reddy Attunuri [1963] Director [Indian]; Raveendranatha Reddy Kambham [1960] Director [Indian]; Chandramani Panda [1974] Director [Indian]; Manoj Prakash [1963] Director

Ambe Limited
Incorporated: 19 July 1999 *Employees:* 8
Net Worth Deficit: £59,011 *Total Assets:* £272,796
Registered Office: Ambe House, Commerce Way, Edenbridge, Kent, TN8 6ED
Major Shareholder: Sandeep Ashokbhai Patel
Officers: Sandeep Ashokbhai Patel, Secretary; Sandeep Ashokbhai Patel [1974] Director/Chairman

American Distilling & Mfg Limited
Incorporated: 8 November 2007
Registered Office: First Floor, Sterling House, Stroudley Road, Basingstoke, Hants, RG24 8UG
Shareholders: Bryan Edward Jackowitz; Kevin Robert Jackowitz
Officers: Kevin Robert Jackowitz, Secretary/Sales and Marketing Corporate [American]; Bryan Edward Jackowitz [1978] Director/Marketing Corporate Executive [American]; Kevin Robert Jackowitz [1981] Director/Sales and Marketing Corporate [American]

Amneal Pharma UK Holdings Limited
Incorporated: 19 April 2013 *Employees:* 17
Net Worth: £11,836,409 *Total Assets:* £20,340,656
Registered Office: Felsted Business Centre, Cock Green, Felsted, Essex, CM6 3LY
Officers: Chirag Patel [1966] Director/Business Executive [American]

AMO United Kingdom Limited
Incorporated: 24 January 2002 *Employees:* 51
Net Worth: £2,697,000 *Total Assets:* £14,102,000
Registered Office: Pinewood Campus, Nine Mile Ride, Wokingham, Berks, RG40 3EW
Officers: Daniel Penhorwood Gleed, Secretary; Andrew Graham Crossley [1968] Finance Director; Daniel Penhorwood Gleed [1967] Director

Ampha Limited
Incorporated: 23 September 2016 *Employees:* 3
Net Worth: £3,033 *Total Assets:* £189,953
Registered Office: c/o James Cowper Kreston, 2 Chawley Park, Cumnor Hill, Oxford, OX2 9GG
Major Shareholder: Sriram Nadathur
Officers: Sriram Nadathur [1972] Director [Maltese]; Rolf Stahel [1944] Director/Businessman [Swiss]

Amphastar UK Ltd
Incorporated: 22 April 2016 *Employees:* 5
Net Worth: £2,885,593 *Total Assets:* £6,161,978
Registered Office: First Floor, 10 Temple Back, Bristol, BS1 6FL
Officers: Jacob Liawatidewi, Secretary; Jacob Liawatidewi [1974] Director/Senior VP Corp Admin Center [American]; Mary Luo [1949] Director/Chief Operations Officer [American]; William Peters [1967] Director/Chief Financial Officer [American]; Jason Shandell [1974] Director/President [American]; Jack Zhang [1946] Director/Chief Executive Officer [Chinese]

Amroz Pharm Limited
Incorporated: 3 April 2018
Registered Office: 17 Rosemary Avenue, London, N9 8QX
Officers: Roza Imill Zobedey [1992] Director

Ana Maria Serban Ltd
Incorporated: 10 May 2013 *Employees:* 1
Net Worth: £51,044 *Total Assets:* £51,044
Registered Office: 31 Priory Glade, Yeovil, Somerset, BA21 3SQ
Major Shareholder: Ana Maria Mihaela Ros
Officers: Ana Maria Mihaela Ros [1981] Director [Romanian]

Anatics Life Sciences Limited
Incorporated: 11 February 2015
Registered Office: Unit 3 Sextant Park, Neptune Close, Medway City Estate, Rochester, Kent, ME2 4LU
Shareholders: Saumil Kiritkumar Bhatt; Anwar Ali; Arun Jangra
Officers: Anwar Ali [1969] Director; Saumil Kiritkumar Bhatt [1976] Director; Arun Jangra [1972] Director

Animal Herbals Ltd
Incorporated: 16 February 2017
Registered Office: Unit 10 Terminus Road, Chichester, W Sussex, PO19 8TX
Major Shareholder: Stephen Francis Ashdown
Officers: Stephen Francis Ashdown, Secretary; Stephen Francis Ashdown [1960] Managing Director

Anna-Med (UK) Ltd
Incorporated: 7 February 2005 *Employees:* 2
Net Worth: £8,277 *Total Assets:* £79,376
Registered Office: Suite 105, 116 Ballards Lane, London, N3 2DN
Shareholder: Oleksiy Tarnakin
Officers: Dr Oleksiy Tarnakin [1957] Director [Greek]; Tetyana Tarnakina [1954] Director/Medical Doctor [Greek]

Antibody Store Limited
Incorporated: 26 May 2016
Net Worth Deficit: £7,993 *Total Assets:* £3,855
Registered Office: West Newbiggen Farm, Newbiggen Lane, Lanchester, Co Durham, DH7 0RF
Major Shareholder: D J Schol
Officers: Dick Joanske Schol [1954] Director/Biochemist [Dutch]

Apex Pharmaceuticals Ltd.
Incorporated: 6 September 2002
Registered Office: c/o Wilkins Kennedy LLP, Anglo House, Bell Lane Office Village, Bell Lane, Amersham, Bucks, HP6 6FA
Major Shareholder: George Frederick Prinsloo
Officers: Leonard Samson, Secretary; Georg Frederick Prinsloo [1950] Director/Pharmaceutical Sales & Marketing [South African]; Leonard Samson [1942] Director

Apisera Ltd
Incorporated: 24 July 2017
Registered Office: 152 Albert Road, Leyton Albert Road, London, E10 6PB
Major Shareholder: Adam Thomas Morten
Officers: Adam Thomas Morten [1989] Director

Apobec Discovery Ltd
Incorporated: 1 November 2018
Registered Office: 7 Shilton Road, Burford, Oxon, OX18 4PA
Major Shareholder: Professor James Scott
Officers: Patrick Heininger [1942] Director [British/American]; Professor James Scott [1946] Director/Professor

Apollo Pharma Ltd
Incorporated: 1 October 2015
Net Worth: £146,834 *Total Assets:* £451,909
Registered Office: 1st Floor, 621-629 Liverpool Road, Irlam, Manchester, M44 5BE
Officers: Paul John McConnell, Secretary; Annette Atkins [1961] Director/Production Manager; Shaun Patrick Fahy [1963] Director/Manufacturing Manager; Paul John McConnell [1971] Director/Engineer; Edwina Margaret McMillan [1960] Director/Purchasing Manager; Ian Moore [1965] Director/Quality Manager; Samantha Ormrod [1966] Director/Production Manager; Jeffrey Price [1973] Director

Apollo Prosthetics Limited
Incorporated: 20 April 2007 *Employees:* 2
Net Worth: £4,122 *Total Assets:* £32,536
Registered Office: Buckingham House, 35 Graham Road, Malvern, Worcs, WR14 2HU
Major Shareholder: Kevin Thomas Carter
Officers: Kevin Thomas Carter [1965] Director/Dental Technician

Apotek Services Ltd
Incorporated: 23 March 2016 *Employees:* 1
Net Worth: £6,341 *Total Assets:* £12,703
Registered Office: 41 Malcolm Way, London, E11 1PW
Major Shareholder: Tuong Van Lam
Officers: Tuong Van Lam [1975] Director

Apotheke San Biagio SRL Limited
Incorporated: 19 January 2018
Registered Office: 27 Old Gloucester Street, London, WC1N 3AX
Shareholder: Francesco Cavaliere
Officers: Francesco Cavaliere [1976] Director/Manager [Italian]

Appex Ltd
Incorporated: 20 December 2018
Registered Office: 8 Walworth Road, London, SE1 6SX
Officers: Michael Greer, Secretary; Michael Greer [1975] Director/Research

Approved Pharma Solutions Ltd
Incorporated: 31 July 2014 *Employees:* 2
Net Worth: £7,900 *Total Assets:* £34,111
Registered Office: Mill Farm, Church Street, Bainton, E Yorks, YO25 9NJ
Shareholders: Richard Stuart Eggleston; Renda Eggleston
Officers: Dr Renda Eggleston [1959] Director; Richard Stuart Eggleston [1960] Director

APS/Berk Limited
Incorporated: 29 January 1996
Registered Office: Ridings Point, Whistler Drive, Castleford, W Yorks, WF10 5HX
Parent: Teva UK Holdings Limited
Officers: Dean Michael Cooper [1972] Director/Chartered Accountant; Kim Innes [1968] Director/General Manager

Aptitud Pharma Ltd
Incorporated: 28 December 2017
Registered Office: 35 White City Estate, London, W12 7NE
Officers: Edison Rodolfo Velastegui Suquillo [1985] Managing Director

Aptuit (Oxford) Limited
Incorporated: 19 July 2011 *Employees:* 154
Net Worth: £8,822,988 *Total Assets:* £21,646,620
Registered Office: 111 Innovation Drive, Milton Park, Milton, Abingdon, Oxon, OX14 4RZ
Parent: Evotec AG
Officers: Dr Christian Dargel, Secretary; Dr Petra Dieterich [1967] Director/Vice President and Head of Site [German]; Dr Christophe Muller [1971] Director [French]; Ralph Enno Spillner [1970] Director [German]

Aquabalm Limited
Incorporated: 25 June 2004
Registered Office: No 2, 36 Stratford Road, London, W8 6QA
Major Shareholder: Robin Baker
Officers: Peter John Merritt, Secretary; Robin Baker [1941] Director; Peter John Merritt [1952] Director/Accountant

Aramiss Technology Limited
Incorporated: 26 March 2014
Registered Office: Meduza, 466 Melton Road, Leicester, LE4 7SN
Major Shareholder: Ricky Singh
Officers: Ricky Singh, Secretary; Ricky Singh [1978] Director

Arc Devices (NI) Limited
Incorporated: 9 April 2013
Registered Office: Imperial House, Donegall Square East, Belfast, BT1 5HD
Officers: Amos Alter [1952] Director [Canadian]; Jacob Elzas [1937] Director [Belgian]; Irwin Lee Gross [1943] Director [American]

Arcadia Pharma Limited
Incorporated: 22 April 2013 *Employees:* 22
Net Worth: £219,828 *Total Assets:* £975,709
Registered Office: Unit 3 Felinfach, Fforestfach, Swansea, SA5 4HP
Shareholder: Christopher John Colebrook
Officers: Christopher John Colebrook, Secretary; Christopher John Colebrook [1967] Director/Operations Manager; Jeffery Raymond Albert Everett [1966] Director/Commercial Manager; Michael John Overy [1946] Director; Jason Webb [1969] Director/Head of Hospitals

Arch Chemicals Products Limited
Incorporated: 1 May 1970
Net Worth: £800,671 *Total Assets:* £816,199
Registered Office: Wheldon Road, Castleford, W Yorks, WF10 2JT
Officers: Nicholas Thomas Carter, Secretary; Nicholas Thomas Carter [1981] Director/Financial Accountant; Anthony William Kelly [1963] Director; Peter Joseph Kitchen [1967] Director/Financial Controller

Ardent Pharma Limited
Incorporated: 15 August 2012
Registered Office: The Office, Heath View, Ray Lane, Blindley Heath, Lingfield, Surrey, RH7 6LH
Major Shareholder: Alex James Duckworth
Officers: Alexander James Duckworth [1970] Pharmaceutical Director

Ardilla Technologies UK Ltd
Incorporated: 13 December 2011 *Employees:* 1
Net Worth Deficit: £46,777 *Total Assets:* £27,161
Registered Office: Hanover House, 18 Mount Ephraim Road, Tunbridge Wells, Kent, TN1 1ED
Officers: Dr Juho Jumppanen [1966] Director/Chief Technology Officer [Finnish]

Ardiou Healthcare Ltd
Incorporated: 24 August 2016
Registered Office: 3 Gower Street, London, WC1E 6HA
Officers: Ibrahim Abdelrazik Albayoomi Fouda [1978] Director [Egyptian]

Ariera Pharma Limited
Incorporated: 24 January 2017 *Employees:* 2
Net Worth: £72,854 *Total Assets:* £77,058
Registered Office: Lowton Business Park, Lowton St Mary's, Warrington, Cheshire, WA3 2AP
Officers: Paul Boulton [1959] Director/Accountant; John Nightingale [1945] Director

Ark Technologies Ltd
Incorporated: 18 April 2018
Registered Office: 20-22 Wenlock Road, London, N1 7GU
Shareholders: Simon Thomas Harry Tankel; Gavin Hilary Sathianathan
Officers: Gavin Hilary Sathianathan [1978] Director/Finance; Simon Thomas Harry Tankel [1991] Director/Finance

Aroma World Limited
Incorporated: 9 March 2009 *Employees:* 5
Net Worth Deficit: £34,932 *Total Assets:* £38,114
Registered Office: 63 Bawtry Road, Bramley, Rotherham, S Yorks, S66 2TN
Major Shareholder: Graham Waddicar
Officers: Graeme Boyd Waddicar [1958] Director

Aromesse Limited
Incorporated: 3 December 2002
Net Worth: £177,351 *Total Assets:* £248,377
Registered Office: Croft Farm, Blyton Carr, Gainsborough, Lincs, DN21 3EN
Major Shareholder: Karen Ann Marriott
Officers: Karen Ann Marriott, Secretary; Christopher Bainborough [1968] Director; Karen Ann Marriott [1967] Director

Arrow Generics Limited
Incorporated: 13 December 2000
Net Worth Deficit: £4,748,753 *Total Assets:* £18,901
Registered Office: Whiddon Valley, Barnstaple, Devon, EX32 8NS
Parent: Teva Pharmaceutical Industries Limited
Officers: Dean Michael Cooper [1972] Director/Chartered Accountant; Kim Innes [1968] Director/General Manager

AS Pharma Consultancy Limited
Incorporated: 1 July 2014
Net Worth: £5,115 *Total Assets:* £5,665
Registered Office: Flat 26, Connaught Heights, Uxbridge Road, Uxbridge, Middlesex, UB10 0NT
Officers: Ayesha Mehreen Sharif [1990] Director/Regulatory Affairs

As-Tec Chemicals Limited
Incorporated: 14 April 2000 *Employees:* 3
Net Worth: £926,284 *Total Assets:* £1,049,730
Registered Office: Astec House, Unit 5e Barnfield Way, Millennium City Park, Preston, Lancs, PR2 5DB
Shareholders: Simon Digby Harris; Andrew John Mitchell
Officers: Simon Digby Harris, Secretary; Mary Catherine Harris [1957] Director; Simon Digby Harris [1955] Director/Chemist; Andrew John Mitchell [1950] Director/Chemist; Marjorie Mitchell [1949] Director

Asaya Cosmeceuticals Limited
Incorporated: 11 February 2019
Registered Office: First Floor, 85 Great Portland Street, London, W1W 7LT
Major Shareholder: Natalie Echeverria
Officers: Natalie Echeverria [1970] Director

Ascot Laboratories Limited
Incorporated: 14 January 2011 *Employees:* 20
Net Worth: £535,189 *Total Assets:* £3,542,153
Registered Office: Unit 1 Olds Approach, Tolpits Lane, Watford, Herts, WD18 9TD
Shareholders: Bhavesh Amratlal Radia; Deepak Anantrai Ghelani
Officers: Dr Abdul Munaf Alam [1968] Director; Deepak Anantrai Ghelani [1961] Director; Bhavesh Amratlal Radia [1965] Director

Aspar Pharmaceuticals Limited
Incorporated: 30 October 1991 *Employees:* 70
Net Worth: £9,147,676 *Total Assets:* £14,759,634
Registered Office: York House, Church Lane, Chalfont St Peter, Gerrards Cross, Bucks, SL9 9RE
Major Shareholder: Terence Edward Prudhoe
Officers: Jonathan Edward Prudhoe, Secretary; Jonathan Edward Prudhoe [1978] Director/Manager; Sandra Jean Prudhoe [1946] Director; Terrence Edward Prudhoe [1940] Director

Aspen Medical Europe Limited
Incorporated: 20 September 1947 *Employees:* 41
Net Worth: £9,022,000 *Total Assets:* £11,015,000
Registered Office: Clinitron House, Ashby Park, Ashby De La Zouch, Leics, LE65 1JG
Parent: Hill-Rom UK (Holdings) Ltd
Officers: Stephen Sanders, Secretary; Carlos Alonso [1959] Director/President International [Spanish]; Duncan James Wilson [1969] Director

Aspensnetas Biopharma Ltd
Incorporated: 22 October 2018
Registered Office: 11 Woodlands Road, Trent Vale, Stoke on Trent, Staffs, ST4 6SU
Shareholder: Kiran Reddy Kadari
Officers: Kiran Reddy Kadari [1981] Director/Businessman; Sateesh Reddy Kadari [1977] Director/Businessman [Indian]

Astagen Therapeutics Limited
Incorporated: 3 November 2015
Registered Office: 5th Floor, Ashford Commercial Quarter, 1 Dover Place, Ashford, Kent, TN23 1FB
Major Shareholder: Martine Dupont
Officers: Dr Jean Daniel Aubert [1944] Director [French]

Asterisk LifeSciences Ltd
Incorporated: 11 November 2014
Net Worth Deficit: £179 *Total Assets:* £870,254
Registered Office: 350 Kilburn Lane, London, W9 3EF
Officers: Gautam Rasiklal Ashra [1956] Director [Indian]; Narsimha Shibroor Kamath [1953] Managing Director [Indian]

Astrazeneca PLC
Incorporated: 17 June 1992 *Employees:* 60,000
Net Worth: £14,960,000,000 *Total Assets:* £63,353,999,360
Registered Office: 1 Francis Crick Avenue, Cambridge Biomedical Campus, Cambridge, CB2 0AA
Officers: Adrian Charles Noel Kemp, Secretary/Company Official; Professor Genevieve Bernadette Berger [1955] Director/Chief Research and Development Officer [Swiss]; Philip Arthur John Broadley [1961] Director; Graham Chipchase [1963] Director/Chief Executive; Marc Pierre Jean Dunoyer [1952] Director/Chief Financial Officer [French]; Deborah Disanzo Eldracher [1960] Board Director [American]; Leif Valdemar Johansson [1951] Director/Chairman [Swedish]; Rudolph Harold Peter Markham [1946] Director; Sherilyn Dawn McCoy [1958] Director [American]; Tony Shu Kam Mok [1960] Director/Professor [Canadian]; Sabera Nazneen Rahman [1967] Director; Pascal Claude Roland Soriot [1959] Director/Chief Executive Officer [French]; Marcus Wallenberg [1956] Director [Swedish]

Atlantia UK Ltd
Incorporated: 13 November 2012
Net Worth Deficit: £64,023 *Total Assets:* £3,651
Registered Office: 10 Grove Hill Road, London, SE5 8DG
Major Shareholder: Brian Andrerw Wilkinson
Officers: Brian Andrew Wilkinson [1968] Director/Marketing

Atlantis Research Limited
Incorporated: 8 June 2016
Registered Office: Richmond House, 29 Parkfield Avenue, Ashton on Ribble, Preston, Lancs, PR2 1JB
Major Shareholder: Andrew Croft
Officers: Andrew Croft [1966] Director/Consultant

Atlantis Skincare Ltd
Incorporated: 26 October 2015 *Employees:* 1
Net Worth: £27 *Total Assets:* £939
Registered Office: Equinox House, Clifton Park Avenue, Shipton Road, York, YO30 5PA
Major Shareholder: Zane Piese
Officers: Zane Piese [1970] Director/Wholesaler [Latvian]

Atnahs Pharma US Limited
Incorporated: 26 January 2016
Net Worth: £2,583,085 *Total Assets:* £3,258,626
Registered Office: Suite 1, 3rd Floor, 11-12 St James's Square, London, SW1Y 4LB
Parent: Atnahs Pharma UK Limited
Officers: Mark John Cotterill [1965] Director; Amit Vijaykumar Patel [1978] Director; Bhikhu Chhotabhai Patel [1949] Director; Dipen Vijaykumar Patel [1979] Director/Accountant; Vijaykumar Chhotabhai Patel [1947] Director

Aucure Medical Technologies Limited
Incorporated: 25 May 2018
Registered Office: 71-75 Shelton Street, London, WC2H 9JQ
Major Shareholder: Sumit Lal
Officers: Dr Sumit Lal [1981] Director/Scientist [Indian]

Auden McKenzie (Pharma Division) Limited
Incorporated: 2 September 1999
Net Worth: £157,626,992 *Total Assets:* £166,636,032
Registered Office: Whiddon Valley, Barnstaple, Devon, EX32 8NS
Parent: Auden McKenzie Holdings Limited
Officers: Dean Michael Cooper [1972] Director/Chartered Accountant; Kim Innes [1968] Director/General Manager

Aura Fragrances Limited
Incorporated: 21 April 1995
Net Worth: £5,894 *Total Assets:* £25,023
Registered Office: 25 The Maltings, Liphook, Hants, GU30 7DG
Officers: Michael Norman Woodrow, Secretary; Margaret Evelyn Anne Woodrow [1946] Director/Perfumer; Michael Norman Woodrow [1937] Director/Flavourist

Aura-Soma Products Limited
Incorporated: 6 February 1987 *Employees:* 40
Net Worth: £9,007,875 *Total Assets:* £9,999,667
Registered Office: South Road, Tetford, Horncastle, Lincs, LN9 6QB
Major Shareholder: John Michael Booth
Officers: Malcolm Edmund Robinson, Secretary; Claudia Gwendoline Forster Booth [1948] Director; John Michael Booth [1950] Director/Consultant

Auralis Limited
Incorporated: 18 January 2005
Net Worth: £7,405,000 *Total Assets:* £7,632,000
Registered Office: 1 Kingdom Street, London, W2 6BD
Parent: Shire Pharmaceuticals Group
Officers: Damien Rodolphe Edmond Bailly [1966] Commercial Director [French]; Nicholas Hugh Meryon Insall [1982] Director/Accountant; Jonathan Clark Neal [1971] Managing Director; Kentaro Shirahata [1976] Director/Accountant [Japanese]

Auramedicann Ltd
Incorporated: 31 August 2018
Registered Office: 71-75 Shelton Street, London, WC2H 9JQ
Officers: Steven Davies [1973] Director

Aurum Pharmaceuticals Limited
Incorporated: 8 February 1991
Registered Office: Bampton Road, Romford, Essex, RM3 8UG
Parent: Macarthys Laboratories Limited
Officers: Bertrand Deluard [1961] Director/Chief Executive Officer [French]; Philip Edward Parry [1965] Director/Quality Assurance Professional; Emmanuel Schmidt [1969] Director/Chief Finance Officer [French]

Automation Control Expertise Limited
Incorporated: 25 June 2009
Net Worth: £7,681 *Total Assets:* £27,787
Registered Office: 35 Primrose Way, Chestfield, Whitstable, Kent, CT5 3QW
Major Shareholder: Martin McKelvie
Officers: Martin McKelvie [1954] Director

Avacare Limited
Incorporated: 15 April 2016 *Employees:* 3
Net Worth Deficit: £26,015 *Total Assets:* £66,536
Registered Office: Stevenage Bioscience Catalyst, Gunnels Wood Road, Stevenage, Herts, SG1 2FX
Shareholders: Rahul Mahendra Shah; Relton John Phillip Herron; Khilan Mahendra Shah
Officers: Relton John Phillip Herron [1973] Director; Khilan Mahendra Shah [1973] Director; Rahul Mahendra Shah [1977] Director

Avanor Healthcare Ltd
Incorporated: 22 February 2006
Net Worth: £11,920 *Total Assets:* £206,200
Registered Office: 1a Wendover Road, Rackheath, Norwich, NR13 6LH
Shareholders: Scott Duffy; Justine Ellen Duffy
Officers: Justine Ellen Duffy, Secretary; Justine Ellen Duffy [1976] Director/Sales Manager; Scott Duffy [1978] Managing Director

Avanzcare Limited
Incorporated: 15 June 2017
Net Worth Deficit: £100,905 *Total Assets:* £35,101
Registered Office: c/o Riverbank House, 2 Swan Lane, London, EC4R 3TT
Officers: Mohamed Ahmed Shafiek Mohamed Ahmed [1966] Managing Director [Egyptian]; John Adel Youssef Tabdros Botros [1968] Director/General Manager [Egyptian]

Aventa International Corporation Ltd
Incorporated: 2 November 2018
Registered Office: 3 Gower Street, London, WC1E 6HA
Shareholders: Ahmed Hassan Ahmed Albahnasawy; Mohamed Hussein Mohamed Mohamed Soliman
Officers: Ahmed Hassan Ahmed Albahnasawy [1976] Director [Egyptian]

AVI BioPharma International Limited
Incorporated: 9 January 2007
Registered Office: Tower Bridge House, St Katharine's Way, London, E1W 1DD
Parent: Sarepta Therapeutics, Inc
Officers: Joseph Bratica [1963] Director/Controller [American]; Matthew Garrett Gall [1976] Director/Treasurer [American]; Andrew Howard Robertson [1964] Director/VP & GM, Europe

Avicenna Herbal Products Limited
Incorporated: 1 April 2016
Net Worth: £199,220 *Total Assets:* £441,551
Registered Office: Bidarren, Cilcennin, Lampeter, Dyfed, SA48 8RL
Major Shareholder: Youssef Izzat Nasr
Officers: Yoessef Izzat Nasr [1955] Director/Medical Herbalist

Avisius Research Limited
Incorporated: 3 March 2003 *Employees:* 1
Net Worth: £16,048 *Total Assets:* £20,198
Registered Office: 3Mc Siskin Drive, Middlemarch Business Park, Coventry, Warwicks, CV3 4FJ
Major Shareholder: Ian Whelan
Officers: Ian Whelan [1965] Director

Avista Holding Co., Ltd.
Incorporated: 11 July 2017
Registered Office: c/o CMS Cameron McKenna Nabarro Olswang LLP, 1 West Regent Street, Glasgow, G2 1AP
Shareholders: Pacific Western Bank; Avista Pharma Solutions, Inc.
Officers: Jon David Jacobs, Secretary; Eric Wayne Evans [1956] Director [American]; Patrick D Walsh [1960] Director [American]

The Top UK Pharmaceutical Manufacturers

Avix Pharmaceuticals Limited
Incorporated: 9 April 2018
Registered Office: 15 Clayton Road, Brighton, BN2 9ZP
Major Shareholder: Md Arif Sheikh
Officers: Dr Nasrin Jahan, Secretary; Dr MD Arif Sheikh [1981] Director/Research Scientist

AWA Export Limited
Incorporated: 21 June 2011
Net Worth: £1 *Total Assets:* £403
Registered Office: 74 Lairgate, Beverley, E Yorks, HU17 8EU
Major Shareholder: Andrew Keith Waide
Officers: Roy Dunsmore Fitzsimmons [1944] Director; Wendy Richings Barrow [1954] Director; Andrew Keith Waide [1958] Director

AXG Ltd
Incorporated: 18 March 2014
Net Worth: £14,595 *Total Assets:* £81,133
Registered Office: 25 Potters Grove, New Malden, Surrey, KT3 5DF
Major Shareholder: Gebray Gebreyesus Biadglgne
Officers: Gebray Gebreyesus Biadglgne [1960] Director

Ayrton Saunders and Company Ltd
Incorporated: 11 June 2010 *Employees:* 10
Net Worth: £261,742 *Total Assets:* £658,492
Registered Office: Ayrton House, Commerce Way, Liverpool, L8 7BA
Officers: Philip Didlick, Secretary; Philip Didlick [1976] Director/Accountant; Generald Francis O'Brien [1949] Director; Padraic Marc Obrien [1979] Director

Ayrton Saunders Limited
Incorporated: 30 September 1997
Net Worth Deficit: £292,305 *Total Assets:* £6,504,914
Registered Office: Parliament Business Park, Ayrton House, 38 Commerce Way, Liverpool, L8 7BA
Major Shareholder: Gerald Francis Obrien
Officers: Philip Didlick, Secretary; Philip Didlick [1976] Director/Accountant; Padraic Marc O'Brien [1979] Director; Generald Francis O'Brien [1949] Director/Chemist

Ayurmedics Clinic Limited
Incorporated: 19 July 2013
Net Worth Deficit: £7,519 *Total Assets:* £14,785
Registered Office: 505 London Road, Thornton Heath, Croydon, Surrey, CR7 6AR
Officers: Natarajan Chellappan [1940] Director

Ayush Ayurveda Care Limited
Incorporated: 2 April 2008
Net Worth Deficit: £16,407 *Total Assets:* £134,613
Registered Office: 69 Great Hampton Street, Birmingham, B18 6EW
Major Shareholder: Girjadevi Gohil
Officers: Girjadevi Gohil [1951] Director/Merchant [Indian]

Mark Aziz Limited
Incorporated: 18 December 2007
Net Worth: £2,410 *Total Assets:* £9,938
Registered Office: Flat 41, Brickdale House, Swingate Street, Stevenage, Herts, SG1 1AS
Major Shareholder: Mark Aziz
Officers: Andrew Aziz, Secretary; Mark Aziz [1988] Director/Pharmacist

B.C. Medical Limited
Incorporated: 19 February 1986
Registered Office: 9 Limes Avenue, Mill Hill, London, NW7 3NY
Officers: Colin Lennox Bywater, Secretary; Colin Lennox Bywater [1943] Director/Solicitor; Gordon Webster Catto [1936] Director/Pharmacist

Baby Face Cosmetics Limited
Incorporated: 18 December 2006
Registered Office: 32 Parsonage Brow, Upholland, Skelmersdale, Lancs, WN8 0JG
Shareholders: Louise Ramsey; Peter Ramsey
Officers: Peter Ramsey, Secretary; Louise Ramsey [1968] Director; Peter Ramsey [1963] Director

Bach Flower Remedies Limited
Incorporated: 8 April 1993
Net Worth: £10,089,000 *Total Assets:* £14,821,000
Registered Office: Nelsons House, 83 Parkside, Wimbledon, London, SW19 5LP
Parent: A Nelson & Co Limited
Officers: Claire Ferguson [1977] Director; Patrick Russell Wilson [1965] Director; Robert Nelson Wilson [1962] Director/Chairman

Bacvacc Ltd
Incorporated: 2 July 2018
Registered Office: 17 Mascotte Road, London, SW15 1NN
Major Shareholder: Caroline Janet Hardwicke
Officers: Caroline Janet Hardwicke [1958] Director/Consultant [Australian]

Badgequo Limited
Incorporated: 4 December 1984 *Employees:* 47
Net Worth: £6,149,694 *Total Assets:* £16,825,688
Registered Office: Units B & C, Orbital Forty Six, The Ridgeway Trading Estate, Iver, Bucks, SL0 9HW
Parent: Retra Holdings Limited
Officers: Samuel Bazini [1963] Director; Matthew David Goldstein [1972] Director/Chartered Accountant; Eoin Alan MacLeod [1962] Director; Steve Richardson [1973] Operations Director; Neil Rodol [1962] Director

Penny Badger Limited
Incorporated: 29 June 2010
Registered Office: Kemp House, 152 City Road, London, EC1V 2NX
Major Shareholder: Penelope Anne Lomatschinsky
Officers: Taras Lomatschinsky, Secretary; Penny Lomatschinsky [1960] Director

Balmy Fox Ltd
Incorporated: 1 May 2018
Registered Office: Dunsdon Farm, Pancrasweek, Holsworthy, Devon, EX22 7JW
Major Shareholder: Paul David Stenning
Officers: Paul David Stenning [1967] Director

Bam Balm Ltd
Incorporated: 3 August 2018
Registered Office: 63 Cannon Lane, Luton, Beds, LU2 8BJ
Shareholders: Wesley Geoffrey Scott; James Lawrence
Officers: James Lawrence [1982] Director/Entrepreneur

Bamford & Wolfe Ltd
Incorporated: 10 March 2017
Net Worth: £8,070 *Total Assets:* £52,830
Registered Office: Berners Mansions, 34-36 Berners Street, London, W1T 3LU
Major Shareholder: Vaughn Wolfe
Officers: Vaughn Wolfe [1979] Director/Entrepreneur [American]

Bandfiled Ltd
Incorporated: 18 July 2018
Registered Office: 214a Kettering Road, Northampton, NN1 4BN
Shareholders: Alma Andal; Abbey Huelin
Officers: Alma Andal [1978] Director [Filipino]

Bard Pharmaceuticals Limited
Incorporated: 21 August 1970 *Employees:* 426
Net Worth: £73,193,000 *Total Assets:* £100,001,000
Registered Office: Unit 191 Cambridge Science Park, Milton Road, Cambridge, CB4 0AB
Parent: Napp Pharmaceutical Group Limited
Officers: Stuart David Baker [1935] Director/Attorney [American]; Colm Joseph Moody [1965] Director of Production and Supply Chain [Irish]; Ake Gunnar Wikstrom [1951] Director/Advisor [Swedish]

Batchable Enterprises Limited
Incorporated: 20 September 1993 *Employees:* 15
Net Worth: £79,463 *Total Assets:* £584,016
Registered Office: 84-90 Stanley Street, Openshaw, Manchester, M11 1LE
Officers: Deborah Jane Kantilal Agravat [1963] Director/Pharmacy Manager; Ken Agravat [1952] Director; Daka Divel Nazael [1952] Director [Ghanaian]

Batel Limited
Incorporated: 20 February 2019
Registered Office: South Staffs Freight Building, Lynn Lane, Shenstone, Lichfield, Staffs, WS14 0ED
Major Shareholder: Christopher Douglas Lee
Officers: Christopher Douglas Lee [1956] Director

Bateman Quality Associates Limited
Incorporated: 3 June 2008
Net Worth: £20,253 *Total Assets:* £43,144
Registered Office: The Smiddy, 2 Blacksmiths End, Bluntisham, Cambs, PE28 3JH
Officers: Karen Marion Bateman [1960] Director/Chemist; Dr Tim Bateman [1959] Director/Chemist

Baxalta UK Limited
Incorporated: 3 October 2014 *Employees:* 80
Net Worth: £42,470,000 *Total Assets:* £74,718,000
Registered Office: 1 Kingdom Street, London, W2 6BD
Parent: Takeda Pharmaceutical Company Limited
Officers: Damien Rodolphe Edmond Bailly [1966] Commercial Director [French]; Mark Gibbons [1984] Director/Accountant [South African]; Nicholas Hugh Meryon Insall [1982] Director/Accountant; Jonathan Clark Neal [1971] Managing Director

Baxter Healthcare Limited
Incorporated: 18 November 1948 *Employees:* 1,157
Net Worth: £101,793,000 *Total Assets:* £296,004,992
Registered Office: Caxton Way, Thetford, Norfolk, IP24 3SE
Parent: Baxter Europe Holdings Ltd
Officers: Jon Garay [1973] Finance Director [Spanish]; Andrew Neil Goldney [1968] Director/General Manager; Bo Anders Caspersson Tarras-Wahlberg [1975] Director/Legal Adviser [Swedish]

BBI Solutions OEM Limited
Incorporated: 21 January 2013 *Employees:* 301
Net Worth: £29,980,000 *Total Assets:* £41,639,000
Registered Office: c/o Berry Smith LLP, Haywood House, Dumfries Place, Cardiff, CF10 3GA
Parent: BBI Diagnostics Group Limited
Officers: Richard George Armitt Couzens [1973] Director; Mario Pietro Gualano [1969] Director; Alan Edward Peterson [1947] Director; Liam Mark Taylor [1977] Director [Australian]

BCM Limited
Incorporated: 20 August 1992
Net Worth: £61,600,000 *Total Assets:* £90,600,000
Registered Office: 1 Thane Road West, Nottingham, NG2 3AA
Parent: Fareva UK Limited
Officers: Andrew John Mortimer [1959] Director/Country Manager UK; Christophe Petras [1969] Director/Vice President Global Operations [French]; Richard David Whall [1962] Managing Director

BCM Specials Limited
Incorporated: 24 November 2006 *Employees:* 2
Net Worth: £20,849,000 *Total Assets:* £22,076,000
Registered Office: 1 Thane Road West, Nottingham, NG2 3AA
Parent: Fareva UK Limited
Officers: Andrew John Mortimer [1959] Director/Country Manager UK; Christophe Petras [1969] Director/Vice President Global Operations [French]; Richard David Whall [1962] Managing Director

Beacon Green Limited
Incorporated: 19 February 2014
Registered Office: Forestside, Fielden Road, Crowborough, E Sussex, TN6 1TR
Major Shareholder: Steven Short
Officers: Dr Steven Short [1952] Director

Beacon Pharmaceuticals Limited
Incorporated: 21 March 2000
Registered Office: DCC Vital, Westminster Industrial Estate, Repton Road, Measham, Swadlincote, Derbys, DE12 7DT
Parent: Kent Pharmaceuticals Limited
Officers: Conor Francis Costigan [1963] Director/Chartered Accountant [Irish]; Leslie Deacon [1963] Director/Chartered Accountant [Irish]; Harry Keenan [1959] Managing Director [Irish]; Redmond McEvoy [1964] Director/Chartered Accountant [Irish]

Beautanix Limited
Incorporated: 10 March 2015
Net Worth Deficit: £6,238 *Total Assets:* £756
Registered Office: 82a Vestry Road Oakwood, Derby, DE21 2BN
Major Shareholder: Margaret Frixou
Officers: Margaret Frixou [1966] Director

The Beautiful Splint Company CIC
Incorporated: 28 November 2009
Net Worth: £449 *Total Assets:* £477
Registered Office: 26 Manor Road, Tadcaster, N Yorks, LS24 8HP
Officers: Leesa Jayne Rayton [1972] Director; Karen Jane Ward [1963] Director/Bank Official

Beautylab UK Limited
Incorporated: 8 August 2008
Registered Office: Unit 5 Compass West Industrial Estate, 33 West Road, London, N17 0XL
Major Shareholder: Roger Aoun
Officers: Michelle Aoun, Secretary; Roger Aoun [1957] Director/Marketing

Beckley Labs Limited
Incorporated: 22 November 2016
Registered Office: 71 Queen Victoria Street, London, EC4V 4BE
Major Shareholder: Lady Amanda Marian Claire Feilding
Officers: Lady Amanda Claire Feilding [1943] Director

Beckley Research and Innovations Limited
Incorporated: 21 November 2016
Registered Office: 71 Queen Victoria Street, London, EC4V 4BE
Shareholders: Cosmo Birdie Feilding Mellen; Lady Amanda Marian Claire Feilding
Officers: Lady Amanda Claire Feilding [1943] Director; Cosmo Birdie Feilding Mellon [1985] Director

Beegood Enterprises Limited
Incorporated: 25 February 2013 *Employees:* 4
Net Worth: £42,178 *Total Assets:* £105,829
Registered Office: Ping CA, P O Box 1077, Camberley, Surrey, GU15 9QH
Officers: Hilary Ann Andrews [1961] Director; Simon Rafe Cavill [1960] Director; John Colin LooSeniore [1948] Director [Australian]; David John Parker [1965] Director

Bell, Sons & Co. (Druggists) Limited
Incorporated: 17 April 1939 *Employees:* 148
Net Worth: £5,039,008 *Total Assets:* £13,834,928
Registered Office: Gifford House, Slaidburn Crescent, Southport, Merseyside, PR9 9AL
Parent: Marksans Holdings Limited
Officers: Gillian Jacks, Secretary; Sathish Kumar Konasagar Jayanna [1973] Managing Director; Mark Bosco Saldanha [1972] Director [Indian]; Sandra Saldanha [1971] Director [Indian]; Jitendra Mahavirprasad Sharma [1969] Director [Indian]; Russell David Williams [1968] Director

Bena Cosmetics (UK) Limited
Incorporated: 21 April 2004
Net Worth Deficit: £31,089 *Total Assets:* £1
Registered Office: 7 Delaware Walk, Manchester, M9 5SG
Major Shareholder: Benadette Ezeakune
Officers: Joseph Ezeakunne, Secretary; Benadette Obuneme Ezeakune [1945] Director/Manufacturer [Nigerian]

Beneficial Oils Ltd
Incorporated: 20 March 2013
Registered Office: 167 Cliftonville Road, Belfast, BT14 6JT
Major Shareholder: Edijs Rumbenieks
Officers: Maura Canavan, Secretary; Edijs Rumbenieks [1980] Director/Student [Latvian]

Berhael Trading Limited
Incorporated: 24 November 2017
Registered Office: Ground Floor, 25 Darling Street, Enniskillen, Co Fermanagh, BT74 7DP
Major Shareholder: Michael Quinn
Officers: Micheal Quinn [1965] Director [Irish]

Bescot Healthcare UK Limited
Incorporated: 10 April 2014
Net Worth: £2 *Total Assets:* £2
Registered Office: 272 Bath Street, Glasgow, G2 4JR
Parent: Bescot Healthcare International Ltd
Officers: Dr Alan Davis [1955] Director/Pharmacologist [Canadian]; Martin Fisher [1963] Director/Pharmaceutical Manager [Canadian]

Bespak Europe Limited
Incorporated: 24 February 1998 *Employees:* 734
Net Worth: £107,336,000 *Total Assets:* £155,496,992
Registered Office: Suite B Breakspear Park, Breakspear Way, Hemel Hempstead, Herts, HP2 4TZ
Parent: Consort Medical PLC
Officers: Andrew Leonard Jackson, Secretary; Dr Keyvan Djamarani [1961] Director; Jonathan Martin Glenn [1968] Company Director; Paul Andrew Hayes [1966] Director

Better Call Paul Limited
Incorporated: 20 May 2016 *Employees:* 1
Net Worth: £35,962 *Total Assets:* £62,794
Registered Office: 2 Lime Tree Grove, Birmingham, B31 3DF
Major Shareholder: Paul Mackey
Officers: Paul Mackey [1970] Director/Pharmaceutical Consultant

BHR Pharmaceuticals Limited
Incorporated: 17 January 1990 *Employees:* 23
Net Worth: £226,897 *Total Assets:* £1,293,107
Registered Office: Centenary Business Centre, Hammond Close, Attleborough Fields Industrial Estate, Nuneaton, Warwicks, CV11 6RY
Major Shareholder: Rameshkumar Jerambhai Patel
Officers: Rameshkumar Jerambhai Patel [1956] Director/Pharmaceutical Sales; Bharat Jivan Vadukul [1958] Director/Business Executive

Bio & Pharma Ltd.
Incorporated: 14 November 2017
Registered Office: 3rd Floor, 207 Regent Street, London, W1B 3HH
Shareholder: Marian Chodacki
Officers: Marian Chodacki [1971] Director [Polish]

Bio Farma Ltd
Incorporated: 28 January 2010
Net Worth: £36,047 *Total Assets:* £52,539
Registered Office: 44 Alberta Street, Bolton, Lancs, BL3 5JD
Officers: Osama Bhatia [1978] Director

Bio Provide 18 Ltd
Incorporated: 10 February 2015
Net Worth: £2 *Total Assets:* £5,329
Registered Office: 5 Meteor Road, Kate Reed Wood, West Malling, Kent, ME19 4TH
Parent: Bio Provide Ltd
Officers: Johannes Robertus Van Herwijnen [1962] Director [Dutch]

Bio Provide 19 Ltd
Incorporated: 10 February 2015
Net Worth: £2 *Total Assets:* £2
Registered Office: 5 Meteor Road, Kate Reed Wood, West Malling, Kent, ME19 4TH
Parent: Bio Provide Ltd
Officers: Johannes Robertus Van Herwijnen [1962] Director [Dutch]

Bio Provide 20 Ltd
Incorporated: 10 February 2015
Net Worth: £2 *Total Assets:* £1
Registered Office: 5 Meteor Road, Kate Reed Wood, West Malling, Kent, ME19 4TH
Parent: EVL Biologicals Ltd
Officers: Johannes Robertus Van Herwijnen [1962] Director [Dutch]

Bio Provide Ltd
Incorporated: 9 February 2015
Net Worth: £2 *Total Assets:* £7
Registered Office: 5 Meteor Road, Kate Reed Wood, West Malling, Kent, ME19 4TH
Parent: EVL Biologicals Ltd
Officers: Johannes Robertus Van Herwijnen [1962] Director [Dutch]

Bio Pure Technology Ltd
Incorporated: 10 November 1998 *Employees:* 62
Net Worth: £2,809,121 *Total Assets:* £3,785,923
Registered Office: Watson Marlow Limited, Bickland Water Road, Tregoniggie, Falmouth, Cornwall, TR11 4RU
Parent: Spirax-Sarco Investments Limited
Officers: Andrew John Robson, Secretary; Steven Robert Feasey [1971] Sales Director; Susan Mary Godzicz [1956] Director; Christopher Andrew Magor [1961] Director; James Lawrence Whalen [1956] Director [American]

Bio-Health Limited
Incorporated: 24 March 1981 *Employees:* 10
Net Worth: £335,161 *Total Assets:* £381,357
Registered Office: The Herb Place, Culpeper Close, Medway City Estate, Rochester, Kent, ME2 4HU
Parent: Sabemonoi Limited
Officers: Victor Daniel Perfitt, Secretary/Manufacturer; Jason Daniel Perfitt [1968] Director/Strategy Consultant; Raoul John Perfitt [1966] Director/Production Manager; Victor Daniel Perfitt [1944] Director/Manufacturer

Bio-Life International Limited
Incorporated: 24 November 2006
Net Worth Deficit: £184,791 *Total Assets:* £271,949
Registered Office: Unit 5a Brailes Industrial Estate, Winderton Road, Lower Brailes, Banbury, Oxon, OX15 5JW
Shareholders: Graham Francis Warmington; Mary Doreen Lloyd
Officers: Graham Francis Warmington, Secretary/Accountant; Mary Doreen Lloyd [1952] Director/Animal Production Scientist; Graham Francis Warmington [1949] Director Accountant

The Bio-Medical Engineering Ltd
Incorporated: 13 August 2014
Net Worth: £22,372 *Total Assets:* £3,426,955
Registered Office: 3rd Floor, Vyman House, 104 College Road, Harrow, Middlesex, HA1 1BQ
Officers: Professor Zhi Li Wang [1950] Director/Doctor [Chinese]

Bio-Medical Services Limited
Incorporated: 27 February 1981
Registered Office: 3 The Grange, Flaxby, Knaresborough, N Yorks, HG5 0RJ
Parent: Neoceuticals Limited
Officers: Susan Proctor, Secretary; Dr Rodney Harry Adams [1944] Director; Dr Andrew Brodrick [1951] Director

Bio-Rad AbD Serotec Ltd
Incorporated: 16 December 1981 *Employees:* 81
Net Worth: £19,591,092 *Total Assets:* £23,531,758
Registered Office: Endeavour House, Langford Lane, Kidlington, Oxon, OX5 1GE
Parent: Bio-Rad Laboratories, Inc.
Officers: Lee Keron Marles [1977] Director; Norman David Schwartz [1950] Director/C.E.O. & President [American]

Bio-Sync International Limited
Incorporated: 19 October 2004 *Employees:* 2
Net Worth: £19,722 *Total Assets:* £20,188
Registered Office: Sentosa, Ankerbold Road, Old Tupton, Chesterfield, Derbys, S42 6BX
Shareholder: Heather Mary Hill
Officers: Heather Mary Hill, Secretary; Norman Hill [1950] Director

Bio-Tech Solutions Limited
Incorporated: 8 October 2002 *Employees:* 13
Net Worth: £303,788 *Total Assets:* £719,453
Registered Office: Kelleythorpe Industrial Estate, Kellythorpe, Driffield, E Yorks, YO25 9DJ
Major Shareholder: Harry Ian Moulds
Officers: Susan Jane Moulds, Secretary; Harry Ian Moulds [1950] Director; Susan Jane Moulds [1953] Director/Doctor; John Tharratt [1953] Director/Manager at Bio-Tech

Bioactive Health Ltd
Incorporated: 22 March 2018
Registered Office: Haacombe House, The Street, Hascombe, Godalming, Surrey, GU8 4JA
Major Shareholder: Timothy John Inskip
Officers: Timothy John Inskip [1957] Director/Designer

Bioavexia Ltd
Incorporated: 1 June 2016 *Employees:* 1
Net Worth: £164,523 *Total Assets:* £1,170,247
Registered Office: Unit 20 Phoenix Business Park, Avenue Close, Birmingham, B7 4NU
Officers: Mohammed Abrar [1978] Director

Biocentra Limited
Incorporated: 6 July 2012
Registered Office: Flat 6, Florence House, 162 Main Street, Ely, Cambs, CB6 2HP
Major Shareholder: Garry Dubickas
Officers: Dr Garry Dubickas, Secretary; Dr Garry Dubickas [1963] Director/Pharmaceuticals & Biotechnology

Bioceuticals Group Ltd
Incorporated: 7 June 2018
Registered Office: 20-22 Wenlock Road, London, N1 7GU
Major Shareholder: Mitesh Soma
Officers: Mitesh Soma [1976] Director

Bioceuticals Limited
Incorporated: 11 July 2012 *Employees:* 1
Net Worth: £15,647 *Total Assets:* £27,895
Registered Office: Brandon House, Marlowe Way, Croydon, Surrey, CR0 4XS
Parent: Interport Limited
Officers: Harshadrai Ishwarbhai Ashabhai Patel [1944] Director/Pharmacist

Bioceutics UK Ltd
Incorporated: 26 September 2014
Registered Office: Advantage Business Centre, 132-134 Great Ancoats Street, Manchester, M4 6DE
Officers: Dr Mohamed Shawki El Morsy Yousef [1977] Director/Pharmacist [Egyptian]

Biocolor Limited
Incorporated: 1 October 1992 *Employees:* 3
Net Worth: £1,573,076 *Total Assets:* £1,631,405
Registered Office: Units 35 & 39 Carrickfergus Enterprise Park, 8 Meadowbank Road, Carrickfergus, Co Antrim, BT38 8YF
Major Shareholder: Gary Elliott
Officers: Gary Elliott [1969] Director/Project Manager

The Top UK Pharmaceutical Manufacturers

Biocon Pharma UK Limited
Incorporated: 7 December 2018
Registered Office: 16 Great Queen Street, Covent Garden, London, WC2B 5AH
Officers: Kiran Mazumdar Shaw [1953] Director [Indian]; John McCallum Marshall Shaw [1949] Director; Abhijit Zutshi [1975] Director [American]

Biocryst UK Limited
Incorporated: 8 May 2007
Registered Office: Condor House, 5-10 St Paul's Churchyard, London, EC4M 8AL
Parent: Biocryst Pharmaceuticals Inc
Officers: Dr Yarlagadda Sudhakara Babu [1952] Director [American]; Alane P Barnes [1965] Director [American]; Philip John Collis [1961] Director; Dr William Patrick Sheridan [1954] Director [Australian]

Biodan Ltd.
Incorporated: 11 July 2018
Registered Office: Institute of Translational Medicine, Heritage Building, Mindelsohn Way, Edgbaston, Birmingham, B15 2TH
Major Shareholder: Alfredo Manuel Brisac
Officers: Alfredo Manuel Brisac [1960] Director [Spanish]

Bioextractions Wales Limited
Incorporated: 29 November 2013 *Employees:* 4
Net Worth: £79,966 *Total Assets:* £339,104
Registered Office: Unit 30 Tafarnaubach Industrial Estate, Tafarnaubach, Tredegar, Gwent, NP22 3AA
Officers: John Richard Jenkins [1963] Director/Accountant; Sir Roger Spencer Jones [1942] Director/Entrepreneur; Kevin Marc Stephens [1966] Director/Manager

Biofortuna Ltd
Incorporated: 26 February 2008 *Employees:* 27
Net Worth: £753,958 *Total Assets:* £1,202,620
Registered Office: Bluebell House, Brian Johnson Way, Preston, Lancs, PR2 5PE
Shareholder: Foresight 4 VCT PLC-O Pool
Officers: Geoffrey Michael Orme, Secretary; Simon Gorgon Douglas [1958] Director; Mark Gordon Delap Hurley [1957] Director; Geoffrey Michael Orme [1957] Finance Director; David John Turner [1981] Director/Senior Investment Manager

Biokemix Worldwide Ltd
Incorporated: 17 April 2015
Previous: Biokemix Europe Ltd
Net Worth: £1 *Total Assets:* £1
Registered Office: 1 Doughty Street, London, WC1N 2PH
Major Shareholder: Dynshaw Fareed Italia
Officers: Dynshaw Fareed Italia [1970] Director/Chartered Accountant

Biologix Laboratories Limited
Incorporated: 9 July 2002 *Employees:* 5
Net Worth: £71,531 *Total Assets:* £432,251
Registered Office: Blackwell Barn, 92 Low Road, Burwell, Cambridge, CB25 0EJ
Parent: Smartec Solutions Ltd
Officers: Kenneth Richardson [1953] Director; John Strauss [1949] Director [Swiss]; Guy James Roger Westcott [1968] Sales Director

Biolyse Pharma Europe Limited
Incorporated: 16 March 2018
Registered Office: Croylands, Church Lane, Averham, Newark, Notts, NG23 5RB
Major Shareholder: Brigette Kiecken
Officers: Brigette Kiecken [1957] Director [French]

Biomed Supplies Limited
Incorporated: 25 October 2004
Registered Office: 28 Robert Street, Williton, Taunton, Somerset, TA4 4PG
Shareholders: Ian Charles Aldridge; Josephine Mary Strzelecki
Officers: Ian Charles Aldridge, Secretary; Ian Charles Aldridge [1953] Director; Josephine Mary Strzelecki [1985] Director

Biomedical Nutrition Ltd
Incorporated: 18 September 2014
Net Worth Deficit: £26,383 *Total Assets:* £11,704
Registered Office: c/o Hentons & Co LLP, Northgate, 118 North Street, Leeds, LS2 7PN
Major Shareholder: Christopher Szymanski
Officers: Phillip Maurice Byrne [1958] Director; Christopher Szymanski [1956] Director

Biomimetic Therapeutics Limited
Incorporated: 7 October 2005
Registered Office: c/o Arnold & Porter (UK) LLP, Tower 42, 25 Old Broad Street, London, EC2N 1HQ
Parent: Wright Medical Group N.V.
Officers: James Lightman, Secretary; Walter Dean Morgan [1966] Director/Vice President, Tax and Treasury [American]

Bioneb PVT Limited
Incorporated: 4 August 2015
Previous: Bioneb Limited
Net Worth: £2,000,000 *Total Assets:* £2,661,241
Registered Office: 82 St John Street, London, EC1M 4JN
Major Shareholder: Nicholas Anthony Havercroft
Officers: Gavin Havercroft [1973] Director; Nick Anthony Havercroft [1965] Director; Stephen Howard Patrick May [1960] Director/Advisor; Dr Michael Spuza [1958] Director/Doctor [American]; Derek Martin Williamson [1944] Director/Accountant

Bionet Research Limited
Incorporated: 31 March 1988
Registered Office: 12 Upper Belgrave Street, London, SW1X 8BA
Parent: Key Organics Limited
Officers: Rosemary Janet Jordan, Secretary; William Paul Alexander [1954] Director; Dr Joseph Carey [1964] Managing Director; Andrew Clive Gingell [1954] Director

Biopharm (U.K.) Limited
Incorporated: 18 November 1983
Net Worth: £144,122 *Total Assets:* £176,362
Registered Office: Bryngelen House, 2 Bryngwili Road, Hendy, Carmarthenshire, SA4 0XT
Officers: Doctor Roy Thomas Sawyer, Secretary; Lorna Mary Elizabeth Sawyer [1948] Director; Doctor Roy Thomas Sawyer [1942] Director/Biologist [American]

Biopharma Laboratories (UK) Limited
Incorporated: 25 September 2007 *Employees:* 3
Net Worth Deficit: £235,243 *Total Assets:* £236,877
Registered Office: Belfry House, Bell Lane, Hertford, SG14 1BP
Major Shareholder: Michael Chambers
Officers: Matthew Douglas Chambers [1975] Director; Michael Chambers [1946] Director

Biopharma Stability Testing Laboratory Limited
Incorporated: 11 May 2012
Net Worth Deficit: £148,774 *Total Assets:* £68,707
Registered Office: Biocity, Pennyfoot Street, Nottingham, NG1 1GF
Shareholders: Michael Charles Allwood; Alan Shaun Wilkinson
Officers: Dr Alan Shaun Wilkinson [1971] Director/Research Scientist

Bioplus Tech Ltd
Incorporated: 19 November 2013 *Employees:* 5
Net Worth: £5,410 *Total Assets:* £229,940
Registered Office: 1 Parkshot, Richmond, Surrey, TW9 2RD
Major Shareholder: Marie Linda Shirley Pavlou
Officers: Danielle Nicole Pavlou [1984] R&D Director; James Paul Pavlou [1986] Production Director; Marie Linda Shirley Pavlou [1959] Director

Bioreactor Corporation Limited
Incorporated: 17 April 2014
Net Worth: £1 *Total Assets:* £1
Registered Office: Celixir House, Stratford upon Avon Business & Technology Park, Innovation Way, Stratford upon Avon, Warwicks, CV37 7GZ
Parent: Cell Therapy Limited
Officers: Trevor Reginald, Secretary; Trevor Reginald [1972] Director

Biostatus Ltd
Incorporated: 12 July 1995 *Employees:* 7
Net Worth: £467,672 *Total Assets:* £827,393
Registered Office: 56a Charnwood Road, Shepshed, Loughborough, Leics, LE12 9NP
Shareholders: Stefan Ogrodzinski; Laurence Hylton Patterson; Professor Paul James Smith
Officers: Stefan Ogrodzinski, Secretary/Commercial Director; Doctor Rachel Jane Errington [1966] Director/Researcher; Michael Stuart Leyland [1949] Director/Chartered Accountant; Stefan Ogrodzinski [1964] Director; Prof Laurence Hylton Patterson [1952] Director/Professor; Professor Paul James Smith [1953] Director/Professor

Biosuspensions Limited
Incorporated: 24 December 2008
Net Worth Deficit: £167,537 *Total Assets:* £1,124
Registered Office: 56a Charnwood Road, Shepshed, Leics, LE12 9NP
Parent: Biostatus Ltd
Officers: Stefan Ogrodzinski [1964] Director

Biosynth Europe Limited
Incorporated: 5 December 2005
Net Worth: £224 *Total Assets:* £3,511
Registered Office: Suite 1, Lower Ground Floor, One George Yard, London, EC3V 9DF
Officers: David Ross McEwan, Secretary; David Ross McEwan [1960] Director

Biotanical Ltd
Incorporated: 5 July 2018
Registered Office: 7 Sandy Court, Ashleigh Way, Langage Business Park, Plymouth, PL7 5JX
Major Shareholder: Richard Corsie
Officers: Richard Corsie [1966] Director

Biotech Design and Validation Ltd.
Incorporated: 24 May 1995
Registered Office: Ardencote, New Road, Norton Lindsey, Warwick, CV35 8JB
Major Shareholder: Philip David Aidan James
Officers: Pauline Stephanie James, Secretary; Pauline Stephanie James [1963] Director/Company Secretary; Doctor Philip David Aidan James [1965] Director/Pharmaceutical Engineer

Biotechflow Ltd
Incorporated: 29 November 2010
Net Worth: £76,512 *Total Assets:* £146,561
Registered Office: Chedworth House, 8 Lansdown, Stroud, Glos, GL5 1BD
Major Shareholder: Martin John Hofmann
Officers: Dr Martin John Hofmann [1957] Managing Director

Biotherics Limited
Incorporated: 26 May 2009
Net Worth Deficit: £2,949 *Total Assets:* £923
Registered Office: 56a Charnwood Road, Shepshed, Leics, LE12 9NP
Parent: Biostatus Ltd
Officers: Stefan Ogrodzinski [1964] Director

Birchwood Pharma Ltd
Incorporated: 17 June 2011 *Employees:* 3
Net Worth: £859,179 *Total Assets:* £950,473
Registered Office: Regus House, Victory Way, Admirals Park, Crossways, Dartford, Kent, DA2 6QD
Shareholders: Henley Laboratories Limited; John Keith Fisher
Officers: John Keith Fisher [1972] Director

Bisurall Ltd
Incorporated: 18 July 2018
Registered Office: Unit 3 Trinity Centre, Park Farm Industrial Estate, Wellingborough, Northants, NN8 6ZB
Major Shareholder: Aimee Heenan
Officers: Maricia Borja [1999] Director [Filipino]

Biteback Products Ltd
Incorporated: 6 March 2017
Net Worth: £8,840 *Total Assets:* £25,060
Registered Office: The Cottage, High Stree Rowde, Devizes, Wilts, SN10 2PL
Shareholders: Kathleen Margaret Shaw; Colin Anthony Shaw
Officers: Colin Anthony Shaw [1948] Director; Fiona Victoria Shaw [1975] Director; Kathleen Margaret Shaw [1947] Managing Director

R & R Black Brilliant Ventures PLC
Incorporated: 14 October 2018
Registered Office: 3rd Floor, 120 Baker Street, London, W1U 6TU
Major Shareholder: Jose Antonio Romero de Souza
Officers: Jose Antonio Romero de Souza, Secretary; Jose Antonio Romero de Souza [1951] Director/President and CEO [Brazilian]; Pedro Durao Romero de Souza [1994] Director/Vice-President and Vice-CEO [Brazilian]

Blackburn Distributions Ltd
Incorporated: 12 July 2007
Net Worth: £169,203 *Total Assets:* £302,300
Registered Office: Unit D, Vision Park, Bell Way, Burnley, Lancs, BB12 0AN
Major Shareholder: Ben Blackburn
Officers: Ben Blackburn [1986] Director/Manager

Blackley 2010 Limited
Incorporated: 2 December 2010
Net Worth Deficit: £58,004 *Total Assets:* £14,734
Registered Office: Douglas Bank House, Wigan Lane, Wigan, Lancs, WN1 2TB
Parent: Blackley Holdings Limited
Officers: Julian Viggars [1968] Director

Blackpool Medicines Limited
Incorporated: 17 May 2018
Registered Office: Unit 2b Premier House, Cornford Road, Blackpool, Lancs, FY4 4QQ
Officers: Dr Daniel Thomas Bennett [1979] Director; Stephanie Louise Milne [1983] Director; Samir Vohra [1971] Director

Blackrock Pharmaceuticals Limited
Incorporated: 20 December 2007 *Employees:* 5
Net Worth Deficit: £548,812 *Total Assets:* £345,957
Registered Office: Abbey Place, 24-28 Easton Street, High Wycombe, Bucks, HP11 1NT
Shareholders: Peter William Griffin; Una Mary Loughrey
Officers: Rupert Adam John Davies [1968] Global Commercial Director; Peter William Griffin [1968] Director; Una Mary Loughrey [1968] Charity Director; Philip William Shaw McFerran [1968] Managing Director; Desmond McMahon [1966] Director/Regulatory Consultant

Blend & Glow Limited
Incorporated: 10 October 2016
Registered Office: Seddon Smith, Milton House, Aylesbury, Bucks, HP19 8EA
Officers: Charlotte Anne Franek [1990] Director

Blends for Massage Limited
Incorporated: 1 February 2017 *Employees:* 1
Net Worth Deficit: £16,177 *Total Assets:* £2,346
Registered Office: 613 London Road, Westcliff on Sea, Essex, SS0 9PE
Major Shareholder: Patricia Mary Muzalewski
Officers: Patricia Mary Muzalewski [1955] Director

Blistex Limited
Incorporated: 18 December 1963 *Employees:* 2
Net Worth: £1,212,561 *Total Assets:* £1,612,094
Registered Office: 94 Rickmansworth Road, Watford, Herts, WD18 7JJ
Shareholder: D.D.D. Limited
Officers: Justin Arch [1979] Director/Chief Executive Officer [American]; Carl Atkinson [1974] Director

Bodeli Consultants Limited
Incorporated: 16 November 2017
Registered Office: Brunel House, 340 Firecrest Court, Centre Park, Warrington, Cheshire, WA1 1RG
Shareholders: Isaac Adebayo; Elizabeth Okoria
Officers: Elizabeth Okoria [1983] Director

Bodywise Limited
Incorporated: 9 April 1980
Net Worth: £1,273,559 *Total Assets:* £1,395,130
Registered Office: Unit 8 Enterprise Way, Somerton Trading Estate, Newport Road, Cowes, Isle of Wight, PO31 8AP
Major Shareholder: David John Craddock
Officers: Kate Ann Yaxley, Secretary; David John Craddock [1953] Director/Chemist

Boehringer Ingelheim Animal Health UK Limited
Incorporated: 20 November 1985 *Employees:* 183
Previous: Merial Animal Health Limited
Net Worth: £15,859,000 *Total Assets:* £62,210,000
Registered Office: c/o Boehringer Ingelheim Limited, Ellesfield Avenue, Bracknell, Berks, RG12 8YS
Officers: Uday Kumar Bose [1975] Director; Richard James Butson [1965] Director; Benjamin James Moynihan [1972] Director

Boehringer Ingelheim Limited
Incorporated: 1 January 1962 *Employees:* 530
Net Worth: £45,469,000 *Total Assets:* £157,427,008
Registered Office: Ellesfield Avenue, Bracknell, Berks, RG12 8YS
Officers: Uday Kumar Bose [1975] Director; Benjamin James Moynihan [1972] Director/Accountant

Bohemia Pharmaceuticals Ltd.
Incorporated: 14 December 2016
Registered Office: Kemp House, 152 City Road, London, EC1V 2NX
Officers: David RAC [1981] Director [Slovak]

Boley Nutraceuticals Ltd.
Incorporated: 13 May 2016
Net Worth Deficit: £43,810 *Total Assets:* £60,100
Registered Office: 6 Tellisford, Esher, Surrey, KT10 8AE
Major Shareholder: Anita Louise Eyles
Officers: Anita Louise Eyles [1960] Founder, Director

The Bolton Pharmaceutical Company 100 Ltd
Incorporated: 27 October 2003 *Employees:* 3
Net Worth Deficit: £3,506 *Total Assets:* £823
Registered Office: Allenby Laboratories, Wigan Road, Westhoughton, Bolton, Lancs, BL5 2AL
Parent: CD Medical Limited
Officers: Lee Fairbrother, Secretary; Elsie Maureen Armstrong [1951] Director; Michael Gatenby [1942] Director; Gerard Michael Dominic Pessagno [1952] Director

Gary Boon Ltd
Incorporated: 27 November 2017
Registered Office: Cannon House, Rutland Road, Sheffield, S3 8DP
Major Shareholder: Gary Boon
Officers: Gary Boon [1961] Director

Boost Hair Limited
Incorporated: 2 November 2017
Registered Office: 36 High Street, Cleethorpes, N E Lincs, DN35 8JN
Parent: Brandhaus Holdings Ltd
Officers: Martin John Schiele [1983] Director

Booteatox Limited
Incorporated: 17 May 2018
Registered Office: Unit G25, Waterfront Studios, 1 Dock Road, London, E16 1AH
Major Shareholder: Bingjie Li
Officers: Bingjie Li [1996] Director [Chinese]

Boothmasked Ltd
Incorporated: 28 April 2018
Registered Office: Office 3, 146-148 Bury Old Road, Whitefield, Manchester, M45 6AT
Shareholders: Deo Anthony Javier; Michael Wolfendale
Officers: Deo Anthony Javier [1981] Director [Filipino]

Botanica International Limited
Incorporated: 30 June 2005 *Employees:* 4
Net Worth: £2,285 *Total Assets:* £107,313
Registered Office: Forsyth House, Cromac Square, Belfast, BT2 8LA
Major Shareholder: Sean Cooney
Officers: Sean Cooney [1954] Director [Irish]

Bowmed Limited
Incorporated: 6 February 2004
Net Worth Deficit: £1,814,391
Registered Office: Ridings Point, Whistler Drive, Castleford, W Yorks, WF10 5HX
Parent: Arrow Group ApS
Officers: Dean Michael Cooper [1972] Director/Chartered Accountant; Kim Innes [1968] Director/General Manager

J.L.Bragg (Ipswich) Limited
Incorporated: 4 November 1971 *Employees:* 8
Net Worth: £386,711 *Total Assets:* £532,982
Registered Office: c/o John Phillips & Co Ltd, 81 Centaur Court, Claydon Business Park, Great Blakenham, Ipswich, Suffolk, IP6 0NL
Parent: Realistic Limited
Officers: John Briggs, Secretary; John Albert Briggs [1961] Director; Vanessa Briggs [1967] Director

Brainpower Group Ltd.
Incorporated: 9 February 2016 *Employees:* 1
Net Worth: £1,348 *Total Assets:* £27,691
Registered Office: 44 High Ash Mount, Leeds, LS17 8RW
Major Shareholder: Ashley Ross Peat
Officers: Ashley Ross Peat [1991] Director

Brainstorm Cell Therapeutics UK Ltd
Incorporated: 19 February 2013
Registered Office: Suite 1, 3rd Floor, 11-12 St James's Square, London, SW1Y 4LB
Parent: Brainstorm Cell Therapeutics Inc.
Officers: Uri Yablonka [1976] Director [Czech]

Brassard Limited
Incorporated: 9 September 2008
Net Worth Deficit: £12,615 *Total Assets:* £657
Registered Office: 1 Leacroft Avenue, Wandsworth Common, London, SW12 8NF
Major Shareholder: Inghua Ting
Officers: Dr Susan Alexander [1971] Director/Orthopaedic Surgeon; Inghua Ting [1974] Director/Designer

Braun International Limited
Incorporated: 31 July 1995
Net Worth Deficit: £17,101 *Total Assets:* £399
Registered Office: Unit 11b-11c Harrier Road, Humber Bridge Industrial Estate, Barton upon Humber, N Lincs, DN18 5RP
Major Shareholder: Barry Roy Shepherd
Officers: Tracey Marie Shepherd, Secretary; Barry Roy Shepherd [1949] Director

Bray Group Limited
Incorporated: 27 October 1978 *Employees:* 30
Net Worth: £942,165 *Total Assets:* £1,772,642
Registered Office: Unit 1 Regal Way, Faringdon, Oxon, SN7 7BX
Parent: Bray Holdings Limited
Officers: Randal Joseph Pakeman, Secretary/Director; Nicholas Barritt Jones [1951] Director; Randal Joseph Pakeman [1953] Director

Brazilian Kimberlite Clay Ltd
Incorporated: 13 November 2018
Registered Office: 13 Newbury Road, London, E4 9JH
Major Shareholder: Bianca Tavares Veloso
Officers: Bianca Tavares Veloso [1978] Director [Portuguese]

Breath Limited
Incorporated: 9 March 2000
Net Worth: £51,837,332 *Total Assets:* £52,331,824
Registered Office: Whiddon Valley, Barnstaple, Devon, EX32 8NS
Parent: Arrow Group ApS
Officers: Dean Michael Cooper [1972] Director/Chartered Accountant; Kim Innes [1968] Director/General Manager

Breckland International Ltd.
Incorporated: 30 March 1995 *Employees:* 1
Net Worth: £19,904 *Total Assets:* £20,597
Registered Office: Grange Farm, Cockley Cley Road, Hilbrough, Thetford, Norfolk, IP26 5BT
Parent: Agrifutura Limited
Officers: Philip Geoffrey Charlton-Smith [1958] Director

Brewtaal Ltd
Incorporated: 30 May 2018
Registered Office: 20-22 Wenlock Road, London, N1 7GU
Officers: Adrian Dulgher [1986] Director; Dr Karen Yvonne Sumser Lupson [1959] Director/PhD - Health & Maritime

Bristol-Myers Squibb Pharmaceuticals Limited
Incorporated: 2 April 1990 *Employees:* 414
Net Worth: £165,060,992 *Total Assets:* £276,734,016
Registered Office: Uxbridge Business Park, Sanderson Road, Uxbridge, Middlesex, UB8 1DH
Parent: Bristol-Myers Squibb Holdings 2002 Limited
Officers: Bertrand Pierre Marie Grosjean [1969] Finance Director [French]; Veronique Maguin EP Walsh [1961] Director/General Manager (UK & Ireland) [French]

Britanica Medicines & Medical Equipment Ltd
Incorporated: 16 August 2016
Registered Office: Zaj Associates, 41-A Mill Lane, West Hampstead, London, NW6 1NB
Major Shareholder: Ashrf Elhoush
Officers: Ashrf Elhoush [1973] Director/Trade [Libyan]

Britpharma UK Limited
Incorporated: 25 August 2018
Registered Office: 71-75 Shelton Street, London, WC2H 9JQ
Shareholders: Mamta Chachan; Prasanna Chachan
Officers: Mamta Chachan, Secretary; Mamta Chachan [1980] Director [Indian]; Prasanna Chachan [1978] Director [Indian]

Brosis Ltd
Incorporated: 23 October 2018
Registered Office: Kemp House, 160 City Road, London, EC1V 2NX
Shareholder: Jaymini Patel
Officers: Jaymini Patel, Secretary; Jaymini Patel [1968] Director/Pharmacist; Nikhil Patel [1996] Director/Student; Sajan Patel [2000] Director/Student; Shayli Patel [1995] Director/Vendor Administrator

Brown & Burk UK Limited
Incorporated: 2 October 2000 *Employees:* 7
Net Worth: £2,455,673 *Total Assets:* £12,304,449
Registered Office: Micro House, 5 Marryat Close, Hounslow, Middlesex, TW4 5DQ
Officers: Preetham Sharma Hiremat [1973] Director [Indian]; Badarinath Ibrampur [1966] Director [Indian]; Ashok Kumar Jain [1956] Director [Indian]

Brown Exclusive (Worldwide) Limited
Incorporated: 2 January 2018
Registered Office: H5 Ash Tree Court, Nottingham Business Park, Nottingham, NG8 6PY
Shareholder: Eckhard Franz Heinrich Emde
Officers: Eckhard Emde, Secretary; Eckhard Emde [1957] Director/IT Analyst [German]; Patrik Heider [1990] Director/Product Development [Austrian]

Brunel Healthcare Manufacturing Limited
Incorporated: 6 August 2002 *Employees:* 389
Net Worth: £5,113,000 *Total Assets:* £33,375,000
Registered Office: William Nadin Way, Swadlincote, Derbys, DE11 0BB
Shareholder: Liang Chang
Officers: James David Amery, Secretary; James David Amery [1975] Finance Director; Richard Henry Fielding [1968] OTC Director; John Edward Hackett [1967] Director; Robert Andrew Jeremy Haytack [1978] Commercial Director; Matthew Robert Woodings [1970] Operations Director

BtechLaboratories (UK) Ltd.
Incorporated: 19 April 2017 *Employees:* 2
Net Worth Deficit: £483 *Total Assets:* £30,015
Registered Office: Ambiya House, 25 Burgess Wood Road South, Beaconsfield, Bucks, HP9 1EX
Shareholder: Heinrich Kunz
Officers: Heinrich Kunz [1972] Director [German]; Sundip Singh Shihn [1969] Director/Investment Professional

Bulgarian Healthy Products Limited
Incorporated: 4 July 2018
Registered Office: Flat 7, 145 Commonside East, Mitcham, Surrey, CR4 2QB
Officers: Vasil Stefanov [1987] Director [Bulgarian]

BVM Medical Limited
Incorporated: 12 July 1989 *Employees:* 24
Net Worth: £4,894,851 *Total Assets:* £6,019,489
Registered Office: B V M House, Trinity Lane, Hinckley, Leics, LE10 0BL
Officers: Chhotalal Chhaganlal Patel, Secretary/Pharmacist; Haroon Al Rashid Dawood Atchia [1960] Director/Medical Device Specialist; Ronald Andrew Eagle [1962] Director/Solicitor; Anthony Hyett [1941] Director; Chhotalal Chhaganlal Patel [1953] Director/Pharmacist; Jayesh Dulabh Tailor [1959] Director/Sales Consultant; Jayshree Jayesh Tailor [1960] Director/Finance Controller

Byrom (South Wales) Limited
Incorporated: 10 October 1997 *Employees:* 15
Net Worth: £699,989 *Total Assets:* £865,794
Registered Office: Rhoose Pharmacy, 53 Fontygary Road, Rhoose, S Glamorgan, CF62 3DT
Major Shareholder: Peter Williams
Officers: Diane Williams, Secretary; Diane Williams [1964] Director/Assistant; Peter Williams [1962] Director/Pharmacist

C 3 Innovations Limited
Incorporated: 3 October 2018
Registered Office: 10 Station Road, Henley on Thames, Oxon, RG9 1AY
Shareholders: John Hywel Davies; John Edward Moses
Officers: John Hywel Davies [1949] Director; John Edward Moses [1975] Director/University Professor

C P Pharmaceuticals Limited
Incorporated: 13 May 1950 *Employees:* 320
Net Worth: £19,766,000 *Total Assets:* £54,467,000
Registered Office: Ash Road North, Wrexham Industrial Estate, Wrexham, Clwyd, LL13 9UF
Officers: James Patrick Higgins, Secretary; Ravindra Kamalakar Limaye [1964] Managing Director [Indian]; Neil Wynne [1958] Director

Caithness Biotechnologies Limited
Incorporated: 19 January 2015 *Employees:* 1
Net Worth Deficit: £548 *Total Assets:* £12,018
Registered Office: 72 Boston Road, Leicester, LE4 1HB
Major Shareholder: Clett Erridge
Officers: Clett Erridge [1973] Director/Scientist

Calea UK Limited
Incorporated: 30 May 1990 *Employees:* 494
Net Worth: £23,250,000 *Total Assets:* £30,017,000
Registered Office: Cestrian Court, Eastgate Way, Manor Park, Runcorn, Cheshire, WA7 1NT
Parent: FHC (Holdings) Limited
Officers: Marc James Gerard Crouton [1959] Director [French]; Christopher Paul Harrison [1966] Managing Director; David Michael Kehoe [1984] Finance Director; Mark Henry Kirkup [1969] Director; Frank Lucassen [1972] Director [German]; Niamh Matic [1973] Director [Irish]; Rezzan Newton [1972] Director [Turkish]

Calla Lily Personal Care Ltd
Incorporated: 3 February 1998
Net Worth: £1,571,954 *Total Assets:* £1,601,679
Registered Office: 10 Rose & Crown Yard, King Street, London, SW1Y 6RE
Shareholders: Keir McGuinness; Vinh-Thang Vo-Ta
Officers: Keir McGuinness [1949] Director/Consultant; Vinh-Thang Vo-TA [1976] Director [Canadian]

Cambcol Ltd
Incorporated: 11 December 2014
Net Worth Deficit: £58,037 *Total Assets:* £18,640
Registered Office: P O Box 727, 15 Station Road, Wilburton, Ely, Cambs, CB7 9RP
Major Shareholder: Jonathan Michael Fitton
Officers: Michael Maloney, Secretary; Jonathan Michael Fitton [1970] Director; Michael Maloney [1958] Finance Director

Cambridge Advanced Technologies Ltd
Incorporated: 24 March 2017
Registered Office: St John's Innovation Centre, Cowley Road, Cambridge, CB4 0WS
Shareholder: Mariusz Czernik
Officers: Mariusz Czernik, Secretary; Mariusz Czernik [1976] Director [Polish]; Monika Czernik [1977] Director [Polish]

Cambridge Collagen Company (UK) Ltd
Incorporated: 31 March 2011
Previous: The Chinese Pancake Company Ltd
Registered Office: P O Box 727, 15 Station Road, Wilburton, Ely, Cambs, CB7 9RP
Major Shareholder: Jonathan Michael Fitton
Officers: Jonathan Fitton, Secretary; Jonathan Fitton [1970] Director

Cambridge Healthcare Supplies 2012 Limited
Incorporated: 29 October 2012 *Employees:* 3
Net Worth: £1,545,746 *Total Assets:* £1,546,776
Registered Office: Unit 1-2 Wymondham Business Park, Chestnut Drive, Wymondham, Norfolk, NR18 9SB
Major Shareholder: Yashvantrai Vallabhji Ondhia
Officers: Aruna Yashvantrai Ondhia [1951] Director; Punam Ondhia [1980] Director; Yashvantrai Vallabhji Ondhia [1948] Director/Chartered Accountant

Cambridge Healthcare Supplies Limited
Incorporated: 11 November 1997 *Employees:* 9
Net Worth: £2,084,170 *Total Assets:* £3,763,750
Registered Office: Unit 1 Wymondham Business Park, Chestnut Drive, Wymondham, Norfolk, NR18 9SB
Officers: Yashvantrai Vallabhji Ondhia, Secretary/Chartered Accountant; Aruna Yashvantrai Ondhia [1951] Director; Punam Ondhia [1980] Director; Yashvantrai Vallabhji Ondhia [1948] Director/Chartered Accountant

Cambridge Innovation Group Limited
Incorporated: 30 August 2016
Registered Office: 73 Eyot House, Sun Passage, London, SE16 4BP
Major Shareholder: Petros Tyrakis
Officers: Petros Tyrakis [1988] Director/Researcher [Greek]

Cambridge Sensors Ltd
Incorporated: 4 December 1991 *Employees:* 34
Net Worth: £4,957,981 *Total Assets:* £5,299,370
Registered Office: 9 Cardinal Park, Godmanchester, Huntingdon, Cambs, PE29 2XG
Shareholders: James Michael McCann; Christopher Robin Lowe
Officers: Nicholas John Diss, Secretary; Nicholas John Diss [1958] Director/Chartered Accountant; Prof Christopher Robin Lowe [1945] Director/Scientist; James Michael McCann [1957] Director/Engineer [Irish]; Karen Susan Skelham [1971] Director/Sales Manager; Dr Bernadette Yon Hin [1957] Director Operations

Cancer Genetics Ltd
Incorporated: 18 July 2017
Registered Office: 21 Vincent Court Green Lane, London, NW4 2AN
Officers: Zvi Suissa [1968] Director

Candles UK Ltd
Incorporated: 17 September 2003
Net Worth: £10,000,000 *Total Assets:* £10,000,000
Registered Office: Apartment 615, 7 Baltimore Wharf, London, E14 9EY
Major Shareholder: Igor Portonenko
Officers: Igor Portonenko [1964] General Director [Belarusian]

Canna Care Limited
Incorporated: 20 February 2018
Registered Office: 13-17 Paradise Square, Sheffield, S1 2DE
Officers: Amy Emma Barker [1985] Director/Member; Anwar Mohamed [1966] Director/Member

Cannabidiol UK Ltd
Incorporated: 7 June 2018
Registered Office: Charnwood Science Centre, 103 High Street, Syston, Leicester, LE7 1GQ
Shareholders: Susan Ruth Huntley-Copeman; Anthony Paul Carter
Officers: Anthony Paul Carter [1964] Director/Consultant; Susan Ruth Huntley-Copeman [1970] Director

Cannacureyou Ltd
Incorporated: 23 April 2018
Registered Office: Unit 2a Gate C, Midland Road, Wednesbury, W Midlands, WS10 8HE
Officers: Jason Ferguson [1974] Director; David Anthony Lavender [1979] Director

Cannerald Group Ltd
Incorporated: 20 December 2018
Registered Office: Suite 41, Victoria House, 38 Surrey Quays Road, London, SE16 7DX
Shareholders: Maik Marcel Pietrowski; Sascha Adrian Waeschle; Levin Kim Amweg
Officers: Levin Kim Amweg [1994] Director/Entrepreneur [Swiss]; Maik Marcel Pietrowski [1993] Director/Entrepreneur [Polish]; Sascha Adrian Waeschle [1995] Director/Entrepreneur [German]

Capa Vision Limited
Incorporated: 24 May 2012
Net Worth: £306,944 *Total Assets:* £400,007
Registered Office: Calder & Co, 16 Charles II Street, London, SW1Y 4NW
Shareholders: Andrea Elizabeth Reading; Clive Henry Reading
Officers: Andrea Elizabeth Reading [1946] Director; Clive Henry Reading [1944] Director

Captium Limited
Incorporated: 7 May 2015 *Employees:* 1
Net Worth Deficit: £53,872 *Total Assets:* £46,282
Registered Office: 5 Bow Road, London, E3 2AD
Major Shareholder: Kevin John Wilkinson
Officers: Kevin John Wilkinson [1960] Director/Manager [Canadian]

Cardiome UK Limited
Incorporated: 6 July 2007
Net Worth Deficit: £36,233 *Total Assets:* £488,073
Registered Office: Lakeside House, 1 Furzeground Way, Stockley Park, Uxbridge, Middlesex, UB11 1BD
Parent: Correvio Pharma Corp
Officers: Sheila Mary Grant [1964] Director/Operations Manager [British/Canadian]; Justin Andrew Renz [1971] Director [American]

Care and Wear Collection Limited
Incorporated: 13 June 2016
Registered Office: 6 Kingswood House, Cyprus Street, Bethnal Green, London, E2 0NL
Officers: Isatou N'jie [1976] Director

Carefusion U.K. 244 Limited
Incorporated: 7 July 2006
Net Worth: £1,563,872 *Total Assets:* £1,902,221
Registered Office: The Crescent, Jays Close, Basingstoke, Hants, RG22 4BS
Parent: Becton, Dickinson and Company
Officers: Michael John Fairbourn [1959] Director/VP International Marketing; Edward Daniel Hopkin [1973] Director/Senior Counsel; John Konrad Neat [1967] Director/Finance Controller

Carmel Herbals Limited
Incorporated: 15 May 1990 *Employees:* 3
Net Worth: £20,469 *Total Assets:* £42,416
Registered Office: 20 Sinclair Street, Thurso, Caithness, Sutherland, KW14 7AQ
Shareholder: Brian Lamb
Officers: Brian Victor Lamb [1937] Director/Herbalist

Cartell UK Limited
Incorporated: 6 May 2008
Net Worth Deficit: £49,706 *Total Assets:* £3,109,127
Registered Office: 56 Causeway Road, Earlstrees Industrial Estate, Corby, Northants, NN17 4DU
Shareholders: Lodovico Branchetti; Yin-Hsien Chen
Officers: Lodovico Branchetti [1946] Director [Italian]; Yin Hsien Chen [1988] Director/Chemical Engineer [New Zealander]; Dr Robert Paul Filik [1972] Director

Casra Consultancy (UK) Limited
Incorporated: 2 April 2007 *Employees:* 1
Net Worth: £5,715 *Total Assets:* £37,674
Registered Office: 6 Camellia Drive, Leyland, Lancs, PR25 5RW
Major Shareholder: Simon Cash
Officers: Olga Maria Gomez-Cash, Secretary; Simon Cash [1966] Director

S.L.Cassidy Limited
Incorporated: 28 May 2015
Net Worth: £173 *Total Assets:* £14,183
Registered Office: 20 Headborough Walk, Aldridge, Walsall, W Midlands, WS9 8SA
Officers: Sally Louise Cassidy [1980] Director/Pharmacy Technician

Cast Healthcare Ltd
Incorporated: 20 September 2010 *Employees:* 10
Net Worth Deficit: £33,226 *Total Assets:* £76,034
Registered Office: Unit E, The Business Centre, 5-7 Tobermore Road, Draperstown, Co Londonderry, BT45 7AG
Parent: iMed (NI) Limited
Officers: Paul Murphy [1967] Director; Laurence Gregory O'Kane [1960] Director

Castex Products Limited
Incorporated: 7 December 1982 *Employees:* 23
Net Worth: £5,161,847 *Total Assets:* £6,165,279
Registered Office: Woodside Mill, Woodside Street, New Mills, High Peak, Derbys, SK22 3HF
Major Shareholder: Martin John Whitehead
Officers: Martin John Whitehead, Company Secretary Engineer; Martin John Whitehead [1955] Director/Company Secretary Engineer; Thomas James Whitehead [1986] Production Director

Castpol Ltd
Incorporated: 6 July 2017
Registered Office: 41 Argyle Place, Edinburgh, EH9 1JT
Major Shareholder: Nektarios Bogris
Officers: Nektarios Bogris [1984] Director/Inventor [Greek]

Catalent CTS (Edinburgh) Limited
Incorporated: 4 November 2004 *Employees:* 238
Net Worth: £70,045,720 *Total Assets:* £79,866,568
Registered Office: Frankland Road, Blagrove, Swindon, Wilts, SN5 8YG
Officers: Shaileshbhai Madhavbhai Patel, Secretary; Wetteny Joseph [1972] Director/VP Finance [American]; Shaileshbhai Madhavbhai Patel [1967] Global Director

Catalent Micron Technologies Limited
Incorporated: 17 September 1980 *Employees:* 45
Previous: Micron Technologies Limited
Net Worth: £7,638,594 *Total Assets:* £10,539,052
Registered Office: Frankland Road, Blagrove, Swindon, Wilts, SN5 8YG
Officers: Nyssa Forde, Secretary; Jonathan Arnold [1965] Director/President, Oral Drug Delivery; Steven Fasman [1962] Director [American]; Wetteny Joseph [1972] Director/SVP, CFO [American]

Catalent MTI Pharma Solutions Limited
Incorporated: 20 December 2012
Previous: MTI Pharma Solutions Ltd
Net Worth Deficit: £1,276,264 *Total Assets:* £4,602,633
Registered Office: Frankland Road, Blagrove, Swindon, Wilts, SN5 8YG
Officers: Nyssa Forde, Secretary; Jonathan Arnold [1965] Director/President, Oral Drug Delivery; Steven Fasman [1962] Director [American]; Wetteny Joseph [1972] Director/SVP, CFO [American]

Catalent U.K. Swindon Encaps Limited
Incorporated: 27 November 1937
Registered Office: Frankland Road, Blagrove, Swindon, Wilts, SN5 8YG
Officers: Kirk Walsh, Secretary; Barry Littlejohns [1966] Director/Business Executive

Catalent U.K. Swindon Zydis Limited
Incorporated: 20 February 1980 *Employees:* 472
Net Worth: £220,927,008 *Total Assets:* £266,815,008
Registered Office: Tenth Floor, Capella Building, 60 York Street, Glasgow, G2 8JX
Officers: Alex Reed, Secretary; Jonathan Arnold [1965] Director/President Oral Drug Delivery; Alessandro Maselli [1972] Director/General Manager [Italian]; Kirk Walsh [1980] Finance Director

Catalent UK Supply Chain Limited
Incorporated: 25 September 1989
Previous: Juniper Pharmaceuticals UK Limited
Net Worth: £2,414,691 *Total Assets:* £15,276,553
Registered Office: 8 Orchard Place, Nottingham Business Park, Nottingham, NG8 6PX
Parent: Juniper Pharmaceuticals, Inc.
Officers: Kirk Walsh, Secretary; Jonathan Arnold [1965] Director/President Oral Drug Delivery; Alessandro Maselli [1972] Director/SVP Operations [Italian]; Dr Nikin Patel [1972] Director/Chief Operating Officer; Kirk Walsh [1980] Director/VP Finance

CB Doctor UK Ltd
Incorporated: 19 October 2018
Registered Office: 95 Church Road, Erdington, Birmingham, B24 9BE
Shareholders: Jake Adam Bytheway; Samuel Raymond Cartwright
Officers: Jake Adam Bytheway [1988] Director; Samuel Raymond Cartwright [1987] Director

CBD Biotech Limited
Incorporated: 16 October 2018
Registered Office: Warlies Park House, Horseshoe Hill, Waltham Abbey, Essex, EN9 3SL
Officers: Zulfiqar Khan [1968] Director/Pharmaceuticals

CBD Grow Tech Ltd
Incorporated: 20 December 2018
Registered Office: Office 13, Sycamore Trading Estate, Squires Gate Lane, Blackpool, Lancs, FY4 3RL
Major Shareholder: Carl Deacon
Officers: Carl Deacon, Secretary; Carl Deacon [1983] Director

CBD Pharma Ltd
Incorporated: 17 January 2018
Registered Office: 20-22 Wenlock Road, London, N1 7GU
Major Shareholder: Jose Luis Triguero
Officers: Jose Luis Triguero [1984] Director/Lawyer [Spanish]

CBDHealthcare Ltd
Incorporated: 30 April 2018
Registered Office: 67 Loughborough Road, Nottingham, NG2 7LA
Officers: Daniel Patrick Hembery [1968] Director; Geoffrey Robert Hunter [1957] Director/Surveyor; Lance Antony Shaw [1961] Director

CBPlus Ltd
Incorporated: 9 October 2018
Registered Office: 5 & 6 Miltons Yard, West Street, Axminster, Devon, EX13 5FE
Major Shareholder: Hayley Elizabeth Bromley
Officers: Hayley Elizabeth Bromley [1983] Sales Director

Celadon Pharma Ltd
Incorporated: 3 September 2018
Registered Office: 71-75 Shelton Street, London, WC2H 9JQ
Shareholders: Cormac Short; Paul Allen
Officers: Paul Allen [1991] Director; Cormac Short [1997] Director

Celadon Pharmaceuticals Ltd
Incorporated: 28 January 2019
Registered Office: 23 Vicarage Road, Edgbaston, Birmingham, B15 3HB
Major Shareholder: Paul Allen
Officers: Paul Allen [1991] Director

Celex Oncology Innovations Limited
Incorporated: 28 November 2017
Registered Office: 9th Floor, The Royal Liver Building, Pier Head, Liverpool, L3 1JH
Shareholders: Laurence John Cohen; Professor Mustafa Bilgin Ali Djamgoz
Officers: Laurence John Cohen [1951] Director/Solicitor; Professor Mustafa Bilgin Ali Djamgoz [1952] Director/University Professor

Celgene UK Manufacturing (II) Limited
Incorporated: 16 August 2001
Net Worth: £9,400,358 Total Assets: £12,935,121
Registered Office: 7 Albemarle Street, London, W1S 4HQ
Parent: Celgene UK Manufacturing Limited
Officers: David Walter Pignolet [1963] Director [Swiss]; Nakisa Serry [1965] Director [American]

Celgene UK Manufacturing (III) Limited
Incorporated: 18 October 2006
Net Worth Deficit: £259,237 Total Assets: £792,012
Registered Office: 7 Albemarle Street, London, W1S 4HQ
Parent: Celgene UK Manufacturing (II) Limited
Officers: David Walter Pignolet [1963] Director [Swiss]; Nakisa Serry [1965] Director [American]

Celgene UK Manufacturing Limited
Incorporated: 18 October 2004
Net Worth: £20,280,292 Total Assets: £20,968,104
Registered Office: 7 Albemarle Street, London, W1S 4HQ
Parent: Celgene UK Holdings Limited
Officers: David Walter Pignolet [1963] Director [Swiss]; Nakisa Serry [1965] Director [American]

Cell Medica Limited
Incorporated: 11 November 2005 Employees: 69
Net Worth: £41,248,000 Total Assets: £80,010,000
Registered Office: 1 Canal Side Studios, 8-14 St Pancras Way, London, NW1 0QG
Shareholder: Invesco Ltd
Officers: Mirza Zafar Iskander Qadir, Secretary; Dr Nigel Robert Burns [1960] Director/Independent Consultant; Julia Paige Gregory [1952] Director [American]; Dr Thomas Hecht [1951] Director/Biotechnology Consultant [German]; Annalisa Jenkins [1965] Director; Allan Patrick Marchington [1966] Director/Investor; Christopher John Nowers [1963] Director

Cellon UK Limited
Incorporated: 14 March 2002 Employees: 1
Net Worth: £4,660,214 Total Assets: £4,957,396
Registered Office: 61 Dublin Street, Edinburgh, EH3 6NL
Officers: Elizabeth Mary Scott, Secretary; Richard Paul Fry [1961] Director; Elizabeth Mary Scott [1962] Director

Cellpath USA Limited
Incorporated: 7 April 2011 Employees: 1
Net Worth Deficit: £34,080 Total Assets: £54,666
Registered Office: Unit 80 Mochdre Industrial Estate, Mochdre, Newtown, Powys, SY16 4LE
Officers: Paul James Hatton Webber [1964] Director; Peter James Webber [1935] Director; Philip Leslie John Webber [1966] Director; Clement Trevor Wheatley [1943] Director

Celtic Wellbeing Ltd
Incorporated: 5 July 2011
Previous: Pharma Nutrition Ltd
Net Worth: £11,514 Total Assets: £48,432
Registered Office: 10a Morfa Enterprise Park, Parc Caer Seion, Conwy, LL32 8FA
Major Shareholder: Richard Rhys Owen
Officers: Richard Rhys Owen [1956] Managing Director

Centaur Healthcare Limited
Incorporated: 12 July 2012 Employees: 131
Net Worth: £2,659,303 Total Assets: £7,735,275
Registered Office: Unit 2b Bretby Business Park, Bretby, Burton on Trent, Staffs, DE15 0YZ
Officers: Julian America [1963] Director; Andrew Corbett [1955] Director; Julian James Anthony Richardson [1966] Director

Chafred Consultancy Limited
Incorporated: 25 November 2015
Net Worth: £16 Total Assets: £20,122
Registered Office: 15 Phipps Avenue, Rugby, Warwicks, CV21 4JA
Major Shareholder: Charles Ayamba Ashu
Officers: Charles Ayamba Ashu [1972] Director/Validation Engineering [Irish]

Chalpharm Consultancy Limited
Incorporated: 22 April 2013
Net Worth: £16,680 Total Assets: £28,995
Registered Office: 25 Fieldway, Chalfont St Peter, Gerrards Cross, Bucks, SL9 9SQ
Shareholder: Roland John Collicott
Officers: Dr Roland John Collicott [1954] Director/Chalpharm Consultancy; Wendy Collicott [1956] Director/Chalpharm Consultancy

Chamcotec Ltd
Incorporated: 15 June 2009
Net Worth: £139,000 *Total Assets:* £139,000
Registered Office: Unit 4 Crossville Buildings, Flint Trade Park, Holywell Road, Flint, CH6 5RR
Officers: Paul Morris, Secretary; Paul Morris [1954] Director

Chaos Businezz Solutions Ltd
Incorporated: 3 May 2016
Registered Office: 20-22 Wenlock Road, London, N1 7GU
Major Shareholder: Gurdev Singh Ruprai
Officers: Gurdev Singh Ruprai [1960] Director/Pharmacist

Chapar 2016 Ltd
Incorporated: 2 March 2017
Registered Office: 85 Yarmouth Road, Blofield, Norwich, NR13 4LQ
Major Shareholder: Chandrakant Vallabhdas Ondhia
Officers: Chandrakant Vallabhdas Ondhia [1954] Managing Director

Chapar 2017 Ltd
Incorporated: 2 March 2017
Registered Office: 85 Yarmouth Road, Blofield, Norwich, NR13 4LQ
Major Shareholder: Chandrakant Vallabhdas Ondhia
Officers: Chandrakant Vallabhdas Ondhia [1954] Managing Director

Charis Consult Limited
Incorporated: 16 October 2014
Net Worth Deficit: £5,922 *Total Assets:* £3,740
Registered Office: 4 Richardson Close, Greenhithe, Kent, DA9 9QG
Officers: Mavis Stella Anim Yeboah [1973] Director/Consultant [Ghanaian]; Stephen Anim Yeboah [1973] Director/Pharmacy [Ghanaian]

Charnwood Molecular Limited
Incorporated: 22 April 1998 *Employees:* 44
Net Worth: £2,322,348 *Total Assets:* £2,761,419
Registered Office: The Heritage Building, Beaumont Court, Prince William Road, Loughborough, Leics, LE11 5GA
Shareholders: Professor Steven Mark Allin; Professor Philip Charles Bulman Page
Officers: Dr Steven Mark Allin, Secretary; Professor Steven Mark Allin [1968] Director/Academic; Professor Philip Charles Bulman Page [1955] Director/Academic

Chatfield Pharmaceuticals Limited
Incorporated: 3 March 1971 *Employees:* 2
Net Worth Deficit: £16,121 *Total Assets:* £563,914
Registered Office: 66 Prescot Street, London, E1 8NN
Shareholders: David Louis Charles Solomon; Jane Celia Frances Soloman
Officers: Charmian Solomon, Secretary; Charmian Solomon [1936] Director/Secretary; Dr David Louis Charles Solomon [1970] Director

Chela Animal Health Limited
Incorporated: 21 July 2014
Registered Office: First Floor, Roxburghe House, 273-287 Regent Street, London, W1B 2HA
Parent: Orion Holdings (UK) Limited
Officers: Minal Shah [1984] Director; Rajiv Bharat Kumar Shah [1985] Director

Chelsea Drug & Chemical Company Limited
Incorporated: 6 March 1963
Registered Office: 66 Prescot Street, London, E1 8NN
Major Shareholder: Charmian Solomon
Officers: Charmian Solomon, Secretary; Charmian Solomon [1936] Director/Secretary; Dr David Louis Charles Solomon [1970] Director

Chemagain Limited
Incorporated: 19 May 2014
Net Worth Deficit: £10,855 *Total Assets:* £153
Registered Office: 40 High Street, Northwood, Middlesex, HA6 1BN
Shareholder: Adam Walker
Officers: Melinda Knudsen [1982] Director/Researcher [Australian]; Cynthia Renee Rhoades [1970] Director [American/British]; Nicholas Richard Ryan [1957] Director; Adam Walker [1977] Director/Consultant

Chembinoid Pharma Limited
Incorporated: 24 April 2018
Registered Office: 14 Greaves Street Great Harwood, Blackburn, BB6 7DY
Officers: Shahid Aziz, Secretary; Shahid Aziz [1987] Director/Pharmacist; Faisal Chaudry [1984] Director/Pharmacist; Mohammed Abu-Bakre Chaudry [1987] Director

Chemidex Pharma Limited
Incorporated: 8 November 1982 *Employees:* 20
Net Worth: £29,905,596 *Total Assets:* £48,929,356
Registered Office: Chemidex House, Unit 7 Egham Business Village, Crabtree Road, Egham, Surrey, TW20 8RB
Shareholders: Navinchandra Jamnadas; Varsha Navinchandra
Officers: Nikesh Engineer [1985] Director/Doctor

Chempro Limited
Incorporated: 6 May 1968
Registered Office: 94 Rickmansworth Road, Watford, Herts, WD18 7JJ
Parent: D.D.D. Limited
Officers: Carl Atkinson [1974] Director; Charles Philip Wadsworth [1962] Finance Director

Chemvet UK Limited
Incorporated: 1 April 2014
Registered Office: 183 High Street, Blackwood, Gwent, NP12 1ZF
Major Shareholder: Frank Arve Christensen
Officers: Frank Arve Christensen [1974] Director [Danish]; Peter Arve Christensen [1951] Director [Danish]

Cherwell Therapeutics Ltd.
Incorporated: 27 February 2017
Registered Office: 48 Mill Stream House, Norfolk Street, Oxford, OX1 1EB
Officers: Dr Felix Clanchy, Secretary; Dr Richard Williams, Secretary; Dr Felix Clanchy [1974] Director/Post Doctoral Research Associate [Australian]; Dr Richard Williams [1956] Director/Associate Professor

Chimerix UK Limited
Incorporated: 9 October 2014 *Employees:* 2
Net Worth Deficit: £292,030 *Total Assets:* £23,305
Registered Office: 5th Floor, 6 St Andrew Street, London, EC4A 3AE
Officers: Timothy Trost [1957] Director/Chief Financial Officer, Senior Vice President [American]

Chiropody Express Limited
Incorporated: 21 July 2000   Employees: 2
Net Worth: £3,364   Total Assets: £63,081
Registered Office: 18 Thornhills Lane, Clifton, Brighouse, W Yorks, HD6 4JG
Shareholders: Alan Fletcher; Janine Elizabeth Churchill-Wilding
Officers: Janine Elizabeth Churchill-Kenningham, Secretary; Janine Elizabeth Churchill-Wilding [1971] Director/Customer Service Manager; Alan Fletcher [1954] Director/Product Manager

Chirotech Technology Limited
Incorporated: 3 December 1991
Registered Office: Chirotech Technology Centre, 410 Cambridge Science Park, Milton Road, Cambridge, CB4 0PE
Parent: Reddys Laboratories (EU) Ltd
Officers: Sumit Kushwaha, Secretary; Subir Kohli [1978] Director; Venkata Narsimham Mannam [1968] Finance Director [Indian]; Clemens Johannes Troche [1965] Director/MD, Beta Pharm [German]

Chitomerics Limited
Incorporated: 26 June 2012
Registered Office: 14 Approach Road, St Albans, Herts, AL1 1SR
Shareholders: Ijeoma Florence Uchegbu; Andreas Gerhard Schatzlein
Officers: Dr Andreas Gerhard Schatzlein [1963] Director [German]

Cho Consulting Ltd.
Incorporated: 13 August 2009   Employees: 2
Net Worth: £187,626   Total Assets: £227,176
Registered Office: 3 Coates Place, Edinburgh, EH3 7AA
Major Shareholder: Bonita Ho-Asjoe
Officers: Bonita Ho-Asjoe, Secretary/Business Consultant; Bonita Ho-Asjoe [1967] Director/Business Consultant

Chrome Surgical Ltd.
Incorporated: 4 March 2015
Registered Office: 22 Amherst Street, Cardiff, CF11 7DR
Major Shareholder: Ali Amjad
Officers: Ali Amjad [1987] Director/Surgical and Cosmetic Products [Pakistani]

Church & Dwight UK Limited
Incorporated: 27 August 1942   Employees: 272
Net Worth: £52,386,000   Total Assets: £77,353,000
Registered Office: Wear Bay Road, Folkestone, Kent, CT19 6PG
Parent: Church & Dwight Co. Inc.
Officers: Paul Fair, Secretary; David James Upton, Secretary; Steven Paul Cugine [1962] Director [American]; Robert David Dancy [1962] Director; Michael Robinsohn [1968] Director [French]; David James Upton [1977] Finance Director

Cingem Ltd
Incorporated: 27 July 2018
Registered Office: 4 Harley Street, London, W1G 9PB
Parent: LEH Global Ltd
Officers: Dr Muhammad Ali Qureshi [1970] Director/Doctor

Circassia Pharmaceuticals PLC
Incorporated: 19 May 2006   Employees: 366
Net Worth: £224,800,000   Total Assets: £402,400,000
Registered Office: The Magdalen Centre, Robert Robinson Avenue, Oxford Science Park, Oxford, OX4 4GA
Officers: Julien Fabrice Cotta, Secretary; Julien Fabrice Cotta [1964] Director/Chief Financial Controller; Russell Cummings [1964] Director; Sharon Curran [1968] Director/Business Executive [Irish]; Dr Francesco Granata [1950] Director/Executive in Residence Warburg Pincus [Italian]; Roderick Peter Hafner [1965] Director/R&D Biotechnology; Steven Charles Andrew Harris [1966] Director; Jo Susan Le Couilliard [1963] Director/Business Executive

CKC Aromatherapy Beauty Products Limited
Incorporated: 14 March 2017
Net Worth: £96   Total Assets: £2,890
Registered Office: 25 Crosscavanagh Road, Galbally, Dungannon, Co Tyrone, BT70 3BJ
Officers: Christina Kelly [1975] Director/Beauty Therapist

CKS Scientific Limited
Incorporated: 11 February 2019
Registered Office: S G House, 6 St Cross Road, Winchester, Hants, SO23 9HX
Major Shareholder: Christopher Mark Davies
Officers: Christopher Mark Davies [1986] Director/Senior Process Engineer

Claris LifeSciences (UK) Limited
Incorporated: 4 August 2003
Net Worth: £5,123   Total Assets: £6,283
Registered Office: Golden Gate Lodge, Crewe Hall, Weston Road, Crewe, Cheshire, CW1 6UL
Officers: Bo Anders Caspersson Tarras-Wahlberg, Secretary; Jon Garay [1973] Finance Director [Spanish]; Andrew Neil Goldney [1968] Director/General Manager; Bo Anders Caspersson Tarras-Wahlberg [1975] Director/Attorney [Swedish]

Clarke Pharma Consulting Limited
Incorporated: 18 August 2017   Employees: 2
Net Worth: £41,830   Total Assets: £72,489
Registered Office: 7 Shawbrow View, Darlington, Co Durham, DL3 8UG
Officers: John Generald Clarke, Secretary; Annette Julie Clarke [1961] Director/Administrator; John Generald Clarke [1957] Director/Pharmaceutical Consultant

Clarornell Consulting and Trading Ltd
Incorporated: 12 December 2011
Net Worth: £194   Total Assets: £982
Registered Office: Dr Colbert, La Maison Medicale, 10 Cromwell Place, South Kensington, London, SW7 2JN
Major Shareholder: Jules Colbert Feuhouo
Officers: Jules Colbert Feuhouo [1970] Director/Doctor [French]

Clean Beauty Co Limited
Incorporated: 25 September 2015   Employees: 5
Net Worth: £135,495   Total Assets: £310,663
Registered Office: Studio 311, Record Hall, 16-16a Baldwin's Gardens, London, EC1N 7RJ
Shareholders: Dominika Minarovic; Elsie Jane Rutterford
Officers: Dominika Minarovic [1987] Director/Co-Founder [Slovak]; Elsie Jane Rutterford [1986] Director/Co-Founder

Clickhealth Limited
Incorporated: 9 November 2011
Net Worth: £5,987 *Total Assets:* £5,987
Registered Office: Plot 1, 5J Green Acre Park, Slapton Road, Little Billington, Leighton Buzzard, Beds, LU7 9BP
Officers: Efe Ekakitie [1976] Director/Pharmacist [Nigerian]

Clinigen Group PLC
Incorporated: 12 December 2008 *Employees:* 727
Net Worth: £311,386,304 *Total Assets:* £594,351,360
Registered Office: Pitcairn House, Crown Square, Centrum 100, Burton on Trent, Staffs, DE14 2WW
Officers: Amanda Miller, Secretary; Martin James Abell [1974] Executive Director; Peter Vance Allen [1956] Director; Alan Keith Boyd [1954] Director; Shaun Edward Chilton [1967] Director/Chief Operating Officer; John Hartup [1951] Director; Anne Philomena Hyland [1960] Director; Ian James Nicholson [1960] Director

Clothopharma Limited
Incorporated: 16 January 2010
Registered Office: 8 Broadway Close, Prestbury, Cheltenham, Glos, GL52 3EA
Major Shareholder: Professor Michael Robert Withington Brown
Officers: Paul Robert Brown, Secretary; Professor Michael Robert Withington Brown [1931] Director/University Professor

Clyde Chemist Limited
Incorporated: 4 November 2008
Registered Office: 44 Adelaide Terrace, Benwell, Newcastle upon Tyne, NE4 8BL
Parent: Farah Chemists
Officers: Mohammed Mushtaq Ahmed [1953] Director/Pharmacist; Shakeel Ahmed [1979] Director/Manager; Shakeela Ahmed [1957] Director/Pharmacist

Clyde Valley Cannaceuticals Ltd
Incorporated: 16 January 2019
Registered Office: 54 Vulcan Street, Motherwell, N Lanarks, ML1 1HB
Major Shareholder: Mark Leaning
Officers: Mark Leaning [1977] Director and Company Secretary

CM & D Pharma Limited
Incorporated: 7 August 2008
Registered Office: Elder House, St Georges Business Park, 207 Brooklands Road, Weybridge, Surrey, KT13 0TS
Officers: Luis Cantarell Rocamora [1952] Director/President and CEO, Nestle Health Science SA [Spanish]; Claudio Kuoni [1967] Director/General Counsel [Swiss]

Coast Science UK Limited
Incorporated: 14 August 2017
Registered Office: Hyde Park House, Cartwright Street, Hyde, Cheshire, SK14 4EH
Major Shareholder: Bruce Thomsen
Officers: Gareth John Cross [1966] Director; Bruce Thomsen [1965] Director [American]

Coating Systems (International) Limited
Incorporated: 3 February 1994
Net Worth: £187,376 *Total Assets:* £318,268
Registered Office: Unit 18 Woolpit Business Park, Woolpit, Bury St Edmunds, Suffolk, IP30 9UP
Parent: Lark Technology Group Ltd
Officers: Jon Collard, Secretary; Sean Andrew Stuteley [1968] Director/Electrician

Cocodentax Ltd
Incorporated: 12 April 2018
Registered Office: 20-22 Wenlock Road, London, N1 7GU
Major Shareholder: Grzegorz Guzek
Officers: Grzegorz Guzek [1977] Director [Polish]

Cod Beck Blenders Limited
Incorporated: 30 August 1988 *Employees:* 112
Previous: Gallows Green Services Limited
Net Worth: £4,703,321 *Total Assets:* £9,919,414
Registered Office: Cod Beck Estate, Dalton, Thirsk, N Yorks, YO7 3HR
Shareholders: Keith Boardall; June Mary Boardall; Marcus Keith Boardall; Rowena June Mary Barlow
Officers: Marcus Keith Boardall, Secretary/Chartered Accountant; Keith Boardall [1934] Director/Chartered Accountant; Marcus Keith Boardall [1962] Director/Chartered Accountant; Leslie Brown [1949] Director; Steven James Meyer [1979] Director

Cognitive Bioscience Limited
Incorporated: 26 May 2010
Net Worth: £18,033 *Total Assets:* £28,572
Registered Office: 3 Ivybridge Close, Uxbridge, Middlesex, UB8 3TT
Major Shareholder: Sunil Pratap Jansen
Officers: Lori Miller, Secretary; Sunil Pratap Jansen [1965] Director

Colorcon Limited
Incorporated: 7 January 1971 *Employees:* 252
Net Worth: £35,843,076 *Total Assets:* £81,699,008
Registered Office: Flagship House, Victory Way, Crossways, Dartford, Kent, DA2 6QD
Parent: Colorcon European Holdings (No.5) Limited
Officers: Stephen John Bachelor, Secretary; David Francis Bain [1971] Managing Director - EMEA; Stephen John Bachelor [1967] Finance Director; Martti Tapani Hedman [1958] Director/Chief Executive Officer [Finnish]

Columbia Laboratories (UK) Limited
Incorporated: 15 January 2015
Registered Office: 8 Orchard Place, Nottingham Business Park, Nottingham, NG8 6PX
Parent: Juniper Pharmaceuticals UK Limited
Officers: Jonathan Arnold [1965] Director/President Oral Drug Delivery; Alessandro Maselli [1972] Director/SVP Operations [Italian]; Dr Nikin Patel [1972] Director; Kirk Walsh [1980] Director/VP Finance

Combe International Limited
Incorporated: 13 March 1974 *Employees:* 10
Net Worth: £3,571,132 *Total Assets:* £8,769,294
Registered Office: Cedar Court, Guildford Road, Leatherhead, Surrey, KT22 9RX
Officers: Adrian McCulloch, Secretary; Keech Combe-Shetty [1977] Director/Co-Chief Executive Officer [American]; Akshay Anand Shetty [1977] Director/SVP Global Operations Co-Head Asia & Latin America [Indian]; Clare Want [1966] Managing Director

Comed Healthcare UK Ltd
Incorporated: 25 February 2019
Registered Office: Kemp House, 160 City Road, London, EC1V 2NX
Major Shareholder: Parvez Salman
Officers: Parvez Salman, Secretary; Bushra Patel [1991] Director [Indian]; Parvez Salman [1985] Director/Pharmacist [Fijian]

Comfort Ventures Limited
Incorporated: 16 May 2007
Net Worth Deficit: £1,373 *Total Assets:* £8,500
Registered Office: 29 Westfield Road, Bexleyheath, Kent, DA7 6LS
Officers: Patience Olufunke Idowu, Secretary; Emmanuel Olukayode Idowu [1966] Director/Pharmaceuticals

Commercial and Academic Services Limited
Incorporated: 9 April 1992 *Employees:* 7
Net Worth: £71,096 *Total Assets:* £202,415
Registered Office: Kimbolton House, Mount Beacon, Lansdown, Bath, BA1 5QP
Major Shareholder: Stephen Humphrey Moss
Officers: Dr Stephen Humphrey Moss, Secretary/University Senior Lecturer; Dr Abdel Rahman Ahmed [1952] Director; Susannah Mary Boyd [1978] Director/Software Developer; Feroze Issa Ismail Janmohamed [1946] Director/Pharmacist; Dr Stephen Humphrey Moss [1947] Director/Pharmacist; Dr Colin William Pouton [1955] Director/University Professor

Compliance & Validation Solutions Ltd
Incorporated: 19 May 2015
Net Worth: £15,909 *Total Assets:* £40,092
Registered Office: 23 Pen Y Wen, Coed Mawr, Bangor, Gwynedd, LL57 4TS
Major Shareholder: Nicholas Hardman
Officers: Dr Nicholas Hardman [1968] Director

Concentrates Warehouse Limited
Incorporated: 7 February 2017
Registered Office: 2 Dewar Court, Astmoor Industrial Estate, Runcorn, Cheshire, WA7 1PT
Officers: Anthony Charles Bowman [1981] Director; Serge Jon Davies [1990] Director

Concorde Perfumery and Cosmetics Limited
Incorporated: 10 April 1959
Registered Office: 94 Ricksmansworth Road, Watford, Herts, WD18 7JJ
Parent: D.D.D. Limited
Officers: Carl Atkinson [1974] Director

Confidence Plus Ltd
Incorporated: 27 February 2019
Registered Office: 9 Honeycomb Place, Netherburn, Larkhall, S Lanarks, ML9 3DB
Major Shareholder: Anne Hocknull Inch
Officers: Anne Hocknull Inch [1954] Director

Connoisseur Clouds Ltd
Incorporated: 15 June 2017
Registered Office: 67 Bankton Green, Livingston, W Lothian, EH54 9EB
Officers: Stuart Donoghue [1987] Director

Contura Holdings Limited
Incorporated: 6 May 2016 *Employees:* 39
Net Worth: £5,186,203 *Total Assets:* £14,137,711
Registered Office: 14 Took's Court, London, EC4A 1LB
Shareholder: Ian Jacobson
Officers: Patrick John Banks, Secretary; Patrick John Banks [1962] Director/Chartered Accountant; Graham Julian Fraser-Pye [1968] Managing Director; Ian Jacobson [1960] Director [Canadian/British]; Rakesh Chhaganlal Tailor [1974] Director/General Manager

Contura Limited
Incorporated: 11 January 1996 *Employees:* 12
Previous: Speciality European Pharma Limited
Net Worth Deficit: £1,357,271 *Total Assets:* £6,162,399
Registered Office: 14 Took's Court, London, EC4A 1LB
Parent: Speciality European Pharma Holdings Limited
Officers: Patrick John Banks, Secretary/CFO; Patrick John Banks [1962] Director; Graham Julian Fraser-Pye [1968] Managing Director; Ian Jacobson [1960] Director [Canadian/British]; Debra Joy Roberts [1962] Director/Accountant; Rakesh Chhaganlal Tailor [1974] Director/Marketing Executive

Cool Gell Limited
Incorporated: 29 April 1999
Net Worth: £104,283 *Total Assets:* £134,916
Registered Office: The Maltings, Burton Row, Leeds, LS11 5NX
Officers: Martin Stead, Secretary; Robert Anthony Deegan [1946] Director; Joseph Orbell [1998] Director/Accounts Manager; Martin Stead [1980] Company Secretary/Director; Chloe Stead Deegan [1994] Director; Hannah Stead Deegan [1998] Director; Nathan Lee Telford [1993] Director

Cool Herbals Limited
Incorporated: 10 October 2006 *Employees:* 3
Net Worth Deficit: £160,374 *Total Assets:* £567,579
Registered Office: 386 Green Lane, Ilford, Essex, IG3 9JU
Shareholders: Rabinder Nath Bhanot; Sushma Bhanot
Officers: Sushma Bhanot, Secretary; Rabinder Nath Bhanot [1961] Director/Pharmacist

Corcept Therapeutics UK Limited
Incorporated: 28 March 2017
Net Worth: £1,290 *Total Assets:* £1,290
Registered Office: c/o Legalinx Limited, 1 Fetter Lane, London, EC4A 1BR
Parent: Corcept Therapeutics Incorporated
Officers: Gary Charles Robb [1962] Director/Chief Financial Officer [American]

Cornish Lavender Limited
Incorporated: 16 November 2017
Registered Office: Great Carnbargus Farm, Carnbargus, Perranporth, Cornwall, TR6 0JG
Major Shareholder: Tina Louise Bessell
Officers: Tina Louise Bessell [1969] Director

Corpus Nostrum Limited
Incorporated: 26 April 1989 *Employees:* 31
Net Worth: £38,794 *Total Assets:* £1,417,190
Registered Office: Unit 1 Cardinal Way, Godmanchester, Huntingdon, Cambs, PE29 2XN
Major Shareholder: Karol Pazik
Officers: David Thomas Brazier, Secretary; David Thomas Brazier [1967] Director/Business Manager; Karol Pazik [1964] Managing Director

Cosmana Limited
Incorporated: 30 October 1984
Registered Office: 94 Rickmansworth Road, Watford, Herts, WD18 7JJ
Parent: D.D.D. Limited
Officers: Carl Atkinson [1974] Director

Cosmarida 2010 Limited
Incorporated: 9 August 2010 *Employees:* 55
Net Worth: £684,928 *Total Assets:* £1,509,333
Registered Office: 176-178 Pontefract Road, Cudworth, Barnsley, S Yorks, S72 8BE
Shareholder: Hothouse (IOM) Limited
Officers: Melanie Brownlow [1967] Director; Dean Garth Cook [1963] Director

Cost Saving Solutions Limited
Incorporated: 11 May 2010 *Employees:* 2
Net Worth: £8,548 *Total Assets:* £28,252
Registered Office: 9 Turnbull Road, Fradley, Lichfield, Staffs, WS13 8TB
Shareholder: Andrew Robert Thain
Officers: Andrew Robert Thain [1974] Director; Debbie Sheila Thain [1974] Director

Cotswold Health Limited
Incorporated: 31 August 2011 *Employees:* 2
Previous: Sarniamedica Limited
Net Worth: £1,077 *Total Assets:* £95,060
Registered Office: Harbour Key Ltd, Midway House, Staverton Technology Park, Staverton, Cheltenham, Glos, GL51 6TQ
Shareholders: Thomas Jenkins; Kathryn Anne Jenkins
Officers: Kathryn Jane Jenkins [1959] Director; Dr Thomas Jenkins [1973] Director

Cottage Garden Cosmetics and Gifts Limited
Incorporated: 21 March 1978
Registered Office: Low Leas House, Lea, Matlock, Derbys, DE4 5JR
Major Shareholder: Fiona Margaret Home King
Officers: Fiona Margaret Home King, Secretary/Administration Executive; Fiona Margaret Home King [1943] Director/Administration Executive; Rupert Saulez King [1965] Sales Director

Courtin and Warner Limited
Incorporated: 31 January 1950 *Employees:* 3
Net Worth: £169,297 *Total Assets:* £421,968
Registered Office: Unit F, Malling Brooks, Brooks Road, Lewes, E Sussex, BN7 2QG
Parent: John Gosnell & Co Limited
Officers: David Alan Warner, Secretary; Matthew Peter Fry [1977] Director [Irish]; Nicola Lesley Tickner [1969] Director; Christopher Robert Warner [1972] Director; David Alan Warner [1942] Director

Covestus Limited
Incorporated: 8 November 2018
Registered Office: 100 Longwater Avenue, Green Park, Reading, Berks, RG2 6GP
Parent: Covestus Holdings Limited
Officers: Anthony Richard Booley [1957] Director

Cox Pharmaceutical Ltd
Incorporated: 22 January 2010
Net Worth Deficit: £1,576,995 *Total Assets:* £522,514
Registered Office: Elscot House, Arcadia Avenue, London, N3 2JU
Shareholders: Ibraheem Al-Bajari; Taife Al-Allaq
Officers: Taife Al-Allaq [1974] Managing Director; Ibraheem Al-Bajari [1958] Director

CPT Science Ltd
Incorporated: 5 March 2004
Net Worth Deficit: £67,368 *Total Assets:* £26,793
Registered Office: Owners Business Centre, High Street, Newburn, Newcastle upon Tyne, NE15 8LN
Major Shareholder: Paul Armstrong
Officers: Roland William Miles Beevor, Secretary; Paul Armstrong [1962] Director; Roland William Miles Beevor [1958] Director

Craintern (UK) Limited
Incorporated: 24 October 2003 *Employees:* 14
Net Worth: £187,844 *Total Assets:* £715,867
Registered Office: Suites 17 & 18 Riverside House, Lower Southend Road, Wickford, Essex, SS11 8BB
Shareholders: Terence Roy Catling; Ann Marie Catling
Officers: Ann Marie Catling, Secretary; Ann Marie Catling [1947] Director/IT Manager; Neal Anthony Catling [1974] Director/Engineering; Paul James Catling [1969] Director/Operations Manager; Terence Roy Catling [1945] Director/Engineering

The Crane Bag Limited
Incorporated: 21 March 2018
Registered Office: 237 Southill, Staple Fitzpaine, Taunton, Somerset, TA3 5SJ
Shareholders: Daniel Spencer; Mechteld Afga Van Heck
Officers: Daniel Spencer [1969] Company Secretary/Director; Mechteld Afga Van Heck [1981] Director and Company Secretary [Dutch]

Crawford Healthcare (R & D) Limited
Incorporated: 9 July 2009
Registered Office: King Edward Court, King Edward Road, Knutsford, Cheshire, WA16 0BE
Parent: Crawford Healthcare Holdings PLC
Officers: Christiaan Jan Otto Pool [1972] Director/Financial Controller [Dutch]; Peter Robert Rhodes [1976] Director/In-House Legal Counsel

Crawford Manufacturing Limited
Incorporated: 4 July 2012 *Employees:* 16
Net Worth Deficit: £2,643,803 *Total Assets:* £936,289
Registered Office: King Edward Court, King Edward Road, Knutsford, Cheshire, WA16 0BE
Parent: Crawford Healthcare Holdings PLC
Officers: John Elwood [1969] Director/SVP, Operations [Irish]; Jonathan Robert Lasparini [1980] Director/Vice President, Finance; Peter Robert Rhodes [1976] Director/In-House Legal Counsel

Crescent API Limited
Incorporated: 13 November 2012 *Employees:* 1
Net Worth Deficit: £712 *Total Assets:* £1,376
Registered Office: Units 3-4 Quidhampton Business Units, Polhampton Lane, Overton, Basingstoke, Hants, RG25 3ED
Major Shareholder: Laith Aldoori
Officers: Laith Aldoori [1989] Director/Marketing Executive

Crescent Manufacturing Limited
Incorporated: 9 December 2015
Net Worth Deficit: £2,775,687 *Total Assets:* £1,560,729
Registered Office: Unit 3-4 Quidhampton Business Units, Polhampton Lane, Overton, Basingstoke, Hants, RG25 3ED
Major Shareholder: Mohammed Khalid Aldoori
Officers: Mohammed Khalid Aldoori [1965] Director

Crescent Pharma Limited
Incorporated: 1 May 2003 *Employees:* 42
Net Worth: £17,988,892 *Total Assets:* £47,265,104
Registered Office: Units 3-4 Quidhampton Business Units, Polhampton Lane, Overton, Basingstoke, Hants, RG25 3ED
Officers: Mohammed Al-Doori [1965] Director/Engineer

Crichton Consultancy Services Limited
Incorporated: 12 March 2015
Registered Office: 11 Kirklands Drive, Newton Mearns, Glasgow, G77 5FF
Officers: John Stuart Crichton [1972] Director/Project Manager

Cross Chemicals UK Limited
Incorporated: 15 September 1978
Net Worth: £534,743 *Total Assets:* £718,412
Registered Office: 54 Portland Place, London, W1B 1DY
Shareholder: Donal Thomas Martin Tierney
Officers: Paul Brady, Secretary [Irish]; Paul Declan Brady [1967] Director/Company Secretary [Irish]; Donal Thomas Martin Tierney [1965] Director [Irish]

Cross Healthcare Limited
Incorporated: 11 June 2003 *Employees:* 41
Net Worth: £1,465,563 *Total Assets:* £5,331,699
Registered Office: Tower Bridge House, St Katherines Way, London, E1W 1DD
Shareholders: Alexander Douglas Miller Cruickshank; Carmelo Stamato
Officers: Katie Embrey, Secretary; Alexander Douglas Miller Cruickshank [1975] Director/Sales Executive; Carmelo Stamato [1971] Director

CT-You Ltd
Incorporated: 13 February 2014
Net Worth: £2,809 *Total Assets:* £9,361
Registered Office: 47 Durand Road, Earley, Reading, Berks, RG6 5YU
Major Shareholder: Olayinka Cole
Officers: Olayinka Elizabeth Balogun, Secretary; Dr Olayinka Elizabeth Balogun [1972] Director/Biochemist

CTI Life Sciences Limited
Incorporated: 27 March 2008 *Employees:* 1
Net Worth: £770,791 *Total Assets:* £1,717,657
Registered Office: Highlands House, Basingstoke Road, Spencers Wood, Reading, Berks, RG7 1NT
Officers: Bruce Seeley [1963] Director/Chief Comms Officer [American]

Cupid Peptide Company Limited
Incorporated: 28 June 2012
Net Worth: £25,733 *Total Assets:* £59,798
Registered Office: 30 Elm Street, Cardiff, CF24 3QS
Major Shareholder: William Jonathan Ryves
Officers: Dr William Ryves, Secretary; Dr William Jonathan Ryves [1964] Director/Scientific Researcher; Andrew William Speirs [1965] Director/Corporate Development Specialist

Curis Life Ltd
Incorporated: 6 December 2016
Registered Office: 56 Ashurst Road, West Moors, Dorset, BH22 0LS
Shareholder: Paul Cousineau Massey
Officers: Paul Cousineau Massey, Secretary; Paul Cousineau Massey [1976] Director/Scientist; Alexandra Grainey [1980] Director/Scientist

Curx Pharma (UK) Limited
Incorporated: 13 January 2015
Net Worth: £100 *Total Assets:* £100
Registered Office: 7th Floor, 16 St Martin's-le-Grand, London, EC1A 4EE
Shareholder: Dinendra Mohan Sen
Officers: Dinendra SEN [1949] Director/Biopharmaceutical Company Worker

Custom Pharmaceuticals Limited
Incorporated: 20 June 1979 *Employees:* 173
Net Worth: £4,969,765 *Total Assets:* £8,963,656
Registered Office: Tecore House, Conway Street, Hove, E Sussex, BN3 3LW
Parent: Cheremy Capital LLC
Officers: Michael Jacobs [1960] Technical Director; Veronica Leahy [1972] Finance Director; Nigel Anthony Richardson [1953] Director/Chartered Surveyor; Eva Torok [1954] Business Development Director

Custom Powders Limited
Incorporated: 7 December 1979 *Employees:* 23
Net Worth: £6,695,658 *Total Assets:* £7,411,054
Registered Office: Gateway, Crewe, Cheshire, CW1 6YT
Major Shareholder: Peter Colyer
Officers: Mark Ardern Chadwick [1965] Operations Director; Peter Colyer [1942] Director/Chemist; Nicholas David Kemp Hopper [1960] Director/Engineer; Pascal Jean Jacques Petronelle Van Wegberg [1967] Commercial Director [Dutch]

Cutera Limited
Incorporated: 22 January 2002 *Employees:* 7
Net Worth: £267,150 *Total Assets:* £339,636
Registered Office: P O Box 501, The Nexus Building, Broadway, Letchworth Garden City, Herts, SG6 9BL
Officers: Darren Wayne Alch [1965] Director [American]; Sandra Gardiner [1965] Director/Business Executive [American]

Cutman Ltd
Incorporated: 22 November 2018
Registered Office: Parwich Hall, Parwich, Ashbourne, Derbys, DE6 1QD
Major Shareholder: David AG Shields

Cuttlefish Limited
Incorporated: 14 January 2005 *Employees:* 3
Net Worth: £63,319 *Total Assets:* £223,861
Registered Office: Fircroft, Blackberry Road, Felcourt, East Grinstead, W Sussex, RH19 2LH
Shareholders: Graeme Parkinson; Teresa Parkinson
Officers: Teresa Parkinson, Secretary; Graeme Parkinson [1966] Director

Cycle Pharmaceuticals Ltd
Incorporated: 2 February 2012 *Employees:* 20
Net Worth Deficit: £2,394,546 *Total Assets:* £7,528,174
Registered Office: Bailey Grundy Barrett Building, Little St Mary's Lane, Cambridge, CB2 1RR
Major Shareholder: James Alexander Harrison
Officers: Antonio Benedetti [1969] Director [Italian]; James Alexander Harrison [1974] Director/Executive Chairman; Allen Lefkowitz [1964] Director/Investment Banker [American]; Dr Duncan Charles McNaught Moore [1959] Director; William John Robinson [1948] Director/Deputy Chairman

Cytetech Limited
Incorporated: 21 April 2016
Net Worth Deficit: £129,056 *Total Assets:* £131,187
Registered Office: 2-3 Oak House, Woodland Office Park, Albert Drive, Burgess Hill, W Sussex, RH15 9TN
Shareholders: Wayne Matthew Channon; Jeffrey Drew
Officers: Wayne Matthew Channon [1958] Director; Dr Jeffrey Drew [1963] Director

D.D.D. Limited
Incorporated: 16 May 1912 *Employees:* 304
Net Worth: £4,715,009 *Total Assets:* £27,138,234
Registered Office: 94 Rickmansworth Road, Watford, Herts, WD18 7JJ
Parent: DDD Investments Limited
Officers: Carl Atkinson [1974] Director; Hanna Joy Coonagh [1972] Director; Digby Lawrence Spence Halsby [1976] Non Executive Director; Roger Harrison [1969] Managing Director; Simon Morris [1973] HR Director; Charles Philip Wadsworth [1962] Finance Director

D.D.S.A.Pharmaceuticals Limited
Incorporated: 29 September 1961 *Employees:* 2
Net Worth: £524,564 *Total Assets:* £533,468
Registered Office: 66 Prescot Street, London, E1 8NN
Parent: Chelsea Drug & Chemical Company Limited
Officers: Charmian Solomon, Secretary; Charmian Solomon [1936] Director/Secretary; Dr David Louis Charles Solomon [1970] Director

Dach Cosmeceutics Limited
Incorporated: 20 September 2017
Registered Office: 118 Richmond Road, Southampton, SO15 8FS
Officers: Dr Chidinma Udegbunam Ibie [1984] Director/Pharmaceutical Scientist [Nigerian]

Dalkeith Laboratories Limited
Incorporated: 29 January 1999 *Employees:* 12
Net Worth: £1,974,385 *Total Assets:* £2,869,766
Registered Office: c/o KJA Group, Network House, West 26, Stubs Back Lane, Cleckheaton, W Yorks, BD19 4TT
Shareholders: Ian John Kirk; Peter Noel Miller Cox
Officers: Peter Noel Miller Cox, Secretary/Chemist; Peter Noel Miller Cox [1946] Director/Chemist; Ian John Kirk [1957] Director; Lynne Whiteley [1972] Director/Office Manager

Dana's Creations Ltd
Incorporated: 11 January 2012
Registered Office: 71 Norbury Avenue, Thornton Heath, Surrey, CR7 8AL
Officers: Valerie Jacqueline Dana Peter [1964] Creative Director

Edward Daniel Limited
Incorporated: 1 November 2007
Previous: Groupe Daniel & Daniel Limited
Net Worth Deficit: £41,206 *Total Assets:* £4,432
Registered Office: 50b Elfort Road, Highbury, London, N5 1AZ
Major Shareholder: Edward Daniel
Officers: Rory Anthony Desch, Secretary; Edward Daniel [1968] Director

Dark Knight Holdings Limited
Incorporated: 8 January 2019
Registered Office: 170 Whitchurch Road, Cardiff, CF14 3NA
Major Shareholder: Marc Robinson
Officers: Marc Robinson [1983] Commercial Director

Daz Solutions Ltd.
Incorporated: 23 November 2012
Net Worth: £11,048 *Total Assets:* £17,945
Registered Office: Phoenix House, 2 Phoenix Park, Eaton Socon, St Neots, Cambs, PE19 8EP
Major Shareholder: Darren James Kember
Officers: Darren James Kember [1978] Director/Pharmaceutical Development

DCMP 8E Cepac Limited
Incorporated: 2 January 2019
Registered Office: 121 Silver Street, Edmonton, London, N18 1RG
Major Shareholder: Andree Exner
Officers: Andree Exner, Secretary; Andree Exner [1964] Director/Entrepreneur [Australian]

Dechra Limited
Incorporated: 16 August 2002 *Employees:* 249
Net Worth: £306,510,016 *Total Assets:* £355,960,992
Registered Office: Snaygill Industrial Estate, Keighley Road, Skipton, N Yorks, BD23 2RW
Parent: Dechra Investments Limited
Officers: Melanie Jane Hall, Secretary; Richard John Cotton [1961] Director; Anthony Gerard Griffin [1963] Director [Irish]; Ian David Page [1961] Director

Delta Diagnostics (UK) Ltd
Incorporated: 18 September 2013 *Employees:* 25
Net Worth: £2,135,064 *Total Assets:* £3,006,092
Registered Office: Citylabs, Nelson Street, Manchester, M13 9NQ
Shareholder: Michael Brian Timbrell Webb
Officers: Edward Peter Henry Farquhar [1966] Director; Gregory John Fitzgibbon [1979] Director; Tony Gee [1963] Finance Director; Dr Ian David Gilham [1960] Director; Mark Andrew Street-Docherty [1984] Sales & Marketing Director

Dendron Limited
Incorporated: 24 July 1895
Registered Office: 94 Rickmansworth Road, Watford, Herts, WD18 7JJ
Parent: D.D.D. Limited
Officers: Carl Atkinson [1974] Director; Charles Philip Wadsworth [1962] Finance Director

Derma Bathe Limited
Incorporated: 27 July 2016
Registered Office: 35 Minster View, Wimborne, Dorset, BH21 1BA
Shareholder: Rebecca Elise Il Ghany
Officers: Morad Khalid Il Ghany [1972] Director; Rebecca Elise Il Ghany [1979] Director

The Derma Hair and Body Shop Limited
Incorporated: 6 November 2018
Registered Office: 71-75 Shelton Street, Covent Garden, London, WC2H 9JQ
Shareholders: Lynne MacGregor; Rose Vero
Officers: Lynne MacGregor, Secretary; Lynne MacGregor [1963] Director; Rose Vero [1991] Director

Derma Solutions Ltd
Incorporated: 21 February 2013
Net Worth Deficit: £1,744 *Total Assets:* £5,300
Registered Office: 18 The Broadway, Stoneleigh, Epsom, Surrey, KT17 2HU
Shareholders: Deon Ross Van Niekerk; Scott David Van Niekerk
Officers: Deon Ross Van Niekerk [1967] Director; Scott David Van Niekerk [1976] Director

Dermaco Limited
Incorporated: 2 April 1996
Net Worth: £81,871 *Total Assets:* £90,017
Registered Office: 8c Market Square, Toddington, Dunstable, Beds, LU5 6BS
Major Shareholder: Joanna Jacqueline Gray
Officers: Joanna Jacqueline Gray [1974] Director/Manager

Dermal Laboratories Limited
Incorporated: 2 November 1981 *Employees:* 146
Net Worth: £30,581,380 *Total Assets:* £40,770,980
Registered Office: Haslers, Old Station Road, Loughton, Essex, IG10 4PL
Parent: Diomed Developments Limited
Officers: Andrew James Head, Secretary; Michael Jonathan Yarrow [1947] Director

Dermaperfetca Ltd
Incorporated: 7 August 2018
Registered Office: Appt 1, 7 Cumberland Road, London, E13 8LH
Major Shareholder: Wagma Ismail
Officers: Dr Wagma Ismail [1981] Director/Doctor [Pakistani]

Dermapharm Skincare Limited
Incorporated: 29 September 2003
Registered Office: The Roothings, 45 Foley Road, Claygate, Surrey, KT10 0LU
Major Shareholder: Timothy James Lovett
Officers: Timothy James Lovett, Secretary/Director; Jennifer Margaret Lovett [1949] Director/Retired Teacher; Timothy James Lovett [1948] Director

Dermatek Limited
Incorporated: 14 February 2019
Registered Office: 61 Lone Tree Avenue, Impington, Cambridge, CB24 9PG
Officers: Kiera Donovan [1966] Sales and Marketing Director; Bjorn Godfrey [1985] Finance Director; Dr Duncan Ross Purvis [1960] Director/Scientist; Dr Janette Ann Thomas [1961] Director/Scientist

Dermato Logical Limited
Incorporated: 3 September 2007 *Employees:* 1
Net Worth: £1,700,034 *Total Assets:* £1,963,435
Registered Office: 102 High Street, Godalming, Surrey, GU7 1DS
Parent: Aspire Pharma Limited
Officers: Debra Joy Roberts, Secretary; Graham Julian Fraser-Pye [1968] Director/Pharmaceuticals; Debra Joy Roberts [1962] Financial Director

Dermatologix Ltd
Incorporated: 15 June 2009
Registered Office: 116 Everton Road, Potton, Sandy, Beds, SG19 2PD
Major Shareholder: Philip Douglas Carroll
Officers: Philip Douglas Carroll [1964] Director/Head of Marketing

Derms Development Limited
Incorporated: 17 August 2004 *Employees:* 2
Net Worth: £45,809 *Total Assets:* £1,058,250
Registered Office: King Edward Court, King Edward Road, Knutsford, Cheshire, WA16 0BE
Parent: Crawford Healthcare Holdings Limited
Officers: Christiaan Jan Otto Pool [1972] Director/Financial Controller [Dutch]; Peter Robert Rhodes [1976] Director/In-House Legal Counsel

Designerx Europe Limited
Incorporated: 27 April 2011
Net Worth: £1 *Total Assets:* £1
Registered Office: Cannon Place, 78 Cannon Street, London, EC4N 6AF
Parent: Polaris Group
Officers: John Stephen Bomalaski [1952] Director/Executive Vice President Medical Affairs [American]; Bor-Wen Wu [1956] Director/Chief Executive Officer [American]

Detraxi Ltd
Incorporated: 3 June 2016
Registered Office: 14 Old Queen Street, London, SW1H 9HP
Shareholders: Philip John Rogers; Anthony Keith King
Officers: Philip John Rogers [1963] Director/Solicitor

Dextra Laboratories Limited
Incorporated: 15 June 2016
Net Worth: £552,267 *Total Assets:* £1,801,955
Registered Office: 1 Glass Wharf, Bristol, BS2 0ZX
Officers: Dr Karen June Etherington [1968] Director/General Manager; Dr Alexander Charles Weymouth-Wilson [1968] Director/Chief Scientific Officer

DHTD Limited
Incorporated: 26 April 1999 *Employees:* 3
Previous: Microimmune Limited
Net Worth: £588,455 *Total Assets:* £628,795
Registered Office: Prospect House, 67 Boston Manor Road, Brentford, Middlesex, TW8 9JQ
Major Shareholder: Deborah Lynn Samuel
Officers: Deborah Lynn Samuel, Secretary; Deborah Lynn Samuel [1957] Director; Hannah Louise Samuel [1986] Director/Nurse; Thomas Peter Samuel [1989] Director/Accountant

Diagnostic Reagents Limited
Incorporated: 4 October 1961 *Employees:* 7
Net Worth: £712,434 *Total Assets:* £766,052
Registered Office: Wenman Road, Thame, Oxon, OX9 3NY
Shareholders: Anthony Kenneth Denson; Anthony Kenneth Denson
Officers: Dr Anthony Kenneth Denson, Secretary; Dr Anthony Kenneth Denson [1948] Managing Director; Stephen Vaughan Reed [1958] Director

Diana Drummond Limited
Incorporated: 14 November 1983
Net Worth: £21,295 *Total Assets:* £24,241
Registered Office: The Machair, Main Road, Cardross, Argyll, G82 5NY
Shareholders: Elspeth Anne Gibb; Charles James Gibb
Officers: Charles James Gibb [1950] Director/Retired; Elspeth Anne MacLean Gibb [1953] Director/Inspector with SCSWIS

Diba Industries Limited
Incorporated: 5 October 1973 *Employees:* 26
Net Worth: £3,301,890 *Total Assets:* £3,840,090
Registered Office: 2 College Park, Coldhams Lane, Cambridge, CB1 3HD
Parent: Halma PLC
Officers: David Marcus Smoley, Secretary; Adam Meyers [1961] Director [American]; Tim O'Sullivan [1967] Director [American]; Kathleen Reilly [1985] Director [American]; David Marcus Smoley [1966] Finance Director

Diep Tran Consultancy Ltd
Incorporated: 28 September 2012 Employees: 2
Net Worth: £22,669 Total Assets: £72,794
Registered Office: 7 Ross Street, Cambridge, CB1 3BP
Shareholders: Diep Duc Tran; Hoa My Thi Vo
Officers: Diep Duc Tran [1963] Director [Dutch]; Hoa MY Thi Vo [1976] Director [Vietnamese]

Dil More Remedies UK Ltd
Incorporated: 7 November 2017
Registered Office: 170 Draycott Avenue, Harrow, Middlesex, HA3 0BZ
Major Shareholder: Diliprao Pandurang More
Officers: Neeta Avinash Mavani [1958] Director; Dr Diliprao Pandurang More [1970] Director [Indian]

Diomed Developments Limited
Incorporated: 2 January 1963 Employees: 238
Net Worth: £54,324,936 Total Assets: £66,227,728
Registered Office: Haslers, Old Station Road, Loughton, Essex, IG10 4PL
Major Shareholder: Michael Jonathan Yarrow
Officers: Heather Jennifer Yarrow, Secretary; Heather Jennifer Yarrow [1949] Director; Michael Jonathan Yarrow [1947] Director; Nicola Irene Yarrow [1987] Director

Dista Products Limited
Incorporated: 13 December 1962
Registered Office: Lilly House, Priestley Road, Basingstoke, Hants, RG24 9NL
Shareholders: Elanco UK AH Limited; Eli Lilly and Company Limited
Officers: Tina Hunt [1969] Director; Christopher Lewis [1978] Director/Finance Manager

Doctor Pharma Manufacturing UK Limited
Incorporated: 23 February 2007
Registered Office: 10 Laud Close, Reading, Berks, RG1 6RD
Major Shareholder: Arun Datwani
Officers: Marty Chakravarti, Secretary; Arun Datwani [1959] Director/Business Investor [Indian]

Dodi Enterprise Ltd
Incorporated: 17 December 2012
Net Worth: £21,651 Total Assets: £21,651
Registered Office: 33 Unity Park, Plymouth, PL3 6NW
Major Shareholder: James Shwarpshaka Yusufu
Officers: Yitmwadi James, Secretary; James Shwarpshaka Yusufu [1977] Director/Pharmacists

Dolphins Limited
Incorporated: 23 January 1996
Net Worth: £2 Total Assets: £24,101
Registered Office: 9 Broadway, London, SW1H 0AZ
Major Shareholder: Philomena Oji Ogboru
Officers: Juliet Joyce Ogboru, Secretary; Philomena Oji Ogboru [1964] Director/Pharmacist

Dong Hwa UK Ltd
Incorporated: 9 November 2018
Registered Office: Suite 31, Second Floor, 107 Cheapside, London, EC2V 6DN
Major Shareholder: Sung Eun Kim
Officers: Sung Eun Kim [1964] Representative Director [South Korean]

Donglun Limited
Incorporated: 9 February 1989 Employees: 4
Net Worth: £514,566 Total Assets: £827,787
Registered Office: 24 Lyndhurst Gardens, London, N3 1TB
Shareholders: Yu Wang; Shunqi Wang
Officers: Yu Wang, Secretary; Tingyu Ke [1944] Director [Chinese]; Shunqi Wang [1944] Director [Chinese]; Yu Wang [1977] Director [Chinese]

Dr Pradeep Reddy's Laboratories (UK & EU) Limited
Incorporated: 25 September 2018
Registered Office: Crown House, 27 Old Gloucester Street, London, WC1N 3AX
Shareholders: Bhavani Potlapadu; Pradeep Kumar Reddy Potlapadu
Officers: Bhavani Potlapadu [1981] Director/Finance Analyst; Dr Pradeep Kumar Reddy Potlapadu [1979] Director/Doctor

Dr Reddy's Laboratories (UK) Limited
Incorporated: 3 June 1983 Employees: 82
Net Worth: £27,312,298 Total Assets: £36,693,180
Registered Office: 6 Riverview Road, Beverley, E Yorks, HU17 0LD
Parent: Reddys Laboratories (EU) Ltd
Officers: Ramanjaneyulu Sane, Secretary; Subir Kohli [1978] Director; Venkata Narsimham Mannam [1968] Director/Vice President - Finance [Indian]; Satish Reddy [1967] Director/Industrialist [Indian]; Clemens Johannes Troche [1965] Director [German]

Dr Russo Cosmetics Limited
Incorporated: 15 October 2018
Registered Office: Flat A, 102 Harley Street, London, W1G 7JB
Officers: Dr Mario Luca Russo [1962] Director/Doctor [Italian]

Dr. Max Pharma Limited
Incorporated: 29 November 2010 Employees: 1
Net Worth: £127,791 Total Assets: £262,845
Registered Office: First Floor, Roxburghe House, 273-287 Regent Street, London, W1B 2HA
Officers: Tomas Fecko [1982] Director [Slovak]

Dr. Reddy's Laboratories (EU) Limited
Incorporated: 13 October 1987 Employees: 200
Net Worth: £70,178,232 Total Assets: £84,630,296
Registered Office: Riverview Road, Beverley, E Yorks, HU17 0LD
Officers: Sumit Kushwaha, Secretary; Subir Kohli [1978] Director; Venkata Narsimham Mannam [1968] Director/VP Finance [Indian]; Clemens Johannes Troche [1965] Managing Director, Betapharm BA [German]

Dr. Tuhin Dev Skin Care Limited
Incorporated: 15 February 2007
Net Worth Deficit: £536,689 Total Assets: £621
Registered Office: 46 St Ina Road, Heath, Cardiff, CF14 4LT
Major Shareholder: Tuhin Kumar Dev
Officers: Brian Neil Cruickshank, Secretary; Dr Tuhin Kumar Development [1969] Managing Director [Malaysian]

Dreamskin Health Limited
Incorporated: 5 October 2004
Net Worth Deficit: £334,184 Total Assets: £104,260
Registered Office: 4 Carters Row, Hatfield Park, Hatfield, Herts, AL9 5NB
Major Shareholder: George Costa
Officers: Eve Kyriacou, Secretary; Egli Gabrielle Costa [1970] Director; George Costa [1963] Director; Eve Kyriacou [1966] Director/Chartered Accountant

Druglab118 Ltd
Incorporated: 15 March 2013
Net Worth Deficit: £146,274 *Total Assets:* £33,827
Registered Office: 43 Coniscliffe Road, Darlington, Co Durham, DL3 7EH
Shareholder: Colin Lyon
Officers: Kylie Christine Bergman [1967] Director [Australian]; Colin Lyon [1957] Director/Company Owner

Drugsdirect Global Ltd
Incorporated: 13 March 2015 *Employees:* 1
Net Worth: £41,861 *Total Assets:* £157,215
Registered Office: Unit 4, 12 Emery Road, Brislington, Bristol, BS4 5PF
Major Shareholder: Alona Courtney
Officers: Dr Alona Courtney [1987] Director

DSP Beauty Development Ltd
Incorporated: 20 July 2017
Registered Office: 19 Cottesmore Court, Stanford Road, London, W8 5QN
Officers: Aldo Masi [1990] Director/Manager [Danish]

DTR Medical Limited
Incorporated: 14 March 2002
Net Worth: £732,891 *Total Assets:* £1,624,281
Registered Office: 17 Clarion Court, Enterprise Park, Swansea, SA6 8RF
Major Shareholder: John Richard Salvage
Officers: Judith Mary Maddock, Secretary; Andrew Robert Davidson [1957] Director; Judith Mary Maddock [1949] Director/Accountant; John Richard Salvage [1959] Managing Director

Duffy Assets Ltd
Incorporated: 22 February 2011
Previous: Duffy Healthcare Ltd
Net Worth: £25,478 *Total Assets:* £243,977
Registered Office: 1a Wendover Road, Rackheath, Norwich, NR13 6LH
Shareholders: Scott Duffy; Justine Ellen Duffy
Officers: Justine Ellen Duffy [1976] Director; Scott Duffy [1978] Managing Director

Durja Pharma Limited
Incorporated: 29 December 2014 *Employees:* 1
Net Worth: £4,386 *Total Assets:* £14,452
Registered Office: 17 Copymoor Close, Wootton, Northampton, NN4 6BL
Major Shareholder: Nishant Shirishkumar Shah
Officers: Jalpa Shah [1985] Director; Nishant Shah [1980] Director

Dushey Limited
Incorporated: 30 January 2019
Registered Office: Accounts Office, Cunliffe House Farm, Longsight Road, Langho, Blackburn, Lancs, BB6 8AD
Shareholders: Kevin Gallagher; Jane Belshaw
Officers: Jane Belshaw [1975] Director; Kevin Gallagher [1964] Director; Brett Andrew Heaps [1987] Director

Dushey Med Limited
Incorporated: 6 February 2019
Registered Office: Accounts Office, Cunliffe House Farm, Longsight Road, Langho, Blackburn, BB6 8AD
Officers: Damien Jonathan Bove [1976] Director; Dr Dorothy Jane Frizelle [1967] Director

DX Products Limited
Incorporated: 14 May 2010 *Employees:* 35
Net Worth: £804,603 *Total Assets:* £3,858,872
Registered Office: Unit 1 Horbury Junction Industrial Park, Calder Vale Road, Horbury, W Yorks, WF4 5ER
Parent: Ultramax Products Ltd
Officers: Joseph Mozalski, Secretary; Carl Alan Pallister [1964] Director

Dynamic Development Laboratories Co Ltd
Incorporated: 16 November 2016
Net Worth: £293 *Total Assets:* £1,454
Registered Office: 316 Beulah Hill, Upper Norwood, London, SE19 3HF
Officers: Serhii Kucherenko [1974] Director [Ukrainian]

Dynamik Products Ltd
Incorporated: 25 February 2016
Registered Office: Canalside House, 5 May's Walk, Alrewas, Burton on Trent, Staffs, DE13 7DT
Officers: Natalie White [1981] Director

E-Breathe Ltd.
Incorporated: 7 October 2016
Net Worth: £5,838 *Total Assets:* £5,838
Registered Office: Ormeau Baths, 18 Ormeau Avenue, Belfast, BT2 8HS
Major Shareholder: David McLaughlin
Officers: Dr David William John McLaughlin, Secretary; Dr David William John McLaughlin [1973] Director

E.P.G Pharma Ltd
Incorporated: 27 September 2018
Registered Office: Medicity Nottingham, D6 Building, Thane Road, Nottingham, NG90 6BH
Major Shareholder: Sherif Mohamed Aboelnaga Mohamed Elmasry
Officers: Sherif Mohamed Aboelnaga Mohamed Elmasry [1972] Director [Egyptian]

T.G. Eakin Limited
Incorporated: 26 October 1973 *Employees:* 73
Net Worth: £27,898,514 *Total Assets:* £32,058,536
Registered Office: Kathleen Drive, 15 Ballystockart Road, Comber, Co Down, BT23 5QY
Shareholders: Paul Andrew Eakin; Jeremy David Eakin; Thomas George Eakin; Violet Pattison Eakin; Richard Gray
Officers: Jeremy David Eakin [1967] Director; Paul Andrew Eakin [1962] Director; Thomas George Eakin [1933] Director; Violet P Eakin [1936] Director

East West Naturals Limited
Incorporated: 10 December 2018
Registered Office: Willow Cottage, Green End, Little Staughton, Bedford, MK44 2BU
Shareholders: Parveen Bhatarah; Richard Charles Finch
Officers: Lisa Tomblin, Secretary; Dr Parveen Bhatarah [1964] Scientific Director; Richard Charles Finch [1960] Managing Director

Eaststone Limited
Incorporated: 25 October 2007 *Employees:* 37
Net Worth: £855,390 *Total Assets:* £1,853,162
Registered Office: Unit 1 Barrs Fold Road, Wingates Industrial Estate, Westhoughton, Bolton, Lancs, BL5 3XP
Parent: Walkboost Limited
Officers: Craig Bernard Fishwick, Secretary; Craig Bernard Fishwick [1974] Director/Accountant

Eclipse Pharma Ltd
Incorporated: 1 February 2019
Registered Office: 413 Hoe Street, London, E17 9AP
Major Shareholder: Mohammed Umar Mahmood
Officers: Mohammed Umar Mahmood [1988] Director/Pharmacist

Eco Animal Health Ltd.
Incorporated: 22 November 1991 *Employees:* 51
Net Worth: £26,555,696 *Total Assets:* £84,152,288
Registered Office: 78 Coombe Road, New Malden, Surrey, KT3 4QS
Officers: Julia Trouse, Secretary; Andrew Buglass [1972] Global Sales Director; Brett Timothy Clemo [1962] Director; Peter Anthony Lawrence [1948] Director; Marc Denham Loomes [1961] Managing Director; Kevin Anthony Stockdale [1965] Finance Director

Ecobrands Limited
Incorporated: 10 June 1991 *Employees:* 1
Net Worth Deficit: £593,627 *Total Assets:* £65,191
Registered Office: No 2, 36 Stratford Road, London, W8 6QA
Major Shareholder: Robin Cambell Baker
Officers: Christine Baker, Secretary; Christine Baker [1952] Director/Publisher [French]; Robin Baker [1941] Director

Ecohydra Technologies Limited
Incorporated: 1 October 2004 *Employees:* 3
Net Worth: £125,433 *Total Assets:* £230,094
Registered Office: College House, 17 King Edwards Road, Ruislip, Middlesex, HA4 7AE
Officers: Brian Richard Warneford, Secretary; John Steven Appleby [1958] Director/Management Consultant; Leslie Christopher Barber [1957] Director; Dr Charles Goodson-Wickes [1945] Director/Consultant; Nicholas Matthew Amadeus May [1954] Director/IT Consultant; Clifton Adrian Melvin [1954] Director/Actuary; Brian Richard Warneford [1950] Director/Accountant; Charles Whait [1954] Commercial Director

Ectomedica Limited
Incorporated: 18 January 2012 *Employees:* 2
Net Worth: £46,878 *Total Assets:* £53,545
Registered Office: 6 Quy Court, Colliers Lane, Stow-Cum-Quy, Cambridge, CB25 9AU
Officers: Elizabeth Rachel Brunton [1973] Director/Medical Entomologist; Ian F Burgess [1949] Director/Medical Entomologist

Edinburgh Nano Limited
Incorporated: 21 September 2017
Registered Office: Ztply, 4/4a Bloomsbury Square, London, WC1A 2RP
Major Shareholder: Ke Wang
Officers: Ke Wang [1978] Director [Chinese]

Edinburgh Nanotechnology Ltd
Incorporated: 6 September 2017
Registered Office: Ztplt 4/4a Bloomsbury Square, London, WC1A 2RP
Major Shareholder: Ke Wang
Officers: Ke Wang [1978] Director [Chinese]

Edwards' Analytical Limited
Incorporated: 13 August 2012 *Employees:* 8
Net Worth: £29,274 *Total Assets:* £62,842
Registered Office: 9 Academy Gardens, Gainford, Darlington, Co Durham, DL2 3EN
Major Shareholder: David John Hugh Edwards
Officers: David John Hugh Edwards [1941] Director/Chemist

Eezilean International Limited
Incorporated: 11 October 2016
Registered Office: 14 Holly Tree Close, London, SW19 6EA
Shareholder: Murray Rhys Bunn
Officers: Murray Rhys Bunn [1970] Director

Egalet Limited
Incorporated: 15 July 2010 *Employees:* 20
Net Worth Deficit: £76,336,800 *Total Assets:* £4,843,679
Registered Office: Dechert LLP, 160 Queen Victoria Street, London, EC4V 4QQ
Parent: Egalet Corporation
Officers: Robert Samuel Radie [1963] Director/President and CEO [American]; Mark Strobeck [1970] Director/Executive VP and COO of Egatel Corporation [American]

EHB Limited
Incorporated: 28 March 2013 *Employees:* 2
Net Worth: £3,914 *Total Assets:* £9,719
Registered Office: 17 Copeland Road, Birstall, Leicester, LE4 3AB
Shareholders: Bhavik Jayendra Naran; Hina Patel-Naran
Officers: Bhavik Jayendra Naran [1980] Director/Pharmacist; Hina Patel-Naran [1979] Director/Pharmacist

Eisai Manufacturing Limited
Incorporated: 1 March 2007 *Employees:* 105
Net Worth: £74,089,208 *Total Assets:* £454,234,976
Registered Office: European Knowledge Centre, Mosquito Way, Hatfield, Herts, AL10 9SN
Parent: Eisai Europe Limited
Officers: Simon Gerard Thomas, Secretary; Nicholas Conrad Burgin [1973] Director; Alex John Felthouse [1973] Director; Yoshiteru Kato [1960] Director [Japanese]; Shin Ujiie [1980] Director [Japanese]; Tatsuyuki Yasuno [1968] Director/Corporate Officer, VP [Japanese]

Ekom Pharma Ltd
Incorporated: 23 April 2018
Registered Office: 79 College Road, Harrow, Middlesex, HA1 1BD
Parent: Harman Finochem Limited
Officers: Sabeena Kaur Bagol, Secretary; Sabeena Kaur Bagol [1973] Director/Entrepreneur

Elanco Animal Vaccines Limited
Incorporated: 15 November 1979
Previous: Novartis Animal Vaccines Ltd
Registered Office: Lilly House, Priestley Road, Basingstoke, Hants, RG24 9NL
Parent: Eli Lilly and Company Limited
Officers: Kristina Mary Hunt [1969] Director; Christopher Lewis [1978] Director/Finance Manager

Elanco Europe Ltd.
Incorporated: 16 April 1963
Previous: Elanco Products Limited
Registered Office: Lilly House, Priestley Road, Basingstoke, Hants, RG24 9NL
Parent: Eli Lilly and Company Limited
Officers: Eamon Flahive [1959] Director/Pharmaceutical Executive [Irish]; Kristina Mary Hunt [1969] Director; Christopher Lewis [1978] Director/Finance Manager

Elanco UK AH Limited
Incorporated: 23 May 2018
Registered Office: Lilly House, Priestley Road, Basingstoke, Hants, RG24 9NL
Parent: Eli Lilly and Company Limited
Officers: Kristina Mary Hunt [1969] Director; Christopher Lewis [1978] Director/Finance Manager; Peter Troutt [1966] Director/General Manager

Elemis Limited
Incorporated: 22 July 1988 *Employees:* 505
Net Worth: £41,931,088 *Total Assets:* £61,136,348
Registered Office: Unit D, Poplar Way East, Cabot Park, Avonmouth, Bristol, BS11 0DD
Parent: Nemo (UK) Holdco, Ltd
Officers: Daniel Michael Chambers, Secretary; Michael Stephan Haringman, Secretary; Oriele Anne Dunbar [1965] Director/Chief Marketing Officer [Canadian]; Noella Gabriel [1956] Managing Director [Irish]; Michael Stephan Haringman [1944] Director/Solicitor; Sean Harrington [1966] Director; Christopher Vieth [1965] Director [American]

Elena's Nature Collection Limited
Incorporated: 21 February 2001
Net Worth: £226 *Total Assets:* £7,021
Registered Office: Woodmans Farm, Perrymans Lane, Burwash, E Sussex, TN19 7DN
Major Shareholder: Elena Joyce
Officers: Elena Joyce [1954] Director [Danish]

Eleosinc Limited
Incorporated: 20 March 2007
Registered Office: 199 Bishopsgate, London, EC2M 3UT
Officers: Joseph Daugherty [1950] Director [American]; Dayton Thomas Reardan [1955] Director/VP Regulatory [American]

Elixir Pure UK Limited
Incorporated: 12 June 2017
Registered Office: 13 Park Road Estate, Timperley, Altrincham, Cheshire, WA14 5QH
Officers: Tracy Irene Martin [1961] Director; Cindy Smith [1964] Director

Emerald Kalama Chemical Limited
Incorporated: 13 March 2001 *Employees:* 86
Previous: Innospec Widnes Limited
Net Worth: £25,620,000 *Total Assets:* £34,191,000
Registered Office: Emerald Kalama Chemical Limited, Dans Road, Widnes, Cheshire, WA8 0RF
Officers: Wayne Thomas Byrne [1963] Director/EVP/CFO [American]; Paul Lawrence Hogan [1969] Director/Vice President, General Manager [Irish]; Graham Robert Smith [1962] Site Director

Emerge Biotech Ltd
Incorporated: 21 March 2013
Net Worth Deficit: £7,145 *Total Assets:* £26,826
Registered Office: Stevenage Bioscience Catalyst, Gunnels Wood Road, Stevenage, Herts, SG1 2FX
Major Shareholder: Peter Christian Kloehn
Officers: Peter Christian Kloehn [1964] Director/Assistant Professor [German]

Emergencypharm Ltd.
Incorporated: 14 October 2014
Net Worth: £6,626 *Total Assets:* £19,456
Registered Office: 68 Hazelhurst Brow, Bradford, BD9 6AQ
Major Shareholder: Muneeb Ur-Rehman
Officers: Muneeb Ur-Rehman [1991] Director/Pharmacist

Emergent Countermeasures International Ltd
Incorporated: 6 July 2015 *Employees:* 5
Net Worth Deficit: £444,000 *Total Assets:* £18,005,000
Registered Office: Parkshot House, 5 Kew Road, Richmond, Surrey, TW9 2PR
Parent: Emergent Biosolutions Inc
Officers: Eric Burt, Secretary; Atul Saran, Secretary; Adam Robert Havey [1971] Director/Executive Vice President [American]; Robert Gregory Kramer [1957] Director/Chief Financial Officer [American]; Richard Scott Lindahl [1963] Director/Executive Vice President, Chief Financial Officer [American]; Atul Saran [1973] Director/Executive Vice President, Business Development, GE [American]; Dr Christopher James Sinclair [1973] Director/Vice-President, Global Commercial Operations [Canadian]

EN RUS Group Limited
Incorporated: 3 April 2018
Registered Office: 27 Old Gloucester Street, London, WC1N 3AX
Officers: Reezberg Malcolm [1970] Director

Encapsula Limited
Incorporated: 10 November 2008 *Employees:* 1
Net Worth: £5,157 *Total Assets:* £165,949
Registered Office: Rowan House, Funston's Industrial Estate, Arkesden Road, Clavering, Saffron Walden, Essex, CB11 4QU
Major Shareholder: Lee Wright
Officers: Lee Wright, Secretary; Lee Wright [1962] Director

Enchanted Brave Limited
Incorporated: 1 October 2013 *Employees:* 1
Net Worth Deficit: £14,694 *Total Assets:* £7,582
Registered Office: 469 Kingsway, Manchester, M19 1NR
Major Shareholder: Vincent William Taylor
Officers: Alan Malova [1977] Director/Trader; Vincent Taylor [1977] Director/Trader

Engelpharma UK Limited
Incorporated: 15 December 2006 *Employees:* 1
Net Worth: £28,858 *Total Assets:* £31,183
Registered Office: 269 Farnborough Road, Farnborough, Hants, GU14 7LY
Major Shareholder: Zsolt Vas
Officers: Zsolt Vas [1970] Director [Hungarian]

Enn-Muk Limited
Incorporated: 29 August 2017
Registered Office: 10 New Laithe Road, Huddersfield, W Yorks, HD4 6PW
Officers: Stephenson Tauya Mukoko [1972] Director/Medicinal Herbs [Zimbabwean]

Ennogen Healthcare Ltd
Incorporated: 14 October 2011 *Employees:* 10
Net Worth: £21,729,260 *Total Assets:* £29,465,110
Registered Office: Unit G4, Riverside Way, Dartford, Kent, DA1 5BS
Major Shareholder: Gurdev Singh Rurai
Officers: Gurdev Singh Ruprai [1960] Director/Pharmacist

Ennogen Pharma Ltd
Incorporated: 24 August 2011 *Employees:* 9
Net Worth: £545,149 *Total Assets:* £2,487,233
Registered Office: Unit G4, Riverside Industrial Estate, Riverside Way, Dartford, Kent, DA1 5BS
Major Shareholder: Gurdev Singh Ruprai
Officers: Gurdev Singh Ruprai [1960] Director/Pharmacist

Envigo RMS (UK) Limited
Incorporated: 30 September 1976 Employees: 190
Previous: Harlan Laboratories U.K. Ltd.
Net Worth: £48,683,000 Total Assets: £60,876,000
Registered Office: Shaw's Farm, Station Road, Blackthorn, Bicester, Oxon, OX25 1TP
Shareholders: Envigo Holdings Limited; Envigo Holdings Limited
Officers: Michael Gregory O'Reilly, Secretary; Michael Gregory O'Reilly [1966] Director/Legal Adviser; Stephen Daniel Symonds [1974] Director/Financial Controller

Epax Pharma UK Ltd
Incorporated: 26 April 2011
Net Worth: £3,578,000 Total Assets: £3,847,000
Registered Office: Gilbey Road, Grimsby, S Humbers, DN31 2SL
Parent: Epax Pharma UK Holdings Unlimited
Officers: Michael McEllone, Secretary; Rolf Andersen [1968] Director [Norwegian]; Egil Magne Haugstad [1957] Director [Norwegian]; Michael McEllone [1974] Director/Scotland [Irish]

Equalbrief Limited
Incorporated: 12 May 1988
Net Worth Deficit: £18,833,766 Total Assets: £15,318,588
Registered Office: Goleigh Farm, Selborne, Alton, Hants, GU34 3SE
Shareholders: CRE Fiduciary Services Inc. as Trustee of CRE Trust; Longbow Finance SA
Officers: Neville George Pope [1953] Director; Sandra Kaye Smith [1962] Director/Q A Manager [Australian]

Erimol Ltd
Incorporated: 12 November 2018
Registered Office: Suit 140, 21 Botanic Avenue, Belfast, BT7 1JJ
Shareholders: Peter Mollison; Ka Yan Che
Officers: Ka Yan Che [1980] Director/Pharmacist; Peter Mollison [1980] Director/Pharmacist

Essenfuture Ltd
Incorporated: 28 February 2019
Registered Office: 18a Sunnyhill Road, London, SW16 2UH
Shareholders: Kyaw Zay Lin; Wai Aung Chan Myo
Officers: Kyaw Zay Lin [1988] Director [Burmese]; Wai Aung Chan Myo [1985] Director [Burmese]

Essential Generics Limited
Incorporated: 8 April 2003
Registered Office: Chemidex House, Unit 7 Egham Business Village, Egham, Surrey, TW20 8RB
Shareholders: Navinchandra Jamnadas; Varsha Navinchandra
Officers: Dr Nikesh Engineer, Secretary; Nikesh Engineer [1985] Director/Doctor

Essential Health Products Limited
Incorporated: 9 March 2000 Employees: 2
Net Worth: £530,174 Total Assets: £594,911
Registered Office: 1 Brassey Road, Old Potts Way, Shrewsbury, Salop, SY3 7FA
Shareholder: Nigel Charles Hawkins
Officers: Graham Carr Smith, Secretary; Graham Carr Smith [1954] Director; Nigel Charles Hawkins [1958] Director

Essential Nutrition Limited
Incorporated: 24 July 1989 Employees: 15
Net Worth: £2,234,547 Total Assets: £2,308,159
Registered Office: Bank House, Saltgrounds Road, Brough, E Yorks, HU15 1EF
Officers: Anne Pauline Parker, Secretary; Andrew Parker [1965] Director; Anne Pauline Parker [1939] Director; Christopher Parker [1966] Director; Timothy Parker [1967] Director/Production Manager

Essential Pharma Limited
Incorporated: 2 February 2011 Employees: 1
Net Worth: £10,300,627 Total Assets: £30,423,222
Registered Office: 7 Egham Business Village, Crabtree Road, Egham, Surrey, TW20 8RB
Shareholders: Navinchandra Jamnadas; Varsha Navinchandra
Officers: Nikesh Engineer [1985] Director/Doctor

Essential Pharmaceuticals Limited
Incorporated: 24 November 2010
Net Worth: £772,739 Total Assets: £2,120,814
Registered Office: 7 Egham Business Village, Crabtree Road, Egham, Surrey, TW20 8RB
Shareholders: Navinchandra Jamnadas; Varsha Navinchandra
Officers: Nikesh Engineer [1985] Director

ESW Healthcare Limited
Incorporated: 19 November 2018
Registered Office: 3 George Street, Great Preston, Leeds, LS26 8FT
Shareholders: David Terence Wrighton; Joanne Patricia Wrighton
Officers: David Terence Wrighton [1971] Director; Joanne Patricia Wrighton [1970] Director

Ether Cosmetics Ltd
Incorporated: 9 November 2017
Registered Office: 16 Francis House, Colville Estate, London, N1 5PX
Major Shareholder: Akin Gursoy
Officers: Akin Gursoy [1991] Director/Owner

Ethno Botanical Resources Limited
Incorporated: 15 October 1993 Employees: 3
Net Worth: £490 Total Assets: £7,642
Registered Office: Vine Barn, Village Green, Northchapel, W Sussex, GU28 9HU
Major Shareholder: Elias Bouras
Officers: John Francis Dickens, Company Secretary; Elias Bouras [1946] Director/Inventor/Researcher; John Francis Dickens [1955] Director/Company Secretary; Brian Frederick Mumford [1945] Director/Chartered Accountant

Etmo UK Limited
Incorporated: 2 July 2014
Registered Office: Flat 53, Stourhead House, 79 Tachbrook Street, London, SW1V 2QP
Major Shareholder: Oredola Cynthia Nyamali
Officers: Oredola Cynthia Nyamali [1968] Director/Pharmacy Technician

Eulysis UK Limited
Incorporated: 10 October 2011 Employees: 1
Net Worth Deficit: £100,514 Total Assets: £64,661
Registered Office: 14/2 Hermand Terrace, Edinburgh, EH11 1QZ
Shareholders: Keith John Morris; Spyridon-Edouard Tsakas
Officers: James William Peter King [1985] Director

Euratlantic-Cosmepharm Limited
Incorporated: 1 July 1996 *Employees:* 1
Net Worth: £19,228 *Total Assets:* £21,288
Registered Office: The Courtyard, 30 Worthing Road, Horsham, W Sussex, RH12 1SL
Major Shareholder: Daryl Cumberland
Officers: Daryl Cumberland [1976] Director/Accountant

Euro Diagnostics Limited
Incorporated: 14 April 2015
Net Worth: £2,800 *Total Assets:* £2,800
Registered Office: 31 Lyme Grove, Stockport, Cheshire, SK2 6SG
Officers: Shahid Hussain [1974] Director [German]

Euro Medical Equipment Limited
Incorporated: 2 September 1991
Registered Office: 48 Welbeck Road, West Harrow, Middlesex, HA2 0RW
Shareholder: Saraj Rajnikant Dhanani
Officers: Paryantrai Dharmashi Punja, Secretary; Saraj Rajnikant Dhanani [1944] Director; Pervez Rajanikant Punja [1964] Director

Euro OTC Pharma UK Limited
Incorporated: 4 February 2014 *Employees:* 5
Net Worth Deficit: £377,746 *Total Assets:* £144,420
Registered Office: 1 King's Court, Harwood Road, Horsham, W Sussex, RH13 5UR
Major Shareholder: Jurgen Franz Beyer
Officers: Jurgen Franz Beyer [1955] Director [German]; Markus Wulfert [1976] Managing Director [German]

Euroclinical Ltd
Incorporated: 8 March 2018
Registered Office: GF10 Oxford House, Sixth Avenue, Doncaster Finningley Airport, Doncaster, S Yorks, DN9 3GG
Major Shareholder: Efe Ekakitie
Officers: Efe Ekakitie, Secretary; Benita Ezete Onyiaorah [1993] Director/Nursing [Nigerian]

Europa-Technia Limited
Incorporated: 25 July 1994
Net Worth: £72,047 *Total Assets:* £219,080
Registered Office: 107 Dutch Barn Close, Stanwell, Staines upon Thames, Middlesex, TW19 7NG
Major Shareholder: Barry Roy Shepherd
Officers: Susanna Allenby, Secretary; Barry Roy Shepherd [1949] Director/Chairman; Tracey Marie Shepherd [1966] Director

European First Aid Limited
Incorporated: 16 March 1995
Net Worth: £20,000 *Total Assets:* £20,000
Registered Office: 1 Windward Drive, Speke, Liverpool, L24 8QR
Parent: Kays Medical Ltd
Officers: Darren Jon Biddlecombe, Secretary; Benjamin Mathew Ludzker [1979] Managing Director

Europharma Limited
Incorporated: 20 October 1998
Registered Office: 16 Southway, London, NW11 6RU
Officers: Mazen Batterjee, Secretary/Director [Saudi Arabian]; Ibrahim Batterjee [1973] Director [Saudi Arabian]; Mahmoud Batterjee [1966] Director [Saudi Arabian]; Mazen Batterjee [1961] Director [Saudi Arabian]; Mohamed Batterjee [1933] Director [Saudi Arabian]

EV Pharma Solutions Ltd
Incorporated: 3 February 2016
Net Worth: £30,161 *Total Assets:* £46,631
Registered Office: 1st Floor, Healthaid House, Marlborough Hill, Harrow, Middlesex, HA1 1UD
Major Shareholder: Evgenia Mengou
Officers: Evgenia Mengou [1972] Director [Greek]

EVC Compounding Ltd
Incorporated: 10 March 2016
Net Worth Deficit: £1,293 *Total Assets:* £33,294
Registered Office: Big Picture House, Pontefract Road, Snaith, E Yorks, DN14 0DE
Officers: Damien Cain [1976] Director [Australian]; Richard Coppack [1961] Director; Angela Marie Lacey [1963] Director; Ann Walker [1969] Director

Everything for Eczema Limited
Incorporated: 1 December 2010
Net Worth Deficit: £43,918 *Total Assets:* £4,590
Registered Office: 99 Eldred Avenue, Brighton, BN1 5EL
Major Shareholder: Gail Palmer
Officers: Gail Palmer [1967] Director

Evida Ltd
Incorporated: 21 November 2017
Registered Office: 46b Dalmeny Road, Bournemouth, BH6 4BW
Officers: Dr Jeremy Eve [1987] Director; Sneha Jethwa [1991] Director/Pharmacist

EVL Biologicals 23 Ltd
Incorporated: 9 February 2015
Net Worth: £13,238 *Total Assets:* £17,747
Registered Office: 5 Meteor Road, Kate Reed Wood, West Malling, Kent, ME19 4TH
Parent: EVL Biologicals Ltd
Officers: Johannes Robertus Van Herwijnen [1962] Director [Dutch]

EVL Biologicals Ltd
Incorporated: 12 December 2014
Net Worth: £1,864 *Total Assets:* £164,105
Registered Office: 5 Meteor Road, Kate Reed Wood, West Malling, Kent, ME19 4TH
Shareholders: J P Van Herwijnen; Jr Van Herwijnen
Officers: Jan Paul Van Herwijnen [1963] Director [Dutch]; Johannes Robertus Van Herwijnen [1962] Director [Dutch]

Evopharm Limited
Incorporated: 19 February 2018
Registered Office: 5 Trinity Close, Ryton on Dunsmore, Coventry, Warwicks, CV8 3FA
Major Shareholder: Kiran Shur
Officers: Dr Jagdeep Singh Shur [1980] Director; Kiran Shur [1993] Director/Pharmacist

Evorin Pharma Limited
Incorporated: 30 January 2014
Net Worth: £1,000 *Total Assets:* £1,000
Registered Office: 3 Gower Street, London, WC1E 6HA
Shareholders: Ibrahim Abdelrazik Albayoomi Fouda; Ahmed Sami
Officers: Ahmed Sami, Secretary; Ibrahim Abdelrazik Albayoomi Fouda [1978] Director [Egyptian]

Exactmer Limited
Incorporated: 13 December 2017
Registered Office: 52 Princes Gate Exhibition Road, London, SW7 2PG
Shareholder: Professor Andrew Guy Livingston
Officers: Dr Piers Robert James Gaffney [1963] Director/Engineering Chemist; Professor Andrtew Guy Livingston [1962] Director/Professor

Exonate Limited
Incorporated: 5 December 2013 *Employees:* 12
Net Worth Deficit: £891,649 *Total Assets:* £1,076,488
Registered Office: Unit 23 Cambridge Science Park, Milton Road, Cambridge, CB4 0EY
Officers: Professor David Owen Bates [1968] Director/University Professor; Mohammad Sohail Fazeli [1964] Director; Dr Steven James Harper [1959] Director/Professor; John Kurek [1967] Director/Investment Manager [Australian]; Dr Catherine Susan Minshull-Beech [1957] Director/Independent Biotechnology Consultant; Andrew James Naylor [1972] Director/Consultant; Sunil Rajen Shah [1973] Director; Dr Christopher John Torrance [1969] Director

Extruded Pharmaceuticals Ltd
Incorporated: 8 March 2016
Net Worth Deficit: £31,800 *Total Assets:* £127,200
Registered Office: First Floor Offices, 332 Marsh Lane, Erdington, Birmingham, B23 6HP
Major Shareholder: David Keith Lawton
Officers: David Keith Lawton [1958] Director; Brian Murray [1947] Director/Retired

Ezoogle UK Limited
Incorporated: 13 May 2015 *Employees:* 2
Net Worth: £939 *Total Assets:* £13,243
Registered Office: 17 Priory Lane, Penwortham, Preston, Lancs, PR1 0AR
Shareholder: Stephen Dominic Martin
Officers: Stephen Dominic Martin, Secretary; Christine Ann Martin [1956] Director; Stephen Dominic Martin [1952] Director

Pierre Fabre Limited
Incorporated: 12 August 1970 *Employees:* 74
Net Worth: £1,734,371 *Total Assets:* £7,420,965
Registered Office: Eversheds House, 70 Great Bridgewater Street, Manchester, M1 5ES
Officers: Xavier Pierre Marie Benoist [1966] Director/Pierre Fabre Dermo Cosmetique FC Manager [French]; Michael Frederic Danon [1969] Pierre Fabre SA General Director [French]; Frederic Marie Duchesne [1959] Pierre Fabre Medicament General Director [French]; Vincent Henri Francois Guiraud-Chaumeil [1964] Ethics Franchise & Europe Region Director [French]; Laura Adele McMullin [1973] Director/General Manager

Fairywire Ltd
Incorporated: 8 June 2018
Registered Office: Suite 1, Fielden House, 41 Rochdale Road, Todmorden, W Yorks, OL14 6LD
Shareholders: Mylene Tagarao; Julie Watson
Officers: Mylene Tagarao [1978] Director [Filipino]

Falls Care Limited
Incorporated: 17 July 2012
Net Worth: £1,164 *Total Assets:* £5,065
Registered Office: 193 Downs Road, Hastings, Kent, TN34 2DY
Major Shareholder: Peter Justin Bennetts
Officers: Peter Justin John Bennetts, Secretary; Mahireen Bennetts [1993] Research and Development Director

Farasha-Cosmetics Ltd
Incorporated: 26 June 2018
Registered Office: 27 Old Gloucester Street, London, WC1N 3AX
Major Shareholder: Massimo Serra
Officers: Massimo Serra, Secretary; Massimo Serra [1965] Director/Self Employed [Italian]

Farm Bionics Ltd
Incorporated: 31 January 2019
Registered Office: Kemp House, 160 City Road, London, EC1V 2NX
Officers: Marshal Patel [1988] Director [Indian]

Farmigea UK Ltd
Incorporated: 8 September 2014
Net Worth: £9,377 *Total Assets:* £147,677
Registered Office: c/o IBC, 10th Floor, 88 Wood Street, London, EC2V 7RS
Officers: Mario Federighi [1965] Director/Businessman [Italian]

Fendall's Ltd.
Incorporated: 28 September 2017
Registered Office: 6 Marefield Close, Barnwood, Gloucester, GL4 3TU
Officers: Helen Maxwell-Clarke [1980] Director

Fermenta Biotech (UK) Limited
Incorporated: 27 January 1997
Net Worth: £41,111 *Total Assets:* £41,772
Registered Office: Lall Ondhia, Charter House, 8-10 Station Road, Manor Park, London, E12 5BT
Officers: Srikant Sharma, Secretary; Srikant Sharma [1964] Director [Indian]; Satish Varma [1970] Director [Indian]

Ferndale Pharmaceuticals Limited
Incorporated: 2 April 2003 *Employees:* 24
Net Worth: £1,758,179 *Total Assets:* £2,920,641
Registered Office: Unit 740 Thorp Arch Estate, Street 2, Wetherby, W Yorks, LS23 7FX
Shareholders: Roger Mark Bloxham; Ferndale Pharma Group Inc
Officers: Roisin Wood, Secretary; Roger Mark Bloxham [1964] Managing Director; Doctor Michael John Burns [1955] Director & President; Sem Lloyd Davies [1965] International Director; James Thayer McMillan II [1946] Chairman & Director [American]

Fernhurst Pharmacy Limited
Incorporated: 22 May 2007 *Employees:* 2
Net Worth: £22,551 *Total Assets:* £161,133
Registered Office: 19 Edinburgh Drive, Staines upon Thames, Middlesex, TW18 1PJ
Officers: Sui Nin Lau [1970] Director/Pharmacist

Fernsoft Limited
Incorporated: 7 July 1992
Net Worth Deficit: £978,613 *Total Assets:* £132,753
Registered Office: Syence House, Owens Road, Skippers Lane Industrial Estate, Middlesbrough, Cleveland, TS6 6HE
Major Shareholder: Sean Campbell
Officers: Sean-Robbie Campbell, Secretary; Sean-Robbie Campbell [1965] Director

Festus Olatoye & Onyekachi Uka London Ltd
Incorporated: 15 February 2018
Registered Office: 32 Glimpsing Green, Erith, London, DA18 4HE
Major Shareholder: Onyekachi Uka
Officers: Onyekachi Uka [1978] Director/Businessman [Nigerian]

Finca Skin Organics Limited
Incorporated: 17 August 2018
Registered Office: 50 Crossan Road, Mayobridge, Newry, Co Down, BT34 2HY
Major Shareholder: Finola Fegan
Officers: Finola Fegan, Secretary; Finola Fegan [1967] Director [Irish]; Catherine McCartan [1967] Director [Irish]

Fine Contract Research Limited
Incorporated: 10 September 2010
Registered Office: c/o Fine Organics Limited, Seal Sands, Middlesbrough, Cleveland, TS2 1UB
Parent: Lianhe Chemical Technology Co. Ltd
Officers: Lee Paul Kingsbury [1972] Director; Dr Nigel Christopher Parkinson [1968] Director; Minghui Xu [1971] Finance Director [Chinese]

Fine Organics Limited
Incorporated: 3 December 1980 *Employees:* 232
Net Worth: £5,385,000 *Total Assets:* £47,671,000
Registered Office: Seal Sands, Middlesbrough, Cleveland, TS2 1UB
Parent: Lianhe Chemical Technology Co. Ltd
Officers: Nigel James Bartley, Secretary; Lee Paul Kingsbury [1972] Operations Director; Dr Nigel Christopher Parkinson [1968] Director; Minghui Xu [1971] Finance Director [Chinese]

Fine Treatment Limited
Incorporated: 14 April 2014
Net Worth: £666 *Total Assets:* £7,022
Registered Office: Pounsley House, Pounsley Road, Dunton Green, Sevenoaks, Kent, TN13 2XP
Officers: Dr Simon Allen [1948] Director/MD

Finer Feet Ltd
Incorporated: 29 March 2010
Net Worth Deficit: £3,452
Registered Office: 5 Phelps Way, Hayes, Middlesex, UB3 4LH
Officers: Jalmeen Lall [1978] Director

First Impressions Denture Centre Ltd
Incorporated: 13 August 2012 *Employees:* 2
Net Worth: £9,605 *Total Assets:* £21,746
Registered Office: 33 New Forest Enterprise Centre, Chapel Lane, Totton, Southampton, SO40 9LA
Shareholders: Toni Dorothy Martin; Steven Daniel Martin
Officers: Steven Daniel Martin [1976] Director/Dental; Toni Dorothy Martin [1969] Director/Medical

Fisons Limited
Incorporated: 23 July 1895 *Employees:* 431
Net Worth: £597,932,032 *Total Assets:* £771,542,016
Registered Office: One Onslow Street, Guildford, Surrey, GU1 4YS
Parent: Sanofi-Aventis UK Holdings Limited
Officers: Francois-Xavier Duhalde [1965] Director/Chief Financial Officer [French]; Hugo Rupert Alexander Fry [1970] Director

Flavour Maker Limited
Incorporated: 2 May 2017
Net Worth Deficit: £17,290 *Total Assets:* £126,700
Registered Office: Lower Ground Floor, 49 Blatchington Road, Hove, E Sussex, BN3 3YJ
Officers: Michael Byron-Cooper [1975] Director; Antony Eely [1975] Director; Richard Marc O'Connell [1977] Director; Christopher Page [1979] Director; Michael Page [1982] Director

Flavour-Tech UK Limited
Incorporated: 10 June 2015
Net Worth: £15,011 *Total Assets:* £73,287
Registered Office: 11 Hedon Road, Hull, HU9 1LH
Shareholder: Philip Glenn Stephenson
Officers: Philip Glenn Stephenson [1962] Director

Fleet Laboratories Limited
Incorporated: 1 January 1949
Registered Office: 94 Rickmansworth Road, Watford, Herts, WD18 7JJ
Parent: D.D.D. Limited
Officers: Carl Atkinson [1974] Director; Charles Philip Wadsworth [1962] Finance Director

Florence Health & Beauty Limited
Incorporated: 21 November 2017
Registered Office: 3 Shining Bank, Sheffield, S13 9DJ
Shareholders: Muthana Obeed; Fatima Aloum
Officers: Fatima Aloum [1982] Director [Syrian]; Muthana Obeed [1976] Director [Iraqi]

Flourish Products Ltd
Incorporated: 6 February 2019
Registered Office: 1st Floor, 25 Lexington Street, London, W1F 9AH
Major Shareholder: Paul Martin Barnes
Officers: Paul Martin Barnes [1953] Director/Certified Chartered Accountant

Flourish Ventures Ltd
Incorporated: 26 April 2011
Net Worth: £1,955 *Total Assets:* £6,256
Registered Office: 75 North Parkway, Leeds, LS14 1JD
Shareholders: Victor Olorunleke Olobaniyi; Adebesi Olobaniyi
Officers: Victor Olorunleke Olobaniyi [1974] Director/Pharmacy Technician [Nigerian]

Fluidx Limited
Incorporated: 14 October 2005
Registered Office: Northbank Industrial Park, Gilchrist Road, Irlam, Manchester, M44 5AY
Officers: Jason Joseph [1970] Director [American]; David Francis Pietrantoni [1972] Director [American]; Lindon Robertson [1961] Director [American]

Fluss Limited
Incorporated: 15 May 2018
Registered Office: 71-75 Shelton Street, London, WC2H 9JQ
Shareholders: Mariana Abbott Ferreira; Bruno Ferreira Silva
Officers: Mariana Abbott Ferreira [1978] Director/Researcher [Brazilian]; Bruno Ferreira Silva [1978] Director/Sales Vice President [Brazilian]; Veronika Stoyanova Nesheva [1990] Director/Engineer [Bulgarian]

Focus Pharma Holdings Limited
Incorporated: 18 July 2007
Net Worth: £6,045,422 *Total Assets:* £6,046,418
Registered Office: Capital House, 85 King William Street, London, EC4N 7BL
Parent: Mercury Pharma Group Limited
Officers: Robert Sully, Secretary; Adeel Ahmad [1973] Director/Chief Financial Officer [Canadian]; Graeme Neville Duncan [1973] Director/Chief Executive Officer; Vikram Laxman Kamath [1977] Director/Vice President Finance and Group Controller [Indian]

Focus Pharmaceuticals Limited
Incorporated: 30 August 2002
Net Worth: £4,404,425 *Total Assets:* £18,041,368
Registered Office: Capital House, 85 King William Street, London, EC4N 7BL
Parent: Focus Pharma Holdings Limited
Officers: Robert Sully, Secretary; Adeel Ahmad [1973] Director/Chief Financial Officer [Canadian]; Graeme Neville Duncan [1973] Director/Chief Executive Officer; Vikram Laxman Kamath [1977] Director/Vice President Finance and Group Controller [Indian]

Follifix Ltd
Incorporated: 4 February 2019
Registered Office: 71-75 Shelton Street, London, WC2H 9JQ
Major Shareholder: Victoria Royle
Officers: Victoria Royle [1980] Operations Director

Fontridge Pharmaceutical Research and Development Limited
Incorporated: 15 June 2000
Net Worth Deficit: £33,027 *Total Assets:* £836
Registered Office: 20 Havelock Road, Hastings, Kent, TN34 1BP
Shareholders: Hendrik Jurjen Gerardus Kruisinga; Hugo Pieter Johannes Kruisinga
Officers: Hugo Pieter Johannes Kruisinga, Secretary [Dutch]; Hendrik Jurjen Gerardus Kruisinga [1953] Director/Social Geographer [Dutch]; Hugo Pieter Johannes Kruisinga [1961] Director/Economist [Dutch]

Fontus Health Ltd
Incorporated: 17 May 2012 *Employees:* 20
Net Worth: £4,454,077 *Total Assets:* £5,603,802
Registered Office: 60 Lichfield Street, Walsall, W Midlands, WS4 2BX
Major Shareholder: Navdeep Birdi
Officers: Navdeep Birdi [1969] Director

Forbleries Ltd
Incorporated: 23 July 2018
Registered Office: 214a Kettering Road, Northampton, NN1 4BN
Shareholders: Cristino Osmundo; Amy Noble
Officers: Cristino Osmundo [1959] Director [Filipino]

Forensic Rescue Limited
Incorporated: 11 May 2001
Net Worth Deficit: £13,097 *Total Assets:* £9,442
Registered Office: 57 Hill Street, Hilperton, Trowbridge, Wilts, BA14 7RX
Major Shareholder: Christopher Huw Braham
Officers: Christopher Huw Braham [1961] Director

Fortingall Advanced Therapeutics Ltd.
Incorporated: 13 April 2018
Registered Office: 7 / 4 Meggetland View, Edinburgh, EH14 1XT
Officers: Professor Marc Leighton Turner [1959] Director/Medical Practitioner

Fortingall Therapeutics International Limited
Incorporated: 13 April 2018
Registered Office: 7 / 4 Meggetland View, Edinburgh, EH14 1XT
Major Shareholder: Marc Turner
Officers: Professor Marc Leighton Turner [1959] Director/Medical Practitioner

Four Pharmaceuticals Limited
Incorporated: 5 September 1997
Net Worth: £335,188 *Total Assets:* £365,517
Registered Office: 23 Upper Green Road, Tewin, Welwyn, Herts, AL6 0LE
Shareholders: Philip Raine; Jane Elizabeth Raine
Officers: Jane Elizabeth Raine, Secretary; Jane Elizabeth Raine [1955] Director/Pharmacist; Philip Raine [1956] Director/Pharmacist

Fourrts (UK) Pharmacare Ltd
Incorporated: 1 February 2011
Registered Office: 5 Braemore Court, Cockfoster Road, Barnet, Herts, EN4 0AE
Major Shareholder: Sekharipuramviswanathan Veerramani
Officers: Radha Veirramani Veerramani [1954] Director [Indian]; Sekharipuram Viswanathan Veerramani [1949] Director [Indian]

FPL - Formulating Partnership Limited
Incorporated: 20 March 2018
Registered Office: Farnham Park House, Farnham Park Lane, Farnham Royal, Bucks, SL2 3LU
Officers: Colin Douglas Ryan [1959] Finance Director; Vivien Ryan [1959] Operations Director

FR Products Limited
Incorporated: 16 March 2016
Net Worth Deficit: £560 *Total Assets:* £9,540
Registered Office: 33b Beauchamp Place, London, SW3 1NU
Major Shareholder: Frederic Elie Roscop
Officers: Frederic Elie Roscop [1975] Director/Osteopath [French]

Fresenius Kabi DG Limited
Incorporated: 20 March 2018
Registered Office: 41-A Mill Lane, West Hampstead, London, NW6 1NB
Major Shareholder: Ashrf Elhoush
Officers: Ashrf Elhoush [1973] Director [Libyan]

Fresenius Kabi Limited
Incorporated: 22 October 1987 *Employees:* 341
Net Worth: £5,464,000 *Total Assets:* £60,723,000
Registered Office: Cestrian Court, Eastgate Way, Manor Park, Runcorn, Cheshire, WA7 1NT
Parent: FHC (Holdings) Limited
Officers: Marc James Gerard Crouton [1959] Director [French]; John Robert Ducker [1960] Director; Christopher Paul Harrison [1966] Managing Director; David Michael Kehoe [1984] Finance Director; Mark Henry Kirkup [1969] Director; Frank Lucassen [1972] Director [German]; Niamh Matic [1973] Director [Irish]; Rezzan Newton [1972] Director [Turkish]

Fresenius Kabi Oncology PLC
Incorporated: 10 December 1998 *Employees:* 47
Net Worth Deficit: £2,692,000 *Total Assets:* £25,414,000
Registered Office: Lion Court, Farnham Road, Bordon, Hants, GU35 0NF
Parent: Fresenius SE & Co KGaA
Officers: Tanja Greve [1972] Director/Executive Vice President - CFO [German]; Michael James Newson [1963] Director [French]

Frontline Trading Limited
Incorporated: 7 September 2005
Net Worth Deficit: £2,302 *Total Assets:* £1,401
Registered Office: 3 Sawyers Crescent, Chelveston, Wellingborough, Northants, NN9 6AD
Major Shareholder: Peter Michael Joseph Brown
Officers: Peter Michael Joseph Brown [1962] Director/IT Consultant [Irish]

Fujifilm Diosynth Biotechnologies UK Limited
Incorporated: 3 May 2006 Employees: 557
Net Worth: £136,100,000 Total Assets: £198,200,000
Registered Office: Fujifilm Diosynth Biotechnologies, Belasis Avenue, Billingham, Cleveland, TS23 1LH
Parent: Fujifilm Holdings Corporation
Officers: Neil Llewellyn Denham, Secretary; Stephen Bagshaw [1964] Director/Engineer; Takatoshi Ishikawa [1954] Director [Japanese]; Akira Kase [1963] Director/Employee [Japanese]; Kenji Orihashi [1962] Director/Employee [Japanese]; Masato Yamamoto [1963] Director [Japanese]

Fulhold Pharma Limited
Incorporated: 25 February 2014
Previous: Fulhold Pharma PLC
Net Worth: £5,490,130 Total Assets: £5,499,010
Registered Office: Suite 1, M6 Motorway House, Charter Way, Macclesfield, Cheshire, SK10 2NY
Officers: Christine Roberta McGee, Secretary; Stephen William Leivers [1960] Director/Scientist; David Nicholas Squire [1961] Director; Hans Jurgen Peter Wederman [1956] Director [South African]

Furoid Ltd
Incorporated: 18 February 2019
Registered Office: Hytec House, Burgess Wood Road South, Beaconsfield, Bucks, HP9 1EX
Parent: BTechLaboratories (UK) Ltd
Officers: Heinrich Kunz [1972] Director [German]; Sundip Singh Shihn [1969] Director/Investment Manager

FV Supplement Ltd
Incorporated: 6 February 2018
Registered Office: 20-22 Wenlock Road, London, N1 7GU
Major Shareholder: Owusu Akyiaw Bempah
Officers: Cecilia Armah [1946] Director/Computer Scientist; Kodjo Agyeman Bempah [1975] Director/Engineer; Dr Owusu Akyiaw Bempah [1940] Director/Scientist [Ghanaian]

G.A.S. Vets (UK) Limited
Incorporated: 23 January 2006
Registered Office: The Old Coach House, rear of Eastville Terrace, Ripon Road, Harrogate, N Yorks, HG1 3HJ
Major Shareholder: Paul Anthony Carter
Officers: Paul Anthony Carter [1962] Director

Ganges Thames Pharmaceuticals & Chemicals Ltd.
Incorporated: 6 December 2017
Registered Office: 130 Old Street, London, EC1V 9BD
Officers: Yogeshkumar Jagjivandas Doshi [1969] Director [Indian]

GB QP Services Limited
Incorporated: 12 September 2005
Net Worth: £1,132 Total Assets: £68,794
Registered Office: 25 Potters Grove, New Malden, Surrey, KT3 5DF
Major Shareholder: Gebray Gebreyesus Biadglgne
Officers: Gebray Gebreyesus Biadglgne [1960] Director

GB Quality Consulting Services Limited
Incorporated: 28 March 2017 Employees: 1
Net Worth: £38,031 Total Assets: £54,730
Registered Office: 5 McIntosh Place, Kirkcaldy, Fife, KY2 6RB
Officers: Gary Brown [1968] Director/Quality & Assurance Consultant

GBBC Ltd
Incorporated: 31 May 2013
Previous: EBK Skincare Ltd
Net Worth Deficit: £6,237 Total Assets: £34,677
Registered Office: 80 High Street, Winchester, Hants, SO23 9AT
Major Shareholder: Benjamin Douglas Swift
Officers: Benjamin Swift [1979] Director

GE Healthcare Limited
Incorporated: 16 February 1971 Employees: 851
Net Worth: £736,966,976 Total Assets: £932,070,016
Registered Office: Amersham Place, Little Chalfont, Bucks, HP7 9NA
Parent: GE Industrial Consolidation Limited
Officers: William Henry Bushill-Matthews, Secretary; Tricia Ann Clark [1976] Director/Executive EHS, GE Healthcare [American]; Ian Alistair Dale [1963] Director/General Manager; Michael Joseph Murphy [1965] Director/General Manager [Irish]; Kevin Michael O'Neill [1968] Director/Accountant

GE Healthcare UK Limited
Incorporated: 17 March 1997 Employees: 270
Net Worth: £430,340,000 Total Assets: £748,172,032
Registered Office: Amersham Place, Little Chalfont, Bucks, HP7 9NA
Parent: GE Medical Systems Limited
Officers: Judit Kalman, Secretary; Maria de Los Angeles Khoury Gonzalo [1970] Director/Financial Management [American]; Emmanuel Francois Joel Ligner [1970] Director/Management Executive [French]; Kevin Michael O'Neill [1968] Director/Accountant

Geistlich Sons Limited
Incorporated: 1 March 1960 Employees: 16
Net Worth: £1,386,167 Total Assets: £2,377,402
Registered Office: 1st Floor, Thorley House, Bailey Lane, Manchester Airport, Manchester, M90 4AB
Officers: Julie Jones, Secretary; Matthias Peter Hermann Dunkel [1966] Director/Deputy Chief Operating Officer [Swiss]; Rolf Franz Jeger [1955] Director/Chief Financial Officer [Swiss]; Paul Druon Michael Note [1956] Director [French]; Frank Sellers [1963] Director

Gelu Life Limited
Incorporated: 22 May 2017
Registered Office: Thames House, Bourne End Business Park, Cores End Road, Bourne End, Bucks, SL8 5AS
Shareholders: George Michel Haddad; Luca Stefano Benati
Officers: Asmir Begovic [1987] Director; Luca Stefano Benati [1970] Director [Italian]; Dr George Michel Haddad [1968] Director

Generics (U.K.) Limited
Incorporated: 29 April 1981 Employees: 262
Net Worth: £45,680,000 Total Assets: £85,286,000
Registered Office: Station Close, Potters Bar, Herts, EN6 1TL
Parent: Mylan Group BV
Officers: Caroline Rebecca Louise Dixon, Finance Director; Jean-Yves Brault [1967] Director/Area Head Northern Europe [Canadian]; Jose Javier Cotarelo [1972] Director/Commercial Head of Northern & Western Europe [American]; Caroline Rebecca Louise Dixon [1968] Finance Director; Balwant Singh Heer [1959] Director/Global Head - Product Safety & Risk Management

Genetis PLC
Incorporated: 13 December 2018
Registered Office: 12th Floor, 6 New Street Square, London, EC4A 3BF
Major Shareholder: Jean Jacques Pierre Chalopin
Officers: Jean Jacques Pierre Chalopin [1950] Director/Bank Executive [French]; Gregory Pepin [1983] Director/Executive Manager [French]

Genomix Ltd
Incorporated: 11 February 2019
Registered Office: No 7 Imperial Wharf, London, SW2 2EX
Major Shareholder: Gholamreza Taheripak
Officers: Gholamreza Taheripak [1972] Director [Iranian]; Mohammad Taheripak [1983] Director [Iranian]; Mehdi Tahripak [1966] Director [Iranian]

Genotact Ltd
Incorporated: 11 July 2018
Registered Office: Suite 6, First Floor, Wordsworth Mill, Wordsworth Street, Bolton, Lancs, BL1 3ND
Shareholders: Paulo Balatbat; Craig Fothringham
Officers: Paulo Balatbat [1962] Director [Filipino]

Genus Pharmaceuticals Limited
Incorporated: 6 February 1986
Net Worth: £44,653,000 *Total Assets:* £58,685,000
Registered Office: Manchester Road, Linthwaite, Huddersfield, W Yorks, HD7 5QH
Parent: Genus Pharmaceutical Holdings Ltd
Officers: Edwin Charles Blythe, Secretary; Charles Ashley Brierley [1963] Director

Genzyme Limited
Incorporated: 21 April 1981 *Employees:* 255
Net Worth: £163,684,000 *Total Assets:* £205,024,992
Registered Office: 37 Hollands Road, Haverhill, Suffolk, CB9 8PU
Parent: Sanofi
Officers: Sara Morrish, Secretary; Francois Xavier Duhalde [1965] Director [French]; James Moretta [1966] Director/Site Head

Geoorganics Limited
Incorporated: 19 December 2018
Registered Office: 48 Gray's Inn Road, London, WC1X 8LT
Major Shareholder: George Kukhaleishvili
Officers: George Kukhaleishvili [1964] Director/Businessman

Geoprep Limited
Incorporated: 28 July 2009
Registered Office: 241a Magdalen Road, London, SW18 3PA
Officers: Philip Safwan Clancy [1968] Director/Geologist; Mohammad Reza Sarabandi [1963] Director/Engineer

Georganics Ltd
Incorporated: 12 November 2014 *Employees:* 3
Net Worth: £110,234 *Total Assets:* £170,919
Registered Office: Lynwood House, Crofton Road, Orpington, Kent, BR6 8QE
Shareholders: Charles Henry Van Boxmeer; Alessandro Rocchi
Officers: Alessandro Rocchi, Secretary; Alessandro Rocchi [1985] Director/Retailer [Italian]; Charles Henry Van Boxmeer [1986] Director/Entrepreneur [Belgian]

Geotek Coring Limited
Incorporated: 20 April 1993 *Employees:* 4
Previous: Geotek Communications Limited
Net Worth: £4,234,650 *Total Assets:* £9,263,396
Registered Office: Lynton House, 7-12 Tavistock Square, London, WC1H 9LT
Shareholders: Quentin James Huggett; Peter John Schultheiss
Officers: Anthony James Bosley [1966] Director; Richard Alan Watson Chamberlain [1974] Technical Director; Dr Quentin James Huggett [1956] Director/Geologist; Dr John Anthony Roberts [1969] Director/Geologist; Peter John Schultheiss [1951] Director/Geophysicist

Geryon Pharma Limited
Incorporated: 1 July 2013
Net Worth: £108,797 *Total Assets:* £285,358
Registered Office: 25 Compass West, Spindus Road, Speke Hall Industrial Estate, Liverpool, L24 1YA
Shareholders: Mark John Dignum; Pamela Ann Turner
Officers: Mark John Dignum [1974] Director; Pamela Ann Turner [1968] Director

Gesco Cosmetics Limited
Incorporated: 12 January 2017
Registered Office: Unit 3 Apollo Trade Center, 124 Lupton Avenue, Leeds, LS9 6ED
Major Shareholder: Radjabu Mbumbu Stonris
Officers: Radjabu Mbumbu Stonris [1963] Director [Norwegian]

Getinge UK Limited
Incorporated: 17 February 1983 *Employees:* 195
Net Worth: £11,598,000 *Total Assets:* £27,519,000
Registered Office: 14-15 Burford Way, Boldon Business Park, Boldon Colliery, Co Durham, NE35 9PZ
Parent: Getinge Extended Care UK Limited
Officers: Martin Forbister, Secretary; Avril Ann Forde [1974] Director/Regional President [Irish]; Karin Soderlund [1981] Director/Chairman [Finnish]; Jon Barrie Yard [1967] QA Director

GFC Diagnostics Limited
Incorporated: 4 July 2007
Net Worth: £49,342 *Total Assets:* £99,620
Registered Office: 5 Minton Place, Victoria Road, Bicester, Oxon, OX26 6QB
Officers: Bruce Savage, Secretary; Graham Cope [1954] Director; Bruce Savage [1948] Director

Gimews Welding Limited
Incorporated: 4 July 2017 *Employees:* 1
Net Worth: £3,824 *Total Assets:* £8,631
Registered Office: 22 Watson Avenue, South Shields, Tyne & Wear, NE34 7QX
Major Shareholder: Graeme Mews
Officers: Graeme David Mews [1990] Director/Tig Welder

Gitflex Ltd
Incorporated: 6 February 2018
Registered Office: 56 St James Road, Salford, M7 4XE
Officers: Kawan Williams [1992] Director/Sale of Sport Supplements [Iranian]

Glacier Nutrition Ltd
Incorporated: 20 February 2018
Registered Office: 115 Oxford Road, Oxford, OX4 2ES
Parent: Ahmeys Limited
Officers: Adnaan Ahmad [1986] Director; Faheem Ahmad [1988] Director; Wasim Ahmed [1985] Director; Egzona Makolli [1991] Director

Glasport Bio UK Limited
Incorporated: 13 July 2018
Registered Office: 2nd Floor, 2 Woodberry Grove, North Finchley, London, N12 0DR
Officers: Ruairi Friel [1976] Director [Irish]; Killian O'Briain [1972] Director [Irish]; Vincent O'Flaherty [1972] Director [Irish]

Glasstomato Ltd
Incorporated: 22 July 2018
Registered Office: Unit 4 Conbar House, Mead Lane, Hertford, SG13 7AP
Major Shareholder: Jodie McClelland
Officers: Consolacion Dela Cruz [1957] Director [Filipino]

Glaxo Operations UK Limited
Incorporated: 1 January 1962 *Employees:* 4,160
Net Worth: £858,684,032 *Total Assets:* £1,324,759,040
Registered Office: 980 Great West Road, Brentford, Middlesex, TW8 9GS
Parent: Glaxo Group Limited
Officers: Victoria Anne Whyte, Secretary; Alan George Burns [1975] Director; Freek Jongen [1980] Director [Dutch]; Regis Jean-Pierre Simard [1965] Director/Head of Supply Chain [French]

GlaxoSmithKline Consumer Healthcare (UK) Trading Limited
Incorporated: 26 September 2014 *Employees:* 1,379
Net Worth: £201,250,000 *Total Assets:* £685,875,968
Registered Office: 980 Great West Road, Brentford, Middlesex, TW8 9GS
Parent: GlaxoSmithKline Consumer Healthcare Holdings Limited
Officers: Richard Green [1974] Director; Aidan Lynch [1964] Managing Director - Trading Partners [Irish]; Terence O'Neill [1965] Finance Director; Eugene Prokopchuk [1981] Finance Director [Ukrainian]

Gley Skincare Limited
Incorporated: 20 December 2013
Registered Office: Embla House, Town Street, Rawdon, Leeds, LS19 6PU
Major Shareholder: Ian William Shaw
Officers: Ian William Shaw [1953] Managing Director

Global Healthcare Innovations Limited
Incorporated: 13 February 2018
Registered Office: Unit 12 The Brunel Centre, Newton Road, Crawley, W Sussex, RH10 9TU
Major Shareholder: Orobola Feyisola Lafe
Officers: Orobola Feyisola Lafe [1966] Director/Finance Manager

Global Herbs Holdings Ltd
Incorporated: 15 February 2017
Registered Office: Unit 10 Terminus Road, Chichester, W Sussex, PO19 8TX
Major Shareholder: Stephen Francis Ashdown
Officers: Stephen Francis Ashdown, Secretary; Stephen Francis Ashdown [1960] Managing Director

Glycanova UK Limited
Incorporated: 18 August 2017
Registered Office: 3a Clavering Walk, Bexhill on Sea, E Sussex, TN39 4TW
Officers: Jonathan James Aldwinckle [1975] Director; Dr Bjorn Kristiansen [1947] Director [Norwegian]

GM Biopharma Ltd
Incorporated: 23 November 2017
Registered Office: 30-31 Furnival Street, London, EC4A 1JQ
Major Shareholder: Ashraf Uddin
Officers: Ashraf Uddin [1975] Director/Company Owner

GM Globalhealth Ltd
Incorporated: 4 February 2019
Registered Office: 27 Old Gloucester Street, London, WC1N 3AX
Major Shareholder: Ghazi Abbass Mohammed Ali Hussein
Officers: Dr Ghazi Abbass Mohammed Ali Hussein, Secretary; Dr Mohamed Ahmed Fadlallah Elsheikh [1980] Director/Veterinary Surgeon [Sudanese]; Dr Ghazi Abbass Mohammed Ali Hussein [1981] Director/Veterinarian

GMP Manufacturing Ltd
Incorporated: 6 September 2018
Registered Office: Park Royal House, Valletta Street, Hull, HU9 5NP
Major Shareholder: Giby George
Officers: Giby George [1976] Managing Director [Indian]

Go-Kyo Science Limited
Incorporated: 26 November 2009 *Employees:* 2
Net Worth Deficit: £5,179 *Total Assets:* £31,287
Registered Office: Kings House Business Centre, St Johns Square, Wolverhampton, W Midlands, WV2 4DT
Shareholders: Lakhveer Singh Sahota; Gurpreet Kaur Sahota
Officers: Gurpreet Kaur Sahota [1978] Director; Lakhveer Singh Sahota [1974] Director

Goat Nutrition Limited
Incorporated: 15 April 1982 *Employees:* 9
Net Worth: £220,229 *Total Assets:* £271,710
Registered Office: Unit B & C, Smarden Business Estate, Smarden, Ashford, Kent, TN27 8QL
Shareholders: Bruce Dolby; Margaret Anne Dolby
Officers: Bruce Dolby, Secretary; Benjamin Dolby [1977] Director; Bruce Dolby [1948] Director/Chartered Chemist; Margaret Anne Dolby [1949] Director/Secretary; Rebecca Goldswain [1973] Director

Graviti Healthcare Limited
Incorporated: 1 October 2018
Registered Office: 209 The Heights, Northolt, Middlesex, UB5 4BX
Major Shareholder: Sridhar Rao Sampalli
Officers: Sridhar Rao Sampalli [1966] Director

The Great British Bee Company Ltd
Incorporated: 24 February 2017
Registered Office: 26 Victoria Road, Devizes, Wilts, SN10 1ET
Officers: Ben Swift [1979] Director

The Great Northern Apothecary Co. Limited
Incorporated: 14 August 2006
Registered Office: 26 Green Close, Stannington, Northumberland, NE61 6PE
Officers: Moya Anne Graham, Secretary; Stuart David Graham [1962] Director/Pharmacist

Greeco Arab Products Ltd.
Incorporated: 9 March 2015 *Employees:* 1
Net Worth: £4,285 *Total Assets:* £7,510
Registered Office: Unit 18 Campus Road, Listerhills Science Park, Bradford, BD7 1HR
Major Shareholder: Muhammad Bilal
Officers: Muhammad Bilal [1980] Director/Business Consultant

Green Groot Limited
Incorporated: 12 April 2017
Net Worth: £11,360 *Total Assets:* £20,680
Registered Office: 47 Costons Avenue, Greenford, Middlesex, UB6 8RJ
Major Shareholder: Amin Khan
Officers: Amin Khan [1990] Director

Green House Monitoring Limited
Incorporated: 18 February 2010
Net Worth: £52,279 *Total Assets:* £71,318
Registered Office: Unit 85 Waterhouse Business Centre, 2 Cromar Way, Chelmsford, Essex, CM1 2QE
Major Shareholder: Suhkdev Dhesi
Officers: Suhkdev Dhesi, Secretary; Suhkdev Dhesi [1970] Director/Programmer

Green Manufacturing Partners Limited
Incorporated: 26 July 2010
Registered Office: Meadow Park Industrial Estate, Essendine, Stamford, Lincs, PE9 4LT
Major Shareholder: David James Carter
Officers: David James Carter [1950] Director

Greenfield Pharmaceuticals Limited
Incorporated: 21 December 1970
Registered Office: Lilly House, Priestley Road, Basingstoke, Hants, RG24 9NL
Parent: Eli Lilly and Company Limited
Officers: Hamish John Carmichael Bennett, Secretary; Hamish John Carmichael Bennett [1974] Director; Nicholas Lemen [1974] Finance Director [American]

Greenova Healthcare UK Ltd.
Incorporated: 14 September 2012
Registered Office: 4 Kenbury Drive, Slough, SL1 5FX
Officers: Girish Shrikrishna Karnataki [1979] Director/Consultant [Indian]; Nahush Shrikrishna Karnataki [1984] Director/Sales & Marketing [Indian]; Shrikrishna Karnataki [1952] Director [Indian]

Grip Enterprises Limited
Incorporated: 14 October 2009
Registered Office: 4 Michaels Mount, Little Bealings, Woodbridge, Suffolk, IP13 6LS
Major Shareholder: David Craddock
Officers: David John Craddock [1953] Director/Chemist

Guerbet Argentina Limited
Incorporated: 29 January 1924   *Employees:* 11
Previous: Mallinckrodt Medical Argentina Limited
Net Worth: £3,580,000   *Total Assets:* £4,426,000
Registered Office: Avon House, 435 Stratford Road, Shirley, Solihull, W Midlands, B90 4AA
Parent: Guerbert Laboratories Limited
Officers: Jean-Francois Le Martret [1958] Director [French]; Antoine Mazraani [1952] Director [French]

GW Pharma Limited
Incorporated: 29 January 1999   *Employees:* 123
Net Worth: £12,442,472   *Total Assets:* £84,644,096
Registered Office: Sovereign House, Vision Park, Chivers Way, Histon, Cambridge, CB24 9BZ
Parent: GW Pharmaceuticals PLC
Officers: Adam David George, Secretary; Adam David George [1970] Director/Chartered Accountant; Dr Geoffrey William Guy [1954] Director/Doctor; Christopher John Tovey [1965] Director/Chief Operating Officer

Gynopharma Ltd
Incorporated: 15 March 2017
Registered Office: The Long Lodge, 265-269 Kingston Road, Wimbledon, London, SW19 3NW
Major Shareholder: Francesco Ciro Guerrieri
Officers: Francesco Ciro Guerrieri [1948] Director [Italian]

Hadley Rose Limited
Incorporated: 23 May 2018
Registered Office: 2a Banks Road, Sandbanks, Poole, Dorset, BH13 7QB
Major Shareholder: Hadley Rose Hellmers-White
Officers: Hadley Rose Hellmers-White [1991] Director/Hairdresser

Hahydra Technologies Ltd
Incorporated: 25 April 2013
Registered Office: 77 High Street, Littlehampton, W Sussex, BN17 5AG
Major Shareholder: Istvan Novak
Officers: Istvan Novak [1976] Director [Hungarian]

Hairblends Limited
Incorporated: 8 January 2016
Net Worth: £65   *Total Assets:* £1,179
Registered Office: 3 Daws Leas, High Wycombe, Bucks, HP11 1QG
Shareholders: Martin Olayinka Ekundayo; Oladele Olanrewaju Ekundayo
Officers: Martin Ekundayo, Secretary; Martin Olayinka Ekundayo [1967] Director

Halewood Chemicals Ltd
Incorporated: 19 September 1951
Previous: Halewood Chemicals Limited
Net Worth: £68,522   *Total Assets:* £530,408
Registered Office: The Mill, Horton Road, Stanwell Moor, Staines upon Thames, Middlesex, TW19 6BJ
Officers: Robin Faber, Secretary; Susan Elizabeth de Zulueta [1957] Director

Halligarth Bioadvisors Ltd
Incorporated: 8 October 2018
Registered Office: 20-22 Wenlock Road, London, N1 7GU
Major Shareholder: Simon James Yvon Saxby
Officers: Simon James Yvon Saxby [1958] Director

Handiskin Limited
Incorporated: 16 January 2014
Net Worth: £12,074   *Total Assets:* £21,074
Registered Office: 170 Upper New Walk, Leicester, LE1 7QA
Shareholders: Nikesh Patel; Pravesh Ganda; Keith Fawdington
Officers: Keith Rodney Fawdington [1960] Director; Praveshkumar Kantilal Ganda [1967] Director; Nikesh Patel [1965] Director

Hannah and Hugh Ltd
Incorporated: 9 November 2012
Registered Office: 2 Surrey House, Stratton Close, Edgware, Middlesex, HA8 6PX
Major Shareholder: Pamela Orji
Officers: Pamela Orji [1971] Director/Business Consultant

Hannah V Limited
Incorporated: 17 March 2009
Registered Office: 47 Elm Walk, Radlett, Herts, WD7 8DP
Major Shareholder: Kimiko Veale
Officers: Kimiko Veale [1953] Director [Japanese]

HARC Therapeutics Limited
Incorporated: 7 February 2019
Registered Office: 65a East Dulwich Grove, London, SE22 8PR
Major Shareholder: Robert Charles Horsewood Chisholm
Officers: Robert Charles Horsewood Chisholm [1972] Director/Pharmaceutical Executive

Harlequin BPI Ltd
Incorporated: 6 July 2012
Net Worth: £22,690   *Total Assets:* £389,701
Registered Office: Unit 2 Falcon Court, Manners Avenue, Manners Industrial Estate, Ilkeston, Derbys, DE7 8EF
Shareholders: Ronald Ian Hopkinson; Beverley Gail Hopkinson
Officers: Ronald Ian Hopkinson [1966] Director/Industrial Chemist

Hartington Pharma Limited
Incorporated: 2 March 2007
Net Worth Deficit: £366,530 *Total Assets:* £382,010
Registered Office: 1 Northumberland Avenue, Trafalgar Square, London, WC2N 5BW
Officers: Dr Dimitri Mtchedlidze, Secretary; Alexander Levdanski [1961] Director [Spanish]; Archil Mtchedlidze [1963] Managing Director [Georgian]

Hashmats Health Ltd
Incorporated: 17 March 2010
Previous: Abagee Limited
Net Worth Deficit: £14,448 *Total Assets:* £4,303
Registered Office: Hashmats House, 123a-125a The Broadway, Southall, Middlesex, UB1 1LW
Officers: Akhtar Ali [1960] Director; Dilshad Ali [1996] Director; Fahid Ali [1987] Director

HAV Vaccines Limited
Incorporated: 15 July 2009
Net Worth: £1,159,830 *Total Assets:* £1,161,696
Registered Office: 11 Parkside Avenue, Wimbledon, London, SW19 5ES
Shareholders: Professor John Hermon-Taylor; Michael Thomas Gwynfor Paynter
Officers: Professor John Hermon-Taylor [1936] Director; Michael Thomas Gwynfor Paynter [1957] Director/Solicitor; Michael James Dahl Stallibrass [1951] Director/Retired

HBNatura Ltd
Incorporated: 24 June 2016
Registered Office: 71-75 Shelton Street, London, WC2H 9JQ
Major Shareholder: Herve Sczerbyna
Officers: Herve Sczerbyna [1955] Director/Engineer [French]

Healing Fusions Ltd
Incorporated: 19 September 2008
Registered Office: 29 Gray Avenue, Sherburn Village, Co Durham, DH6 1JE
Officers: Anthony Frederick William Grossi [1983] Director

Health + Plus Limited
Incorporated: 24 April 1980 *Employees:* 4
Net Worth: £307,504 *Total Assets:* £711,817
Registered Office: G1 Chaucer Business Park, Dittons Road, Polegate, E Sussex, BN26 6QH
Shareholder: Janet Frances Bandy
Officers: Brian Edward Bandy, Secretary; Brian Edward Bandy [1943] Director/Accountant; Janet Frances Bandy [1943] Director

Health Innovations (UK) Limited
Incorporated: 3 April 2007 *Employees:* 63
Net Worth: £181,631 *Total Assets:* £4,387,863
Registered Office: Airedale Business Centre, Millennium Road, Skipton, N Yorks, BD23 2TZ
Shareholder: Michael John Davies
Officers: Richard Doyle, Secretary; Clare Campbell [1975] Director; Michael John Davies [1951] Director

Health Marque Ltd
Incorporated: 28 February 2018
Registered Office: Black Country House, Rounds Green Road, Oldbury, W Midlands, B69 2DG
Major Shareholder: Uzma Hashmat
Officers: Uzma Hashmat [1980] Director [Pakistani]

Health Plus Limited
Incorporated: 26 November 1991
Net Worth: £137 *Total Assets:* £29,166
Registered Office: G1 Chaucer Business Park, Dittons Road, Polegate, E Sussex, BN26 6QH
Major Shareholder: Brian Edward Bandy
Officers: Brian Edward Bandy, Secretary/Accountant; Brian Edward Bandy [1943] Director/Accountant; Janet Frances Bandy [1943] Director/Sales Assistant

Health Remit Limited
Incorporated: 8 May 2018
Registered Office: 33 Richards Way, Slough, SL1 5EU
Officers: Fawad Basheer, Secretary; Fawad Basheer [1970] Director/Accountant

Healthbiotics Ltd
Incorporated: 19 March 2018
Registered Office: Unit 5 Progress Industrial Park, Progress Way, Croydon, Surrey, CR0 4XD
Parent: Nileshkumar Indubhai Patel
Officers: Nileshkumar Indubhai Patel [1974] Managing Director [Indian]

Healthcare Consortium Ltd
Incorporated: 13 March 2015
Registered Office: 37 Willenhall Road, Bilston, W Midlands, WV14 6NW
Major Shareholder: Narinder Singh Khakh
Officers: Narinder Singh Khakh [1978] Director/Pharmacist

Heavenly Group of Company Limited
Incorporated: 4 May 2018
Registered Office: The House Beyond, The Avenue, Farnham Common, Bucks, SL2 3JY
Shareholder: Francis Fernandes
Officers: Margareta Kulcsar [1979] Director [Hungarian]

The Heavenly Herb Company Ltd.
Incorporated: 24 October 2016
Net Worth: £12 *Total Assets:* £12
Registered Office: Steel Farm Cottage, Steel, Hexham, Northumberland, NE47 0LG
Shareholders: Katrina Padmore; Ross McPherson Menzies
Officers: Ross McPherson Menzies [1967] Director/Herbalist; Katrina Padmore [1964] Director/Project Co-ordinator

Hedgarth Ltd
Incorporated: 23 February 2018
Registered Office: 71-75 Shelton Street, London, WC2H 9JQ
Officers: Amine Belmejdoub [1983] Director/Business Development Manager [Moroccan]

Hemma Healthcare Teronta Ltd
Incorporated: 2 May 2018
Registered Office: Kemp House, 160 City Road, London, EC1V 2NX
Shareholder: Aveen Hasan
Officers: Darra Ali, Secretary; Aveen Hasan, Secretary; Darra Mohamed Ali [1969] Director/Development Manager [Irish]; Aveen Hasan [1974] Director/Accounting [Irish]

The Hemp Broker Ltd
Incorporated: 20 May 2016
Registered Office: 46 Nova Road, Croydon, Surrey, CR0 2TL
Major Shareholder: Michal Takac
Officers: Michal Takac [1979] Director/Trader [Czech]

Herbal Concepts Limited
Incorporated: 4 November 1998 Employees: 3
Net Worth Deficit: £560,625 Total Assets: £377,384
Registered Office: Network House, West 26 Industrial Estate, Cleckheaton, W Yorks, BD19 4TT
Shareholders: Peter Noel Miller Cox; Ian John Kirk; Ian Charles Gardner
Officers: Peter Noel Miller Cox, Secretary/Chemist; Peter Noel Miller Cox [1946] Director/Chemist; Ian Charles Gardner [1949] Director; Ian John Kirk [1957] Director

The Herbal Factory Ltd
Incorporated: 3 July 2012
Net Worth Deficit: £13,417 Total Assets: £109,210
Registered Office: Unit 28 Vulcan Way, New Addington, Croydon, Surrey, CR0 9UG
Major Shareholder: Soe Lu Gyaw
Officers: Soe Lu Gyaw [1941] Director

Herbal Food Life Limited
Incorporated: 17 October 2017
Registered Office: 87 Watersmeet Road, Coventry, Warwicks, CV2 3HT
Shareholder: Thangarajah Gunabalsinkam
Officers: Thangarajah Gunabalsinkam [1961] Director [German]

Herbal Republic Ltd
Incorporated: 16 May 2018
Registered Office: 5 Windmill Cottages, Colton, Leeds, LS15 9JG
Major Shareholder: James McCartney
Officers: James McCartney [1991] Director/General Manager

Herbal Right UK Limited
Incorporated: 7 March 2006
Net Worth Deficit: £4,051 Total Assets: £6,215
Registered Office: 317 Dickenson Road, Manchester, M13 0NR
Shareholder: Muhammad Zubair Ayub
Officers: Ch Muhammad Ayub, Secretary; Muhammad Zubair Ayub [1981] Director/Business Risk Analyst

Herbapharmedica Limited
Incorporated: 15 March 2012
Net Worth: £4,105 Total Assets: £10,192
Registered Office: 78 York Street, London, W1H 1DP
Major Shareholder: Tariq Sadeq
Officers: Dr Tariq Sadeq [1980] Director [Iraqi]

IM Herd Ltd
Incorporated: 11 August 2014
Net Worth: £26,342 Total Assets: £52,790
Registered Office: 35 Stamford New Road, Altrincham, Cheshire, WA14 1EB
Major Shareholder: Ian Malcolm Herd
Officers: Ian Malcolm Herd [1974] Director

Herman Claude Ltd
Incorporated: 1 May 2007
Net Worth Deficit: £22,067 Total Assets: £72
Registered Office: Farthings, Misbourne Avenue, Chalfont St Peter, Gerrards Cross, Bucks, SL9 0PD
Shareholder: Ann-Marie Watson
Officers: Janet Lawrence, Secretary; Ann-Marie Watson [1977] Director

Hermes Pharma Limited
Incorporated: 9 February 2018
Registered Office: Fairview House, 3 Gosse Close, Hoddesdon, Herts, EN11 9FG
Officers: Zulfiqar Ali Khan [1968] Director/Pharmaceutical Manufacturing

Hermes Pharmaceutical Limited
Incorporated: 15 September 1994
Registered Office: c/o Laytons LLP, Level 5, More London Riverside, London, SE1 2AP
Major Shareholder: Johannes Franz Burges
Officers: Johannes Franz Burges [1939] Director [German]

Herrco Cosmetics Limited
Incorporated: 17 February 2009 Employees: 156
Net Worth: £5,627,319 Total Assets: £9,066,244
Registered Office: 5 Broadway Drive, Halesworth, Suffolk, IP19 8QR
Officers: Susan Herrmann, Secretary; Derek Herrmann [1982] Director; Nigel Kurt Herrmann [1951] Director; Susan Herrmann [1950] Director

Hewlett Healthcare Limited
Incorporated: 5 September 1995
Net Worth Deficit: £58,590 Total Assets: £83,590
Registered Office: 1 Princes Court, Royal Way, Loughborough, Leics, LE11 5XR
Officers: Margaret Bell, Secretary; Margaret Bell [1955] Director/Secretary; Alexander James Wigmore [1951] Director/Advertising Executive

Hexa-Halers Ltd
Incorporated: 7 March 2018
Registered Office: Daresbury Innovation Centre, Keckwick Lane, Daresbury, Warrington, Cheshire, WA4 4FS
Shareholder: Michael Howell
Officers: Catherine Howell [1982] Director/Educationalist; Michael Howell [1982] Director/Engineer

Hexagon Therapeutics Limited
Incorporated: 11 January 2019
Registered Office: 26 Whittaker Lane, Prestwich, Manchester, M25 1FX
Major Shareholder: Marc Saul Borson
Officers: Marc Saul Borson [1978] Director/Pharmacist

Hexpress Healthcare Limited
Incorporated: 12 April 2011 Employees: 1
Net Worth: £2,119,366 Total Assets: £3,810,796
Registered Office: 144 Mitcham Road, London, SW17 9NH
Shareholders: Chetan Vinodrai Shukla; Kaushika Chetan Shukla
Officers: Kaushika Shukla, Secretary; Vijay Kumar Harendra Patel [1974] Director; Chetan Vinodrai Shukla [1962] Director

HFA Healthcare Products Limited
Incorporated: 8 September 2014
Net Worth Deficit: £34,805 Total Assets: £1,214,447
Registered Office: 7 Greenfield Crescent, Edgbaston, Birmingham, B15 3EE
Shareholders: Faisal Kibria Janjua; Ambreen Janjua
Officers: Ambreen Janjua, Secretary; Faisal Kibria Janjua [1967] Director/General Manager

Hichrom Limited
Incorporated: 21 December 1984 *Employees:* 91
Net Worth: £13,010,257 *Total Assets:* £15,070,568
Registered Office: Hichrom Limited, Hunter Boulevard, Magna Park, Lutterworth, Leics, LE17 4XN
Parent: VWR Holdco Limited
Officers: Karen Jane Pulford, Secretary; William Patrick Hogan [1959] Managing Director [Irish]; Karen Jane Pulford [1968] Director/Accountant; Andrew Smith [1972] Operations Director

Hickson W.A. Chemicals Limited
Incorporated: 29 February 1988
Registered Office: Wheldon Road, Castleford, W Yorks, WF10 2JT
Officers: Nicholas Thomas Carter, Secretary; Nicholas Thomas Carter [1981] Director/Financial Accountant; Anthony William Kelly [1963] Director

Higgs Pharma Private Limited
Incorporated: 8 November 2017
Registered Office: Unit E5, Telford Road, Bicester, Oxon, OX26 4LD
Major Shareholder: Dipesh Parikh
Officers: Dr Dipesh Parikh [1975] Director

Hikma Pharmaceuticals International Limited
Incorporated: 23 June 2011 *Employees:* 3
Previous: West-Ward Pharmaceuticals International Limited
Net Worth: £274,979,232 *Total Assets:* £1,053,292,032
Registered Office: 1 New Burlington Place, London, W1S 2HR
Parent: Hikma UK Limited
Officers: Peter Alexander Speirs, Secretary; Dr Basel Ibrahim Bakir Awad [1955] Director/VP Quality and Regulatory Affairs [Dutch]; Natheer Masarweh [1971] Director/Chief Operating Officer [Jordanian]; Riad Mishlawi [1964] Director [Portuguese]; Frank Louis Savastano [1975] Director/Executive Management [American]; Peter Alexander Speirs [1979] Director/Chartered Secretary

Hikma Pharmaceuticals Public Limited Company
Incorporated: 8 September 2005 *Employees:* 8,521
Net Worth: £1,099,012,736 *Total Assets:* £2,459,349,504
Registered Office: 1 New Burlington Place, London, W1S 2HR
Officers: Peter Alexander Speirs, Secretary; Ali Mohammed Al Husry [1935] Director [Jordanian]; Patrick Noel Butler [1960] Director [Irish]; John Julius Castellani [1951] Director [American]; Mazen Samih Darwazah [1958] Director [Jordanian]; Said Samih Darwazah [1957] Director/Chief Executive Officer [Jordanian]; Jochen Gann [1964] Finance Director [German]; Mary Regina Henderson [1950] Director [American]; Dr Pamela Josephine Kirby [1953] Director; Sigurdur Oli Olafsson [1968] Director/Chief Executive Officer [Icelander]; Robert Mark Pickering [1959] Director/Investment Banker and Financial Consultant

Hikma UK Limited
Incorporated: 3 July 2005
Previous: Hikma Ventures Limited
Net Worth: £1,511,870,464 *Total Assets:* £1,696,593,792
Registered Office: 1 New Burlington Place, London, W1S 2HR
Parent: Hikma Holdings (UK) Limited
Officers: Peter Alexander Speirs, Secretary; Gurpal Singh Atwal [1964] Director/Tax Consultant; Peter Alexander Speirs [1979] Director/Company Secretary

Hikmacure Limited
Incorporated: 26 June 2013
Net Worth: £3,395,749 *Total Assets:* £3,402,692
Registered Office: 1 New Burlington Place, London, W1S 2HR
Shareholders: Hikma Pharmaceuticals PLC; Mohammed Hussein Al Amoudi
Officers: Peter Alexander Speirs, Secretary; Bassam Felix Aburdene [1948] Director; Sheikh Mohammed Hussein Al Amoudi [1946] Director [Saudi Arabian]; Mazen Samih Taleb Darwazah [1958] Director/Vice Chairman [Jordanian]; Bashar Basel Yacoub Shomali [1978] Director of M&A [Jordanian]

Hipra UK and Ireland Limited
Incorporated: 20 July 2010 *Employees:* 19
Previous: Hipra UK Ltd
Net Worth: £1,166,637 *Total Assets:* £1,828,547
Registered Office: Foxhall Business Centre, Foxhall Lodge, Foxhall Road, Nottingham, NG7 6LH
Parent: Laboratorious Hipra S.A
Officers: Carlos Montanes Estupina [1963] Director/Veterinary Surgeon [Spanish]; David Nogareda Estivill [1965] Director/Veterinary Surgeon [Spanish]; Maria Del Mar Nogareda Estivill [1966] Director/Economist [Spanish]

HK Pharma Limited
Incorporated: 23 January 1998
Registered Office: 25a Becher Close, Renhold, Bedford, MK41 0LP
Officers: Sara Jane Kettleborough [1989] Director/Head of Business Operations

Hlinka Pharma Ltd
Incorporated: 18 January 2019
Registered Office: Flat 19, Camellia Apartments, 87 Hill Top Avenue, London, NW10 8RY
Major Shareholder: Daniel Hlinka
Officers: Dr Daniel Hlinka, Secretary; Dr Daniel Hlinka [1979] Director/Doctor [Czech]

HMS Vilgo UK Ltd
Incorporated: 6 January 2015
Net Worth Deficit: £18,962 *Total Assets:* £44,929
Registered Office: French Chamber of Commerce in GB, 4th Floor, Lincoln House, 300 High Holborn, London, WC1V 7JH
Major Shareholder: Patrick Jude
Officers: Christian Jude [1973] Director [French]

HOCL Limited
Incorporated: 30 August 2011
Registered Office: Studio 9, The Greenhouse, Mannings Heath Road, Poole, Dorset, BH12 4NQ
Major Shareholder: Paul Robin Booker
Officers: Hannah Marie Booker, Secretary; Paul Robin Booker [1960] Managing Director; Ross John Thornley [1979] Brand Director

Hollins Denture Clinic Limited
Incorporated: 3 April 2013 *Employees:* 2
Previous: Hollins Dental Laboratory Limited
Net Worth: £6,791 *Total Assets:* £21,065
Registered Office: 54 Bury Old Road, Whitefield, Manchester, M45 6TL
Major Shareholder: Robert William Carey
Officers: Genieve Carey [1982] Director/Air Steward; Robert Carey [1978] Director

Hologic Ltd.
Incorporated: 11 June 1992 *Employees:* 243
Net Worth: £36,445,000 *Total Assets:* £52,481,000
Registered Office: Heron House, Oaks Business Park, Crewe Road, Wythenshawe, Manchester, M23 9HZ
Parent: Hologic Inc
Officers: John Joseph O'Shea, Secretary; John Joseph O'Shea [1967] Director/Business Executive [Irish]; Michelangelo Stefani [1966] Director/International Counsel [Italian]; Jan Valeer Verstreken [1967] Director [Belgian]

Home Health Limited
Incorporated: 22 January 2015
Registered Office: 53 Charlbert Court, Mackennal Street, St John's Wood, London, NW8 7DB
Major Shareholder: Joanne Stoller
Officers: Joanne Stoller [1966] Director

Homicon Prime International Limited
Incorporated: 9 February 2018
Registered Office: 161 Park Road, London, NW4 3TH
Officers: Maureen Raymond [1954] Director

Hope Pharmaceuticals, Ltd.
Incorporated: 22 April 2013
Net Worth: £80,477 *Total Assets:* £800,029
Registered Office: 3rd Floor, 120 Baker Street, London, W1U 6TU
Shareholders: Craig Sherman; Hope Sherman
Officers: Hope Sherman, Secretary; Craig Sherman [1961] Director/Physician [American]; Hope Sherman [1963] Director/Attorney [American]

Horizon Medical Supplies UK Ltd
Incorporated: 9 March 2018
Registered Office: Myrtle House, High Street, Henfield, W Sussex, BN5 9DA
Major Shareholder: Angela Mary McConnell
Officers: Angela McConnell, Secretary; Angela Mary McConnell [1960] Director/Audiologist

Hospira Aseptic Services Limited
Incorporated: 12 November 1997
Registered Office: Horizon, Honey Lane, Hurley, Maidenhead, Berks, SL6 6RJ
Parent: Hospira UK Limited
Officers: Ian Eric Franklin [1965] Director/Accountant; Edwin James Pearson [1974] Director; Susan Rienow [1979] Director [American]

Hospira UK Limited
Incorporated: 18 June 1985 *Employees:* 70
Net Worth: £25,724,000 *Total Assets:* £30,085,000
Registered Office: Horizon, Honey Lane, Hurley, Maidenhead, Berks, SL6 6RJ
Parent: Pfizer Limited
Officers: Ian Eric Franklin [1965] Director/Accountant; Ben John Osborn [1977] Director; Edwin James Pearson [1974] Director/Solicitor

Huayawei Biomedical Company Ltd
Incorporated: 15 January 2018
Registered Office: c/o LL & Co, Office 201, 10 Courtenay Road, East Lane Business Park, Wembley, Middlesex, HA9 7ND
Major Shareholder: Xueli Wei
Officers: Xueli Wei [1980] Director

Humn Pharmaceuticals (UK) Ltd
Incorporated: 12 March 2012
Registered Office: 22 St Johns Road, Corstorphine, Edinburgh, EH12 6NZ
Officers: Brian Nigel Herron [1948] Director/Retired; Blair McInnes [1952] Director/Businessman [Canadian]; Adam Topp [1966] Director/COO Winnipeg Health Sciences Centre [Canadian]

Hunger Control Limited
Incorporated: 20 June 2000 *Employees:* 2
Net Worth: £248,013 *Total Assets:* £335,209
Registered Office: 104 Iffley Road, London, W6 0PF
Shareholder: Robert James Weir
Officers: Caroline Liddell, Secretary; Caroline Liddell [1948] Director; Robert James Weir [1937] Director

Hutrade Ltd.
Incorporated: 17 June 2013
Previous: Une Limited
Net Worth: £871 *Total Assets:* £871
Registered Office: 71 Edmonds Road, Oldbury, W Midlands, B68 9AT
Major Shareholder: Anne Stephanie Rita Huckert
Officers: Anne Stephanie Rita Huckert [1972] Director/Providing and Selling Goods and Services [French]

Hydranure Ltd
Incorporated: 28 July 2016
Net Worth Deficit: £3,961 *Total Assets:* £9,243
Registered Office: c/o D M McNaught & Co Ltd, 166 Buchanan Street, Glasgow, G1 2LW
Major Shareholder: Paul John McGregor
Officers: Laura Taylor McGregor [1968] Director; Paul John McGregor [1968] Director

Hydro Fresh Ltd
Incorporated: 9 April 2018
Registered Office: 87 Gortree Road, Drumahoe, Co Londonderry, BT47 3LL
Officers: Zita Bertha, Secretary; Dr Terence McIvor [1970] Director [Irish]

Hygieia Medical Ltd
Incorporated: 22 August 2013 *Employees:* 6
Net Worth: £79,588 *Total Assets:* £327,866
Registered Office: Marlborough House, 30 Victoria Street, Belfast, BT1 3GG
Officers: Eran Bashan [1971] Director [Israeli]; Matthew James McWilliams [1986] Director/Pharmacist/Hygieia Northern Ireland Manager

Hygitech Limited
Incorporated: 4 September 2015
Net Worth: £47,847 *Total Assets:* £170,398
Registered Office: c/o Chambre De Commerce Francaise De Grande Bretagne, Lincoln House, 300 High Holborn, London, WC1V 7JH
Major Shareholder: Michael Stemmer
Officers: Michael Stemmer [1979] Director [French]

Hyperbiotics Corp Ltd
Incorporated: 20 October 2016 *Employees:* 6
Net Worth: £308,058 *Total Assets:* £1,631,282
Registered Office: First Floor, 10 Temple Back, Bristol, BS1 6FL
Parent: Hyperbiotics PLC
Officers: Jamie Marie Amaral [1980] Director [American]; Lucas Abel Morea [1981] Director [Argentinian]; Rohit Nair [1984] Director [Indian]

Hyperbiotics PLC
Incorporated: 20 October 2016 *Employees:* 20
Net Worth: £5,409,919 *Total Assets:* £5,944,005
Registered Office: First Floor, 10 Temple Back, Bristol, BS1 6FL
Officers: Jamie Marie Amaral [1980] Director [American]; Lucas Abel Morea [1981] Director [Argentinian]; Rohit Nair [1984] Director [Indian]

Hyperdrug Pharmaceuticals Ltd
Incorporated: 21 March 1985 *Employees:* 24
Net Worth: £71,105 *Total Assets:* £1,587,031
Registered Office: Hyperdrug Pharmaceuticals Ltd, Station Industrial Estate, Barnard Castle, Co Durham, DL12 0NG
Shareholder: Christine Jennifer Watson
Officers: Christine Jennifer Watson, Secretary; Benjamin Nicholas Watson [1974] Director; Christine Jennifer Watson [1946] Director; Geoffrey Walton Watson [1938] Director/Pharmacist; John Geoffrey Frederick Watson [1971] Director/Sales Manager

Hyperion Biotechnology Limited
Incorporated: 20 May 2009
Net Worth Deficit: £24,913 *Total Assets:* £16,339
Registered Office: 79 Magheraconluce Road, Hillsborough, Co Down, BT26 6PR
Shareholders: William Renest Walker; Kyle Matthew Walker
Officers: William Ernest Walker, Secretary; Kyle Matthew Walker [1981] Director/Manager; William Ernest Walker [1953] Director/Manager

Hyperion Catalysis EU Limited
Incorporated: 21 October 2008
Net Worth Deficit: £11,745
Registered Office: 3rd Floor, 1 Ashley Road, Altrincham, Cheshire, WA14 2DT
Officers: Nadine Wohlstadter [1945] Managing Director [American]; Samuel Wohlstadter [1941] Managing Director [American]

Ibeautify Ltd
Incorporated: 1 June 2017
Registered Office: 516 Oxo Tower Wharf, South Bank, London, SE1 9GY
Major Shareholder: Jeannette Lahai-Taylor
Officers: Dr Jeannette Lahai-Taylor [1971] Director/Aesthetic & Surgical Doctor

iCell Therapeutics Ltd
Incorporated: 8 November 2018
Registered Office: 20-22 Wenlock Road, London, N1 7GU
Major Shareholder: Yuchun Gu
Officers: Prof Yuchun Gu [1972] Director/Professor

Iceni Pharmaceuticals Limited
Incorporated: 15 April 2016
Registered Office: 22 G3 Forth Street, Edinburgh, EH1 3LH
Parent: Bigdna Ltd
Officers: David Bremner Sowersby, Secretary; Dr John Bernard March [1962] Director/Business Executive

Ideal Manufacturing Limited
Incorporated: 24 June 1980 *Employees:* 33
Net Worth: £925,826 *Total Assets:* £2,007,665
Registered Office: Atlas House, Burton Road, Finedon, Wellingborough, Northants, NN9 5HX
Shareholders: Michael Kalli; Philip Kalli
Officers: Darren Lee Booker [1968] Operations Director; David Goodger [1951] Director/Production Manager; Michael Kalli [1942] Director/Chemist; Phillip Kalli [1978] Director

Idrolabs Limited
Incorporated: 4 September 2015
Net Worth: £11,873 *Total Assets:* £12,088
Registered Office: Europa Tool House, Springbank Park, Dunmurry, Belfast, BT17 0QL
Major Shareholder: Peter Philip Cook
Officers: Peter Cook [1954] Director/Engineer

IGMA Limited
Incorporated: 10 July 1995
Net Worth: £467,288 *Total Assets:* £797,653
Registered Office: Unit 5 Compass West Industrial Estate, 33 West Road, London, N17 0XL
Major Shareholder: Roger Aoun
Officers: Michelle Helen Aoun, Secretary; Roger Aoun [1957] Director/Marketing

Ilody Skincare Ltd
Incorporated: 30 November 2015
Net Worth: £1 *Total Assets:* £6,061
Registered Office: 130 Old Street, London, EC1V 9BD
Major Shareholder: Deepika Patel
Officers: Deepika Patel [1974] Director/Producer and Founder of Ilody Skincare

Immbio Therapeutics Limited
Incorporated: 10 August 2006
Net Worth Deficit: £6,362 *Total Assets:* £5,010
Registered Office: Meditrina Babraham Research Campus, Babraham, Cambridge, CB22 3AT
Shareholders: Camilo Anthony Colaco; Graham John Clarke
Officers: Graham John Clarke, Secretary; Graham John Clarke [1956] Director/Manager; Dr Camilo Anthony Selwyn Leo Colaco [1956] Director/Scientist

Impact Pharma Solutions Ltd
Incorporated: 13 February 2019
Registered Office: 20-22 Wenlock Road, London, N1 7GU
Major Shareholder: Bahijja Abraham
Officers: Dr Bahijja Abraham [1985] Director/Pharmacist

Imphatec Ltd
Incorporated: 17 September 2018
Registered Office: Oak Cottage, Langley Bridge, Liss, Hants, GU33 7JP
Shareholders: James Peter Catt; Hassan Oliver James Morad
Officers: James Peter Catt [1991] Director/Assistant Underwriter; Hassan Oliver James Morad [1992] Director/PhD Student

Incepta Blackrock Limited
Incorporated: 22 March 2016
Registered Office: Winterhill House, Station Approach, Marlow, Bucks, SL7 1NT
Major Shareholder: Philip William Shaw McFerran
Officers: Philip William Shaw McFerran, Secretary; Peter William Griffin [1968] Director; Philip William Shaw McFerran [1968] Managing Director; Abdul Muktadir [1957] Director [Bangladeshi]; Hasneen Muktadir [1959] Director [Bangladeshi]

Incepta Pharma UK Limited
Incorporated: 28 July 2015
Registered Office: 29 Lincoln's Inn Fields, London, WC2A 3EG
Shareholder: Abdul Muktadir
Officers: Abdul Muktadir [1957] Director [Bangladeshi]; Akther Jahan Hasneen Muktadir [1959] Director [Bangladeshi]

Incline Therapeutics Europe Ltd.
Incorporated: 17 October 2012 *Employees:* 1
Net Worth: £1,687 *Total Assets:* £347,378
Registered Office: First Floor, 10 Temple Back, Bristol, BS1 6FL
Parent: The Medicines Company
Officers: Andre Reinhold Heer [1970] Director/Head of Finance [German]

Indigo Diagnostics Limited
Incorporated: 14 January 2016
Net Worth: £84,738 *Total Assets:* £110,380
Registered Office: 168 Church Road, Hove, E Sussex, BN3 2DL
Officers: Dr Andrew Timothy Sweet [1964] Director; Dr Ruth Margaret Sweet [1962] Director

Indivior EU Limited
Incorporated: 28 June 2012
Previous: RB Pharmaceuticals (EU) Limited
Net Worth: £21,049,536 *Total Assets:* £45,776,016
Registered Office: The Chapleo Building, Henry Boot Way, Priory Park, Hull, HU4 7DY
Parent: Indivior UK Limited
Officers: Kathryn Barbara Hudson, Secretary; Gilles Picard [1962] Director [French]; Thomas Weis [1980] Finance Director [German]

Indivior PLC
Incorporated: 26 September 2014
Net Worth Deficit: £152,919,024 *Total Assets:* £1,087,758,976
Registered Office: 103-105 Bath Road, Slough, Berks, SL1 3UH
Officers: Kathryn Barbara Hudson, Secretary; Mark Wesley Crossley [1969] Director [American]; Dr Yvonne Greenstreet [1962] Director; Tatjana Anni Hilde May [1965] Director; Dr Andrew Thomas McLellan [1948] Director [American]; Lorna Mary Southcombe Parker [1959] Director; Daniel Joseph Phelan [1949] Director [American]; Howard Hao Pien [1957] Director [American]; Christian Stanton Schade [1961] Director [American]; Daniel Tasse [1960] Director [Canadian]; Shaun Thaxter [1967] Director [British/American]; Lizabeth Herbst Zlatkus [1958] Director [American]

Indivior UK Limited
Incorporated: 9 March 2010 *Employees:* 170
Previous: RB Pharmaceuticals Limited
Net Worth: £747,916,992 *Total Assets:* £848,174,016
Registered Office: The Chapleo Building, Henry Boot Way, Priory Park, Hull, HU4 7DY
Parent: RBP Global Holdings Limited
Officers: Kathryn Barbara Hudson, Secretary; Katherine Julie Beard [1979] Director/Chartered Tax Advisor; Massimo D'Angelo [1972] Director [Italian]; Gilles Picard [1962] Director [French]; Ms Amei W Shank [1963] Director [American]; Richard Simkin [1970] Director; Frank Stier [1959] Director [German]; Thomas Weis [1980] Finance Director [German]

Infection Monitoring and Control Ltd
Incorporated: 18 December 2012 *Employees:* 2
Net Worth Deficit: £55,337 *Total Assets:* £19,789
Registered Office: 24 Second Avenue, Horbury, Wakefield, W Yorks, WF4 6HB
Major Shareholder: Thomas Brian Chapman
Officers: Thomas William Chapman [1976] Director/Chef; Janet Matthews [1953] Director

Infinitus Enterprise Limited
Incorporated: 10 March 2011
Previous: Kobil Consultancy Limited
Net Worth: £30,533 *Total Assets:* £81,859
Registered Office: 5 Sackville Close, Harrow, Middlesex, HA2 0NJ
Major Shareholder: Anish Shah
Officers: Anish Shah [1984] Director/Pharmacist

Infirst Healthcare Limited
Incorporated: 21 May 2012 *Employees:* 18
Net Worth: £5,496,860 *Total Assets:* £7,689,849
Registered Office: 265 Strand, London, WC2R 1BH
Shareholder: Biocopea Limited
Officers: Kimbell Rush Duncan [1965] Director; Carol Isabel L'heveder [1959] Director/Lawyer; Manfred Scheske [1951] Director [German]; Gregory Alan Stoloff [1961] Director [Australian]

Infirst Limited
Incorporated: 8 February 2019
Registered Office: Central Point, 45 Beech Street, London, EC2Y 8AD
Parent: Infirst Healthcare Limited
Officers: Philip Edmund Lindsell [1953] Director/Chartered Accountant

Inflazome UK Limited
Incorporated: 13 December 2016
Net Worth Deficit: £724,112 *Total Assets:* £26,600
Registered Office: D6 Grain House, Mill Court, Great Shelford, Cambridge, CB22 5LD
Officers: Matthew Cooper [1969] Director [Australian]; Angus MacLeod [1958] Research Director

Infohealth Laboratories Limited
Incorporated: 18 February 1935
Registered Office: Samanvaya Cultural Centre, Milton Road, Harrow, Middlesex, HA1 1ST
Parent: Infohealth Limited
Officers: Amish Patel [1972] Director; Rajive Patel [1973] Director

Infohealth Limited
Incorporated: 31 May 2000 *Employees:* 19
Net Worth: £251,094 *Total Assets:* £1,198,344
Registered Office: Samanvaya Cultural Centre, 1st Floor Office, Milton Road, Harrow, Middlesex, HA1 1ST
Parent: Infohealth Holdings Ltd
Officers: Amish Patel [1972] Director/Pharmacist; Rajive Patel [1973] Director/Pharmacist

Ingel Technologies Limited
Incorporated: 16 November 2000
Registered Office: Starpol Technology Centre, North Road, Marchwood Industrial Park, Southampton, SO40 4BL
Parent: Biome Technologies PLC
Officers: Donna Simpson-Strange, Secretary; Declan Linsay Brown [1974] Finance Director; Paul Robert Mines [1963] Director/Chief Executive

Inkhancement Limited
Incorporated: 28 January 2019
Registered Office: 96 Kings Drive, Edgware, Middlesex, HA8 8EG
Major Shareholder: Harry Avraam
Officers: Harry Avraam [1981] Director

Innov8tor Limited
Incorporated: 2 February 2016
Net Worth Deficit: £1,462 *Total Assets:* £5,368
Registered Office: Tudor House, Northgate, Northwood, Middlesex, HA6 2TH
Major Shareholder: Alison Stevenson
Officers: Alison Stevenson [1963] Director

Innova Biosciences Ltd
Incorporated: 12 April 2002 *Employees:* 24
Net Worth: £2,255,910 *Total Assets:* £2,699,841
Registered Office: 25 Norman Way, Over, Cambridge, CB24 5QE
Parent: Sygnis AG
Officers: Heikki Lanckriet [1977] Director [Belgian]; David John Roth [1967] Director [German]

Insense Limited
Incorporated: 2 November 2000 *Employees:* 4
Net Worth: £322,273 *Total Assets:* £362,373
Registered Office: Colworth Park, Sharnbrook, Bedford, MK44 1LQ
Shareholder: Unilever UK Holdings Limited
Officers: Paul James Davis [1947] Director/Scientist; Christopher David Hunt [1959] Director/Manager; Stewart Worth Newton [1941] Director

Inskin Skincare Ltd
Incorporated: 19 July 2011
Net Worth Deficit: £15,643 *Total Assets:* £241
Registered Office: 53 Hough, Halifax, W Yorks, HX3 7BU
Shareholders: Paul Radcliffe; Elizabeth Anne Radcliffe
Officers: Paul Radcliffe, Secretary; Elizabeth Radcliffe [1967] Director/MD; Paul Radcliffe [1965] Director/MD

Insmed Limited
Incorporated: 19 June 2007 *Employees:* 2
Net Worth: £92,629 *Total Assets:* £315,312
Registered Office: 3rd Floor, 207 Regent Street, London, W1B 3HH
Parent: Insmed Incorporated
Officers: Christine Pellizzari [1967] Director/General Counsel [American]; Christel Elisabeth Rossig [1972] Director/Corporate Counsel Europe [French/German]; Jamie Lee Sale [1977] Director

Inspire Flavours Ltd
Incorporated: 24 October 2016
Registered Office: Unit G3, Carrowreagh Road, Dundonald, Belfast, BT16 1QT
Major Shareholder: Steven George Mealey
Officers: Steven George Mealey [1984] Director

Instavit Limited
Incorporated: 6 August 2013 *Employees:* 8
Net Worth: £307,254 *Total Assets:* £936,964
Registered Office: 4 Devonshire Street, London, W1W 5DT
Officers: Sonia Joshi, Secretary; Dr Jatin Rajnikant Joshi [1975] Director/Doctor; Dr Sonia Joshi [1978] Director/Dentist; Robert Kennedy [1966] Director/Investor [American]; Paul Clifford Luke [1953] Director; Scott James Perkins [1972] Director

Instrument Research Company Limited
Incorporated: 20 June 2014
Net Worth: £24,544 *Total Assets:* £42,069
Registered Office: 11 Montrose Avenue, Welling, Kent, DA16 2QP
Major Shareholder: Martyn Dawson
Officers: Sarah Joanne Dawson, Secretary; Martyn John Dawson [1969] Managing Director; Sarah Joanne Dawson [1976] Director/Secretary

Insuphar Laboratories Limited
Incorporated: 7 March 2011
Net Worth: £22,652 *Total Assets:* £22,952
Registered Office: Ground Floor, Gadd House, Arcadia Avenue, Finchley, London, N3 2JU
Major Shareholder: Raushan Tahiyeu
Officers: Zafer Karaman, Secretary; Zafer Karaman [1958] Director/Account/Law

Intapharm Laboratories Limited
Incorporated: 29 June 2017
Registered Office: Globe House, Eclipse Park, Sittingbourne Road, Maidstone, Kent, ME14 3EN
Major Shareholder: Mehdi Muradi
Officers: Mehdi Muradi [1975] Director

Integrated Pharma Services (UK) Ltd
Incorporated: 25 July 2017
Registered Office: Globe Square, Dukinfield, Cheshire, SK16 4RF
Major Shareholder: Matthew John Lewis
Officers: Matthew John Lewis [1987] Director

Integrated Pharmaceutical Services (IPS) Limited
Incorporated: 23 December 2009 *Employees:* 4
Net Worth Deficit: £16,963,000 *Total Assets:* £2,359,000
Registered Office: 41 Central Avenue, West Molesey, Surrey, KT8 2QZ
Parent: Ipsco Limited
Officers: Ashokkumar Patel, Secretary; Soimitra Tony Dutta [1963] Director/Chief Executive; Vishal Patani [1977] Finance Director; Ashokkumar Dahyabhai Patel [1956] Director/Pharmacist; Jonathan Mark Penfold [1962] Director/Chartered Accountant

Intelligent Fabric Technologies Holdings Limited
Incorporated: 7 January 2016
Registered Office: 4 Carters Row, Hatfield Park, Hatfield, Herts, AL9 5NB
Major Shareholder: George Costa
Officers: George Costa [1963] Director; Anthony Leonard Wilson [1953] Director

Interaction Chempharm Ltd
Incorporated: 20 May 2017
Net Worth: £2,000 *Total Assets:* £2,000
Registered Office: 463 Basingstoke Road, Reading, Berks, RG2 0JF
Major Shareholder: Muhammad Yaqoob
Officers: Dr Muhammad Yaqoob [1968] Director

International Medication Systems (U.K.) Limited
Incorporated: 3 June 1975 *Employees:* 5
Net Worth Deficit: £223,000 *Total Assets:* £174,000
Registered Office: First Floor, 10 Temple Back, Bristol, BS1 6FL
Parent: Amphastar UK Ltd
Officers: Jacob Liawatidewi, Secretary; Jacob Liawatidewi [1974] Director/Senior VP Corp Admin Center [American]; Mary Luo [1949] Director/Chief Operations Officer [American]; William Peters [1967] Director/Chief Financial Officer [American]; Jason Shandell [1974] Director/President [American]; Jack Zhang [1946] Director/Chief Executive Officer [Chinese]

International Scientific Supplies Limited
Incorporated: 13 February 2002
Net Worth: £1,212,900 *Total Assets:* £2,276,886
Registered Office: Richmond House, Canal Road, Bradford, W Yorks, BD2 1AL
Major Shareholder: John Barry Trowbridge
Officers: Michael William Brighten, Secretary; Christopher Buckley [1950] Director; John Barry Trowbridge [1942] Director

International Technidyne Corporation Limited
Incorporated: 25 March 1988 *Employees:* 1
Net Worth: £134,273 *Total Assets:* £217,826
Registered Office: 71 Queen Victoria Street, London, EC4V 4BE
Officers: Gregory Tibbitts, Secretary; Martin Lipman [1959] Director/General Counsel, Instrumentation Laboratory [American]

Intervet UK Production Limited
Incorporated: 13 May 1996 Employees: 192
Net Worth: £61,146,000 Total Assets: £118,581,000
Registered Office: Walton Manor, Walton, Milton Keynes, Bucks, MK7 7AJ
Parent: Intervet UK Limited
Officers: Ebru Can Temucin [1972] Director [Turkish]; Allen Harberg Jr [1971] Director [American]; Jan Moehlenbrock [1970] Managing Director [German]

Intrapharm Laboratories Limited
Incorporated: 27 June 1997 Employees: 14
Net Worth: £3,780,355 Total Assets: £11,116,160
Registered Office: The Courtyard Barns, Choke Lane, Maidenhead, Berks, SL6 6PT
Parent: Riemser Pharma UK Limited
Officers: Rene Just [1967] Director [Danish]; Dr Mohammed Choudhary Shafiq [1964] Sales & Marketing Director; Konstantin Von Alvensleben [1957] Director/Manager [German]

Invictus R & D Ltd
Incorporated: 25 April 2016
Net Worth Deficit: £92,496 Total Assets: £82
Registered Office: Alpha House, 646c Kingsbury Road, Kingsbury, London, NW9 9HN
Shareholders: Hitesh Govind Vaghjiani; Kamlesh Govind Vaghjiani; Govind Samji Vaghjiani
Officers: Govind Samji Vaghjiani [1945] Director; Hitesh Govind Vaghjiani [1966] Director/Pharmacist; Kamlesh Govind Vaghjiani [1968] Director/Pharmacist

Invitrohair Ltd
Incorporated: 12 February 2019
Registered Office: c/o Shihn & Co, Hytec House, Beaconsfield, Bucks, HP9 1EX
Parent: BTechLaboratories Ltd
Officers: Heinrich Kunz [1972] Director [German]; Sundip Singh Shihn [1969] Director/Investment Professional

Invizius Limited
Incorporated: 26 January 2018
Registered Office: 5th Floor, 125 Princes Street, Edinburgh, EH2 4AD
Shareholders: Andy Herbert; Edinburgh Technology Fund Limited
Officers: Richard Graham Boyd [1967] Director/Engineer; Andrew Herbert [1972] Director/Scientist; Dr Magnus Nicolson [1960] Director

Invos Ltd
Incorporated: 1 June 2018
Registered Office: New Bridge Street House, 30-34 New Bridge Street, London, EC4V 6BJ
Major Shareholder: Antonios Papathanasiou
Officers: Jason Hughes [1970] Director/Administrator; Antonios Papathanasiou [1970] Director [Greek]

IOLAMD Ltd
Incorporated: 23 June 2016
Net Worth: £50,612 Total Assets: £62,207
Registered Office: c/o LEH Pharma Ltd, Park House, 116 Park Street, London, W1K 6SS
Officers: Dr Muhammad Ali Qureshi [1970] Director

Ipca Laboratories UK Limited
Incorporated: 4 November 2003
Net Worth: £5,367,133 Total Assets: £5,369,833
Registered Office: Units 97-98 Silverbriar, Sunderland Enterprise Park East, Sunderland, Tyne & Wear, SR5 2TQ
Parent: Ipca Ltd
Officers: Nathan Vincent Lane, Secretary; Denise Bowser [1971] Commercial Director; Manish Jain [1974] Director/Vice President - Business Development [Indian]; Dr Derek John Londesbrough [1970] R&D Director

IPS International Corporation Ltd
Incorporated: 28 December 2018
Registered Office: c/o Talat Qazi Consulting, 58b Ilford Lane, Ilford, Essex, IG1 2JZ
Major Shareholder: Ahmed Ibrahim Fadel Abdelgalil
Officers: Ahmed Ibrahim Fadel Abdelgalil [1981] Director [Egyptian]

Ipsco Limited
Incorporated: 23 October 2014 Employees: 72
Net Worth Deficit: £25,266,000 Total Assets: £4,689,000
Registered Office: 41 Central Avenue, West Molesey, Surrey, KT8 2QZ
Major Shareholder: Ashokkumar Dahyabhai Patel
Officers: Soimitra Tony Dutta [1963] Director/Chief Executive; Vishal Patani [1977] Finance Director; Ashokkumar Dahyabhai Patel [1956] Director/Pharmacist; Jonathan Mark Penfold [1962] Director/Chartered Accountant

Ipsen Biopharm Limited
Incorporated: 23 July 1982 Employees: 475
Net Worth: £373,100,992 Total Assets: £561,416,000
Registered Office: Ash Road, Wrexham Industrial Estate, Wrexham, Clwyd, LL13 9UF
Parent: Ipsen Developments Limited
Officers: Catherine Lamb, Secretary; Asad Mohsin Ali [1975] Director/GM; Isobel Louise Boyne [1969] Director/Accountant; Dr John Andrew Chaddock [1968] Director/Manager; Nicholas Davis [1975] Director; Catherine Lamb [1978] Director/Solicitor

IQ Pharmatech Limited
Incorporated: 15 April 2016
Registered Office: 125 Wood Street, London, EC2V 7AW
Major Shareholder: Mohammad Mokhlis Abdullatif
Officers: Mohammad Mokhlis Abdullatif [1972] Director/Pharmacist [Iraqi]

IQ5 Consultancy Limited
Incorporated: 26 January 2017
Registered Office: Legacy Business Centre, Town Hall Approach Road, Tottenham Town Hall, London, N15 4RY
Officers: Dr Delphine Tiku Oben [1979] Director/Scientist - Nano (Chemist)

Iroko Products Limited
Incorporated: 1 March 2007 Employees: 2
Net Worth Deficit: £452,499 Total Assets: £2,743,691
Registered Office: c/o Hackwood Secretaries Limited, One Silk Street, London, EC2Y 8HQ
Major Shareholder: Nicolas Maurice
Officers: Jeremy Peter Anthony Fletcher [1954] Director/Investment Banker; Fred C Krieger [1947] Director/CFO of Iroko Pharmaceuticals, LLC [American]

IS Pharmaceuticals Limited
Incorporated: 10 February 1992
Registered Office: Eden House, Lakeside, Chester Business Park, Chester, CH4 9QT
Parent: IS Pharma Ltd
Officers: Jason Rodney Tate, Secretary; Jayne Katherine Burrell [1974] Director; Alan Musgrave Olby [1971] Director; Christopher Paul Spooner [1968] Director

Isca Biochemicals Limited
Incorporated: 7 October 2011 *Employees:* 2
Net Worth: £1,240 *Total Assets:* £31,746
Registered Office: 26 Hanover Road, Heavitree, Exeter, EX1 2TL
Shareholders: Clifford Peter Rush; Sean Edwin Leonard George Webb
Officers: Clifford Peter Rush [1968] Director/Biochemist; Sean Edwin Leonard George Webb [1970] Director

Isola Manufacturing Co.(Wythenshawe) Limited
Incorporated: 2 September 1937 *Employees:* 6
Net Worth: £389,559 *Total Assets:* £677,537
Registered Office: Unit 7 Spectrum Way, Cheadle Heath, Stockport, Cheshire, SK3 0SA
Shareholders: David Michael Tonge; Peter Richard Tonge; Christine Margaret Tonge
Officers: Peter Richard Tonge, Secretary; David Michael Tonge [1957] Director/Chemist; Peter Richard Tonge [1960] Director/Office Manager

Isopath Limited
Incorporated: 6 June 1996
Registered Office: 2 Oak Hill, Lisburn, Co Antrim, BT27 5UE
Officers: Patricia Ann Forbes, Secretary; James Keiron Hugh Forbes [1958] Director/Agricultural Consultant; Nigel Joseph Forbes [1955] Director/Location Photographer; Patricia Anne Forbes [1963] Director/Housewife; Patricia Ann Forbes [1954] Director/Teacher; Karen Elizabeth Jennings [1968] Director/Nurse; Russell Edward Jennings [1965] Director [Irish]

Isovitality Nutriceuticals Limited
Incorporated: 21 November 2016
Net Worth Deficit: £7,983 *Total Assets:* £17,114
Registered Office: Office 415, 275 Deansgate, Manchester, M3 4EL
Officers: Tahir Mahmood [1987] Director/Pharmacist

Ithonpharma Ltd
Incorporated: 20 June 2017
Registered Office: Rhos Farm, Llanbadarn Fynydd, Llandrindod Wells, Powys, LD1 6YN
Officers: Alan Cecil Watson [1958] Director; Emma Watson [1993] Director; Julie Ann Watson [1964] Director/Secretary; Paul Aaron Watson [1989] Director; Ryan Watson [1991] Director

Itreatskin Limited
Incorporated: 16 February 2017
Net Worth: £14,199 *Total Assets:* £23,200
Registered Office: 2 Innings Way, Rochdale, Lancs, OL11 3DE
Officers: Razna Rani [1981] Director/Researcher

J J Design and Engineering Limited
Incorporated: 20 March 2005
Net Worth Deficit: £363 *Total Assets:* £118
Registered Office: Churchdown Chambers, Bordyke, Tonbridge, Kent, TN9 1NR
Major Shareholder: Jasper John Day
Officers: Emma Jane Wallaker, Secretary; Jasper John Day [1971] Director/Engineer

Jac+Q Limited
Incorporated: 31 December 2015 *Employees:* 2
Net Worth: £47,529 *Total Assets:* £86,631
Registered Office: 25 High Street, Wolviston, Billingham, Cleveland, TS22 5JY
Shareholders: Sally Louise Adamson; John Stanley George Adamson
Officers: John Stanley George Adamson [1963] Director

Henri L.Jaccaz & Co. Limited
Incorporated: 3 September 2002
Net Worth: £4,915 *Total Assets:* £14,763
Registered Office: 23 Fulford Road, Epsom, Surrey, KT19 9QZ
Officers: Jen Ann Mitchell [1962] Director

Ernest Jackson & Co. Limited
Incorporated: 20 June 1916 *Employees:* 117
Net Worth: £6,829,000 *Total Assets:* £11,159,000
Registered Office: Cadbury House, Sanderson Road, Uxbridge, Middlesex, UB8 1DH
Parent: Kraft Foods UK IP & Production Holdings Limited
Officers: Louise Anne Stigant [1967] Category Development & Market Activation Director; David Mark Walter [1971] Director/General Manager

Jai Clinical Services Limited
Incorporated: 31 October 2017
Registered Office: 109 Cranbrook Drive, Maidenhead, Berks, SL6 6SR
Major Shareholder: Ruchika Ahuja
Officers: Ruchika Ahuja [1984] Director/Medical Safety Specialist

Jai Pharma Limited
Incorporated: 10 February 2012
Net Worth: £95,829 *Total Assets:* £136,047
Registered Office: 6 Headington Close, Basingstoke, Hants, RG22 4LN
Major Shareholder: Jatinder Kapur
Officers: Jatinder Kapur [1967] Director [Indian]

M Jallow Ltd
Incorporated: 24 April 2016
Net Worth: £8 *Total Assets:* £2,328
Registered Office: 41 Mercator Close, Southampton, SO16 4HW
Major Shareholder: Mamadou Salieu Jallow
Officers: Mamadou Salieu Jallow [1982] Director/Pharmacist

Janssen-Cilag Limited
Incorporated: 19 October 1971 *Employees:* 939
Net Worth: £266,952,000 *Total Assets:* £415,416,992
Registered Office: 50-100 Holmers Farm Way, High Wycombe, Bucks, HP12 4EG
Parent: Johnson & Johnson
Officers: Liesbeth Aerts [1979] Finance Director [Belgian]; Shelagh Mary Anderson [1960] Regulatory Affairs Director; Mark Iain Hicken [1971] Director/Business Executive; Nicholas George Hodges [1972] Director/Vice President, Global Clinical Operations; Clare Sicklen [1971] HR Director; Bernardo Soares [1974] Director [Portuguese]

Jasan Technical Services Limited
Incorporated: 13 December 2005
Registered Office: Jasan House, 12 Syston Road, Queniborough, Leics, LE7 3FX
Officers: Bhadra Kumari Juj, Secretary; Arwinder Paul Singh Juj [1957] Director/Cosmetic Chemist

Jasmine.Touch Ltd
Incorporated: 6 February 2018
Registered Office: 48 Lanntara, Ballymena, Co Antrim, BT42 3BE
Major Shareholder: Ciprian Ionut Boboia
Officers: Andreea Mihaela Boboia [1993] Director/Administrator [Romanian]; Ciprian Ionut Boboia [1988] Director [Romanian]

Jela Pharm Limited
Incorporated: 8 April 2013 *Employees:* 1
Net Worth: £612 *Total Assets:* £11,601
Registered Office: 50 Woodgate, Leicester, LE3 5GF
Officers: Romin Tayub [1984] Director/Pharmacist

Jellyhills Ltd
Incorporated: 25 June 2018
Registered Office: Suite 6, First Floor, Wordsworth Mill, Wordsworth Street, Bolton, Lancs, BL1 3ND
Major Shareholder: Bradley Blunt
Officers: Ismael Duran [1986] Director [Filipino]

Jenarron Therapeutics Limited
Incorporated: 27 March 2012
Net Worth Deficit: £82,922 *Total Assets:* £7,441
Registered Office: 8 Dermont Crescent, Newtownabbey, Co Antrim, BT36 4NZ
Shareholder: Innovation Ulster Limited
Officers: Dr Mark Godfrey Jenkins [1966] Director/Doctor; Dr Norry McBride [1961] Director; Professor Paul Anthony McCarron [1965] Director/Pharmacist; Samuel William John Rusk [1952] Director/Investor

JGPSK Limited
Incorporated: 25 November 2010 *Employees:* 2
Net Worth: £886 *Total Assets:* £11,153
Registered Office: 16 Regency Drive, Coventry, Warwicks, CV3 6QA
Major Shareholder: Jasbinder Singh Heer
Officers: Harsimran Kaur Heer [1997] Director; Jasbinder Singh Heer [1964] Director/Pharmacist

Jim & Sheila Ltd.
Incorporated: 27 April 2004
Net Worth Deficit: £17,242 *Total Assets:* £6,626
Registered Office: XL Business Solutions Ltd, Catcraig Quarry, Craigie, Kilmarnock, E Ayrshire, KA1 5NB
Major Shareholder: Sheila Joyce Steele
Officers: Sheila Joyce Steele [1950] Director/Customer Resource Manager

Jini Ltd
Incorporated: 17 May 2018
Registered Office: Flat 19, 199 Old Marylebone Road, London, NW1 5QR
Major Shareholder: Ali Raza Awan
Officers: Dr Ali Raza Awan [1981] Director/Biologist

JIT Laboratories Limited
Incorporated: 31 October 2003
Net Worth: £67,157 *Total Assets:* £426,538
Registered Office: Somerford House, Somerford Place, Willenhall, W Midlands, WV13 3DT
Parent: 8pm Chemist Limited
Officers: Mukesh Aggarwal, Secretary; Mukesh Aggarwal [1966] Director/Pharmacist

JNRMCL Ltd
Incorporated: 14 August 2018
Registered Office: 46 Victoria Square, Rostrevor, Newry, Co Armagh, BT34 3EU
Major Shareholder: Henry McLaughlin
Officers: Henry McLaughlin [1994] Director/Pharmacist [Irish]

Jones Balm Limited
Incorporated: 19 September 2018
Registered Office: 130 Old Street, London, EC1V 9BD
Officers: Sarah Alisha Jones [1985] Director/Teaching Assistant

Joribunda Limited
Incorporated: 18 February 2002
Registered Office: Green Farm, Wichling, Sittingbourne, Kent, ME9 0DH
Officers: Robert Alexander Jardine-Rose, Secretary; Paula Kay Jardine Rose [1966] Director/Herbalist & Holistic Therapist

Joyce Pharmac Services Ltd
Incorporated: 6 December 2012 *Employees:* 1
Net Worth Deficit: £879 *Total Assets:* £265
Registered Office: 4th Floor, Radius House, 51 Clarendon Road, Watford, Herts, WD17 1HP
Shareholders: Henry Ezenwa Olekanma; Joyce Ijeme Olekanma
Officers: Joyce Ijeme Olekanma [1982] Director [Austrian]

JPI Care Limited
Incorporated: 9 October 2018
Registered Office: 54 Frensham Close, Southall, Middlesex, UB1 2YG
Officers: Ibrahim Akel [1986] Director/Lawyer [Jordanian]

JSN Chemicals Limited
Incorporated: 13 April 2017
Registered Office: 8 Gainsborough Gardens, Edgware, Middlesex, HA8 5TB
Shareholder: Rahul Rathod
Officers: Rahul Rathod [1991] Director

R Judge Consultancy Ltd
Incorporated: 9 October 2015 *Employees:* 1
Net Worth: £8,257 *Total Assets:* £17,639
Registered Office: 8 Shire Close, Bagshot, Surrey, GU19 5RA
Major Shareholder: Rajinder Judge
Officers: Rajinder Judge [1988] Director/IT Professional

Juice Sauz Ltd
Incorporated: 30 November 2015 *Employees:* 15
Net Worth: £96,321 *Total Assets:* £366,669
Registered Office: 3 Pioneer Way, Doddington Road, Lincoln, LN6 3DH
Shareholders: Liam Chapman; Julie Chapman
Officers: Julie Chapman [1974] Director/Businesswoman; Liam Martin Chapman [1988] Finance Director

Juno Britain Ltd
Incorporated: 12 February 2019
Registered Office: 18 Rutland Street, London, SW7 1EF
Parent: Juno Laboratories Pty Ltd
Officers: Garry Watts [1956] Director

Kaizen Ceramics Ltd
Incorporated: 15 January 2013 *Employees:* 12
Net Worth: £168,743 *Total Assets:* £202,921
Registered Office: 30 Chapel Street, Pemberton, Wigan, Lancs, WN5 8JR
Officers: David Ashcroft [1963] Director; Kate Silcock [1973] Director

Kalfar Health Ltd
Incorporated: 1 December 2015
Net Worth Deficit: £4,763 *Total Assets:* £2,458
Registered Office: 10 Hambleton Road, Heald Green, Cheadle, Cheshire, SK8 3DW
Shareholders: Mohamad Ismail Farhat; Abdenour Khalfaoui
Officers: Mohamad Ismail Farhat [1988] Director; Abdenour Kalfaoui [1988] Director

Kalms Limited
Incorporated: 4 August 1981
Registered Office: c/o G R Lane Holdings Ltd, Sisson Road, Gloucester, GL2 0GR
Parent: G. R. Lane Holdings Ltd
Officers: Paul Charles Whatley, Secretary; Janet Margaret Groves [1982] Director; Jonathan Groves [1980] Director

Kalula Cosmetics Ltd
Incorporated: 30 January 2019
Registered Office: Suite A, 82 James Carter Road, Mildenhall, Bury St Edmunds, Suffolk, IP28 7DE
Major Shareholder: Justice Marie Bynoe
Officers: Justice Marie Bynoe [1994] Director/Recruitment Consultant

Kamada Biopharma Limited
Incorporated: 29 January 2014
Net Worth: £1,684 *Total Assets:* £1,684
Registered Office: Riverbank House, 2 Swan Lane, London, EC4R 3TT
Parent: Kamada Limited
Officers: Nir Livneh, Secretary; Amir London [1969] Director [Israeli]; Chaime Orlev [1970] Director [Israeli]

Karnot Limited
Incorporated: 31 March 2006
Registered Office: 8 Mitchell Street, Leven, Fife, KY8 4HJ
Major Shareholder: Stuart Edmund Cox
Officers: Stuart Edmund Cox [1964] Director/Engineer

Kee Logic Limited
Incorporated: 22 June 2006
Net Worth: £17,762 *Total Assets:* £57,104
Registered Office: 111a Neilston Road, Paisley, Renfrewshire, PA2 6ER
Shareholders: Robert Marshall; Alison Marshall
Officers: Alison Marshall, Secretary; Robert Marshall [1962] Director

Kenmare Medical Limited
Incorporated: 2 November 2018
Registered Office: Lytchett House, Wareham Road, Lytchett Matravers, Poole, Dorset, BH16 6FA
Major Shareholder: Joseph Sheehan
Officers: Joseph Sheehan [1984] Director/Doctor [Irish]

Kensington Pharma Ltd
Incorporated: 15 April 2015
Net Worth Deficit: £79,676 *Total Assets:* £213,240
Registered Office: Unit A, Newlands House, 60 Chain House Lane, Whitestake, Preston, Lancs, PR4 4LG
Major Shareholder: Iqbal Moosa
Officers: Iqbal Moosa [1963] Director

Kent Pharmaceuticals Limited
Incorporated: 15 May 1997 *Employees:* 43
Net Worth Deficit: £1,369,000 *Total Assets:* £14,979,000
Registered Office: DCC Vital, Westminster Industrial Estate, Repton Road, Measham, Swadlincote, Derbys, DE12 7DT
Parent: DCC Vital UK Limited
Officers: Conor Francis Costigan [1971] Director/Chartered Accountant [Irish]; Leslie Deacon [1963] Director/Chartered Accountant [Irish]; Harry Keenan [1959] Managing Director [Irish]; Redmond McEvoy [1964] Director [Irish]

The Kentish Soap Company Limited
Incorporated: 14 March 2018
Registered Office: Lynwood House, Crofton Road, Orpington, Kent, BR6 8QE
Shareholders: Jayne Lisa Waddy; John Barrie Waddy
Officers: Jayne Lisa Waddy [1968] Director; John Barrie Waddy [1966] Director

Kerbina, Limited
Incorporated: 19 February 1938
Registered Office: c/o Bio Health Ltd, Culpeper Close, Medway City Estate, Rochester, Kent, ME2 4HU
Officers: Victor Daniel Perfitt, Secretary; Victor Daniel Perfitt [1944] Managing Director

Kew Health and Beauty Limited
Incorporated: 6 January 2004 *Employees:* 2
Net Worth: £527,716 *Total Assets:* £1,097,569
Registered Office: Jubilee House, 3 The Drive, Great Warley, Brentwood, Essex, CM13 3FR
Officers: Mary Joan Tate, Secretary; Mary Joan Tate [1945] Director/Manager; Simon Robert Geoffrey Tate [1977] Director/Manager

Kew Organic Limited
Incorporated: 9 April 2018
Registered Office: 18 Gary Court 189 London Road, Croydon, Surrey, CR0 2DR
Shareholders: Manojkumar Kalugachalapuram Krishnasamy; Ramya Manojkumar
Officers: Manojkumar Kalugachalapuram Krishnasamy [1979] Director/CEO & Founder; Ramya Manojkumar [1980] Director/Operations Manager

Key Empire Resources (UK) Limited
Incorporated: 18 July 2011
Registered Office: Flat 7, Drive House, 337 London Road, Mitcham, Surrey, CR4 4BE
Officers: Samuel Antwi [1988] Director

Key Organics Limited
Incorporated: 17 September 1986 *Employees:* 32
Net Worth: £2,545,000 *Total Assets:* £3,107,000
Registered Office: 12 Upper Belgrave Street, London, SW1X 8BA
Parent: Tennants Consolidated Limited
Officers: Rosemary Janet Jordan, Secretary; William Paul Alexander [1954] Director; Dr Joseph Carey [1964] Managing Director; Andrew Clive Gingell [1954] Director

Keybiotech Ltd
Incorporated: 29 March 2017
Registered Office: 142 Uxbridge Road Hanwell, London, W7 3SL
Officers: Gurjot Singh Patwalia [1982] Director

Keziah Ltd
Incorporated: 12 April 2018
Registered Office: 105 Easedale House, 71 Summerwood Road, Isleworth, Middlesex, TW7 7QF
Major Shareholder: Priscilla Adwoa Asamaniwa McKing
Officers: Priscilla Adwoa Asamaniwa McKing [1979] Director/Social Worker

Khattak Resolution Ltd
Incorporated: 16 October 2018
Registered Office: 90 Swanshurst Lane, Birmingham, B13 0AL
Major Shareholder: Shukria Khan
Officers: Dr Shukria Khan [1971] Director/Drug Safety Manager

Kinerva Ltd
Incorporated: 28 February 2018
Registered Office: Black Country House, Rounds Green Road, Oldbury, W Midlands, B69 2DG
Major Shareholder: Uzma Hashmat
Officers: Uzma Hashmat [1980] Director [Pakistani]

Kiniksa Pharmaceuticals (UK), Ltd.
Incorporated: 6 December 2018
Registered Office: 11th Floor, Whitefriars, Lewins Mead, Bristol, BS1 2NT
Parent: Kiniksa Pharmaceuticals, Ltd.
Officers: Thomas Beetham, Secretary; Thomas Beetham [1969] Director/Secretary [American]; Christopher Heberlig [1974] Director/Treasurer [American]; Stephen Mahoney [1970] Director/President [American]

KKG Consulting Limited
Incorporated: 16 September 2016
Net Worth: £31,229 *Total Assets:* £45,003
Registered Office: 1 Ford Lane, Allestree, Derby, DE22 2EX
Major Shareholder: Karanjit Gill
Officers: Karanjit Gill [1989] Director

Klinge Chemicals Limited
Incorporated: 21 December 1976 *Employees:* 48
Net Worth: £3,678,700 *Total Assets:* £5,697,768
Registered Office: One Fleet Place, London, EC4M 7WS
Officers: Robert Templeton, Secretary; Michael Klinge [1950] Director; Stephan Klinge [1954] Director

KMCI Services Ltd
Incorporated: 20 February 2017
Net Worth: £26,346 *Total Assets:* £46,954
Registered Office: 418 Jersey Road, Bonymaen, Swansea, SA1 7DW
Major Shareholder: Kieran McInerney
Officers: Kieran McInerney [1992] Director/Statistical Analyst

KMX Healthcare Ltd
Incorporated: 14 September 2016
Net Worth Deficit: £1,378 *Total Assets:* £49,946
Registered Office: 20-22 Wenlock Road, London, N1 7GU
Parent: White Rhino Property Investments Ltd
Officers: Michael Williamson [1969] Director

Knoll UK Investments Unlimited
Incorporated: 23 November 2004 *Employees:* 3
Net Worth: £146,945,552 *Total Assets:* £146,950,176
Registered Office: Abbott House, Vanwall Business Park, Vanwall Road, Maidenhead, Berks, SL6 4XE
Parent: Abbott Laboratories
Officers: Kevan Gogay, Secretary; Neil Harris [1974] Director/General Manager; Georgios Mountrichas [1977] Director/General Manager [Greek]; Brian Yoor [1969] Director/Business Executive [American]

Koasta Limited
Incorporated: 22 August 2005
Net Worth Deficit: £49,122 *Total Assets:* £359,501
Registered Office: Banbury House, 121 Stonegrove, Edgware, Middlesex, HA8 7TJ
Shareholder: Olubukola Taofik Shodunke
Officers: Olubukola Taofik Shodunke [1971] Director

Kohilam Limited
Incorporated: 4 December 2017
Registered Office: 105 Friern Barnet Lane, London, N20 0XZ
Major Shareholder: Kumar Kandasamy
Officers: Nigel Haniff [1963] Director/Sales Consultant; Kumar Kandasamy [1962] Director

Koolpak Limited
Incorporated: 13 April 1993
Net Worth: £22,886 *Total Assets:* £216,661
Registered Office: Greenway House, Sugarswell Business Park, Shenington, Banbury, Oxon, OX15 6HW
Parent: Poole Bay Holdings Limited
Officers: Kenneth James Adnams, Secretary; Martyn Andrew Bright [1955] Director; Hugh Michael McKenna [1953] Director

Kowa Pharmaceutical Europe Co. Ltd.
Incorporated: 26 September 2000 *Employees:* 9
Net Worth: £16,039,077 *Total Assets:* £22,979,906
Registered Office: 105 Wharfedale Road, Winnersh, Wokingham, Berks, RG41 5RB
Officers: Dr Roderick Joseph Coombs [1963] Director/Vice President Marketing Affairs EU & MENA; Dr Junichi Kawagoe [1964] Director [Japanese]; Takashi Narusawa [1971] Director/Manager of European Department, International Business [Japanese]; Koichi Shiraishi [1947] Director [Japanese]; Dr Sohei Tanabe [1952] Director/Corporate Officer (Kowa Co, Ltd) [Japanese]; Dr Ralph Antonius Zaat [1958] Director/President, Medical Doctor [Dutch]

KR Regulatory Limited
Incorporated: 6 December 2016
Net Worth: £312 *Total Assets:* £44,792
Registered Office: 27 The Chase, Watford, Herts, WD18 7JQ
Officers: Fardoss Begum, Secretary; Khalil Rehman [1973] Director

KVK Limited
Incorporated: 29 March 2004
Net Worth: £2,187 *Total Assets:* £10,571
Registered Office: 29 Old School Place, Croydon, Surrey, CR0 4GA
Major Shareholder: Catherine Namatovu Kalanzi
Officers: Catherine Namatovu Kalanzi [1975] Director

Lab 21 Healthcare Limited
Incorporated: 9 August 1994 *Employees:* 20
Net Worth: £54,000 *Total Assets:* £1,248,000
Registered Office: Unit 1 Watchmoor Point, Watchmoor Road, Camberley, Surrey, GU15 3AD
Parent: Lab21 Ltd
Officers: Anthony William Dyer [1972] Finance Director; Graham David Mullis [1962] Director; Phillip Bryan Sefton [1960] Managing Director

Laboratoire Mergens (UK) Ltd
Incorporated: 15 December 2010
Registered Office: 14 Hackwood, Robertsbridge, E Sussex, TN32 5ER
Parent: Laboratoire Mergens SA
Officers: John Clive Andrews [1947] Director/Accountant

Ladysystems International Limited
Incorporated: 12 December 2006
Net Worth: £15,595 *Total Assets:* £38,481
Registered Office: Unit 1 Cambridge House, Camboro Business Park, Oakington Road, Girton, Cambridge, CB3 0QH
Major Shareholder: Zainuddin Dawoodi
Officers: Sarfaraz Hussein Dawoodi, Company Secretary; Dr Zain Dawoodi [1956] Director

Lamicare Health Ltd
Incorporated: 29 June 2012
Net Worth Deficit: £39,563 *Total Assets:* £26,550
Registered Office: New Derwent House, 69-73 Theobalds Road, London, WC1X 8TA
Officers: Dr Nigel David Christie [1948] Director/Marine Biologist (PhD); Francesco Maccioni [1963] Director [Italian]

G.R. Lane Health Products Limited
Incorporated: 1 April 1965 *Employees:* 177
Net Worth: £8,646,956 *Total Assets:* £35,044,788
Registered Office: G R Lane Health Products Limited, Sisson Road, Gloucester, GL2 0GR
Parent: G R Lane Holdings Ltd
Officers: Paul Charles Whatley, Secretary; David Cole [1969] Director; Janet Margaret Groves [1952] Director; Jonathan Roger Groves [1980] Commercial Director; Paul Henly [1962] Technical Director; Mark Horan [1973] Operations Director; Trevor Edward Howard [1962] Director; Aden Craig Kelly [1974] Sales Director; Hilary Lynn [1967] Marketing Director; Paul Charles Whatley [1958] Director

Langdales Limited
Incorporated: 3 September 1996
Net Worth: £10,417 *Total Assets:* £18,646
Registered Office: 1 High Street, Thatcham, Berks, RG19 3JG
Major Shareholder: George Mitchell Sutherland
Officers: Sheena Sukumaran [1971] Director

Langeland Ltd
Incorporated: 21 November 2017
Registered Office: Gibson House, 800 High Road, London, N17 0DH
Shareholder: Jason Krupp
Officers: Jason Krupp [1973] Director/Businessman [American]

Lawrance Pharma Limited
Incorporated: 18 December 2012
Net Worth Deficit: £2,924 *Total Assets:* £12
Registered Office: 100 Mile End Road, London, E1 4UN
Officers: Muhammad Farhan Arif [1983] Director/Business Person [Pakistani]

Laxmi BNS Holdings Limited
Incorporated: 10 February 2010 *Employees:* 646
Net Worth: £22,051,180 *Total Assets:* £109,609,696
Registered Office: Unit 4 Bradfield Road, Ruislip, Middlesex, HA4 0NU
Officers: Govindji Hathi, Secretary; Alpa Hathi [1968] Director/HR; Govindji Thakershi Hathi [1941] Director; Samit Govindji Hathi [1967] Director

LDN Pharma Limited
Incorporated: 22 January 2015
Net Worth: £1,146,603 *Total Assets:* £1,454,918
Registered Office: Locke Lord (UK) LLP, 201 Bishopsgate, London, EC1M 3AB
Shareholders: Paul Joseph Sweeney; Ian Thompson
Officers: Graham Henry Burton [1950] Director/Consultant [American]; Dr Angus George Dalgleish [1950] Director/Professor of Oncology, London; Michael Dennis Mitchell [1950] Director; Paul Joseph Sweeney [1968] Director/Consultant/Advisor [Irish]; Ian Thompson [1981] Director/Consultant/Advisor [Irish]

Lea Pharma Limited
Incorporated: 19 January 2018
Registered Office: 1st Floor, Midas House, 62 Goldsworth Road, Woking, Surrey, GU21 6LQ
Shareholders: Bernard Robert Filippi; Charbel Wardini
Officers: Bernard Robert Filippi [1951] Director [French]; Charbel Wardini [1955] Director [French]

Leap Pharma Ltd
Incorporated: 30 May 2012
Net Worth Deficit: £188,895 *Total Assets:* £6,841
Registered Office: 13 The Causeway, Teddington, Middlesex, TW11 0JR
Major Shareholder: Francis Kwame Essuman
Officers: Francis Essuman, Secretary; Francis Kwame Essuman [1970] Director [Ghanaian]

Leeds Industries (UK) Ltd
Incorporated: 12 January 2016
Net Worth: £383 *Total Assets:* £644,510
Registered Office: 55a Palmerston Road, Sutton, Surrey, SM1 4QL
Major Shareholder: Abhijnan Mukherjee
Officers: Abhijnan Mukherjee [1985] Director

LEH Pharma Ltd
Incorporated: 12 April 2011
Previous: London Eye Hospital Pharma Ltd
Net Worth: £836,541,376 *Total Assets:* £850,437,888
Registered Office: Park House, 116 Park Street, London, W1K 6SS
Officers: Dr Muhammad Ali Qureshi [1970] Director/Doctor

Leptrex Ltd.
Incorporated: 28 September 2011
Net Worth Deficit: £24,353 *Total Assets:* £68,222
Registered Office: 135 Church Road, Folkestone, Kent, CT20 3ER
Parent: Allicin International Ltd
Officers: Carol Ann Coleman, Secretary; Norman John Bennett [1946] Director; Dr Edward Ramsey [1955] Director/Professor

Letdrop Ltd
Incorporated: 16 May 2018
Registered Office: Room 320, Engineering Building, Mile End Road, London, E1 4NS
Major Shareholder: Stoyan Smoukov
Officers: Dr. Stoyan Smoukov [1972] Director/Engineer [Bulgarian]

Lewtress Natural Health Limited
Incorporated: 7 July 2004
Net Worth Deficit: £67,255 *Total Assets:* £106,276
Registered Office: Unit 4 Wervil Grange, Pentregat, Llandysul, Ceredigion, SA44 6HW
Shareholders: Cathay Ann Wootres; Robert John Lewis; Robert John Lewis
Officers: Robert John Lewis, Secretary; Robert John Lewis [1960] Director; Cathay Ann Wootres [1962] Director [American]

Life Molecular Imaging Limited
Incorporated: 8 July 2003 *Employees:* 4
Previous: Piramal Imaging Limited
Net Worth Deficit: £41,892,120 *Total Assets:* £7,825,845
Registered Office: ICENI Centre, Warwick Technology Park, Warwick, CV34 6DA
Parent: Alliance Medical Acquisition Co Limited
Officers: Nico Francois Beukman [1968] Director; Dr Ludger Maria Theodor Dinkelborg [1962] Director [German]; Edward Henry Lunt [1977] Finance Director; Howard Alexander David Marsh [1974] Director

Life on Healthcare Ltd
Incorporated: 5 March 2009 *Employees:* 2
Net Worth: £78,586 *Total Assets:* £324,916
Registered Office: Unit C, Arlington Building, Bow Quarter, Fairfield Road, London, E3 2UB
Major Shareholder: Ganesh Krishna
Officers: Srinivas Gudipati [1976] Director/Businessman; Ganesh Krishna [1977] Director/Business Person

Life Technologies BPD UK Limited
Incorporated: 25 February 1999 *Employees:* 144
Previous: Hyclone UK Limited
Net Worth: £96,059,000 *Total Assets:* £99,384,000
Registered Office: 3rd Floor, 1 Ashley Road, Altrincham, Cheshire, WA14 2DT
Parent: Thermo Fisher Scientific Inc.
Officers: Rhona Gregg, Secretary; Nicole Aspinall [1978] Director; Euan Daney Ross Cameron [1976] Director; Lucie Mary Katja Grant [1976] Director/Solicitor; David John Norman [1960] Director/Chartered Accountant; Anthony Hugh Smith [1962] Director/Vice President, Tax and Treasury [American]

Lifeplan Products Limited
Incorporated: 28 August 1984 *Employees:* 80
Net Worth: £2,248,002 *Total Assets:* £5,748,236
Registered Office: Elizabethan Way, Lutterworth, Leics, LE17 4ND
Officers: Vincent Jamie Gosling, Secretary; Rodney Graham Bray [1970] Director; Sarah Jane Brockhurst [1970] Director; Michael Conrad Jackson [1933] Director; Nicholas Adrian Mead [1966] Director/Sales Manager; Jacqueline Robinson [1965] Director/Accounts Manager; Melvyn Warren Sadofsky [1949] Director/Chartered Accountant

Lifeshield Limited
Incorporated: 7 September 1998 *Employees:* 2
Net Worth: £21,374 *Total Assets:* £161,652
Registered Office: 3 Old Estate Yard, North Stoke Lane, Upton Cheyney, Bristol, BS30 6ND
Major Shareholder: Irina Ananina
Officers: Steven John Blackmore [1968] Director

Lifetime Products Limited
Incorporated: 9 September 2013
Registered Office: 134 Hugh Road, Smethwick, W Midlands, B67 7JR
Major Shareholder: Chalak Mala
Officers: Chalak Mala, Secretary; Chalak Mala [1974] Director

Lift Health Limited
Incorporated: 11 August 2017
Registered Office: 64 Hillside Gardens, Barnet, Herts, EN5 2NL
Officers: Anna Jane Lewis [1984] Director/Account Manager

Eli Lilly (Basingstoke) Limited
Incorporated: 26 November 1987
Registered Office: Lilly House, Priestley Road, Basingstoke, Hants, RG24 9NL
Parent: Eli Lilly and Company Limited
Officers: Hamish John Carmichael Bennett, Secretary; Hamish John Carmichael Bennett [1974] Director; Nicholas Lemen [1974] Finance Director [American]

Eli Lilly and Company Limited
Incorporated: 5 February 1934 *Employees:* 1,513
Net Worth: £645,555,008 *Total Assets:* £1,206,620,032
Registered Office: Lilly House, Priestley Road, Basingstoke, Hants, RG24 9NL
Parent: Eli Lilly Group Limited
Officers: Hamish John Carmichael Bennett, Secretary; Karen Ann Alexander [1967] Director; Hamish John Carmichael Bennett [1974] Director; Ashley Diaz-Granados [1976] Director/General Manager [American]; Dr Susan Renee Forda [1958] Director/VP Global Regulatory Affairs - International; Nicholas Lemen [1974] Finance Director [American]

Eli Lilly Group Limited
Incorporated: 10 September 1979
Net Worth: £55,074,000 *Total Assets:* £108,451,000
Registered Office: Lilly House, Priestley Road, Basingstoke, Hants, RG24 9NL
Parent: Eli Lilly and Company
Officers: Hamish John Carmichael Bennett, Secretary; Hamish John Carmichael Bennett [1974] Director; Ashley Diaz-Granados [1976] Director/General Manager [American]; Nicholas Lemen [1974] Finance Director [American]

Eli Lilly Holding Company Limited
Incorporated: 7 November 2001
Registered Office: Lilly House, Priestley Road, Basingstoke, Hants, RG24 9NL
Parent: Eli Lilly and Company Limited
Officers: Hamish John Carmichael Bennett, Secretary; Hamish John Carmichael Bennett [1974] Director; Nicholas Lemen [1974] Finance Director [American]

Eli Lilly Holdings Limited
Incorporated: 14 December 1983
Registered Office: Lilly House, Priestley Road, Basingstoke, Hants, RG24 9NL
Parent: Eli Lilly and Company
Officers: Hamish John Carmichael Bennett, Secretary; Hamish John Carmichael Bennett [1974] Director; Nicholas Lemen [1974] Finance Director [American]

Lilly Industries Limited
Incorporated: 9 April 1963
Registered Office: Lilly House, Priestley Road, Basingstoke, Hants, RG24 9NL
Parent: Eli Lilly and Company Limited
Officers: Hamish John Carmichael Bennett, Secretary; Hamish John Carmichael Bennett [1974] Director; Nicholas Lemen [1974] Finance Director [American]

Eli Lilly Leasing Limited
Incorporated: 5 January 1994
Registered Office: Lilly House, Priestley Road, Basingstoke, Hants, RG24 9NL
Parent: Eli Lilly and Company Limited
Officers: Hamish John Carmichael Bennett, Secretary; Hamish John Carmichael Bennett [1974] Director; Nicholas Lemen [1974] Finance Director [American]

Lilly Property Limited
Incorporated: 8 May 2002
Registered Office: Lilly House, Priestley Road, Basingstoke, Hants, RG24 9NL
Parent: Eli Lilly and Company Limited
Officers: Hamish John Carmichael Bennett, Secretary; Hamish John Carmichael Bennett [1974] Director; Nicholas Lemen [1974] Finance Director [American]

Eli Lilly Property Limited
Incorporated: 8 May 2002
Registered Office: Lilly House, Priestley Road, Basingstoke, Hants, RG24 9NL
Parent: Eli Lilly and Company Limited
Officers: Hamish John Carmichael Bennett, Secretary; Hamish John Carmichael Bennett [1974] Director; Nicholas Lemen [1974] Finance Director [American]

Lilly Research Centre Limited
Incorporated: 22 April 1963
Registered Office: Lilly House, Priestley Road, Basingstoke, Hants, RG24 9NL
Parent: Eli Lilly and Company Limited
Officers: Hamish John Carmichael Bennett, Secretary; Hamish John Carmichael Bennett [1974] Director; Nicholas Lemen [1974] Finance Director [American]

Lilly Resources Limited
Incorporated: 8 May 2002
Registered Office: Lilly House, Priestley Road, Basingstoke, Hants, RG24 9NL
Parent: Eli Lilly and Company Limited
Officers: Hamish John Carmichael Bennett, Secretary; Hamish John Carmichael Bennett [1974] Director; Nicholas Lemen [1974] Finance Director [American]

Eli Lilly Resources Limited
Incorporated: 8 May 2002
Registered Office: Lilly House, Priestley Road, Basingstoke, Hants, RG24 9NL
Parent: Eli Lilly and Company Limited
Officers: Hamish John Carmichael Bennett, Secretary; Hamish John Carmichael Bennett [1974] Director; Nicholas Lemen [1974] Finance Director [American]

Limehurst Limited
Incorporated: 3 September 1992 *Employees:* 2
Net Worth: £129,395 *Total Assets:* £135,317
Registered Office: c/o Evans Weir, The Victoria, 25 St Pancras, Chichester, W Sussex, PO19 7LT
Major Shareholder: Philippe Maurice Henri Wanty
Officers: Michael John Howlett, Secretary; Michael Howlett [1963] Director; Philippe Maurice Henri Wanty [1954] Director/Botanist [French]

Limitless Med Ltd
Incorporated: 5 July 2018
Registered Office: 88 Russell Road, Hall Green, Birmingham, B28 8SG
Shareholders: Nadim Razaq; Julian Cooper
Officers: Julian Cooper [1977] Director; Nadim Razaq [1977] Director

Lincoln Medical Limited
Incorporated: 14 June 2000
Net Worth: £947 *Total Assets:* £3,048,369
Registered Office: Unit B, Stanley Court, Glenmore Business Park, Telford Road, Churchfields, Salisbury, Wilts, SP2 7GH
Parent: Bioprojet Pharma SARL
Officers: Jean-Guillaume Lecomte [1960] Director/Consultant [French]; Jeanne-Marie Lecomte [1935] Director/Consultant [French]

Linnaeus Herbals Limited
Incorporated: 12 October 2017
Registered Office: 3 Gosse Close, Hoddesdon, Herts, EN11 9FG
Officers: Zulfiqar Ali Khan [1968] Director/Pharmaceuticals

Linosa Limited
Incorporated: 1 April 1974 *Employees:* 1
Net Worth: £268,972 *Total Assets:* £383,493
Registered Office: Batchworth House, Batchworth Place, Church Street, Rickmansworth, Herts, WD3 1JE
Major Shareholder: Sudesh Sharma
Officers: Sudesh Sharma, Secretary; Pushpinder Sharma [1939] Director/Sales Manager; Sudesh Sharma [1943] Director/Economic Analyst

Lipcote & Co Limited
Incorporated: 30 November 2017
Registered Office: Unit 4 Forest Works, Forest Road, Charlbury, Oxon, OX7 3HH
Major Shareholder: Ben Peter Woodward
Officers: Ben Peter Woodward [1969] Director/Chartered Accountant; Charles Edward Woodward [1943] Director

Lipidev Ltd
Incorporated: 23 June 2014
Net Worth Deficit: £59,149 *Total Assets:* £103,073
Registered Office: Science and Technology Centre, Earley Gate, Whiteknights Road, Reading, Berks, RG6 6BZ
Major Shareholder: Derek Wyndham Clissold
Officers: Derek Wyndham Clissold [1945] Director

Lipsy Couture Limited
Incorporated: 3 December 2018
Registered Office: 2b Paragon House, Michigan Avenue, Salford Quays, Manchester, M50 2GY
Officers: Maxine Hopley, Secretary; Maxine Hopley [1978] Director

The Liquid Comb Limited
Incorporated: 28 January 2015
Registered Office: Flat 53, Charlbert Court, MacKennal Street, London, NW8 7DB
Major Shareholder: Joanne Stoller
Officers: Joanne Stoller [1966] Director

Lisoma International Limited
Incorporated: 24 December 1998 *Employees:* 1
Net Worth Deficit: £182,053 *Total Assets:* £305,915
Registered Office: Forum House, Stirling Road, Chichester, W Sussex, PO19 7DN
Major Shareholder: Pia Gunborg Anette Rabe
Officers: Thomas Wayne Atkinson, Secretary [New Zealander]; Thomas Wayne Atkinson [1946] Director [New Zealander]; Pia Gunborg Anette Rabe [1956] Director [Swedish]

Little Green Beehive Ltd
Incorporated: 23 April 2018
Registered Office: 7 Potts Close, Kenilworth, Warwicks, CV8 2SD
Shareholders: Josephine Cassell; Nikki Lee
Officers: Dr Josephine Cassell [1987] Director/Co-Founder; Dr Nikki Lee [1989] Director/Co-Founder [Canadian]

Livbio Limited
Incorporated: 27 July 2018
Registered Office: Kemp House, 160 City Road, London, EC1V 2NX
Major Shareholder: Takashi Takenoshita
Officers: Takashi Takenoshita [1970] Director [Japanese]

Living Skin Care Limited
Incorporated: 5 May 2015
Registered Office: 26 Dukeswood Drive, Dibden Purlieu, Southampton, SO45 4NJ
Shareholders: Paul Stephenson; Lynn Stephenson
Officers: Paul Stephenson, Secretary; Lynn Stephenson [1964] Director/Aromatherapist; Paul Stephenson [1961] Director/IT Project Manager

Milton Lloyd Limited
Incorporated: 22 December 1975 *Employees:* 16
Net Worth: £4,210,043 *Total Assets:* £14,223,723
Registered Office: 42-44 Norwood High Street, London, SE27 9NR
Parent: Jackson Trading Company PLC
Officers: Alison Jackson, Secretary; Alison Jackson [1952] Director; Charles Peter Christopher Howard Jackson [1983] Sales Director; Christopher William John Jackson [1954] Director; Daniel William John Jackson [1982] Director; Jemma Audrey Ilse Jackson [1986] Director; Jodie Alison Caroline Victoria Jackson [1988] Media Director; Howard Walters [1947] Director/Accountant

LMP (UK) Limited
Incorporated: 14 February 2011
Net Worth Deficit: £4,554 *Total Assets:* £788
Registered Office: North Lodge, Hawkesyard, Armitage Lane, Rugeley, Staffs, WS15 1PS
Parent: Links Medical Products Inc
Officers: Glenn Alex Brosche [1952] Director [American]; Thomas Buckley [1941] Director [American]; Andrew Robert Thain [1974] Director

Lochview Pharm Ltd.
Incorporated: 4 February 2010 *Employees:* 3
Net Worth: £36,953 *Total Assets:* £122,362
Registered Office: Dalmally Pharmacy, Main Road, Dalmally, Argyll & Bute, PA33 1AX
Shareholders: Rukhsana Akbar; Isma Yaqoob
Officers: Ruksana Akbar, Secretary; Rukhsana Akbar [1982] Director/Tax Officer/Manager; Isma Yaqoob [1980] Director/Pharmacy & Healthcare

Lofthouse of Fleetwood Limited
Incorporated: 18 November 1963 *Employees:* 385
Net Worth: £79,805,056 *Total Assets:* £97,787,144
Registered Office: Maritime Street, Fleetwood, Lancs, FY7 7LP
Shareholders: Doreen Wilson Lofthouse OBE; Duncan Charles Lofthouse
Officers: Duncan Charles Lofthouse, Secretary; Doreen Wilson Lofthouse [1930] Director; Duncan Charles Lofthouse [1951] Director

London Pharma Capital Limited
Incorporated: 10 March 2015
Net Worth Deficit: £4,926 *Total Assets:* £264,052
Registered Office: First Floor, Roxburghe House, 273-287 Regent Street, London, W1B 2HA
Major Shareholder: Ivan Berkes
Officers: Ivan Berkes [1968] Director [Slovak]; Dr Simon James Dorris [1971] Director; Jonathan George Farrington [1969] Director

The London Specialist Pharmacy Limited
Incorporated: 11 February 2009 *Employees:* 14
Net Worth: £763,071 *Total Assets:* £1,050,060
Registered Office: Unit 3 Cedar Court, 1 Royal Oak Yard, London, SE1 3GA
Parent: Gluck Holdings Limited
Officers: Dr Marion Sylwia Gluck [1950] Director/Medical Doctor [Polish]

London Surgical Limited
Incorporated: 29 October 2009
Registered Office: Flat 3, Aldersgate Court, 30 Bartholomew Close, London, EC1A 7ES
Shareholders: Daniel Calladine; Henry Barnabas Smith
Officers: Daisy Raven, Secretary; Daniel Calladine [1979] Director/Doctor of Medicine; Henry Barnabas Smith [1973] Director/Doctor of Medicine; Richard Zaltzman [1972] Director/Consultant

Longshawe Packaging Limited
Incorporated: 23 August 1984 *Employees:* 40
Net Worth: £1,155,300 *Total Assets:* £1,512,588
Registered Office: Unit 1 Leekbrook Way, Leek, Staffs, ST13 7AP
Officers: Liam Joseph McDermott [1992] Managing Director; Patrick John McDermott [1957] Director/Manufacturers Agent

Longwood Medevice Ltd
Incorporated: 1 March 2016
Registered Office: 3 Moss Gardens, Southport, Merseyside, PR8 4JD
Officers: Kenneth Kan Li Lam [1956] Director

Lothian Laboratories Ltd
Incorporated: 26 October 2017
Registered Office: 66 Westwood Park, Deans, Livingston, W Lothian, EH54 8QW
Major Shareholder: Jennifer Margaret Davidson
Officers: Jennifer Margaret Davidson, Secretary; Jennifer Margaret Davidson [1977] Director/Dental Technician; Kenneth Nairn Davidson [1967] Director/Consultant

LPC Medical (UK) Limited
Incorporated: 1 November 2001 *Employees:* 7
Net Worth Deficit: £618,384 *Total Assets:* £1,115,289
Registered Office: Unit 3 Nursery Court, Kibworth Business Park, Kibworth, Leics, LE8 0EX
Parent: In2 Healthcare Ltd
Officers: Ian David Waring, Secretary; Satnam Singh Butter [1961] Director/Pharmacist; Shirazali Sharif Dharamshi [1949] Director; Amirali Sharif Tejani [1954] Director; Karim Sharif Dharamshi Tejani [1959] Director; Nazirali Sharif Dharamshi Tejani [1952] Director; Salim Sharif Dharamshi Tejani [1950] Director

LRC Products Limited
Incorporated: 14 July 1961
Net Worth: £634,280,000 *Total Assets:* £776,812,032
Registered Office: 103-105 Bath Road, Slough, Berks, SL1 3UH
Parent: London International Group Limited
Officers: Christine Anne-Marie Logan, Secretary; John Dixon [1956] Director/SVP Tax; Charles David Everitt [1973] Director; Harminder Singh Virdi [1978] Finance Director

Lucy Annabella Ltd
Incorporated: 16 May 2011
Net Worth: £5,698 *Total Assets:* £60,257
Registered Office: 175 Ballygawley Road, Dungannon, Co Tyrone, BT70 1RX
Major Shareholder: Colleen Harte
Officers: Colleen Harte [1983] Director/Complementary Therapist [Irish]; Shannon Quinn [1990] Director/Chartered Accountant

Lukas Lab Limited
Incorporated: 10 January 2018
Registered Office: 364-368 Cranbrook Road, Ilford, Essex, IG2 6HY
Officers: Ranjan Singh [1972] Director [Indian]

Lumibio Ltd
Incorporated: 22 July 2010 *Employees:* 1
Net Worth Deficit: £36,058 *Total Assets:* £3,465
Registered Office: St Helens Farm, St Helens Hill, Dalton in Furness, Cumbria, LA15 8GD
Major Shareholder: Mark Andrew Wilding
Officers: Mark Andrew Wilding [1968] Director

Luoda UK Limited
Incorporated: 8 March 2016
Registered Office: Bailey House, 4-10 Barttelot Road, Horsham, W Sussex, RH12 1DQ
Parent: Luoda Pharma Pty Limited
Officers: Nicholas Patrick Bova [1982] Director/Pharmacist [Australian]; Stephen Walter Page [1954] Director/Veterinarian [Australian]; Brett Alan Watkins [1983] Director [Australian]

Lux Viridis Services Ltd
Incorporated: 28 November 2017
Registered Office: 3 Greenhalgh Walk, London, N2 0DJ
Shareholder: Carlos Eduardo Pavesio
Officers: Sonia de Lara Gonsalez [1961] Director/Ophthalmologist [Brazilian]; Carlos Eduardo Pavesio [1959] Director/Ophthalmologist [Brazilian]

Luxury CBD Oils Ltd
Incorporated: 9 August 2018
Registered Office: 8 Harlech Court, Vauxhall Lane, Chepstow, Monmouthshire, NP16 5PZ
Shareholder: Richard Wright
Officers: Richard Wright [1978] Director

M & A Pharmachem Limited
Incorporated: 1 February 1977 *Employees:* 139
Net Worth: £9,661,144 *Total Assets:* £21,316,352
Registered Office: Allenby Laboratories, Wigan Road, Westhoughton, Bolton, Lancs, BL5 2AL
Shareholder: CD Medical Limited
Officers: Lee Fairbrother, Secretary; Elsie Maureen Armstrong [1951] Director; Michael Gatenby [1942] Sales & Marketing Director; Gerard Michael Dominic Pessagno [1952] Director

M D M Healthcare Ltd
Incorporated: 18 April 2008 *Employees:* 2
Net Worth: £681,065 *Total Assets:* £1,039,737
Registered Office: Granite Building, 6 Stanley Street, Liverpool, L1 6AF
Shareholders: Daniel Bracey; Marcus Fritze; Marco Wolfgang Huelsbeck
Officers: Daniel Bracey [1974] Director; Marcus Fritze [1974] Director [German]; Marco Wolfgang Huelsbeck [1975] Director [German]

M V Locums Limited
Incorporated: 14 December 2011
Net Worth: £59 *Total Assets:* £412
Registered Office: Staffordshire House, Beechdale Road, Nottingham, NG8 3FH
Major Shareholder: Mahesh Kumar Verma
Officers: Mahesh Kumar Verma [1984] Director

M3 Cosmetics Limited
Incorporated: 26 October 2012
Registered Office: Weller House, 58-60 Longbridge Road, Barking, Essex, IG11 8RT
Officers: Ngozi Muoneke [1965] Director/Pharmacy Technician; Victor Muoneke [1968] Director/Construction

Macarthys Laboratories Limited
Incorporated: 30 January 1959 *Employees:* 440
Net Worth: £112,461,000 *Total Assets:* £137,148,992
Registered Office: Bampton Road, Harold Hill, Romford, Essex, RM3 8UG
Parent: Orphea Limited
Officers: Paul Joseph Concannon [1959] Commercial Director; Bertrand Deluard [1961] Director/Chief Executive Officer [French]; Philip Edward Parry [1965] Director/Quality Assurance Professional; Emmanuel Schmidt [1969] Director/Chief Finance Officer [French]

MacFarlan Smith Limited
Incorporated: 12 September 1960 *Employees:* 362
Net Worth Deficit: £600,000 *Total Assets:* £219,838,000
Registered Office: Wheatfield Road, Edinburgh, EH11 2QA
Parent: Meconic Limited
Officers: Simon Farrant, Secretary; Terrence Bernard Cooke [1967] Director; Simon Farrant [1961] Director/Solicitor; David Martin Payne [1980] Director

MacFarlane Martin Ltd
Incorporated: 18 June 2014
Net Worth Deficit: £21,412 *Total Assets:* £2,308
Registered Office: Peter McKinney Associates, 14 West Terrace, South Queensferry, Edinburgh, EH30 9LL
Shareholder: Grant Martin
Officers: Pamela Martin, Secretary; Grant Martin [1978] Director/Transport Planner; Pamela Martin [1978] Director/Podiatrist

MacLeods Pharma UK Limited
Incorporated: 17 December 2007 *Employees:* 2
Net Worth Deficit: £2,430,348 *Total Assets:* £2,208,099
Registered Office: Wynyard Park House, Wynyard Avenue, Wynyard, Billingham, Cleveland, TS22 5TB
Officers: Vijay Girdharilal Agarwal [1977] Director/Service [Indian]

Maco Edge Limited
Incorporated: 30 August 2017
Registered Office: 8th Floor, 11 Old Jewry, London, EC2R 8DU
Parent: Groupe Maco Pharma International S.A.S.
Officers: Yvan Malepart [1965] Director [Canadian]

Macopharma (UK) Limited
Incorporated: 7 February 1986 *Employees:* 9
Net Worth: £1,788,796 *Total Assets:* £5,246,038
Registered Office: 8th Floor, 11 Old Jewry, London, EC2R 8DU
Officers: Caroline Christiane Paule Hernu, Secretary; Yvann Malepart [1965] Director [Canadian]

Maculeh Ltd
Incorporated: 10 April 2016
Registered Office: 4 Harley Street, London, W1G 9PB
Major Shareholder: Muhammad Ali Qureshi
Officers: Dr Muhammad Ali Qureshi [1970] Director

Made in Nature Ltd
Incorporated: 28 April 2016
Registered Office: 85 Heyes Lane, Alderley Edge, Cheshire, SK9 7LN
Officers: Mark Christopher Roger Duffy [1964] Director; Charlotte Fellows [1990] Director

Madhusudhana Solutions Limited
Incorporated: 19 September 2018
Registered Office: 85a Heigham Road, London, E6 2JJ
Major Shareholder: Sharath Kumar Reddy Mallareddy
Officers: Sharath Kumar Reddy Mallareddy [1988] Director [Indian]

Maelor Laboratories Limited
Incorporated: 22 April 1997
Net Worth: £6,584,000 *Total Assets:* £16,086,000
Registered Office: Avonbridge House, Bath Road, Chippenham, Wilts, SN15 2BB
Parent: Alliance Pharmaceuticals Limited
Officers: Chrysanthos Theocus Chrysanthou, Secretary; Peter Jonathan Butterfield [1975] Executive Director; Alexander James Hanbury Duggan [1970] Director/Chief Commercial Officer; Andrew Timothy Franklin [1966] Finance Director; Stephen Martin Kidner [1968] Director/Chief Scientific & Operations Officer

Magna Pharmaceuticals Ltd
Incorporated: 4 July 2007
Registered Office: 75 Woodbourne, Edgbaston, Birmingham, B15 3PJ
Officers: Valerie Chamberlain, Secretary; Iftekhar Ahmed [1970] Director

Maia Pharma Ltd
Incorporated: 19 March 2018
Registered Office: 26 Gurney Road, London, E15 1SH
Shareholders: Iftikhar Ahmed; Irum Iftikhar
Officers: Zafran Iftikhar Ahmed, Secretary; Iftikhar Ahmed [1971] Managing Director; Irum Iftikhar [1975] Marketing Director

Mak Health Limited
Incorporated: 26 January 2016
Registered Office: Crossings, Bickley Road, Bromley, Kent, BR1 2NF
Shareholder: Hadeel Haddad
Officers: Hadeel Haddad, Secretary; Hadeel Haddad [1970] Director; Morad Kara [1956] Director

Make Skincare Ltd.
Incorporated: 9 January 2012
Net Worth Deficit: £8,801 *Total Assets:* £15,551
Registered Office: Thorney House, Thorney, Langport, Somerset, TA10 0DR
Major Shareholder: Mary Clementine Temperley
Officers: Jacob Motley [1974] Director/Contracts Manager; Mary Clementine Temperley [1978] Director/Consultant

Makjay Pharmaceutical Limited
Incorporated: 13 October 1999
Registered Office: 89 Burdon Lane, Sutton, Surrey, SM2 7BZ
Officers: Surendra Patel, Secretary/Accountant; Makarand Mohan Mulherkar [1969] Director/Pharmaceutical Mfg [Indian]; Mohan Madhukar Mulherkar [1948] Director/Businessman [Indian]; Surendra Patel [1947] Director

Maklary Ltd
Incorporated: 28 August 2014
Registered Office: 20-22 Wenlock Road, London, N1 7GU
Major Shareholder: Zoltan Akos Maklari
Officers: Zoltan Akos Maklari [1982] Director [Hungarian]

F.Maltby & Sons Limited
Incorporated: 21 January 1949
Registered Office: Stanley Bett House, 15-23 Tentercroft Street, Lincoln, LN5 7DB
Parent: Lincolnshire Co-operative Ltd
Officers: Jane Powell, Secretary; Stephen Robert Hughes [1961] Director/Pharmacist; Reverend Barbara Anne Hutchinson [1955] Director/Reverend; David Frank Maltby [1956] Director/Retired; Jane Moate [1957] Director/Retired Bank Manager; Susan Neal [1951] Director/Medical Records Admin Data Clerk and Phlebotomist; Claudia Nel [1966] Director/Solicitor & Data Protection Officer; Stuart William Parker [1958] Director/Engineer; Julia Anne Romney [1956] Director/Security Officer; Margaret Williamson Tranter [1947] Director/Retired

Maltron International Limited
Incorporated: 15 October 1996 *Employees:* 6
Net Worth: £13,358 *Total Assets:* £111,471
Registered Office: Lodge Park, Lodge Lane, Langham, Colchester, Essex, CO4 5NE
Major Shareholder: Anjum Mohanum Malik
Officers: Anjum Mohanum Malik [1957] Director/Manager

The Mammoet Cannabis Limited
Incorporated: 15 May 2017
Net Worth: £1,940 *Total Assets:* £8,850
Registered Office: 10k Craufurdland Road, Kilmarnock, E Ayrshire, KA3 2HT
Major Shareholder: Mariusz Biniak
Officers: Katarzyna Wit-Biniak [1980] Director/Finance Sales [Polish]

Man Oil Company Limited
Incorporated: 23 February 2017
Registered Office: 8 Helen Cottages, Dedworth Road, Windsor, Berks, SL4 4JZ
Officers: Matthew George Prince [1984] Director/MD; Emma Sadler [1981] Director

Man Pharma Limited
Incorporated: 9 January 2018
Registered Office: 472 Greenford Road, Greenford, Middlesex, UB6 8SQ
Officers: Abdullah Issac [1982] Director

Mandeville Medicines Limited
Incorporated: 27 March 2001
Registered Office: Mandeville Medicines, Stoke Mandeville Hospital, Mandeville Road, Aylesbury, Bucks, HP21 8AL
Officers: David Thomas Brazier, Secretary/Director; David Thomas Brazier [1967] Director; Karol Pazik [1964] Director

Manta - Cognitive Fuels Ltd
Incorporated: 9 August 2018
Registered Office: 31b Lexden Road, Colchester, Essex, CO3 3PX
Major Shareholder: David William Higgins
Officers: David William Higgins [1990] Director

Mantiza Ltd
Incorporated: 23 July 2018
Registered Office: 214a Kettering Road, Northampton, NN1 4BN
Shareholders: Prima de Lugar; Paul Noble
Officers: Prima de Lugar [1962] Director [Filipino]

Manx Healthcare Limited
Incorporated: 3 March 1994 *Employees:* 24
Net Worth: £2,401,544 *Total Assets:* £9,309,355
Registered Office: Taylor Group House, Wedgnock Lane, Warwick, CV34 5YA
Parent: Richard's Pharma Limited
Officers: Laurence Dudley Taylor, Secretary; Malcolm Clive Ramsay [1964] Director; Simone Elizabeth Taylor [1958] Director

Manx Pharma Ltd
Incorporated: 24 September 1996
Net Worth Deficit: £249,618 *Total Assets:* £195,131
Registered Office: Taylor Group House, Wedgnock Lane, Warwick, CV34 5YA
Parent: Richard's Pharma Limited
Officers: Laurence Dudley Taylor, Secretary; Malcolm Clive Ramsay [1964] Director; Simone Elizabeth Taylor [1958] Director

Marigold Projects Jamaica Limited
Incorporated: 22 August 2017
Registered Office: c/o Hillier Hopkins LLP, First Floor, Radius House, 51 Clarendon Road, Watford, Herts, WD17 1HP
Major Shareholder: Laban Edward Roomes
Officers: Laban Edward Roomes [1969] Director/Entrepreneur

Marine Labs Limited
Incorporated: 31 January 2018
Registered Office: Vantage Point, 2 High View Close, Leicester, LE4 9LJ
Shareholders: Mitesh Soma; Ji Li
Officers: Ji Li [1986] Director [Chinese]; Mitesh Soma [1976] Director

Marlborough Pharmaceuticals Limited
Incorporated: 24 January 2005
Net Worth: £3,675,708 *Total Assets:* £10,607,300
Registered Office: Suite 1, 3rd Floor, 11-12 St James's Square, London, SW1Y 4LB
Parent: Atnahs Pharma UK Limited
Officers: Mark John Cotterill [1965] Director; Amit Vijaykumar Patel [1978] Director; Bhikhu Chhotabhai Patel [1947] Director; Dipen Vijaykumar Patel [1979] Director; Vijay Kumar Chhotabhai Patel [1949] Director

Bob Martin (UK) Limited
Incorporated: 25 February 2002 *Employees:* 396
Net Worth: £1,128,330 *Total Assets:* £50,035,164
Registered Office: Wemberham Lane, Yatton, Bristol, BS49 4BS
Parent: Martin & Martin Holdings
Officers: Andrew Mark Cooke [1974] Director; Andrew Michael Ford [1964] Director; Daniel Sebastian Fromm [1975] Director; Georgina Melissa Martin [1974] Director; William James Steele [1971] Director; Jeremy Paul Warne [1963] Director

Martini International Ltd
Incorporated: 5 October 2018
Registered Office: 7 Hillside Road, Radcliffe on Trent, Nottingham, NG12 2GZ
Shareholders: Flavia Martini; Valerio Martini; Alessandra Giannelli
Officers: Alessandra Giannelli [1964] Director/Nurse [Italian]; Flavia Martini [2001] Director/Student [Italian]; Valerio Martini [1970] Director/Businessman [Italian]

Masters Pharmaceuticals Limited
Incorporated: 17 October 1984 *Employees:* 85
Net Worth: £485,273 *Total Assets:* £9,841,748
Registered Office: 380 Centennial Avenue, Centennial Park, Elstree, Herts, WD6 3TJ
Officers: Suzad Masters [1958] Director; Zulfikar Masters [1956] Director/Chairman

Materia Prima Ltd
Incorporated: 18 September 2017
Registered Office: The Oak, Wix Road, Beaumont-Cum-Moze, Essex, CO16 0AT
Shareholders: Professor Mark William Lowdell; Afshin Mosahebi
Officers: Professor Mark William Lowdell [1962] Director/University Professor; Afshin Mosahebi [1967] Director/Consultant

Matthews & Wilson Limited
Incorporated: 15 February 1946 *Employees:* 9
Net Worth: £1,204,659 *Total Assets:* £1,439,577
Registered Office: Unit 4 Forest Works, Forest Road, Charlbury, Oxon, OX7 3HH
Parent: M & W Holdings Limited
Officers: Ben Peter Woodward, Secretary; Charles Edward Woodward [1943] Director

Max Medical Products Ltd
Incorporated: 15 December 2010 *Employees:* 1
Net Worth Deficit: £354,122 *Total Assets:* £29,718
Registered Office: 3 Shortlands, Hammersmith, London, W6 8DA
Major Shareholder: Muneer Aqel
Officers: Muneer Aqel, Secretary; Muneer Aqel [1968] Director [Jordanian]

Maxearn Limited
Incorporated: 10 January 2001 *Employees:* 67
Net Worth: £460,116 *Total Assets:* £819,693
Registered Office: Unit 29 Devonshire Road, Worsley, Manchester, M28 3PT
Parent: Walkboost Limited
Officers: Craig Bernard Fishwick, Secretary; Craig Bernard Fishwick [1974] Director/Accountant

Maxvac Ltd
Incorporated: 9 January 2019
Registered Office: Unit 8 Starborough Farm, Starborough Road, Marsh Green, Edenbridge, Kent, TN8 5RB
Major Shareholder: Adrian Endacott
Officers: Adrian Endacott [1976] Director

Maxwellia Ltd
Incorporated: 18 June 2013
Net Worth: £84,681 *Total Assets:* £243,922
Registered Office: 20F38 Alderley Park, Alderley Edge, Cheshire, SK10 4TG
Shareholders: GM & C Life Sciences Fund LP; Anna Helen Blackledge
Officers: Anna Helen Maxwell [1964] Director; Robert Nelson Wilson [1962] Director/Chairman

May & Baker Limited
Incorporated: 7 December 1989 *Employees:* 4
Net Worth: £130,619,000 *Total Assets:* £157,120,992
Registered Office: One Onslow Street, Guildford, Surrey, GU1 4YS
Parent: Sanofi-Aventis UK Holdings Limited
Officers: Francois-Xavier Duhalde [1965] Director/Chief Financial Officer [French]; Hugo Rupert Alexander Fry [1970] Director/UK Country Chair

Maycross Sports Limited
Incorporated: 14 March 2005
Net Worth Deficit: £5,430 *Total Assets:* £3,316
Registered Office: 256 Martin Way, Morden, Surrey, SM4 4AW
Officers: Mona Mehta, Secretary; Deepak Mehta [1963] Director

Mayfair & Hayes Pharmaceuticals Ltd
Incorporated: 24 February 2015 *Employees:* 1
Net Worth: £8,730 *Total Assets:* £26,024
Registered Office: 11 Portland Road, Edgbaston, Birmingham, B16 9HN
Major Shareholder: Farhan Sharif
Officers: Lubna Sharif [1980] Director

Mayfair Ventures Management Ltd
Incorporated: 30 January 2018
Registered Office: 6 Hampshire House, 12 Hyde Park Place, London, W2 2LH
Major Shareholder: Saba Yussouf
Officers: Saba Yussouf [1988] Director

Mayuveda R & D Limited
Incorporated: 17 November 2017
Registered Office: 467 Great Horton Road, Bradford, BD7 3DL
Shareholders: Mayuri Patel; Birju Rach
Officers: Mayuri Patel [1980] Director/Clinical Psychologist & Ayurvedic Practitioner; Birju Rach [1979] Director/Consultant

MB UN Ltd
Incorporated: 17 October 2012
Net Worth Deficit: £59,175
Registered Office: 11 Ravenspoint Road, Trearddur Bay, Holyhead, Anglesey, LL65 2AX
Major Shareholder: Martin Brook
Officers: Martin Brook [1944] Director

MC2 Therapeutics Limited
Incorporated: 1 February 2005 *Employees:* 10
Previous: Drug Delivery Solutions Limited
Net Worth Deficit: £8,253,964 *Total Assets:* £3,161,694
Registered Office: James House, Emlyn Lane, Leatherhead, Surrey, KT22 7EP
Parent: MC2 Therapeutics ApS
Officers: Richard William Twydell, Secretary; Mads Jorgen Nohr Clausen [1984] Director/Engineer [Danish]; Dr Nigel Crutchley [1977] Director/Business Executive; Jesper Jorn Lange [1967] Director/Lawyer [Danish]; Dr Stephen John Lenon [1956] Director/Scientist; Morten Praestegaard [1971] Director/Business Executive [Danish]

McAleer & Donnelly Pharmacy Limited
Incorporated: 25 February 2000
Net Worth: £1,582,989 *Total Assets:* £1,793,918
Registered Office: 105 Edendoit Road, Pomeroy, Co Tyrone, BT70 2RG
Shareholder: Emos Patrick Donnelly
Officers: Michael McAleer, Secretary; Emos Patrick Donnelly [1968] Director/Pharmacist [Irish]; Michael McAleer [1960] Director/Construction [Irish]

MDI Medical (N.I.) Limited
Incorporated: 29 September 1989
Net Worth Deficit: £176,926 *Total Assets:* £313,460
Registered Office: Unit 4 Windsor Business Park, Boucher Place, Belfast, BT12 6HT
Officers: John Lyng, Secretary; Sean Kiernan [1963] Director [Irish]; John Lyng [1981] Director [Irish]

MDX Healthcare Ltd
Incorporated: 20 October 2011 *Employees:* 11
Net Worth: £245,047 *Total Assets:* £1,193,625
Registered Office: 3rd Floor, The Heights, 59-65 Lowlands Road, Harrow, Middlesex, HA1 3AW
Major Shareholder: Daniel Chun Ying Cheung
Officers: Daniel Chun Ying Cheung [1980] Director; Fung Ha Sharan Chiu [1974] Director [Chinese]; Ho Ching Chung [1984] Director [Chinese]; Shuk Han Poon [1974] Director [Hong Kong]

Medi-Cure Bio Ergonomics Ltd
Incorporated: 13 September 2016
Registered Office: 6-10 Headgate, Colchester, Essex, CO3 3BY
Major Shareholder: Leon Francis
Officers: Leon Sinclair [1973] Director

Medical Ethics UK Limited
Incorporated: 9 August 2017
Registered Office: 2 Sovereign Quay, Havannah Street, Cardiff, CF10 5SF
Officers: Allan Bruce Giffard [1963] Director [Australian]; Meredith Louise Sheil [1964] Director [Australian]

Medical Export Company Limited
Incorporated: 1 October 1981 *Employees:* 3
Net Worth: £816,926 *Total Assets:* £1,108,841
Registered Office: Unit 1 The I O Centre, Valley Drive, Rugby, Warwicks, CV21 1TW
Parent: Chemox Pound Limited
Officers: David George Barnby [1963] Director; Philip Charles Hinton [1967] Director; Gavin David Westley [1970] Director

Medical Regulatory Consulting Ltd
Incorporated: 23 June 2011 *Employees:* 1
Net Worth Deficit: £2,389 *Total Assets:* £6,468
Registered Office: Suite 4, 2 Mannin Way, Lancaster Business Park, Caton Road, Lancaster, LA1 3SU
Major Shareholder: Javeed Anjum Mirza
Officers: Maryam Barlas Mirza, Secretary; Javeed Anjum Mirza [1972] Director/Regulatory Specialist

The Medical Supply Company Limited
Incorporated: 13 February 1962
Registered Office: Aston Down Business Park, Aston Down, Minchinhampton, Stroud, Glos, GL6 8GA
Officers: David Robert Cole, Secretary; David Robert Cole [1948] Director; Richard John Henry Seymour [1942] Director

Medical Technologies Limited
Incorporated: 30 October 2003
Net Worth: £56,148 Total Assets: £61,228
Registered Office: Suite 2, Rosehill, 165 Lutterworth Road, Blaby, Leicester, LE8 4DY
Shareholders: Jeffrey Martin Bucksey; Neil Graham Johnson
Officers: Jeffrey Martin Bucksey, Secretary; Jeffrey Martin Bucksey [1951] Engineering Director; Neil Graham Johnson [1961] Managing Director

Medicaleaf Limited
Incorporated: 4 February 2019
Registered Office: Suite 13, 23 Mount Pleasant Road, Tunbridge Wells, Kent, TN1 1NT
Shareholders: Anthony Ellis; Philip Mark Cox
Officers: Anthony Ellis [1948] Director/Business Consultant; Paul Anthony Ford [1964] Director

Medicam Limited
Incorporated: 2 August 1999
Registered Office: Betsoms Farmhouse, Pilgrims Way, Westerham, Kent, TN16 2DP
Shareholders: Marek Czosnyka; Professor John Douglas Pickard
Officers: Dr David Brian Ashton Hutchinson, Secretary; Marek Czosnyka [1955] Director/Senior Research Associate; Professor Peter John Ashton Hutchinson [1965] Director/Professor of Neurosurgery; Professor John Douglas Pickard [1946] Director/Emeritus Professor of Neurosurgery

Medicann Pharma (UK) Ltd
Incorporated: 16 August 2018
Registered Office: 8 Wellington Gardens, Greenwich, London, SE7 7PH
Shareholder: Ross Smith
Officers: Ross Smith [1963] Director [New Zealander]

Medicareplus International Ltd
Incorporated: 23 January 2007 Employees: 31
Net Worth: £443,995 Total Assets: £2,495,702
Registered Office: Chemilines House, Alperton Lane, Wembley, Middlesex, HA0 1DX
Shareholders: Kamlesh Palana; Chemilines Group Holdings Limited
Officers: Ravindra Prabhudas Karia, Secretary; Jagdish Prabhudas Karia [1958] Director; Ravindra Prabhudas Karia [1953] Director; Kamlesh Pallana [1955] Director

Medicareplus Limited
Incorporated: 20 September 2012
Registered Office: Chemilines House, Alperton Lane, Wembley, Middlesex, HA0 1DX
Parent: Medicareplus International Limited
Officers: Jagdish Prabhudas Karia [1958] Director; Ravindra Prabhudas Karia [1953] Director; Kamlesh Pallana [1955] Director

Medicleanse Limited
Incorporated: 17 March 2017
Registered Office: Unit 5a, Brailes Industrial Estate, Winderton Lane, Brailes, Banbury, Oxon, OX15 5JW
Shareholders: Graham Francis Warmington; Mary Doreen Lloyd
Officers: Graham Francis Warmington, Secretary; Mary Doreen Lloyd [1952] Director and Scientist; Graham Francis Warmington [1949] Director

Medicol Limited
Incorporated: 27 May 1988
Net Worth: £303,320 Total Assets: £428,545
Registered Office: Churchdown Chambers, Bordyke, Tonbridge, Kent, TN9 1NR
Shareholder: Mohammed Hanif Rahman
Officers: Nasreen Rahman, Secretary; Mahammed Usmaan Hanif Rahman [1988] Director; Mahammed Armaan Hanif Rahman [1990] Director; Mahommed Hanif Rahman [1965] Director/Consultant; Dr Sakhawhat Hussain Rahman [1973] Director/Registrar of Medicine

Medics Kingdom Limited
Incorporated: 31 January 2019
Registered Office: 150 Aldersgate Street, London, EC1A 4AB
Parent: Win-Medics Holdings Limited
Officers: Takahisa Karita [1970] Director [Japanese]; Shigeru Shiraki [1977] Director [Japanese]

Medicus Integrated Medicine Limited
Incorporated: 12 November 2014
Registered Office: 10 Hangerfield Court, Northampton, NN3 8LL
Major Shareholder: Adam Przygoda
Officers: Adam Przygoda [1972] Director

Medina Corp. Ltd
Incorporated: 27 November 2013
Net Worth: £1,000 Total Assets: £1,000
Registered Office: 20-22 Wenlock Road, London, N1 7GU
Major Shareholder: Aquilar Cuevas Yeuby Sohanna
Officers: Aquilar Cuevas Yeuby Sohanna [1982] Director [Dominican]

Medisante Limited
Incorporated: 11 June 2010 Employees: 3
Net Worth: £121,403 Total Assets: £273,248
Registered Office: 37 Great Pulteney Street, Bath, BA2 4DA
Major Shareholder: Stephen William Riley
Officers: Stephen William Riley, Secretary; Stephen William Riley [1948] Director; Dr Christopher Smejkal [1976] Director/Regulatory Consultant

Mediskills Limited
Incorporated: 4 August 1998
Net Worth: £64,086 Total Assets: £108,034
Registered Office: Summit House, 4-5 Mitchell Street, Edinburgh, EH6 7BD
Major Shareholder: John Terence Kelly
Officers: John Terence Kelly, Secretary; John Terence Kelly [1948] Director/Marketing Consultant; Pushparani Kelly [1953] Director/Administrator

Medison Pharma Limited
Incorporated: 3 October 2013
Net Worth: £5,422 Total Assets: £23,045
Registered Office: 1a Crown Lane, London, SW16 6AY
Major Shareholder: Alexey Egorov
Officers: Alexey Egorov [1961] Director [Russian]

Medlabs Europe Ltd
Incorporated: 29 April 2016 Employees: 1
Net Worth: £100 Total Assets: £100
Registered Office: Craven House, 40-44 Uxbridge Road, Ealing, London, W5 2BS
Major Shareholder: Marian Rozewicki
Officers: Marian Rozewicki [1957] Director [Polish]

Medley Pharma Limited
Incorporated: 30 August 2014 Employees: 6
Net Worth: £794,245 Total Assets: £1,342,462
Registered Office: Unit 2a Olympic Way, Sefton Business Park, Bootle, Merseyside, L30 1RD
Major Shareholder: Sarosh Sami Khatib
Officers: Sarosh Sami Khatib [1964] Managing Director [Indian]

Medlock Medical Limited
Incorporated: 26 November 2003 Employees: 168
Net Worth: £5,538,000 Total Assets: £18,744,000
Registered Office: Unity House, Medlock Street, Oldham, Lancs, OL1 3HS
Parent: MHC UK Ltd
Officers: Christopher John Stubbs, Secretary; Stefan Ulf Fristedt [1966] Finance Director [Swedish]; Phil Anthony Hague [1962] Director/Factory Manager; Richard Twomey [1964] Director

Medpro Health Limited
Incorporated: 13 August 2013
Previous: Pragen Pharma Limited
Net Worth Deficit: £35,144 Total Assets: £27,356
Registered Office: First Floor, Roxburghe House, 273-287 Regent Street, London, W1B 2HA
Parent: London Pharma Capital Limited
Officers: Dr Simon James Dorris [1971] Director; Jonathan George Farrington [1969] Director

Medtrack Ltd
Incorporated: 25 February 2019
Registered Office: 20-22 Wenlock Road, London, N1 7GU
Major Shareholder: Pervez Akhter
Officers: Wajid Ali [1961] Director

A. Menarini Diagnostics Limited
Incorporated: 7 April 1987 Employees: 75
Net Worth: £3,528,276 Total Assets: £9,254,251
Registered Office: 405 Wharfedale Road, Winnersh, Wokingham, Berks, RG41 5RA
Officers: Gianni Masselli, Secretary; Gianni Masselli [1965] Director/Controller [Italian]; Nico Noel Andre Samaille [1971] Director [Belgian]; Paul Tolan [1960] Director

Mendelikabs Europe Limited
Incorporated: 8 July 2015
Registered Office: Unit G.07, The Light Box, 111 Power Road, Chiswick, London, W4 5PY
Parent: Mendelikabs Inc
Officers: Bruno Maranda [1975] Director/Physician [Canadian]

Mentholatum Company Limited (The)
Incorporated: 7 April 1924 Employees: 98
Net Worth: £17,919,000 Total Assets: £25,760,000
Registered Office: Tricor Suite, 4th Floor, 50 Mark Lane, London, EC3R 7QR
Officers: Linda Anne McColgan, Secretary; Colin Martin Brown [1967] Director of R&QD; Steve Hossenlopp [1965] Director/Chief Financial Officer [American]; Linda Anne McColgan [1972] Finance Director; Maciej Adam Misztak [1972] Business Development Director [Polish]; Masaya Saito [1963] Director/Company Executive [Japanese]; Robert William Yateman [1960] Managing Director

Mento-Neem International Ltd
Incorporated: 1 February 2012
Net Worth Deficit: £10,165
Registered Office: Old Bakery, 22 Beaumont Road, Headington, Oxford, OX3 8JN
Major Shareholder: Henrik Blicher Hansen
Officers: Cecilia Anita Bradshaw [1958] Director; Henrik Blicher Hansen [1956] Director [Danish]

Merad Pharmaceuticals Limited
Incorporated: 29 June 2000 Employees: 4
Net Worth: £12,531 Total Assets: £83,608
Registered Office: Lewis House, Great Chesterford Court, Great Chesterford, Essex, CB10 1PF
Shareholders: Narinder Kumar; Rajinder Kumar
Officers: Narinder Kumar, Secretary; Narinder Kumar [1961] Director; Dr Rajinder Kumar [1955] Director/Physician

Merck Serono Europe Limited
Incorporated: 28 March 1995 Employees: 5
Net Worth: £832,662 Total Assets: £1,333,400
Registered Office: 56 Marsh Wall, London, E14 9TP
Parent: Merck KGaA
Officers: Peter Biro [1967] Director/US Certified Public Accountant [Dutch]; Sandrine Courtheoux Batilliet [1957] Director [French]; Andrew Galazka [1955] Director [Swiss]

Merck Sharp & Dohme Limited
Incorporated: 25 September 1964 Employees: 1,162
Net Worth: £440,820,992 Total Assets: £607,619,008
Registered Office: Hertford Road, Hoddesdon, Herts, EN11 9BU
Parent: Merck Sharp & Dohme (Holdings) Limited
Officers: Richard Robinski, Secretary; Louise Jane Houson [1976] Director; Simon Nicholson [1975] Director; Ebru Can Temucin [1972] Director [Turkish]

Mercury Pharma Group Limited
Incorporated: 23 December 1988
Net Worth: £126,976,456 Total Assets: £202,432,240
Registered Office: Capital House, 85 King William Street, London, EC4N 7BL
Parent: Concordia Investment Holdings (UK) Limited
Officers: Robert Sully, Secretary; Adeel Ahmad [1973] Director/Vice-President, Finance [Canadian]; Graeme Neville Duncan [1973] Director/Chief Executive Officer; Vikram Laxman Kamath [1977] Director/Vice President Finance and Group Controller [Indian]

Mercury Pharmaceuticals Limited
Incorporated: 12 June 1991 Employees: 13
Net Worth: £6,743,635 Total Assets: £44,843,036
Registered Office: Capital House, 85 King William Street, London, EC4N 7BL
Parent: Mercury Pharma Group Limited
Officers: Robert Sully, Secretary; Adeel Ahmad [1973] Director/Chief Financial Officer [Canadian]; Graeme Neville Duncan [1973] Director/Chief Executive Officer; Vikram Laxman Kamath [1977] Director/Vice President Finance and Group Controller [Indian]

Merial Limited
Incorporated: 7 March 1997
Net Worth: £194,750,848 Total Assets: £272,727,264
Registered Office: Ellesfield Avenue, Bracknell, Berks, RG12 8YS
Officers: Marshall Burke Barton, Secretary; Christian Orth [1962] Director/Senior Vice President Finance & CFO [Swiss]

Merrimack Pharmaceuticals U.K. Limited
Incorporated: 16 June 2010
Registered Office: 21 Holborn Viaduct, London, EC1A 2DY
Parent: Merrimack Pharmaceuticals, Inc.
Officers: Jeffrey a Munsie, Secretary; Jeffrey a Munsie [1977] Director/Corporate Counsel [American]; Michael Robert Slater [1946] Director/Head of Regulatory Affairs [American]

Mexichem Medical HFA Trading Limited
Incorporated: 7 February 2014
Registered Office: c/o Medichem UK Limited, The Heath Business & Technical Park, Runcorn, Cheshire, WA7 4QX

MHR Pharmacy Ltd
Incorporated: 8 September 2018
Registered Office: 65 Broadway, Haslingden, Rossendale, Lancs, BB4 4ES
Major Shareholder: Muhammad Hamza Rahman
Officers: Muhammad Hamza Rahman [1994] Director

Microbiome Technologies Limited
Incorporated: 31 July 2017
Registered Office: 50 Galley Hill View, Bexhill on Sea, E Sussex, TN40 1SX
Major Shareholder: Hon Adam Smith
Officers: Hon Adam Smith [1964] Director

Microfluidx Ltd
Incorporated: 25 October 2018
Registered Office: Flat 4, 36 Clifton Gardens, London, W9 1AU
Major Shareholder: Antoine Jean Espinet
Officers: Dr. Antoine Jean Espinet [1987] Director/Chief Executive [French]

Microgenetics Limited
Incorporated: 11 December 2014 *Employees:* 1
Net Worth Deficit: £255,005
Registered Office: 3 Corsham Science Park, Park Lane, Corsham, Wilts, SN13 9FU
Parent: Qualasept Pharmaxo Holdings Limited
Officers: Christopher James Fountain [1966] Director/Chartered Accountant; Tamryn Jo Hassel [1982] Director; Christopher Dean Watt [1968] Director

Micropharm Limited
Incorporated: 18 August 1998 *Employees:* 45
Net Worth: £2,702,750 *Total Assets:* £6,670,762
Registered Office: Units F & G, Station Road Industrial Estate, Station Road, Newcastle Emlyn, Carmarthenshire, SA38 9BY
Parent: Flynn Pharma (Holdings) Limited
Officers: Ian Fergus Cameron [1961] Director; Doctor Ruth Elizabeth Coxon [1943] Director/Clinical Research Scientist; Dr David William Fakes [1960] Director; Professor John Landon [1931] Director/Doctor of Medicine; David Edward Walters [1951] Director

Microsens Biophage Limited
Incorporated: 28 June 1999 *Employees:* 7
Net Worth Deficit: £1,204,927 *Total Assets:* £362,622
Registered Office: LBIC, 2 Royal College Street, London, NW1 0NH
Officers: Dr Stuart Mark Wilson, Secretary; William Alan Hyde [1936] Director/Microbiologist Consultant; Dr Stuart Mark Wilson [1963] Director/Scientist

Microskin PLC
Incorporated: 11 December 2012 *Employees:* 7
Net Worth: £12,656,676 *Total Assets:* £14,849,522
Registered Office: 27 Old Gloucester Street, London, WC1N 3AX
Shareholders: Barry Charles Amor; Barry Sean Lowndes
Officers: Barry Charles Amor [1949] Director/Consultant [Australian]; Barry Sean Lowndes [1969] Director/Manager [Australian]; Scott Malcolm McTaggart [1947] Director/Geophysicist [Australian]; David Tom Merson [1941] Director [Australian]

Microspec Ltd
Incorporated: 14 July 2005 *Employees:* 15
Net Worth: £37,675 *Total Assets:* £488,539
Registered Office: 10 Stadium Court, Stadium Road, Wirral, Merseyside, CH62 3RP
Major Shareholder: Alan Christie
Officers: Jennifer Louise Caldwell [1987] Director; Alan Christie [1968] Director/Biologist

Microvisk Technologies International Limited
Incorporated: 23 March 2016
Net Worth: £100 *Total Assets:* £100
Registered Office: Innovation House, Unit 4 Ffordd Richard Davies, St Asaph Business Park, St Asaph, Denbighshire, LL17 0LJ
Shareholder: Nilesh Nathwani
Officers: Parag Khiroya [1963] Director/Chartered Accountant; Nilesh Nathwani [1961] Director/Pharmacist

Milepitch Ltd
Incorporated: 23 July 2018
Registered Office: 214a Kettering Road, Northampton, NN1 4BN
Shareholders: Kimberly Morales; William Bernard Morrell
Officers: Kimberly Morales [1997] Director [Filipino]

Milewackers Ltd
Incorporated: 23 July 2018
Registered Office: Unit 3 Trinity Centre, Park Farm Industrial Estate, Wellingborough, Northants, NN8 6ZB
Shareholders: Alexander Garcia; William Bernard Morrell
Officers: Alexander Garcia [1957] Director [Filipino]

Millbrook (NI) Limited
Incorporated: 17 September 1982
Registered Office: Old Belfast Road, Millbrook, Larne, Co Antrim, BT40 2SH
Parent: Chilcott UK Limited
Officers: Dean Michael Cooper [1972] Director/Chartered Accountant; Kim Innes [1968] Director/General Manager

Millicent Pharma (NI) Limited
Incorporated: 7 June 2018
Registered Office: Old Belfast Road, Millbrook, Larne, Co Antrim, BT40 2SH
Parent: Millicent Pharma Ltd
Officers: Dr Anthony John David Jackson [1957] Director/Business Consultant

Millpledge Limited
Incorporated: 10 May 1976 *Employees:* 46
Net Worth: £5,118,770 *Total Assets:* £5,821,375
Registered Office: 1 Holly Street, Sheffield, S1 2GT
Officers: Ian Patrick Campbell [1955] Director/Chartered Accountant; Nathan James Smith [1976] Director/Commercial Manager; Leah Jane Styring [1978] Director/Operations Manager; Richard Ian Talbot [1978] Director/Finance Manager; Philip Neil Wood [1965] Director/Group Production Manager

Miltenyi Biotec Limited
Incorporated: 30 August 1995 Employees: 32
Net Worth: £483,259 Total Assets: £3,925,877
Registered Office: Miltenyi Biotec Ltd, Almac House, Church Lane, Bisley, Woking, Surrey, GU24 9DR
Parent: Miltenyi Biotec GmbH
Officers: Michele Louise Giroux, Secretary; Stefan Gyorgy Miltenyi [1961] Managing Director [German]

Milton Pharmaceutical Company UK Limited
Incorporated: 4 April 2001
Net Worth: £1,290,471 Total Assets: £2,509,607
Registered Office: Mitchells, 41 Rodney Road, Cheltenham, Glos, GL50 1HX
Major Shareholder: Christian Laine
Officers: Christian Laine [1963] Managing Director [French]

Mineral Pharma Limited
Incorporated: 21 February 2018
Registered Office: 2nd Floor, College House, 17 King Edwards Road, Ruislip, Middlesex, HA4 7AE
Major Shareholder: Afrasyiab Hashimi
Officers: Sabir Khan [1987] Director [Afghan]; Shuokat Khan [1977] Director [Afghan]

Miongam Ltd
Incorporated: 20 August 2018
Registered Office: 83 Coney Crescent, Crosby, Liverpool, L23 9YW
Major Shareholder: Domonic Robertini
Officers: Domonic Robertini [1957] Director/Consultant

Miracol Ltd
Incorporated: 31 October 2016
Registered Office: 1st Floor Office, Aspen House, West Terrace, Folkestone, Kent, CT20 1TH
Officers: Paul Pearson [1957] Director

Mirroman Ltd
Incorporated: 26 January 2017
Registered Office: 29 Alexandra Gardens, Chiswick, London, W4 2RY
Major Shareholder: Djan Ivan Mirroman
Officers: Lady Mimi Kassie Mirroman, Secretary; Lord El Elohim [1988] Director/Mechatronic Engineer Plumber; Lady Sandra Karpinska [1995] Company Secretary/Director [Polish]; Lord Djan Ivan Mirroman [1988] Director; Dr Roman Sabirov [1961] Director/Underwriter

Mirror 5 Ltd
Incorporated: 14 September 2015
Net Worth Deficit: £6,299
Registered Office: 16 Graham Road, West Kirby, Wirral, Merseyside, CH48 5DW
Major Shareholder: Michael James Howell
Officers: Catherine Moya Howell [1982] Director/Teacher; Michael James Howell [1982] Director/Engineer

Miss Derriere Ltd
Incorporated: 2 October 2015
Registered Office: 13 Broadway, Leyland, Lancs, PR25 3EH
Major Shareholder: Andrew Roland Brown
Officers: Andrew Roland Brown [1956] Director

MK Ventures Limited
Incorporated: 24 May 2004
Net Worth: £634 Total Assets: £9,638
Registered Office: 50 Lillie Road, London, SW6 1TN
Major Shareholder: Madhu Kapisthalam
Officers: Dr Manisha Kulkarni, Secretary; Madhu Kapisthalam [1966] Director/Management Consultant

Molecular Profiles Ltd
Incorporated: 16 January 2015
Registered Office: 8 Orchard Place, Nottingham Business Park, Nottingham, NG8 6PX
Parent: Juniper Pharma Services Limited
Officers: Kirk Walsh, Secretary; Jonathan Arnold [1965] Director/President Oral Drug Delivery; Dr Claire Elizabeth Madden-Smith [1973] Director; Alessandro Maselli [1972] Director/SVP Operations [Italian]; Dr Nikin Patel [1972] Director; Kirk Walsh [1980] Director/VP Finance

Molnlycke Health Care Limited
Incorporated: 12 January 1998 Employees: 168
Net Worth: £2,379,000 Total Assets: £23,249,000
Registered Office: Unity House, Medlock Street, Oldham, Lancs, OL1 3HS
Officers: Christopher John Stubbs, Secretary; Stefan Ulf Fristedt [1966] Finance Director [Swedish]; Nicholas Andrew Rothwell [1973] Director/General Manager; Richard Twomey [1964] Director

Morar Design Limited
Incorporated: 27 November 2013 Employees: 1
Net Worth: £61,682 Total Assets: £102,328
Registered Office: Morar, Closeburn, Thornhill, Dumfries, DG3 5HW
Major Shareholder: Jaqueline Jessie Carson
Officers: Jaqueline Jessie Carson [1966] Director

More Poland Limited
Incorporated: 16 November 2016
Net Worth Deficit: £6,129 Total Assets: £169
Registered Office: 2a South Street, Southville, Bristol, BS3 3AX
Major Shareholder: Katarzyna Koziak
Officers: Professor Katarzyna Koziak [1967] Director/Biologist [Polish]

Morningside Healthcare Limited
Incorporated: 14 March 2001 Employees: 7
Net Worth: £8,162,035 Total Assets: £12,387,210
Registered Office: Morningside House, Unit C Harcourt Way, Meridian Business Park, Leicester, LE19 1WP
Officers: Danesh Vinodkumar Gadhia [1965] Director; Sanjay Kishan Gadhia [1978] Director

Morningside Pharmaceuticals Limited
Incorporated: 18 December 1991 Employees: 50
Net Worth: £6,005,035 Total Assets: £20,841,896
Registered Office: Nene House, 4 Rushmills, Northampton, NN4 7YB
Parent: Remedi Medical Holdings Limited
Officers: Monisha Nikesh Kotecha, Secretary; Monisha Nikesh Kotecha [1969] Director; Dr Nikesh Rasiklal Kotecha [1966] Director

Moroccan Natural Resources Limited
Incorporated: 26 March 2010 Employees: 1
Net Worth Deficit: £26,612 Total Assets: £17,071
Registered Office: Flat D, 138-140 Shirland Road, London, W9 2BT
Major Shareholder: Carole Fraser
Officers: Raymond Charles Verrall, Secretary; Carole Fraser [1940] Director; Raymond Charles Verrall [1944] Director

Mr Derriere Ltd
Incorporated: 26 November 2015
Registered Office: 13 Broadway, Leyland, Lancs, PR25 3EH
Major Shareholder: Andrew Roland Brown
Officers: Andrew Roland Brown [1956] Director

Muamko Uzuri Limited
Incorporated: 22 September 2017
Registered Office: 1b Harcourt Road, London, SE4 2AJ
Major Shareholder: Asmara Mitchell
Officers: Asmara Mitchell [1990] Director

Mudd By Alix Ltd.
Incorporated: 13 April 2017
Net Worth: £1,900 *Total Assets:* £1,900
Registered Office: Faraday Wharf, Holt Street, Birmingham, B7 4BB
Major Shareholder: Alixzondra Samuda
Officers: Alixzondra Samuda [1987] Director

Muhammad 786 Limited
Incorporated: 1 December 2015
Net Worth Deficit: £34,285 *Total Assets:* £26,723
Registered Office: 2 Meadow Court, Allerton, Bradford, W Yorks, BD15 9JZ
Officers: Mohammed Yaqoob [1949] Director

Mumma Love Organics Limited
Incorporated: 27 January 2015
Net Worth Deficit: £18,510 *Total Assets:* £546
Registered Office: Mayfield, Avisford Park Road, Walberton, Arundel, W Sussex, BN18 0AP
Shareholders: Sam Leon Quinn; Clifford Moss; Samantha Quinn
Officers: Sam Leon Quinn [1977] Director/Carpenter; Samantha Quinn [1981] Director/Skincare Provider

Musclemantra Ltd
Incorporated: 6 May 2016
Previous: Spier Welt Ltd
Registered Office: 71-75 Shelton Street, Covent Garden, London, WC2H 9JQ
Officers: Munit Sachdeva [1976] Director [Indian]; Rahib Sachdeva [1990] Director [Indian]

MW Encap (Holdings) Limited
Incorporated: 29 February 1996 *Employees:* 135
Net Worth: £631,496 *Total Assets:* £13,716,701
Registered Office: Suite 1, 3rd Floor, 11-12 St James's Square, London, SW1Y 4LB
Officers: Richard Paul Coop, Secretary; Christian Steven Dowdeswell [1966] Director; Dr Jane Fraser [1973] Director

MW Encap Limited
Incorporated: 6 January 1994 *Employees:* 128
Net Worth Deficit: £910,532 *Total Assets:* £11,825,646
Registered Office: Suite 1, 3rd Floor, 11-12 St James's Square, London, SW1Y 4LB
Parent: MW Encap (Holdings) Ltd
Officers: Richard Paul Coop, Secretary; Christian Steven Dowdeswell [1966] Director; Dr Jane Fraser [1973] Director; Olivier Gregory J. Van Hoorebeke [1972] Director/Head of Value Chain Management [Belgian]

My Shea Limited
Incorporated: 3 August 2011
Net Worth: £6,124 *Total Assets:* £19,600
Registered Office: 65 Navarre Gardens, Romford, Essex, RM5 2HL
Officers: Rosemary Agyeman-Kuma [1975] Director/Chemical Engineer [Ghanaian]

MyHairDoctor Ltd
Incorporated: 14 January 2015
Net Worth Deficit: £159,683 *Total Assets:* £2,778
Registered Office: 44 Hardinge Road, London, NW10 3PJ
Major Shareholder: Guy Dominic Parsons
Officers: Guy Parsons [1965] Director/Hair Product Development

Myoproducts Limited
Incorporated: 2 April 2012
Net Worth: £485 *Total Assets:* £3,400
Registered Office: 115 Brunswick Park Road, London, N11 1EA
Shareholders: David Lintonbon; Stefania Gwendolin Lintonbon
Officers: David Lintonbon [1959] Director/Osteopath; Stefania Gwendolin Lintonbon [1952] Director [American]

N.T. Laboratories Limited
Incorporated: 23 June 1982 *Employees:* 15
Net Worth: £509,970 *Total Assets:* £696,199
Registered Office: Unit B, Manor Farm, Tonbridge Road, Wateringbury, Kent, ME18 5PP
Parent: Milava Limited
Officers: Paul Richard Hooper [1978] Director/Sales Manager

N2SA Limited
Incorporated: 11 August 2017
Registered Office: 130 Old Street, London, EC1V 9BD
Officers: Srikanth Injarapu [1984] Director/Consultant [Indian]; Ndabezinhle Ndlovu [1973] Director/Consultant

N9NE Cosmetics Ltd
Incorporated: 17 September 2016
Net Worth: £445 *Total Assets:* £445
Registered Office: 22 Ludlow Close, St Pauls, Bristol, BS2 9JQ
Major Shareholder: Charmaine Lynette Angela Lawrence
Officers: Charmaine Lynette Angela Lawrence [1984] Director/Cosmetic Beauty Products

Nabros Pharma (UK) Ltd
Incorporated: 8 October 2018
Registered Office: 79 College Road, Harrow, Middlesex, HA1 1BD
Major Shareholder: Narendrakumar Laxmansingh Darbar
Officers: Narenrdakumar Laxmansingh Darbar, Secretary; Narendrakumar Laxmansingh Darbar [1980] Director/Business Development Consultant [Indian]

Nacur Healthcare Ltd
Incorporated: 8 July 2005
Net Worth Deficit: £103,619 *Total Assets:* £13,162
Registered Office: Suite 1, 3rd Floor, 11-12 St James's Square, London, SW1Y 4LB
Major Shareholder: Jonny Spendler
Officers: Kubilay Spendler, Company Secretary [German]; Jonny Spendler [1967] Director [German]

Nagashree Ltd
Incorporated: 13 October 2011
Net Worth: £2,370 *Total Assets:* £8,495
Registered Office: Flat 8 Wrights Court, 6 Jefferson Place, Bromley, Kent, BR2 9FX
Major Shareholder: Srinath Nagaraj
Officers: Vasudha Chandrashekar [1983] Director [Indian]; Srinath Nagaraj [1977] Director [Indian]

Naia (London) Limited
Incorporated: 9 June 2015
Net Worth: £10 Total Assets: £10
Registered Office: c/o Lord Razzall, 7th Floor, 39 St James' Street, London, SW1A 1JD
Officers: Mark Nicholas Kenneth Bagnall [1957] Director; Hector Daniel Perez [1949] Director [American]

Nano and Nature Pharma Ltd
Incorporated: 28 December 2017
Registered Office: Kemp House, 152-160 City Road, London, EC1V 2NX
Shareholders: Ibrahim Alhariri; Mohammad Al Hariri
Officers: Ahmad Alhariri, Secretary; Dr Mohammad Al Hariri [1984] Director/Operation Manager [German]; Dr Ibrahim Alhariri [1971] Director/Executive Manager [Syrian]

Nanomed Ltd
Incorporated: 17 January 2017
Registered Office: Flat 15, 39 Bramham Gardens, London, SW5 0HG
Shareholders: Jeremy Llewellyn Smith; Matei Foit
Officers: Matei Foit [1989] Director/Business Consultant [Romanian]; Jeremy Llewellyn Smith [1994] Director/Engineer

Nanopharm Limited
Incorporated: 11 February 2002 Employees: 7
Net Worth: £1,632,085 Total Assets: £1,692,641
Registered Office: Fiveways, 57-59 Hatfield Road, Potters Bar, Herts, EN6 1HS
Shareholders: SBMS Enterprises Limited; Silures Limited
Officers: Mark Rowland Clement, Secretary; Prof Robert Price [1970] Director/Scientist; Dr Jagdeep Singh Shur [1980] Director

Nanotherapeutics UK Limited
Incorporated: 22 November 2016
Registered Office: 16th Floor, Citypoint, One Ropemaker Street, London, EC2Y 9AW
Officers: James Michael Matthew [1953] Director/Chief Financial Officer [American]

Napp Pharmaceutical Group Limited
Incorporated: 27 July 1966
Net Worth: £82,254,000 Total Assets: £87,942,000
Registered Office: Unit 196 Cambridge Science Park, Milton Road, Cambridge, CB4 0AB
Parent: Napp Pharmaceutical Holdings Limited
Officers: Stuart David Baker [1935] Director/Lawyer [American]; Ake Gunnar Wikstrom [1951] Director/Advisor [Swedish]

Napp Pharmaceutical Holdings Limited
Incorporated: 19 December 1997 Employees: 612
Net Worth: £191,744,000 Total Assets: £304,665,984
Registered Office: Unit 196 Cambridge Science Park, Milton Road, Cambridge, CB4 0AB
Shareholder: Stuart David Baker
Officers: Stuart David Baker [1935] Director/Lawyer [American]; Ake Gunnar Wikstrom [1951] Director/Advisor [Swedish]

Naturafam Limited
Incorporated: 16 August 2018
Registered Office: 71-75 Shelton Street, Covent Garden, London, WC2H 9JQ
Major Shareholder: John Edem Yao Afeeva
Officers: John Edem Yao Afeeva, Secretary; John Edem Yao Afeeva [1981] Director/Engineer [Ghanaian]

The Natural Cornish Company Ltd
Incorporated: 12 July 2011
Net Worth Deficit: £6,277 Total Assets: £6
Registered Office: Bohemia, Nancledra, Penzance, Cornwall, TR20 8LP
Parent: Abra Cosmetics & Services S.L.
Officers: William Douglas Clarke, Secretary; William Douglas Clarke [1949] Director; Jaime Jauregui [1960] Director [Spanish]

Natural Dermatology Ltd
Incorporated: 28 December 2011
Net Worth Deficit: £8,632 Total Assets: £2,008
Registered Office: Kilsby Wiliams, Cedar House, Hazell Drive, Newport, NP10 8FY
Major Shareholder: Jordan Marc Sully
Officers: Jordan Marc Sully [1984] Director/Natural Dermatology

Natural Miracles Limited
Incorporated: 5 February 2019
Registered Office: 6 Cameron Road, Widnes, Cheshire, WA8 7LA
Major Shareholder: Leon Phillips
Officers: Steven Leadbetter [1993] Director; Leon Phillips [1982] Director

Natural Way Limited
Incorporated: 7 January 1997
Net Worth: £3,823 Total Assets: £6,023
Registered Office: Beechwood House, 25 Ralliwood Road, Ashtead, Surrey, KT21 1DD
Officers: Brennig Jonathan Bryan Davis, Secretary; Brennig Jonathan Bryan Davis [1973] Director/Engineering; Rosemary Jane Davis [1970] Finance Director; Dr Walter Bryan Davis [1943] Director/Consultant

Nature + Nurture Limited
Incorporated: 31 July 2017
Registered Office: 10 Edenfield Close, Redditch, Worcs, B97 6TP
Officers: Azeem Mohammed [1980] Director

ND Pharma & Biotech Ltd
Incorporated: 30 October 2012
Registered Office: Kemp House, 152-160 City Road, London, EC1V 2NX
Major Shareholder: Jose Manuel Lopez
Officers: Dr. Jose Manuel Lopez [1966] Director/Consultant [Spanish]; Miquel Vericat Vidal [1978] Director/Businessman [Spanish]

Nejati Dental Instruments and Supplies (UK) Ltd
Incorporated: 14 July 2005
Registered Office: Latif House, First Way, Wembley, Middlesex, HA9 0JD
Major Shareholder: Amir Reza Latif

Nektar Therapeutics UK Limited
Incorporated: 5 December 1994
Net Worth Deficit: £83,844 Total Assets: £16,113
Registered Office: Elizabeth House, 13-19 Queen Street, Leeds, LS1 2TW
Parent: Nektar Therapeutics
Officers: Gil Labrucherie, Secretary/Director [American]; Carlo Difonzo [1951] Director [American]; Gil Labrucherie [1971] Director [American]; Jillian Thomsen [1965] Director [American]

Nelovy Healthcare Ltd
Incorporated: 24 August 2016
Registered Office: 3 Gower Street, London, WC1E 6HA
Officers: Ibrahim Abdelrazik Albayoomi Fouda [1978] Director [Egyptian]

A Nelson & Co Limited
Incorporated: 1 August 1930 *Employees:* 168
Net Worth: £5,714,000 *Total Assets:* £33,033,000
Registered Office: Nelsons House, 83 Parkside, Wimbledon, London, SW19 5LP
Parent: Nelson & Russell Holdings Limited
Officers: Claire Ferguson [1977] Director; Gary McGaghey [1968] Director/Chief Financial Officer [South African]; Patrick Russell Wilson [1965] Director; Robert Nelson Wilson [1962] Director/Chairman

Nelson & Russell Holdings Limited
Incorporated: 18 November 1999 *Employees:* 274
Net Worth: £9,158,000 *Total Assets:* £31,932,000
Registered Office: Nelsons House, 83 Parkside, Wimbledon, London, SW19 5LP
Shareholders: Robert Nelson Wilson; Patrick Russell Wilson
Officers: Claire Ferguson [1977] Director; Gary McGaghey [1968] Director/Chief Financial Officer [South African]; Patrick Russell Wilson [1965] Director; Robert Nelson Wilson [1962] Director/Chairman

Nelsons Aura Limited
Incorporated: 18 November 1999
Registered Office: Nelsons House, 83 Parkside, Wimbledon, London, SW19 5LP
Officers: Robert Nelson Wilson [1962] Director/Chairman

Neo Laboratories Limited
Incorporated: 26 July 1957 *Employees:* 3
Net Worth: £81,794 *Total Assets:* £84,823
Registered Office: Jubilee House, 3 The Drive, Great Warley, Brentwood, Essex, CM13 3FR
Shareholders: Simon Robert Geoffrey Tate; Mary Joan Tate
Officers: Mary Joan Tate, Secretary; Mary Joan Tate [1945] Director; Simon Robert Geoffrey Tate [1977] Director; Richard Earl Warriner [1956] Director

Neoceuticals Limited
Incorporated: 12 April 2005 *Employees:* 4
Net Worth: £434,991 *Total Assets:* £683,471
Registered Office: The Innovation Centre, Innovation Way, Heslington, York, YO10 5DG
Officers: Susan Proctor, Secretary; Brenda Margaret Adams [1942] Director; Dr Rodney Harry Adams [1944] Director; Dr Andrew Brodrick [1951] Director; Deborah Jane Brodrick [1953] Director

Neomedic Limited
Incorporated: 4 November 1997
Net Worth: £667,587 *Total Assets:* £1,256,184
Registered Office: 97 High Street, Rickmansworth, Herts, WD3 1EF
Shareholders: Husein Mohamedraza Sultanali Gulamhusein; Fatema Gulamhusein
Officers: Fatema Gulamhusein, Secretary; Husein Mohamedraza Sultanali Gulamhusein [1972] Director

New Cheshire Salt Works Limited
Incorporated: 18 December 1923
Net Worth: £1,870,000 *Total Assets:* £1,870,000
Registered Office: Mond House, Winnington, Northwich, Cheshire, CW8 4DT
Parent: British Salt Limited
Officers: Jonathan Laurence Abbotts [1964] Director; Dr Ladan Iravanian [1960] Director

New Directions Europe Ltd
Incorporated: 14 February 2012 *Employees:* 2
Net Worth: £55,353 *Total Assets:* £129,612
Registered Office: 19 Sandleheath Industrial Estate, Fordingbridge, Hants, SP6 1PA
Major Shareholder: Patricia Ann Gilbert
Officers: Patricia Ann Gilbert, Secretary; Domenic Anthony Ardino [1966] Director [Australian]; Patricia Ann Gilbert [1956] Director; Robert Patrick Gilbert [1996] Director/Operations Manager; Kamal Jit Kaur Gill [1966] Director [Australian]

New Eleusis Limited
Incorporated: 15 July 2013
Registered Office: 71 Queen Victoria Street, London, EC4V 4BE
Officers: Lady Amanda Claire Feilding [1943] Director

New Nordic Limited
Incorporated: 29 December 1995 *Employees:* 3
Net Worth: £2,181,220 *Total Assets:* £2,740,352
Registered Office: 19a Golding Gardens, East Peckham, Tonbridge, Kent, TN12 5PB
Officers: Karl Kristian Jensen, Secretary; Karl Kristian Jensen [1962] Director [Danish]; Marinus Soerensen [1951] Director/Marketing [Danish]

Newmed Consultancy Limited
Incorporated: 30 October 2017
Net Worth Deficit: £4,990 *Total Assets:* £12,170
Registered Office: Saxon Lodge, Ferry Road, Bawdsey, Woodbridge, Suffolk, IP12 3AW
Officers: Karen Whitehouse [1955] Director/Housewife; Norman Whitehouse [1953] Director

Nextpharma Technologies Holding Limited
Incorporated: 2 January 2003 *Employees:* 4
Net Worth Deficit: £89,095 *Total Assets:* £8,285,816
Registered Office: 1 Tannery House, Tannery Lane, Send, Woking, Surrey, GU23 7EF
Officers: Alan Jonathan Dodsworth, Secretary; Peter Arend William Burema [1958] Director/Chief Executive [Dutch]

NHC Limited
Incorporated: 14 July 2000 *Employees:* 2
Net Worth: £36,630 *Total Assets:* £43,007
Registered Office: 113 Parchmore Road, Thornton Heath, Surrey, CR7 8LZ
Officers: Brian Dart, Secretary; Akosua Yamoa [1967] Director

Nia Nova Ltd
Incorporated: 2 November 2001
Net Worth Deficit: £5,644
Registered Office: 34 Bateson Road, Cambridge, CB4 3HF
Shareholders: Stephen Michael O'Connor; Eugenia Borissova Parvanova
Officers: Stephen Michael O'Connor, Secretary; Stephen Michael O'Connor [1968] Director/Consultant; Eugenia Borissova Parvanova [1971] Director/Designer

Niche Generics Limited
Incorporated: 15 January 2002 *Employees:* 83
Net Worth Deficit: £6,219,016 *Total Assets:* £5,714,967
Registered Office: 1 The Cam Centre, Wilbury Way, Hitchin, Herts, SG4 0TW
Parent: Unichem Laboratories Limited
Officers: Christopher Moss, Secretary; Gerard Majella Cole [1954] Managing Director; Dilip Janardan Kunkolienkar [1950] Director [Indian]; Christopher Moss [1970] Director

Nicobrand Limited
Incorporated: 19 November 1997 *Employees:* 29
Net Worth: £26,734,932 *Total Assets:* £28,111,060
Registered Office: 189 Castleroe Road, Coleraine, Co Londonderry, BT51 3RP
Parent: Teva Pharmaceutical Industries Limited
Officers: Helen Doreen Boyd, Secretary; Helen Doreen Boyd [1968] Director/Accountant; Dean Michael Cooper [1972] Director/Chartered Accountant; Mark McQuillan [1976] Director/Chemical Engineer [Irish]

Nicofix (Europe) Limited
Incorporated: 20 April 2007
Net Worth Deficit: £7,097 *Total Assets:* £8,757
Registered Office: Syence House, Owens Road, Skippers Lane Industrial Estate, Middlesbrough, Cleveland, TS6 6HE
Major Shareholder: Sean Campbell
Officers: Sean-Robbie Campbell [1965] Director

Nikkiso UK Co., Ltd.
Incorporated: 21 November 2013 *Employees:* 26
Net Worth: £332,587 *Total Assets:* £1,366,738
Registered Office: Unit 2 Ashfields Farm, Priors Court Road, Hermitage, Thatcham, Berks, RG18 9XY
Officers: Benjamin Ryan Houston [1976] Director/Global Vice President of Operations; Yoshiro Ueda [1969] Managing Director [Japanese]

Nillergen Limited
Incorporated: 28 April 2009
Registered Office: Unit 5a Brailes Industrial Estate, Winderton Road, Lower Brailes, Banbury, Oxon, OX15 5JW
Shareholders: Graham Francis Warmington; Mary Doreen Lloyd
Officers: Graham Francis Warmington, Secretary; Mary Doreen Lloyd [1952] Director/Scientist; Graham Francis Warmington [1949] Director/Accountant and Manufacturer

Nimasol Limited
Incorporated: 11 October 2012
Net Worth Deficit: £2,480 *Total Assets:* £2,537
Registered Office: 104 Allerburn Lea, Alnwick, Northumberland, NE66 2QP
Shareholders: Roland Jurke; Michael Andrew Carroll
Officers: Roland Jurke [1960] Director

NKCell Plus PLC
Incorporated: 28 November 2018
Registered Office: 3rd Floor, 207 Regent Street, London, W1B 3HH
Officers: Lidell Page, Secretary; Malcolm Groat [1961] Director/Executive; Lidell Page [1971] Director/Attorney [American]

NKK Investments Limited
Incorporated: 25 September 2018
Registered Office: 71-75 Shelton Street, London, WC2H 9JQ
Major Shareholder: Rahesh Jivan
Officers: Rahesh Jivan, Secretary; Rahesh Jivan [1976] Director

Nnadi's Healthcare and Pharmaceuticals Ltd
Incorporated: 23 October 2015
Registered Office: Third Floor, 35-37 Ludgate Hill, London, EC4M 7JN
Major Shareholder: Sonny Armstrong Marizu Ume
Officers: Sonny Armstrong Marizu Ume [1988] Director

Noble Green (Essex) Limited
Incorporated: 7 December 2018
Registered Office: 977 London Road, Leigh on Sea, Essex, SS9 3LB
Major Shareholder: Fraser Andrew Gourley
Officers: Fraser Andrew Gourley [1990] Director/Resourcing Operations Manager

Nocov Ltd
Incorporated: 6 March 2018
Registered Office: Kemp House, 160 City Road, London, EC1V 2NX
Officers: Muhammad Zukermi Bin Edi [1991] Director [Malaysian]

Nonivlok Limited
Incorporated: 24 May 2016
Registered Office: Mandeville Medicines, Stoke Mandeville Hospital, Aylesbury, Bucks, HP21 8AL
Major Shareholder: Karol Pazik
Officers: David Brazier, Secretary; David Thomas Brazier [1967] Director; Karol Pazik [1964] Managing Director

The Noohra Limited
Incorporated: 27 April 2018
Registered Office: Innovation Centre Medway, Maidstone Road, Chatham, Kent, ME5 9FD
Major Shareholder: Ononuju Nkem Chukwumah
Officers: Ononuju Nkem Chukwumah [1976] Director/Pharmacist

Noorik Biopharmaceuticals Limited
Incorporated: 4 January 2011
Registered Office: Suite 1, 3rd Floor, 11-12 St James's Square, London, SW1Y 4LB
Major Shareholder: Iker Navarro
Officers: Iker Navarro [1969] Director/Physician [American]

Norbrook Laboratories Limited
Incorporated: 22 July 1969 *Employees:* 1,614
Net Worth: £99,235,000 *Total Assets:* £171,416,992
Registered Office: Station Works, Camlough Road, Newry, Co Down, BT35 6JP
Shareholders: Lady Ballyedmond; Robert William Roy McNulty; Philip Charles Cornwallis Trousdell
Officers: Martin Patrick Murdock, Secretary; Lady Mary Gordon Ballyedmond [1947] Director; Sir Ian Gibson [1947] Director; The Honourable Edward Gordon Shannon Haughey [1979] Director; James Quinton Stewart Haughey [1981] Director/Medical Doctor; John Paul McGrath [1972] Director [Irish]; Liam Nagle [1962] Director [Irish]

Norgine Limited
Incorporated: 14 August 1926 *Employees:* 572
Net Worth: £38,287,000 *Total Assets:* £56,208,000
Registered Office: New Rd, Tiryberth, Hengoed, Mid Glamorgan, CF82 8SJ
Parent: Norgine B.V.
Officers: Francis Andrew Blackmore, Secretary; Christopher William Bath [1974] Director/Chief Financial Officer; Tara Bussey [1974] Director/Vice President, Human Resources [Canadian]; Jean-Roch Guy Nicolas Ledouble [1969] Site Director [French]; Peter Martin [1956] Director/Chief Operating Officer; Paul William Pay [1954] Director/Chief Business Development Officer

Norma Chemicals (U K) Ltd
Incorporated: 26 October 2017
Registered Office: c/o Neville & Stocker, Jubilee House, 3 The Drive, Great Warley, Brentwood, Essex, CM13 3FR
Major Shareholder: Simon Tate
Officers: Simon Tate [1977] Director/Manager

Norma Chemicals Limited
Incorporated: 23 October 1947 Employees: 3
Net Worth: £56,226 Total Assets: £56,908
Registered Office: Jubilee House, 3 The Drive, Great Warley, Brentwood, Essex, CM13 3FR
Major Shareholder: Mary Joan Tate
Officers: Mary Joan Tate, Secretary; Mary Joan Tate [1945] Director; Simon Robert Geoffrey Tate [1977] Director; Richard Earl Warriner [1956] Director

North Star Healthcare Limited
Incorporated: 4 February 2016
Net Worth Deficit: £1,267 Total Assets: £198,019
Registered Office: Unit 6 The IO Centre, Salbrook Road Industrial Estate, Salfords, Surrey, RH1 5GJ
Major Shareholder: Kalvinder Singh Ruprai
Officers: Kalvinder Singh Ruprai [1969] Director/Businessman

Northumbria Pharma Ltd
Incorporated: 5 December 2016 Employees: 4
Net Worth: £516,545 Total Assets: £685,320
Registered Office: Netpark, Thomas Wright Way, Sedgefield, Co Durham, TS21 3FD
Shareholder: Paul Watson
Officers: Dr Samer Taslaq [1980] Director; Paul Watson [1972] Director

Norton Healthcare (1998) Limited
Incorporated: 26 May 1998
Net Worth: £73,701,000 Total Assets: £73,701,000
Registered Office: Ridings Point, Whistler Drive, Castleford, W Yorks, WF10 5HX
Parent: Norton Healthcare Limited
Officers: Dean Michael Cooper [1972] Director/Chartered Accountant; Kim Innes [1968] Director/General Manager

Norton Healthcare Limited
Incorporated: 13 February 1969 Employees: 421
Net Worth: £1,411,873,792 Total Assets: £1,498,274,944
Registered Office: Ridings Point, Whistler Drive, Castleford, W Yorks, WF10 5HX
Parent: Ivax UK Limited
Officers: Dean Michael Cooper [1972] Director/Chartered Accountant; Stephen Llanon Forrester-Coles [1960] Site Director; David Vrhovec [1967] Director [Slovenian]

Nova Bio-Pharma Technologies Limited
Incorporated: 17 June 2009 Employees: 3
Net Worth Deficit: £443,941 Total Assets: £526,751
Registered Office: Martin House, Gloucester Crescent, Wigston, Leics, LE18 4YL
Parent: Nova Bio-Pharma Holdings Limited
Officers: Clement Roger Staniforth, Secretary; Samooh Dishal de Costa [1974] Technical Director; Dr Peter John Pitt White [1948] Director/Pharmacist

Nova Laboratories Limited
Incorporated: 25 November 1993 Employees: 217
Net Worth: £14,533,310 Total Assets: £26,162,616
Registered Office: Martin House, Gloucester Crescent, Wigston, Leics, LE18 4YL
Parent: Nova Bio-Pharma Holdings Limited
Officers: Clement Roger Staniforth, Secretary; Dr Peter John Pitt White [1948] Director/Pharmacist

Novartis Grimsby Limited
Incorporated: 11 September 1920 Employees: 381
Net Worth: £281,785,984 Total Assets: £348,511,008
Registered Office: Frimley Business Park, Frimley, Camberley, Surrey, GU16 7SR
Parent: Novartis UK Limited
Officers: Rebecca Ann Weston, Secretary; Haseeb Ahmad [1976] Director/CPO Head UK & Ireland; Cynthia Helena Chiaramitara [1976] Managing Director [Brazilian]; Jeremiah Carmel Collins [1965] Director/Head of Chemical Operations and NIPBI [Irish]; Oriane Fanny Lacaze [1979] Director/Country Chief Financial Officer [French]

Novartis Pharmaceuticals UK Limited
Incorporated: 8 December 1911 Employees: 821
Net Worth: £72,936,000 Total Assets: £303,975,008
Registered Office: Frimley Business Park, Frimley, Camberley, Surrey, GU16 7SR
Parent: Novartis UK Limited
Officers: Rebecca Ann Weston, Secretary; Haseeb Ahmad [1976] Director/CPO Head UK & Ireland; Oriane Fanny Lacaze [1979] Director/Country Chief Financial Officer [French]; Dr Anna Mari Scheiffele [1974] Director/General Manager, Oncology UK & Ireland [Finnish]; Marie-France Tschudin [1971] Director/Head Novartis Pharma Region Europe [Swiss]

Novo Nordisk Holding Limited
Incorporated: 7 September 1977
Net Worth: £3,430,000 Total Assets: £3,432,000
Registered Office: 3 City Place, Beehive Ring Road, Gatwick, W Sussex, RH6 0PA
Parent: Novo Nordisk A/S
Officers: Matthew O'Flynn, Secretary; Jesper Brandgaard [1963] Director/Chief Financial Officer [Danish]; Tomas Haagen [1966] Director [Danish]; Matt Joseph Regan [1971] Director/General Manager [Irish]

NSK Locums Limited
Incorporated: 19 January 2005
Net Worth: £22,459 Total Assets: £30,439
Registered Office: 37 Willenhall Road, Bilston, W Midlands, WV14 6NW
Shareholder: Narinder Singh Khakh
Officers: Aninder Kaur Khakh, Secretary; Narinder Singh Khakh [1978] Director/Pharmacist

Nunataq Limited
Incorporated: 2 August 2013
Net Worth: £1,017,471 Total Assets: £1,180,021
Registered Office: Level 17, Dashwood House, 69 Old Broad Street, London, EC2M 1QS
Major Shareholder: Robert F Ryan
Officers: Dr. Robert Ryan, Secretary; Dr. Robert F Ryan [1960] Chairman, Director, President and CEO [American]

Nuradec Ltd
Incorporated: 3 July 2018
Registered Office: 7 Blythe Way, Highfields Caldecote, Cambridge, CB23 7NR
Major Shareholder: Sulaiman Mubashir Ahmad
Officers: Sulaiman Mubashir Ahmad [1973] Director/Entrepreneur [Swiss]

Nutra Aid Ltd.
Incorporated: 19 October 2015
Registered Office: Galla House, 695 High Road, North Finchley, London, N12 0BT
Shareholders: Anish Patel; Mikesh Patel
Officers: Anish Patel [1995] Director; Mikesh Patel [1990] Director

Nutramax Ltd
Incorporated: 2 January 2019
Registered Office: 2nd Floor, College House, 17 King Edwards Road, Ruislip, Middlesex, HA4 7AE
Major Shareholder: Dip Thakkar
Officers: Dip Thakkar, Secretary; Dip Thakkar [1987] Director/Sales

Nutrapharm Ltd
Incorporated: 9 May 2017
Registered Office: 9 Denton Drive, West Bridgford, Nottingham, NG2 7FS
Officers: Gavin Gresswell [1972] Director; Paul Settle [1970] Director; Simon Wills [1969] Director

Nutrasulin Ltd.
Incorporated: 13 October 2016
Net Worth: £1,068 *Total Assets:* £5,687
Registered Office: Silverwood, 48 The Rise, Sevenoaks, Kent, TN13 1RL
Major Shareholder: Jessika Hildegard Kuhne
Officers: Jessika Hildegard Kuhne [1965] Director [German]

Nutridote Ltd
Incorporated: 5 July 2017
Registered Office: 9 Charles Lakin Close, Shilton, Coventry, Warwicks, CV7 9LB
Officers: Jay Bhardwa [1996] Director

Nutripharm Limited
Incorporated: 6 April 2010
Net Worth Deficit: £3,541 *Total Assets:* £114,209
Registered Office: 7 Lansdowne Court, Carlisle, CA3 9HW
Shareholder: Philip Thomas Jobson
Officers: Philip Thomas Jobson [1960] Director

Nutrition Group PLC
Incorporated: 11 December 2007 *Employees:* 112
Net Worth: £8,462,679 *Total Assets:* £11,890,243
Registered Office: 316 Blackpool Road, Fulwood, Preston, Lancs, PR2 3AE
Major Shareholder: Peter Greathead
Officers: John Hartley Smith, Secretary; John David Atkinson [1966] Director; Sean Anthony Carey [1966] Director [Irish]; Peter Greathead [1943] Director; Richard Lewis Greathead [1984] Director; John Hartley Smith [1955] Director/Accountant

Nuvision Biotherapies Limited
Incorporated: 7 April 2015 *Employees:* 10
Net Worth: £338,306 *Total Assets:* £517,857
Registered Office: Medicity, D6 Building, Thane Road, Nottingham, NG90 6BH
Shareholder: The University of Nottingham
Officers: Dr Andrew Hopkinson [1976] Director; Roger Peter Teasdale [1967] Managing Director; Dr Jonathan Mark Treherne [1961] Director/Scientist

NZP UK Limited
Incorporated: 8 September 1989
Previous: Dextra Laboratories Limited
Net Worth: £2,679,547 *Total Assets:* £4,205,742
Registered Office: One Glass Wharf, Bristol, BS2 0ZX
Officers: Dr Karen June Etherington [1968] Director/General Manager; Dr Alexander Charles Weymouth-Wilson [1968] Director/Chief Scientific Officer

Oat Services Limited
Incorporated: 23 August 2001 *Employees:* 8
Net Worth: £521,546 *Total Assets:* £747,780
Registered Office: 226 Bassett Avenue, Southampton, SO16 7FU
Shareholders: Miranda Elizabeth Maunsell; Carteret Hunter Maunsell
Officers: Miranda Elizabeth Maunsell, Secretary/Director; Timothy Hugh Fielder [1952] Director; Cara Alison Maunsell [1984] Director/Manager; Carteret Hunter Maunsell [1949] Director/Manager; Hannah Maunsell [1982] Director; Mark Hugo Maunsell [1986] Director/Student; Miranda Elizabeth Maunsell [1955] Director

OBG Holding Limited
Incorporated: 11 January 2016 *Employees:* 333
Net Worth: £20,707,284 *Total Assets:* £58,080,152
Registered Office: Ayrton House, Commerce Way, Liverpool, L8 7BA
Shareholder: Gerald Francis Obrien
Officers: Philip Didlick, Secretary; Philip Didlick [1976] Director/Chartered Accountant; Generald Francis O'Brien [1949] Director; Padraic Marc O'Brien [1979] Director; Brigid Christina Obrien [1946] Director

Occidem Biotech Limited
Incorporated: 18 February 2004
Registered Office: The Maples, 17 Pembroke Road, Moorpark, Northwood, Middlesex, HA6 2HP
Major Shareholder: Husein Mohamedraza Sultanali Gulamhusein
Officers: Fatema Gulamhusein, Secretary; Fatema Gulamhusein [1977] Director; Husein Mohamedraza Sultanali Gulamhusein [1972] Managing Director

Ochil Skincare Company Ltd
Incorporated: 26 January 2015
Net Worth: £8,324 *Total Assets:* £24,315
Registered Office: Unit 1 Carsebridge Court, Whins Road, Alloa, Clackmannanshire, FK10 3LQ
Shareholder: Fiona Ritchie
Officers: Fiona Ritchie [1971] Director

Octapharma Limited
Incorporated: 17 April 1989 *Employees:* 22
Net Worth: £5,093,525 *Total Assets:* £14,170,924
Registered Office: The Zenith Building, 26 Spring Gardens, Manchester, M2 1AB
Shareholder: Wolfgang Marguerre
Officers: Cornelius Marguerre, Secretary; Cornelius Marguerre [1958] Director/General Counsel [German]; Wolfgang Marguerre [1941] Director/General Manager [German]

Offit Nootropics Limited
Incorporated: 10 July 2018
Registered Office: 130 Old Street, London, EC1V 9BD
Officers: Donna Marie Anderson, Secretary; Anthony William Anderson [1977] Director/Manager; William Sydney Anderson [1982] Director/Manager

Ohemaa's Skincare Ltd.
Incorporated: 26 February 2018
Registered Office: 34 Devonshire Road, London, E16 3NB
Officers: Jonette Mills [1992] Director [British/American]

Olbas Limited
Incorporated: 29 June 1995
Registered Office: G R Lane, Sisson Road, Gloucester, GL2 0GR
Parent: G. R. Lane Holdings Ltd
Officers: Paul Charles Whatley, Secretary; Janet Margaret Groves [1952] Director; Jonathan Groves [1980] Director

Omega Pharma Limited
Incorporated: 14 November 1967 *Employees:* 135
Net Worth: £33,898,000 *Total Assets:* £67,744,000
Registered Office: First Floor, 32 Vauxhall Bridge Road, London, SW1V 2SA
Parent: Omega Pharma Holding (Nederland) BV
Officers: Annette Corcoran, Secretary; Neil Thomas Lister [1975] Managing Director; Dominic James Rivers [1977] Director; Christopher Allan Rudd [1980] Commercial Director

Oncoparp Ltd
Incorporated: 29 August 2017
Registered Office: 4 Tycehurst Hill, Loughton, Essex, IG10 1BU
Officers: Syed Omar Ali [1995] Director/Entrepreneur

One Second Supplements Limited
Incorporated: 25 June 2018
Registered Office: 135 Hendon Lane, London, N3 3PR
Parent: Instavit Limited
Officers: Scott James Perkins [1972] Director

One Stop 15 Limited
Incorporated: 3 November 2016
Net Worth: £1,940 *Total Assets:* £3,004
Registered Office: 10 Beaumont Close, Ifield, Crawley, W Sussex, RH11 0RN
Major Shareholder: Ezim Adesola Eneli
Officers: Ezim Adesola Eneli [1967] Director/Pharmacist

Onipede Clinical Research Ltd
Incorporated: 29 May 2009 *Employees:* 1
Net Worth: £27,292 *Total Assets:* £27,292
Registered Office: 18 Rodney Place, Walthamstow, London, E17 5NN
Shareholders: Tonisha Annette Russell; Terry Efeosa Egheosa Egharevba
Officers: Terry Efeosa Egheosa Egharevba [1982] Director

Ono Pharma UK Ltd.
Incorporated: 23 January 1998 *Employees:* 42
Net Worth: £7,178,002 *Total Assets:* £8,618,626
Registered Office: Midcity Place, 71 High Holborn, London, WC1V 6EA
Parent: Ono Pharmaceutical Co. Ltd
Officers: Teruo Tsurui, Secretary; Toshiomi Minamide [1964] Managing Director [Japanese]

Onsite Diagnostics Limited
Incorporated: 11 March 2016 *Employees:* 2
Net Worth Deficit: £38,741 *Total Assets:* £4,694
Registered Office: City Gates, 2-4 Southgate, Chichester, W Sussex, PO19 8DJ
Parent: Wildrush Limited
Officers: Paul Jeremy Rush [1967] Director; Howard John Wilder [1959] Director

Onyx Scientific Limited
Incorporated: 14 March 2000 *Employees:* 52
Net Worth: £3,030,826 *Total Assets:* £4,226,662
Registered Office: Units 97 & 98 Silverbriar, Sunderland Enterprise Park East, Sunderland, Tyne & Wear, SR5 2TQ
Parent: Ipca Laboratories Ltd
Officers: Denise Bowser [1971] Commercial Director; Pranay Godha [1972] Executive Director [Indian]; Nathan Vincent Lane [1972] Finance Director; Derek John Londesbrough [1970] Director of Chemistry

Opal IP Limited
Incorporated: 12 February 2016
Net Worth: £50,100 *Total Assets:* £50,100
Registered Office: 28 Edenside, Cumbernauld, N Lanarks, G68 0ER
Major Shareholder: Peter Charles Brown
Officers: Linda Ann Brown [1958] Director/Paralegal; Peter Charles Brown [1959] Sales Director

Opiant Pharmaceuticals UK Limited
Incorporated: 4 November 2016 *Employees:* 4
Net Worth Deficit: £1,001,074 *Total Assets:* £230,235
Registered Office: 19 North Street, Ashford, Kent, TN24 8LF
Shareholders: Geoffrey Charles Wolf; Roger Crystal; Michael Jeffrey Sinclair
Officers: Roger Crystal [1976] Director; David O'Toole [1958] Director [American]

Opix Ltd
Incorporated: 4 January 2019
Registered Office: 71-75 Shelton Street, London, WC2H 9JQ
Major Shareholder: Raj Gill
Officers: Dr Raj Gill, Secretary; Dr Raj Gill [1964] Director/Scientist

Optronica Limited
Incorporated: 13 August 2014
Registered Office: 21 East Central, 127 Olympic Avenue, Milton Park, Abingdon, Oxon, OX14 4SA
Major Shareholder: Andrew Nadeem Obeid
Officers: Doctor Andrew Nadeem Obeid, Secretary; Dr Andrew Nadeem Obeid [1961] Director

Orb Global Ltd
Incorporated: 30 October 2012
Registered Office: 24th Floor, The Shard, 32 London Bridge Street, London, SE1 9SG
Major Shareholder: Nima Golsharifi
Officers: Dr Nima Golsharifi [1987] Director

Orbus Therapeutics Ltd
Incorporated: 25 January 2013
Net Worth Deficit: £27,047
Registered Office: 12 New Fetter Lane, London, EC4A 1JP
Officers: Jason Daniel Levin [1970] Director/Executive [American]; Robert Mackie Myers [1963] Director/Executive [American]

Organic CBD Products Limited
Incorporated: 28 November 2018
Registered Office: Ground Floor, 25 Darling Street, Enniskillen, Co Fermanagh, BT74 7DP
Major Shareholder: Padraig Corby
Officers: Padraig Corby [1961] Director [Irish]

Organic Hemp Oils Limited
Incorporated: 14 November 2018
Registered Office: Ground Floor, 25 Darling Street, Enniskillen, Co Fermanagh, BT74 7DP
Major Shareholder: Padraig Corby
Officers: Padraig Corby [1961] Director [Irish]

Organic Herbs for Health Limited
Incorporated: 30 July 2001
Registered Office: Trevarno Farm, Prospidnick, Helston, Cornwall, TR13 0RY
Parent: Killiow Estates Limited
Officers: Michael Roy Sagin [1950] Director

Organic Herbs for Life Limited
Incorporated: 27 July 2001
Registered Office: Trevarno Farm, Prospidnick, Helston, Cornwall, TR13 0RY
Parent: Killiow Estates Limited
Officers: Michael Roy Sagin [1950] Director

Organic Lifecare Ltd.
Incorporated: 20 December 2016
Net Worth Deficit: £680 *Total Assets:* £26
Registered Office: 176a Ealing Road, Wembley, Middlesex, HA0 4QD
Officers: Santosh Kumar Tiwari [1987] Director [Indian]

The Organic Pharmacy Limited
Incorporated: 28 June 2000
Net Worth: £1,986,948 *Total Assets:* £3,790,621
Registered Office: Units 7 & 8 Vision Industrial Park, Kendal Avenue, London, W3 0AF
Major Shareholder: Domenico Ganassini Di Camerati
Officers: Giuseppe Ganassini di Camerati [1976] Director [Italian]; Daniel White [1975] Executive Managing Director

Oriel Therapeutics Limited
Incorporated: 10 September 2008
Net Worth Deficit: £344,000 *Total Assets:* £2,029,000
Registered Office: c/o Novartis Pharmaceuticals UK Limited, Frimley Business Park, Frimley, Camberley, Surrey, GU16 7SR
Parent: Oriel Therapeutics Inc
Officers: Rebecca Ann Weston, Secretary; Timothy Charles de Gavre [1974] Director; Oriane Fanny Lacaze [1979] Director/Country Chief Financial Officer [French]; Carol Lesley Lynch [1967] Director/President

Ortho-Clinical Diagnostics
Incorporated: 18 October 1990 *Employees:* 418
Net Worth: £148,832,000 *Total Assets:* £253,118,000
Registered Office: Felindre Meadows, Pencoed, Bridgend, Mid Glamorgan, CF35 5PZ
Officers: Paul Jonathan Hackworth [1970] Country Director; Richard John Jenkins [1979] Finance Director

Ortholese Limited
Incorporated: 27 August 2013
Net Worth: £9,820 *Total Assets:* £49,272
Registered Office: Basepoint Business & Innovation Centre, 110 Butterfield, Great Marlings, Luton, Beds, LU2 8DL
Shareholders: Samantha Evans; Lee Edward Evans
Officers: Lee Edward Evans [1968] Director; Samantha Evans [1972] Director

Osgen Ltd.
Incorporated: 13 October 2015
Registered Office: Galla House, 695 High Road, North Finchley, London, N12 0BT
Shareholders: Anish Patel; Mikesh Patel
Officers: Anish Patel [1995] Director; Mikesh Patel [1990] Director; Nutan Patel [1965] Director

Osgen Pharmaceuticals Limited
Incorporated: 9 April 2016 *Employees:* 2
Net Worth Deficit: £449,983 *Total Assets:* £61,191
Registered Office: Galla House, 695 High Road, North Finchley, London, N12 0BT
Shareholders: Mikesh Patel; Anish Patel
Officers: Anish Patel [1995] Director; Mikesh Patel [1990] Director

Osteoporosis Research Ltd
Incorporated: 1 February 2012 *Employees:* 3
Net Worth: £318,716 *Total Assets:* £372,162
Registered Office: 1st Floor, Sackville House, 143-149 Fenchurch Street, London, EC3M 6BN
Shareholders: Derek Richard Gray; Professor John Anthony Kanis
Officers: Derek Richard Gray [1933] Director/Fiscal Advisor; Professor John Anthony Kanis [1944] Director/Medical Professor; Rebecca Louise Kanis-Buck [1975] Director/Programme Manager

OTC Concepts Limited
Incorporated: 28 October 2002
Net Worth Deficit: £45,180 *Total Assets:* £245,821
Registered Office: Network House, West 26, Stubs Beck Lane, Cleckheaton, W Yorks, BD19 4TT
Shareholders: Ian John Kirk; Peter Noel Miller Cox
Officers: Ian John Kirk, Secretary/Chemist; Peter Noel Miller Cox [1946] Director/Chemist; Ian John Kirk [1957] Director/Chemist

Oxbridge Pharma Limited
Incorporated: 5 September 2002 *Employees:* 3
Net Worth Deficit: £396,884 *Total Assets:* £42,607
Registered Office: The St Botolph Building, 138 Houndsditch, London, EC3A 7AR
Major Shareholder: Jae-Young Ha
Officers: Dr Jai Jun Choung [1959] Director [South Korean]; Jae-Young Ha [1960] Director

Oxford Biodynamics PLC
Incorporated: 25 April 2007 *Employees:* 31
Previous: Oxford Biodynamics Limited
Net Worth: £20,030,000 *Total Assets:* £20,941,000
Registered Office: 26 Beaumont Street, Oxford, OX1 2NP
Officers: Alexandre Akoulitchev [1962] Director/Research Fellow; Stephen Charles Diggle [1964] Director; Christian Gurth Hoyer Millar [1959] Director; Alison Caroline Kibble [1969] Director/Consultant; Paul Leslie Stockdale [1975] Director/Chartered Accountant; David Jeffreys Williams [1952] Director

Oxford Immunotec Global PLC
Incorporated: 16 August 2013 *Employees:* 454
Net Worth: £64,888,136 *Total Assets:* £108,605,648
Registered Office: 94c Innovation Drive, Milton Park, Milton, Abingdon, Oxon, OX14 4RZ
Officers: Elizabeth Keiley, Secretary; Ronald Andrews [1959] Director/Consultant [American]; Patrick Balthrop Snr [1956] Director/Retired CEO, Principal of Apalachee Ventures [American]; Mark Klausner [1965] Director/Investor Relations [American]; Patricia Randall [1950] Director/Attorney [American]; Herman Rosenman [1947] Director/Senior Executive [American]; Richard Alvin Sandberg [1942] Director/Entrepreneur [American]; James Tobin [1944] Director/Consultant [American]; Andrew Scott Walton [1967] Director/Business Executive [American]; Dr Peter James Wrighton-Smith [1974] Director

Oxford Immunotec Limited
Incorporated: 21 August 2002 *Employees:* 86
Net Worth: £97,352,000 *Total Assets:* £115,932,000
Registered Office: 94c Innovation Drive, Milton Park, Milton, Abingdon, Oxon, OX14 4RZ
Parent: Oxford Immunotec Global PLC
Officers: Elizabeth Keiley, Secretary; Richard Alvin Sandberg [1942] Director/Entrepreneur [American]; Dr Peter James Wrighton-Smith [1974] Director

Oxford Pharmaceuticals Limited
Incorporated: 6 October 2015
Registered Office: 60a Keighley Road, Halifax, W Yorks, HX2 8AL
Officers: Shahid Malik [1967] Director/Chairman; Faisal Shoukat [1987] Director/Pharmacists

Oxford Supramolecular Biotechnology Limited
Incorporated: 30 January 2019
Registered Office: Connaught House, 15-17 Upper George Street, Luton, Beds, LU1 2RD
Shareholders: Robert Tobias Steffen; Fangqian Wang
Officers: Robert Tobias Steffen [1973] Director [German]; Fangqian Wang [1976] Director [Chinese]

P & S Nano Limited
Incorporated: 26 April 2012
Net Worth Deficit: £21,450 *Total Assets:* £3,628
Registered Office: 7 Ashleigh Gardens, Pembroke, SA71 4AR
Major Shareholder: Alan Geoffrey Marsh
Officers: Alan Geoffrey Marsh [1953] Director

P.I.E. Pharma Limited
Incorporated: 8 January 1996
Net Worth: £139,906 *Total Assets:* £10,276,358
Registered Office: 39a Joel Street, Northwood Hills, Northwood, Middlesex, HA6 1NZ
Major Shareholder: Anuj Somchand Shah
Officers: Anuj Somchand Shah [1966] Director/Actuary

P2 Healthcare Limited
Incorporated: 25 November 2014
Net Worth: £4,688 *Total Assets:* £57,760
Registered Office: 3 Young Place, Kelvin Industrial Estate, East Kilbride, G75 0TD
Major Shareholder: Richard de Souza
Officers: Richard de Souza [1952] Director; Stuart John Overend [1970] Director

P2-Molteni Pharma Limited
Incorporated: 10 March 2016
Registered Office: 3 Young Place, Kelvin Industrial Estate, East Kilbride, G75 0TD
Shareholders: L.Molteni & C. Deif.Lli Alitti Societa Di Esercizio SpA; P2 Healthcare Limited
Officers: Richard de Souza [1952] Director/Pharmacist; Stuart John Overend [1970] Director/Accountant; Federico Seghi Recil [1969] Director [Italian]

PAB Apothecary Ltd
Incorporated: 30 June 2014 *Employees:* 1
Net Worth: £472 *Total Assets:* £13,902
Registered Office: 15 Old Masters Close, Walsall, W Midlands, WS1 2QP
Major Shareholder: Paul Andrew Blaylock
Officers: Paul Andrew Blaylock [1962] Director

Pacific Height Limited
Incorporated: 1 August 2007
Net Worth Deficit: £11,296 *Total Assets:* £2,468
Registered Office: 3 Cranwell Court, Fieldmead Barnet, London, NW9 5SF
Shareholder: Eileen Onumonu
Officers: Angela Onyekauwazulu Onumonu, Secretary; Eileen Onumonu [1963] Director/Income Recovery Consultant

Panaomics Limited
Incorporated: 30 October 2017
Registered Office: Lower Ground Floor, 40 Bloomsbury Way, London, WC1A 2SE
Major Shareholder: Nima Golsharifi
Officers: Dr Nima Golsharifi [1987] Director/Chief Executive Officer

Panpharma UK Limited
Incorporated: 31 March 2015 *Employees:* 4
Net Worth: £55,254 *Total Assets:* £786,139
Registered Office: Cotton Exchange, Bixteth Street, Liverpool, L3 9LQ
Officers: Jean-Louis Andre Gauthier [1958] Director [French]; Marie-Helene Daniele Madelpuech Dick [1964] Director [French]

Paradox Omega Oils Ltd
Incorporated: 31 August 2007 *Employees:* 3
Net Worth: £493,459 *Total Assets:* £804,343
Registered Office: 207 Belmont Road, Belfast, BT4 2AG
Shareholders: Alan Geoffrey Hayhurst; Michelle Hayhurst
Officers: Dr Alan Geoffrey Hayhurst [1958] Technical Director; Michelle Denise Hayhurst [1960] Sales Director [Canadian]

Parakill Limited
Incorporated: 10 February 2011
Registered Office: Cardale House, Cardale Park, Beckwith Head Road, Harrogate, N Yorks, HG3 1RY
Shareholder: Tim Parkinson
Officers: Timothy Andrew Parkinson, Secretary; Peter Robert Wilkinson [1954] Director

Parbold Therapeutics Limited
Incorporated: 16 January 2017
Registered Office: Kingsway House, 365 Atherton Road, Hindley Green, Wigan, Lancs, WN2 3XD
Shareholders: Nicholas Ralphe Rogerson; Paul Boulton
Officers: Paul Boulton, Secretary; Paul Boulton [1959] Director; Nicholas Ralphe Rogerson [1955] Director

The Top UK Pharmaceutical Manufacturers

Pari Medical Limited
Incorporated: 10 June 1994 Employees: 14
Net Worth: £3,543,026 Total Assets: £4,119,982
Registered Office: 5 New Street Square, London, EC4A 3TW
Major Shareholder: Stephan Brugger
Officers: Malcolm John Apter [1972] Director/Country Manager Pari Medical Ltd; Juergen Mueller [1959] Director [German]

Parkacre Enterprises Limited
Incorporated: 16 September 2005 Employees: 174
Net Worth: £2,559,167 Total Assets: £10,942,910
Registered Office: Hangar 2, Learoyd Road, Caenby Corner Estate, Hemswell Cliff, Gainsborough, Lincs, DN21 5TJ
Officers: James Caseley [1976] Sales Director; Charles Stern [1976] Finance Director; John Stern [1979] Director

Patheon UK Limited
Incorporated: 29 April 1999 Employees: 312
Net Worth: £31,208,536 Total Assets: £130,475,168
Registered Office: Kingfisher Drive, Swindon, Wilts, SN3 5BZ
Parent: Thermo Fisher Scientific Inc.
Officers: Nicholas Roger Clive Plummer, Secretary; Luca Andretta [1974] Director [Italian]; Nicholas Roger Clive Plummer [1970] Director and Company Secretary; Andrew Robinson [1972] Finance Director

Paxvax Ltd
Incorporated: 3 October 2013 Employees: 1
Net Worth: £1,807,997 Total Assets: £3,241,071
Registered Office: 1 Victoria Square, Birmingham, B1 1BD
Parent: Emergent International Inc.
Officers: Robert Gregory Kramer [1957] Director/President & COO [American]; Richard Scott Lindahl [1963] Director/Executive Vice President, CFO & Treasurer [American]; Mark Meltz [1973] Director/Lawyer [American]; Atul Saran [1973] Director/Executive VP, Corporate Development and Lawyer [American]

PCCA (UK) Holdings Limited
Incorporated: 28 January 2014 Employees: 78
Net Worth Deficit: £126,779 Total Assets: £13,744,165
Registered Office: Unit 2 Regents Drive, Low Prudhoe Industrial Estate, Prudhoe, Northumberland, NE42 6PX
Parent: PCCA
Officers: Sharon Clift [1976] Managing Director; Jimmy Ray Smith [1960] Director/Company President [American]; Lester David Sparks [1943] Director [American]

PCCA Limited
Incorporated: 14 May 1999 Employees: 78
Previous: The Specials Laboratory Limited
Net Worth: £1,432,901 Total Assets: £4,557,221
Registered Office: Unit 2 Regents Drive, Low Prudhoe Industrial Estate, Low Prudhoe, Northumberland, NE42 6PX
Parent: PCCA (UK) Holdings Limited
Officers: Sharon Clift [1976] Director; Jimmy Ray Smith [1960] Director/Company President [American]; Lester David Sparks [1943] Director [American]

PCI Penn UK Holdco Limited
Incorporated: 14 July 2014
Net Worth: £51,104,000 Total Assets: £177,702,000
Registered Office: Capital Building, Tyndall Street, Cardiff, CF10 4AZ
Parent: Pioneer UK Holdings Limited
Officers: Salim Haffar [1973] Director [French]; Remy Hauser [1967] Director/MD - Industry Value Creation Partners Group [Swiss]; Sujit John [1983] Director/Finance [American]; III Mitchell [1954] Director/Chief Executive Officer [American]

Peakdale Chemistry Services Limited
Incorporated: 16 October 2009
Registered Office: One St Peter's Square, Manchester, M2 3DE
Parent: Peakdale Molecular Limited
Officers: Dr Paul Martin Doyle [1956] Director; Paul McCluskey [1963] Director/Consultant

Peckforton Pharmaceuticals Limited
Incorporated: 11 April 1995 Employees: 4
Net Worth: £2,991,654 Total Assets: £4,014,318
Registered Office: The Courtyard Barns, Choke Lane, Maidenhead, Berks, SL6 6PT
Parent: Riemser Pharma UK Limited
Officers: Shafiq Choudhary [1964] Financial Director; Rene Just [1967] Director [Danish]; Konstantin Von Alvensleben [1957] Director/Manager [German]

Pegasus Equine Diagnostics Limited
Incorporated: 9 May 2006
Net Worth Deficit: £758 Total Assets: £14,508
Registered Office: 8 Teal Farm Way, Teal Farm Park, Washington, Tyne & Wear, NE38 8BG
Shareholders: East Midlands Early Growth Fund Limited; Susan Jane Alexia Haritou
Officers: Christos Sotirious Haritou [1956] Director

Pegasus Pharma Limited
Incorporated: 18 March 2015
Registered Office: Suite B, Fairgate House, Kings Road, Tyseley, Birmingham, B11 2AA
Officers: Heny Lachman Mahtani [1964] Director/Businessman

Pellis Care Limited
Incorporated: 10 October 2017
Registered Office: St John's Innovation Centre, Cowley Road, Cambridge, CB4 0WS
Officers: Kiera Donovan [1986] Director of Sales, Marketing & Communication; Bjorn Godfrey [1985] Finance Director; Dr Duncan Ross Purvis [1960] Technical Director; Dr Janette Thomas [1961] Director

Penlan Healthcare Limited
Incorporated: 11 September 2002
Net Worth: £456,387 Total Assets: £1,539,291
Registered Office: Chiltlee Manor, Haslemere Road, Liphook, Hants, GU30 7AZ
Shareholder: Pharmaceuticals Investments Ltd
Officers: Simon Paul Raynor, Secretary; Stephen Jeremy Martin [1965] Director/Pharmacist; Simon Paul Raynor [1966] Director

Penn Pharma Group Limited
Incorporated: 8 January 2007
Net Worth Deficit: £8,348,000 Total Assets: £89,409,000
Registered Office: Capital Building, Tyndall Street, Cardiff, CF10 4AZ
Parent: PCI Penn UK Holdco Limited
Officers: Salim Haffar [1973] Director [French]; Remy Hauser [1967] Director/MD - Industry Value Creation Partners Group [Swiss]; Sujit John [1983] Director/Finance [American]; III Mitchell [1954] Director [American]

Penn Pharmaceutical Services Limited
Incorporated: 26 September 1977 *Employees:* 357
Net Worth: £16,098,000 *Total Assets:* £50,982,000
Registered Office: Capital Building, Tyndall Street, Cardiff, CF10 4AZ
Parent: Penn Pharma Group Limited
Officers: Salim Haffar [1973] Director [French]; Remy Hauser [1967] Director/MD - Industry Value Creation Partners Group [Swiss]; Sujit John [1983] Director/Finance [American]; III Mitchell [1954] Director [American]

Pentail Enzymes Limited
Incorporated: 10 July 2018
Registered Office: 28 Consort Avenue, Trumpington, Cambridge, CB2 9AF
Shareholders: Paulo de Paiva Rosa Amaral; Ka Hing Che
Officers: Dr Paulo de Paiva Rosa Amaral [1982] Director/Biochemist [Brazilian]

Pentonova Limited
Incorporated: 1 July 2014
Registered Office: 75 Woodbourne, Augustus Road, Edgbaston, Birmingham, B15 3PJ
Officers: Iftekhar Ahmed, Secretary; Muhammad Abdullah Majid [1981] Director [Pakistani]; Muhammad Ali Majid [1972] Director [Pakistani]; Humera Jawwad [1976] Director [Pakistani]; Sarah Omar [1974] Director [Pakistani]; Amna Raza [1970] Director [Pakistani]

Peptone Ltd
Incorporated: 6 April 2018
Registered Office: 20-22 Wenlock Road, London, N1 7GU
Shareholders: Master Kamil Tamiola; Matthew Michael Heberling
Officers: Dr Matthew Michael Heberling [1978] Director/Researcher [American]; Kamil Tamiola [1982] Director/Researcher [Polish]

Percuro Medica Ltd
Incorporated: 22 July 2008
Net Worth Deficit: £6,013,002 *Total Assets:* £2,295,998
Registered Office: Alpha House, 646c Kingsbury Road, London, NW9 9HN
Officers: Govind Samji Vaghjiani [1945] Director

Personal Care Packs Limited
Incorporated: 1 February 2013
Net Worth: £103 *Total Assets:* £84,528
Registered Office: 92 Burleys Way, Leicester, LE1 3BD
Officers: Rama Bhalla [1958] Project Director; Sujata Bhalla [1967] Director/Resource Development Manager; Anita Patel [1960] Director/Supervisor

Petbiocell UK Ltd
Incorporated: 13 June 2016
Net Worth: £500 *Total Assets:* £500
Registered Office: Mansour Makki, 2 Lamerton Way, Wilmslow, Cheshire, SK9 3UN
Shareholders: Thomas Grammel; Simon Grammel
Officers: Simon Grammel [1986] Director/Business Administrator [German]

Pfertec Limited
Incorporated: 20 August 1996
Net Worth: £9,446 *Total Assets:* £14,096
Registered Office: c/o Blanche & Co, 3b The Lanterns, 16 Melbourn Street, Royston, Herts, SG8 7BX
Major Shareholder: Dorothea Janice Stockham
Officers: Dorothea Janice Stockham, Secretary/Pharmacist; Dorothea Janice Stockham [1939] Director/Pharmacist; Michael Arthur Stockham [1937] Director/Registered Pharmacist

Pfylori Limited
Incorporated: 8 April 1999
Net Worth: £64,343 *Total Assets:* £65,814
Registered Office: c/o Blanche & Co, 3 The Lanterns, 16 Melbourn Street, Royston, Herts, SG8 7BX
Shareholders: Michael Arthur Stockham; Dorothea Janice Stockham
Officers: Dorothea Janice Stockham, Secretary/Pharmaceutical Locum; Sally Rust [1970] Director; Ben Michael Paul Stockham [1972] Director; Michael Arthur Stockham [1937] Director

PG Pharma Ltd
Incorporated: 21 June 2016
Net Worth: £34,562 *Total Assets:* £59,250
Registered Office: Unit A, Alpha House, Peacock Street, Gravesend, Kent, DA12 1DW
Officers: Pardeep Marwaha [1988] Director/Pharmacist

Phamar Limited
Incorporated: 20 June 2013 *Employees:* 2
Net Worth: £620,002 *Total Assets:* £620,002
Registered Office: Suite F2, The Officers Mess, Coldstream Road, Caterham, Surrey, CR3 5QX
Shareholders: Pheadra Runacres; Andrew Peter Runacres
Officers: Andrew Peter Runacres [1965] Director/Sales Manager; Pheadra Runacres [1968] Director/Office Manager

Pharm E-Cig Ltd
Incorporated: 16 August 2013
Registered Office: 61 Rodney Street, Liverpool, L1 9ER
Shareholders: Paul Brennan; Patrick Philip Joseph Higgins
Officers: Paul Brennan [1965] Director

Pharm Recon Ltd
Incorporated: 15 February 2019
Registered Office: 196 High Road, London, N22 8HH
Major Shareholder: Dmitrii Sharov
Officers: Dmitrii Sharov [1971] Director [Russian/Canadian]

Pharm-Assist (Regulatory Services) Limited
Incorporated: 14 February 2005 *Employees:* 1
Net Worth: £37,602 *Total Assets:* £55,844
Registered Office: 150 High Street, Sevenoaks, Kent, TN13 1XE
Major Shareholder: Julie Ann Turner
Officers: Paul Andrew Lee, Secretary; Julie Ann Turner [1971] Director

Pharma Device Delivery Limited
Incorporated: 2 May 2018
Registered Office: Holly Tree Barn, Rotten Row Farm, Hambleden, Henley on Thames, Oxon, RG9 6NB
Major Shareholder: Marc Franken
Officers: Marc Franken [1963] Director [Dutch]

Pharma Future Ltd
Incorporated: 24 March 2011
Registered Office: 3rd Floor, 120 Baker Street, London, W1U 6TU
Officers: Petra Otepkova [1992] Director [Czech]

Pharma Maiden Ltd
Incorporated: 14 June 2018
Registered Office: 152 Empress Avenue, London, E12 5HW
Major Shareholder: Doreen Bennett Cooke
Officers: Doreen Bennett Cooke [1979] Director/Pharmacist

Pharma Pack Limited
Incorporated: 9 December 2003
Net Worth: £1,165,550 *Total Assets:* £2,143,835
Registered Office: Unit 10a Conwy Morfa Enterprise Park, Parc Caer Seion, Conwy, LL32 8FA
Parent: Pharma Group Holdings Limited
Officers: Dr Aron Rhys Owen [1985] Director/Merchant; Marian Owen [1960] Director; Richard Rhys Owen [1956] Director/Chief Executive

Pharma QP Solutions Ltd
Incorporated: 3 June 2010
Net Worth: £29,559 *Total Assets:* £30,932
Registered Office: Nightingale House, 4 Homestall Crescent, Withersfield, Haverhill, Suffolk, CB9 7SP
Major Shareholder: Elizabeth Whyard
Officers: Elizabeth Whyard, Secretary; Stephen Whyard [1954] Director/Pharmaceutical Manager

Pharma Syntech Ltd
Incorporated: 30 July 2014
Registered Office: 49 Station Road, Polegate, E Sussex, BN26 6EA
Shareholder: Shuxiang Wang
Officers: Shuxiang Wang [1964] Director/Manager

Pharma XP Consulting Ltd
Incorporated: 27 January 2014
Net Worth: £2,184 *Total Assets:* £2,184
Registered Office: Billingscroft, 2 Farquhar Street, Hertford, SG14 3BP
Major Shareholder: Christian Seiler
Officers: Justine Clare Stansall-Seiler, Secretary; Christian Seiler [1970] Director/Chemical Engineer

Pharma Zad Ltd
Incorporated: 4 January 2019
Registered Office: 254 Goldhawk Road, London, W12 9PE
Major Shareholder: Maher Abueleinin Mohammad Badawy
Officers: Maher Abueleinin Mohammad Badawy [1985] Director [Egyptian]

Pharmacann Ltd
Incorporated: 26 July 2018
Registered Office: 31-37 Friar Lane, Nottingham, NG1 6DD
Major Shareholder: Oliver Charles-Richards
Officers: Oliver Charles-Richards [1977] Director

Pharmacare International Ltd
Incorporated: 28 December 2018
Registered Office: 96-98 Baker Street, London, W1U 6TJ
Major Shareholder: Sanaa Al-Hadethee
Officers: Sanaa Al-Hadethee [1964] Director

Pharmacell Medication Systems Limited
Incorporated: 11 February 2015
Net Worth: £16,591 *Total Assets:* £537,741
Registered Office: Market House, 10 Market Walk, Saffron Walden, Essex, CB10 1JZ
Officers: Stefan Gal [1969] Director/General Manager [German]; Ralf Mackensen [1960] Director/General Manager [German]; Adrian Christopher John Milne [1948] Director; Caroline Tremayne Milne [1950] Director

Pharmacenna Ltd
Incorporated: 17 April 2012
Net Worth: £25,004 *Total Assets:* £25,004
Registered Office: 158 Gilson Place, Coppetts Road, London, N10 1BJ
Major Shareholder: Amin Nazem Ashoora
Officers: Amin Nazem Ashoora [1984] Director

Pharmaceutical Equipment Ltd
Incorporated: 6 April 2006
Registered Office: Unit 4b Earley Works, Butts Pond Industrial Estate, Sturminster Newton, Dorset, DT10 1AZ
Parent: Caleva Process Solutions Ltd
Officers: Dr Stephen William Robinson, Secretary; Raj Kumar Budhraja [1946] Director [Indian]; Dr Stephen William Robinson [1946] Director/Manager

Pharmach Ltd
Incorporated: 3 September 2018
Registered Office: Kemp House, 160 City Road, London, EC1V 2NX
Major Shareholder: Salvatore de Furia
Officers: Salvatore de Furia, Secretary; Salvatore de Furia [1974] Director/Manager [Italian]

Pharmaclarity Limited
Incorporated: 21 April 2015 *Employees:* 1
Net Worth Deficit: £103,488 *Total Assets:* £177,162
Registered Office: Bemin House, Cox Lane, Chessington Industrial Estate, Chessington, Surrey, KT9 1SG
Major Shareholder: Bemal Patel
Officers: Bemal Patel [1973] Director

Pharmaco Group Limited
Incorporated: 6 April 2018
Registered Office: Kemp House, 160 City Road, London, EC1V 2NX
Shareholders: Roy Salmons; Nutresco Limited
Officers: Roy Salmons [1945] Director

Pharmacy Advisory Services Limited
Incorporated: 18 March 2003
Net Worth: £528,889 *Total Assets:* £582,602
Registered Office: North Ives Farm, Marsh Oxenhope, Keighley, W Yorks, BD22 9RP
Officers: Jeffrey Alan Cox, Secretary; Jeffrey Alan Cox [1950] Director/Pharmacist; Maria Cox [1953] Director/Pharmacist

Pharmacy Business Consultancy Limited
Incorporated: 26 July 2017
Registered Office: 27 Montreal Road, Blackburn, BB2 7BY
Officers: Adam Esa, Secretary; Adam Esa [1992] Director/Pharmacist Business Consultant

Pharmacy Medicines Ltd
Incorporated: 15 November 2011
Net Worth: £36,743 *Total Assets:* £106,463
Registered Office: 20 Allen Road, Peterborough, Cambs, PE1 3BT
Shareholder: Fiaz Kauser
Officers: Fiaz Kauser [1975] Director/Dispenser; Riaz Kauser [1976] Director/Pharmacist

Pharmacy Warehouse Limited
Incorporated: 13 November 2012
Net Worth: £2,937 *Total Assets:* £3,217
Registered Office: Unit 3, 2 Somerset Road, London, N17 9EJ
Major Shareholder: Ahmed Said
Officers: Mohamed Abdiaziz Hashi [1982] Director/Businessman [Dutch]

Pharmadynamics UK Limited
Incorporated: 14 May 2008
Net Worth: £63,121 *Total Assets:* £98,490
Registered Office: Unit 36 Thomas Way, Lakesview International Business Park, Hersden, Canterbury, Kent, CT3 4JZ
Major Shareholder: Tony Irechukwu
Officers: Patricia Georgina Martha Black, Secretary; Leon Irechukwu [1996] Director/Bioscientist; Tony Irechukwu [1965] Director/Industrial Pharmacist

Pharmagen Direct Limited
Incorporated: 18 May 2016
Registered Office: Garlands, Croft Road, Gerrards Cross, Bucks, SL9 9AF
Officers: Barun Batra [1986] Director; Manav Maratha [1990] Director

Pharmakrysto Ltd
Incorporated: 23 October 2017
Registered Office: RMT Accountants & Business Advisors Ltd, Gosforth Park Avenue, Newcastle upon Tyne, NE12 8EG
Officers: Julian David Howell [1966] Director; Carl Andrew Sterritt [1968] Director

Pharmapac (U.K.) Limited
Incorporated: 21 May 1996 *Employees:* 219
Net Worth: £4,280,452 *Total Assets:* £8,128,585
Registered Office: Unit 22 Valley Road Business Park, Bidston, Wirral, Merseyside, CH41 7EL
Officers: Geoffrey Elliott [1952] Director; John Pugh [1980] Director/Chief Executive Officer; Andrew Michael Sampson [1958] Director

Pharmaserve (North West) Limited
Incorporated: 12 September 2007 *Employees:* 107
Net Worth: £3,871,062 *Total Assets:* £13,113,160
Registered Office: Ayrton House, Parliament Business Park, Commerce Way, Liverpool, L8 7BA
Officers: Philip Didlick, Secretary; Philip Didlick [1976] Director/Accountant; Padraic Marc O'Brien [1979] Director; Generald Francis Obrien [1949] Director [Irish]

Pharmaserve Limited
Incorporated: 17 May 1988 *Employees:* 3
Net Worth: £67,867 *Total Assets:* £379,783
Registered Office: Ayrton House, Commerce Way, Liverpool, L8 7BA
Shareholders: Gerald Francis Obrien; Brigid Christina Obrien
Officers: Philip Didlick, Secretary; Philip Didlick [1976] Director/Accountant; Generald Francis O'Brien [1949] Director; Padraic Marc O'Brien [1979] Director

Pharmasol Limited
Incorporated: 25 April 2002 *Employees:* 65
Net Worth Deficit: £2,814,884 *Total Assets:* £5,107,678
Registered Office: Ayrton House, Parliament Business Park, Commerce Way, Liverpool, L8 7BA
Officers: Philip Didlick, Secretary; Philip Didlick [1976] Director/Accountant; Generald Francis O'Brien [1949] Director/Retail Pharmacist; Padraic Marc Obrien [1979] Director

Pharmaspec Limited
Incorporated: 3 February 2004 *Employees:* 2
Net Worth: £741,085 *Total Assets:* £820,418
Registered Office: Unit 31 Bordesley Trading Estate, Bordesley Green Road, Bordesley Green, Birmingham, B8 1BZ
Shareholder: Majad Hussain
Officers: Dr Majad Hussain, Secretary; Dr Majad Hussain [1975] Director; Dr Qamar Nawaz [1973] Director

Pharmau Healthcare Ltd
Incorporated: 19 October 2018
Registered Office: Suite 3c, Chapel Allerton House, 114 Harrogate Road, Leeds, LS7 4NY
Parent: Hereford Holdings Ltd
Officers: Andrew John Lenney [1972] Director

Pharmax Limited
Incorporated: 11 November 1960
Registered Office: Ridings Point, Whistler Drive, Castleford, W Yorks, WF10 5HX
Parent: Teva Laboratories UK Limited
Officers: Dean Michael Cooper [1972] Director/Chartered Accountant; Kim Innes [1968] Director/General Manager

Pharmaxo Pharmacy Services Limited
Incorporated: 5 August 2009 *Employees:* 33
Net Worth: £1,964,968 *Total Assets:* £7,044,014
Registered Office: 3 Corsham Science Park, Park Lane, Corsham, Wilts, SN13 9FU
Parent: Qualasept Pharmaxo Holdings Limited
Officers: Alison Maria Davis [1973] Director; Christopher James Fountain [1966] Director/Chartered Accountant; Christopher Dean Watt [1968] Director

PharmaYouth Ltd.
Incorporated: 23 November 2015
Registered Office: 284 Kingsway, Manchester, M19 1QA
Shareholders: Hussain Abdeh; Mehraan Sattar; Omar Hosam Noori
Officers: Hussain Abdeh [1992] Director [French]; Omar Noori [1991] Director; Mehraan Sattar [1991] Director

Pharmazy Limited
Incorporated: 28 March 2018
Registered Office: 17 Rosemary Avenue, London, N9 8QX
Major Shareholder: Yasmin Wessal Zobedey
Officers: Husham Jawad Kadhim [1979] Director [Iraqi]; Yasmin Wessal Zobedey [1989] Director

Pharmcom Trading Limited
Incorporated: 17 July 2018
Registered Office: First Floor, 85 Great Portland Street, London, W1W 7LT
Officers: Lajos Balog [1994] Director [Hungarian]

Pharmlife Industry Ltd
Incorporated: 11 July 2018
Registered Office: Ground Floor, Studentwise, Abchurch Chambers, 24 St Peters Road, Bournemouth, BH1 2LN
Parent: My Family Holding Ltd
Officers: Massimo Berti [1958] Director [Italian]

Pharmvit Limited
Incorporated: 23 October 1979 *Employees:* 24
Net Worth: £120,960 *Total Assets:* £5,199,113
Registered Office: 177 Bilton Road, Greenford, Middlesex, UB6 7HQ
Major Shareholder: Khalid Latif
Officers: Khalid Latif [1954] Director/Management Accountant

Phetalz Ltd
Incorporated: 19 February 2013 *Employees:* 4
Net Worth Deficit: £32,643 *Total Assets:* £34,752
Registered Office: 4 Ives Way, Hopton on Sea, Great Yarmouth, Norfolk, NR31 9TN
Shareholders: Waheedat Owodeyi; Jamiu Owodeyi
Officers: Jamiu Owodeyi, Secretary; Dr Jamiu Owodeyi [1973] Director [Nigerian]; Waheedat Owodeyi [1979] Director [Nigerian]

Phico Therapeutics Limited
Incorporated: 30 August 2000 *Employees:* 25
Net Worth Deficit: £2,763,897 *Total Assets:* £2,222,978
Registered Office: Bertarelli Building, Bourn Hall, High Street, Bourn, Cambs, CB23 2TN
Officers: David Colin Beadle [1968] Director/Biotechnology Executive; Heather Marie Fairhead [1956] Director; Allan Jerome Hirst [1949] Director/Financial Services [American]; Dr Anthony Francis Martin [1954] Director/Consultant [Irish]; Robert Dwyer Nolan [1943] Director [Irish]; Professor Mark Harvey Wilcox [1962] Director/Hospital Consultant

Phytacol Limited
Incorporated: 24 February 2009 *Employees:* 1
Net Worth Deficit: £106,728 *Total Assets:* £152,552
Registered Office: 10 Station Road, Henley on Thames, Oxon, RG9 1AY
Major Shareholder: Michael John Allaway
Officers: Michael John Allaway, Secretary; Michael John Allaway [1947] Director

Phyto Products Limited
Incorporated: 19 January 1981
Net Worth: £541,235 *Total Assets:* £630,571
Registered Office: Unit 2 Sherbrook Enterprise, 100 Sherbrook Road, Daybrook, Nottingham, NG5 6AB
Shareholders: Dawn Parkin; Exors of Hein Hidde Zeylstra
Officers: Dawn Parkin [1959] Director/Medical Herbalist

Phytoceutical Limited
Incorporated: 1 September 1998
Net Worth Deficit: £44,824 *Total Assets:* £46,953
Registered Office: The Harrow Cottage, North Street, Midhurst, W Sussex, GU29 9DJ
Major Shareholder: William Andrew Buchanan
Officers: William Andrew Buchanan [1957] Director Herbal Cosmetics

Phytovation Limited
Incorporated: 2 December 2004 *Employees:* 16
Net Worth: £754,678 *Total Assets:* £1,059,008
Registered Office: Overshot, Badger Lane, Oxford, OX1 5BL
Shareholders: Roger Spencer Jones; Brian Kay Shand; Andrew Paul Beggin
Officers: Andrew Paul Beggin [1954] Director; Roy Dunsmore Fitzsimmons [1944] Director; Sir Roger Spencer Jones [1943] Director; Bryan Kay Shand [1941] Director

Pine Technologies Limited
Incorporated: 5 February 2018
Registered Office: Mfm 32 Mitcham Lane, London, SW16 6NW
Shareholder: Sampson Sule
Officers: Sampson Sule [1963] Director [Nigerian]

Pinewood Healthcare Limited
Incorporated: 23 November 2012 *Employees:* 2
Net Worth: £14,000 *Total Assets:* £16,000
Registered Office: c/o Wockhardt UK Limited, Ash Road North, Wrexham Industrial Estate, Wrexham, Clwyd, LL13 9UF
Officers: Jason Wainwright, Secretary; Ajay Sahni [1966] Director [Belgian]; Gopalakrishnan Venkatesan [1964] Director [Indian]

Pioneer UK Holdings Limited
Incorporated: 2 June 2016
Net Worth: £218,100 *Total Assets:* £219,060
Registered Office: Capital Building, Tyndall Street, Cardiff, CF10 4AZ
Parent: Pioneer UK Midco 2 Limited
Officers: Salim Haffar [1973] Director [French]; Remy Hauser [1967] Director/MD - Industry Value Creation Partners Group [Swiss]; Sujit John [1983] Director/Finance [American]; III Mitchell [1954] Director [American]

Pioneer UK Midco 1 Limited
Incorporated: 1 June 2016 *Employees:* 3,121
Net Worth: £282,002,912 *Total Assets:* £893,723,520
Registered Office: Capital Building, Tyndall Street, Cardiff, CF10 4AZ
Officers: Salim Haffar [1973] Director [French]; Remy Hauser [1967] Director/MD - Industry Value Creation Partners Group [Swiss]; Sujit John [1983] Director/Finance [American]; III Mitchell [1954] Director [American]

Pioneer UK Midco 2 Limited
Incorporated: 2 June 2016
Net Worth: £340,309,856 *Total Assets:* £340,309,856
Registered Office: Capital Building, Tyndall Street, Cardiff, CF10 4AZ
Parent: Pioneer UK Midco 1 Limited
Officers: Salim Haffar [1973] Director [French]; Remy Hauser [1967] Director/MD - Industry Value Creation Partners Group [Swiss]; Sujit John [1983] Director/Finance [American]; William T Mitchell III [1954] Director [American]

Piramal Critical Care Limited
Incorporated: 22 June 2004 *Employees:* 16
Previous: Piramal Life Sciences (UK) Limited
Net Worth: £18,122,694 *Total Assets:* £276,387,680
Registered Office: Ground Floor, Suite 4, Heathrow Boulevard East Wing, 280 Bath Road, West Drayton, Middlesex, UB7 0DQ
Officers: Kaushik Upadhyay, Secretary; Peter Daniel Deyoung [1978] Director/Chief Executive Officer of Piramal Critical Care B [American]; William John Hargan [1958] Director/VP Sales and Marketing; Kaushik Upadhyay [1980] Director [Indian]

Mimi Pisano Limited
Incorporated: 26 April 2005
Registered Office: 64 Green Lane, Imperial Road, Windsor, Berks, SL4 3SA
Officers: Dr Anthony Pisano [1963] Director/Scientist [Italian]

Placebex Ltd
Incorporated: 29 April 2015
Previous: The Bees Knees Honey Company Ltd
Net Worth: £100 *Total Assets:* £100
Registered Office: Flat 34, 68 Vincent Square, London, SW1P 2NU
Major Shareholder: Michael Louis Conitzer
Officers: Michael Louis Conitzer, Secretary; Daniel John Alexander Conitzer [1971] Director

Plackett Limited
Incorporated: 6 December 2016
Net Worth: £100 *Total Assets:* £100
Registered Office: 31 Edward Road, Eastwood, Nottingham, NG16 3EU
Major Shareholder: Michael Plackett
Officers: Michael Plackett [1953] Director/Aromatherapy

Plantgenic Ltd
Incorporated: 16 November 2018
Registered Office: 20 Donns Close, Patchway, Bristol, BS34 5JW
Major Shareholder: Adrian Szekeres
Officers: Adrian Szekeres [1990] Director/Entrepreneur [Hungarian]

Pliva Pharma Limited
Incorporated: 10 August 1989
Registered Office: Ridings Point, Whistler Drive, Castleford, W Yorks, WF10 5HX
Parent: Teva UK Holdings Limited
Officers: Dean Michael Cooper [1972] Director/Chartered Accountant; Kim Innes [1968] Director/General Manager

PLS Microbiology Limited
Incorporated: 9 February 2010 *Employees:* 1
Net Worth: £60,748 *Total Assets:* £66,029
Registered Office: Wiston House, 1 Wiston Avenue, Worthing, W Sussex, BN14 7QL
Officers: Linda Mary Lovegrove Saville [1961] Director; Paul Dominic Lovegrove Saville [1957] Director/Microbiology Consultant; Linda Mary Lovegrove-Saville [1961] Director; Paul Dominic Lovegrove-Saville [1957] Director/Microbiologist

Plus Orthopedics (UK) Limited
Incorporated: 17 November 1993
Registered Office: 15 Adam Street, London, WC2N 6LA
Parent: Smith & Nephew Trading Group Limited
Officers: Timothy John Allison [1970] Director; Susan Margaret Swabey [1961] Director/Chartered Secretary

Pneumoflex E.U. Limited
Incorporated: 9 March 2009
Registered Office: First Floor, 10 Temple Back, Bristol, BS1 6FL
Officers: Dr William Robert Addington II [1962] Director/Physician [American]; Dr Stuart Perry Miller [1954] Director/Physician [American]

Point International Limited
Incorporated: 31 May 1988
Registered Office: 27-28 Eastcastle Street, London, W1W 8DH
Major Shareholder: Scot Frederick von Bergen
Officers: Facundo Ganin [1971] Director [Argentinian]; Scot Frederick Von Bergen [1946] Director [American]

Pollenase Limited
Incorporated: 13 October 2014
Registered Office: Unit 2a, Old Dalby Business Park, Station Road, Old Dalby, Melton Mowbray, Leics, LE14 3NJ
Officers: Jayanti Chimanbhai Patel [1984] Executive Director; Kirit Chimanbhai Tulsibhai Patel [1980] Executive Director

Polychem Limited
Incorporated: 27 May 1980
Net Worth: £320,613 *Total Assets:* £2,453,003
Registered Office: 17 Warren Road, Purley, Surrey, CR8 1AF
Officers: Rizvan Kassam, Secretary; Kain Kassam [1988] Director/Self Employed; Rizwanali Noorali Kassam [1949] Director; Zain Kassam [1982] Director/Self Employed

N Popov Ltd
Incorporated: 2 July 2018
Registered Office: First Floor Flat, 33 Edith Road, London, W14 0SU
Major Shareholder: Nikolay Popov
Officers: Dr Nikolay Popov [1983] Director [Bulgarian]

Portola Pharma UK Limited
Incorporated: 29 April 2015
Net Worth Deficit: £565,839
Registered Office: Suite 1, 3rd Floor, 11-12 St James's Square, London, SW1Y 4LB
Officers: Michael Ouimette, Secretary; Janice Castillo [1947] Director/Vice President [American]; Mardi Dier [1964] Director/Executive Vice President; Michael Ouimette [1973] Director/Corporate Counsel [American]

Porton Biopharma Limited
Incorporated: 27 November 2014 *Employees:* 313
Net Worth: £78,866,000 *Total Assets:* £102,041,000
Registered Office: Manor Farm Road, Porton, Salisbury, Wilts, SP4 0JG
Parent: Secretary of State for Health
Officers: Nigel Richard Mowbray Mackie, Secretary; Michael Brodie [1969] Finance and Commercial Director; Nigel Stanley Brooksby [1950] Director; Barry Clare [1953] Director; Donald Richard Gleave [1963] Director/Deputy Chief Executive; Martin Hindle [1943] Director/Independent Chairman; Roger James Hinton [1958] Director/Manager

Porvair PLC
Incorporated: 3 September 1982 *Employees:* 819
Net Worth: £74,869,000 *Total Assets:* £127,947,000
Registered Office: 7 Regis Place, Bergen Way, Kings Lynn, Norfolk, PE30 2JN
Officers: Christopher Patric Tyler, Finance Director; Paul David Dean [1961] Director; Sarah Jean Martin [1965] Director [Irish]; John Edward Nicholas [1956] Director; Benjamin Denys William Stocks [1962] Director; Christopher Patric Tyler [1962] Finance Director

Positive Diagnostics Ltd
Incorporated: 5 December 2003
Net Worth: £24,607 *Total Assets:* £52,275
Registered Office: 13 Barn Crescent, Margate, Kent, CT9 5HF
Officers: Helen Rees Jones, Secretary; Dawn Margaret Gallimore [1941] Director/Chemical Analyst

Premax Europe Limited
Incorporated: 17 August 2016
Net Worth Deficit: £2,602 *Total Assets:* £37,085
Registered Office: 23 Ansdell Street, London, W8 5BN
Shareholders: Randall Lyall Cooper; Peter Damian Brucker
Officers: Peter Damian Brukner [1952] Director [Australian]; Randall Lyall Cooper [1974] Director [Australian]; Cameron John Tudor [1975] Director [Australian]

Prep Skincare Products Limited
Incorporated: 14 August 2012
Net Worth Deficit: £24,346 *Total Assets:* £28,371
Registered Office: Camden 255, Brooklands Road, Weybridge, Surrey, KT13 0RN
Officers: Ross John Richardson [1967] Director/Marketing Manager [Irish]

Shirley Price Aromatherapy Limited
Incorporated: 15 August 2006 *Employees:* 4
Net Worth Deficit: £32,579 *Total Assets:* £83,766
Registered Office: 8 Hawley Road, Hinckley, Leics, LE10 0PR
Major Shareholder: Peter Ian Brealey
Officers: Peter Ian Brealey, Secretary; Peter Ian Brealey [1958] Director/Accountant; Mun Yue Chang [1964] Director [Chinese]; Joon Lian Wong [1960] Director [Malaysian]

Primal Core UK Ltd
Incorporated: 28 August 2018
Registered Office: 20-22 Wenlock Road, London, N1 7GU
Major Shareholder: Michael McCartney
Officers: Michael McCartney [1985] Director

Prime Medical Equipment Ltd
Incorporated: 20 June 2018
Registered Office: 71-75 Shelton Street, London, WC2H 9JQ
Major Shareholder: Mohamed Ali Mohamed Dermish
Officers: Mohamed Dermish, Secretary; Mohamed Ali Mohamed Dermish [1994] Director [Libyan]

Prime Test Limited
Incorporated: 28 March 2013
Net Worth: £78,696 Total Assets: £78,696
Registered Office: 98 Swallow Road, Ipswich, Suffolk, IP2 0TS
Major Shareholder: Karl Wright
Officers: Karl Wright, Secretary; Karl Wright [1957] Director; Sam Wright [1997] Director

Primetonic Ltd
Incorporated: 27 April 2018
Registered Office: 129 Burnley Road, Padiham, Burnley, Lancs, BB12 8BA
Shareholders: Josephine Miranda; Domonic Robertini
Officers: Josephine Miranda [1964] Director [Filipino]

Primius Lab Limited
Incorporated: 5 December 2011
Net Worth Deficit: £8,869,655 Total Assets: £1,539,422
Registered Office: 48 Britannia Street, London, WC1X 9BS
Major Shareholder: Perry Bourkas
Officers: Eric Yvan Thierry [1968] Director [French]

Principle Healthcare International Limited
Incorporated: 20 January 2004 Employees: 139
Net Worth: £4,431,476 Total Assets: £9,670,585
Registered Office: Principle Healthcare International Ltd, Airedale Business Centre, Millennium Road, Skipton, N Yorks, BD23 2TZ
Major Shareholder: Michael John Davies
Officers: Richard Howard Doyle, Secretary/Chartered Accountant; Andrew Michael Davies [1982] Director; Michael John Davies [1951] Director; Philip Benjamin Davies [1977] Director

Principle Healthcare Limited
Incorporated: 7 September 2001 Employees: 23
Net Worth: £1,711,821 Total Assets: £4,341,947
Registered Office: Airedale Business Centre, Millennium Road, Skipton, N Yorks, BD23 2TZ
Shareholders: Principle Healthcare International; Principle Healthcare International Ltd
Officers: Richard Doyle, Secretary; Clare Campbell [1975] Director; Andrew Michael Davies [1982] Director; Michael John Davies [1951] Director; Philip Benjamin Davies [1977] Director

Private Trichology Clinic Ltd
Incorporated: 29 May 2018
Registered Office: 3 Towers Square, Meanwood, Leeds, LS6 4PN
Major Shareholder: Agnes Marufu
Officers: Agnes Marufu [1973] Director/Trichologist

Pro Bono Bio Limited
Incorporated: 6 December 2018
Registered Office: Leverton House, 13 Bedford Square, London, WC1B 3RA
Major Shareholder: Biresh Roy
Officers: Biresh Roy [1962] Director

G. & M. Procter Limited
Incorporated: 31 March 1989 Employees: 103
Net Worth: £26,308,000 Total Assets: £28,281,000
Registered Office: 3 Fountain Drive, Inchinnan Business Park, Paisley, Renfrewshire, PA4 9RF
Parent: Oxoid Limited
Officers: Rhona Gregg, Secretary; Euan Daney Ross Cameron [1976] Director; Claude Georgette Emilie Dartiguelongue [1959] Director/President of Microbiology Division [French]; Lucie Mary Katja Grant [1976] Director/Solicitor; David John Norman [1960] Director/Chartered Accountant; Anthony Hugh Smith [1962] Director/Vice President, Tax and Treasury [American]

Prometic Pharma SMT Limited
Incorporated: 11 December 2015 Employees: 11
Net Worth: £55,836,120 Total Assets: £82,372,512
Registered Office: Prometic Pharma SMT Limited, Horizon Park, Barton Road, Comberton, Cambridge, CB23 7AJ
Parent: Prometic Pharma SMT Holdings Limited
Officers: Prof. Simon Geoffrey Best [1956] Director; Kurt Stefan Victor Clulow [1970] Director [Canadian/British]; Kenneth Harry Galbraith [1962] Director [Canadian]; David John Jeans [1950] Director; Dr John Edward Moran [1945] Director/Chief Medical Officer [American/Canadian]; Bruce Philip Pritchard [1972] Director; Patrick Sartore [1974] Director and Company Secretary [Canadian]; Bruce Jeffrey Wendel [1953] Director [American]

Promtain Ltd
Incorporated: 8 June 2018
Registered Office: 546 Chorley Old Road, Bolton, Lancs, BL1 6AB
Shareholders: Michael Peter Ang; Gary Owen
Officers: Michael Peter Ang [1990] Director [Filipino]

Protak Scientific Limited
Incorporated: 19 November 2014 Employees: 4
Net Worth: £313,183 Total Assets: £1,069,487
Registered Office: Luminox House, 48 Holmethorpe Avenue, Redhill, Surrey, RH1 2NL
Officers: Phillip Robert Charles Godden [1977] Director

Proteintech Europe Limited
Incorporated: 16 May 2006 Employees: 9
Net Worth: £939,352 Total Assets: £1,105,635
Registered Office: 4 Greek Street, Stockport, Cheshire, SK3 8AB
Parent: Proteintech Group, Inc
Officers: Zhihua BA, Secretary; Dr Jianxun Li [1962] Director [American]; Kier Timothy Wilkinson [1986] Director

Protezione Herbals PVT Ltd
Incorporated: 26 February 2018
Registered Office: 27 Old Gloucester Street, London, WC1N 3AX
Major Shareholder: Amit Mandal
Officers: Amit Mandal, Secretary; Amit Mandal [1984] Director [Indian]

Prothea-X Limited
Incorporated: 11 July 2018
Registered Office: 7-8 Eghams Court, Boston Drive, Bourne End, Bucks, SL8 5YS
Officers: Mark Bradley [1962] Director; Kanwaldeep Dhaliwal [1975] Director; Maziar Zarrehparvar [1968] Director [Danish]

Protherics UK Limited
Incorporated: 12 November 1997 *Employees:* 108
Net Worth: £278,511,008 *Total Assets:* £283,756,000
Registered Office: Blaenwaun Ffostrasol, Llandysul, Ceredigion, SA44 5JT
Parent: BTG Management Services Limited
Officers: Elaine Maureen Johnston, Secretary; Anthony Higham [1966] Operations Director; Elaine Maureen Johnston [1976] Director/Lawyer [Irish]; Timothy John Martel [1975] Director/Accountant

Protiaso Ltd
Incorporated: 28 May 2012
Net Worth: £42 *Total Assets:* £42
Registered Office: Brickfield Cottage, Hurn, Christchurch, Dorset, BH23 6AR
Officers: Professor John Patrick Baldwin [1935] Director/Scientist; Hugh Smallman [1948] Director/Scientist; Dr Christopher Wood [1957] Director/Scientist

Proveca Limited
Incorporated: 15 July 2010 *Employees:* 8
Net Worth Deficit: £3,717,171 *Total Assets:* £2,439,543
Registered Office: Neo Building, Charlotte Street, Manchester, M1 4ET
Officers: Simon Barter [1958] Commercial Director; Christopher David Brinsmead [1959] Director; Simon Peter Bryson [1968] Director; Christoph Oliver Ruedig [1976] Director/Investor Manager [German]; Dr Helen Margaret Shaw [1962] Director

Provita Eurotech Ltd
Incorporated: 19 February 1990 *Employees:* 22
Net Worth: £1,386,735 *Total Assets:* £2,331,792
Registered Office: 21 Bankmore Road, Omagh, Co Tyrone, BT79 0EU
Major Shareholder: Michael Kerr
Officers: Stacey Lorraine McAleer, Secretary; Michael Kerr [1961] Director/Management

Prozomix Limited
Incorporated: 28 February 2008 *Employees:* 16
Net Worth: £242,565 *Total Assets:* £648,337
Registered Office: Unit 3 Station Court, Haltwhistle, Northumberland, NE49 9HN
Shareholders: Simon James Charnock; Ruth Marie Lloyd
Officers: Simon James Charnock, Secretary; Simon James Charnock [1973] Director; Ruth Marie Lloyd [1971] Director

Prulab Pharma Ltd
Incorporated: 27 February 2017
Net Worth: £3,460 *Total Assets:* £37,810
Registered Office: Victoria Square, Victoria Street, St Albans, Herts, AL1 3TF
Shareholders: Alan Cheshire; Mumtaz Cheshire
Officers: Alan Cheshire [1949] Director; Mumtaz Cheshire [1953] Director

PSR Analytical Services Ltd
Incorporated: 15 July 2002
Net Worth: £8,137 *Total Assets:* £64,056
Registered Office: 13 Finch Street, Brindley Ford, Stoke on Trent, Staffs, ST8 7QQ
Officers: Ashley Rabone, Secretary; Philip Stephen Rabone [1954] Director/Analytical Consultant

PT Direct Limited
Incorporated: 8 June 2015 *Employees:* 2
Net Worth: £98 *Total Assets:* £36,633
Registered Office: Coopers Farm, Newton, Thornbury, Bristol, BS35 1LG
Shareholders: Nicola Juliette Barnes; Thomas Richard Barnes
Officers: Thomas Richard Barnes, Secretary; Thomas Richard Barnes [1969] Director

PTC Therapeutics, Limited
Incorporated: 24 February 2012 *Employees:* 10
Net Worth: £401,417 *Total Assets:* £1,489,343
Registered Office: Hill House, 1 Little New Street, London, EC4A 3TR
Parent: PTC Therapeutics, Inc.
Officers: Mark Elliott Boulding, Secretary; Adrian James Haigh [1959] Director/Senior Vice President & General Manager EMEA; Stuart Walter Peltz [1959] Director [American]

PTGO Sever UK Limited
Incorporated: 23 May 2008
Registered Office: 6 St David's Square, Westferry Road, London, E14 3WA
Major Shareholder: Dmitry Sokolov
Officers: Dmitry Sokolov [1965] Director [Russian]

Pulmeze Limited
Incorporated: 29 January 2014
Registered Office: York House, Winkfield Lane, Winkfield, Windsor, Berks, SL4 4RU
Major Shareholder: Stephen Charles Appelbee
Officers: Stephen Charles Appelbee [1956] Director

Purce Associates Limited
Incorporated: 11 June 1971
Registered Office: 453-455 Antrim Road, Belfast, BT15 3BL
Major Shareholder: Gwendoline Maria Purce
Officers: Gwendoline Maria Purce, Secretary; Gwendoline Maria Purce [1963] Director

Pure Peace Ltd
Incorporated: 20 February 2017 *Employees:* 1
Net Worth Deficit: £3,814 *Total Assets:* £5,036
Registered Office: 57 Darwin Drive, Tonbridge, Kent, TN10 4SA
Officers: Denice Cartwright [1973] Director/Candle and Bath Product Maker

Purely Health Ltd
Incorporated: 22 January 2019
Registered Office: Imperial House, Butts Close, Thornton-Cleveleys, Lancs, FY5 4HT
Officers: Graham Ian Butler [1960] Director

Purple Healthcare Limited
Incorporated: 23 July 2018
Registered Office: 20 Rushall Manor Road, Walsall, W Midlands, WS4 2HF
Officers: Jitendrakumar Desai [1974] Director/Pharmacist

PVR Works Ltd
Incorporated: 25 November 2016 *Employees:* 2
Net Worth Deficit: £38,733 *Total Assets:* £53,789
Registered Office: The Old Surgery, 43 Derbe Road, Lytham St Annes, Lancs, FY8 1NJ
Shareholders: Helen Paula Erichsen; Espen Erichsen
Officers: Helen Paula Erichsen [1966] Director

PW Green UK II Limited
Incorporated: 11 September 2018
Registered Office: 8 Hanover Square, London, W1S 1HQ
Shareholders: Bertrand Perrodo; Andrew Wynn
Officers: Dario Marenghi [1978] Director; Andrew Thomas Wynn [1984] Director

Q Health Direct Ltd
Incorporated: 9 August 2017
Registered Office: 29 Ambergate Drive, Pontprennau, Cardiff, CF23 8AX
Officers: Muthanna Albaldawi [1977] Director of Research and Development [Iraqi]; Colin John Conrad Cunningham [1974] Director

Qiagen Manchester Limited
Incorporated: 14 February 2001 *Employees:* 238
Net Worth: £23,218,536 *Total Assets:* £47,177,324
Registered Office: Skelton House, Lloyd Street North, Manchester, M15 6SH
Parent: Qiagen NV
Officers: Paul Jonathan Birch, Secretary; Thierry Bernard [1964] Director/Senior VP Head of Business Area Molecular Diagnostics [French]; Roland Sackers [1968] Director [German]; Peer Michael Schatz [1965] Director [Austrian]; Thomas Schweins [1967] Director/Senior Vice President Life Sciences [German]

QOL Therapeutics UK Limited
Incorporated: 24 January 2013
Net Worth Deficit: £15,977 *Total Assets:* £2,336
Registered Office: 5 The Green, Richmond, Surrey, TW9 1PL
Officers: Jamie Nicholas Bradshaw [1976] Director; David Spencer Tuomey [1970] Director [Irish]

Qualasept Holdings Limited
Incorporated: 20 April 2016 *Employees:* 208
Net Worth: £13,619,092 *Total Assets:* £45,933,204
Registered Office: 3 Corsham Science Park, Park Lane, Corsham, Wilts, SN13 9FU
Shareholders: Christopher Dean Watt; Richard John Wastnage
Officers: Richard John Wastnage [1965] Director/Pharmacist; Christopher Dean Watt [1968] Director; Maria Ann Watt [1970] Director/Pharmacist

Qualasept Limited
Incorporated: 30 August 2005 *Employees:* 169
Net Worth: £13,716,244 *Total Assets:* £34,878,516
Registered Office: 3 Corsham Science Park, Park Lane, Corsham, Wilts, SN13 9FU
Parent: Qualasept Pharmaxo Holdings Limited
Officers: Christopher James Fountain [1966] Director/Chartered Accountant; Richard John Wastnage [1965] Director/Pharmacist; Christopher Dean Watt [1968] Director

Quality Products 360 Ltd
Incorporated: 30 November 2016
Registered Office: 20-22 Wenlock Road, London, N1 7GU
Major Shareholder: Patrizio Gastaldo
Officers: Patrizio Gastaldo [1960] Director/GP [Italian]

Quality Skincare Ltd
Incorporated: 9 April 2018
Registered Office: 68 Medlicott Road, Birmingham, B11 1PY
Officers: Sehra Khan [1991] Director/Self Employed; Saqiba Najum [1992] Director/Self Employed

Quantum Biomed Farms PLC
Incorporated: 7 February 2019
Registered Office: 3rd Floor, 207 Regent Street, London, W1B 3HH
Officers: Arnold Leonard Gustafson, Secretary; Arnold Leonard Gustafson [1955] Director/Agronomist [Canadian]; John Tourette [1952] Director/Financial Consultant [Greek]

Quantum Pharma 2014 Limited
Incorporated: 17 October 2014 *Employees:* 6
Net Worth: £20,258,000 *Total Assets:* £49,960,000
Registered Office: Quantum House, Hobson Industrial Estate, Burnopfield, Co Durham, NE16 6EA
Parent: Quantum Pharma Holdings Limited
Officers: Amanda Miller, Secretary; David John Bryant [1967] Director/Chief Business Officer; Richard John Paling [1970] Director/Group Financial Controller

Quantum Pharma Holdings Limited
Incorporated: 17 October 2014 *Employees:* 5
Previous: Quantum Pharma Holdings PLC
Net Worth: £97,339,000 *Total Assets:* £121,374,000
Registered Office: Quantum House, Hobson Industrial Estate, Burnopfield, Co Durham, NE16 6EA
Parent: Clinigen Group PLC
Officers: Amanda Miller, Secretary; David John Bryant [1967] Director/Chief Business Officer; Richard John Paling [1970] Director/Group Financial Controller

Quantum Pharmaceutical Limited
Incorporated: 24 September 2004 *Employees:* 257
Net Worth: £7,469,000 *Total Assets:* £55,414,000
Registered Office: Quantum House, Hobson Industrial Estate, Burnopfield, Co Durham, NE16 6EA
Parent: Quantum Pharma Group Limited
Officers: Amanda Miller, Secretary; Andrew Paul Matthews [1976] Operations Director; David Alan Sanson [1959] Technical Director; Michael James Tagg [1982] Finance Director

Quay Pharmaceuticals Limited
Incorporated: 19 January 2001 *Employees:* 105
Net Worth: £5,038,255 *Total Assets:* £8,695,925
Registered Office: Quay House, 28 Parkway, Deeside Industrial Park, Deeside, Flintshire, CH5 2NS
Shareholders: Professor Michael Henry Rubinstein; Rudolph David Patterson
Officers: David Hugh Patterson, Secretary; David Hugh Patterson [1965] Commercial Director; Maireadh Anne Pedersen [1967] Director/Business Development; Professor Michael Henry Rubinstein [1944] Director/Research Pharmacist

Quest HC Limited
Incorporated: 3 November 2015
Net Worth: £29,761 *Total Assets:* £3,707,726
Registered Office: Alexander House, 60-61 Tenby Street North, Birmingham, B1 3EG
Major Shareholder: Majad Hussain
Officers: Dr Majad Hussain [1975] Director

Quest Healthcare Aseptics Limited
Incorporated: 6 September 2013
Registered Office: Alexander House, 60-61 Tenby Street North, Birmingham, B1 3EG
Major Shareholder: Majad Hussain
Officers: Yasar Hussain [1976] Director/Pharmacist

Quest Healthcare Injectables Limited
Incorporated: 6 September 2013
Registered Office: Alexander House, 60-61 Tenby Street North, Birmingham, B1 3EG
Major Shareholder: Majad Hussain
Officers: Yasar Hussain [1976] Director/Pharmacist

Quest Healthcare Non-Injectables Limited
Incorporated: 6 September 2013
Registered Office: Alexander House, 60-61 Tenby Street North, Birmingham, B1 3EG
Shareholders: Isma Naz; Shazia Akhtar; Naseeba Sabir
Officers: Yasar Hussain [1976] Director/Pharmacist

Quest Healthcare Solutions Limited
Incorporated: 11 June 2013
Registered Office: Alexander House, 60-61 Tenby Street North, Birmingham, B1 3EG
Shareholders: Majad Hussain; Azmat Begum; Sabar Hussain
Officers: Dr Majad Hussain [1975] Director

Quest Ingredients Limited
Incorporated: 25 August 2000 *Employees:* 33
Previous: Flavex International Limited
Net Worth: £512,984 *Total Assets:* £3,689,597
Registered Office: Units 1-4 Gooses Foot Industrial Estate, Kingstone, Hereford, HR2 9HY
Shareholders: Mohamed Abbas Hassam; Ahmed Gulamabbas Hassam
Officers: Neil Brett Dainty [1960] Finance Director; Dr Ahmed Gulamabbas Hassam [1948] Director/Biochemist; Mohamed Abbas Hassam [1980] Director/Lawyer

Quest Pharm Limited
Incorporated: 21 March 2018
Registered Office: Alexander House, 60-61 Tenby Street North, Birmingham, B1 3EG
Officers: Yasar Hussain [1976] Director/Pharmacist

Quicksilver Scientific Europe Limited
Incorporated: 1 March 2013
Previous: Kazakh Healthcare Limited
Net Worth: £100 *Total Assets:* £100
Registered Office: First Floor, Roxburghe House, 273-287 Regent Street, London, W1B 2HA
Shareholder: Ann Julie Mary Edwards
Officers: Ivan Berkes [1968] Director/Strategy Consultant [Slovak]; Ann Julie Mary Edwards [1956] Director; Tim Charles Jackson [1959] Director

Quotient Diagnostics Limited
Incorporated: 6 December 2002
Net Worth: £141,604 *Total Assets:* £141,604
Registered Office: Avon House, 19 Stanwell Road, Penarth, Cardiff, CF64 2EZ
Parent: EKF Diagnostics Holdings PLC
Officers: Salim Hamir, Secretary; Julian Huw Baines [1964] Director; Richard Anthony Evans [1957] Director

Qures Healthcare Limited
Incorporated: 24 May 2011
Net Worth: £66 *Total Assets:* £66
Registered Office: Bank Chambers, Brook Street, Bishops Waltham, Hants, SO32 1AX
Major Shareholder: Richard George Stead
Officers: Richard George Stead, Secretary; Richard George Stead [1949] Director

R D T Technology Limited
Incorporated: 22 December 2005 *Employees:* 9
Net Worth: £52,295 *Total Assets:* £142,795
Registered Office: 2 The Pantiles, Ferringham Lane, Ferring, Worthing, W Sussex, BN12 5NE
Shareholders: Derren Neve; Trevor Howard Neve
Officers: Derren Neve [1971] Director; Trevor Howard Neve [1946] Director/Engineer

Rainbow Engineering Services Limited
Incorporated: 17 March 2010
Registered Office: Shaftesbury Industrial Centre, Icknield Way, Letchworth Garden City, Herts, SG6 1RR
Major Shareholder: Alan Lynford Profit
Officers: Alan Lynford Profit [1950] Director/Engineer

Pete Randle Grinding & Son Limited
Incorporated: 18 April 2003
Net Worth: £18,130 *Total Assets:* £39,994
Registered Office: Unit 9 Enterprise Workshops, 28 Heming Road, Washford Industrial Estate, Redditch, Worcs, B98 0DH
Shareholder: Neil Raymond Randle
Officers: Samantha Barrass, Secretary; Luke Randle [1994] Director; Neil Raymond Randle [1966] Director/Grinding

Ranir (Holdings) Limited
Incorporated: 11 February 2010
Net Worth Deficit: £4,552,085 *Total Assets:* £15,928,748
Registered Office: 4th Floor, Charles House, 100-110 Finchley Road, London, NW3 5JJ
Parent: Ranir LLC
Officers: Lucas Caspar Schwinner [1977] Finance Director [Austrian]

Ranir Limited
Incorporated: 16 February 1971 *Employees:* 22
Net Worth: £6,385,089 *Total Assets:* £28,971,104
Registered Office: 4th Floor, Charles House, 108-110 Finchley Road, London, NW3 5JJ
Shareholders: Ranir LLC; Ranir Holdings Limited
Officers: Nicki Marchant [1959] Director; Lucas Caspar Schwinner [1977] Finance Director [Austrian]; Richard Sorota [1963] Director/Chairman [American]

Ransom Naturals Limited
Incorporated: 24 January 2011 *Employees:* 38
Net Worth: £2,038,814 *Total Assets:* £3,996,917
Registered Office: Ayrton Saunders House, Parliament Business Park, Commerce Way, Liverpool, L8 7BA
Officers: Philip Didlick, Secretary; Philip Didlick [1976] Director/Accountant; Generald Francis O'Brien [1949] Director; Padraic Marc O'Brien [1979] Director

Rapid Nutrition PLC
Incorporated: 11 January 2012 *Employees:* 3
Net Worth: £6,928,913 *Total Assets:* £8,777,363
Registered Office: 20-22 Wenlock Road, London, N1 7GU
Officers: Shayne Anthony Kellow [1959] Director/Healthcare [Australian]; Simon St Ledger [1983] Director [Australian]; Vesta Venderbeken [1976] Director [Australian]

Rapidscan Pharma Solutions EU Limited
Incorporated: 17 August 2010
Net Worth Deficit: £352,000 *Total Assets:* £6,254,000
Registered Office: The Grove Centre, White Lion Road, Amersham, Bucks, HP7 9LL
Parent: General Electric Company
Officers: Emmanuel Francois Joel Ligner [1970] Director/Management Executive [French]; Etienne Louis Marie Robert Montagut [1975] Director/Global Product Leader [French]; Adrian Ashwin Narayan [1973] Director/Accountant

Raught Limited
Incorporated: 27 July 1973
Net Worth: £1,048 *Total Assets:* £59,352
Registered Office: 39 The Grove, Edgware, Middlesex, HA9 8QA
Shareholders: Jack Lassman; Israelith Sheila Lassman
Officers: Israelith Sheila Lassman, Secretary; Israelith Sheila Lassman [1943] Director; Jack Lassman [1931] Director

Re-Vire Limited
Incorporated: 9 January 2017
Registered Office: 1 Oakwood Rise, Leeds, LS8 2QY
Officers: Anthony Brown [1958] Director/Lecturer; Heiko Wurdak [1972] Director/Biochemist [German]

Reaxa Limited
Incorporated: 2 September 2003 *Employees:* 2
Net Worth: £419,501 *Total Assets:* £1,474,072
Registered Office: Biohub, Alderley Park, Macclesfield, Cheshire, SK10 4TG
Officers: Tanmay Naimish Godiawala [1986] Director [Indian]; Arunkumar Chhaganbhai Patel [1953] Director/Businessman

Recassa Limited
Incorporated: 3 October 2017
Registered Office: Suite 47, 95 Wilton Road, London, SW1V 1DW
Officers: Anthony William Slack [1963] Director/Businessman

Recentia Limited
Incorporated: 13 January 2015 *Employees:* 1
Net Worth Deficit: £247,119 *Total Assets:* £102,382
Registered Office: 21 Elthiron Road, London, SW6 4BN
Major Shareholder: Stephanie Capuano
Officers: Stephanie Capuano [1971] Director/Consultant

Recipharm HC Limited
Incorporated: 3 May 2018
Registered Office: London Road, Holmes Chapel, Cheshire, CW4 8BE
Parent: Recipharm Holdings Limited
Officers: Thomas Bengt Eldered [1960] Director/CEO at Recipharm AB [Swedish]; Mark Royston Quick [1966] Director/Executive Vice President Corporate Development

Recipharm Limited
Incorporated: 10 August 2012 *Employees:* 137
Net Worth Deficit: £2,515,000 *Total Assets:* £7,638,000
Registered Office: Bardsley Vale Mills, Oldham Road, Ashton under Lyne, Lancs, OL7 9RR
Parent: Recipharm Holdings Limited
Officers: Thomas Bengt Eldered [1960] Director [Swedish]; Mark Royston Quick [1966] Director

Reddy Quality Services Ltd
Incorporated: 10 January 2019
Registered Office: 16 Sullivan Way, Elstree, Borehamwood, Herts, WD6 3DH
Major Shareholder: Srujan Yakkati
Officers: Srujan Yakkati [1984] Director/Quality Assurance Consultant

Redlight Exchange Ltd
Incorporated: 5 June 2018
Registered Office: 42 Hampden Road, London, N17 0AY
Major Shareholder: Muhammad Abdul Qaiyum
Officers: Fatimah Begum, Secretary; Muhammad Abdul Qaiyum [1989] Director/Lawyer

Redrose Manufacturing Limited
Incorporated: 31 January 1995 *Employees:* 38
Net Worth: £1,021,056 *Total Assets:* £1,546,502
Registered Office: Unit 21A/B Cherry Way, Dubmire Industrial Estate, Houghton-le-Spring, Co Durham, DH4 5RJ
Major Shareholder: Nadia Mahan
Officers: David Goodings [1966] Managing Director; Nadia Mahan [1977] Director; Thomas Mahan [1943] Director

Redrose Nutraceuticals Limited
Incorporated: 21 February 2017
Registered Office: 21 A/B Cherry Way, Dubmire Industrial Estate, Fencehouses, Co Durham, DH4 5RJ
Shareholders: Thomas Mahan; Nadia Mahan
Officers: David Goodings [1966] Director/Operations Manager; Nadia Mahan [1977] Director; Thomas Mahan [1943] Director

Reelvision Print Limited
Incorporated: 4 July 2006
Net Worth: £3,911,774 *Total Assets:* £5,243,202
Registered Office: Reelvision Print Ltd, Carrs Industrial Estate, Commerce Street, Haslingden, Rossendale, Lancs, BB4 5JT
Officers: Michael John Davies, Secretary; Richard Doyle, Secretary; Gareth Clayton Bakewell [1968] Director; Kelvin John Reece [1967] Director/Secretary

Reem Tanning Company Limited
Incorporated: 25 June 2012
Net Worth Deficit: £1,815 *Total Assets:* £15,039
Registered Office: 212 Upholland Road, Billinge, Wigan, Lancs, WN5 7DJ
Shareholder: Philip Anthony Fouracre
Officers: Philip Anthony Fouracre [1972] Director/Business Development Chemist; Pauline Morley [1967] Operations Director

Regent Generics Limited
Incorporated: 26 July 2002
Registered Office: Lincoln House, 137-143 Hammersmith Road, London, W14 0QL
Officers: Arif Husain, Secretary/Chartered Accountant; Arif Husain [1945] Director/Chartered Accountant

Regent Pharmaceuticals Limited
Incorporated: 27 November 2013
Net Worth Deficit: £110,493 *Total Assets:* £976,710
Registered Office: 5 Darlington Close, Sandy, Beds, SG19 1RW
Officers: Samuel Akonwubel Atsu, Secretary; Faiz Juneja, Secretary; Rehan Ullah [1978] Commercial Director

Reig Jofre UK Limited
Incorporated: 7 November 2014 *Employees:* 2
Net Worth: £5,051,563 *Total Assets:* £5,463,440
Registered Office: Unit 9A Caddsdown Business Support Centre, Caddsdown Industrial Park, Bideford, Devon, EX39 3DX
Shareholders: Laboratorio Reig Jofre SA; Compania Espanola de Financiacion Del Desarrollo
Officers: Ignasi Biosca Reig [1968] Director [Spanish]; Gabriel Roig Zapatero [1972] Director/Chief Financial Officer [Spanish]

Rejuvenile Ltd
Incorporated: 16 October 2018
Registered Office: 78 Thomas Street, Rochdale, Lancs, OL12 8DG
Major Shareholder: Chris Salford
Officers: Chris Salford [1990] Director/Retired

Reld Tech Ltd
Incorporated: 13 November 2018
Registered Office: 2 Hazelwood Grove, South Croydon, Surrey, CR2 9DU
Major Shareholder: Reuben Luke Dawkins
Officers: Reuben Luke Dawkins [1987] Director/Founder

Remedi Medical Holdings Limited
Incorporated: 16 October 2013 *Employees:* 50
Net Worth: £6,007,621 *Total Assets:* £20,844,708
Registered Office: Nene House, 4 Rushmills, Northampton, NN4 7YB
Shareholders: Monisha Nikesh Kotecha; Nikesh Rasiklal Kotecha; Blue Skies Investments Limited
Officers: Monisha Nikesh Kotecha, Secretary; Monisha Nikesh Kotecha [1969] Director; Dr Nikesh Rasiklal Kotecha [1966] Director

Rena Specials Limited
Incorporated: 24 October 2014
Net Worth: £187 *Total Assets:* £899
Registered Office: Mill Farm, Church Street, Bainton, E Yorks, YO25 9NJ
Major Shareholder: Richard Stuart Eggleston
Officers: Dr Renda Eggleston [1959] Physician Clinical Director; Richard Stuart Eggleston [1960] Director/Pharmacist CEO; Ashwin Thacker [1954] Director [Indian]; Raju Thacker [1957] Director [Indian]

Renascience Pharma Limited
Incorporated: 4 February 2015
Net Worth: £7,236 *Total Assets:* £91,135
Registered Office: 11 George Street West, Luton, Beds, LU1 2BJ
Officers: Mobeen Akhtar [1981] Director; Ka Yan Che [1980] Director; Peter Mollison [1980] Director; Haziq Patel [1974] Director

Renew Medical UK Limited
Incorporated: 11 September 2014 *Employees:* 5
Net Worth Deficit: £16,888 *Total Assets:* £45,921
Registered Office: ATB Accounting Ltd, 850 Oxford Road, Reading, Berks, RG30 1EL
Officers: Tidhar Shalon [1965] Director/Business Executive [American]

Rescued By Nature Limited
Incorporated: 9 February 2018
Registered Office: 21 Morton Road, London, E15 4AN
Major Shareholder: Imtishal Whitney Zina Zeine
Officers: Imtishal Whitney Zina Zeine [1989] Director [Dutch]

Resok Healthcare Ltd
Incorporated: 24 August 2016
Registered Office: 3 Gower Street, London, WC1E 6HA
Officers: Ibrahim Abdelrazik Albayoomi Fouda [1978] Director [Egyptian]

Resolution Chemicals Limited
Incorporated: 3 June 1985 *Employees:* 7
Net Worth: £4,032,179 *Total Assets:* £5,262,351
Registered Office: 930 High Road, London, N12 9RT
Parent: Reso Holdings Limited
Officers: Nitanj Patel, Secretary; Nitanj Patel [1972] Director; Michael John Frederick Sparrow [1948] Director; Lawrence Stolzenberg [1947] Director

Resolution Generics Limited
Incorporated: 15 September 2011
Registered Office: 930 High Road, London, N12 9RT
Parent: Reso Holdings Limited
Officers: Nitanj Patel, Secretary; Nitanj Patel [1972] Director; Michael John Frederick Sparrow [1948] Director

Retrobot Ltd
Incorporated: 28 April 2018
Registered Office: Office 3, 146-148 Bury Old Road, Whitefield, Manchester, M45 6AT
Shareholders: Leny Villanueva; Ian Jones
Officers: Leny Villanueva [1971] Director [Filipino]

Retrogrow Limited
Incorporated: 19 February 2018
Registered Office: 39 Monks Avenue, Barnet, Herts, EN5 1BZ
Major Shareholder: William Stojan Cutting
Officers: William Stojan Cutting [1993] Director

Revive Herbal UK Ltd
Incorporated: 17 August 2016
Registered Office: 77 Galloway Drive, Kennington, Ashford, Kent, TN25 4QQ
Shareholder: Gregory Juan
Officers: Errol Juan [1973] Director/Herbalist [South African]; Gregory Juan [1974] Director

Revive Us Limited
Incorporated: 30 August 2017
Registered Office: Flat 2, 189 Holdenhurst Road, Bournemouth, BH8 8DG
Officers: Christopher Pane [1988] Director

RG and Co Limited
Incorporated: 12 April 2012
Net Worth: £66,563 *Total Assets:* £93,822
Registered Office: 23 Parish Ghyll Drive, Ilkley, W Yorks, LS29 9PT
Major Shareholder: Rajashekhar Rao
Officers: Geeta Suryanarayan, Secretary; Rajashekhar Rao [1967] Director/Doctor; Geeta Suryanarayan [1972] Director/Doctor

RGCC Pharma Limited
Incorporated: 15 June 2011
Net Worth Deficit: £3,352
Registered Office: Suite 1, 3rd Floor, 11-12 St James's Square, London, SW1Y 4LB
Major Shareholder: Ioannis Papasotiriou
Officers: Dr Ioannis Papasotiriou [1973] Director/Doctor [Greek]

The Top UK Pharmaceutical Manufacturers

Rhino Education Ltd
Incorporated: 19 March 2012
Previous: Chemate Laboratories (UK) Limited
Net Worth Deficit: £7,940 *Total Assets:* £73,432
Registered Office: 85 Great Portland Street, London, W1W 7LT
Major Shareholder: Chen Chen
Officers: Chen Chen [1972] Director [Chinese]

Rhodia Pharma Solutions Limited
Incorporated: 26 August 1965
Registered Office: 34 Clarendon Road, Watford, Herts, WD17 1JJ
Parent: Rhodia Pharma Solutions (Holdings) Limited
Officers: Alison Murphy, Secretary; Tom Dutton [1964] Director/Health, Safety & Environment Manager; Alison Murphy [1965] Director/Financial Controller

Ria Generics Limited
Incorporated: 20 September 1999
Net Worth: £55,980 *Total Assets:* £415,742
Registered Office: 36 Ingleby Way, Wallington, Surrey, SM6 9LR
Parent: Kanchanlal Naginbhai Patel
Officers: Krishnamurthy Balasubramanian [1958] Director/Company Executive [Indian]; Kanchanlal Naginbhai Patel [1951] Director

Rimmerdax Limited
Incorporated: 8 August 1973
Net Worth: £439,906 *Total Assets:* £440,670
Registered Office: 17 Warren Road, Purley, Surrey, CR8 1AF
Shareholder: Rizwanali Noorali Kassam
Officers: Mohamedali Noorali Bharwani, Secretary; Mohamedali Noorali Bharwani [1946] Director/Pharmacist; Rizwanali Noorali Kassam [1949] Director/Pharmacist

Ripple MC Pharma Ltd
Incorporated: 18 February 2019
Registered Office: 2 Fosseway Court, North Hykeham, Lincs, LN6 8FG
Major Shareholder: Hedley Andrew Appleby
Officers: Hedley Andrew Appleby [1947] Director

RLC Technology Limited
Incorporated: 10 April 2006 *Employees:* 1
Net Worth: £32,494 *Total Assets:* £102,216
Registered Office: Atic Innovation Centre, Oakwood Drive, Loughborough, Leics, LE11 3QF
Major Shareholder: Mark Jones
Officers: Mark Jones [1964] Director

RLS Pharma Ltd
Incorporated: 14 September 2018
Registered Office: 2 Stamford Square, London, SW15 2BF
Major Shareholder: Rachid Aichaoui
Officers: Rachid Aichaoui [1976] Director/Pharmacist [French]

RM Medical Care Ltd
Incorporated: 8 August 2015
Net Worth: £25,053 *Total Assets:* £25,053
Registered Office: 68 Old Road, Frinton on Sea, Essex, CO13 9BY
Major Shareholder: Al Mohammed Rafique Miah
Officers: Al Mohammed Rafique Miah [1992] Director

RMW Laboratories Limited
Incorporated: 4 April 2018
Registered Office: RMW Laboratories, Unit 7 Lufton Trading Estate, 10 Armoury Road, Yeovil, Somerset, BA22 8RL
Major Shareholder: Isaac Merriman
Officers: Isaac Merriman, Secretary; Isaac Merriman [1995] Director

Roche Products Limited
Incorporated: 14 December 1908 *Employees:* 1,460
Net Worth: £247,339,008 *Total Assets:* £474,462,016
Registered Office: 6 Falcon Way, Shire Park, Welwyn Garden City, Herts, AL7 1TW
Parent: Roche Holding (UK) Limited
Officers: Scott Davis, Secretary; Richard William Erwin [1967] Director/General Manager; Beat Christoph Kraehenmann [1957] Director/Attorney at Law [Swiss]; Geoffrey John Twist [1971] Managing Director; Kezia Jayn Vitug [1976] Finance & Corporate Services Director [American]

Rojal Pharm USA Limited
Incorporated: 7 September 2016
Registered Office: 483 Green Lanes, London, N13 4BS
Officers: Dr Marko Kohek [1971] Director/Manager [Slovenian]

Roma Pharmaceuticals Limited
Incorporated: 7 June 2016 *Employees:* 2
Net Worth Deficit: £1,060,645 *Total Assets:* £473,433
Registered Office: First Floor, 10 Temple Back, Bristol, BS1 6FL
Shareholders: Mark Cresswell; Roland Alexander Brown
Officers: Roland Alexander Brown [1971] Director; Mark Cresswell [1967] Director

Roonivoolin Naturals Ltd
Incorporated: 17 August 2011
Net Worth: £13,075 *Total Assets:* £38,923
Registered Office: 18 Bayview Road, Ballycastle, Co Antrim, BT54 6BT
Shareholder: Liam McBride
Officers: Caroline O'Doherty, Secretary; Liam McBride [1964] Director/Shopkeeper [Irish]; Sinead Marie McBride [1983] Director/Factory Worker [Irish]

Root2tip Haircare Solutions Ltd
Incorporated: 27 July 2010
Net Worth: £1 *Total Assets:* £23,551
Registered Office: 4 Whitchurch Parade, Whitchurch Lane, Edgware, Middlesex, HA8 6LR
Major Shareholder: Salem Ayesha Wynter
Officers: Salem Ayesha Wynter [1979] Director/Self Employed

Rosalique Skincare Limited
Incorporated: 2 November 2017
Registered Office: 36 High Street, Cleethorpes, N E Lincs, DN35 8JN
Parent: Bradhaus Holdings Ltd
Officers: Martin John Schiele [1983] Director; Claudia Talsma [1983] Director [Dutch]

Rosemont Pharmaceuticals Limited
Incorporated: 14 December 1967 *Employees:* 193
Net Worth: £37,358,000 *Total Assets:* £46,942,000
Registered Office: Wrafton, Braunton, Devon, EX33 2DL
Parent: Acacia Biopharma Limited
Officers: Annette Corcoran, Secretary; Neil Thomas Lister [1975] Director; Dominic James Rivers [1977] Director; Christopher Allan Rudd [1980] Director; Howard Taylor [1966] Director

Rotapharm Limited
Incorporated: 19 October 2005 *Employees:* 1
Net Worth: £651,824 *Total Assets:* £1,222,298
Registered Office: Ground Floor, Gadd House, Arcadia Avenue, Finchley, London, N3 2JU
Major Shareholder: Raushan Tahiyeu
Officers: Tony Jack Douglas, Secretary; Tony Jack Douglas [1942] Director

Rotapharm Pharmaceutical Limited
Incorporated: 29 March 2011
Registered Office: Ground Floor, Gadd House, Arcadia Avenue, Finchley, London, N3 2JU
Officers: Serkan Uysal, Secretary; Serkan Uysal [1975] Director/Financial Consultant [Turkish]

Rowblast Ltd
Incorporated: 28 April 2018
Registered Office: Office 3, 146-148 Bury Old Road, Whitefield, Manchester, M45 6AT
Shareholders: Leo Nathaniel Adriano; Jack Catlow
Officers: Leo Nathaniel Adriano [1996] Director [Filipino]

Royce Health Sciences Ltd
Incorporated: 21 September 2017
Registered Office: 58 Aldfield Green, Hamilton, Leicester, LE5 1BP
Shareholders: Sinnan Fazwani; Rizwan Ladak
Officers: Sinnan Fazwani [1993] Director [Pakistani]; Rizwan Ladak [1982] Director

RP & MP Investments Limited
Incorporated: 21 July 2014
Net Worth: £204,599 *Total Assets:* £337,054
Registered Office: 25 Thorncliffe, Two Mile Ash, Milton Keynes, Bucks, MK8 8DT
Major Shareholder: Usha Shantilal Patel
Officers: Usha Shantilal Patel [1939] Director

RPH Innovations Limited
Incorporated: 2 September 2014
Net Worth Deficit: £3,573 *Total Assets:* £499
Registered Office: 71-75 Shelton Street, Covent Garden, London, WC2H 9JQ
Major Shareholder: Akindayo Habeeb Adegbesan
Officers: Akindayo Habeeb Adegbesan [1991] Director/Pharmacist

RPL (UK) Limited
Incorporated: 15 June 2004
Net Worth: £1,000 *Total Assets:* £4,100
Registered Office: 316 Blackpool Road, Fulwood, Preston, Lancs, PR2 3AE
Parent: Nutrition Group PLC
Officers: Peter Greathead [1943] Director

RRA Green Cross Limited
Incorporated: 26 April 2006
Net Worth: £1,162 *Total Assets:* £11,326
Registered Office: 136 Carlyon Avenue, South Harrow, Middlesex, HA2 8SW
Shareholder: Vinayagar Rajasingam
Officers: Vinayagar Rajasingam [1966] Director

RSH QP Services Limited
Incorporated: 1 December 2017
Registered Office: 17 Fairbanks, Haywards Heath, W Sussex, RH16 3JN
Major Shareholder: Rodney Stephen Henry
Officers: Dr Rodney Stephen Henry [1946] Director

RSI Chemrep Limited
Incorporated: 22 February 2019
Registered Office: Floor LG 12, Blake Tower, Barbican, London, EC2Y 8BR
Major Shareholder: Andrew Burgess
Officers: Andrew Burgess [1972] Director

RSR Limited
Incorporated: 7 May 1999 *Employees:* 117
Net Worth: £17,973,888 *Total Assets:* £19,709,656
Registered Office: 7 Robin Lane, High Bentham, Lancaster, LA2 7AB
Major Shareholder: Bernard Rees-Smith
Officers: Jenny Louise Barwise, Secretary; Janet Bradbury [1966] Director/Scientist; Dr Shu Chen [1966] Director/Scientist; Dr Jadwiga Furmaniak [1951] Director/Scientist; Dr Michael Powell [1960] Director/Scientist; Dr Bernard Rees Smith [1944] Director; Dr Jane Sanders [1966] Director/Scientist

Rubyquartz Ltd
Incorporated: 20 August 2018
Registered Office: 48 St Phillips Drive, Royton, Oldham, Lancs, OL2 6AE
Major Shareholder: MacAulay Ravenscroft
Officers: MacAulay Ravenscroft [1995] Director/Consultant

Rucals Ltd
Incorporated: 12 October 2017
Registered Office: 213a Rochdale Road, Greetland, Halifax, W Yorks, HX4 8JE
Major Shareholder: David Charles Margison
Officers: David Charles Margison [1954] Director/Online Sales

Rusco Limited
Incorporated: 15 December 1950
Registered Office: Unit 3 Nursery Court, Kibworth Business Park, Kibworth, Leics, LE8 0EX
Parent: In2 Healthcare Ltd
Officers: Ian David Waring, Secretary; Satnam Singh Butter [1961] Director; Karim Sharif Dharamshi Tejani [1959] Director; Salim Sharif Dharamshi Tejani [1950] Director

Russell and Denver Ltd
Incorporated: 28 August 2008
Registered Office: 3 Addlestone House, Sutton Way, London, W10 5HE
Officers: Alan Russell [1970] Director/Trader

Rutland Biodynamics Limited
Incorporated: 23 May 2002
Net Worth: £368,155 *Total Assets:* £507,999
Registered Office: Town Park Farm, Oakham Road, Oakham, Rutland, LE15 8DG
Major Shareholder: Paul Nigel Chenery
Officers: Paul Nigel Chenery [1951] Director

S M Consultancy (MK) Limited
Incorporated: 4 September 2007
Net Worth: £578,482 *Total Assets:* £640,010
Registered Office: 25 Thorncliffe, Two Mile Ash, Milton Keynes, Bucks, MK8 8DT
Officers: Usha Shantilal Patel, Secretary; Shantilal Maganbhai Patel [1938] Director

S.C.A.C. Limited
Incorporated: 13 June 2006
Registered Office: Unit 2a Bandeath Industrial Estate, Throsk, Stirling, FK7 7NP
Shareholders: Alexander Douglas Miller Cruickshank; Carmelo Stamato
Officers: Alexander Douglas Miller Cruickshank [1975] Director; Carmelo Stamato [1971] Director

Sage Therapeutics Limited
Incorporated: 1 March 2017 *Employees:* 4
Net Worth: £50,854 *Total Assets:* £143,230
Registered Office: 100 New Bridge Street, London, EC4V 6JA
Parent: Sage Therapeutics, Inc.
Officers: Anne Marie Cook [1961] Director/Business Executive [American]; Kimi Ellen Iguchi [1962] Director/Business Executive [American]

Sahara Biomedix Ltd
Incorporated: 18 December 2018
Registered Office: Milton Hall, Ely Road, Milton, Cambridge, CB24 6WZ
Major Shareholder: Abiola Okubanjo
Officers: Abiola Okubanjo [1979] Director

Saifee Healthcare Limited
Incorporated: 21 January 2016 *Employees:* 2
Net Worth Deficit: £128,141 *Total Assets:* £295,977
Registered Office: 46 High Street, Lye, Stourbridge, W Midlands, DY9 8LQ
Shareholders: Aliasghar Shiraz Porbanderwalla; Yusuf Abdulali
Officers: Yusuf Abdulali [1988] Director/Pharmacist; Aliasghar Shiraz Porbanderwalla [1978] Director/Pharmacist

Salcura Limited
Incorporated: 25 April 2002 *Employees:* 6
Net Worth: £5,630 *Total Assets:* £417,175
Registered Office: 36 High Street, Cleethorpes, N E Lincs, DN35 8JN
Parent: Brandhaus Holdings Ltd
Officers: Martin John Schiele, Secretary/Student; Martin John Schiele [1983] Sales Director; Claudia Talsma [1983] Director [Dutch]

Salenco Limited
Incorporated: 5 December 2014
Net Worth Deficit: £36,618
Registered Office: First Floor, Aspen House, West Terrace, Folkestone, Kent, CT20 1TH
Officers: Paul Davidson Pearson [1957] Director; Raymond Gerard Rohrbach [1961] Director

Salicin Healthcare Limited
Incorporated: 8 August 2016
Registered Office: 23 Pilmore Mews, Hurworth Place, Darlington, Co Durham, DL2 2BQ
Major Shareholder: Keith Martin MacGregor
Officers: Keith Martin MacGregor [1950] Director/Chemist

Salutem Supplements Ltd
Incorporated: 9 June 2016 *Employees:* 1
Net Worth Deficit: £21,153 *Total Assets:* £12,615
Registered Office: P J Molloy & Co Ltd, Nursery Cottage, Beckley, Hinton, Christchurch, Dorset, BH23 7ED
Major Shareholder: Simon John Lewis Meads
Officers: Andrew Paul Larwood [1959] Director; Simon John Lewis Meads [1965] Director

Samritz Healthcare Ltd
Incorporated: 31 December 2013
Previous: Samritz Health Care Ltd
Registered Office: 54 Clarendon Road, Watford, Herts, WD17 1DU
Officers: Dr Ramiz Amin [1969] Director/Pharmacist; Sherif Mohamed Aboelnaga Mohamed Elmasry [1972] Director [Egyptian]

Sandine Zartaux Holding Ltd
Incorporated: 25 November 2014
Net Worth Deficit: £3,722 *Total Assets:* £3,544
Registered Office: 27 Old Gloucester Street, London, WC1N 3AX
Major Shareholder: Kyriaki Zartaloudi
Officers: Kyriaki Zartaloudi [1973] Director/Trader [Greek]

Sandoz Limited
Incorporated: 24 February 1981 *Employees:* 119
Net Worth: £10,852,000 *Total Assets:* £47,303,000
Registered Office: Frimley Business Park, Frimley, Camberley, Surrey, GU16 7SR
Shareholder: Novartis AG
Officers: Rebecca Ann Weston, Secretary; Haseeb Ahmad [1976] Director/CPO Head; Francesco Balestrieri [1969] Director/Head Sandoz Region Europe [Italian]; Timothy Charles de Gavre [1974] Director; Oriane Fanny Lacaze [1979] Director/Country Chief Financial Officer [French]

Sands Fulton Limited
Incorporated: 20 April 2015
Registered Office: 61 Hymers Avenue, Kingston upon Hull, HU3 1LL
Shareholders: Jean Collingwood; Paul Colin Milner
Officers: Jean Collingwood [1958] Managing Director; Paul Colin Milner [1963] Art Director

Sanhak Ltd
Incorporated: 22 November 2018
Registered Office: 8 Rosslyn Mews, Sunderland, Tyne & Wear, SR4 7DA
Shareholders: Sudhakar Bathala; Sandhya Mohan Bathala
Officers: Sudhakar Bathala [1986] Director [Indian]

Sanofi-Synthelabo Limited
Incorporated: 3 September 1990
Registered Office: One Onslow Street, Guildford, Surrey, GU1 4YS
Parent: Sanofi-Aventis UK Holdings Limited
Officers: Francois-Xavier Duhalde [1965] Director/Chief Financial Officer [French]; Hugo Rupert Alexander Fry [1970] Director/UK Country Chair

Sarakan Limited
Incorporated: 21 October 1971
Registered Office: G R Lane, Sisson Road, Gloucester, GL2 0GR
Parent: G R Lane Health Products Ltd
Officers: Paul Charles Whatley, Secretary; Janet Margaret Groves [1952] Director; Paul Charles Whatley [1958] Director

Sarepta International UK Ltd.
Incorporated: 29 September 2017
Registered Office: Hill House, 1 Little New Street, London, EC4A 3TR
Parent: Sarepta Therapeutics, Inc
Officers: Joseph Bratica [1963] Director/Accountant [American]; Enrico Maria Dolfini [1970] Executive Director - International Legal Affairs [Italian]; Matthew Garrett Gall [1976] Director/Businessman [American]

Sarissa Biomedical Limited
Incorporated: 4 November 2002 *Employees:* 6
Net Worth: £427,168 *Total Assets:* £1,048,218
Registered Office: 14 Harvey Road, Bedford, MK41 9LF
Shareholder: Mercia Fund Management Limited
Officers: Nicholas Egerton Dale, Secretary; Quentin Mark Compton-Bishop [1958] Director; Nicholas Egerton Dale [1960] Director; Professor Bruno Generald Frenguelli [1967] Director/Professor of Neuroscience; Dr Everard Joseph Philip Mascarenhas [1960] Director; William Penn Moffitt [1946] Director [American]; George Thomas Zajicek [1949] Director

SAS Pharma Limited
Incorporated: 27 September 2017
Registered Office: Companies House, Default Address, Cardiff, CF14 8LH
Major Shareholder: Christine Jung
Officers: Dr Christine Jung, Secretary; Dr Christine Jung [1948] Director/Nurse [German]

Satelec (UK) Limited
Incorporated: 24 June 1999 *Employees:* 16
Net Worth: £446,782 *Total Assets:* £1,788,970
Registered Office: Acteon House, Phoenix Park, Eaton Socon, St Neots, Cambs, PE19 8EP
Parent: Satelec SAS
Officers: Constance Coughlan [1982] Sales Director; Marie-Laure Jeanne Antoinette Dore WW Pochon [1959] Director/Chief Executive Officer [French]

Sauflon (Manufacturing) Limited
Incorporated: 23 October 1986
Net Worth: £100 *Total Assets:* £100
Registered Office: Delta Park, Concorde Way, Segensworth North, Fareham, Hants, PO15 5RL
Parent: CooperVision Lens Care Limited
Officers: Brian George Andrews [1978] Director/Corporate Executive [American]; Richard Michael Cheshire [1969] Finance Director; Randal Louis Golden [1961] Director/Corporate Executive [American]; Mark Stephen Harty [1962] Director/President, Europe; Agostino Ricupati [1967] Director/Corporate Executive [American]

Savoo Care Limited
Incorporated: 4 October 2018
Registered Office: 54 Frensham Close, Southall, Middlesex, UB1 2YG
Officers: Ibrahim Akel [1986] Director/Lawyer [Jordanian]

Savoy Laboratories (International) Limited
Incorporated: 27 August 1965 *Employees:* 3
Net Worth: £347,033 *Total Assets:* £347,033
Registered Office: Jubilee House, 3 The Drive, Great Warley, Brentwood, Essex, CM13 3FR
Major Shareholder: Mary Joan Tate
Officers: Mary Joan Tate, Secretary; Mary Joan Tate [1945] Director; Simon Robert Geoffrey Tate [1977] Director; Richard Earl Warriner [1956] Director

Schering-Plough Limited
Incorporated: 31 December 1884
Net Worth: £10,558,000 *Total Assets:* £14,245,000
Registered Office: Walton Manor, Walton, Milton Keynes, Bucks, MK7 7AJ
Parent: Merck & Co., Inc.
Officers: Richard Robinski, Secretary; Ebru Can Temucin [1972] Director [Turkish]; Martin Ian Rogers [1968] Director

Scipac Limited
Incorporated: 5 March 1986
Registered Office: Haywood House, Dumfries Place, Cardiff, CF10 3GA
Parent: BBI Solutions OEM Limited
Officers: Richard George Armitt Couzens [1973] Director; Mario Pietro Gualano [1969] Director; Alan Edward Peterson [1947] Director

Scottish Bioenergy Cooperative Ventures Limited
Incorporated: 28 September 2007 *Employees:* 5
Net Worth Deficit: £90,001 *Total Assets:* £248,793
Registered Office: Biocity Scotland, Bo'ness Road, Motherwell, N Lanarks, ML1 5UH
Parent: Tantillus Synergy Limited
Officers: Thomas Kirk Craig [1951] Director/Chartered Accountant; David Ian Dobbins [1958] Director; Dr Matthew Kaser [1956] Director/Patent Attorney; Thomas Anthony McHolmes [1967] Director/Company Owner [Irish]; Martyn Charles Mulcahy [1956] Director; Nicholas Mark Trott [1964] Finance Director; David Christian Daniel Van Alstyne [1963] Managing Director [Irish]; Polly Marston Van Alstyne [1971] Director/Chief Operating Officer

Seacross Pharmaceuticals Ltd
Incorporated: 31 May 2011 *Employees:* 1
Net Worth: £610,276 *Total Assets:* £2,809,240
Registered Office: Bedford Business Centre, 61-63 St Peters Street, Bedford, MK40 2PR
Shareholders: Zhao Ding; Qianyi Huang
Officers: Ping HE, Secretary; Dr Zhao Ding [1985] Director [Chinese]; Ping HE [1972] Director [Chinese]

Seadbincold Ltd
Incorporated: 17 August 2018
Registered Office: 7 Freeland Place, Kirkintilloch, Glasgow, G66 1NB
Major Shareholder: Nicole Smith
Officers: Nicole Smith [1992] Director/Consultant

G.D.Searle & Co.Limited
Incorporated: 2 March 1953
Registered Office: c/o Pfizer Ltd, Ramsgate Road, Sandwich, Kent, CT13 9NJ
Parent: Pfizer Inc
Officers: Ian Eric Franklin [1965] Director; David Ian Highton [1968] Director; Jacqueline Ann Mount [1963] Director

Seborgo Limited
Incorporated: 16 January 2019
Registered Office: Lancaster House, Amy Johnson Way, Blackpool, Lancs, FY4 2RP
Parent: Patient Guard Ltd
Officers: David Raymond Small [1983] Director

Sedigel Limited
Incorporated: 15 August 2012
Registered Office: 18 West Park Crescent, Leeds, LS8 2HF
Major Shareholder: Burrinder Singh Grewal
Officers: Dr Burrinder Singh Grewal [1970] Director

Selborne Biological Services Limited
Incorporated: 16 February 1978 *Employees:* 13
Net Worth Deficit: £1,315,803 *Total Assets:* £1,493,572
Registered Office: Goleigh Farm, Selborne, Alton, Hants, GU34 3SE
Parent: Equalbrief Limited
Officers: Neville George Pope, Secretary; Jane Judith Harvey [1950] Director; Louise Gladys Phillips [1946] Director; Neville George Pope [1953] Director

Selepharm Ltd
Incorporated: 18 July 2017
Registered Office: Carpenter Court, 1 Maple Road, Bramhall, Stockport, Cheshire, SK7 2DH
Major Shareholder: Abderrahim Benmakhlouf
Officers: Asmae Benmakhlouf, Secretary; Abderrahim Benmakhlouf [1961] Director [Swedish]

Sentinel Health Limited
Incorporated: 7 March 2011
Registered Office: 9 Hamilton Close, St John's Wood, London, NW8 8QY
Major Shareholder: Mariam Moussavi Satrap
Officers: Mariam Moussavi Satrap [1978] Director

Sepal Pharma PLC
Incorporated: 10 June 2005 *Employees:* 3
Net Worth Deficit: £342,172
Registered Office: One New Change, London, EC4M 9AF

Seqirus Vaccines Limited
Incorporated: 11 April 2000 *Employees:* 475
Previous: Novartis Vaccines and Diagnostics Limited
Net Worth: £196,200,000 *Total Assets:* £263,800,000
Registered Office: Point, 29 Market Street, Maidenhead, Berks, SL6 8AA
Parent: Seqirus Vaccines Holdings Limited
Officers: John Andrew Goodman Levy, Secretary; Martin Thomas Quinn, Secretary; John Andrew Goodman Levy [1959] Director/Business Executive [Australian]; Kian Meng Lim [1973] Director/Business Executive [Australian]; Stephen Michael Marlow [1971] Director/Business Executive; Dr Laura Elizabeth O'Brien [1968] Director/Business Executive

Sequana LifeSciences Ltd
Incorporated: 25 February 2019
Registered Office: Alpha House, 646c Kingsbury Road, Kingsbury, London, NW9 9HN
Major Shareholder: Avni Sameer Motla
Officers: Avni Sameer Motla [1981] Director

Sestri (Sales) Limited
Incorporated: 3 January 1979
Net Worth: £148,641 *Total Assets:* £200,052
Registered Office: York House, Church Lane, Chalfont St Peter, Bucks, SL9 9RE
Officers: Jonathan Edward Prudhoe, Secretary; Terence Edward Prudhoe [1940] Director

Seven Days Vitamin Company Limited
Incorporated: 3 January 2017
Registered Office: Seven Days Vitamin Company Limited, Airedale Business Centre, Millennium Road, Skipton, N Yorks, BD23 2TZ
Parent: Health & Well Being Brands
Officers: Andrew Michael Davies [1982] Director

Seven Seas Healthcare Limited
Incorporated: 11 October 2016
Registered Office: Chestnut Lodge, Woodland Rise, North Ferriby, E Yorks, HU14 3JT
Major Shareholder: Seethal Susan Mark
Officers: Dr Seethal Susan Mark [1980] Director/Dentist [Indian]

Seven Seas Limited
Incorporated: 6 April 1939 *Employees:* 44
Net Worth Deficit: £25,302,000 *Total Assets:* £16,648,000
Registered Office: Bedfont Cross, Stanwell Road, Feltham, Middlesex, TW14 8NX
Parent: Merck Consumer Healthcare Limited
Officers: Anthony Joseph Appleton [1962] Director & General Counsel; James David Binnington [1968] Director; Alexander George Buckthorp [1973] Finance Director; Heidrun Gresle [1966] Director/General Manager UK & Ireland [German]; Vijay Indroo Sitlani [1975] Finance Director [Singaporean]; Christopher John Young [1974] HR Director

Severn Biotech Limited
Incorporated: 27 November 1989 *Employees:* 9
Net Worth: £212,366 *Total Assets:* £308,940
Registered Office: Unit 2 Park Lane, Kidderminster, Worcs, DY11 6TJ
Major Shareholder: Andrew John Smart
Officers: Andrew John Smart, Secretary/Biochemist; Andrew John Smart [1961] Managing Director Biochemist

SH Snakes UK Ltd.
Incorporated: 22 January 2018
Registered Office: The Workshop, 19 Drake Close, New Milton, Hants, BH25 5LR
Major Shareholder: Simon Edward Harry Hyett
Officers: Simon Edward Harry Hyett [1989] Director/Herpetologist

Shabelle Ltd
Incorporated: 8 May 2018
Registered Office: 95 Harlington Road, Uxbridge, Middlesex, UB8 3HZ
Major Shareholder: Mohamed Mahmoud Dugsiye
Officers: Mohamed Mahmoud Dugsiye [1991] Director/Consultant

Shah-British Enterprises Limited
Incorporated: 3 April 1995
Net Worth Deficit: £199,143
Registered Office: Rockware Business Centre, 5 Rockware Avenue, Greenford, Middlesex, UB6 0AA
Major Shareholder: Shokat Munir Sayed Shah
Officers: Dr Sh Shah [1950] Director/Clinical Pathologist [Indian]

Shanghai Neopharm Co., Ltd
Incorporated: 17 January 2014
Registered Office: 8 Standard Road, London, NW10 6EU
Major Shareholder: Lihua Zhu
Officers: Lihua Zhu, Secretary; Lihua Zhu [1982] Director [Chinese]

Shanmonrie Services Limited
Incorporated: 15 November 2004 *Employees:* 1
Net Worth Deficit: £19,049 *Total Assets:* £25,236
Registered Office: 23 Banim Street, Hammersmith, London, W6 0DN
Major Shareholder: Rosemarie Smith
Officers: Monique Wilson, Secretary; Rosemarie Smith [1967] Director/Financial Controller

Sharp Clinical Services (UK) Limited
Incorporated: 23 March 1988 *Employees:* 70
Net Worth: £2,420,435 *Total Assets:* £8,185,346
Registered Office: Ashfield House, Resolution Road, Ashby De La Zouch, Leics, LE65 1HW
Parent: Sharp Clinical Services (UK) Holdings Limited
Officers: Damien Moynagh, Secretary; Simon Hayes [1972] Director [Irish]; Ian Christopher Morgan [1957] Director

Shea By Day Ltd
Incorporated: 22 October 2012
Registered Office: 109 Brighton Road, Moseley, Birmingham, B12 8QJ
Officers: Kevin Jones, Secretary; Lorrenda Waite [1977] Director

Shekinah Health Consultancy Limited
Incorporated: 11 August 2017
Registered Office: 200 B Long Lane, Bexleyheath, Kent, DA7 5AG
Major Shareholder: Evelyn Tawiah
Officers: Evelyn Tawiah [1961] Director/Medical Doctor

Shellmarks Limited
Incorporated: 3 July 2017
Registered Office: 20-22 Wenlock Road, London, N1 7GU
Major Shareholder: Hany Mohamed Abdelhady Mohamed Ghoneim
Officers: Hany Mohamed Abdelhady Mohamed Ghoneim [1976] Director [Egyptian]

Sher Limited
Incorporated: 17 March 2005
Net Worth: £402,439 Total Assets: £477,405
Registered Office: 176 Melton Road, West Bridgford, Nottingham, NG2 6FJ
Shareholders: Karrar Ahmad Khan; Asma Khan
Officers: Asma Khan, Secretary; Asma Khan [1955] Director/Company Secretary; Karrar Ahmad Khan [1943] Director/Pharmaceutical Consultant

Shiraz Pharm Limited
Incorporated: 1 July 2009
Net Worth: £3,889 Total Assets: £13,554
Registered Office: 30 The Pastures, Beardwood, Blackburn, BB2 7QR
Major Shareholder: Shiraz Mohammed Mirza
Officers: Shiraz Mohammed Mirza [1970] Director/Chemist

Shire Pharmaceuticals Limited
Incorporated: 26 June 1986 Employees: 102
Net Worth: £47,738,000 Total Assets: £75,774,000
Registered Office: 1 Kingdom Street, London, W2 6BD
Parent: Baxalta UK Limited
Officers: Damien Rodolphe Edmond Bailly [1966] Commercial Director [French]; Mark Gibbons [1984] Director/Accountant [South African]; Nicholas Hugh Meryon Insall [1982] Director/Accountant; Jonathan Clark Neal [1971] Managing Director

Sic Services Ltd
Incorporated: 17 April 2018
Registered Office: 1 Shepperton Marina, Felix Lane, Shepperton, Surrey, TW17 8NS
Major Shareholder: Michael Stephenson
Officers: Michael Stephenson [1953] Director/Pharmacist

Siga Pharmaceuticals (Europe) Limited
Incorporated: 4 January 2008
Registered Office: Suite 1, 3rd Floor, 11-12 St James's Square, London, SW1Y 4LB
Parent: Siga Technologies, Inc.
Officers: Daniel Luckshire, Secretary; Phillip Louis Gomez [1967] Director/Chief Executive [American]

Silver Shell Limited
Incorporated: 28 April 2016
Net Worth Deficit: £60,697 Total Assets: £45,310
Registered Office: Hema Works, Station Lane, Chesterfield, Derbys, S41 9QX
Officers: Matthew Taylor [1976] Director; Sheena Taylor [1948] Director

Simcere UK Limited
Incorporated: 20 December 2017
Registered Office: King Court Business Centre, London Road, Stevenage, Herts, SG1 2NG
Officers: Dr Yuehua Cong [1975] Executive Director [Chinese]; Matthew Kraman [1967] Director/Business Development [British/American]

Simkar Healthcare Ltd
Incorporated: 28 June 2018
Registered Office: 59 Morris Road, Leicester, LE2 6BR
Officers: Kavaljeet Singh Hundle [1981] Director

Sina Pharm Limited
Incorporated: 14 January 2019
Registered Office: 107 China House, Edgware Road, London, NW2 6GY
Major Shareholder: Ayoub Shirvani
Officers: Dr Ayoub Shirvani [1962] Research Director

Sinclair Animal and Household Care Limited
Incorporated: 13 May 2002 Employees: 57
Net Worth: £3,362,342 Total Assets: £3,824,774
Registered Office: Ropery Road, Gainsborough, Lincs, DN21 2QB
Major Shareholder: Daan Aa
Officers: Lee Robert Wallhead, Secretary; Daan AA [1976] Director [Dutch]; Johannes Hendrikus Lifgerus AA [1948] Director [Dutch]

Sinclair Pharmaceuticals Limited
Incorporated: 6 April 1971 Employees: 79
Net Worth: £13,659,000 Total Assets: £43,112,000
Registered Office: Eden House, Lakeside, Chester Business Park, Chester, CH4 9QT
Parent: Sinclair Pharma Holdings Ltd
Officers: Jason Rodney Tate, Secretary; Jayne Katherine Burrell [1974] Director; Alan Musgrave Olby [1971] Director; Christopher Paul Spooner [1968] Director

Sinduram Healthcare International Ltd
Incorporated: 23 March 2018
Registered Office: 56 Weighton Road, Harrow, Middlesex, HA3 6HZ
Major Shareholder: Sindhupriya Chintalapudi
Officers: Sindhupriya Chintalapudi [1986] Director

Sizwe Limited
Incorporated: 10 April 2012
Net Worth: £1,302 Total Assets: £1,626
Registered Office: 16 Longthorpe Court, Invermead Close, London, W6 0QH
Major Shareholder: Jabulile Gumede
Officers: Jabulile Gumede [1956] Director/Nurse

SK Network Ltd
Incorporated: 3 December 2018
Registered Office: 20-22 Wenlock Road, London, N1 7GU
Major Shareholder: Salma Karolia
Officers: Salma Karolia [1982] Director/Self Employed

Skin Cell Labs Limited
Incorporated: 23 February 2017
Net Worth Deficit: £160,980 *Total Assets:* £31,060
Registered Office: Parkhill Studio, Walton Road, Wetherby, W Yorks, LS22 5DZ
Major Shareholder: Krzysztof Mariusz Wronski
Officers: Krzysztof Mariusz Wronski [1981] Director [Polish]

Skin Defence Limited
Incorporated: 22 December 2014
Registered Office: 88 The Martlets, Rustington, Littlehampton, W Sussex, BN16 2UF
Major Shareholder: Richard Patrick Sinnott
Officers: Richard Patrick Sinnott [1993] Director

Skin Euphoria Limited
Incorporated: 14 May 2018
Registered Office: 207 Regent Street, London, W1B 3HH
Major Shareholder: Emma Osman
Officers: Emma Osman [1965] Director [British/Australian]

Skin Naturale Ltd
Incorporated: 2 February 2012
Net Worth: £83 *Total Assets:* £1,312
Registered Office: 187 Northenden Road, Sale, Cheshire, M33 2JB
Major Shareholder: Jonathan William Brokenbrow
Officers: Jonathan William Brokenbrow [1967] Director

Skincare Innovation Ltd
Incorporated: 8 March 2016
Registered Office: 1st Floor, Portland House, Belmont Business Park, Durham, DH1 1TW
Shareholder: Glenn Jones
Officers: Glenn Jones [1959] Director

Skindoc Formula Limited
Incorporated: 26 September 2014
Net Worth Deficit: £106,030 *Total Assets:* £169,000
Registered Office: First Floor, 85 Great Portland Street, London, W1W 7LT
Major Shareholder: Dirk Kremer
Officers: Dirk Dr. Kremer [1970] Director/Medical Doctor [German]

Skinlikes Limited
Incorporated: 9 December 2016
Registered Office: 3 Craiksland Court, by Loans, Troon, S Ayrshire, KA10 7HN
Major Shareholder: James Andrew Steele
Officers: James Andrew Steele [1948] Director

Skinnytan UK Limited
Incorporated: 22 December 2014 *Employees:* 6
Net Worth: £1,497,919 *Total Assets:* £3,681,050
Registered Office: 27 Old Gloucester Street, London, WC1N 3AX
Parent: Innovaderma PLC
Officers: Joseph John Bayer [1957] Director [Australian]; Haris Altaf Chaudhry [1972] Director [Australian]

Skinska Pharmaceutica Limited
Incorporated: 24 December 2018
Registered Office: 34 Ingledew Court, Leeds, LS17 8TP
Major Shareholder: Sindhupriya Chintalapudi
Officers: Sindhupriya Chintalapudi [1986] Director

SKN-RG Ltd
Incorporated: 30 August 2011 *Employees:* 2
Previous: B2 Beauty Ltd
Net Worth Deficit: £113,994 *Total Assets:* £42,945
Registered Office: Winnington House, 2 Woodberry Grove, North Finchley, London, N12 0DR
Major Shareholder: Deborah Annette Scott
Officers: Deborah Annette Scott, Secretary; Deborah Annette Scott [1971] Director; Robert Scott [1973] Director

SKN-RG Research & Development Ltd
Incorporated: 16 July 2015
Registered Office: Marshlands, The Street, Salcott, Maldon, Essex, CM9 8HJ
Shareholders: Deborah Annette Scott; Robert James Scott
Officers: Deborah Annette Scott [1971] Director; Robert Scott [1973] Director

Skyrocket Phytopharma (UK) Limited
Incorporated: 6 December 2012
Net Worth: £64,062 *Total Assets:* £64,862
Registered Office: Redwoods, 2 The Drive, Brookmans Park, Hatfield, Herts, AL9 7BD
Major Shareholder: John Andrew Simpson
Officers: John Andrew Simpson [1956] Managing Director

Slo Drinks Limited
Incorporated: 21 October 2005
Net Worth Deficit: £48,014 *Total Assets:* £23,685
Registered Office: Alpha House, 4 Greek Street, Stockport, Cheshire, SK3 8AB
Major Shareholder: Edward Mathew Done
Officers: Linda Carolyn Done, Secretary/Draughtswoman; Edward Mathew Done [1967] Director/Marketeer

Smart Formula Limited
Incorporated: 13 June 2005
Registered Office: 185 Knella Road, Welwyn Garden City, Herts, AL7 3NT
Major Shareholder: Osama Ahmed Aswania
Officers: Dr Kirsty Margaret Brown MacKay, Secretary; Dr Osama Ahmed Aswania [1967] Director/Pharmaceutical Scientist

Smart Instruments UK Limited
Incorporated: 21 June 2011
Net Worth: £12,892 *Total Assets:* £19,360
Registered Office: 78 Lumley Avenue, South Shields, Tyne & Wear, NE34 7DL
Major Shareholder: Waqas Shahid
Officers: Waqas Shahid [1980] Director/Businessman

Smith & Nephew PLC
Incorporated: 17 February 1937 *Employees:* 16,333
Net Worth: £3,371,080,192 *Total Assets:* £5,709,930,496
Registered Office: 15 Adam Street, London, WC2N 6LA
Officers: Susan Margaret Swabey, Secretary; Graham Timothy Baker [1968] Director/Chief Financial Officer; Vinita Bali [1955] Director [Indian]; Ian Edward Barlow [1951] Director/Chartered Accountant; Baroness Virginia Hilda Brunette Maxwell Bottomley [1948] Director/Executive Search; Roland Daniel Diggelmann [1967] Director [Swiss]; Erik Engstrom [1963] Director [Swedish]; Robin Anthony David Freestone [1958] Finance Director; Michael Allen Friedman [1943] Director [American]; Namal Sasrika Nawana [1970] Director/Chief Executive Officer [Australian/French]; Marc Ellis Owen [1959] Director; Roberto Quarta [1949] Director/Chairman [Italian/American]; Angela Susan Risley [1958] Director

Smith Kline & French Laboratories Limited
Incorporated: 21 April 1897
Net Worth: £464,864,000 *Total Assets:* £464,873,984
Registered Office: 980 Great West Road, Brentford, Middlesex, TW8 9GS
Parent: SmithKline Beecham Limited
Officers: Simon Paul Dingemans [1963] Director; Charalampos Panagiotidis [1977] Director/Financial Controller, Corporate Entities [Greek]

SmithKline Beecham Limited
Incorporated: 24 January 1989 *Employees:* 1,333
Net Worth: £1,310,000,000 *Total Assets:* £2,496,000,000
Registered Office: 980 Great West Road, Brentford, Middlesex, TW8 9GS
Parent: GlaxoSmithKline Finance PLC
Officers: Victoria Anne Whyte, Secretary; Simon Paul Dingemans [1963] Director

Snor-Ring Limited
Incorporated: 12 September 2006
Registered Office: Atwood House, Claremount Gardens, Epsom, Surrey, KT18 5XF
Major Shareholder: Roger Philip Whitaker
Officers: Roger Philip Whitaker, Secretary; Michael Carter Smith [1947] Director; Roger Philip Whitaker [1953] Director

SNS Limited
Incorporated: 21 May 1997
Net Worth: £322,465 *Total Assets:* £322,517
Registered Office: 1B, First Floor, 142 Johnson Street, Southall, Middlesex, UB2 5FD
Major Shareholder: Amit Hasmukh Raojibjai Patel
Officers: Amit Hasmukh Raojibhai Patel, Secretary/Accountant; Amit Hasmukh Raojibhai Patel [1975] Director/Accountant

Soft Coughs Ltd
Incorporated: 11 June 2018
Registered Office: 4 Normandy House, Southview Road, Crowborough, E Sussex, TN6 1HW
Major Shareholder: Danny Taylor
Officers: Danny Taylor [1990] Director/Designer

Softgel Solutions Ltd
Incorporated: 21 May 2018
Registered Office: 48 Parc Gellifaelog, Tonypandy, Mid Glamorgan, CF40 1DU
Officers: Dean Clive Marsh [1978] Director/Engineer

Sogeval UK Limited
Incorporated: 10 June 1994
Net Worth: £2,392,214 *Total Assets:* £2,425,692
Registered Office: Unit 3 Anglo Office Park, White Lion Road, Amersham, Bucks, HP7 9FB
Officers: Yan Pierre Francois Gabe, Secretary; Yan Pierre Francois Gabe [1978] Finance Director [French]; Marc Dominique Prikazsky [1959] EU MoTI Africa Director [French]

Solarius UK & Overseas Limited
Incorporated: 15 January 2018
Registered Office: The Gate Business Centre, Keppoch Street, Cardiff, CF24 3JW
Shareholder: Tamer Mohamed Hassan Elzokrod
Officers: Tamer Aly Emam Aly Elkaramany [1975] Director [Egyptian]; Tamer Mohamed Hassan Elzokrod [1976] Director/Pharmacist [Egyptian]

Soleaero Limited
Incorporated: 21 November 2002
Net Worth: £100 *Total Assets:* £60,100
Registered Office: 2 Silvermere, Basildon, Essex, SS16 6RA
Major Shareholder: Abbas Abdulhusein Nurbhai
Officers: Abbas Abdulhusein Nurbhai [1955] Director [Indian]

Solent Oral Care Ltd
Incorporated: 14 June 2017 *Employees:* 6
Net Worth: £3,155,319 *Total Assets:* £6,321,358
Registered Office: 4th Floor, Charles House, 108-110 Finchley Road, London, NW3 5JJ
Parent: Ranir Limited
Officers: Gijsbert Dezaire [1966] Managing Director [Dutch]; Shakil Lalani [1975] Director/European Operations Manager; Lucas Caspar Schwinner [1977] Director/Head of Finance [Austrian]

Sonifar Pharma Expert Limited
Incorporated: 23 November 2017
Registered Office: 2 Bartle Green, Burnley, Lancs, BB11 5BF
Shareholders: Songul Emritte; Nizam Mohamed Emritte
Officers: Zohra Allimah Shadoobuccus [1985] Director

South Wales Specials Limited
Incorporated: 13 June 1935
Net Worth: £2,617,871 *Total Assets:* £4,370,433
Registered Office: c/o Howard and Palmer Ltd, Castell Close, Swansea Enterprise Park, Llansamlet, Swansea, SA7 9FH
Major Shareholder: Jacqueline Mary Racey
Officers: Christopher Stephen Racey, Secretary; Christopher Stephen Racey [1958] Director; Jacqueline Mary Racey [1954] Director

Sparsanctuary Limited
Incorporated: 14 November 2016
Registered Office: 18 Chevalier Grove, Crownhill, Milton Keynes, Bucks, MK8 0EJ
Officers: Shontell Sparvelyn Stephen [1979] Director/Therapist/Practitioner [Grenadian]

Speakers at The Limits Ltd.
Incorporated: 4 August 2017
Registered Office: Holly Tree Barn, Rotten Row Farm, Hambleden, Henley on Thames, Oxon, RG9 6NB
Major Shareholder: Miroslava Kroslakova
Officers: David Hetherington, Secretary; David Andrew Jones [1965] Director/Event Producer; Miroslava Kroslakova [1981] Director/Procurement Manager [Czech]

Spear Therapeutics Limited
Incorporated: 12 June 2002
Registered Office: 76 King Street, Manchester, M2 4NH
Parent: Incanthera Limited
Officers: Timothy Paul McCarthy [1956] Director; Dr Simon Julian Ward [1967] Director

Spectrum Biomedical UK Limited
Incorporated: 30 August 2018
Registered Office: The Pinnacle, 170 Midsummer Boulevard, Milton Keynes, Bucks, MK9 1FE
Officers: Dr Pierre Debs [1966] Managing Director [American]; Cosmo Feilding Mellen [1985] Managing Director, Beckley Canopy Therapeutics; Phillip Stephen Shaer [1973] Director/Chief Legal Officer [Canadian]; Marc Wayne [1966] Director/Business Executive [Canadian]

Spey Limited
Incorporated: 7 February 2017
Registered Office: Astra House, Arklow Road, London, SE14 6EB
Parent: Abstragan Limited
Officers: Sadullo Abdulloev [1980] Director/Pharmaceutical Business [Tajikistani]

Spey Pharma Limited
Incorporated: 8 February 2017
Registered Office: Astra House, Arklow Road, London, SE14 6EB
Parent: Abstragan Limited
Officers: Sadullo Abdulloev [1980] Director/Pharmaceutical Business [Tajikistani]

E.R.Squibb & Sons Limited
Incorporated: 29 August 1949
Registered Office: Uxbridge Business Park, Sanderson Road, Uxbridge, Middlesex, UB8 1DH
Parent: Bristol-Myers Squibb Holdings Limited
Officers: Bruno Marie Pierre Lauras [1961] Director/Head of Business and Finance Services, Europe [French]; Joanne Elizabeth Rishworth [1977] Director

SS Products International Limited
Incorporated: 6 December 2004
Net Worth Deficit: £3,438
Registered Office: 3rd Floor, 120 Baker Street, London, W1U 6TU
Major Shareholder: Aleksandr Ter Hovakimyan
Officers: Aleksandr Ter Hovakimyan [1969] Director/Manager [Armenian]

St Andrews Botanics Limited
Incorporated: 10 September 2018
Registered Office: 28 Graemeslea View, Aberuthven, Auchterarder, Perth & Kinross, PH3 1FG
Major Shareholder: Shona Robertson Geddes
Officers: Shona Robertson Geddes [1980] Director/Owner

St Labs Limited
Incorporated: 4 October 2018
Registered Office: Room 4, 1st Floor, 50 Jermyn Street, London, SW1Y 6LX
Shareholders: Timothy Vincent Le Druillenec; Adrian Richard Thorpe Beeston
Officers: Adrian Richard Thorpe Beeston [1969] Director

St. George Technology Limited
Incorporated: 15 August 1995
Net Worth: £2,123 *Total Assets:* £9,101
Registered Office: Wyndham, Hophurst Hill, Crawley Down, Crawley, W Sussex, RH10 4LP
Shareholders: David John Clements; Stephanie Joyce Clements
Officers: Stephanie Clements, Secretary; David John Clements [1947] Director/Consultant

Stablepharma Limited
Incorporated: 26 January 2012
Net Worth Deficit: £394,075 *Total Assets:* £185,308
Registered Office: 3 Pierrepont Street, Bath, BA1 1LB
Shareholder: Bruce Joseph Roser
Officers: Nicola Jane Smith, Secretary; Nicholas Edward Child [1961] Director; Martin Carrick Powell [1956] Director; Dr Bruce Joseph Roser [1935] Director; Robert John Shepherd [1958] Director

Star Pharmaceuticals Limited
Incorporated: 16 February 2000
Net Worth: £786 *Total Assets:* £3,741,231
Registered Office: 39a Joel Street, Northwood Hills, Northwood, Middlesex, HA6 1NZ
Major Shareholder: Anuj Somchand Shah
Officers: Anuj Somchand Shah [1966] Director

Starkwell Validation Limited
Incorporated: 30 May 2013 *Employees:* 1
Net Worth: £82,017 *Total Assets:* £97,934
Registered Office: Bollin House, Bollin Link, Wilmslow, Cheshire, SK9 1DP
Major Shareholder: Ashok Barua
Officers: Ashok Barua [1975] Director/Pharmaceuticals

Stegram Pharmaceuticals Limited
Incorporated: 20 October 1989
Net Worth: £243,572 *Total Assets:* £375,203
Registered Office: 72 High Beeches, Banstead, Surrey, SM7 1NW
Officers: Peter William Ellson, Secretary; Peter William Ellson [1935] Director/Accountant; Paul George Margetts [1974] Director/Doctor; Lyn Janet Pugh [1970] Director/Doctor

Stem Cell Technology Ltd
Incorporated: 27 June 2018
Registered Office: The Oak, Wix Road, Beaumont-Cum-Moze, Essex, CO16 0AT
Shareholders: Professor Mark William Lowdell; Afshin Mosahebi
Officers: Professor Mark William Lowdell [1962] Director/University Professor; Afshin Mosahebi [1967] Director/Consultant

Sterling Pharma Solutions Limited
Incorporated: 16 February 2006 *Employees:* 366
Previous: Shasun Pharma Solutions Limited
Net Worth: £17,489,000 *Total Assets:* £49,927,000
Registered Office: Dudley, Cramlington, Northumberland, NE23 7QG
Parent: Saffron Bidco Limited
Officers: Tushar Jain Bahadur [1986] Finance and Procurement Director [Indian]; Kevin Peter Cook [1964] Director/President

Sterling Pharmaceuticals Limited
Incorporated: 4 June 2007 *Employees:* 44
Net Worth: £157,718 *Total Assets:* £1,900,247
Registered Office: 458 Belchers Lane, Bordesley Green, Birmingham, B9 5SX
Shareholder: Qamar Nawaz
Officers: Dr Qamar Nawaz, Secretary/Director; Dr Qamar Nawaz [1973] Director

Stockcare Limited
Incorporated: 26 May 1983 *Employees:* 15
Net Worth: £442,258 *Total Assets:* £590,150
Registered Office: 83 West Street, Leven, Hull, HU17 5LR
Officers: Amanda Jayne Good [1965] Director

Stride-Davies Pharma Limited
Incorporated: 16 September 2015
Registered Office: 1a Heol Don, Cardiff, CF14 2AR
Officers: Dr John Stephen Davies, Secretary; Dr John Stephen Davies [1964] Director/Doctor; Victoria Hammond [1976] Director/Regulatory Affairs; Paul Martin Southern [1959] Director/Pharmaceutical Adviser

Strides Pharma UK Ltd
Incorporated: 20 December 1993 Employees: 7
Previous: Strides Shasun (UK) Ltd
Net Worth: £3,396,219 Total Assets: £4,940,967
Registered Office: Unit 4 The Metro Centre, Dwight Road, Watford, Herts, WD18 9SS
Shareholders: Strides Arcolab International Limited; Strides Pharma Global (UK) Limited
Officers: Vikesh Kumar [1984] Director/Service [Indian]; Krishnan Tirucherai Parthasarathy [1971] Director [Indian]; Mohana Kumar Pillai [1956] Director [Indian]; Visvanathan Rajasekar [1961] Director/Accountant

H.E. Stringer (Perfumery) Limited
Incorporated: 3 July 1962
Registered Office: c/o H E Stringer Ltd, Icknield Way, Tring, Herts, HP23 4JZ
Parent: H. E. Stringer Limited
Officers: Stephen David Baxter, Secretary; Gwendoline Harriette Baxter [1946] Director/Businesswoman; Stephen David Baxter [1952] Director/Consultant

Stuckola-Pharma Limited
Incorporated: 25 October 2010
Net Worth Deficit: £3,621 Total Assets: £1,474
Registered Office: 85 Brookdene Road, London, SE18 1EH
Major Shareholder: Adebukonla Olusanya
Officers: Adebukonla Olusanya [1977] Director/Pharmacy Technician

Sultan & Sons Enterprises Limited
Incorporated: 30 January 2008
Net Worth Deficit: £3,724 Total Assets: £4,505
Registered Office: 51 Wadhurst Avenue, Luton, Beds, LU3 1UQ
Major Shareholder: Shaukat Pervez Awan
Officers: Shaukat Pervez Awan [1969] Director/Pharmacy

Summan International Limited
Incorporated: 23 May 1996
Registered Office: 99 Castle Road, Tipton, W Midlands, DY4 8EA
Officers: Kc Summan, Secretary; Dev Raj Summan [1947] Director; Kc Summan [1968] Director; Madhu Bala Summan [1971] Director

Summer Healthcare Limited
Incorporated: 3 July 2008
Net Worth: £13,323 Total Assets: £48,537
Registered Office: Unit 2 Blackburn Technology Management Centre, Challenge Way, Blackburn, BB1 5QB
Shareholders: Mujahid Ali; Amjid Malik Khan; Tabassum Zabier
Officers: Mujahid Ali [1979] Director; Amjid Malik Khan [1975] Director/Business Executive; Tabassam Zabier [1978] Director

Summit Veterinary Pharmaceuticals Limited
Incorporated: 12 August 2009 Employees: 21
Net Worth: £1,164,977 Total Assets: £2,558,834
Registered Office: 4th Floor, New Penderel House, 283-288 High Holborn, London, WC1V 7HP
Shareholders: Stephen Daniel Organ; Laura Michiko Organ
Officers: Laura Michiko Organ [1957] Director [Canadian]; Stephen Daniel Organ [1957] Director/Business Owner [Canadian]

Supamed Limited
Incorporated: 24 July 2002
Net Worth: £432,000 Total Assets: £432,000
Registered Office: 95 Broad Street, Birmingham, B15 1AU
Officers: Ravindar Singh Banga [1951] Director

Supersun Nutrition Limited
Incorporated: 12 February 1958
Registered Office: c/o G R Lane Health Products Ltd, Sisson Road, Gloucester, GL2 0GR
Parent: G R Lane Health Products Ltd
Officers: Paul Charles Whatley, Secretary; Janet Margaret Groves [1952] Director; Jonathan Groves [1980] Director

Surepharm Services Limited
Incorporated: 27 July 1982 Employees: 131
Net Worth: £5,771,951 Total Assets: £10,754,378
Registered Office: Unit 2b Bretby Business Park, Ashby Road, East Bretby, Burton on Trent, Staffs, DE15 0YZ
Parent: Centaur Healthcare Ltd
Officers: Julian America [1963] Director; Andrew Corbett [1955] Director; Julian James Anthony Richardson [1966] Director

Surrey Pharma Ltd
Incorporated: 22 October 2012 Employees: 1
Net Worth Deficit: £187,229 Total Assets: £70,912
Registered Office: 52 Bedford Square, Bloomsbury, London, WC1B 3DP
Major Shareholder: Misha
Officers: Misha Engineer [1983] Director

Sussex Biologicals Ltd
Incorporated: 26 March 2014
Net Worth: £138,466 Total Assets: £441,739
Registered Office: 2nd Floor, Stanford Gate, South Road, Brighton, BN1 6SB
Shareholders: Susan Ann Nest; Peter Gerard Nest
Officers: Peter Gerard Nest [1960] Director; Susan Ann Nest [1960] Director; Nicholas Stringer [1948] Director/Retired

Sutherland Health Limited
Incorporated: 6 February 1991 Employees: 4
Net Worth: £22,810 Total Assets: £340,311
Registered Office: Unit 1 Rivermead, Pipers Way, Thatcham, Berks, RG19 4EP
Officers: Stephen John Coke, Secretary/Chartered Accountant; Stephen John Coke [1961] Director/Chartered Accountant; Sheena Sukumaran [1971] Director

Suzie Who Limited
Incorporated: 31 October 1990
Net Worth: £173,738 Total Assets: £226,033
Registered Office: Woodside Cottage, 146a Higher Green Lane, Astley, Wigan, Lancs, M29 7JB
Officers: Susan Crook, Secretary; Michael Crook [1948] Director/Health Food Advisor

Swann-Morton (Europe) Limited
Incorporated: 24 August 1990 Employees: 2
Net Worth: £213,062 Total Assets: £213,062
Registered Office: Owlerton Green, Sheffield, S6 2BJ
Shareholder: W R Swann & Co Ltd
Officers: Michael Ian Hirst, Secretary; Michael Ian Hirst [1959] Director/Chartered Accountant; Richard John Whiteley [1964] Director

Swedish Orphan Biovitrum Ltd
Incorporated: 8 February 2002 Employees: 32
Net Worth: £3,969,071 Total Assets: £16,528,444
Registered Office: Suite 2, Building 3, Riverside Suite, Granta Park, Great Abington, Cambridge, CB21 6AD
Parent: Swedish Orphan Biovitrum International AB
Officers: Neil Alan Dugdale [1971] Director/Sales and Marketing; Hege Hellstrom [1965] Director/President Emenar [Norwegian]; Henrik Stenqvist [1967] Finance Director [Swedish]

Swift Dent Engineering Services Limited
Incorporated: 8 October 2013 *Employees:* 2
Net Worth: £55,975 *Total Assets:* £126,067
Registered Office: Charter House, 103-105 Leigh Road, Leigh on Sea, Essex, SS9 1JL
Major Shareholder: Anthony Stone
Officers: Jane Stone, Secretary; Anthony Stone [1961] Director/Engineer; Jane Stone [1969] Director/Office Manager

Swiss Pharma Dynamic Ltd
Incorporated: 18 February 2016
Registered Office: 27 Old Gloucester Street, London, WC1N 3AX
Major Shareholder: Kiriaki Zartaloudi
Officers: Kyriaki Zartaloudi [1973] Director [Greek]

Symbiosis Pharmaceutical Services Limited
Incorporated: 24 February 2010 *Employees:* 43
Net Worth: £1,474,428 *Total Assets:* £3,259,841
Registered Office: Unit 10 Scion House, Stirling University, Innovation Park, Stirling, FK9 4NF
Shareholder: Scottish Enterprise
Officers: Sukhpal Singh Bal [1976] Director; Colin Smith MacKay [1968] Director/Sales and Marketing; Gerry Merten [1956] Director; Dr Robert Morris Reekie [1956] Director

Syner-Med Pharmaceuticals (Kenya) Limited
Incorporated: 27 October 1995
Net Worth: £1,607,409 *Total Assets:* £2,405,535
Registered Office: DS House, 306 High Street, Croydon, Surrey, CR0 1NG
Officers: Pratima Dipak Bhatti, Secretary; Dipak Devji Bhatti [1956] Director; Pratima Dipak Bhatti [1960] Director

Synergetic Global Limited
Incorporated: 5 February 2019
Registered Office: 56 Moat View, Roslin, Midlothian, EH25 9NZ
Major Shareholder: Jaskarn Singh Nottay
Officers: Jaskarn Singh Nottay [1985] Director/Chief Executive

Synergy Biologics Limited
Incorporated: 23 August 2010 *Employees:* 23
Net Worth: £3,903,107 *Total Assets:* £4,931,767
Registered Office: 1st Floor, 61-63 Alexandra Road, Walsall, W Midlands, WS1 4DX
Shareholders: Robin Kumar Deb; Zahida Parveen Khurshid
Officers: Robin Kumar Deb, Secretary; Robin Kumar Deb [1963] Director; Zahida Parveen Khurshid [1975] Director

Synergy Pharma Consultancy Ltd
Incorporated: 9 March 2018
Registered Office: 79 College Road, Harrow, Middlesex, HA1 1BD
Major Shareholder: Shonar Mistry
Officers: Shonar Mistry, Secretary; Shonar Mistry [1987] Director/Senior Quality Assurance Officer [Indian]

Synergy Specials Limited
Incorporated: 14 July 2011
Net Worth: £229,738 *Total Assets:* £284,068
Registered Office: 109 Percy Road, Sparkhill, Birmingham, B11 3NQ
Officers: Murtaza Roshanali Master [1968] Director/Pharmacist; Mussadiq Roshanali Master [1957] Director/Pharmacist

Synnion Limited
Incorporated: 5 June 2018
Registered Office: Kings Court Business Centre, London Road, Stevenage, Herts, SG1 2NG
Major Shareholder: Yuehua Cong
Officers: Dr Yuehua Cong [1975] Director [Chinese]

Syri Limited
Incorporated: 1 December 2010
Net Worth: £11,851 *Total Assets:* £311,732
Registered Office: 4 Bradfield Road, Ruislip, Middlesex, HA4 0NU
Officers: Alpa Hathi [1968] Director/HR; Govindji Thakershi Hathi [1941] Director; Samit Hathi [1967] Director

T-In Medical Limited
Incorporated: 20 March 2017
Registered Office: 4th Floor, Park Gate, 161-163 Preston Road, Brighton, BN1 6AF
Shareholders: David Jonathan Redfern; Joel Didier Claude Vernois; Paul Jonathan Winsor
Officers: David Jonathan Redfern [1969] Director/Surgeon; Joel Didier Claude Vernois [1966] Director/Doctor [French]; Paul Jonathan Winsor [1974] Director

Taisho Pharmaceutical (Europe) Limited
Incorporated: 8 September 1998 *Employees:* 2
Net Worth: £7,299,721 *Total Assets:* £26,349,054
Registered Office: Hays Galleria, 1 Hays Lane, London, SE1 2RD
Parent: Taisho Pharmaceutical Holdings Co Ltd
Officers: Naoaki Sugano [1966] Director/Chairman [Japanese]; Kenichi Yamaguchi [1965] Director [Japanese]

Tal Pharma and Chemicals Limited
Incorporated: 2 March 2011
Net Worth Deficit: £3,963 *Total Assets:* £103
Registered Office: The Hart Shaw Building, Europa Link, Sheffield Business Park, Sheffield, S9 1XU
Major Shareholder: Taranjeet Singh Minhas
Officers: Taranjeet Singh Minhas [1983] Director/Pharmacist

Talley Environmental Care Limited
Incorporated: 27 March 2007 *Employees:* 10
Net Worth Deficit: £1,004,243 *Total Assets:* £634,092
Registered Office: Premier Way, Abbey Park Industrial Estate, Romsey, Hants, SO51 9DQ
Parent: Aspire Technology Group Ltd
Officers: Martin Barry Webb, Secretary/Accountant; Gary Brierley [1960] Technical Director; Christopher Peter Evans [1962] Director; John James Henry Evans [1966] Director; Kevin Peter Mearns [1963] Director; Robert William Thornton [1949] Director/Chartered Accountant; Martin Barry Webb [1956] Director

Tantillus Synergy Limited
Incorporated: 12 September 2007
Net Worth: £446,944 *Total Assets:* £485,357
Registered Office: The Apex, 2 Sheriffs Orchard, Coventry, Warwicks, CV1 3PP
Officers: Thomas Kirk Craig [1951] Director/Chartered Accountant; David Ian Dobbins [1958] Director; Dr Matthew Kaser [1956] Director/Patent Attorney; Thomas Anthony McHolmes [1967] Director [Irish]; Martyn Charles Mulcahy [1956] Director; Nicholas Mark Trott [1964] Finance Director; David Christian Daniel Van Alstyne [1963] Managing Director [Irish]; Polly Marston Van Alstyne [1971] Director/Chief Operating Officer

Tate Pharma Ltd
Incorporated: 28 January 2016
Registered Office: 21 Holystone Avenue, Gosforth, Newcastle upon Tyne, NE3 3HN
Officers: Susan Clare Tate [1964] Director

Tawil Co Limited
Incorporated: 19 July 2007
Registered Office: 73 Vicarage Road, Smethwick, W Midlands, B67 7AQ
Major Shareholder: Ahmed Mhs El-Tawil
Officers: Dr Abid Karim, Secretary; Dr Allah Detta [1960] Director Assistant; Amhs El-Tawil [1957] General Director [Egyptian]

Taylor of London Limited
Incorporated: 17 February 2010
Net Worth: £684,601 *Total Assets:* £902,441
Registered Office: 42-44 Norwood High Street, London, SE27 9NR
Parent: Jackson Trading Company PLC
Officers: Alison Jackson, Secretary; Alison Jackson [1952] Director; Charles Peter Christopher Howard Jackson [1983] Sales Director; Daniel William John Jackson [1982] Sales Director; Jemma Audrey Ilse Jackson [1986] Director; Jodie Alison Caroline Victoria Jackson [1988] Director; Howard Walters [1947] Director/Accountant

TCS Biosciences Limited
Incorporated: 1 October 1987 *Employees:* 48
Net Worth: £6,403,373 *Total Assets:* £12,692,194
Registered Office: Botolph Farm, Botolph Claydon, Buckingham, MK18 2LR
Major Shareholder: Lynda Jane Preston
Officers: Ruth Vanessa Toombs, Secretary; Dr Kate Langston [1973] Director/Doctor; James Eley Preston [1987] Director/Financial Analyst; Lynda Jane Preston [1947] Director/Farmer; Ruth Vanessa Toombs [1969] Director/Finance Manager; Emily Jane Utley [1971] Director/Solicitor; Gareth Arran Williams [1977] Sales and Marketing Director

Technical & General Limited
Incorporated: 4 March 1986 *Employees:* 8
Net Worth: £1,291,885 *Total Assets:* £1,756,937
Registered Office: 2 Albion Place, London, W6 0QT
Major Shareholder: Ahmad Youssef
Officers: Dr Abir Youssef, Secretary; Dr Ahmad Youssef [1946] Director/Engineer

Technical Textile Services Limited
Incorporated: 2 January 1992 *Employees:* 66
Net Worth: £1,147,167 *Total Assets:* £5,219,491
Registered Office: Units 7 & 8 Rhodes Business Park, Silburn Way, Middleton, Manchester, M24 4NE
Parent: Techtex Holdings Limited
Officers: David John Beardsworth, Secretary; David John Beardsworth [1960] Director/Business Manager; Stephen John Oldfield [1963] Director/Chartered Accountant; Brian John Whitney [1967] Director

Teisen Products Limited
Incorporated: 1 April 1987 *Employees:* 4
Net Worth: £667,635 *Total Assets:* £823,749
Registered Office: Droitwich Road, Bradley Green, Redditch, Worcs, B96 6RP
Shareholders: Peter Henrik Teisen; Elizabeth Anne Teisen
Officers: Elizabeth Anne Teisen, Secretary; Elizabeth Anne Teisen [1958] Director/Secretary; Peter Henrik Teisen [1946] Director/Heating Engineer Agriculturist; Sven Christian Teisen [1986] Director/Sales Manager

Teklab (ML) Ltd
Incorporated: 23 March 1961 *Employees:* 8
Net Worth: £21,013 *Total Assets:* £68,548
Registered Office: 9 Dorothy Terrace, Sacriston, Co Durham, DH7 6LG
Shareholders: Anne Margaret Hay; Jean Carol Metcalfe
Officers: Jean Carol Metcalfe, Secretary; Anne Margaret Hay [1940] Director/Technical Manager; Jean Carol Metcalfe [1950] Director/Office Manager

Telix Life Sciences (UK) Ltd
Incorporated: 9 August 2017
Registered Office: 11 Staple Inn, London, WC1V 7QH
Officers: Melanie Louise Farris, Secretary; Dr Christian Peter Behrenbruch [1975] Director [Australian]; Douglas Ernest Charles Cubbin [1961] Director [Australian]

Tell Products,Limited
Incorporated: 2 September 1947
Net Worth: £106,930 *Total Assets:* £163,440
Registered Office: 93 Cobbold Road, London, NW10 9SU
Major Shareholder: Werner Tell
Officers: Werner Tell, Secretary; David Hewer [1957] Director/Tablet Maker; Delroy George Morrison [1958] Director/Tablet Maker; Werner Tell [1921] Director/Chemist

Temag Pharma Ltd
Incorporated: 19 December 2008 *Employees:* 28
Net Worth: £214,790 *Total Assets:* £533,385
Registered Office: Biopark, Broadwater Road, Welwyn Garden City, Herts, AL7 3AX
Parent: The Saltire Group Limited
Officers: Lewis Campbell [1993] Director; Stephen Peter Duncan [1986] Director

E J Templeton Limited
Incorporated: 23 January 2012 *Employees:* 10
Net Worth: £117,610 *Total Assets:* £445,595
Registered Office: Smith & Wallace & Co Chartered Accountants, 1 Simonsburn Road, Kilmarnock, E Ayrshire, KA1 5LA
Shareholder: Elizabeth Janet Templeton
Officers: Alan Templeton [1974] Director; Colin Templeton [1969] Director; Elizabeth Janet Templeton [1941] Director; John Barrie Templeton [1941] Director; Sheena Templeton [1970] Director

Tersan Pharmaceuticals Ltd.
Incorporated: 3 December 1997
Registered Office: York House, Church Lane, Chalfont St Peter, Gerrards Cross, Bucks, SL9 9RE
Major Shareholder: Terence Edward Prudhoe
Officers: Sandra Jean Prudhoe, Secretary; Terence Edward Prudhoe [1940] Director

Terumo BCT Ltd.
Incorporated: 18 February 2004 *Employees:* 326
Net Worth: £10,472,179 *Total Assets:* £30,228,952
Registered Office: Old Belfast Road, Millbrook, Larne, Co Antrim, BT40 2SH
Parent: Terumo BCT Europe NV
Officers: Stephen Brunt, Secretary; Scott Charles Henderson [1960] Director/General Manager; Russell Bevier Spinney [1966] Finance Director [American]

Testfield UK Ltd
Incorporated: 3 March 2015
Net Worth: £1,372 *Total Assets:* £14,943
Registered Office: First Floor, 427 Green Lanes, London, N4 1EY
Major Shareholder: Behcet Bicakci
Officers: Behcet Bicakci [1980] Director

Tetraphase UK Limited
Incorporated: 11 January 2017
Registered Office: 21 Holborn Viaduct, London, EC1A 2DY
Officers: Maria Sophie Gawryl [1953] Director/Vice President, Regulatory Affairs and Quality [American]; Guy MacDonald [1959] Director/Business Professional, Chief Executive Officer [American]; Maria Delourdes Stahl [1970] Director/Attorney [American]

Teva Laboratories UK Limited
Incorporated: 3 May 1954
Previous: Forest Laboratories UK Limited
Net Worth: £29,107,372 *Total Assets:* £32,736,420
Registered Office: Ridings Point, Whistler Drive, Castleford, W Yorks, WF10 5HX
Parent: Teva Pharma Holdings Limited
Officers: Dean Michael Cooper [1972] Director/Chartered Accountant; Kim Innes [1968] Director/General Manager

Teva NI Limited
Incorporated: 14 November 1989 *Employees:* 145
Previous: Warner Chilcott UK Limited
Net Worth: £82,234,600 *Total Assets:* £97,861,032
Registered Office: Old Belfast Road, Millbrook, Larne, Co Antrim, BT40 2SH
Parent: Chilcott UK Limited
Officers: Peter Vincent Chestnutt [1960] Engineering Director; Dean Michael Cooper [1972] Director/Chartered Accountant; Brendan Christopher Oliver Muldoon [1976] Director [Irish]

Teva Pharma Holdings Limited
Incorporated: 12 April 2016
Net Worth: £309,742 *Total Assets:* £471,293
Registered Office: Ridings Point, Whistler Drive, Castleford, W Yorks, WF10 5HX
Parent: Teva Pharmaceuticals Industries Limited
Officers: Dean Michael Cooper [1972] Director/Chartered Accountant; Kim Innes [1968] Director/General Manager; David Vrhovec [1967] Director [Slovenian]

Teva Pharmaceuticals Limited
Incorporated: 19 October 1972
Registered Office: Ridings Point, Whistler Drive, Castleford, W Yorks, WF10 5HX
Parent: Teva UK Holdings Limited
Officers: Dean Michael Cooper [1972] Director/Chartered Accountant; Kim Innes [1968] Director/General Manager; David Vrhovec [1967] Director [Slovenian]

Teva Research Laboratories (NI) Limited
Incorporated: 8 September 1975
Previous: Warner Chilcott Research Laboratories Limited
Registered Office: Old Belfast Road, Millbrook, Larne, Co Antrim, BT40 2SH
Parent: Chilcott UK Limited
Officers: Dean Michael Cooper [1972] Director/Chartered Accountant; Kim Innes [1968] Director/General Manager

Teva UK Limited
Incorporated: 1 July 1935 *Employees:* 792
Net Worth: £66,836,000 *Total Assets:* £561,601,984
Registered Office: Ridings Point, Whistler Drive, Castleford, W Yorks, WF10 5HX
Parent: Teva UK Holdings Limited
Officers: Dean Michael Cooper [1972] Director/Chartered Accountant; Kim Innes [1968] Director/General Manager; David Vrhovec [1967] Director [Slovenian]

That Cream Ltd
Incorporated: 6 December 2013
Registered Office: 14 Belgrave Road, London, SW1V 1QD
Officers: Mervyn John Keynes [1955] Director/Security

Therakind Limited
Incorporated: 14 July 2006
Net Worth: £2,159,589 *Total Assets:* £2,573,014
Registered Office: Third Floor, 314 Regents Park Road, London, N3 2JX
Shareholder: Ipso Management Limited
Officers: Samantha Race, Secretary; Dr Susan Esther Conroy [1970] Director/Consultant; Professor David Seymour Latchman [1956] Director/Professor; Matthew John Valentine [1969] Director/Investment Manager; Jacqueline Winslade [1959] Director

Theramit Limited
Incorporated: 14 April 2010
Net Worth Deficit: £1,068 *Total Assets:* £9,503
Registered Office: 30 Plough Gardens, Broughton, Stockbridge, Hants, SO20 8AF
Shareholders: Joanna Binks; Colin Binks
Officers: Colin Binks [1958] Director; Joanna Binks [1958] Director

Therapi Natural Products Ltd
Incorporated: 9 March 2006
Net Worth Deficit: £102,619 *Total Assets:* £82,019
Registered Office: Hillside, Cooks Lane, Salford, Chipping Norton, Oxon, OX7 5FG
Major Shareholder: Katharine Tanya Hawkes
Officers: Esme Hawkes [1991] Director; Katharine Tanya Hawkes [1965] Director

Thermo Fisher Scientific Life Holdings Limited
Incorporated: 27 November 2013
Net Worth: £418,814,016 *Total Assets:* £1,730,963,968
Registered Office: 3rd Floor, 1 Ashley Road, Altrincham, Cheshire, WA14 2DT
Parent: Thermo Fisher Scientific Life Technologies Investment UK II Limited
Officers: Rhona Gregg, Secretary; Euan Daney Ross Cameron [1976] Director; Lucie Mary Katja Grant [1976] Director/Solicitor; David John Norman [1960] Director/Chartered Accountant; Anthony Hugh Smith [1962] Director/Vice President, Tax and Treasury [American]

Thexo Pharmacial Limited
Incorporated: 22 November 2017
Registered Office: 27 Old Gloucester Street, London, WC1N 3AX
Major Shareholder: Jrid Talal Elmarghni Omran
Officers: Jrid Talal Elmarghni Omran [1972] Director/Businessman [Libyan]

Think Noo Limited
Incorporated: 2 May 2017
Registered Office: Flat A, 214 Queenstown Road, Wandsworth, London, SW8 3NR
Shareholders: Shannon John O'Brien; Steven Austin
Officers: Steven Austin [1990] Director [Australian]; Shannon John O'Brien [1990] Director [Australian]

This Product Ltd
Incorporated: 15 November 2018
Registered Office: Room 2, 43a Summerisland Road, Loughgall, Co Armagh, BT61 8LG
Shareholders: Turlough Malachy Hamill; David Michael Hill; Hugh Colm McGrath; Killian Joseph Johnston
Officers: Killian Joseph Johnston, Secretary; Dr Turlough Malachy Hamill [1981] Director/Pharmacist; David Michael Hill [1967] Director/Regulatory Affairs Specialist; Killian Joseph Johnston [1981] Director/Pharmacist [Irish]; Hugh Colm McGrath [1980] Director/Pharmacist [Irish]

Thistle Soaps Ltd
Incorporated: 13 March 2013
Registered Office: Unit 3G Coopies Field, Coopies Lane, Morpeth, Northumberland, NE61 6JT
Major Shareholder: Alan Edwards
Officers: Denise Edwards, Secretary; Alan Edwards [1943] Director/Company Owner

Thompson and Capper Limited
Incorporated: 21 December 1928 *Employees:* 254
Net Worth: £39,143,000 *Total Assets:* £46,262,000
Registered Office: 9-12 Hardwick Road, Astmoor Industrial Estate, Runcorn, Cheshire, WA7 1PH
Parent: DCC Health & Beauty Solutions Limited
Officers: Karen Michelle Leay, Secretary; Conor Francis Costigan [1971] Director [Irish]; John Downey [1952] Director; Matthew Richard Dyal [1963] Operations Director; Karen Michelle Leay [1972] Director/Accountant; Redmond McEvoy [1964] Director [Irish]; Stephen Clifford O'Connor [1964] Director/Chartered Accountant; Reginald Laurence Kenneth Witheridge [1941] Director

Thornit Canker Ltd.
Incorporated: 25 January 2012 *Employees:* 2
Net Worth: £23,610 *Total Assets:* £47,880
Registered Office: 9 High Street, Ixworth, Bury St Edmunds, Suffolk, IP31 2HH
Shareholder: Michael Henry Archdale Bett
Officers: Janet Rosemary Bett [1941] Director; Michael Henry Archdale Bett [1939] Director/Retired; Carrie Wotton [1965] Director

Thornton & Ross Limited
Incorporated: 23 November 1922 *Employees:* 590
Net Worth: £35,706,000 *Total Assets:* £119,136,000
Registered Office: Linthwaite, Huddersfield, W Yorks, HD7 5QH
Parent: Stada UK Holdings Ltd
Officers: Edwin Charles Blythe, Secretary; Edwin Charles Blythe [1968] Director/Chartered Accountant; Charles Ashley Brierley [1963] Director

Thorpe Laboratories Limited
Incorporated: 18 June 2003 *Employees:* 37
Net Worth Deficit: £1,175,423 *Total Assets:* £342,466
Registered Office: Network House, Stubs Beck Lane, West 26 Industrial Estate, Cleckheaton, W Yorks, BD19 4TT
Shareholder: Ian John Kirk
Officers: James Ritchie Kilner, Secretary/Accountant; Ian John Kirk [1957] Director/Chemist

Thread and Co UK Limited
Incorporated: 26 February 2018
Registered Office: Kemp House, 160 City Road, London, EC1V 2NX
Major Shareholder: Charmilla Herath
Officers: Charmilla Herath, Secretary; Charmilla Herath [1978] Director [Australian]

Tickletec Limited
Incorporated: 7 June 2016
Net Worth Deficit: £14,524 *Total Assets:* £9,105
Registered Office: 1 Malthouse Cottages, Chanctonbury Ring Road, Wiston, Steyning, W Sussex, BN44 3DP
Officers: Elisabeth Bailey [1957] Director; Ralph-Peter Steven Bailey [1951] Director/Inventor; Christopher James Kennedy [1984] Director; Orobola Feyisola Lafe [1966] Director

Tips & Tricks Ltd
Incorporated: 21 December 2015
Registered Office: Spectrum House, Dunstable Road, Redbourn, Herts, AL3 7PR
Shareholder: Katrina Appie
Officers: Katrina Appie [1986] Director; Natasha Hangyal [1985] Director

Tithonus Ltd
Incorporated: 22 September 2017
Registered Office: 37 Connaught Street, London, W2 2AZ
Major Shareholder: Geoffrey Patrick Mullan
Officers: Dr Geoffrey Patrick Mullan [1975] Director/Entrepreneur

TLD Sachets Limited
Incorporated: 2 May 2007
Net Worth: £137,011 *Total Assets:* £174,314
Registered Office: 7 Hecham Way, Higham Ferrers, Rushden, Northants, NN10 8LX
Officers: Rosalyn Moya McIlroy [1966] Operations Director; Stuart Robert James McIlroy [1965] Director/European Business Manager

Tomorrow Biotech Ltd
Incorporated: 22 November 2018
Registered Office: 71-75 Shelton Street, Covent Garden, London, WC2H 9JQ
Major Shareholder: Sophie-Louise Schofield
Officers: Sophie-Louise Schofield [1998] Director

The Toothsmith Limited
Incorporated: 8 August 2012
Registered Office: 15 Lane End Drive, Knaphill, Woking, Surrey, GU21 2QQ
Major Shareholder: Stuart Christopher Smith
Officers: Stuart Christopher Smith [1963] Director

Torbet Laboratories Limited
Incorporated: 9 November 1964 *Employees:* 5
Net Worth Deficit: £130,804 *Total Assets:* £283,956
Registered Office: 10th Floor, 133 Finnieston Street, Glasgow, G3 8HB
Shareholder: Yashvantrai Vallabhji Ondhia
Officers: Yashvantrai Vallabhji Ondhia, Secretary/Chartered Accountant; Aruna Yashvantrai Ondhia [1951] Director; Punam Ondhia [1980] Director; Yashvantrai Vallabhji Ondhia [1948] Director/Chartered Accountant

Total Pharma Ltd
Incorporated: 26 May 2009
Net Worth: £10 *Total Assets:* £5,718
Registered Office: Belvoir House, 1 Rous Road, Newmarket, Suffolk, CB8 8DH
Major Shareholder: Stephen Scott
Officers: Julie Scott, Secretary; Stephen Scott [1962] Director

Total Pharmacare Ltd
Incorporated: 12 January 2015 Employees: 1
Net Worth: £1,041 Total Assets: £11,140
Registered Office: 20-22 Wenlock Road, London, N1 7GU
Major Shareholder: Gurdev Singh Ruprai
Officers: Gurdev Singh Ruprai [1960] Director

Traditional Pure Potions Ltd
Incorporated: 1 June 2015
Net Worth Deficit: £274 Total Assets: £37
Registered Office: Suite 5, 1 Market Square, Horsham, W Sussex, RH12 1EU
Major Shareholder: Amanda Jane Taylor
Officers: Amanda Jane Taylor [1974] Director/Customer Service Advisor

Transdermal Technology & Systems (TTS) Limited
Incorporated: 10 August 2006
Net Worth Deficit: £879,236 Total Assets: £96,169
Registered Office: Liverpool Science Park, 131 Mount Pleasant, Liverpool, L3 5TF
Parent: TTS Pharma Ltd
Officers: Mark Rupert Tucker, Secretary; Samuel Redcliffe Sneddon [1944] Director; Mark Rupert Tucker [1965] Director

Trauma Trays Limited
Incorporated: 19 April 2016
Net Worth: £36,954 Total Assets: £38,051
Registered Office: Park House, 37 Clarence Street, Leicester, LE1 3RW
Major Shareholder: Rajesh Gupta
Officers: Keith Rodney Fawdington [1960] Director

Trecona Limited
Incorporated: 18 December 2015 Employees: 3
Net Worth: £415,430 Total Assets: £502,029
Registered Office: 26 Leslie Way, Dunbar, E Lothian, EH42 1GP
Shareholders: Leslie Patmore; Paul Gerald Fagan; Peter Dennis Fenn
Officers: Dr Paul Generald Fagan [1968] Director/Consultant; Dr Peter Dennis Fenn [1961] Director/Consultant

Tregenna Technical Services Limited
Incorporated: 21 February 2015
Net Worth: £737 Total Assets: £23,428
Registered Office: 43 Coniscliffe Road, Darlington, Co Durham, DL3 7EH
Major Shareholder: Declan Michael McGuckin
Officers: Declan Michael McGuckin [1958] Director/Project Engineer

Tribe Therapeutics UK Limited
Incorporated: 13 July 2018
Registered Office: 2nd Floor, 2 Woodberry Grove, North Finchley, London, N12 0DR
Officers: Ruairi Friel [1976] Director [Irish]; Killian O'Briain [1972] Director [Irish]; Vincent O'Flaherty [1972] Director [Irish]

Trintech Services Limited
Incorporated: 18 May 1988
Net Worth: £23,789 Total Assets: £72,968
Registered Office: 222 North Allington, Bridport, Dorset, DT6 5EF
Officers: John Edward Budden [1947] Director/Engineer

Triumph Pharma Ltd
Incorporated: 29 August 2018
Registered Office: 71-75 Shelton Street, London, WC2H 9JQ
Major Shareholder: Pasha Khan
Officers: Pasha Khan [1973] Director

Trogon Regulatory Ltd
Incorporated: 7 January 2015
Net Worth: £25,600 Total Assets: £37,666
Registered Office: Devon View, 9 Homer Rise, Elburton, Plymouth, PL9 8NE
Major Shareholder: Claire Naomi Levee
Officers: Dr. Claire Naomi Levee [1982] Director/Regulatory Affairs (Biotechnology)

TTS Manufacturing Limited
Incorporated: 11 September 2017
Registered Office: Shoulder Way House, Tidmington, Shipston on Stour, Warwicks, CV36 5LP
Parent: TTS Pharma Ltd
Officers: Mark Tucker, Secretary; Samuel Redcliffe Sneddon [1944] Director; Mark Rupert Tucker [1965] Director

Tuscania Consulting Limited
Incorporated: 3 October 2018
Registered Office: Tuscania Consulting, 272 Bath Street, Glasgow, G2 4JR
Major Shareholder: Leonardo Mancini
Officers: Leonardo Mancini [1952] Director/Manager [Italian]

Twisbee (UK) Limited
Incorporated: 21 November 2013
Registered Office: 56 Bevis Close, Stone, Dartford, Kent, DA2 6HB
Major Shareholder: Abayomi Opeyemi Abiodun
Officers: Abayomi Opeyemi Abiodun [1950] Director [Nigerian]; Victoria Eileen Abiodun [1945] Director/Retired

Tyne Care Limited
Incorporated: 12 December 1990
Registered Office: 44 Adelaide Terrace, Benwell, Newcastle upon Tyne, NE4 8BL
Parent: Tyne Care Holdings Limited
Officers: Mohammed Mushtaq Ahmed [1953] Director/Pharmacist; Shakeel Ahmed [1979] Director/Manager; Shakeela Ahmed [1957] Director/Pharmacist

Typharm Developments Limited
Incorporated: 29 October 2012 Employees: 2
Net Worth: £1,569,660 Total Assets: £2,354,344
Registered Office: Unit 39 Mahoney Green, Green Lane West, Rackheath, Norwich, NR13 6JY
Major Shareholder: Chandrakant Vallabhdas Ondhia
Officers: Chandrakant Vallabhdas Ondhia [1954] Director/Pharmacist; Parveen Chandrakant Ondhia [1954] Director/Pharmacist

Typharm Limited
Incorporated: 22 December 1966
Net Worth: £5,058,890 Total Assets: £8,434,921
Registered Office: Unit 14d Wendover Road, Rackheath Industrial Estate, Norwich, NR13 6LH
Officers: Amrisha Chandrakant Ondhia [1992] Director/Dentist; Chandni Chandrakant Ondhia [1986] Director/Doctor; Chandrakant Vallabhdas Ondhia [1954] Director/Pharmacist; Deepesh Chandrakant Ondhia [1989] Director/Doctor

UCB Pharma Limited
Incorporated: 24 November 1925 *Employees:* 193
Net Worth: £88,308,000 *Total Assets:* £141,030,000
Registered Office: 208 Bath Road, Slough, Berks, SL1 3WE
Parent: Celltech Group Limited
Officers: Mark Glyn Hardy, Secretary; Willy Constant Cnops [1961] Director/Head of EMEA Operations [Belgian]; Dan Coombes [1975] Area Head, British & Irish Isles (Managing Director); Mark Glyn Hardy [1953] Director/Solicitor; Yogesh Khatri [1965] Director/Head of Finance and Administration; Steven Craig Price [1969] Director, Financial Control UK & Ireland

UK Animal Products Limited
Incorporated: 2 June 1999
Net Worth: £93,649 *Total Assets:* £93,649
Registered Office: The Rivendell Centre, White Horse Lane, Maldon, Essex, CM9 5QP
Major Shareholder: Lee Richard Joseph Fribbins
Officers: Lee Richard Joseph Fribbins [1972] Managing Director

UK Biopharma Ltd
Incorporated: 18 July 2012
Net Worth Deficit: £25,005 *Total Assets:* £10,316
Registered Office: 22 Worcester Street, Wolverhampton, W Midlands, WV2 4LD
Major Shareholder: Gayane Chobanyan
Officers: Dr Gayane Chobanyan [1965] Director/Doctor

UK Healthcare Pharma Limited
Incorporated: 28 September 2010
Registered Office: 61 Marlands Road, Ilford, Essex, IG5 0JJ
Major Shareholder: Sohail Shahzad
Officers: Sohail Shahzad [1963] Director/Doctor [Irish]

UK Seven Seas Pharma Limited
Incorporated: 20 February 2017
Registered Office: 18 Gilpin Close, Mitcham, Surrey, CR4 3QR
Shareholder: Mohammed Zakirullah
Officers: Mohammed Zakirullah [1982] Director/Export and Import

UK Steriles Ltd
Incorporated: 5 April 2018
Registered Office: 20-22 Wenlock Road, London, N1 7GU
Major Shareholder: Brendan Stuart Walsh
Officers: Brendan Stuart Walsh [1977] Director/Chemist

Ukann Limited
Incorporated: 13 November 2018
Registered Office: Memery Crystal LLP, 165 Fleet Street, London, EC4A 2DY
Parent: Clinicann Limited
Officers: David Colin Wheeler [1958] Director [Australian]

Ultrasound Enterprises Limited
Incorporated: 11 April 2018
Registered Office: Abercorn School, Newton, Broxburn, W Lothian, EH52 6PZ
Officers: Hans-Juergen Gassert, Secretary; Hans-Juergen Gassert [1944] Director [German]

Unconventional E & P Services Limited
Incorporated: 25 March 2014 *Employees:* 2
Net Worth: £2 *Total Assets:* £3,932
Registered Office: 21-27 Lambs Conduit Street, London, WC1N 3GS
Shareholders: Geraint Richard Lloyd; Florence Marie Milka Carissan-Lloyd
Officers: Dr Florence Marie Milka Carissan-Lloyd [1969] Director/Medical Science Officer [French]; Geraint Richard Lloyd [1971] Director/Consultant

Uni Health Distribution Ltd
Incorporated: 12 May 2015 *Employees:* 3
Net Worth: £1,145,983 *Total Assets:* £2,576,881
Registered Office: Unit G4, Riverside Industrial Estate, Riverside Way, Dartford, Kent, DA1 5BS
Major Shareholder: Gurdev Singh Ruprai
Officers: Gursharan Singh Panesar [1975] Director/Pharmaceutical Trade; Davide Eduardo Rinaldi [1980] Purchase Director [Italian]; Gurdev Singh Ruprai [1960] Managing Director

Unicomm Pro Limited
Incorporated: 1 February 2007
Previous: Miracle Pharma Group Ltd
Net Worth: £45,893 *Total Assets:* £312,089
Registered Office: Suite 12, 2nd Floor, Queens House, 180 Tottenham Court Road, London, W1T 7PD
Major Shareholder: Oleg Degtyarev
Officers: Oleg Degtyarev [1968] Director

Unigreg Worldwide Limited
Incorporated: 27 May 2011
Net Worth: £1 *Total Assets:* £1
Registered Office: Ellenborough House, Wellington Street, Cheltenham, Glos, GL50 1YD
Shareholders: Lap Fung Ho; Shui Chee Ho
Officers: Anthony Booley [1957] Director; Lap Fung Ho [1979] Director [Chinese]; Shui Chee Ho [1946] Director [Chinese]

Unir Unlimited
Incorporated: 6 July 2018
Registered Office: Unit 1685, 109 Vernon House, Friar Lane, Nottingham, NG1 6DQ
Major Shareholder: Jean-Christophe Guy Jacques Nivard
Officers: Jean-Christophe Guy Jacques Nivard [1980] Director [French]

Unit 6 Gateway Limited
Incorporated: 29 May 2018
Registered Office: 217 Halliwell Road, Bolton, Lancs, BL1 3NT
Officers: Robert Neil Grant [1949] Director/Manager

United Colors of London (UK) Limited
Incorporated: 26 April 2004
Registered Office: 18c Broadway, London, W13 0SR
Officers: Ecem Avci, Secretary; Ecem Avci [1996] Director/Solicitor; Ergenekon Mustafa Avci [1973] Director

United Pharma Group Limited
Incorporated: 17 October 2017
Registered Office: Zaj Associates, 41A Mill Lane, West Hampstead, London, NW6 1NB
Major Shareholder: Ashrf Elhoush
Officers: Ashrf Elhoush [1973] Director [Libyan]

Universal Business Services UK Limited
Incorporated: 11 April 2014
Net Worth: £41,036 Total Assets: £64,494
Registered Office: 21 Albacore Way, Hayes, Middlesex, UB3 2FS
Major Shareholder: Somendra Singh
Officers: Lalasa Alina Singh [1979] Director; Somendra Singh [1977] Director

Universal Cell Therapeutics Ltd.
Incorporated: 15 March 2017
Net Worth: £100 Total Assets: £100
Registered Office: 78 West Street, Hoole, Chester, CH2 3PS
Major Shareholder: Steven Joseph Mayers
Officers: Steven Joseph Mayers [1988] Director/Chemical Engineer [Irish/Canadian]

Universal Generics Limited
Incorporated: 15 January 2018
Registered Office: 19 Rectory Road, Shoreham-by-Sea, W Sussex, BN43 6EB
Officers: Arthur John Startin Dashwood-Quick [1954] Director/Business Consultant

Univit Ltd
Incorporated: 2 July 2004
Net Worth: £70,671 Total Assets: £132,244
Registered Office: 57a Aneter Road, Coagh, Cookstown, Co Tyrone, BT80 0HZ
Major Shareholder: Gavin Patrick Quinn
Officers: Gavin Quinn, Secretary; Gavin Patrick Quinn [1976] Director/Pharmaceutical Production Manager [Irish]

Unyte Pharma Ltd
Incorporated: 31 December 2018
Registered Office: Bennett Verby Ltd, St Petersgate, Stockport, Cheshire, SK1 1EB
Officers: Craig Brown [1969] Director; Garry Lee Stevens-Smith [1967] Director

The Urban Homestead London Ltd
Incorporated: 30 January 2017
Registered Office: 2 Arnulf Street, London, SE6 3EF
Officers: Catherine O'Brien [1974] Director/Herbalist

Uro Innovations Limited
Incorporated: 29 March 2018
Registered Office: Suite D, Pinbrook Court, Venny Bridge, Exeter, Devon, EX4 8JQ
Major Shareholder: Gary Francis Hunter
Officers: Ronald Halden [1953] Director; Gary Francis Hunter [1959] Director

Uvamed Ltd
Incorporated: 15 May 2014
Net Worth Deficit: £53,730 Total Assets: £37,878
Registered Office: Park House, 37 Clarence Street, Leicester, LE1 3RW
Shareholder: Keith Rodney Fawdington
Officers: Keith Rodney Fawdington [1960] Director

Vaccine Manufacturing and Innovation Centre UK Limited
Incorporated: 27 December 2017
Registered Office: London School of Hygiene and Tropical Medicine, Keppel Street, London, WC1E 7HT
Officers: Lucinda Annabella Parr, Secretary; Steven Neville Chatfield [1957] Director/Consultant; Daria Donati [1973] Director Business Development and Innovation [Italian/Swedish]; Ruxandra Draghia-Akli [1965] Director/VP Public Health & Scientific Affairs, Merck [American]; Dr Matthew John Lee [1964] Director/Chief Operating Officer; Professor Robin John Shattock [1963] Director/Professor, Imperial College London; Johan Van Hoof [1957] Managing Director [Belgian]

Van Vleck and Olivers Limited
Incorporated: 20 September 1967
Registered Office: 94 Rickmansworth Road, Watford, Herts, WD18 7JJ
Parent: D.D.D. Limited
Officers: Carl Atkinson [1974] Director; Charles Philip Wadsworth [1962] Finance Director

Vapour Chef Ltd
Incorporated: 5 May 2015
Registered Office: Suite 1, Store It Building, Nicholson Road, Ryde, Isle of Wight, PO33 1BE
Shareholders: Anastasia Vladova; Anastasia Vladova
Officers: Anastasia Vladova [1989] Director/Sales Administration [Moldovan]

Varydose Limited
Incorporated: 25 January 2011
Net Worth: £48,393 Total Assets: £48,393
Registered Office: Room 204, Queens Building, Mile End Road, London, E1 4NS
Officers: Brian David Barney [1960] Director/Consultant; Dr Adam Charles Daykin [1967] Director; Dr Shoufeng Yang [1972] Director/University Senior Lecturer

Vaxaid Ltd.
Incorporated: 14 May 2010 Employees: 2
Net Worth: £15,814 Total Assets: £27,052
Registered Office: Unit 1 Horbury Junction Industrial Park, Calder Vale Road, Horbury, W Yorks, WF4 5ER
Parent: DX Products Ltd
Officers: Joseph Mozalski, Secretary; Carl Alan Pallister [1964] Director

VBD Drug Safety Ltd
Incorporated: 14 October 2016
Net Worth: £14,302 Total Assets: £28,466
Registered Office: 6 Viewpoint Office Village, Babbage Road, Stevenage, Herts, SG1 2EQ
Major Shareholder: Devashish Mishra
Officers: Devashish Mishra [1983] Director

Vedabio Health Ltd
Incorporated: 23 July 2018
Registered Office: Premier House, Braintree Road, Ruislip, Middlesex, HA4 0EJ
Major Shareholder: Viren Heny Mahtani
Officers: Viren Heny Mahtani [1993] Director

Ventarc Limited
Incorporated: 24 August 2000
Registered Office: Manor Stables, Corsley, Warminster, Wilts, BA12 7QE
Officers: Simon William Waterfield, Secretary; Richard Jeremy Waterfield [1957] Director/Management Consultant

Venture Healthcare Ltd
Incorporated: 7 May 2015
Net Worth Deficit: £11,194 *Total Assets:* £70,522
Registered Office: 5 Bede House, Saxon Close, Surbiton, Surrey, KT6 6BP
Shareholders: Paul Anthony Hawtin; Martina Linda Simone Toby
Officers: Paul Anthony Hawtin [1981] Director/Trader; Martina Linda Simone Toby [1982] Director/Doctor

Veradis Specials Limited
Incorporated: 26 July 2013
Registered Office: 3 Waveney Park, Hewett Road, Great Yarmouth, Norfolk, NR31 0NN
Major Shareholder: Jacqueline Mary Racey
Officers: Jacqueline Mary Racey [1954] Director

Vericore Limited
Incorporated: 22 July 1998
Registered Office: Lilly House, Priestley Road, Basingstoke, Hants, RG24 9NL
Parent: Eli Lilly and Company Limited
Officers: Kristina Mary Hunt [1969] Director; Christopher Lewis [1978] Director/Finance Manager

Vernalis (R & D) Limited
Incorporated: 4 February 1986 *Employees:* 85
Net Worth Deficit: £571,603,968 *Total Assets:* £14,107,000
Registered Office: Granta Park, Great Abington, Cambridge, CB21 6GB
Parent: Vernalis PLC
Officers: Susan Jean Wallcraft, Secretary; Charles Stuart Berkman [1968] Director/Corporate Executive [American]; Matthew William Foehr [1972] Director/Corporate Executive [American]; Matthew Edward Korenberg [1975] Director/Corporate Executive [American]

Vernalis Development Limited
Incorporated: 11 April 1991
Net Worth Deficit: £25,458,000 *Total Assets:* £2,042,000
Registered Office: Granta Park, Great Abington, Cambridge, CB21 6GB
Parent: Vernalis Group Limited
Officers: Susan Jean Wallcraft, Secretary; Charles Stuart Berkman [1968] Director/Corporate Executive [American]; Matthew William Foehr [1972] Director/Corporate Executive [American]; Matthew Edward Korenberg [1975] Director/Corporate Executive [American]

Vertical Pharma Resources Limited
Incorporated: 1 February 2007 *Employees:* 72
Net Worth: £2,382,000 *Total Assets:* £4,686,000
Registered Office: 41 Central Avenue, West Molesey, Surrey, KT8 2QZ
Officers: Ashokkumar Dahyabhai Patel, Secretary; Soimitra Tony Dutta [1963] Director/Chief Executive; Vishal Patani [1977] Finance Director; Ashokkumar Dahyabhai Patel [1956] Director/Pharmacist; Jonathan Mark Penfold [1962] Director/Chartered Accountant

Veterinary Immunogenics Limited
Incorporated: 22 December 1992 *Employees:* 8
Net Worth: £550,012 *Total Assets:* £634,395
Registered Office: Carleton Hill, Penrith, Cumbria, CA11 8TZ
Shareholders: Thomas John Barr; Eileen Barr
Officers: Thomas John Barr, Secretary; Eileen Barr [1954] Director/Credit Controller; Thomas John Barr [1944] Director/Veterinary Surgeon

Viatem Limited
Incorporated: 20 July 2017
Registered Office: 7 The Courtyard, Buntsford Drive, Bromsgrove, Worcs, B60 3DJ
Shareholders: University of Birmingham; George Edward Rainger
Officers: George Edward Rainger [1965] Director/Professor of Chronic Inflammation

Virgo Trade UK Limited
Incorporated: 26 May 2016
Registered Office: 135 Notting Hill Gate, London, W11 3LB
Officers: Mark Simon Harris [1965] Director; Rob Shiper Syed [1972] Director

Viridian Pharma Limited
Incorporated: 20 March 2002
Net Worth: £1,000 *Total Assets:* £1,000
Registered Office: Martindale Pharma, Bampton Road, Harold Hill, Romford, Essex, RM3 8UG
Parent: Macarthys Laboratories Limited
Officers: Bertrand Deluard [1961] Director/Chief Executive Officer [French]; Emmanuel Schmidt [1969] Director/Chief Finance Officer [French]

Virodefense Limited
Incorporated: 23 October 2012
Registered Office: Magdelen Centre, The Oxford Science Park, Robert Robinson Avenue, Oxford, OX4 4GA
Parent: Virodefense Inc
Officers: Dr Marc Collett [1951] Director/Pharmaceutical Development [American]; Jeffrey Hincks [1957] Director/Pharmaceutical Development [American]

Viropharma Limited
Incorporated: 14 May 2007
Registered Office: 1 Kingdom Street, London, W2 6BD
Parent: Shire Pharmaceuticals Limited
Officers: Sarah Lucy Charsley [1974] Director/Assistant Company Secretary; Kentaro Shirahata [1976] Director/Accountant [Japanese]

Virtual Reaction Limited
Incorporated: 16 March 2018
Registered Office: Cariocca Business Park, 2 Sawley Road, Manchester, M40 8BB
Major Shareholder: Jukka Grasten
Officers: Jukka Grasten, Secretary; Jukka Grasten [1981] Director [Finnish]

Vision Laboratories Limited
Incorporated: 18 July 2016
Registered Office: 11 Crammavill Street, Stifford Clays, Grays, Essex, RM16 2AP
Shareholders: Tauqir Hassan; Muhammad Imran Munir; Shaheryar Ashfaque Alam; Waseem Ahmed Syed
Officers: Shaheryar Ashfaque Alam [1978] Director/Pharmacist; Tauqir Hassan [1971] Director/Pharmacist; Muhammad Imran Munir [1975] Director/Pharmacist; Waseem Ahmed Syed [1970] Director/Pharmacist

Vit Supermarket Ltd
Incorporated: 25 June 2009
Net Worth: £485,000 *Total Assets:* £660,654
Registered Office: Unit 2 Airedale Business Centre, Millennium Road, Skipton, N Yorks, BD23 2TZ
Major Shareholder: Michael John Davies
Officers: Richard Howard Doyle, Secretary; Michael John Davies [1951] Director

Vita (Europe) Limited
Incorporated: 6 March 1997 Employees: 10
Net Worth: £2,434,875 Total Assets: £2,655,111
Registered Office: Vita House, London Street, Basingstoke, Hants, RG21 7PG
Shareholders: Jeremy Michael Wells Owen; Maxwell Scott Watkins
Officers: Sebastian David Wells Owen [1981] Commercial Director; Dr Maxwell Scott Watkins [1959] Director

Vita Animal Health Ltd
Incorporated: 21 December 2016
Registered Office: Vita House, London Street, Basingstoke, Hants, RG21 7PG
Shareholder: Jeremy Michael Wells Owen
Officers: Sebastian David Wells Owen [1981] Commercial Director; Dr Max Scott Watkins [1959] Director

Vita Bee Health Ltd
Incorporated: 2 February 2017
Registered Office: Vita House, London Street, Basingstoke, Hants, RG21 7PG
Parent: Vita Europe Ltd
Officers: Sebastian David Wells Owen [1981] Commercial Director; Dr Max Scott Watkins [1959] Director

Vita Sun Ltd
Incorporated: 7 January 2016
Net Worth Deficit: £6,285 Total Assets: £3,441
Registered Office: Suite 1, 2 Station Court, Townmead Road, London, SW6 2PY
Major Shareholder: Anurag Kumar
Officers: Sunil Kumar, Secretary; Anurag Kumar [1976] Director [Indian]

Vitaact Ltd
Incorporated: 25 July 2018
Registered Office: Flat 608 Masshouse Plaza, Birmingham, B5 5JE
Shareholder: Anthony Soroush Rajabi
Officers: Anthony Soroush Rajabi [1995] Director/Pre Registration Pharmacist

Vitabiotics Limited
Incorporated: 25 May 1971 Employees: 90
Net Worth: £94,547,800 Total Assets: £119,392,768
Registered Office: 1 Apsley Way, London, NW2 7HF
Officers: Robert Peter Taylor, Secretary; Prof Ajit Lalvani [1963] Director/Professor; Dr. Kartar Singh Lalvani [1931] Director/Chairman; Tej Lalvani [1974] Director; Rohit Shelatkar [1979] Director; Robert Peter Taylor [1968] Director/Marketing; Peter Stephen Vaines [1950] Director

Vitabonna Development Limited
Incorporated: 12 January 2017
Registered Office: 103 Dawberry Fields Road, Kings Heath, Birmingham, B14 6PQ
Shareholder: Nicola Salisbury
Officers: Nicola Salisbury, Secretary; Andrew Currie [1966] Director/Founder; Nicola Salisbury [1968] Director

Vitactive Limited
Incorporated: 23 January 2018
Registered Office: 11 Tintern Drive, Monksmoor Park, Daventry, Northants, NN11 2LL
Major Shareholder: Mohammed Ahmed
Officers: Mohammed Ahmed [1983] Director

Vitalogic Limited
Incorporated: 21 May 2001
Net Worth Deficit: £96,479 Total Assets: £1,632
Registered Office: 1 Apsley Way, London, NW2 7HF
Parent: Vitabiotics Ltd
Officers: Robert Peter Taylor, Secretary; Dr. Kartar Singh Lalvani [1931] Director/Pharmacist; Robert Peter Taylor [1968] Director/Marketing

Vitame Ltd
Incorporated: 31 January 2014 Employees: 1
Net Worth Deficit: £377,349 Total Assets: £556,800
Registered Office: Unit G4, Riverside Industrial Estate, Riverside Way, Dartford, Kent, DA1 5BS
Major Shareholder: Gurdev Singh Ruprai
Officers: Gurdev Singh Ruprai [1960] Director/Pharmacist

Vitaminiv Franchising Limited
Incorporated: 14 January 2019
Registered Office: 68 Leigham Court Drive, Leigh on Sea, Essex, SS9 1PU
Major Shareholder: Julieann Pollitt
Officers: Julieann Pollitt [1971] Director/Manufacturer

Vitane Pharma Limited
Incorporated: 5 August 2011
Net Worth Deficit: £12,061 Total Assets: £4,817
Registered Office: 49 Peregrine Close, Watford, Herts, WD25 9AP
Parent: Vitane Pharma GmbH
Officers: Mohammed Mohsin Reza Lilani [1969] Director

Vitaxis International Limited
Incorporated: 21 April 2011
Net Worth: £68,728 Total Assets: £71,117
Registered Office: 37 St Margaret's Street, Canterbury, Kent, CT1 2TU
Shareholders: Maxim Eliseev; Ivaylo Vladimirov
Officers: Ivaylo Vladimirov, Secretary; Maxim Eliseev [1983] Director [Russian]

Vitra Pharmaceuticals Ltd
Incorporated: 17 February 1993
Net Worth: £51,861 Total Assets: £53,661
Registered Office: c/o Blanche & Co, 3b The Lanterns, 16 Melbourn Street, Royston, Herts, SG8 7BX
Shareholders: Dorothea Janice Stockham; Michael Arthur Stockham
Officers: Dorothea Janice Stockham, Secretary/Pharmacist; Sally Rust [1970] Director; Ben Michael Paul Stockham [1972] Director; Dorothea Janice Stockham [1939] Director/Pharmacist; Michael Arthur Stockham [1937] Director/Registered Pharmacist

Vitrition UK Ltd.
Incorporated: 6 March 1998 Employees: 27
Net Worth: £591,625 Total Assets: £1,020,005
Registered Office: Unit 26 Victoria Spring Business Park, Wormald Street, Liversedge, W Yorks, WF15 6RA
Parent: Health Innovations (UK) Ltd
Officers: Richard Doyle, Secretary; Clare Campbell [1975] Director; Michael John Davies [1951] Director

Vivalabs Europe Limited
Incorporated: 12 October 2015
Net Worth: £24,655 Total Assets: £265,142
Registered Office: Gladstone House, 77-79 High Street, Egham, Surrey, TW20 9HY
Major Shareholder: Jagadish Subramani
Officers: Jagadish Subramani [1979] Director [Indian]

Vivi Yeah Limited
Incorporated: 16 January 2018
Registered Office: 7 Kennedy Cox House, Burke Street, London, E16 1EU
Shareholders: Wei Ye; Da Mi
Officers: Da Mi [1982] Director [Chinese]; Wei Ye [1995] Director [Chinese]

Vivimed Labs Europe Ltd
Incorporated: 16 April 1901 *Employees:* 22
Net Worth: £9,571,000 *Total Assets:* £13,855,000
Registered Office: P O Box B3, Leeds Road, Huddersfield, W Yorks, HD1 6BU
Parent: Vivimed Labs Ltd
Officers: Rachael Elizabeth Blakey, Secretary; Varalwar Manohar Rao [1936] Director [Indian]; Mark Ian Robbins [1957] Director/Chief Executive; Sandeep Varalwar [1968] Director [Indian]; Sanketh Varalwar [1977] Globe Sales & Marketing Director [American]; Santosh Varalwar [1962] Director [Indian]; Subhash Varalwar [1948] Director [Indian]

Vivonics Preclinical Limited
Incorporated: 16 July 2014
Net Worth Deficit: £17,617 *Total Assets:* £71,510
Registered Office: Biohub at Alderley Park, Alderley Edge, Cheshire, SK10 4TG
Officers: Clare Skinner [1976] Director; Matthew Skinner [1974] Director

Wallace Manufacturing Chemists Limited
Incorporated: 20 June 1947
Net Worth: £1,178,045 *Total Assets:* £2,760,487
Registered Office: Jubilee House, 3 The Drive, Great Warley, Brentwood, Essex, CM13 3FR
Parent: Alinter Limited
Officers: Mary Joan Tate, Secretary; Mary Joan Tate [1945] Director; Simon Robert Geoffrey Tate [1977] Director; Richard Earl Warriner [1956] Director/Pharmacist

Wallace Pharma Limited
Incorporated: 1 September 2000 *Employees:* 2
Net Worth: £283,656 *Total Assets:* £308,656
Registered Office: Jubilee House, 3 The Drive, Great Warley, Brentwood, Essex, CM13 3FR
Shareholders: Simon Robert Geoffrey Tate; Mary Joan Tate
Officers: Mary Joan Tate, Secretary/Director; Mary Joan Tate [1945] Director; Simon Robert Geoffrey Tate [1977] Director

Wallis Laboratory (Sales) Limited
Incorporated: 13 June 1966 *Employees:* 2
Net Worth Deficit: £25,525
Registered Office: 66 Prescot Street, London, E1 8NN
Major Shareholder: Charmian Solomon
Officers: Charmian Solomon, Secretary; Charmian Solomon [1936] Director/Secretary; Dr David Louis Charles Solomon [1970] Director

Wallis Laboratory Limited (The)
Incorporated: 25 August 1951
Net Worth Deficit: £223,739
Registered Office: Ash Road North, Wrexham Industrial Estate, Wrexham, Clwyd, LL13 9UF
Officers: James Patrick Higgins, Secretary; Ravindra Kamalakar Limaye [1964] Managing Director [Indian]; Neil Wynne [1958] Director

Wallis Licensing Limited
Incorporated: 29 April 1994
Net Worth Deficit: £1,130,058 *Total Assets:* £2,893,737
Registered Office: Ash Road North, Wrexham Industrial Estate, Wrexham, Clwyd, LL13 9UF
Officers: James Patrick Higgins, Secretary; Ravindra Kamalakar Limaye [1964] Managing Director [Indian]; Neil Wynne [1958] Director

Ward Surgical & Supplies Ltd
Incorporated: 16 December 1999
Net Worth Deficit: £135,692 *Total Assets:* £771
Registered Office: 533 Rayleigh Road, Benfleet, Essex, SS7 3TN
Major Shareholder: Terrence Fisher
Officers: Marilyn Fisher, Secretary; Terence Martin Fisher [1946] Director

Wark Services Limited
Incorporated: 6 March 2018
Registered Office: 71-75 Shelton Street, Covent Garden, London, WC2H 9JQ
Major Shareholder: John Crichton
Officers: John Crichton [1972] Director/CQV Engineer

Wasdell Manufacturing Limited
Incorporated: 16 July 2014 *Employees:* 57
Net Worth: £7,655,066 *Total Assets:* £9,811,889
Registered Office: Units 6-8 Euro Way, Blagrove, Swindon, Wilts, SN5 8YW
Major Shareholder: Martin John Tedham
Officers: Martin John Tedham [1960] Director

Wave Life Sciences UK Limited
Incorporated: 3 April 2017
Net Worth: £93,830,000 *Total Assets:* £101,130,000
Registered Office: Hays Galleria, 1 Hays Lane, London, SE1 2RD
Parent: Wave Life Sciences Ltd.
Officers: Paul B. Bolno [1974] Director [American]; Dr Michael Panzara [1967] Director/Franchise Lead, Neurology [American]; Linda Rockett [1972] Director/General Counsel [American]

Webottle Ltd
Incorporated: 12 January 2017
Net Worth Deficit: £119,070 *Total Assets:* £382,893
Registered Office: Unit F8, Inspire Business Park, Carrowreagh Road, Dundonald, Belfast, BT16 1QT
Shareholders: Vaping Global Ltd; Vaping Global Ltd; SM Innovation Ltd
Officers: Andrej Kuttruf [1986] Director [German]; Steven George Mealey [1984] Director

Welby Healthcare Limited
Incorporated: 20 January 1995 *Employees:* 8
Net Worth: £592,511 *Total Assets:* £806,679
Registered Office: 29 Brandon Street, Hamilton, S Lanarks, ML3 6DA
Major Shareholder: Anne Welby
Officers: Anne Welby, Secretary; Anne Welby [1949] Director/Secretary; Stephen Michael Welby [1971] Director/Manager

Weleda (U.K.) Limited
Incorporated: 19 January 1925 *Employees:* 77
Net Worth: £5,927 *Total Assets:* £9,472,708
Registered Office: Heanor Road, Ilkeston, Derbys, DE7 8DR
Officers: Robert Keen [1970] Regional Director [American]; Andreas Olaf Sommer [1970] Commercial Director [German]

Well & Well Pharma UK Ltd
Incorporated: 9 March 2010
Net Worth Deficit: £764 *Total Assets:* £200
Registered Office: 102 Bressey Grove, South Woodford, London, E18 2HX
Shareholders: Fazal Nawaz Khan; Fazal Nawaz Khan
Officers: Fazal Nawaz Khan [1956] Director/Executive [Pakistani]; Shahyan Mahmud [1991] Director; Badar Munir [1952] Director [Pakistani]; Khalid Shaukat [1955] Director [Pakistani]

Wellington Unit Limited
Incorporated: 28 September 2016
Registered Office: 32 Clarkson Avenue, Heckmondwike, W Yorks, WF16 9JZ
Officers: Sohaib Saleem [1986] Director/Pharmacy; Safraz Shafqat [1986] Director/Pharmacy

Wellness Lab Ltd
Incorporated: 22 March 2017
Net Worth: £15,555 *Total Assets:* £22,325
Registered Office: 1 Eleanor Crescent, Nottingham, NG9 8BH
Major Shareholder: Elin Traustadottir
Officers: Elin Traustadottir, Secretary; Elin Traustadottir [1989] Director [Icelander]

Wenimed Ltd
Incorporated: 22 February 2019
Registered Office: Pixel Building, 110 Brooker Road, Waltham Abbey, Essex, EN9 1JH
Major Shareholder: Ahmet Murat Cinar
Officers: Ahmet Murat Cinar [1975] Director/Businessman [Turkish]

West Pharmaceutical Services Cornwall Limited
Incorporated: 9 April 1968 *Employees:* 159
Net Worth: £12,068,000 *Total Assets:* £27,493,000
Registered Office: Holmbush Industrial Estate, Bucklers Lane, St Austell, Cornwall, PL25 3JU
Parent: West Pharmaceutical Services Group Ltd
Officers: Darren Pope, Secretary; Ellen Yvette Grose [1970] Operations Director; George Lloyd Miller [1955] Director/Corporate Secretary [American]; Sean Peter Parish [1974] Senior Regional Director of Finance; Dr Stephan Selke [1967] Director/Vice President - Finance [German]

Westech Scientific Instruments Limited
Incorporated: 6 June 2012 *Employees:* 4
Net Worth Deficit: £22,555 *Total Assets:* £225,055
Registered Office: 75 Springfield Road, Chelmsford, Essex, CM2 6JB
Shareholders: Shiraz Manji; Naaz Manji
Officers: Naaz Manji, Secretary; Naaz Manji [1959] Managing Director; Shiraz Abdulmalick Manji [1955] Managing Director

Westway Health UK Limited
Incorporated: 13 July 2018
Registered Office: 2nd Floor, 2 Woodberry Grove, North Finchley, London, N12 0DR
Officers: Ruairi Friel [1976] Director [Irish]; Killian O'Briain [1972] Director [Irish]; Vincent O'Flaherty [1972] Director [Irish]

Wildrush Limited
Incorporated: 10 March 2016
Net Worth Deficit: £13,014 *Total Assets:* £47,486
Registered Office: City Gates, 2-4 Southgate, Chichester, W Sussex, PO19 8DJ
Shareholders: Howard John Wilder; Paul Jeremy Rush
Officers: Paul Jeremy Rush [1967] Director; Howard John Wilder [1959] Director

Wilsons Pharma Limited
Incorporated: 2 October 2017
Registered Office: 79 Robin Hod Lane, London, SW15 3QR
Shareholders: Dheyaa Jaafar Mohammed Samaka; Haider Dheyaa Jaafar Samaka
Officers: Hamzah Ali Hussein Sabzee [1988] Director [Iraqi]; Dheyaa Jaafar Mohammed Samaka [1955] Director; Haider Dheyaa Jaafar Samaka [1985] Director [Iraqi]

Winchpharma (Consumer Healthcare) Ltd
Incorporated: 28 August 2012
Net Worth Deficit: £121 *Total Assets:* £2,538
Registered Office: c/o Byotrol PLC, Building 303, Thornton Science Park, Pool Lane, Chester, CH2 4NU
Parent: Byotrol PLC
Officers: Denise Yvonne Keenan, Secretary; Dr Thomas Trevor Francis [1950] Director; David Thomas Traynor [1965] Director

Winross Limited
Incorporated: 30 August 2011 *Employees:* 13
Net Worth: £533 *Total Assets:* £109,198
Registered Office: 369 Main Street, Wishaw, N Lanarks, ML2 7NG
Shareholders: Ross McNeil; Linda McNeil
Officers: Linda McNeil, Secretary; Ross McNeil [1959] Director/Dental Lab Technician

Winston Laboratories Limited
Incorporated: 16 July 2004
Registered Office: The Roothings, 45 Foley Road, Claygate, Surrey, KT10 0LU
Major Shareholder: Timothy James Lovett
Officers: Timothy James Lovett, Secretary/Director; Doctor Joel Edward Bernstein [1943] Director/Chairman [American]; Timothy James Lovett [1948] Director

Wockhardt UK Limited
Incorporated: 2 June 2006 *Employees:* 71
Net Worth: £12,217,000 *Total Assets:* £65,638,000
Registered Office: Ash Road North, Wrexham Industrial Estate, Wrexham, Clwyd, LL13 9UF
Officers: Jason Wainwright, Secretary; Ajay Sahni [1966] Director [Belgian]; Gopalakrishnan Venkatesan [1964] Director [Indian]

Wogue One Limited
Incorporated: 16 October 2018
Registered Office: Kemp House, 160 City Road, London, EC1V 2NX
Major Shareholder: Khalil Rehman
Officers: Fardoss Begum, Secretary; Khalil Rehman [1973] Director

Wope - Migraine Ltd
Incorporated: 24 February 2016
Registered Office: Wellesley House, Duke of Wellington Avenue, Royal Arsenal, London, SE18 6SS
Shareholders: Peter Kropp; Wolfgang Leonhard Friedrich Meyer
Officers: Dr Wolfgang Leonhard Friedrich Meyer [1949] Director [German]

Workstead Limited
Incorporated: 6 February 2007
Net Worth Deficit: £34,658 *Total Assets:* £26,168
Registered Office: Bank Chambers, Brook Street, Bishops Waltham, Hants, SO32 1AX
Major Shareholder: Richard George Stead
Officers: Richard George Stead, Secretary; Rosalind Lucy Margaret Futter [1979] Director; Richard George Stead [1949] Director

World Max Power Enterprise Ltd
Incorporated: 27 February 2008
Registered Office: 1a Salamander Close, Carlton, Nottingham, NG4 4FJ
Major Shareholder: Rahim Bakhshi
Officers: Rahim Bakhshi, Secretary; Khalil Bakhshi [1974] Director [Iranian]; Rahim Bakhshi [1968] Director

World Medicine Limited
Incorporated: 12 November 2004 Employees: 5
Net Worth: £1,218,859 Total Assets: £2,779,074
Registered Office: Ground Floor, Gadd House, Arcadia Avenue, Finchley, London, N3 2JU
Major Shareholder: Raushan Tahiyeu
Officers: Zafer Karaman, Secretary; Raushan Tahiyeu [1969] Sales and Marketing Director [Belarusian]

World Medicine Ophthalmics Limited
Incorporated: 25 June 2010
Net Worth: £181,940 Total Assets: £229,597
Registered Office: Ground Floor, Gadd House, Arcadia Avenue, Finchley, London, N3 2JU
Officers: Martin Sheward, Secretary; Martin Sheward [1975] Director/Businessman

World Medicine Pharmaceutical Limited
Incorporated: 29 March 2011
Registered Office: Ground Floor, Gadd House, Arcadia Avenue, Finchley, London, N3 2JU
Parent: Trokas Holding Ltd
Officers: Serkan Uysal, Secretary; Serkan Uysal [1975] Director/Financial Consultant [Turkish]

World Technologies for Long Life CN. Limited
Incorporated: 5 April 2018
Registered Office: 12 Ilkley Court, London, N11 3GB
Major Shareholder: Aleksei Margovenko
Officers: Aleksei Margovenko [1965] Director [Russian]

Woundcare Limited
Incorporated: 12 April 2006
Net Worth: £10,246 Total Assets: £66,644
Registered Office: 10 Babylon Lane, Bishampton, Pershore, Worcs, WR10 2NN
Major Shareholder: Joe Patrick Hartley
Officers: Joe Patrick Hartley, Secretary; Joe Patrick Hartley [1941] Director; Julia Margaret Hartley [1941] Director

Woundil Limited
Incorporated: 31 December 2007
Net Worth: £2 Total Assets: £150,002
Registered Office: 14 Hackwood, Robertsbridge, E Sussex, TN32 5ER
Parent: Laboratoire Mergens
Officers: John Clive Andrews, Secretary; John Clive Andrews [1947] Director/Accountant

Wrafton Laboratories Limited
Incorporated: 16 August 1991 Employees: 500
Net Worth: £17,128,000 Total Assets: £45,168,000
Registered Office: Wrafton, Braunton, Devon, EX33 2DL
Parent: Perrigo UK Acquisition Limited
Officers: Annette Corcoran, Secretary; Neil Thomas Lister [1975] Director; Dominic James Rivers [1977] Director; Christopher Allan Rudd [1980] Director

Wren Hygiene Limited
Incorporated: 10 November 2014
Registered Office: Court of Noke, Pembridge, Herefords, HR6 9HW
Parent: Gent Fairhead Holdings Limited
Officers: Emma Katherine Bulmer, Secretary; Emma Katherine Bulmer [1963] Director; Robert William Thomas Fairhead [1937] Director/Farmer; Thomas Edwin Fairhead [1958] Director; Leslie Alan Jordan [1930] Director

Wychem Limited
Incorporated: 13 June 1969 Employees: 25
Net Worth: £2,322,212 Total Assets: £3,637,020
Registered Office: Eldo House, Kempson Way, Suffolk Business Park, Bury St Edmunds, Suffolk, IP32 7AR
Parent: MRG Holdings Limited
Officers: Gerhard Engleder [1968] Director [Austrian]

John Wyeth & Brother Limited
Incorporated: 20 May 1914 Employees: 272
Net Worth: £338,726,016 Total Assets: £393,776,992
Registered Office: Pfizer, Ramsgate Road, Sandwich, Kent, CT13 9NJ
Parent: Pfizer Limited
Officers: Jacqueline Ann Mount, Secretary; Sukhdave Singh Aujla [1975] Director/Site Leader; Ian Eric Franklin [1965] Director; Denise Jean Harnett [1964] Director; Jacqueline Ann Mount [1963] Director; Hendrikus Hermannus Nordkamp [1969] UK Managing Director, Pfizer [Dutch]; Edwin James Pearson [1974] Director/Solicitor; Colin Malcolm Seller [1963] Director

Xanadu Valley Limited
Incorporated: 17 May 2011
Net Worth: £1 Total Assets: £1
Registered Office: 64 New Cavendish Street, London, W1G 8TB
Major Shareholder: Barry Clare
Officers: Bibi Rahima Ally, Secretary; Barry Clare [1953] Director

Xcelonce Limited
Incorporated: 3 July 2014
Registered Office: 1 Beech Road, Drury, Buckley, Flintshire, CH7 3EG
Major Shareholder: Keith Thomas Wharton
Officers: Keith Wharton, Secretary; Keith Thomas Wharton [1952] Director

Xeal Pharma Ltd
Incorporated: 14 April 2016 Employees: 4
Net Worth Deficit: £3,712 Total Assets: £125,211
Registered Office: Unit 13 Vauxhall Trading Estate, Dollman Street, Nechells, Birmingham, B7 4RA
Officers: Haidar Abdullah Mohammed Al-Bukhari [1977] Director; Azhar Zafeer Chughtai [1979] Director; Husam Amer Hisham Jafar [1986] Director; Ibraar Mahmood Sultan [1986] Director

Xersizer Limited
Incorporated: 14 July 2016
Registered Office: Unit 1 Calder Vale Road, Horbury, Wakefield, W Yorks, WF4 5ER
Shareholder: Carl Alan Pallister
Officers: Jozef Stanislaw Mosalski, Secretary; Carl Alan Pallister [1964] Managing Director

Xinax Ltd
Incorporated: 9 March 2018
Registered Office: 7 Abbey Crescent, Oldbury, W Midlands, B68 9HH
Officers: Ryan Anthony Anderson [1992] Director/Therapeutic Practitioner

Xylomed Pharmaceuticals Limited
Incorporated: 2 June 2016
Registered Office: 13 Hillier Close, Stroud, Glos, GL5 1XS
Shareholders: Emmanuel Nyaradzo Garaipasi Chisadza; Mkhululi Patrick William Palane
Officers: Emmanuel Nyaradzo Garaipasi Chisadza [1969] Director/Pharmacist; Mkhululi Patrick Palane [1970] Director/Pharmacist [Zimbabwean]

Y Consultancy Ltd
Incorporated: 1 March 2001
Net Worth Deficit: £1,064 *Total Assets:* £1,975
Registered Office: Flat 4, 4 Brownswood Road, London, N4 2XU
Shareholder: Ade Yinka Shittu
Officers: Adebisi Shittu, Secretary; Ade Yinka Shittu [1974] Director/Data Manager

Y4U Limited
Incorporated: 13 October 1999
Net Worth Deficit: £981 *Total Assets:* £15,409
Registered Office: 70 Upper Richmond Road, London, SW15 2RP
Major Shareholder: Thomas Slator
Officers: Thomas Slator [1953] Director/Chartered Accountant

Yic Bio Ltd.
Incorporated: 21 July 2017
Registered Office: Janet Poole House, 105 Gower Street, London, WC1E 6AA
Officers: Yichen Wang [1997] Director [Chinese]

Yorkshire Hygiene Solutions Limited
Incorporated: 1 August 2012
Net Worth: £82,151 *Total Assets:* £120,088
Registered Office: 8 Omega Industrial Village, Thurston Road, Northallerton, N Yorks, DL6 2NL
Major Shareholder: Andrew David James Best
Officers: Andrew David James Best [1981] Operational Director

Your Noo Edge Ltd.
Incorporated: 2 May 2017
Registered Office: Flat A, 214 Queenstown Road, Wandsworth, London, SW8 3NR
Shareholders: Shannon John O'Brien; Steven Austin
Officers: Steven Austin [1990] Director [Australian]; Shannon John O'Brien [1990] Director [Australian]

G.H. Zeal Limited
Incorporated: 27 February 1990 *Employees:* 14
Net Worth: £310,257 *Total Assets:* £642,830
Registered Office: 8 Deer Park Road, London, SW19 3UU
Officers: Chin Kan Wilmot, Secretary; Joseph Tidboald Coles [1960] Director; Geoffrey Robert Excell [1955] Director; Harry More Gordon [1959] Director

Zeltiq Limited
Incorporated: 9 August 2011 *Employees:* 44
Net Worth Deficit: £1,255,332 *Total Assets:* £34,529,580
Registered Office: 1st Floor, Marlow International, The Parkway, Marlow, Bucks, SL7 1YL
Parent: Allergan PLC
Officers: Patricia Haran, Secretary; Judith Tomkins, Secretary; Glen Curran [1973] Director; Nick Hudson [1975] Director; Duncan James Reeves [1978] Director

Zerenex Molecular Limited
Incorporated: 31 May 2006 *Employees:* 1
Net Worth: £209,082 *Total Assets:* £344,318
Registered Office: 32 Westland Avenue, Bolton, Lancs, BL1 5NP
Major Shareholder: Mohamed Hanif Bhatia
Officers: Dr Mohamed Hanif Bhatia [1974] Director

Zindaclin Limited
Incorporated: 5 May 2010
Net Worth: £5,725 *Total Assets:* £5,725
Registered Office: King Edward Court, King Edward Road, Knutsford, Cheshire, WA16 0BE
Parent: Crawford Healthcare Holdings PLC
Officers: Christiaan Jan Otto Pool [1972] Director/Financial Controller [Dutch]; Peter Robert Rhodes [1976] Director/In-House Legal Counsel

Zink Tattoo Care Limited
Incorporated: 6 September 2016
Registered Office: 34 Blaeshill Road, East Kilbride, G75 8PL
Shareholder: Emma Traynor
Officers: Nadia Farah Radmehr [1990] Director; Amy Singh [1994] Director; Emma Traynor [1995] Director; Ellen Ward [1995] Director

ZO-X Ltd
Incorporated: 20 June 2014
Net Worth Deficit: £2,970 *Total Assets:* £51
Registered Office: 4 Cross Street, Beeston, Nottingham, NG9 2NX
Shareholders: John Francis Codd; Stuart John Tideswell
Officers: Mary Caroline Baxter, Secretary; John Francis Codd [1953] Director/General Assistant; Stuart John Tideswell [1970] Director/General Assistant

Zogenix Europe Limited
Incorporated: 7 June 2010 *Employees:* 4
Net Worth: £4,399,528 *Total Assets:* £28,842,276
Registered Office: 11th Floor, Whitefriars, Lewins Mead, Bristol, BS1 2NT
Parent: Zogenix Inc
Officers: Dr Stephen James Farr [1959] Director/President/COO; Michael Patrick Smith [1968] Director/EVP-CFO Zogenix Inc [American]

Zomi Ltd
Incorporated: 3 July 2018
Registered Office: Flat 26, Plamer Court, 34 Charcot Road, London, NW9 5US
Major Shareholder: Efrat Shemesh Idelson
Officers: Avi Idelson, Secretary; Efrat Shemesh Idelson [1974] Director/Lawyer [Canadian/Israeli]

Zota Healthcare Limited
Incorporated: 28 March 2017
Net Worth Deficit: £213 *Total Assets:* £100
Registered Office: 29 Sunningdale Gardens, London, NW9 9NB
Major Shareholder: Moxesh Zota
Officers: Moxesh Zota [1990] Director/Businessman [Indian]

ZVF Pharma Ltd
Incorporated: 27 June 2014 *Employees:* 23
Net Worth: £120,884 *Total Assets:* £856,515
Registered Office: Congress House, 14 Lyon Road, Harrow, Middlesex, HA1 2EN
Shareholders: Mohammed Fahim; Vimal Patel; Zahoor Ahmed Sharif
Officers: Mohammed Fahim [1981] Director/Pharmacist; Vimal Patel [1975] Director/Pharmacist; Zahoor Ahmed Sharif [1975] Director/Pharmacist

This page is intentionally left blank

Index of Directorships

Aa, Daan
Sinclair Animal and Household Care

Aa, Johannes Hendrikus Lifgerus
Sinclair Animal and Household Care

Abbott Ferreira, Mariana
Fluss Limited

Abbotts, Jonathan Laurence
New Cheshire Salt Works Ltd

Abdeh, Hussain
PharmaYouth Ltd.

Abdelgalil, Ahmed Ibrahim Fadel
IPS International Corporation Ltd

Abdulali, Yusuf
Saifee Healthcare Limited

Abdullah Majid, Muhammad
Pentonova Limited

Abdullatif, Mohammad Mokhlis
IQ Pharmatech Limited

Abdulloev, Sadullo
Spey Limited
Spey Pharma Limited

Abell, Martin James
Clinigen Group PLC

Abiodun, Abayomi Opeyemi
Twisbee (UK) Limited

Abiodun, Victoria Eileen
Twisbee (UK) Limited

Abraham, Bahijja, Dr
Impact Pharma Solutions Ltd

Abrar, Mohammed
Bioavexia Ltd

Aburdene, Bassam Felix
Hikmacure Limited

Adams, Brenda Margaret
Neoceuticals Limited

Adams, Rodney Harry, Dr
Bio-Medical Services Limited
Neoceuticals Limited

Adamson, John Stanley George
Jac+Q Limited

Addington II, William Robert, Dr
Pneumoflex E.U. Limited

Adegbesan, Akindayo Habeeb
RPH Innovations Limited

Adriano, Leo Nathaniel
Rowblast Ltd

Adu, Stephanie
S Adu Ltd

Aerts, Liesbeth
Janssen-Cilag Limited

Afeeva, John Edem Yao
Naturafam Limited

Afzal, Zahara
Afzal Pharma Ltd

Agarwal, Vijay Girdharilal
MacLeods Pharma UK Limited

Aggarwal, Mukesh
JIT Laboratories Limited

Agravat, Deborah Jane Kantilal
Batchable Enterprises Limited

Agravat, Ken
Batchable Enterprises Limited

Agyeman-Kuma, Rosemary
My Shea Limited

Ahmad, Adeel
Advanz Pharma Generics (UK) Ltd
Focus Pharma Holdings Limited
Focus Pharmaceuticals Limited
Mercury Pharma Group Limited
Mercury Pharmaceuticals Ltd

Ahmad, Adnaan
Glacier Nutrition Ltd

Ahmad, Faheem
Glacier Nutrition Ltd

Ahmad, Haseeb
Novartis Grimsby Limited
Novartis Pharmaceuticals UK Ltd
Sandoz Limited

Ahmad, Sulaiman Mubashir
Nuradec Ltd

Ahmed, Abdel Rahman, Dr
Commercial and Academic Services Ltd

Ahmed, Almas Khawar, Dr
Acarrier Limited

Ahmed, Iftekhar
Magna Pharmaceuticals Ltd

Ahmed, Iftikhar
Maia Pharma Ltd

Ahmed, Mohamed Ahmed Shafiek Mohamed
Avanzcare Limited

Ahmed, Mohammed Mushtaq
Clyde Chemist Limited
Tyne Care Limited

Ahmed, Mohammed
Vitactive Limited

Ahmed, Shakeel
Clyde Chemist Limited
Tyne Care Limited

Ahmed, Shakeela
Clyde Chemist Limited
Tyne Care Limited

Ahmed, Wasim
Glacier Nutrition Ltd

Ahuja, Ruchika
Jai Clinical Services Limited

Aichaoui, Rachid
RLS Pharma Ltd

Akbar, Rukhsana
Lochview Pharm Ltd.

Akel, Ibrahim
JPI Care Limited
Savoo Care Limited

Akhtar, Mobeen
Renascience Pharma Limited

Akoulitchev, Alexandre
Oxford Biodynamics PLC

Al Amoudi, Mohammed Hussein, Sheikh
Hikmacure Limited

Al Hariri, Mohammad, Dr
Nano and Nature Pharma Ltd

Al Husry, Ali Mohammed
Hikma Pharmaceuticals PLC

Al-Allaq, Taife
Cox Pharmaceutical Ltd

Al-Bajari, Ibraheem
Cox Pharmaceutical Ltd

Al-Bukhari, Haidar Abdullah Mohammed
Xeal Pharma Ltd

Al-Doori, Mohammed
Crescent Pharma Limited

Al-Hadethee, Sanaa
Pharmacare International Ltd

Alam, Abdul Munaf, Dr
Ascot Laboratories Limited

Alam, Shaheryar Ashfaque
Vision Laboratories Limited

Albahnasawy, Ahmed Hassan Ahmed
Aventa International Corporation Ltd

Albaldawi, Muthanna
Q Health Direct Ltd

Alch, Darren Wayne
Cutera Limited

Aldoori, Laith
Crescent API Limited

Aldoori, Mohammed Khalid
Crescent Manufacturing Limited

Aldridge, Ian Charles
Biomed Supplies Limited

Aldwinckle, Jonathan James
Glycanova UK Limited

Alexander, Susan, Dr
Brassard Limited

Alexander, William Paul
Bionet Research Limited
Key Organics Limited

Alhariri, Ibrahim, Dr
Nano and Nature Pharma Ltd

Ali Majid, Muhammad
Pentonova Limited

Ali, Akhtar
Hashmats Health Ltd

Ali, Anwar
Anatics Life Sciences Limited

Ali, Asad Mohsin
Ipsen Biopharm Limited

Ali, Darra Mohamed
Hemma Healthcare Teronta Ltd

Ali, Dilshad
Hashmats Health Ltd

Ali, Fahid
Hashmats Health Ltd

Ali, Mujahid
Summer Healthcare Limited

Ali, Syed Omar
Oncoparp Ltd

Ali, Wajid
Medtrack Ltd

Allaway, Michael John
Phytacol Limited

Allen, Benjamin Frederick
Allen & Jain Industries Ltd

Allen, Paul
Celadon Pharma Ltd
Celadon Pharmaceuticals Ltd

Allen, Peter Vance
Clinigen Group PLC

Allen, Simon, Dr
Fine Treatment Limited

Allin, Steven Mark, Professor
Charnwood Molecular Limited

Allison, Timothy John
Plus Orthopedics (UK) Limited

Almeshal, Talal, Dr
Al Razi Pharma UK Ltd

Alonso, Carlos
Aspen Medical Europe Limited

Aloum, Fatima
Florence Health & Beauty Ltd

Alter, Amos
Arc Devices (NI) Limited

Alwahebi, Abdullah Wahebi
Alhaddag Phrma Ltd

Alzahrani, Saeed Radad
Al Razi Pharma UK Ltd

Amaral, Jamie Marie
Hyperbiotics Corp Ltd
Hyperbiotics PLC

Amaral, Paulo de Paiva Rosa, Dr
Pentail Enzymes Limited

America, Julian
Centaur Healthcare Limited
Surepharm Services Limited

Amery, James David
Brunel Healthcare Manufacturing Ltd

Amin, Ramiz, Dr
Samritz Healthcare Ltd

Amjad, Ali
Chrome Surgical Ltd.

Amor, Barry Charles
Microskin PLC

Amweg, Levin Kim
Cannerald Group Ltd

Andal, Alma
Bandfiled Ltd

Andersen, Rolf
Epax Pharma UK Ltd

Anderson, Anthony William
Offit Nootropics Limited

Anderson, Ryan Anthony
Xinax Ltd

Anderson, Shelagh Mary
Janssen-Cilag Limited

Anderson, Toby Matthew
AAH Pharmaceuticals Limited

Anderson, William Sydney
Offit Nootropics Limited

Andretta, Luca
Patheon UK Limited

Andrews, Brian George
Sauflon (Manufacturing) Ltd

Andrews, Hilary Ann
Beegood Enterprises Limited

Andrews, John Clive
Laboratoire Mergens (UK) Ltd
Woundil Limited

Andrews, Ronald
Oxford Immunotec Global PLC

Ang, Michael Peter
Promtain Ltd

Anim Yeboah, Mavis Stella
Charis Consult Limited

Anim Yeboah, Stephen
Charis Consult Limited

Antwi, Samuel
Key Empire Resources (UK) Ltd

Aoun, Roger
Beautylab UK Limited
IGMA Limited

Appelbee, Stephen Charles
Pulmeze Limited

Appie, Katrina
Tips & Tricks Ltd

Appleby, Hedley Andrew
Ripple MC Pharma Ltd

Appleby, John Steven
Ecohydra Technologies Limited

Appleton, Anthony Joseph
Seven Seas Limited

Apter, Malcolm John
Pari Medical Limited

Aqel, Muneer
Max Medical Products Ltd

Arch, Justin
Blistex Limited

Ardalan, Shahbaz Shoja
Alpex Pharma (UK) Limited

Ardino, Domenic Anthony
New Directions Europe Ltd

Arif, Muhammad Farhan
Lawrance Pharma Limited

Armah, Cecilia
FV Supplement Ltd

Armstrong, Alan David
Almac Pharma Services Limited

Armstrong, Elsie Maureen
M & A Pharmachem Limited

Armstrong, Paul
CPT Science Ltd

Arneja, Gurpreet Singh
Alcott Healthcare Limited

Arneja, Pavneet Kaur
Alcott Healthcare Limited

Arnold, Jonathan
Catalent MTI Pharma Solutions Ltd
Catalent Micron Technologies Ltd
Catalent U.K. Swindon Zydis Ltd
Catalent UK Supply Chain Ltd
Columbia Laboratories (UK) Ltd
Molecular Profiles Ltd

Ashcroft, David
Kaizen Ceramics Ltd

Ashdown, Stephen Francis
Animal Herbals Ltd
Global Herbs Holdings Ltd

Ashoora, Amin Nazem
Pharmacenna Ltd

Ashra, Gautam Rasiklal
Asterisk LifeSciences Ltd

Ashraf, Saadia
Alvinsons Medical (PVT) Ltd

Aspinall, Nicole
Life Technologies BPD UK Ltd

Aswania, Osama Ahmed, Dr
Smart Formula Limited

Atchia, Haroon Al Rashid Dawood
BVM Medical Limited

Atkins, Annette
Apollo Pharma Ltd

Atkinson, Carl
Blistex Limited
Chempro Limited
Concorde Perfumery and Cosmetics Ltd
Cosmana Limited
D.D.D. Limited
Dendron Limited
Fleet Laboratories Limited
Van Vleck and Olivers Limited

Atkinson, John David
Nutrition Group PLC

Atkinson, Thomas Wayne
Lisoma International Limited

Attunuri, Venkata Narasa Reddy
Amarox Limited

Atwal, Gurpal Singh
Hikma UK Limited

Aubert, Jean Daniel, Dr
Astagen Therapeutics Limited

Austin, Steven
Think Noo Limited
Your Noo Edge Ltd.

Avci, Ecem
United Colors of London (UK) Ltd

Avci, Ergenekon Mustafa
United Colors of London (UK) Ltd

Avraam, Harry
Inkhancement Limited

Awad, Basel Ibrahim Bakir, Dr
Hikma Pharmaceuticals International

Awan, Ali Raza, Dr
Jini Ltd

Awan, Shaukat Pervez
Sultan & Sons Enterprises Ltd

Ayamba Ashu, Charles
Chafred Consultancy Limited

Ayub, Muhammad Zubair
Herbal Right UK Limited

Aziz, Mark
Mark Aziz Limited

Aziz, Shahid
Chembinoid Pharma Limited

Babu, Yarlagadda Sudhakara, Dr
Biocryst UK Limited

Bachelor, Stephen John
Colorcon Limited

Badawy, Maher Abueleinin Mohammad
Pharma Zad Ltd

Lomatschinsky, Penny
Penny Badger Limited

Bagnall, Mark Nicholas Kenneth
Naia (London) Limited

Bagol, Sabeena Kaur
Ekom Pharma Ltd

Bagshaw, Stephen
Fujifilm Diosynth Biotechnologies UK

Bahadur, Tushar Jain
Sterling Pharma Solutions Ltd

Bailey, Elisabeth
Tickletec Limited

Bailey, Ralph-Peter Steven
Tickletec Limited

Bailly, Damien Rodolphe Edmond
Auralis Limited
Baxalta UK Limited
Shire Pharmaceuticals Limited

Bain, David Francis
Colorcon Limited

Bainborough, Christopher
Aromesse Limited

Baines, Julian Huw
Quotient Diagnostics Limited

Baker, Christine
Ecobrands Limited

Baker, Graham Timothy
Smith & Nephew PLC

Baker, Robin
Aquabalm Limited
Ecobrands Limited

Baker, Stuart David
Bard Pharmaceuticals Limited
Napp Pharmaceutical Group Ltd
Napp Pharmaceutical Holdings Ltd

Bakewell, Gareth Clayton
Reelvision Print Limited

Bakhshi, Khalil
World Max Power Enterprise Ltd

Bakhshi, Rahim
World Max Power Enterprise Ltd

Bal, Sukhpal Singh
Symbiosis Pharmaceutical Services

Balasubramanian, Krishnamurthy
Ria Generics Limited

Balatbat, Paulo
Genotact Ltd

Baldwin, John Patrick, Professor
Protiaso Ltd

Balestrieri, Francesco
Sandoz Limited

Bali, Vinita
Smith & Nephew PLC

Ballyedmond, Mary Gordon, Lady
Norbrook Laboratories Limited

Balog, Lajos
Pharmcom Trading Limited

Balogun, Olayinka Elizabeth, Dr
CT-You Ltd

Balthrop Snr, Patrick
Oxford Immunotec Global PLC

Bandy, Brian Edward
Health + Plus Limited
Health Plus Limited

Bandy, Janet Frances
Health + Plus Limited
Health Plus Limited

Banga, Ravindar Singh
Supamed Limited

Banks, Patrick John
Contura Holdings Limited
Contura Limited

Barber, Leslie Christopher
Ecohydra Technologies Limited

Barker, Amy Emma
Canna Care Limited

Barlow, Ian Edward
Smith & Nephew PLC

Barnard, Alan
Aid Pharma Limited

Barnby, David George
Medical Export Co Ltd

Barnes, Alane P
Biocryst UK Limited

Barnes, Paul Martin
Flourish Products Ltd

Barnes, Thomas Richard
PT Direct Limited

Barney, Brian David
Varydose Limited

Barr, Eileen
Veterinary Immunogenics Ltd

Barr, Thomas John
Veterinary Immunogenics Ltd

Barrowcliffe, Susan Elizabeth
Aimmune Therapeutics UK Ltd

Barter, Simon
Proveca Limited

Barua, Ashok
Starkwell Validation Limited

Bashan, Eran
Hygieia Medical Ltd

Basheer, Fawad
Health Remit Limited

Bateman, Karen Marion
Bateman Quality Associates Ltd

Bateman, Tim, Dr
Bateman Quality Associates Ltd

Bates, David Owen, Professor
Exonate Limited

Bath, Christopher William
Norgine Limited

Bathala, Sudhakar
Sanhak Ltd

Batra, Barun
Pharmagen Direct Limited

Batterjee, Ibrahim
Europharma Limited

Batterjee, Mahmoud
Europharma Limited

Batterjee, Mazen
Europharma Limited

Batterjee, Mohamed
Europharma Limited

Bawa, Ahsan
Acme Pharmatek Ltd

Bawa, Asim Ismail
Acme Pharmatek Ltd

Bayer, Joseph John
Skinnytan UK Limited

Bazini, Samuel
Badgequo Limited

Beadle, David Colin
Phico Therapeutics Limited

Beard, Katherine Julie
Indivior UK Limited

Beardsworth, David John
Technical Textile Services Ltd

Beatson-Hird, Jonathan Denis
Agroceutical Products Ltd

Beatty, Benjamin Charles
2tonk Limited

Rayton, Leesa Jayne
The Beautiful Splint Company CIC

Ward, Karen Jane
The Beautiful Splint Company CIC

Beeston, Adrian Richard Thorpe
St Labs Limited

Beetham, Thomas
Kiniksa Pharmaceuticals (UK), Ltd.

Beevor, Roland William Miles
CPT Science Ltd

Beggin, Andrew Paul
Phytovation Limited

Begovic, Asmir
Gelu Life Limited

Behrenbruch, Christian Peter, Dr
Telix Life Sciences (UK) Ltd

Bell, Margaret
Hewlett Healthcare Limited

Belmejdoub, Amine
Hedgarth Ltd

Belshaw, Jane
Dushey Limited

Bempah, Kodjo Agyeman
FV Supplement Ltd

Bempah, Owusu Akyiaw, Dr
FV Supplement Ltd

Benati, Luca Stefano
Gelu Life Limited

Benedetti, Antonio
Cycle Pharmaceuticals Ltd

Benmakhlouf, Abderrahim
Selepharm Ltd

Bennett, Daniel Thomas, Dr
Blackpool Medicines Limited

Bennett, Hamish John Carmichael
Greenfield Pharmaceuticals Ltd
Lilly Industries Limited
Lilly Property Limited
Lilly Research Centre Limited
Lilly Resources Limited

Bennett, Norman John
Leptrex Ltd.

Bennetts, Mahireen
Falls Care Limited

Berger, Genevieve Bernadette, Professor
Astrazeneca PLC

Bergman, Kylie Christine
Druglab118 Ltd

Berkes, Ivan
Adpharm Limited
London Pharma Capital Limited
Quicksilver Scientific Europe Ltd

Berkman, Charles Stuart
Vernalis (R & D) Limited
Vernalis Development Limited

Bernard, Thierry
Qiagen Manchester Limited

Bernstein, Joel Edward, Doctor
Winston Laboratories Limited

Berti, Massimo
Pharmlife Industry Ltd

Bessell, Tina Louise
Cornish Lavender Limited

Best, Andrew David James
Yorkshire Hygiene Solutions Ltd

Best, Simon Geoffrey, Prof
Prometic Pharma SMT Limited

Bett, Janet Rosemary
Thornit Canker Ltd.

Bett, Michael Henry Archdale
Thornit Canker Ltd.

Beukman, Nico Francois
Life Molecular Imaging Limited

Beyer, Jurgen Franz
Euro OTC Pharma UK Limited

Bhalla, Rama
Personal Care Packs Limited

Bhalla, Sujata
Personal Care Packs Limited

Bhanot, Rabinder Nath
Cool Herbals Limited

Bhardwa, Jay
Nutridote Ltd

Bharwani, Mohamedali Noorali
Rimmerdax Limited

Bhatarah, Parveen, Dr
East West Naturals Limited

Bhatia, Mohamed Hanif, Dr
Zerenex Molecular Limited

Bhatia, Osama
Bio Farma Ltd

Bhatt, Saumil Kiritkumar
Anatics Life Sciences Limited

Bhatti, Dipak Devji
Syner-Med Pharmaceuticals (Kenya)

Bhatti, Pratima Dipak
Syner-Med Pharmaceuticals (Kenya)

Biadglgne, Gebray Gebreyesus
AXG Ltd
GB QP Services Limited

Bicakci, Behcet
Testfield UK Ltd

Bilal, Muhammad
Greeco Arab Products Ltd.

Binks, Colin
Theramit Limited

Binks, Joanna
Theramit Limited

Binnington, James David
Seven Seas Limited

Wang, Zhi Li, Professor
The Bio-Medical Engineering Ltd

Biosca Reig, Ignasi
Reig Jofre UK Limited

Birdi, Navdeep
Fontus Health Ltd

Biro, Peter
Merck Serono Europe Limited

Bisson, Jean Louis Michel
Active Cosmethics International Ltd

Bjerkholt, Eric Hands Claude
Aimmune Therapeutics UK Ltd

Romero de Souza, Jose Antonio
R & R Black Brilliant Ventures PLC

Romero de Souza, Pedro Durao
R & R Black Brilliant Ventures PLC

Blackburn, Ben
Blackburn Distributions Ltd

Blackmore, Steven John
Lifeshield Limited

Blaylock, Paul Andrew
PAB Apothecary Ltd

Bleasdale, Claire Chan, Dr
21CEC PX Pharm Ltd

Bloxham, Roger Mark
Ferndale Pharmaceuticals Ltd

Blythe, Edwin Charles
Thornton & Ross Limited

Boardall, Keith
Cod Beck Blenders Limited

Boardall, Marcus Keith
Cod Beck Blenders Limited

Boboia, Andreea Mihaela
Jasmine.Touch Ltd

Boboia, Ciprian Ionut
Jasmine.Touch Ltd

Boerman, Manja Hermina Elisabeth Maria, Dr
Aesica Formulation Development Ltd
Aesica Holdco Limited
Aesica Pharmaceuticals Limited
Aesica Queenborough Limited

Bogris, Nektarios
Castpol Ltd

Bolno, Paul B
Wave Life Sciences UK Limited

Armstrong, Elsie Maureen
The Bolton Pharmaceutical Company 100

Gatenby, Michael
The Bolton Pharmaceutical Company 100

Pessagno, Gerard Michael Dominic
The Bolton Pharmaceutical Company 100

Bomalaski, John Stephen
Designerx Europe Limited

Booker, Darren Lee
Ideal Manufacturing Limited

Booker, Paul Robin
HOCL Limited

Booley, Anthony Richard
Covestus Limited

Booley, Anthony
Unigreg Worldwide Limited

Boon, Gary
Gary Boon Ltd

Booth, Claudia Gwendoline Forster
Aura-Soma Products Limited

Booth, John Michael
Aura-Soma Products Limited

Borja, Maricia
Bisurall Ltd

Borodiansky, Charles
Alexi Laboratories Ltd

Borson, Marc Saul
Hexagon Therapeutics Limited

Bose, Uday Kumar
Boehringer Ingelheim Animal Health UK
Boehringer Ingelheim Limited

Bosley, Anthony James
Geotek Coring Limited

Botros, John Adel Youssef Tabdros
Avanzcare Limited

Bottomley, Virginia Hilda Brunette Maxwell, Baroness
Smith & Nephew PLC

Boulton, Paul
Active Medical Technology Ltd
Ariera Pharma Limited
Parbold Therapeutics Limited

Bouras, Elias
Ethno Botanical Resources Ltd

Bouyer, Jerome Stephane
AbbVie Australasia Holdings Ltd

Bova, Nicholas Patrick
Luoda UK Limited

Bove, Damien Jonathan
Dushey Med Limited

Bowie, Susan Elizabeth
ADS Biotec Limited

Bowman, Anthony Charles
Concentrates Warehouse Limited

Bowser, Denise
Ipca Laboratories UK Limited
Onyx Scientific Limited

Boyd, Alan Keith
Clinigen Group PLC

Boyd, Helen Doreen
Nicobrand Limited

Boyd, Richard Graham
Invizius Limited

Boyd, Roland Wheatley
Alba Bioscience Limited

Boyd, Susannah Mary
Commercial and Academic Services Ltd

Boyne, Isobel Louise
Ipsen Biopharm Limited

Bracey, Daniel
M D M Healthcare Ltd

Bradbury, Janet
RSR Limited

Bradley, Mark
Prothea-X Limited

Bradshaw, Cecilia Anita
Mento-Neem International Ltd

Bradshaw, Jamie Nicholas
QOL Therapeutics UK Limited

Brady, Paul Declan
Cross Chemicals UK Limited

Briggs, John Albert
J.L.Bragg (Ipswich) Limited

Briggs, Vanessa
J.L.Bragg (Ipswich) Limited

Braham, Christopher Huw
Forensic Rescue Limited

Branchetti, Lodovico
Cartell UK Limited

Brandgaard, Jesper
Novo Nordisk Holding Limited

Bratica, Joseph
AVI BioPharma International Ltd
Sarepta International UK Ltd.

Brault, Jean-Yves
Generics (U.K.) Limited

Bray, Rodney Graham
Lifeplan Products Limited

Brazier, David Thomas
Corpus Nostrum Limited
Mandeville Medicines Limited
Nonivlok Limited

Brennan, Paul
Pharm E-Cig Ltd

Brierley, Charles Ashley
Genus Pharmaceuticals Limited
Thornton & Ross Limited

Brierley, Gary
Talley Environmental Care Ltd

Bright, Martyn Andrew
Koolpak Limited

Brinsmead, Christopher David
Proveca Limited

Brisac, Alfredo Manuel
Biodan Ltd.

Broadley, Philip Arthur John
Astrazeneca PLC

Brockhurst, Sarah Jane
Lifeplan Products Limited

Brodie, Michael
Porton Biopharma Limited

Brodrick, Andrew, Dr
Bio-Medical Services Limited
Neoceuticals Limited

Brodrick, Deborah Jane
Neoceuticals Limited

Brokenbrow, Jonathan William
Skin Naturale Ltd

Bromley, Hayley Elizabeth
CBPlus Ltd

Brook, Martin
MB UN Ltd

Brooksby, Nigel Stanley
Porton Biopharma Limited

Brosche, Glenn Alex
LMP (UK) Limited

Brown, Andrew Roland
Miss Derriere Ltd
Mr Derriere Ltd

Brown, Anthony
Re-Vire Limited

Brown, Colin Martin
Mentholatum Co Ltd

Brown, Craig
Unyte Pharma Ltd

Brown, Crawford David
Allergan Biologics Limited

Brown, Declan Linsay
Ingel Technologies Limited

Brown, Gary
GB Quality Consulting Services Ltd

Brown, Leslie
Cod Beck Blenders Limited

Brown, Linda Ann
Opal IP Limited

Brown, Michael Robert Withington, Professor
Clothopharma Limited

Brown, Peter Charles
Opal IP Limited

Brown, Peter Michael Joseph
Frontline Trading Limited

Brown, Roland Alexander
Roma Pharmaceuticals Limited

Brownlow, Melanie
Cosmarida 2010 Limited

Brukner, Peter Damian
Premax Europe Limited

Brunton, Elizabeth Rachel
Ectomedica Limited

Bryant, David John
Quantum Pharma 2014 Limited
Quantum Pharma Holdings Ltd

Bryson, Simon Peter
Proveca Limited

Buchanan, William Andrew
Phytoceutical Limited

Buckley, Christopher
International Scientific Supplies

Buckley, Thomas
LMP (UK) Limited

Bucksey, Jeffrey Martin
Medical Technologies Limited

Buckthorp, Alexander George
Seven Seas Limited

Budden, John Edward
Trintech Services Limited

Budhraja, Raj Kumar
Pharmaceutical Equipment Ltd

Buglass, Andrew
Eco Animal Health Ltd.

Bulman Page, Philip Charles, Professor
Charnwood Molecular Limited

Bulmer, Emma Katherine
Wren Hygiene Limited

Bunn, Murray Rhys
Eezilean International Limited

Burema, Peter Arend William
Nextpharma Technologies Holding Ltd

Burges, Johannes Franz
Hermes Pharmaceutical Limited

Burgess, Andrew
RSI Chemrep Limited

Burgess, Ian F
Ectomedica Limited

Burgin, Nicholas Conrad
Eisai Manufacturing Limited

Burke, Steven Keith
Abfero Limited

Burley, Nicholas James
Alliance Medical Radiopharmacy Ltd

Burns, Alan George
Glaxo Operations UK Limited

Burns, Michael John, Doctor
Ferndale Pharmaceuticals Ltd

Burns, Nigel Robert, Dr
Cell Medica Limited

Burrell, Jayne Katherine
IS Pharmaceuticals Limited
Sinclair Pharmaceuticals Ltd

Burt, James, Dr
Accord Healthcare Limited
Accord-UK Ltd

Burton, Graham Henry
LDN Pharma Limited

Bussey, Tara
Norgine Limited

Butler, Graham Ian
Purely Health Ltd

Butler, Patrick Noel
Hikma Pharmaceuticals PLC

Butson, Richard James
Boehringer Ingelheim Animal Health UK

Butter, Satnam Singh
LPC Medical (UK) Limited
Rusco Limited

Butterfield, Peter Jonathan
Alliance Pharmaceuticals Ltd
Maelor Laboratories Limited

Bynoe, Justice Marie
Kalula Cosmetics Ltd

Byrne, Phillip Maurice
Biomedical Nutrition Ltd

Byrne, Wayne Thomas
Emerald Kalama Chemical Ltd

Byron-Cooper, Michael
Flavour Maker Limited

Bytheway, Jake Adam
CB Doctor UK Ltd

Bywater, Colin Lennox
B.C. Medical Limited

Cain, Damien
EVC Compounding Ltd

Caldwell, Jennifer Louise
Microspec Ltd

Calladine, Daniel
London Surgical Limited

Cameron, Euan Daney Ross
Life Technologies BPD UK Ltd
Thermo Fisher Scientific Life Holdings

Cameron, Ian Fergus
Micropharm Limited

Campbell, Clare
Health Innovations (UK) Ltd
Principle Healthcare Limited
Vitrition UK Ltd.

Campbell, Ian Patrick
Millpledge Limited

Campbell, Lewis
Temag Pharma Ltd

Campbell, Sean-Robbie
Fernsoft Limited
Nicofix (Europe) Limited

Campbell, Stephen
Almac Pharma Services Limited

Can Temucin, Ebru
Intervet UK Production Limited
Schering-Plough Limited

Cantarell Rocamora, Luis
CM & D Pharma Limited

Capuano, Stephanie
Recentia Limited

Carey, Genieve
Hollins Denture Clinic Limited

Carey, Joseph, Dr
Bionet Research Limited
Key Organics Limited

Carey, Robert
Hollins Denture Clinic Limited

Carey, Sean Anthony
Nutrition Group PLC

Carissan-Lloyd, Florence Marie Milka, Dr
Unconventional E & P Services Ltd

Carr Smith, Graham
Essential Health Products Ltd

Carroll, Philip Douglas
Dermatologix Ltd

Carson, Jaqueline Jessie
Morar Design Limited

Carter Smith, Michael
Snor-Ring Limited

Carter, Anthony Paul
Cannabidiol UK Ltd

Carter, David James
Green Manufacturing Partners Ltd

Carter, Kevin Thomas
Apollo Prosthetics Limited

Carter, Nicholas Thomas
Arch Chemicals Products Ltd
Hickson W.A. Chemicals Limited

Carter, Paul Anthony
G.A.S. Vets (UK) Limited

Cartwright, Denice
Pure Peace Ltd

Cartwright, Samuel Raymond
CB Doctor UK Ltd

Caseley, James
Parkacre Enterprises Limited

Cash, Simon
Casra Consultancy (UK) Limited

Cassell, Josephine, Dr
Little Green Beehive Ltd

Cassidy, Sally Louise
S.L.Cassidy Limited

Castellani, John Julius
Hikma Pharmaceuticals PLC

Castillo, Janice
Portola Pharma UK Limited

Catling, Ann Marie
Craintern (UK) Limited

Catling, Neal Anthony
Craintern (UK) Limited

Catling, Paul James
Craintern (UK) Limited

Catling, Terence Roy
Craintern (UK) Limited

Catt, James Peter
Imphatec Ltd

Catto, Gordon Webster
B.C. Medical Limited

Cavaliere, Francesco
Apotheke San Biagio SRL Ltd

Cavill, Simon Rafe
Beegood Enterprises Limited

Chachan, Mamta
Britpharma UK Limited

Chachan, Prasanna
Britpharma UK Limited

Chaddock, John Andrew, Dr
Ipsen Biopharm Limited

Chadwick, Mark Ardern
Custom Powders Limited

Chalopin, Jean Jacques Pierre
Genetis PLC

Chamberlain, Richard Alan Watson
Geotek Coring Limited

Chambers, Matthew Douglas
Biopharma Laboratories (UK) Ltd

Chambers, Michael
Biopharma Laboratories (UK) Ltd

Chandrashekar, Vasudha
Nagashree Ltd

Channon, Wayne Matthew
Cytetech Limited

Chapman, Julie
Juice Sauz Ltd

Chapman, Liam Martin
Juice Sauz Ltd

Chapman, Thomas William
Infection Monitoring and Control Ltd

Charachon, Remi
Air Liquide Limited

Charles-Richards, Oliver
Pharmacann Ltd

Charlton-Smith, Philip Geoffrey
Breckland International Ltd.

Charnock, Simon James
Prozomix Limited

Charsley, Sarah Lucy
Viropharma Limited

Chase, William Joseph
AbbVie Australasia Holdings Ltd

Chatfield, Steven Neville
Vaccine Manufacturing and Innovation Centre UK

Chaudhry, Haris Altaf
Skinnytan UK Limited

Chaudry, Faisal
Chembinoid Pharma Limited

Chaudry, Mohammed Abu-Bakre
Chembinoid Pharma Limited

Chavada, Govindsinh, Dr
Abaxon Biologics Ltd

Che, Ka Yan
Erimol Ltd
Renascience Pharma Limited

Chellappan, Natarajan
Ayurmedics Clinic Limited

Chen, Chen
Rhino Education Ltd

Chen, Rongjun, Dr
Alphacells Biotechnologies Ltd

Chen, Shu, Dr
RSR Limited

Chen, Yin Hsien
Cartell UK Limited

Chenery, Paul Nigel
Rutland Biodynamics Limited

Cheshire, Alan
Prulab Pharma Ltd

Cheshire, Mumtaz
Prulab Pharma Ltd

Cheshire, Richard Michael
Sauflon (Manufacturing) Ltd

Chesnutt, Stephen William
Algal Omega 3 Ltd

Chestnutt, Peter Vincent
Teva NI Limited

Cheung, Daniel Chun Ying
MDX Healthcare Ltd

Chiaramitara, Cynthia Helena
Novartis Grimsby Limited

Chick, David Winston
Algal Omega 3 Ltd

Chikhlia, Chetna Harsad
Ace Interventional Medical Ltd

Child, Nicholas Edward
Stablepharma Limited

Chilton, Shaun Edward
Clinigen Group PLC

Chintalapudi, Sindhupriya
Sinduram Healthcare International Ltd
Skinska Pharmaceutica Limited

Chipchase, Graham
Astrazeneca PLC

Chisadza, Emmanuel Nyaradzo Garaipasi
Xylomed Pharmaceuticals Ltd

Chisholm, Robert Charles Horsewood
HARC Therapeutics Limited

Chiu, Fung Ha Sharan
MDX Healthcare Ltd

Chobanyan, Gayane, Dr
UK Biopharma Ltd

Chodacki, Marian
Bio & Pharma Ltd.

Choudhary, Shafiq
Peckforton Pharmaceuticals Ltd

Choung, Jai Jun, Dr
Oxbridge Pharma Limited

Christensen, Frank Arve
Chemvet UK Limited

Christensen, Peter Arve
Chemvet UK Limited

Christie, Alan
Microspec Ltd

Christie, Nigel David, Dr
Lamicare Health Ltd

Chudgar, Binish Hasmukhbhai
Accord Healthcare Limited

Chughtai, Azhar Zafeer
Xeal Pharma Ltd

Chung, Ho Ching
MDX Healthcare Ltd

Churchill-Wilding, Janine Elizabeth
Chiropody Express Limited

Cinar, Ahmet Murat
Wenimed Ltd

Clanchy, Felix, Dr
Cherwell Therapeutics Ltd.

Clancy, Philip Safwan
Geoprep Limited

Clare, Barry
Porton Biopharma Limited
Xanadu Valley Limited

Clark, Tricia Ann
GE Healthcare Limited

Clarke, Annette Julie
Clarke Pharma Consulting Ltd

Clarke, Graham John
Immbio Therapeutics Limited

Clarke, John Generald
Clarke Pharma Consulting Ltd

Clausen, Mads Jorgen Nohr
MC2 Therapeutics Limited

Clements, David John
St. George Technology Limited

Clemo, Brett Timothy
Eco Animal Health Ltd.

Clift, Sharon
PCCA (UK) Holdings Limited
PCCA Limited

Clissold, Derek Wyndham
Lipidev Ltd

Clulow, Kurt Stefan Victor
Prometic Pharma SMT Limited

Cnops, Willy Constant
UCB Pharma Limited

Codd, John Francis
ZO-X Ltd

Cohen, Laurence John
Celex Oncology Innovations Ltd

Cohen, Ron
Acorda Therapeutics Limited

Coke, Stephen John
Sutherland Health Limited

Colaco, Camilo Anthony Selwyn Leo, Dr
Immbio Therapeutics Limited

Cole, Gerard Majella
Niche Generics Limited

Colebrook, Christopher John
Arcadia Pharma Limited

Collett, Marc, Dr
Virodefense Limited

Collicott, Roland John, Dr
Chalpharm Consultancy Limited

Collicott, Wendy
Chalpharm Consultancy Limited

Collingwood, Jean
Sands Fulton Limited

Collins, Jeremiah Carmel
Novartis Grimsby Limited

Collis, Philip John
Biocryst UK Limited

Colyer, Peter
Custom Powders Limited

Combe-Shetty, Keech
Combe International Limited

Compton-Bishop, Quentin Mark
Sarissa Biomedical Limited

Concannon, Paul Joseph
Macarthys Laboratories Limited

Condes, John Joseph
Air Liquide Limited

Cong, Yuehua, Dr
Simcere UK Limited
Synnlon Limited

Conitzer, Daniel John Alexander
Placebex Ltd

Conroy, Susan Esther, Dr
Therakind Limited

Cook, Anne Marie
Sage Therapeutics Limited

Cook, Dean Garth
Cosmarida 2010 Limited

Cook, Kevin Peter
Sterling Pharma Solutions Ltd

Cook, Peter
Idrolabs Limited

Cooke, Doreen Bennett
Pharma Maiden Ltd

Cooke, Terrence Bernard
MacFarlan Smith Limited

Coombes, Dan
UCB Pharma Limited

Coombs, Roderick Joseph, Dr
Kowa Pharmaceutical Europe Co Ltd

Coonagh, Hanna Joy
D.D.D. Limited

Cooney, Sean
Botanica International Limited

Cooper, Dean Michael
APS/Berk Limited
Actavis Holdings UK II Limited
Arrow Generics Limited
Auden McKenzie (Pharma Division) Ltd
Bowmed Limited
Breath Limited
Millbrook (NI) Limited
Nicobrand Limited
Norton Healthcare (1998) Ltd
Norton Healthcare Limited
Pharmax Limited
Pliva Pharma Limited
Teva Laboratories UK Limited
Teva NI Limited
Teva Pharma Holdings Limited
Teva Pharmaceuticals Limited
Teva Research Laboratories (NI) Ltd
Teva UK Limited

Cooper, Julian
Limitless Med Ltd

Cooper, Matthew
Inflazome UK Limited

Cooper, Randall Lyall
Premax Europe Limited

Cope, Graham
GFC Diagnostics Limited

Coppack, Richard
EVC Compounding Ltd

Corbett, Andrew
Centaur Healthcare Limited
Surepharm Services Limited

Corby, Padraig
Organic CBD Products Limited
Organic Hemp Oils Limited

Cordrey, Anthony Leonard
Accord Healthcare Limited

Corsie, Richard
Biotanical Ltd

Costa, Egli Gabrielle
Dreamskin Health Limited

Costa, George
Dreamskin Health Limited
Intelligent Fabric Technologies Holdings

Costigan, Conor Francis [3-1963]
Beacon Pharmaceuticals Limited

Costigan, Conor Francis [1-1971]
Kent Pharmaceuticals Limited

Costigan, Conor Francis
Thompson and Capper Limited

Cotarelo, Jose Javier
Generics (U.K.) Limited

Cotta, Julien Fabrice
Circassia Pharmaceuticals PLC

Cotterill, Mark John
Atnahs Pharma US Limited
Marlborough Pharmaceuticals Ltd

Cotton, Richard John
Dechra Limited

Coughlan, Constance
Satelec (UK) Limited

Courtheoux Batilliet, Sandrine
Merck Serono Europe Limited

Courtney, Alona, Dr
Drugsdirect Global Ltd

Cousineau Massey, Paul
Curis Life Ltd

Couzens, Richard George Armitt
BBI Solutions OEM Limited
Scipac Limited

Cox, Jeffrey Alan
Pharmacy Advisory Services Ltd

Cox, Maria
Pharmacy Advisory Services Ltd

Cox, Peter Noel Miller
Dalkeith Laboratories Limited
Herbal Concepts Limited
OTC Concepts Limited

Cox, Stuart Edmund
Karnot Limited

Coxon, Ruth Elizabeth, Doctor
Micropharm Limited

Coyle, Anthony
AKD Pharma Limited

Craddock, David John
Bodywise Limited
Grip Enterprises Limited

Craig, Thomas Kirk
Scottish Bioenergy Cooperative Ventures
Tantillus Synergy Limited

Spencer, Daniel
The Crane Bag Limited

Van Heck, Mechteld Afga
The Crane Bag Limited

Crane, Thomas
A Shroom with a View Ltd

Cresswell, Mark
Roma Pharmaceuticals Limited

Crichton, John Stuart
Crichton Consultancy Services Ltd

Crichton, John
Wark Services Limited

Croft, Andrew
Atlantis Research Limited

Crook, Michael
Suzie Who Limited

Cross, Gareth John
Coast Science UK Limited

Crossley, Andrew Graham
AMO United Kingdom Limited

Crossley, Mark Wesley
Indivior PLC

Crouton, Marc James Gerard
Calea UK Limited
Fresenius Kabi Limited

Cruickshank, Alexander Douglas Miller
Cross Healthcare Limited
S.C.A.C. Limited

Crutchley, Nigel, Dr
MC2 Therapeutics Limited

Crystal, Roger
Opiant Pharmaceuticals UK Ltd

Cubbin, Douglas Ernest Charles
Telix Life Sciences (UK) Ltd

Cugine, Steven Paul
Church & Dwight UK Limited

Cumberland, Daryl
Euratlantic-Cosmepharm Limited

Cummings, Russell
Circassia Pharmaceuticals PLC

Cunningham, Colin John Conrad
Q Health Direct Ltd

Curran, Glen
Zeltiq Limited

Curran, Sharon
Circassia Pharmaceuticals PLC

Currie, Andrew
Vitabonna Development Limited

Curtis, Nicholas
Acle Urban Gardens Limited

Cutting, William Stojan
Retrogrow Limited

Czernik, Mariusz
Cambridge Advanced Technologies Ltd

Czernik, Monika
Cambridge Advanced Technologies Ltd

Czosnyka, Marek
Medicam Limited

D'angelo, Massimo
Indivior UK Limited

Dainty, Neil Brett
Quest Ingredients Limited

Dale, Ian Alistair
GE Healthcare Limited

Dale, Nicholas Egerton
Sarissa Biomedical Limited

Dalgleish, Angus George, Dr
LDN Pharma Limited

Dancy, Robert David
Church & Dwight UK Limited

Daniel, Edward
Edward Daniel Limited

Darbar, Narendrakumar Laxmansingh
Nabros Pharma (UK) Ltd

Darwazah, Mazen Samih Taleb
Hikmacure Limited

Darwazah, Mazen Samih
Hikma Pharmaceuticals PLC

Darwazah, Said Samih
Hikma Pharmaceuticals PLC

Dashwood-Quick, Arthur John Startin
Universal Generics Limited

Datwani, Arun
Doctor Pharma Manufacturing UK Ltd

Daugherty, Joseph
Eleosinc Limited

Davidson, Andrew Robert
DTR Medical Limited

Davidson, Jennifer Margaret
Lothian Laboratories Ltd

Davidson, Kenneth Nairn
Lothian Laboratories Ltd

Davies, Andrew Michael
Principle Healthcare International
Principle Healthcare Limited
Seven Days Vitamin Co Ltd

Davies, Christopher Mark
CKS Scientific Limited

Davies, John Hywel
C 3 Innovations Limited

Davies, John Stephen, Dr
Stride-Davies Pharma Limited

Davies, Michael John
Health Innovations (UK) Ltd
Principle Healthcare International
Principle Healthcare Limited
Vit Supermarket Ltd
Vitrition UK Ltd.

Davies, Philip Benjamin
Principle Healthcare International
Principle Healthcare Limited

Davies, Rupert Adam John
Blackrock Pharmaceuticals Ltd

Davies, Sem Lloyd
Ferndale Pharmaceuticals Ltd

Davies, Serge Jon
Concentrates Warehouse Limited

Davies, Steven
Auramedicann Ltd

Davis, Alan, Dr
Bescot Healthcare UK Limited

Davis, Alison Maria
Pharmaxo Pharmacy Services Ltd

Davis, Brennig Jonathan Bryan
Natural Way Limited

Davis, Nicholas
Ipsen Biopharm Limited

Davis, Paul James
Insense Limited

Davis, Robert James
Algal Omega 3 Ltd

Davis, Rosemary Jane
Natural Way Limited

Davis, Walter Bryan, Dr
Natural Way Limited

Dawkins, Reuben Luke
Reld Tech Ltd

Dawoodi, Zain, Dr
Ladysystems International Ltd

Dawson, Martyn John
Instrument Research Co Ltd

Dawson, Sarah Joanne
Instrument Research Co Ltd

Day, Jasper John
J J Design and Engineering Ltd

Daykin, Adam Charles, Dr
Varydose Limited

De Costa, Samooh Dishal
Nova Bio-Pharma Technologies Ltd

De Furia, Salvatore
Pharmach Ltd

De Gavre, Timothy Charles
Oriel Therapeutics Limited
Sandoz Limited

De Lara Gonsalez, Sonia
Lux Viridis Services Ltd

De Los Angeles Khoury Gonzalo, Maria
GE Healthcare UK Limited

De Lugar, Prima
Mantiza Ltd

De Souza, Richard
P2 Healthcare Limited
P2-Molteni Pharma Limited

De Zulueta, Susan Elizabeth
Halewood Chemicals Ltd

Deacon, Carl
CBD Grow Tech Ltd

Deacon, Leslie
Beacon Pharmaceuticals Limited
Kent Pharmaceuticals Limited

Dean, Paul David
Porvair PLC

Deb, Robin Kumar
Synergy Biologics Limited

Debethizy, Joseph Donald
Albumedix Ltd

Debs, Pierre, Dr
Spectrum Biomedical UK Limited

Deegan, Robert Anthony
Cool Gell Limited

Degtyarev, Oleg
Unicomm Pro Limited

Dela Cruz, Consolacion
Glasstomato Ltd

Deluard, Bertrand
Aurum Pharmaceuticals Limited
Macarthys Laboratories Limited
Viridian Pharma Limited

Denson, Anthony Kenneth, Dr
Diagnostic Reagents Limited

MacGregor, Lynne
The Derma Hair and Body Shop Ltd

Vero, Rose
The Derma Hair and Body Shop Ltd

Dermish, Mohamed Ali Mohamed
Prime Medical Equipment Ltd

Desai, Jitendrakumar
Purple Healthcare Limited

Dessen, Arne
Algipharma UK Limited

Detta, Allah, Dr
Tawil Co Limited

Dev, Tuhin Kumar, Dr
Dr. Tuhin Dev Skin Care Ltd

Deyoung, Peter Daniel
Piramal Critical Care Limited

Dezaire, Gijsbert
Solent Oral Care Ltd

Dhaliwal, Kanwaldeep
Prothea-X Limited

Dhanani, Saraj Rajnikant
Euro Medical Equipment Limited

Dharamshi, Shirazali Sharif
LPC Medical (UK) Limited

Dhesi, Suhkdev
Green House Monitoring Limited

Dickens, John Francis
Ethno Botanical Resources Ltd

Didlick, Philip
Ayrton Saunders Limited
Ayrton Saunders and Co Ltd
OBG Holding Limited
Pharmaserve (North West) Ltd
Pharmaserve Limited
Pharmasol Limited
Ransom Naturals Limited

Dier, Mardi
Portola Pharma UK Limited

Dieterich, Petra, Dr
Aptuit (Oxford) Limited

Difonzo, Carlo
Nektar Therapeutics UK Limited

Diggelmann, Roland Daniel
Smith & Nephew PLC

Diggle, Stephen Charles
Oxford Biodynamics PLC

Dignum, Mark John
Geryon Pharma Limited

Ding, Zhao, Dr
Seacross Pharmaceuticals Ltd

Dingemans, Simon Paul
Smith Kline & French Laboratories
SmithKline Beecham Limited

Dinkelborg, Ludger Maria Theodor, Dr
Life Molecular Imaging Limited

Diss, Nicholas John
Cambridge Sensors Ltd

Dixon, Caroline Rebecca Louise
Generics (U.K.) Limited

Dixon, John
LRC Products Limited

Djamarani, Keyvan, Dr
Bespak Europe Limited

Djamgoz, Mustafa Bilgin Ali, Professor
Celex Oncology Innovations Ltd

Dobbins, David Ian
Scottish Bioenergy Cooperative Ventures
Tantillus Synergy Limited

Dolby, Benjamin
Goat Nutrition Limited

Dolby, Bruce
Goat Nutrition Limited

Dolby, Margaret Anne
Goat Nutrition Limited

Dolfini, Enrico Maria
Sarepta International UK Ltd.

Donati, Daria
Vaccine Manufacturing and Innovation Centre UK

Done, Edward Mathew
Slo Drinks Limited

Donnelly, Emos Patrick
McAleer & Donnelly Pharmacy Ltd

Donoghue, Stuart
Connoisseur Clouds Ltd

Donovan, Kiera
Dermatek Limited
Pellis Care Limited

Dore WW Pochon, Marie-Laure Jeanne Antoinette
Satelec (UK) Limited

Dorris, Simon James, Dr
London Pharma Capital Limited
Medpro Health Limited

Doshi, Yogeshkumar Jagjivandas
Ganges Thames Pharmaceuticals & Chemicals

Douglas, Simon Gorgon
Biofortuna Ltd

Douglas, Tony Jack
Rotapharm Limited

Douglas-Bell, Adrian
3rd Hour Limited

Douglas-Bell, Stephanie
3rd Hour Limited

Dowdeswell, Christian Steven
MW Encap (Holdings) Limited
MW Encap Limited

Downey, John
Thompson and Capper Limited

Doyle, Paul Martin, Dr
Peakdale Chemistry Services Ltd

Dr. Kremer, Dirk
Skindoc Formula Limited

Draghia-Akli, Ruxandra
Vaccine Manufacturing and Innovation Centre UK

Drew, Jeffrey, Dr
Cytetech Limited

Dube, Vijay
ADS Biotec Limited

Dubickas, Garry, Dr
Biocentra Limited

Dubly, Herve
Acime UK Limited

Ducker, John Robert
Fresenius Kabi Limited

Duckworth, Alexander James
Ardent Pharma Limited

Duffy, Justine Ellen
Avanor Healthcare Ltd
Duffy Assets Ltd

Duffy, Mark Christopher Roger
Made in Nature Ltd

Duffy, Scott
Avanor Healthcare Ltd
Duffy Assets Ltd

Dugdale, Neil Alan
Swedish Orphan Biovitrum Ltd

Duggan, Alexander James Hanbury
Alliance Pharmaceuticals Ltd
Maelor Laboratories Limited

Dugsiye, Mohamed Mahmoud
Shabelle Ltd

Duhalde, Francois Xavier
Genzyme Limited

Duhalde, Francois-Xavier
Fisons Limited
May & Baker Limited
Sanofi-Synthelabo Limited

Dulgher, Adrian
Brewtaal Ltd

Dunbar, Oriele Anne
Elemis Limited

Duncan, Graeme Neville
Advanz Pharma Generics (UK) Ltd
Focus Pharma Holdings Limited
Focus Pharmaceuticals Limited
Mercury Pharma Group Limited
Mercury Pharmaceuticals Ltd

Duncan, Kimbell Rush
Infirst Healthcare Limited

Duncan, Matthew John
Acime UK Limited

Duncan, Stephen Peter
Temag Pharma Ltd

Dunkel, Matthias Peter Hermann
Geistlich Sons Limited

Dunoyer, Marc Pierre Jean
Astrazeneca PLC

Duran, Ismael
Jellyhills Ltd

Dutta, Soimitra Tony
Integrated Pharmaceutical Services (IPS)
Ipsco Limited
Vertical Pharma Resources Ltd

Dutton, Tom
Rhodia Pharma Solutions Ltd

Dyal, Matthew Richard
Thompson and Capper Limited

Dyer, Anthony William
Lab 21 Healthcare Limited

Eagle, Ronald Andrew
BVM Medical Limited

Eakin, Jeremy David
T.G. Eakin Limited

Eakin, Paul Andrew
T.G. Eakin Limited

Eakin, Thomas George
T.G. Eakin Limited

Eakin, Violet P
T.G. Eakin Limited

Echeverria, Natalie
Asaya Cosmeceuticals Limited

Edi, Muhammad Zukermi Bin
Nocov Ltd

Edwards, Alan
Thistle Soaps Ltd

Edwards, Ann Julie Mary
Quicksilver Scientific Europe Ltd

Edwards, David John Hugh
Edwards' Analytical Limited

Eely, Antony
Flavour Maker Limited

Eggleston, Renda, Dr
Approved Pharma Solutions Ltd
Rena Specials Limited

Eggleston, Richard Stuart
Approved Pharma Solutions Ltd
Rena Specials Limited

Egharevba, Terry Efeosa Egheosa
Onipede Clinical Research Ltd

Egorov, Alexey
Medison Pharma Limited

Ekakitie, Efe
Clickhealth Limited

Ekundayo, Martin Olayinka
Hairblends Limited

El-Tawil, Amhs
Tawil Co Limited

Eldered, Thomas Bengt
Recipharm HC Limited
Recipharm Limited

Eldracher, Deborah Disanzo
Astrazeneca PLC

Elhag, Noon Abdelgaffar Hussein, Dr
Almisbar Limited

Elhoush, Ashrf
Britanica Medicines & Medical Equipment
Fresenius Kabi DG Limited
United Pharma Group Limited

Eliseev, Maxim
Vitaxis International Limited

Elkaramany, Tamer Aly Emam Aly
Solarius UK & Overseas Limited

Elliott, Gary
Biocolor Limited

Elliott, Geoffrey
Pharmapac (U.K.) Limited

Ellis, Anthony
Medicaleaf Limited

Ellson, Peter William
Stegram Pharmaceuticals Ltd

Elmasry, Sherif Mohamed Aboelnaga Mohamed
E.P.G Pharma Ltd
Samritz Healthcare Ltd

Elohim, El, Lord
Mirroman Ltd

Elsheikh, Mohamed Ahmed Fadlallah, Dr
GM Globalhealth Ltd

Elwood, John
Crawford Manufacturing Limited

Elzas, Jacob
Arc Devices (NI) Limited

Elzokrod, Tamer Mohamed Hassan
Solarius UK & Overseas Limited

Emde, Eckhard
Brown Exclusive (Worldwide) Ltd

Endacott, Adrian
Maxvac Ltd

Eneli, Ezim Adesola
One Stop 15 Limited

Engineer, Misha
Surrey Pharma Ltd

Engineer, Nikesh
Chemidex Pharma Limited
Essential Generics Limited
Essential Pharma Limited
Essential Pharmaceuticals Ltd

Engleder, Gerhard
Wychem Limited

Engstrom, Erik
Smith & Nephew PLC

Erichsen, Helen Paula
PVR Works Ltd

Erridge, Clett
Caithness Biotechnologies Ltd

Errington, Rachel Jane, Doctor
Biostatus Ltd

Erwin, Richard William
Roche Products Limited

Esa, Adam
Pharmacy Business Consultancy Ltd

Escudie, Philippe Marcel Georges
Air Liquide Limited

Espinet, Antoine Jean, Dr
Microfluidx Ltd

Essuman, Francis Kwame
Leap Pharma Ltd

Etherington, Karen June, Dr
Dextra Laboratories Limited
NZP UK Limited

Evans, Christopher Peter
Talley Environmental Care Ltd

Evans, Eric Wayne
Avista Holding Co., Ltd.

Evans, John James Henry
Talley Environmental Care Ltd

Evans, Lee Edward
Ortholese Limited

Evans, Richard Anthony
Quotient Diagnostics Limited

Evans, Samantha
Ortholese Limited

Eve, Jeremy, Dr
Evida Ltd

Everett, Jeffery Raymond Albert
Arcadia Pharma Limited

Everitt, Charles David
LRC Products Limited

Exner, Andree
DCMP 8E Cepac Limited

Eyles, Anita Louise
Boley Nutraceuticals Ltd.

Ezeakune, Benadette Obuneme
Bena Cosmetics (UK) Limited

Duchesne, Frederic Marie
Pierre Fabre Limited

Danon, Michael Frederic
Pierre Fabre Limited

Benoist, Xavier Pierre Marie
Pierre Fabre Limited

McMullin, Laura Adele
Pierre Fabre Limited

Guiraud-Chaumeil, Vincent Henri Francois
Pierre Fabre Limited

Fagan, Paul Generald, Dr
Trecona Limited

Fahim, Mohammed
ZVF Pharma Ltd

Fahy, Shaun Patrick
Apollo Pharma Ltd

Fairbourn, Michael John
Carefusion U.K. 244 Limited

Fairhead, Heather Marie
Phico Therapeutics Limited

Fairhead, Robert William Thomas
Wren Hygiene Limited

Fairhead, Thomas Edwin
Wren Hygiene Limited

Fakes, David William, Dr
Micropharm Limited

Farhat, Mohamad Ismail
Kalfar Health Ltd

Farquhar, Edward Peter Henry
Delta Diagnostics (UK) Ltd

Farr, Stephen James, Dr
Zogenix Europe Limited

Farrant, Simon
MacFarlan Smith Limited

Farrington, Jonathan George
London Pharma Capital Limited
Medpro Health Limited

Fasman, Steven
Catalent MTI Pharma Solutions Ltd
Catalent Micron Technologies Ltd

Fawdington, Keith Rodney
Handiskin Limited
Trauma Trays Limited
Uvamed Ltd

Fazeli, Mohammad Sohail
Exonate Limited

Fazwani, Sinnan
Royce Health Sciences Ltd

Feasey, Steven Robert
Bio Pure Technology Ltd

Fecko, Tomas
Dr. Max Pharma Limited

Federighi, Mario
Farmigea UK Ltd

Fegan, Finola
Finca Skin Organics Limited

Feilding, Amanda Claire, Lady
Beckley Labs Limited
Beckley Research and Innovations Ltd
New Eleusis Limited

Fellows, Charlotte
Made in Nature Ltd

Felthouse, Alex John
Eisai Manufacturing Limited

Fenn, Peter Dennis, Dr
Trecona Limited

Ferguson, Claire
Bach Flower Remedies Limited
Nelson & Russell Holdings Ltd

Ferguson, Jason
Cannacureyou Ltd

Ferreira Silva, Bruno
Fluss Limited

Feuhouo, Jules Colbert
Clarornell Consulting and Trading Ltd

Field, Clifford Joseph
Allfresh Products Limited

Fielder, Timothy Hugh
Oat Services Limited

Fielding, Richard Henry
Brunel Healthcare Manufacturing Ltd

Filik, Robert Paul, Dr
Cartell UK Limited

Filippi, Bernard Robert
Lea Pharma Limited

Finch, Richard Charles
East West Naturals Limited

Fisher, John Keith
Birchwood Pharma Ltd

Fisher, Martin
Bescot Healthcare UK Limited

Fisher, Terence Martin
Ward Surgical & Supplies Ltd

Fishwick, Craig Bernard
Eaststone Limited
Maxearn Limited

Fitton, Jonathan Michael
Cambcol Ltd

Fitton, Jonathan
Cambridge Collagen Company (UK) Ltd

Fitzgibbon, Gregory John
Delta Diagnostics (UK) Ltd

Fitzsimmons, Roy Dunsmore
AWA Export Limited
Phytovation Limited

Flahive, Eamon
Elanco Europe Ltd.

Fletcher, Alan
Chiropody Express Limited

Fletcher, Jeremy Peter Anthony
Iroko Products Limited

Foehr, Matthew William
Vernalis (R & D) Limited
Vernalis Development Limited

Foit, Matei
Nanomed Ltd

Fontana, Mario
Adam Project Ltd

Forbes, James Keiron Hugh
Isopath Limited

Forbes, Nigel Joseph
Isopath Limited

Forbes, Patricia Ann
Isopath Limited

Forbes, Patricia Anne
Isopath Limited

Ford, Paul Anthony
Medicaleaf Limited

Forde, Avril Ann
Getinge UK Limited

Forrester-Coles, Stephen Llanon
Norton Healthcare Limited

Fouda, Ibrahim Abdelrazik Albayoomi
Ardiou Healthcare Ltd
Evorin Pharma Limited
Nelovy Healthcare Ltd
Resok Healthcare Ltd

Fountain, Christopher James
Microgenetics Limited
Pharmaxo Pharmacy Services Ltd
Qualasept Limited

Fouracre, Philip Anthony
Reem Tanning Co Ltd

Francis, Thomas Trevor, Dr
Winchpharma (Consumer Healthcare) Ltd

Franek, Charlotte Anne
Blend & Glow Limited

Franken, Marc
Pharma Device Delivery Limited

Franklin, Andrew Timothy
Alliance Pharmaceuticals Ltd
Maelor Laboratories Limited

Franklin, Ian Eric
Hospira Aseptic Services Ltd
Hospira UK Limited

Fraser, Carole
Moroccan Natural Resources Ltd

Fraser, Jane, Dr
MW Encap (Holdings) Limited
MW Encap Limited

Fraser-Pye, Graham Julian
Contura Holdings Limited
Contura Limited
Dermato Logical Limited

Freestone, Robin Anthony David
Smith & Nephew PLC

Frenguelli, Bruno Generald, Professor
Sarissa Biomedical Limited

Fribbins, Lee Richard Joseph
UK Animal Products Limited

Friedman, Michael Allen
Smith & Nephew PLC

Friel, Ruairi
Glasport Bio UK Limited
Tribe Therapeutics UK Limited
Westway Health UK Limited

Fristedt, Stefan Ulf
Medlock Medical Limited
Molnlycke Health Care Limited

Fritze, Marcus
M D M Healthcare Ltd

Frixou, Margaret
Beautanix Limited

Frizelle, Dorothy Jane, Dr
Dushey Med Limited

Froggatt, Christopher Mark Davidson
Albany Molecular Research Ltd

Fry, Hugo Rupert Alexander
Fisons Limited
May & Baker Limited
Sanofi-Synthelabo Limited

Fry, Matthew Peter
Courtin and Warner Limited

Fry, Richard Paul
Cellon UK Limited

Furmaniak, Jadwiga, Dr
RSR Limited

Futter, Rosalind Lucy Margaret
Workstead Limited

Gabe, Yan Pierre Francois
Sogeval UK Limited

Gabriel, Noella
Elemis Limited

Gadhia, Danesh Vinodkumar
Morningside Healthcare Limited

Gadhia, Jitesh Kishorekumar, Lord
Accord Healthcare Limited

Gadhia, Sanjay Kishan
Morningside Healthcare Limited

Gadhri, Munish, Dr
AA Zentivus Ltd

Gaffney, Piers Robert James, Dr
Exactmer Limited

Gal, Stefan
Pharmacell Medication Systems Ltd

Galazka, Andrew
Merck Serono Europe Limited

Galbraith, Kenneth Harry
Prometic Pharma SMT Limited

Gall, Matthew Garrett
AVI BioPharma International Ltd
Sarepta International UK Ltd.

Gallagher, Kevin
Dushey Limited

Gallimore, Dawn Margaret
Positive Diagnostics Ltd

Ganda, Praveshkumar Kantilal
Handiskin Limited

Ganin, Facundo
Point International Limited

Gann, Jochen
Hikma Pharmaceuticals PLC

Garay, Jon
Baxter Healthcare Limited
Claris LifeSciences (UK) Ltd

Garcia, Alexander
Milewackers Ltd

Gardiner, Sandra
Cutera Limited

Gardner, Ian Charles
Herbal Concepts Limited

Gassert, Hans-Juergen
Ultrasound Enterprises Limited

Gastaldo, Patrizio
Quality Products 360 Ltd

Gatenby, Michael
M & A Pharmachem Limited

Gauthier, Jean-Louis Andre
Panpharma UK Limited

Gawryl, Maria Sophie
Tetraphase UK Limited

Geddes, Shona Robertson
St Andrews Botanics Limited

Gee, Tony
Delta Diagnostics (UK) Ltd

George, Adam David
GW Pharma Limited

George, Giby
GMP Manufacturing Ltd

Ghelani, Deepak Anantrai
Ascot Laboratories Limited

Giannelli, Alessandra
Martini International Ltd

Gibb, Charles James
Diana Drummond Limited

Gibb, Elspeth Anne MacLean
Diana Drummond Limited

Gibbons, Mark
Baxalta UK Limited
Shire Pharmaceuticals Limited

Gibson, Ian, Sir
Norbrook Laboratories Limited

Giffard, Allan Bruce
Medical Ethics UK Limited

Gilbert, Patricia Ann
New Directions Europe Ltd

Gilbert, Robert Patrick
New Directions Europe Ltd

Gilham, Ian David, Dr
Delta Diagnostics (UK) Ltd

Gill, Kamal Jit Kaur
New Directions Europe Ltd

Gill, Karanjit
KKG Consulting Limited

Gill, Raj, Dr
Opix Ltd

Gingell, Andrew Clive
Bionet Research Limited
Key Organics Limited

Gleave, Donald Richard
Porton Biopharma Limited

Gleed, Daniel Penhorwood
AMO United Kingdom Limited

Glenn, Jonathan Martin
Aesica BC Limited
Aesica Formulation Development Ltd
Aesica Holdco Limited
Aesica M1 Limited
Aesica M2 Limited
Aesica Pharmaceuticals Limited
Aesica Queenborough Limited
Aesica Trustee Co Ltd
Bespak Europe Limited

Goddard, John Geoffrey
Accord Healthcare Limited

Godden, Phillip Robert Charles
Protak Scientific Limited

Godfrey, Bjorn
Dermatek Limited
Pellis Care Limited

Godha, Pranay
Onyx Scientific Limited

Godiawala, Tanmay Naimish
Reaxa Limited

Godzicz, Susan Mary
Bio Pure Technology Ltd

Gohil, Girjadevi
Ayush Ayurveda Care Limited

Golden, Randal Louis
Sauflon (Manufacturing) Ltd

Goldney, Andrew Neil
Baxter Healthcare Limited
Claris LifeSciences (UK) Ltd

Goldstein, Matthew David
Badgequo Limited

Goldswain, Rebecca
Goat Nutrition Limited

Goldsworth, John Graham
Abatron Limited

Golsharifi, Nima, Dr
Orb Global Ltd
Panaomics Limited

Gomez, Phillip Louis
Siga Pharmaceuticals (Europe) Ltd

Good, Amanda Jayne
Stockcare Limited

Goodger, David
Ideal Manufacturing Limited

Goodings, David
Redrose Manufacturing Limited
Redrose Nutraceuticals Limited

Goodson-Wickes, Charles, Dr
Ecohydra Technologies Limited

Gourley, Fraser Andrew
Noble Green (Essex) Limited

Grainey, Alexandra
Curis Life Ltd

Grammel, Simon
Petbiocell UK Ltd

Granata, Francesco, Dr
Circassia Pharmaceuticals PLC

Grant, Lucie Mary Katja
Life Technologies BPD UK Ltd
Thermo Fisher Scientific Life Holdings

Grant, Robert Neil
Unit 6 Gateway Limited

Grant, Sheila Mary
Cardiome UK Limited

Grasten, Jukka
Virtual Reaction Limited

Gray, Derek Richard
Osteoporosis Research Ltd

Gray, Joanna Jacqueline
Dermaco Limited

Swift, Ben
The Great British Bee Co Ltd

Graham, Stuart David
The Great Northern Apothecary Co.

Greathead, Peter
Nutrition Group PLC
RPL (UK) Limited

Greathead, Richard Lewis
Nutrition Group PLC

Green, Richard
GlaxoSmithKline Consumer Healthcare (UK) Trading

Greenstreet, Yvonne, Dr
Indivior PLC

Greer, Michael
Appex Ltd

Gregory, Julia Paige
Cell Medica Limited

Gresle, Heidrun
Seven Seas Limited

Gresswell, Gavin
Nutrapharm Ltd

Greve, Tanja
Fresenius Kabi Oncology PLC

Grewal, Burrinder Singh, Dr
Sedigel Limited

Griffin, Anthony Gerard
Dechra Limited

Griffin, Peter William
Blackrock Pharmaceuticals Ltd
Incepta Blackrock Limited

Groat, Malcolm
NKCell Plus PLC

Grose, Ellen Yvette
West Pharmaceutical Services Cornwall

Grosjean, Bertrand Pierre Marie
Bristol-Myers Squibb Pharmaceuticals

Gross, Irwin Lee
Arc Devices (NI) Limited

Grossi, Anthony Frederick William
Healing Fusions Ltd

Groves, Janet Margaret
Olbas Limited
Sarakan Limited

Groves, Janet Margaret
Supersun Nutrition Limited
Kalms Limited

Groves, Jonathan
Kalms Limited
Olbas Limited
Supersun Nutrition Limited

Gu, Yuchun, Prof
iCell Therapeutics Ltd

Gualano, Mario Pietro
BBI Solutions OEM Limited
Scipac Limited

Gudipati, Srinivas
Life on Healthcare Ltd

Guerrieri, Francesco Ciro
Gynopharma Ltd

Gulamhusein, Fatema
Occidem Biotech Limited

Gulamhusein, Husein Mohamedraza Sultanali
Neomedic Limited
Occidem Biotech Limited

Gumede, Jabulile
Sizwe Limited

Gunabalsinkam, Thangarajah
Herbal Food Life Limited

Gursoy, Akin
Ether Cosmetics Ltd

Gustafson, Arnold Leonard
Quantum Biomed Farms PLC

Guy, Geoffrey William, Dr
GW Pharma Limited

Guzek, Grzegorz
Cocodentax Ltd

Ha, Jae-Young
Oxbridge Pharma Limited

Haagen, Tomas
Novo Nordisk Holding Limited

Habib, Fatima
Albert Pharma Chemicals Ltd

Habib, Khadija
Albert Pharma Chemicals Ltd

Habib, Lubna
Albert Pharma Chemicals Ltd

Habib, Omer
Albert Pharma Chemicals Ltd

Hackett, John Edward
Brunel Healthcare Manufacturing Ltd

Hackworth, Paul Jonathan
Ortho-Clinical Diagnostics

Haddad, George Michel, Dr
Gelu Life Limited

Haddad, Hadeel
Mak Health Limited

Haffar, Salim
PCI Penn UK Holdco Limited
Penn Pharma Group Limited
Penn Pharmaceutical Services Ltd
Pioneer UK Holdings Limited
Pioneer UK Midco 1 Limited
Pioneer UK Midco 2 Limited

Hafner, Roderick Peter
Circassia Pharmaceuticals PLC

Hague, Phil Anthony
Medlock Medical Limited

Haig, Timothy Robert
Algal Omega 3 Ltd

Haigh, Adrian James
PTC Therapeutics, Limited

Halden, Ronald
Uro Innovations Limited

Halsby, Digby Lawrence Spence
D.D.D. Limited

Hamill, Turlough Malachy, Dr
This Product Ltd

Hammond, Victoria
Stride-Davies Pharma Limited

Hangyal, Natasha
Tips & Tricks Ltd

Haniff, Nigel
Kohilam Limited

Hansen, Henrik Blicher
Mento-Neem International Ltd

Harberg Jr, Allen
Intervet UK Production Limited

Hardman, Nicholas, Dr
Compliance & Validation Solutions Ltd

Hardwicke, Caroline Janet
Bacvacc Ltd

Hardy, Mark Glyn
UCB Pharma Limited

Hargan, William John
Piramal Critical Care Limited

Haringman, Michael Stephan
Elemis Limited

Haritou, Christos Sotirious
Pegasus Equine Diagnostics Ltd

Harper, Steven James, Dr
Exonate Limited

Harrington, Sean
Elemis Limited

Harris, Mark Simon
Virgo Trade UK Limited

Harris, Mary Catherine
As-Tec Chemicals Limited

Harris, Neil
Abbott Iberian Investments Ltd
Abbott Vascular Devices (2) Ltd
Knoll UK Investments Unlimited

Harris, Simon Digby
As-Tec Chemicals Limited

Harris, Steven Charles Andrew
Circassia Pharmaceuticals PLC

Harrison, Christopher Paul
Calea UK Limited
Fresenius Kabi Limited

Harrison, James Alexander
Cycle Pharmaceuticals Ltd

Harrison, Roger
D.D.D. Limited

Harte, Colleen
Lucy Annabella Ltd

Hartley, Joe Patrick
Woundcare Limited

Hartley, Julia Margaret
Woundcare Limited

Hartup, John
Clinigen Group PLC

Harty, Mark Stephen
Sauflon (Manufacturing) Ltd

Harvey, Jane Judith
Selborne Biological Services Ltd

Hasan, Aveen
Hemma Healthcare Teronta Ltd

Hashi, Mohamed Abdiaziz
Pharmacy Warehouse Limited

Hashmat, Uzma
Health Marque Ltd
Kinerva Ltd

Hasnip, Matthew John
Air Liquide Limited

Hassam, Ahmed Gulamabbas, Dr
Quest Ingredients Limited

Hassam, Mohamed Abbas
Quest Ingredients Limited

Hassan, Tauqir
Vision Laboratories Limited

Hassel, Tamryn Jo
Microgenetics Limited

Hathi, Alpa
Laxmi BNS Holdings Limited
Syri Limited

Hathi, Govindji Thakershi
Laxmi BNS Holdings Limited
Syri Limited

Hathi, Samit Govindji
Laxmi BNS Holdings Limited

Hathi, Samit
Syri Limited

Haughey, Edward Gordon Shannon, The Honourable
Norbrook Laboratories Limited

Haughey, James Quinton Stewart
Norbrook Laboratories Limited

Haugstad, Egil Magne
Epax Pharma UK Ltd

Hauser, Remy
PCI Penn UK Holdco Limited
Penn Pharma Group Limited
Penn Pharmaceutical Services Ltd
Pioneer UK Holdings Limited
Pioneer UK Midco 1 Limited
Pioneer UK Midco 2 Limited

Havercroft, Gavin
Bioneb PVT Limited

Havercroft, Nick Anthony
Bioneb PVT Limited

Havey, Adam Robert
Emergent Countermeasures International

Hawkes, Esme
Therapi Natural Products Ltd

Hawkes, Katharine Tanya
Therapi Natural Products Ltd

Hawkins, Nigel Charles
Essential Health Products Ltd

Hawkins, Roger, Dr
Amarevida Limited

Hawtin, Paul Anthony
Venture Healthcare Ltd

Hay, Anne Margaret
Teklab (ML) Ltd

Hayburn, Colin
Almac Pharma Services Limited

Hayes, Paul Andrew
Aesica BC Limited
Aesica Formulation Development Ltd
Aesica Holdco Limited
Aesica M1 Limited
Aesica M2 Limited
Aesica Pharmaceuticals Limited
Aesica Queenborough Limited
Aesica Trustee Co Ltd
Bespak Europe Limited

Hayes, Simon
Sharp Clinical Services (UK) Ltd

Hayhurst, Alan Geoffrey, Dr
Paradox Omega Oils Ltd

Hayhurst, Michelle Denise
Paradox Omega Oils Ltd

Haytack, Robert Andrew Jeremy
Brunel Healthcare Manufacturing Ltd

He, Ping
Seacross Pharmaceuticals Ltd

Head, Stephen Christopher
Agroceutical Products Ltd

Heaps, Brett Andrew
Dushey Limited

Menzies, Ross McPherson
The Heavenly Herb Co Ltd.

Padmore, Katrina
The Heavenly Herb Co Ltd.

Heberlig, Christopher
Kiniksa Pharmaceuticals (UK), Ltd.

Heberling, Matthew Michael, Dr
Peptone Ltd

Hecht, Thomas, Dr
Cell Medica Limited

Hedman, Martti Tapani
Colorcon Limited

Heer, Andre Reinhold
Incline Therapeutics Europe Ltd.

Heer, Balwant Singh
Generics (U.K.) Limited

Heer, Harsimran Kaur
JGPSK Limited

Heider, Patrik
Brown Exclusive (Worldwide) Ltd

Heininger, Patrick
Apobec Discovery Ltd

Hellmers-White, Hadley Rose
Hadley Rose Limited

Hellstrom, Hege
Swedish Orphan Biovitrum Ltd

Hembery, Daniel Patrick
CBDHealthcare Ltd

Takac, Michal
The Hemp Broker Ltd

Henderson, Mary Regina
Hikma Pharmaceuticals PLC

Henderson, Scott Charles
Terumo BCT Ltd.

Henry, Rodney Stephen, Dr
RSH QP Services Limited

Herath, Charmilla
Thread and Co UK Limited

Lu Gyaw, Soe
The Herbal Factory Ltd

Herbert, Andrew
Invizius Limited

Herd, Ian Malcolm
IM Herd Ltd

Hermon-Taylor, John, Professor
HAV Vaccines Limited

Herrmann, Derek
Herrco Cosmetics Limited

Herrmann, Nigel Kurt
Herrco Cosmetics Limited

Herrmann, Susan
Herrco Cosmetics Limited

Herron, Brian Nigel
Humn Pharmaceuticals (UK) Ltd

Herron, Relton John Phillip
Avacare Limited

Hewer, David
Tell Products,Limited

Hicken, Mark Iain
Janssen-Cilag Limited

Higgins, David William
Manta - Cognitive Fuels Ltd

Higham, Anthony
Protherics UK Limited

Hilger, Marcus
AAH Pharmaceuticals Limited

Hill, David Michael
This Product Ltd

Hill, Norman
Bio-Sync International Limited

Hincks, Jeffrey
Virodefense Limited

Hindle, Martin
Porton Biopharma Limited

Hinton, Philip Charles
Medical Export Co Ltd

Hinton, Roger James
Porton Biopharma Limited

Hiremat, Preetham Sharma
Brown & Burk UK Limited

Hirst, Allan Jerome
Phico Therapeutics Limited

Hirst, Michael Ian
Swann-Morton (Europe) Limited

Hlinka, Daniel, Dr
Hlinka Pharma Ltd

Ho, Lap Fung
Unigreg Worldwide Limited

Ho, Shui Chee
Unigreg Worldwide Limited

Ho-Asjoe, Bonita
Cho Consulting Ltd.

Hodge, Margaret Ann
& Stuff Naturally Ltd

Hodges, Nicholas George
Janssen-Cilag Limited

Hofmann, Martin John, Dr
Biotechflow Ltd

Hogan, Paul Lawrence
Emerald Kalama Chemical Ltd

Hogan, William Patrick
Hichrom Limited

Holden, Ben William
2tonk Limited

Hooper, Paul Richard
N.T. Laboratories Limited

Hopkin, Edward Daniel
Carefusion U.K. 244 Limited

Hopkinson, Andrew, Dr
Nuvision Biotherapies Limited

Hopkinson, Ronald Ian
Harlequin BPI Ltd

Hopley, Maxine
Lipsy Couture Limited

Hopper, Nicholas David Kemp
Custom Powders Limited

Hoque, Radhwan
Ad Hoque Ltd

Hossenlopp, Steve
Mentholatum Co Ltd

Houson, Louise Jane
Merck Sharp & Dohme Limited

Houston, Benjamin Ryan
Nikkiso UK Co., Ltd.

Howell, Catherine Moya
Mirror 5 Ltd

Howell, Catherine
Hexa-Halers Ltd

Howell, Julian David
Pharmakrysto Ltd

Howell, Michael James
Mirror 5 Ltd

Howell, Michael
Hexa-Halers Ltd

Howlett, Michael
Limehurst Limited

Hoyer Millar, Christian Gurth
Oxford Biodynamics PLC

Huckert, Anne Stephanie Rita
Hutrade Ltd.

Hudson, Nick
Zeltiq Limited

Huelsbeck, Marco Wolfgang
M D M Healthcare Ltd

Huggett, Quentin James, Dr
Geotek Coring Limited

Hughes, Jason
Invos Ltd

Hundle, Kavaljeet Singh
Simkar Healthcare Ltd

Hunt, Christopher David
Insense Limited

Hunt, Kristina Mary
Elanco Animal Vaccines Limited
Elanco Europe Ltd.
Elanco UK AH Limited
Vericore Limited

Hunt, Tina
Dista Products Limited

Hunter, Gary Francis
Uro Innovations Limited

Hunter, Geoffrey Robert
CBDHealthcare Ltd

Huntley-Copeman, Susan Ruth
Cannabidiol UK Ltd

Hurley, Mark Gordon Delap
Biofortuna Ltd

Husain, Arif
Regent Generics Limited

Hussain, Majad, Dr
Pharmaspec Limited
Quest HC Limited
Quest Healthcare Solutions Ltd

Hussain, Mazahar
Ace Direct Ltd

Hussain, Shahid
Euro Diagnostics Limited

Hussain, Yasar
Quest Healthcare Aseptics Ltd
Quest Healthcare Injectables Ltd
Quest Healthcare Non-Injectables Ltd
Quest Pharm Limited

Hussein, Ghazi Abbass Mohammed Ali, Dr
GM Globalhealth Ltd

Hutchinson, Peter John Ashton, Professor
Medicam Limited

Hyde, William Alan
Microsens Biophage Limited

Hyett, Anthony
BVM Medical Limited

Hyett, Simon Edward Harry
SH Snakes UK Ltd.

Hyland, Anne Philomena
Clinigen Group PLC

Ibie, Chidinma Udegbunam, Dr
Dach Cosmeceutics Limited

Ibrampur, Badarinath
Brown & Burk UK Limited

Idowu, Emmanuel Olukayode
Comfort Ventures Limited

Iftikhar, Irum
Maia Pharma Ltd

Iguchi, Kimi Ellen
Sage Therapeutics Limited

Il Ghany, Morad Khalid
Derma Bathe Limited

Il Ghany, Rebecca Elise
Derma Bathe Limited

Inch, Anne Hocknull
Confidence Plus Ltd

Injarapu, Srikanth
N2SA Limited

Innes, Kim
APS/Berk Limited
Actavis Holdings UK II Limited
Arrow Generics Limited
Auden McKenzie (Pharma Division) Ltd
Bowmed Limited
Breath Limited
Millbrook (NI) Limited
Norton Healthcare (1998) Ltd
Pharmax Limited
Pliva Pharma Limited
Teva Laboratories UK Limited
Teva Pharma Holdings Limited
Teva Pharmaceuticals Limited
Teva Research Laboratories (NI) Ltd
Teva UK Limited

Insall, Nicholas Hugh Meryon
Auralis Limited
Baxalta UK Limited
Shire Pharmaceuticals Limited

Inskip, Timothy John
Bioactive Health Ltd

Iravanian, Ladan, Dr
New Cheshire Salt Works Ltd

Irechukwu, Leon
Pharmadynamics UK Limited

Irechukwu, Tony
Pharmadynamics UK Limited

Ishikawa, Takatoshi
Fujifilm Diosynth Biotechnologies UK

Ismail, Wagma, Dr
Dermaperfetca Ltd

Issac, Abdullah
Man Pharma Limited

Italia, Dynshaw Fareed
Biokemix Worldwide Ltd

Mitchell, Jen Ann
Henri L.Jaccaz & Co. Limited

Jackowitz, Bryan Edward
American Distilling & Mfg Ltd

Jackowitz, Kevin Robert
American Distilling & Mfg Ltd

Stigant, Louise Anne
Ernest Jackson & Co. Limited

Walter, David Mark
Ernest Jackson & Co. Limited

Jackson, Alison
Taylor of London Limited

Jackson, Anthony John David, Dr
Millicent Pharma (NI) Limited

Jackson, Charles Peter Christopher Howard
Taylor of London Limited

Jackson, Daniel William John
Taylor of London Limited

Jackson, Jemma Audrey Ilse
Taylor of London Limited

Jackson, Jodie Alison Caroline Victoria
Taylor of London Limited

Jackson, Michael Conrad
Lifeplan Products Limited

Jackson, Tim Charles
Quicksilver Scientific Europe Ltd

Jacobs, Michael
Custom Pharmaceuticals Limited

Jacobson, Ian
Contura Holdings Limited
Contura Limited

Jafar, Husam Amer Hisham
Xeal Pharma Ltd

Jain, Ashok Kumar
Brown & Burk UK Limited

Jain, Manish
Ipca Laboratories UK Limited

Jakes, Nadine
Accord-UK Ltd

Jallow, Mamadou Salieu
M Jallow Ltd

James, Pauline Stephanie
Biotech Design and Validation Ltd.

James, Philip David Aidan, Doctor
Biotech Design and Validation Ltd.

Jangra, Arun
Anatics Life Sciences Limited

Janjua, Faisal Kibria
HFA Healthcare Products Ltd

Janmohamed, Feroze Issa Ismail
Commercial and Academic Services Ltd

Jansen, Sunil Pratap
Cognitive Bioscience Limited

Jardine Rose, Paula Kay
Joribunda Limited

Javier, Deo Anthony
Boothmasked Ltd

Jawwad, Humera
Pentonova Limited

Jeans, David John
Prometic Pharma SMT Limited

Jeger, Rolf Franz
Geistlich Sons Limited

Jenkins, Annalisa
Cell Medica Limited

Jenkins, John Richard
Bioextractions Wales Limited

Jenkins, Kathryn Jane
Cotswold Health Limited

Jenkins, Mark Godfrey, Dr
Jenarron Therapeutics Limited

Jenkins, Richard John
Ortho-Clinical Diagnostics

Jenkins, Thomas, Dr
Cotswold Health Limited

Jennings, Karen Elizabeth
Isopath Limited

Jennings, Russell Edward
Isopath Limited

Jensen, Karl Kristian
New Nordic Limited

Jensen, Peter Sinclair
Allergy Therapeutics PLC

Jethwa, Sneha
Evida Ltd

Jivan, Rahesh
NKK Investments Limited

Jobson, Philip Thomas
Nutripharm Limited

Johansson, Leif Valdemar
Astrazeneca PLC

John, Sujit
PCI Penn UK Holdco Limited
Penn Pharma Group Limited
Penn Pharmaceutical Services Ltd
Pioneer UK Holdings Limited
Pioneer UK Midco 1 Limited
Pioneer UK Midco 2 Limited

Johnson, Edward
Advanced Healthcare Systems Ltd
Advanced Medical Solutions Ltd

Johnson, Neil Graham
Medical Technologies Limited

Johnston, Elaine Maureen
Protherics UK Limited

Johnston, Killian Joseph
This Product Ltd

Jones, David Andrew
Speakers at The Limits Ltd.

Jones, Glenn
Skincare Innovation Ltd

Jones, Mark
RLC Technology Limited

Jones, Nicholas Barritt
Bray Group Limited

Jones, Roger Spencer, Sir
Bioextractions Wales Limited
Agroceutical Products Ltd

Jones, Roger Spencer, Sir
Phytovation Limited

Jones, Sarah Alisha
Jones Balm Limited

Jones, Steven Lewis
4soap Limited

Jongen, Freek
Glaxo Operations UK Limited

Jordan, Leslie Alan
Wren Hygiene Limited

Joseph, Jason
Fluidx Limited

Joseph, Wetteny
Catalent CTS (Edinburgh) Ltd
Catalent MTI Pharma Solutions Ltd
Catalent Micron Technologies Ltd

Joshi, Jatin Rajnikant, Dr
Instavit Limited

Joshi, Sonia, Dr
Instavit Limited

Joyce, Elena
Elena's Nature Collection Ltd

Juan, Errol
Revive Herbal UK Ltd

Juan, Gregory
Revive Herbal UK Ltd

Jude, Christian
HMS Vilgo UK Ltd

Judge, Rajinder
R Judge Consultancy Ltd

Juj, Arwinder Paul Singh
Jasan Technical Services Ltd

Jumppanen, Juho, Dr
Ardilla Technologies UK Ltd

Jung, Christine, Dr
SAS Pharma Limited

Jurke, Roland
Nimasol Limited

Just, Rene
Intrapharm Laboratories Ltd
Peckforton Pharmaceuticals Ltd

Kadari, Kiran Reddy
Aspensnetas Biopharma Ltd

Kadari, Sateesh Reddy
Aspensnetas Biopharma Ltd

Kadhim, Husham Jawad
Pharmazy Limited

Kalanzi, Catherine Namatovu
KVK Limited

Kalfaoui, Abdenour
Kalfar Health Ltd

Kalli, Michael
Ideal Manufacturing Limited

Kalli, Phillip
Ideal Manufacturing Limited

Kalugachalapuram Krishnasamy, Manojkumar
Kew Organic Limited

Kamath, Narsimha Shibroor
Asterisk LifeSciences Ltd

Kamath, Vikram Laxman
Advanz Pharma Generics (UK) Ltd
Focus Pharma Holdings Limited
Focus Pharmaceuticals Limited
Mercury Pharma Group Limited
Mercury Pharmaceuticals Ltd

Kambham, Raveendranatha Reddy
Amarox Limited

Kandasamy, Kumar
Kohilam Limited

Kanis, John Anthony, Professor
Osteoporosis Research Ltd

Kanis-Buck, Rebecca Louise
Osteoporosis Research Ltd

Kapisthalam, Madhu
MK Ventures Limited

Kapur, Jatinder
Jai Pharma Limited

Kara, Morad
Mak Health Limited

Karaman, Zafer
Insuphar Laboratories Limited

Karia, Jagdish Prabhudas
Medicareplus International Ltd
Medicareplus Limited

Karia, Ravindra Prabhudas
Medicareplus International Ltd
Medicareplus Limited

Karita, Takahisa
Medics Kingdom Limited

Karnataki, Girish Shrikrishna
Greenova Healthcare UK Ltd.

Karnataki, Nahush Shrikrishna
Greenova Healthcare UK Ltd.

Karnataki, Shrikrishna
Greenova Healthcare UK Ltd.

Karolia, Salma
SK Network Ltd

Karpinska, Sandra, Lady
Mirroman Ltd

Kase, Akira
Fujifilm Diosynth Biotechnologies UK

Kaser, Matthew, Dr
Scottish Bioenergy Cooperative Ventures
Tantillus Synergy Limited

Kassam, Kain
Polychem Limited

Kassam, Rizwanali Noorali
Polychem Limited
Rimmerdax Limited

Kassam, Zain
Polychem Limited

Kato, Yoshiteru
Eisai Manufacturing Limited

Kauser, Fiaz
Pharmacy Medicines Ltd

Kauser, Riaz
Pharmacy Medicines Ltd

Kawagoe, Junichi, Dr
Kowa Pharmaceutical Europe Co Ltd

Ke, Tingyu
Donglun Limited

Keen, Robert
Weleda (U.K.) Limited

Keenan, Harry
Beacon Pharmaceuticals Limited
Kent Pharmaceuticals Limited

Kehoe, David Michael
Calea UK Limited
Fresenius Kabi Limited

Kellow, Shayne Anthony
Rapid Nutrition PLC

Kelly, Anthony William
Arch Chemicals Products Ltd
Hickson W.A. Chemicals Limited

Kelly, Christina
CKC Aromatherapy Beauty Products Ltd

Kelly, John Terence
Mediskills Limited

Kelly, Pushparani
Mediskills Limited

Kember, Darren James
Daz Solutions Ltd.

Kennedy, Christopher James
Tickletec Limited

Kennedy, Robert
Instavit Limited

Waddy, Jayne Lisa
The Kentish Soap Co Ltd

Waddy, John Barrie
The Kentish Soap Co Ltd

Kerr, Michael
Provita Eurotech Ltd

Kettleborough, Sara Jane
Alpex Pharma (UK) Limited
HK Pharma Limited

Keynes, Mervyn John
That Cream Ltd

Khakh, Narinder Singh
Healthcare Consortium Ltd
NSK Locums Limited

Khan, Amin
Green Groot Limited

Khan, Amjid Malik
Summer Healthcare Limited

Khan, Asma
Sher Limited

Khan, Fazal Nawaz
Well & Well Pharma UK Ltd

Khan, Karrar Ahmad
Sher Limited

Khan, Pasha
Triumph Pharma Ltd

Khan, Sabir
Mineral Pharma Limited

Khan, Sehra
Quality Skincare Ltd

Khan, Shukria, Dr
Khattak Resolution Ltd

Khan, Shuokat
Mineral Pharma Limited

Khan, Zulfiqar Ali
Hermes Pharma Limited
Linnaeus Herbals Limited

Khan, Zulfiqar
CBD Biotech Limited

Khatib, Sarosh Sami
Medley Pharma Limited

Khatri, Yogesh
UCB Pharma Limited

Khiroya, Parag
Microvisk Technologies International

Khurshid, Zahida Parveen
Synergy Biologics Limited

Kibble, Alison Caroline
Oxford Biodynamics PLC

Kidner, Stephen Martin
Alliance Pharmaceuticals Ltd
Maelor Laboratories Limited

Kiecken, Brigette
Biolyse Pharma Europe Limited

Kiernan, Sean
MDI Medical (N.I.) Limited

Kim, Sung Eun
Dong Hwa UK Ltd

King, Fiona Margaret Home
Cottage Garden Cosmetics and Gifts

King, James William Peter
Eulysis UK Limited

King, Rupert Saulez
Cottage Garden Cosmetics and Gifts

Kingsbury, Lee Paul
Fine Contract Research Limited
Fine Organics Limited

Kirby, Pamela Josephine, Dr
Hikma Pharmaceuticals PLC

Kirk, Ian John
Dalkeith Laboratories Limited
Herbal Concepts Limited
OTC Concepts Limited
Thorpe Laboratories Limited

Kirkup, Mark Henry
Calea UK Limited
Fresenius Kabi Limited

Kitchen, Peter Joseph
Arch Chemicals Products Ltd

Klausner, Mark
Oxford Immunotec Global PLC

Klinge, Michael
Klinge Chemicals Limited

Klinge, Stephan
Klinge Chemicals Limited

Kloehn, Peter Christian
Emerge Biotech Ltd

Knudsen, Melinda
Chemagain Limited

Kohek, Marko, Dr
Rojal Pharm USA Limited

Kohli, Subir
Chirotech Technology Limited
Dr Reddy's Laboratories (UK) Ltd
Dr. Reddy's Laboratories (EU) Ltd

Kojima, Tsutomu
ADS Biotec Limited

Konasagar Jayanna, Sathish Kumar
Bell,Sons & Co.(Druggists) Ltd

Korenberg, Matthew Edward
Vernalis (R & D) Limited
Vernalis Development Limited

Kotecha, Monisha Nikesh
Morningside Pharmaceuticals Ltd
Remedi Medical Holdings Ltd

Kotecha, Nikesh Rasiklal, Dr
Morningside Pharmaceuticals Ltd
Remedi Medical Holdings Ltd

Koziak, Katarzyna, Professor
More Poland Limited

Kraehenmann, Beat Christoph
Roche Products Limited

Kraman, Matthew
Simcere UK Limited

Kramer, Robert Gregory
Emergent Countermeasures International
Paxvax Ltd

Krieger, Fred C
Iroko Products Limited

Krishna, Ganesh
Life on Healthcare Ltd

Kristiansen, Bjorn, Dr
Glycanova UK Limited

Kroslakova, Miroslava
Speakers at The Limits Ltd.

Kruisinga, Hendrik Jurjen Gerardus
Fontridge Pharmaceutical Research and Development

Kruisinga, Hugo Pieter Johannes
Fontridge Pharmaceutical Research and Development

Krupp, Jason
Langeland Ltd

Kucherenko, Serhii
Dynamic Development Laboratories Co Ltd

Kuhne, Jessika Hildergard
Nutrasulin Ltd.

Kukhaleishvili, George
Geoorganics Limited

Kulcsar, Margareta
Heavenly Group of Co Ltd

Kumar, Anurag
Vita Sun Ltd

Kumar, Narinder
Merad Pharmaceuticals Limited

Kumar, Rajinder, Dr
Merad Pharmaceuticals Limited

Kumar, Vijay
Abryl Formulations Ltd

Kumar, Vikesh
Strides Pharma UK Ltd

Kunkolienkar, Dilip Janardan
Niche Generics Limited

Kunz, Heinrich
BtechLaboratories (UK) Ltd.
Furoid Ltd
Invitrohair Ltd

Kuoni, Claudio
CM & D Pharma Limited

Kurek, John
Exonate Limited

Kuttruf, Andrej
Webottle Ltd

Kyriacou, Eve
Dreamskin Health Limited

L'heveder, Carol Isabel
Infirst Healthcare Limited

Labrucherie, Gil
Nektar Therapeutics UK Limited

Lacaze, Oriane Fanny
Novartis Grimsby Limited
Novartis Pharmaceuticals UK Ltd
Oriel Therapeutics Limited
Sandoz Limited

Lacey, Angela Marie
EVC Compounding Ltd

Ladak, Rizwan
Royce Health Sciences Ltd

Lafe, Orobola Feyisola
Global Healthcare Innovations Ltd
Tickletec Limited

Lahai-Taylor, Jeannette, Dr
Ibeautify Ltd

Laine, Christian
Milton Pharmaceutical Company UK Ltd

Lal, Sumit, Dr
Aucure Medical Technologies Ltd

Lalani, Shakil
Solent Oral Care Ltd

Lall, Jalmeen
Finer Feet Ltd

Lalta, Shalini Lakshmidevi
Alisha GXP QP Consultancy Ltd

Lalvani, Ajit, Prof
Vitabiotics Limited

Lalvani, Kartar Singh, Dr
Vitabiotics Limited
Vitalogic Limited

Lalvani, Tej
Vitabiotics Limited

Lam, Kenneth Kan Li
Longwood Medevice Ltd

Lam, Tuong Van
Apotek Services Ltd

Lamb, Brian Victor
Carmel Herbals Limited

Lamb, Catherine
Ipsen Biopharm Limited

Lanckriet, Heikki
Innova Biosciences Ltd

Landon, John, Professor
Micropharm Limited

Cole, David
G.R. Lane Health Products Ltd

Groves, Janet Margaret
G.R. Lane Health Products Ltd

Groves, Jonathan Roger
G.R. Lane Health Products Ltd

Henly, Paul
G.R. Lane Health Products Ltd

Horan, Mark
G.R. Lane Health Products Ltd

Howard, Trevor Edward
G.R. Lane Health Products Ltd

Kelly, Aden Craig
G.R. Lane Health Products Ltd

Lynn, Hilary
G.R. Lane Health Products Ltd

Whatley, Paul Charles
G.R. Lane Health Products Ltd

Lane, Nathan Vincent
Onyx Scientific Limited

Lange, Jesper Jorn
MC2 Therapeutics Limited

Langston, Kate, Dr
TCS Biosciences Limited

Larwood, Andrew Paul
Salutem Supplements Ltd

Lasparini, Jonathan Robert
Crawford Manufacturing Limited

Lassman, Israelith Sheila
Raught Limited

Lassman, Jack
Raught Limited

Latchman, David Seymour, Professor
Therakind Limited

Latif, Khalid
Pharmvit Limited

Lau, Sui Nin
Fernhurst Pharmacy Limited

Lavender, David Anthony
Cannacureyou Ltd

Lawrence, Charmaine Lynette Angela
N9NE Cosmetics Ltd

Lawrence, James
Bam Balm Ltd

Lawrence, Peter Anthony
Eco Animal Health Ltd.

Lawton, David Keith
Extruded Pharmaceuticals Ltd

Lazarev, Dmitry
Akvion Limited

Le Couilliard, Jo Susan
Circassia Pharmaceuticals PLC

Le Martret, Jean-Francois
Guerbet Argentina Limited

Leadbetter, Steven
Natural Miracles Limited

Leahy, Veronica
Custom Pharmaceuticals Limited

Leaning, Mark
Clyde Valley Cannaceuticals Ltd

Leay, Karen Michelle
Thompson and Capper Limited

Lecomte, Jean-Guillaume
Lincoln Medical Limited

Lecomte, Jeanne-Marie
Lincoln Medical Limited

Ledouble, Jean-Roch Guy Nicolas
Norgine Limited

Lee, Christopher Douglas
Batel Limited

Lee, Matthew John, Dr
Vaccine Manufacturing and Innovation Centre UK

Lee, Nikki, Dr
Little Green Beehive Ltd

Lee, Sandra
Accord-UK Ltd

Lefkowitz, Allen
Cycle Pharmaceuticals Ltd

Leinenweber, Scott Michael
Allergy Therapeutics PLC

Leivers, Stephen William
Fulhold Pharma Limited

Lemen, Nicholas
Greenfield Pharmaceuticals Ltd
Lilly Industries Limited
Lilly Property Limited
Lilly Research Centre Limited
Lilly Resources Limited

Lenney, Andrew John
Pharmau Healthcare Ltd

Lenon, Stephen John, Dr
MC2 Therapeutics Limited

Lethbridge, Priscilla Anne
Accord-UK Ltd

Levdanski, Alexander
Hartington Pharma Limited

Levee, Claire Naomi, Dr
Trogon Regulatory Ltd

Levin, Jason Daniel
Orbus Therapeutics Ltd

Levy, John Andrew Goodman
Seqirus Vaccines Limited

Lewis, Anna Jane
Lift Health Limited

Lewis, Carmen
A1 Pharmaceuticals Holdings Ltd

Lewis, Christopher
Dista Products Limited
Elanco Animal Vaccines Limited
Elanco Europe Ltd.
Elanco UK AH Limited
Vericore Limited

Lewis, Gary Stephen
A1 Pharmaceuticals Holdings Ltd

Lewis, Matthew John
Integrated Pharma Services (UK) Ltd

Lewis, Robert John
Lewtress Natural Health Ltd

Leyland, Michael Stuart
Biostatus Ltd

Li, Bingjie
Booteatox Limited

Li, Ji
Marine Labs Limited

Li, Jianxun, Dr
Proteintech Europe Limited

Liawatidewi, Jacob
Amphastar UK Ltd
International Medication Systems (U.K.)

Liddell, Caroline
Hunger Control Limited

Ligner, Emmanuel Francois Joel
GE Healthcare UK Limited
Rapidscan Pharma Solutions EU Ltd

Lilani, Mohammed Mohsin Reza
Vitane Pharma Limited

Bennett, Hamish John Carmichael
Eli Lilly (Basingstoke) Ltd

Lemen, Nicholas
Eli Lilly (Basingstoke) Ltd

Bennett, Hamish John Carmichael
Eli Lilly Group Limited

Diaz-Granados, Ashley
Eli Lilly Group Limited

Lemen, Nicholas
Eli Lilly Group Limited

Bennett, Hamish John Carmichael
Eli Lilly Holding Co Ltd

Lemen, Nicholas
Eli Lilly Holding Co Ltd

Bennett, Hamish John Carmichael
Eli Lilly Holdings Limited

Lemen, Nicholas
Eli Lilly Holdings Limited

Bennett, Hamish John Carmichael
Eli Lilly Leasing Limited

Lemen, Nicholas
Eli Lilly Leasing Limited

Bennett, Hamish John Carmichael
Eli Lilly Property Limited

Lemen, Nicholas
Eli Lilly Property Limited

Bennett, Hamish John Carmichael
Eli Lilly Resources Limited

Lemen, Nicholas
Eli Lilly Resources Limited

Alexander, Karen Ann
Eli Lilly and Co Ltd

Bennett, Hamish John Carmichael
Eli Lilly and Co Ltd

Diaz-Granados, Ashley
Eli Lilly and Co Ltd

Forda, Susan Renee, Dr
Eli Lilly and Co Ltd

Lemen, Nicholas
Eli Lilly and Co Ltd

Lim, Kian Meng
Seqirus Vaccines Limited

Limaye, Ravindra Kamalakar
C P Pharmaceuticals Limited
Wallis Laboratory Limited
Wallis Licensing Limited

Lin, Kyaw Zay
Essenfuture Ltd

Lindahl, Richard Scott
Emergent Countermeasures International
Paxvax Ltd

Lindsell, Philip Edmund
Infirst Limited

Lintonbon, David
Myoproducts Limited

Lintonbon, Stefania Gwendolin
Myoproducts Limited

Lipman, Martin
International Technidyne Corporation

Stoller, Joanne
The Liquid Comb Limited

Lister, Neil Thomas
Omega Pharma Limited
Rosemont Pharmaceuticals Ltd
Wrafton Laboratories Limited

Littlejohns, Barry
Catalent U.K. Swindon Encaps Ltd

Livingston, Andrtew Guy, Professor
Exactmer Limited

Llobet, Manuel
Allergy Therapeutics (UK) Ltd
Allergy Therapeutics PLC

Jackson, Alison
Milton Lloyd Limited

Jackson, Christopher William John
Milton Lloyd Limited

Jackson, Charles Peter Christopher Howard
Milton Lloyd Limited

Jackson, Daniel William John
Milton Lloyd Limited

Jackson, Jemma Audrey Ilse
Milton Lloyd Limited

Jackson, Jodie Alison Caroline Victoria
Milton Lloyd Limited

Walters, Howard
Milton Lloyd Limited

Lloyd, Geraint Richard
Unconventional E & P Services Ltd

Lloyd, Mary Doreen
Bio-Life International Limited
Medicleanse Limited
Nillergen Limited

Lloyd, Ruth Marie
Prozomix Limited

Lofthouse, Doreen Wilson
Lofthouse of Fleetwood Limited

Lofthouse, Duncan Charles
Lofthouse of Fleetwood Limited

Londesbrough, Derek John
Onyx Scientific Limited

Londesbrough, Derek John, Dr
Ipca Laboratories UK Limited

Gluck, Marion Sylwia, Dr
The London Specialist Pharmacy Ltd

London, Amir
Kamada Biopharma Limited

LooSeniore, John Colin
Beegood Enterprises Limited

Loomes, Marc Denham
Eco Animal Health Ltd.

Lopez, Jose Manuel, Dr
ND Pharma & Biotech Ltd

Loughrey, Una Mary
Blackrock Pharmaceuticals Ltd

Lovegrove Saville, Linda Mary
PLS Microbiology Limited

Lovegrove Saville, Paul Dominic
PLS Microbiology Limited

Lovegrove-Saville, Linda Mary
PLS Microbiology Limited

Lovegrove-Saville, Paul Dominic
PLS Microbiology Limited

Lovett, Jennifer Margaret
Dermapharm Skincare Limited

Lovett, Timothy James
Dermapharm Skincare Limited
Winston Laboratories Limited

Lowdell, Mark William, Professor
Materia Prima Ltd
Stem Cell Technology Ltd

Lowe, Christopher Robin, Prof
Cambridge Sensors Ltd

Lowndes, Barry Sean
Microskin PLC

Lucassen, Frank
Calea UK Limited
Fresenius Kabi Limited

Ludzker, Benjamin Mathew
European First Aid Limited

Luke, Paul Clifford
Instavit Limited

Lunt, Edward Henry
Life Molecular Imaging Limited

Luo, Mary
Amphastar UK Ltd
International Medication Systems (U.K.)

Lynch, Aidan
GlaxoSmithKline Consumer Healthcare (UK) Trading

Lynch, Carol Lesley
Oriel Therapeutics Limited

Lyng, John
MDI Medical (N.I.) Limited

Lyon, Colin
Druglab118 Ltd

MacDonald, Guy
Tetraphase UK Limited

MacGregor, Keith Martin
Salicin Healthcare Limited

MacKay, Colin Smith
Symbiosis Pharmaceutical Services

MacLeod, Angus
Inflazome UK Limited

MacLeod, Eoin Alan
Badgequo Limited

Maccioni, Francesco
Lamicare Health Ltd

Mackensen, Ralf
Pharmacell Medication Systems Ltd

Mackey, Paul
Better Call Paul Limited

Madden-Smith, Claire Elizabeth, Dr
Molecular Profiles Ltd

Maddock, Judith Mary
DTR Medical Limited

Madelpuech Dick, Marie-Helene Daniele
Panpharma UK Limited

Magor, Christopher Andrew
Bio Pure Technology Ltd

Maguin EP Walsh, Veronique
Bristol-Myers Squibb Pharmaceuticals

Mahan, Nadia
Redrose Manufacturing Limited
Redrose Nutraceuticals Limited

Mahan, Thomas
Redrose Manufacturing Limited
Redrose Nutraceuticals Limited

Mahmood, Mohammed Umar
Eclipse Pharma Ltd

Mahmood, Tahir
Isovitality Nutriceuticals Ltd

Mahmud, Shahyan
Well & Well Pharma UK Ltd

Mahoney, Stephen
Kiniksa Pharmaceuticals (UK), Ltd.

Mahtani, Heny Lachman
Pegasus Pharma Limited

Mahtani, Viren Heny
Vedabio Health Ltd

Maklari, Zoltan Akos
Maklary Ltd

Makolli, Egzona
Glacier Nutrition Ltd

Mala, Chalak
Lifetime Products Limited

Malcolm, Reezberg
EN RUS Group Limited

Malepart, Yvan
Maco Edge Limited

Malepart, Yvann
Macopharma (UK) Limited

Malik, Anjum Mohanum
Maltron International Limited

Malik, Shahid
Oxford Pharmaceuticals Limited

Mallareddy, Sharath Kumar Reddy
Madhusudhana Solutions Limited

Maloney, Michael
Cambcol Ltd

Malova, Alan
Enchanted Brave Limited

Hughes, Stephen Robert
F.Maltby & Sons Limited

Hutchinson, Barbara Anne, Reverend
F.Maltby & Sons Limited

Maltby, David Frank
F.Maltby & Sons Limited

Moate, Jane
F.Maltby & Sons Limited

Neal, Susan
F.Maltby & Sons Limited

Nel, Claudia
F.Maltby & Sons Limited

Parker, Stuart William
F.Maltby & Sons Limited

Romney, Julia Anne
F.Maltby & Sons Limited

Tranter, Margaret Williamson
F.Maltby & Sons Limited

Wit-Biniak, Katarzyna
The Mammoet Cannabis Limited

Mancini, Leonardo
Tuscania Consulting Limited

Mandal, Amit
Protezione Herbals PVT Ltd

Manji, Naaz
Westech Scientific Instruments Ltd

Manji, Shiraz Abdulmalick
Westech Scientific Instruments Ltd

Mannam, Venkata Narsimham
Chirotech Technology Limited
Dr Reddy's Laboratories (UK) Ltd
Dr. Reddy's Laboratories (EU) Ltd

Manojkumar, Ramya
Kew Organic Limited

Maranda, Bruno
Mendelikabs Europe Limited

Maratha, Manav
Pharmagen Direct Limited

March, John Bernard, Dr
Iceni Pharmaceuticals Limited

Marchant, Nicki
Ranir Limited

Marchington, Allan Patrick
Cell Medica Limited

Marenghi, Dario
PW Green UK II Limited

Margetts, Paul George
Stegram Pharmaceuticals Ltd

Margison, David Charles
Rucals Ltd

Margovenko, Aleksei
World Technologies for Long Life CN.

Marguerre, Cornelius
Octapharma Limited

Marguerre, Wolfgang
Octapharma Limited

Mark, Seethal Susan, Dr
Seven Seas Healthcare Limited

Markham, Rudolph Harold Peter
Astrazeneca PLC

Marles, Lee Keron
Bio-Rad AbD Serotec Ltd

Marlow, Stephen Michael
Seqirus Vaccines Limited

Marquilles Escola, Roger
Accord Healthcare Limited

Marriott, Karen Ann
Aromesse Limited

Marsh, Alan Geoffrey
P & S Nano Limited

Marsh, Dean Clive
Softgel Solutions Ltd

Marsh, Howard Alexander David
Alliance Medical Molecular Imaging
Alliance Medical Radiopharmacy Ltd
Life Molecular Imaging Limited

Marshall, Robert
Kee Logic Limited

Martel, Timothy John
Protherics UK Limited

Cooke, Andrew Mark
Bob Martin (UK) Limited

Ford, Andrew Michael
Bob Martin (UK) Limited

Fromm, Daniel Sebastian
Bob Martin (UK) Limited

Martin, Georgina Melissa
Bob Martin (UK) Limited

Steele, William James
Bob Martin (UK) Limited

Warne, Jeremy Paul
Bob Martin (UK) Limited

Martin, Anthony Francis, Dr
Phico Therapeutics Limited

Martin, Christine Ann
Ezoogle UK Limited

Martin, Grant
MacFarlane Martin Ltd

Martin, Pamela
MacFarlane Martin Ltd

Martin, Peter
Norgine Limited

Martin, Sarah Jean
Porvair PLC

Martin, Stephen Dominic
Ezoogle UK Limited

Martin, Stephen Jeremy
Penlan Healthcare Limited

Martin, Steven Daniel
First Impressions Denture Centre Ltd

Martin, Toni Dorothy
First Impressions Denture Centre Ltd

Martin, Tracy Irene
Elixir Pure UK Limited

Martini, Flavia
Martini International Ltd

Martini, Valerio
Martini International Ltd

Marufu, Agnes
Private Trichology Clinic Ltd

Marwaha, Pardeep
PG Pharma Ltd

Masarweh, Natheer
Hikma Pharmaceuticals International

Mascarenhas, Everard Joseph Philip, Dr
Sarissa Biomedical Limited

Maselli, Alessandro
Catalent U.K. Swindon Zydis Ltd
Catalent UK Supply Chain Ltd
Columbia Laboratories (UK) Ltd
Molecular Profiles Ltd

Masi, Aldo
DSP Beauty Development Ltd

Master, Murtaza Roshanali
Synergy Specials Limited

Master, Mussadiq Roshanali
Synergy Specials Limited

Masters, Suzad
Masters Pharmaceuticals Ltd

Masters, Zulfikar
Masters Pharmaceuticals Ltd

Matic, Niamh
Calea UK Limited
Fresenius Kabi Limited

Matthew, James Michael
Nanotherapeutics UK Limited

Matthews, Andrew Paul
Quantum Pharmaceutical Limited

Matthews, Janet
Infection Monitoring and Control Ltd

Maunsell, Cara Alison
Oat Services Limited

Maunsell, Carteret Hunter
Oat Services Limited

Maunsell, Hannah
Oat Services Limited

Maunsell, Mark Hugo
Oat Services Limited

Maunsell, Miranda Elizabeth
Oat Services Limited

Mavani, Neeta Avinash
Dil More Remedies UK Ltd

Maxwell, Anna Helen
Maxwellia Ltd

Maxwell, Peter Colin Eglington
Aim-Straight Limited

Maxwell-Clarke, Helen
Fendall's Ltd.

May, Nicholas Matthew Amadeus
Ecohydra Technologies Limited

May, Stephen Howard Patrick
Bioneb PVT Limited

May, Tatjana Anni Hilde
Indivior PLC

Mayers, Steven Joseph
Universal Cell Therapeutics Ltd.

Mazraani, Antoine
Guerbet Argentina Limited

Mazumdar Shaw, Kiran
Biocon Pharma UK Limited

McAleer, Michael
McAleer & Donnelly Pharmacy Ltd

McBride, Liam
Roonivoolin Naturals Ltd

McBride, Norry, Dr
Jenarron Therapeutics Limited

McBride, Sinead Marie
Roonivoolin Naturals Ltd

McBurney, Graeme
Almac Pharma Services Limited

McCann, James Michael
Cambridge Sensors Ltd

McCarron, Paul Anthony, Professor
Jenarron Therapeutics Limited

McCartan, Catherine
Finca Skin Organics Limited

McCarthy, Timothy Paul
Spear Therapeutics Limited

McCartney, James
Herbal Republic Ltd

McCartney, Michael
Primal Core UK Ltd

McCluskey, Paul
Peakdale Chemistry Services Ltd

McColgan, Linda Anne
Mentholatum Co Ltd

McConnell, Angela Mary
Horizon Medical Supplies UK Ltd

McConnell, Paul John
Apollo Pharma Ltd

McCoy, Sherilyn Dawn
Astrazeneca PLC

McDermott, Catherine
AAH Pharmaceuticals Limited

McDermott, Liam Joseph
Longshawe Packaging Limited

McDermott, Patrick John
Longshawe Packaging Limited

McEllone, Michael
Epax Pharma UK Ltd

McEvoy, Redmond
Beacon Pharmaceuticals Limited

McEvoy, Redmond
Kent Pharmaceuticals Limited
Thompson and Capper Limited

McEwan, David Ross
Biosynth Europe Limited

McFerran, Philip William Shaw
Blackrock Pharmaceuticals Ltd
Incepta Blackrock Limited

McGaghey, Gary
Nelson & Russell Holdings Ltd

McGrath, Hugh Colm
This Product Ltd

McGrath, John Paul
Norbrook Laboratories Limited

McGregor, Laura Taylor
Hydranure Ltd

McGregor, Paul John
Hydranure Ltd

McGuckin, Declan Michael
Tregenna Technical Services Ltd

McGuinness, Keir
Calla Lily Personal Care Ltd

McHolmes, Thomas Anthony
Scottish Bioenergy Cooperative Ventures
Tantillus Synergy Limited

McIlroy, Rosalyn Moya
TLD Sachets Limited

McIlroy, Stuart Robert James
TLD Sachets Limited

McInerney, Kieran
KMCI Services Ltd

McInnes, Blair
Humn Pharmaceuticals (UK) Ltd

McIvor, Terence, Dr
Hydro Fresh Ltd

McKelvie, Martin
Automation Control Expertise Ltd

McKenna, Hugh Michael
Koolpak Limited

McKenzie, Verna Angela
Afro Hair and Beauty International

McKing, Priscilla Adwoa Asamaniwa
Keziah Ltd

McLaughlin, David William John, Dr
E-Breathe Ltd.

McLaughlin, Henry
JNRMCL Ltd

McLaughlin, Jack
Age Reversal Europe Ltd.

McLellan, Andrew Thomas, Dr
Indivior PLC

McMahon, Desmond
Blackrock Pharmaceuticals Ltd

McMillan II, James Thayer
Ferndale Pharmaceuticals Ltd

McMillan, Edwina Margaret
Apollo Pharma Ltd

McMorran, Richard John
Abatron Limited

McMyn, Lisa Charleston
1nhaler Ltd

McNeil, Ross
Winross Limited

McQuillan, Mark
Nicobrand Limited

McTaggart, Scott Malcolm
Microskin PLC

McWilliams, Matthew James
Hygieia Medical Ltd

Mead, Nicholas Adrian
Lifeplan Products Limited

Meads, Simon John Lewis
Salutem Supplements Ltd

Mealey, Steven George
Inspire Flavours Ltd
Webottle Ltd

Mearns, Kevin Peter
Talley Environmental Care Ltd

Cole, David Robert
The Medical Supply Co Ltd

Seymour, Richard John Henry
The Medical Supply Co Ltd

Mehta, Deepak
Maycross Sports Limited

Mellen, Cosmo Feilding
Spectrum Biomedical UK Limited

Mellon, Cosmo Birdie Feilding
Beckley Research and Innovations Ltd

Meltz, Mark
Paxvax Ltd

Melvin, Clifton Adrian
Ecohydra Technologies Limited

Tolan, Paul
A. Menarini Diagnostics Ltd

Samaille, Nico Noel Andre
A. Menarini Diagnostics Ltd

Masselli, Gianni
A. Menarini Diagnostics Ltd

Mengou, Evgenia
EV Pharma Solutions Ltd

Meredith, Christopher
Advanced Healthcare Systems Ltd
Advanced Medical Solutions Ltd

Merriman, Isaac
RMW Laboratories Limited

Merritt, Peter John
Aquabalm Limited

Merson, David Tom
Microskin PLC

Merten, Gerry
Symbiosis Pharmaceutical Services

Metcalfe, Jean Carol
Teklab (ML) Ltd

Mews, Graeme David
Gimews Welding Limited

Meyer, Steven James
Cod Beck Blenders Limited

Meyer, Wolfgang Leonhard Friedrich, Dr
Wope - Migraine Ltd

Meyers, Adam
Diba Industries Limited

Mi, Da
Vivi Yeah Limited

Miah, Al Mohammed Rafique
RM Medical Care Ltd

Miller, George Lloyd
West Pharmaceutical Services Cornwall

Miller, Stuart Perry, Dr
Pneumoflex E.U. Limited

Mills, Jonette
Ohemaa's Skincare Ltd.

Milne, Adrian Christopher John
Pharmacell Medication Systems Ltd

Milne, Caroline Tremayne
Pharmacell Medication Systems Ltd

Milne, Stephanie Louise
Blackpool Medicines Limited

Milner, Paul Colin
Sands Fulton Limited

Miltenyi, Stefan Gyorgy
Miltenyi Biotec Limited

Minamide, Toshiomi
Ono Pharma UK Ltd.

Minarovic, Dominika
Clean Beauty Co Limited

Mines, Paul Robert
Ingel Technologies Limited

Minhas, Taranjeet Singh
Tal Pharma and Chemicals Ltd

Minshull-Beech, Catherine Susan, Dr
Exonate Limited

Miranda, Josephine
Primetonic Ltd

Mirroman, Djan Ivan, Lord
Mirroman Ltd

Mirza, Javeed Anjum
Medical Regulatory Consulting Ltd

Mirza, Shiraz Mohammed
Shiraz Pharm Limited

Mishlawi, Riad
Hikma Pharmaceuticals International

Mishra, Devashish
VBD Drug Safety Ltd

Mistry, Shonar
Synergy Pharma Consultancy Ltd

Misztak, Maciej Adam
Mentholatum Co Ltd

Mitchell III, William T
Pioneer UK Midco 2 Limited

Mitchell, Andrew John
As-Tec Chemicals Limited

Mitchell, Asmara
Muamko Uzuri Limited

Mitchell, Iii
PCI Penn UK Holdco Limited
Penn Pharma Group Limited
Penn Pharmaceutical Services Ltd
Pioneer UK Holdings Limited
Pioneer UK Midco 1 Limited

Mitchell, Marjorie
As-Tec Chemicals Limited

Mitchell, Michael Dennis
LDN Pharma Limited

Moehlenbrock, Jan
Intervet UK Production Limited

Moffitt, William Penn
Sarissa Biomedical Limited

Mohamed Ghoneim, Hany Mohamed Abdelhady
Shellmarks Limited

Mohamed, Anwar
Canna Care Limited

Mohammed, Azeem
Nature + Nurture Limited

Mok, Tony Shu Kam
Astrazeneca PLC

Moller, Jonas Skjodt
Albumedix Ltd

Mollison, Peter
Erimol Ltd
Renascience Pharma Limited

Montagut, Etienne Louis Marie Robert
Rapidscan Pharma Solutions EU Ltd

Montanes Estupina, Carlos
Hipra UK and Ireland Limited

Moody, Colm Joseph
Bard Pharmaceuticals Limited

Moore, Duncan Charles McNaught, Dr
Cycle Pharmaceuticals Ltd

Moore, Ian
Apollo Pharma Ltd

Moosa, Iqbal
Kensington Pharma Ltd

Morad, Hassan Oliver James
Imphatec Ltd

Morales, Kimberly
Milepitch Ltd

Moran, John Edward, Dr
Prometic Pharma SMT Limited

More, Diliprao Pandurang, Dr
Dil More Remedies UK Ltd

Morea, Lucas Abel
Hyperbiotics Corp Ltd
Hyperbiotics PLC

Moretta, James
Genzyme Limited

Morgan, Ian Christopher
Sharp Clinical Services (UK) Ltd

Morgan, Walter Dean
Biomimetic Therapeutics Ltd

Morley, Pauline
Reem Tanning Co Ltd

Morris, Paul
Chamcotec Ltd

Morris, Simon
D.D.D. Limited

Morrison, Delroy George
Tell Products, Limited

Morten, Adam Thomas
Apisera Ltd

Mortimer, Andrew John
BCM Limited
BCM Specials Limited

Mosahebi, Afshin
Materia Prima Ltd
Stem Cell Technology Ltd

Moses, John Edward
C 3 Innovations Limited

Moss, Christopher
Niche Generics Limited

Moss, Stephen Humphrey, Dr
Commercial and Academic Services Ltd

Motla, Avni Sameer
Sequana LifeSciences Ltd

Motley, Jacob
Make Skincare Ltd.

Moulds, Harry Ian
Bio-Tech Solutions Limited

Moulds, Susan Jane
Bio-Tech Solutions Limited

Mountrichas, Georgios
Abbott Iberian Investments Ltd
Knoll UK Investments Unlimited

Moynihan, Benjamin James
Boehringer Ingelheim Animal Health UK
Boehringer Ingelheim Limited

Mtchedlidze, Archil
Hartington Pharma Limited

Mueller, Juergen
Pari Medical Limited

Mukherjee, Abhijnan
Leeds Industries (UK) Ltd

Mukoko, Stephenson Tauya
Enn-Muk Limited

Muktadir, Abdul
Incepta Blackrock Limited
Incepta Pharma UK Limited

Muktadir, Akther Jahan Hasneen
Incepta Pharma UK Limited

Muktadir, Hasneen
Incepta Blackrock Limited

Mulcahy, Martyn Charles
Scottish Bioenergy Cooperative Ventures
Tantillus Synergy Limited

Muldoon, Brendan Christopher Oliver
Teva NI Limited

Mulherkar, Makarand Mohan
Makjay Pharmaceutical Limited

Mulherkar, Mohan Madhukar
Makjay Pharmaceutical Limited

Mullan, Geoffrey Patrick, Dr
Tithonus Ltd

Muller, Christophe, Dr
Aptuit (Oxford) Limited

Mullis, Graham David
Lab 21 Healthcare Limited

Mumford, Brian Frederick
Ethno Botanical Resources Ltd

Munir, Badar
Well & Well Pharma UK Ltd

Munir, Muhammad Imran
Vision Laboratories Limited

Munsie, Jeffrey
Merrimack Pharmaceuticals U.K. Ltd

Muoneke, Ngozi
M3 Cosmetics Limited

Muoneke, Victor
M3 Cosmetics Limited

Muradi, Mehdi
Intapharm Laboratories Limited

Murphy, Alison
Rhodia Pharma Solutions Ltd

Murphy, Michael Joseph
GE Healthcare Limited

Murphy, Paul
Cast Healthcare Ltd

Murray, Brian
Extruded Pharmaceuticals Ltd

Murray, John David
A & E Plasters and Dressings Ltd

Muzalewski, Patricia Mary
Blends for Massage Limited

Myers, Robert Mackie
Orbus Therapeutics Ltd

Myo, Wai Aung Chan
Essenfuture Ltd

N'jie, Isatou
Care and Wear Collection Ltd

Nadathur, Sriram
Ampha Limited

Nagaraj, Srinath
Nagashree Ltd

Nagle, Liam
Norbrook Laboratories Limited

Nahar, Kazi Sharmin
ADC Healthcare Limited

Nailor, Gareth
Accliff Ltd

Nair, Rohit
Hyperbiotics Corp Ltd
Hyperbiotics PLC

Najum, Saqiba
Quality Skincare Ltd

Naran, Bhavik Jayendra
EHB Limited

Narayan, Adrian Ashwin
Rapidscan Pharma Solutions EU Ltd

Narusawa, Takashi
Kowa Pharmaceutical Europe Co Ltd

Nasr, Yoessef Izzat
Avicenna Herbal Products Ltd

Nathwani, Nilesh
Microvisk Technologies International

Clarke, William Douglas
The Natural Cornish Co Ltd

Jauregui, Jaime
The Natural Cornish Co Ltd

Navarro, Iker
Noorik Biopharmaceuticals Ltd

Nawana, Namal Sasrika
Smith & Nephew PLC

Nawaz, Qamar, Dr
Pharmaspec Limited
Sterling Pharmaceuticals Ltd

Naylor, Andrew James
Exonate Limited

Nazael, Daka Divel
Batchable Enterprises Limited

Ndlovu, Ndabezinhle
N2SA Limited

Neal, Jonathan Clark
Auralis Limited
Baxalta UK Limited
Shire Pharmaceuticals Limited

Neat, John Konrad
Carefusion U.K. 244 Limited

Neenan, Thomas Xavier
Abfero Limited

Ferguson, Claire
A Nelson & Co Limited

McGaghey, Gary
A Nelson & Co Limited

Wilson, Patrick Russell
A Nelson & Co Limited

Wilson, Robert Nelson
A Nelson & Co Limited

Nesheva, Veronika Stoyanova
Fluss Limited

Nest, Peter Gerard
Sussex Biologicals Ltd

Nest, Susan Ann
Sussex Biologicals Ltd

Neve, Derren
R D T Technology Limited

Neve, Trevor Howard
R D T Technology Limited

Newson, Michael James
Fresenius Kabi Oncology PLC

Newton, Rezzan
Calea UK Limited
Fresenius Kabi Limited

Newton, Stewart Worth
Insense Limited

Nicholas, John Edward
Porvair PLC

Nichols, Christopher James
Active Cosmetic Ingredients Ltd

Nichols, Jacqueline
Active Cosmetic Ingredients Ltd

Nicholson, Ian James
Clinigen Group PLC

Nicholson, Simon
Merck Sharp & Dohme Limited

Nicolson, Magnus, Dr
Invizius Limited

Nightingale, John
Ariera Pharma Limited

Nivard, Jean-Christophe Guy Jacques
Unir Unlimited

Nogareda Estivill, David
Hipra UK and Ireland Limited

Nogareda Estivill, Maria Del Mar
Hipra UK and Ireland Limited

Nolan, Robert Dwyer
Phico Therapeutics Limited

Chukwumah, Ononuju Nkem
The Noohra Limited

Noori, Omar
PharmaYouth Ltd.

Norman, David John
Life Technologies BPD UK Ltd
Thermo Fisher Scientific Life Holdings

Note, Paul Druon Michael
Geistlich Sons Limited

Nottay, Jaskarn Singh
Synergetic Global Limited

Novak, Istvan
Hahydra Technologies Ltd

Nowers, Christopher John
Cell Medica Limited

Nurbhai, Abbas Abdulhusein
Soleaero Limited

Nyamali, Oredola Cynthia
Etmo UK Limited

O'Briain, Killian
Glasport Bio UK Limited
Tribe Therapeutics UK Limited
Westway Health UK Limited

O'Brien, Generald Francis
Ayrton Saunders Limited
Ayrton Saunders and Co Ltd
OBG Holding Limited
Pharmaserve Limited
Pharmasol Limited
Ransom Naturals Limited

O'Brien, Laura Elizabeth, Dr
Seqirus Vaccines Limited

O'Brien, Padraic Marc
Ayrton Saunders Limited
OBG Holding Limited
Pharmaserve (North West) Ltd
Pharmaserve Limited
Ransom Naturals Limited

O'Brien, Shannon John
Think Noo Limited
Your Noo Edge Ltd.

O'Connell, Richard Marc
Flavour Maker Limited

O'Connor, Stephen Clifford
Thompson and Capper Limited

O'Connor, Stephen Michael
Nia Nova Ltd

O'Flaherty, Vincent
Glasport Bio UK Limited
Tribe Therapeutics UK Limited
Westway Health UK Limited

O'Kane, Laurence Gregory
Cast Healthcare Ltd

O'Neill, Kevin Michael
GE Healthcare Limited
GE Healthcare UK Limited

O'Neill, Terence
GlaxoSmithKline Consumer Healthcare (UK) Trading

O'Reilly, Michael Gregory
Envigo RMS (UK) Limited

O'Shea, John Joseph
Hologic Ltd.

O'Sullivan, Tim
Diba Industries Limited

O'Toole, David
Opiant Pharmaceuticals UK Ltd

Obeed, Muthana
Florence Health & Beauty Ltd

Obeid, Andrew Nadeem, Dr
Optronica Limited

Oben, Delphine Tiku, Dr
IQ5 Consultancy Limited

Obrien, Brigid Christina
OBG Holding Limited

Obrien, Generald Francis
Pharmaserve (North West) Ltd

Obrien, Padraic Marc
Ayrton Saunders and Co Ltd
Pharmasol Limited

Ogboru, Philomena Oji
Dolphins Limited

Ogrodzinski, Stefan
Biostatus Ltd
Biosuspensions Limited
Biotherics Limited

Okoria, Elizabeth
Bodeli Consultants Limited

Okubanjo, Abiola
Sahara Biomedix Ltd

Olafsson, Sigurdur Oli
Hikma Pharmaceuticals PLC

Olby, Alan Musgrave
IS Pharmaceuticals Limited
Sinclair Pharmaceuticals Ltd

Oldfield, Stephen John
Technical Textile Services Ltd

Olekanma, Joyce Ijeme
Joyce Pharmac Services Ltd

Olobaniyi, Victor Olorunleke
Flourish Ventures Ltd

Olusanya, Adebukonla
Stuckola-Pharma Limited

Omar, Sarah
Pentonova Limited

Ondhia, Amrisha Chandrakant
Typharm Limited

Ondhia, Aruna Yashvantrai
Cambridge Healthcare Supplies 2012
Cambridge Healthcare Supplies Ltd
Torbet Laboratories Limited

Ondhia, Chandni Chandrakant
Typharm Limited

Ondhia, Chandrakant Vallabhdas
Chapar 2016 Ltd
Chapar 2017 Ltd
Typharm Developments Limited
Typharm Limited

Ondhia, Deepesh Chandrakant
Typharm Limited

Ondhia, Parveen Chandrakant
Typharm Developments Limited

Ondhia, Punam
Cambridge Healthcare Supplies 2012
Cambridge Healthcare Supplies Ltd
Torbet Laboratories Limited

Ondhia, Yashvantrai Vallabhji
Cambridge Healthcare Supplies 2012
Cambridge Healthcare Supplies Ltd
Torbet Laboratories Limited

Onumonu, Eileen
Pacific Height Limited

Onyiaorah, Benita Ezete
Euroclinical Ltd

Orbell, Joseph
Cool Gell Limited

Organ, Laura Michiko
Summit Veterinary Pharmaceuticals

Organ, Stephen Daniel
Summit Veterinary Pharmaceuticals

Ganassini di Camerati, Giuseppe
The Organic Pharmacy Limited

White, Daniel
The Organic Pharmacy Limited

Orihashi, Kenji
Fujifilm Diosynth Biotechnologies UK

Orji, Pamela
Hannah and Hugh Ltd

Orlev, Chaime
Kamada Biopharma Limited

Orme, Geoffrey Michael
Biofortuna Ltd

Ormrod, Samantha
Apollo Pharma Ltd

Orth, Christian
Merial Limited

Osborn, Ben John
Hospira UK Limited

Osman, Emma
Skin Euphoria Limited

Osmundo, Cristino
Forbleries Ltd

Otepkova, Petra
Pharma Future Ltd

Otulana, Babatunde Adekunle, Dr
Allergy Therapeutics PLC

Ouimette, Michael
Portola Pharma UK Limited

Overend, Stuart John
P2 Healthcare Limited
P2-Molteni Pharma Limited

Overy, Michael John
Arcadia Pharma Limited

Owen, Aron Rhys, Dr
Pharma Pack Limited

Owen, Marc Ellis
Smith & Nephew PLC

Owen, Marian
Pharma Pack Limited

Owen, Richard Rhys
Celtic Wellbeing Ltd
Pharma Pack Limited

Owen, Sebastian David Wells
Vita (Europe) Limited
Vita Animal Health Ltd
Vita Bee Health Ltd

Owodeyi, Jamiu, Dr
Phetalz Ltd

Owodeyi, Waheedat
Phetalz Ltd

Pack, Aaron Junior
Acle Urban Gardens Limited

Page, Christopher
Flavour Maker Limited

Page, Ian David
Dechra Limited

Page, Lidell
NKCell Plus PLC

Page, Michael
Flavour Maker Limited

Page, Stephen Walter
Luoda UK Limited

Pakeman, Randal Joseph
Bray Group Limited

Palane, Mkhululi Patrick
Xylomed Pharmaceuticals Ltd

Paling, Richard John
Quantum Pharma 2014 Limited
Quantum Pharma Holdings Ltd

Pallana, Kamlesh
Medicareplus International Ltd
Medicareplus Limited

Pallister, Carl Alan
DX Products Limited
Vaxaid Ltd.
Xersizer Limited

Palmer, David John
Agroceutical Products Ltd

Palmer, Gail
Everything for Eczema Limited

Panagiotidis, Charalampos
Smith Kline & French Laboratories

Panda, Chandramani
Amarox Limited

Pane, Christopher
Revive Us Limited

Panesar, Gursharan Singh
Uni Health Distribution Ltd

Panzara, Michael, Dr
Wave Life Sciences UK Limited

Papasotiriou, Ioannis, Dr
RGCC Pharma Limited

Papathanasiou, Antonios
Invos Ltd

Parikh, Dipesh, Dr
Higgs Pharma Private Limited

Parish, Sean Peter
West Pharmaceutical Services Cornwall

Parker, Andrew
Essential Nutrition Limited

Parker, Anne Pauline
Essential Nutrition Limited

Parker, Christopher
Essential Nutrition Limited

Parker, David John
Beegood Enterprises Limited

Parker, Lorna Mary Southcombe
Indivior PLC

Parker, Timothy
Essential Nutrition Limited

Parkin, Dawn
Phyto Products Limited

Parkinson, Graeme
Cuttlefish Limited

Parkinson, Nigel Christopher, Dr
Fine Contract Research Limited
Fine Organics Limited

Parmar, Nilesh
Accord Healthcare Limited

Parry, Philip Edward
Aurum Pharmaceuticals Limited
Macarthys Laboratories Limited

Parsons, Guy
MyHairDoctor Ltd

Parthasarathy, Krishnan Tirucherai
Strides Pharma UK Ltd

Parvanova, Eugenia Borissova
Nia Nova Ltd

Pastinelli, Jean Yves
Alexi Laboratories Ltd

Patani, Vishal
Integrated Pharmaceutical Services (IPS)
Ipsco Limited
Vertical Pharma Resources Ltd

Patel, Amish
Infohealth Laboratories Ltd
Infohealth Limited

Patel, Amit Hasmukh Raojibhai
SNS Limited

Patel, Amit Vijaykumar
Atnahs Pharma US Limited
Marlborough Pharmaceuticals Ltd

Patel, Anish
Nutra Aid Ltd.
Osgen Ltd.
Osgen Pharmaceuticals Limited

Patel, Anita
Personal Care Packs Limited

Patel, Arunkumar Chhaganbhai
Reaxa Limited

Patel, Ashokkumar Dahyabhai
Integrated Pharmaceutical Services (IPS)
Ipsco Limited
Vertical Pharma Resources Ltd

Patel, Bemal
Pharmaclarity Limited

Patel, Bhikhu Chhotabhai [8-1947]
Marlborough Pharmaceuticals Ltd

Patel, Bhikhu Chhotabhai [11-1949]
Atnahs Pharma US Limited

Patel, Bushra
Comed Healthcare UK Ltd

Patel, Chhotalal Chhaganlal
BVM Medical Limited

Patel, Chirag
Amneal Pharma UK Holdings Ltd

Patel, Deepika
Ilody Skincare Ltd

Patel, Dipen Vijaykumar
Atnahs Pharma US Limited
Marlborough Pharmaceuticals Ltd

Patel, Harshadrai Ishwarbhai Ashabhai
Bioceuticals Limited

Patel, Haziq
Renascience Pharma Limited

Patel, Jayanti Chimanbhai
Pollenase Limited

Patel, Jaymini
Brosis Ltd

Patel, Kanchanlal Naginbhai
Ria Generics Limited

Patel, Kirit Chimanbhai Tulsibhai
Pollenase Limited

Patel, Marshal
Farm Bionics Ltd

Patel, Mayuri
Mayuveda R & D Limited

Patel, Mikesh
Nutra Aid Ltd.
Osgen Ltd.
Osgen Pharmaceuticals Limited

Patel, Nikesh
Handiskin Limited

Patel, Nikhil
Brosis Ltd

Patel, Nikin, Dr
Catalent UK Supply Chain Ltd
Columbia Laboratories (UK) Ltd
Molecular Profiles Ltd

Patel, Nileshkumar Indubhai
Healthbiotics Ltd

Patel, Nitanj
Resolution Chemicals Limited
Resolution Generics Limited

Patel, Nutan
Osgen Ltd.

Patel, Rajive
Infohealth Laboratories Ltd
Infohealth Limited

Patel, Rameshkumar Jerambhai
BHR Pharmaceuticals Limited

Patel, Sajan
Brosis Ltd

Patel, Sandeep Ashokbhai
Ambe Limited

Patel, Shaileshbhai Madhavbhai
Catalent CTS (Edinburgh) Ltd

Patel, Shantilal Maganbhai
S M Consultancy (MK) Limited

Patel, Shayli
Brosis Ltd

Patel, Surendra
Makjay Pharmaceutical Limited

Patel, Umang Rajendrakumar
Alps Biosciences Limited

Patel, Usha Shantilal
RP & MP Investments Limited

Patel, Vijay Kumar Chhotabhai
Marlborough Pharmaceuticals Ltd

Patel, Vijay Kumar Harendra
Hexpress Healthcare Limited

Patel, Vijaykumar Chhotabhai
Atnahs Pharma US Limited

Patel, Vimal
ZVF Pharma Ltd

Patel-Naran, Hina
EHB Limited

Patterson, David Hugh
Quay Pharmaceuticals Limited

Patterson, Laurence Hylton, Prof
Biostatus Ltd

Patwalia, Gurjot Singh
Keybiotech Ltd

Pavesio, Carlos Eduardo
Lux Viridis Services Ltd

Pavlou, Danielle Nicole
Bioplus Tech Ltd

Pavlou, James Paul
Bioplus Tech Ltd

Pavlou, Marie Linda Shirley
Bioplus Tech Ltd

Pavlovskyi, Illia
AB Biotechnology Limited

Pay, Paul William
Norgine Limited

Payne, David Martin
MacFarlan Smith Limited

Paynter, Michael Thomas Gwynfor
HAV Vaccines Limited

Pazik, Karol
Corpus Nostrum Limited
Mandeville Medicines Limited
Nonivlok Limited

Pearson, Edwin James
Hospira Aseptic Services Ltd
Hospira UK Limited

Pearson, Paul Davidson
Salenco Limited

Pearson, Paul
Miracol Ltd

Peat, Ashley Ross
Brainpower Group Ltd.

Pedersen, Maireadh Anne
Quay Pharmaceuticals Limited

Pellizzari, Christine
Insmed Limited

Peltz, Stuart Walter
PTC Therapeutics, Limited

Penfold, Jonathan Mark
Integrated Pharmaceutical Services (IPS)
Ipsco Limited
Vertical Pharma Resources Ltd

Pepin, Gregory
Genetis PLC

Perez, Hector Daniel
Naia (London) Limited

Perfitt, Jason Daniel
Bio-Health Limited

Perfitt, Raoul John
Bio-Health Limited

Perfitt, Victor Daniel
Bio-Health Limited
Kerbina,Limited

Perkins, Scott James
Instavit Limited
One Second Supplements Limited

Pessagno, Gerard Michael Dominic
M & A Pharmachem Limited

Peter, Valerie Jacqueline Dana
Dana's Creations Ltd

Peters, William
Amphastar UK Ltd
International Medication Systems (U.K.)

Peterson, Alan Edward
BBI Solutions OEM Limited
Scipac Limited

Petras, Christophe
BCM Limited
BCM Specials Limited

Phelan, Daniel Joseph
Indivior PLC

Phillips, Leon
Natural Miracles Limited

Phillips, Louise Gladys
Selborne Biological Services Ltd

Phillips, Stacie
Albany Molecular Research Ltd

Phull, Ravinder Singh
AAA Pharmaceuticals Limited

Picard, Gilles
Indivior EU Limited
Indivior UK Limited

Pickard, John Douglas, Professor
Medicam Limited

Pickering, Robert Mark
Hikma Pharmaceuticals PLC

Pien, Howard Hao
Indivior PLC

Piese, Zane
Atlantis Skincare Ltd

Pietrantoni, David Francis
Fluidx Limited

Pietrowski, Maik Marcel
Cannerald Group Ltd

Pignolet, David Walter
Celgene UK Manufacturing (II) Ltd
Celgene UK Manufacturing (III) Ltd
Celgene UK Manufacturing Ltd

Pillai, Mohana Kumar
Strides Pharma UK Ltd

Pisano, Anthony, Dr
Mimi Pisano Limited

Plackett, Michael
Plackett Limited

Plummer, Nicholas Roger Clive
Patheon UK Limited

Pollitt, Julieann
Vitaminiv Franchising Limited

Pool, Christiaan Jan Otto
Crawford Healthcare (R & D) Ltd
Derms Development Limited
Zindaclin Limited

Poon, Shuk Han
MDX Healthcare Ltd

Pope, Neville George
Equalbrief Limited
Selborne Biological Services Ltd

Popov, Nikolay, Dr
N Popov Ltd

Porbanderwalla, Aliasghar Shiraz
Saifee Healthcare Limited

Portonenko, Igor
Candles UK Ltd

Potlapadu, Bhavani
Dr Pradeep Reddy's Laboratories (UK & EU)

Potlapadu, Pradeep Kumar Reddy, Dr
Dr Pradeep Reddy's Laboratories (UK & EU)

Pouton, Colin William, Dr
Commercial and Academic Services Ltd

Powell, Martin Carrick
Stablepharma Limited

Powell, Michael, Dr
RSR Limited

Powers, Linda Fairing
Advent Bioservices Ltd

Praestegaard, Morten
MC2 Therapeutics Limited

Prakash, Manoj
Amarox Limited

Preston, James Eley
TCS Biosciences Limited

Preston, Lynda Jane
TCS Biosciences Limited

Chang, Mun Yue
Shirley Price Aromatherapy Ltd

Wong, Joon Lian
Shirley Price Aromatherapy Ltd

Brealey, Peter Ian
Shirley Price Aromatherapy Ltd

Price, Jeffrey
Apollo Pharma Ltd

Price, Robert, Prof
Nanopharm Limited

Price, Steven Craig
UCB Pharma Limited

Prikazsky, Marc Dominique
Sogeval UK Limited

Prince, Matthew George
Man Oil Co Ltd

Prinsloo, Georg Frederick
Apex Pharmaceuticals Ltd.

Pritchard, Bruce Philip
Prometic Pharma SMT Limited

Cameron, Euan Daney Ross
G. & M. Procter Limited

Dartiguelongue, Claude Georgette Emilie
G. & M. Procter Limited

Grant, Lucie Mary Katja
G. & M. Procter Limited

Norman, David John
G. & M. Procter Limited

Smith, Anthony Hugh
G. & M. Procter Limited

Profit, Alan Lynford
Rainbow Engineering Services Ltd

Prokopchuk, Eugene
GlaxoSmithKline Consumer Healthcare (UK) Trading

Prudhoe, Jonathan Edward
Aspar Pharmaceuticals Limited

Prudhoe, Sandra Jean
Aspar Pharmaceuticals Limited

Prudhoe, Terence Edward
Sestri (Sales) Limited
Tersan Pharmaceuticals Ltd.

Prudhoe, Terrence Edward
Aspar Pharmaceuticals Limited

Przygoda, Adam
Medicus Integrated Medicine Ltd

Pugh, John
Pharmapac (U.K.) Limited

Pugh, Lyn Janet
Stegram Pharmaceuticals Ltd

Pulford, Karen Jane
Hichrom Limited

Punja, Pervez Rajanikant
Euro Medical Equipment Limited

Purce, Gwendoline Maria
Purce Associates Limited

Purvis, Duncan Ross, Dr
Dermatek Limited
Pellis Care Limited

Qaiyum, Muhammad Abdul
Redlight Exchange Ltd

Quarta, Roberto
Smith & Nephew PLC

Quick, Mark Royston
Recipharm HC Limited
Recipharm Limited

Quinn, Gavin Patrick
Univit Ltd

Quinn, Micheal
Berhael Trading Limited

Quinn, Sam Leon
Mumma Love Organics Limited

Quinn, Samantha
Mumma Love Organics Limited

Quinn, Shannon
Lucy Annabella Ltd

Qureshi, Muhammad Ali, Dr
Cingem Ltd
IOLAMD Ltd
LEH Pharma Ltd
Maculeh Ltd

Rabe, Pia Gunborg Anette
Lisoma International Limited

Rabone, Philip Stephen
PSR Analytical Services Ltd

Rac, David
Bohemia Pharmaceuticals Ltd.

Racey, Christopher Stephen
Aeropax International Limited
South Wales Specials Limited

Racey, Jacqueline Mary
Aeropax International Limited
South Wales Specials Limited
Veradis Specials Limited

Rach, Birju
Mayuveda R & D Limited

Radcliffe, Elizabeth
Inskin Skincare Ltd

Radcliffe, Paul
Inskin Skincare Ltd

Radia, Bhavesh Amratlal
Ascot Laboratories Limited

Radie, Robert Samuel
Egalet Limited

Radmehr, Nadia Farah
Zink Tattoo Care Limited

Rahman, Khondaker Mirazur, Dr
ADC Healthcare Limited

Rahman, Mahammed Armaan Hanif
Medicol Limited

Rahman, Mahammed Usmaan Hanif
Medicol Limited

Rahman, Mahommed Hanif
Medicol Limited

Rahman, Muhammad Hamza
MHR Pharmacy Ltd

Rahman, Sabera Nazneen
Astrazeneca PLC

Rahman, Sakhawhat Hussain, Dr
Medicol Limited

Raine, Jane Elizabeth
Four Pharmaceuticals Limited

Raine, Philip
Four Pharmaceuticals Limited

Rainger, George Edward
Viatem Limited

Rajabi, Anthony Soroush
Vitaact Ltd

Rajasekar, Visvanathan
Strides Pharma UK Ltd

Rajasingam, Vinayagar
RRA Green Cross Limited

Ramsay, Malcolm Clive
Manx Healthcare Limited
Manx Pharma Ltd

Ramsey, Edward, Dr
Leptrex Ltd.

Ramsey, Louise
Baby Face Cosmetics Limited

Ramsey, Peter
Baby Face Cosmetics Limited

Randall, Patricia
Oxford Immunotec Global PLC

Randle, Neil Raymond
Pete Randle Grinding & Son Ltd

Randle, Luke
Pete Randle Grinding & Son Ltd

Rani, Razna
Itreatskin Limited

Rao, Rajashekhar
RG and Co Limited

Rao, Varalwar Manohar
Vivimed Labs Europe Ltd

Rathod, Rahul
JSN Chemicals Limited

Ravenscroft, MacAulay
Rubyquartz Ltd

Rawlinson, Ian Malcolm
A Q V S Limited

Raymond, Maureen
Homicon Prime International Ltd

Raynor, Simon Paul
Penlan Healthcare Limited

Raza, Amna
Pentonova Limited

Razaq, Nadim
Limitless Med Ltd

Reading, Andrea Elizabeth
Capa Vision Limited

Reading, Clive Henry
Capa Vision Limited

Reardan, Dayton Thomas
Eleosinc Limited

Reddy, Satish
Dr Reddy's Laboratories (UK) Ltd

Redfern, David Jonathan
T-In Medical Limited

Reece, Kelvin John
Reelvision Print Limited

Reed, Stephen Vaughan
Diagnostic Reagents Limited

Reekie, Robert Morris, Dr
Symbiosis Pharmaceutical Services

Rees Smith, Bernard, Dr
RSR Limited

Reeves, Duncan James
Zeltiq Limited

Regan, Matt Joseph
Novo Nordisk Holding Limited

Reginald, Trevor
Bioreactor Corporation Limited

Rehman, Khalil
KR Regulatory Limited
Wogue One Limited

Reilly, Kathleen
Diba Industries Limited

Renz, Justin Andrew
Cardiome UK Limited

Rhoades, Cynthia Renee
Chemagain Limited

Rhodes, Peter Robert
Crawford Healthcare (R & D) Ltd
Crawford Manufacturing Limited
Derms Development Limited
Zindaclin Limited

Richardson, Julian James Anthony
Centaur Healthcare Limited
Surepharm Services Limited

Richardson, Kenneth
Biologix Laboratories Limited

Richardson, Nigel Anthony
Custom Pharmaceuticals Limited

Richardson, Ross John
Prep Skincare Products Limited

Richardson, Steve
Badgequo Limited

Richings Barrow, Wendy
AWA Export Limited

Richmond, Alicia Tomora Amylinda
A-Rich Nutrition Ltd

Ricupati, Agostino
Sauflon (Manufacturing) Ltd

Rienow, Susan
Hospira Aseptic Services Ltd

Riley, Stephen William
Medisante Limited

Rinaldi, Davide Eduardo
Uni Health Distribution Ltd

Risley, Angela Susan
Smith & Nephew PLC

Risley, John Carter
Algal Omega 3 Ltd

Ritchie, Fiona
Ochil Skincare Co Ltd

Rivers, Dominic James
Omega Pharma Limited
Rosemont Pharmaceuticals Ltd
Wrafton Laboratories Limited

Rizwan, Raja
Allmarks Products Limited

Robb, Gary Charles
Corcept Therapeutics UK Ltd

Robbins, Mark Ian
Vivimed Labs Europe Ltd

Robertini, Domonic
Miongam Ltd

Roberts, Debra Joy
Contura Limited
Dermato Logical Limited

Roberts, John Anthony, Dr
Geotek Coring Limited

Robertson, Andrew Howard
AVI BioPharma International Ltd

Robertson, Lindon
Fluidx Limited

Robinsohn, Michael
Church & Dwight UK Limited

Robinson, Andrew
Patheon UK Limited

Robinson, Jacqueline
Lifeplan Products Limited

Robinson, Marc
Dark Knight Holdings Limited

Robinson, Stephen William, Dr
Pharmaceutical Equipment Ltd

Robinson, William John
Cycle Pharmaceuticals Ltd

Rocchi, Alessandro
Georganics Ltd

Rockett, Linda
Wave Life Sciences UK Limited

Rodol, Neil
Badgequo Limited

Rogers, Martin Ian
Schering-Plough Limited

Rogers, Philip John
Detraxi Ltd

Rogerson, Nicholas Ralphe
Parbold Therapeutics Limited

Rohrbach, Raymond Gerard
Salenco Limited

Roig Zapatero, Gabriel
Reig Jofre UK Limited

Roomes, Laban Edward
Marigold Projects Jamaica Ltd

Ros, Ana Maria Mihaela
Ana Maria Serban Ltd

Roscop, Frederic Elie
FR Products Limited

Rosenman, Herman
Oxford Immunotec Global PLC

Roser, Bruce Joseph, Dr
Stablepharma Limited

Rosholm, Peter
Albumedix Ltd

Rossig, Christel Elisabeth
Insmed Limited

Roth, David John
Innova Biosciences Ltd

Rothwell, Nicholas Andrew
Molnlycke Health Care Limited

Rougemond, Eric
Aguettant Limited

Roy, Biresh
Pro Bono Bio Limited

Royle, Victoria
Follifix Ltd

Rozewicki, Marian
Medlabs Europe Ltd

Rubinstein, Michael Henry, Professor
Quay Pharmaceuticals Limited

Rudd, Christopher Allan
Omega Pharma Limited
Rosemont Pharmaceuticals Ltd
Wrafton Laboratories Limited

Ruedig, Christoph Oliver
Proveca Limited

Ruffo, Frank
Aclaris Therapeutics International

Rumbenieks, Edijs
Beneficial Oils Ltd

Runacres, Andrew Peter
Phamar Limited

Runacres, Pheadra
Phamar Limited

Ruprai, Gurdev Singh
Uni Health Distribution Ltd
Chaos Businezz Solutions Ltd

Ruprai, Gurdev Singh
Ennogen Healthcare Ltd
Ennogen Pharma Ltd
Total Pharmacare Ltd
Vitame Ltd

Ruprai, Kalvinder Singh
North Star Healthcare Limited

Rush, Clifford Peter
Isca Biochemicals Limited

Rush, Paul Jeremy
Onsite Diagnostics Limited
Wildrush Limited

Rusk, Samuel William John
Jenarron Therapeutics Limited

Russell, Alan
Russell and Denver Ltd

Russo, Mario Luca, Dr
Dr Russo Cosmetics Limited

Rust, Sally
Pfylori Limited
Vitra Pharmaceuticals Ltd

Rutterford, Elsie Jane
Clean Beauty Co Limited

Ryan, Colin Douglas
FPL - Formulating Partnership Ltd

Ryan, Nicholas Richard
Chemagain Limited

Ryan, Robert F, Dr
Nunataq Limited

Ryan, Vivien
FPL - Formulating Partnership Ltd

Rye, Philip Desmond, Dr
Algipharma UK Limited

Ryves, William Jonathan, Dr
Cupid Peptide Co Ltd

Sabirov, Roman, Dr
Mirroman Ltd

Sabzee, Hamzah Ali Hussein
Wilsons Pharma Limited

Sachdeva, Munit
Musclemantra Ltd

Sachdeva, Rahib
Musclemantra Ltd

Sackers, Roland
Qiagen Manchester Limited

Sadeq, Tariq, Dr
Herbapharmedica Limited

Sadler, Emma
Man Oil Co Ltd

Sadofsky, Melvyn Warren
Lifeplan Products Limited

Sagin, Michael Roy
Organic Herbs for Health Ltd
Organic Herbs for Life Limited

Sahni, Ajay
Pinewood Healthcare Limited
Wockhardt UK Limited

Sahota, Gurpreet Kaur
Go-Kyo Science Limited

Sahota, Lakhveer Singh
Go-Kyo Science Limited

Sainz de Mier, Lucia
Air Liquide Limited

Saito, Masaya
Mentholatum Co Ltd

Saldanha, Mark Bosco
Bell,Sons & Co.(Druggists) Ltd

Saldanha, Sandra
Bell,Sons & Co.(Druggists) Ltd

Sale, Jamie Lee
Insmed Limited

Saleem, Sohaib
Wellington Unit Limited

Salford, Chris
Rejuvenile Ltd

Salisbury, Nicola
Vitabonna Development Limited

Salman, Parvez
Comed Healthcare UK Ltd

Salmons, Roy
Pharmaco Group Limited

Salvage, John Richard
DTR Medical Limited

Samaka, Dheyaa Jaafar Mohammed
Wilsons Pharma Limited

Samaka, Haider Dheyaa Jaafar
Wilsons Pharma Limited

Sampalli, Sridhar Rao
Graviti Healthcare Limited

Sampson, Andrew Michael
Pharmapac (U.K.) Limited

Samson, Leonard
Apex Pharmaceuticals Ltd.

Samuda, Alixzondra
Mudd By Alix Ltd.

Samuel, Deborah Lynn
DHTD Limited

Samuel, Hannah Louise
DHTD Limited

Samuel, Thomas Peter
DHTD Limited

Sandberg, Richard Alvin
Oxford Immunotec Global PLC
Oxford Immunotec Limited

Sanders, Jane, Dr
RSR Limited

Sanson, David Alan
Quantum Pharmaceutical Limited

Sarabandi, Mohammad Reza
Geoprep Limited

Saran, Atul
Emergent Countermeasures International
Paxvax Ltd

Sartore, Patrick
Prometic Pharma SMT Limited

Sathianathan, Gavin Hilary
Ark Technologies Ltd
Alta Flora Ltd

Satrap, Mariam Moussavi
Sentinel Health Limited

Sattar, Mehraan
PharmaYouth Ltd.

Savage, Bruce
GFC Diagnostics Limited

Savastano, Frank Louis
Hikma Pharmaceuticals International

Sawyer, Lorna Mary Elizabeth
Biopharm (U.K.) Limited

Sawyer, Roy Thomas, Doctor
Biopharm (U.K.) Limited

Saxby, Simon James Yvon
Halligarth Bioadvisors Ltd

Schade, Christian Stanton
Indivior PLC

Schatz, Peer Michael
Qiagen Manchester Limited

Schatzlein, Andreas Gerhard, Dr
Chitomerics Limited

Scheiffele, Anna Mari, Dr
Novartis Pharmaceuticals UK Ltd

Scheske, Manfred
Infirst Healthcare Limited

Schiele, Martin John
Boost Hair Limited
Rosalique Skincare Limited
Salcura Limited

Schmidt, Emmanuel
Aurum Pharmaceuticals Limited
Macarthys Laboratories Limited
Viridian Pharma Limited

Schofield, Sophie-Louise
Tomorrow Biotech Ltd

Schol, Dick Joanske
Antibody Store Limited

Schultheiss, Peter John
Geotek Coring Limited

Schwartz, Norman David
Bio-Rad AbD Serotec Ltd

Schweins, Thomas
Qiagen Manchester Limited

Schwinner, Lucas Caspar
Ranir (Holdings) Limited
Ranir Limited
Solent Oral Care Ltd

Scott, Deborah Annette
SKN-RG Ltd
SKN-RG Research & Development Ltd

Scott, Elizabeth Mary
Cellon UK Limited

Scott, James, Professor
Apobec Discovery Ltd

Scott, Robert
SKN-RG Ltd
SKN-RG Research & Development Ltd

Scott, Stephen
Total Pharma Ltd

Scotto, Serge
AB Biotechnology Limited

Sczerbyna, Herve
HBNatura Ltd

Franklin, Ian Eric
G.D.Searle & Co.Limited

Highton, David Ian
G.D.Searle & Co.Limited

Mount, Jacqueline Ann
G.D.Searle & Co.Limited

Seeley, Bruce
CTI Life Sciences Limited

Sefton, Phillip Bryan
Lab 21 Healthcare Limited

Seghi Recil, Federico
P2-Molteni Pharma Limited

Seiler, Christian
Pharma XP Consulting Ltd

Selke, Stephan, Dr
West Pharmaceutical Services Cornwall

Sellers, Frank
Geistlich Sons Limited

Semmens, Phillip
Accord Healthcare Limited

Sen, Dinendra
Curx Pharma (UK) Limited

Serra, Massimo
Farasha-Cosmetics Ltd

Serry, Nakisa
Celgene UK Manufacturing (II) Ltd
Celgene UK Manufacturing (III) Ltd
Celgene UK Manufacturing Ltd

Settle, Paul
Nutrapharm Ltd

Shadoobuccus, Zohra Allimah
Sonifar Pharma Expert Limited

Shaer, Phillip Stephen
Spectrum Biomedical UK Limited

Shafiq, Mohammed Choudhary, Dr
Intrapharm Laboratories Ltd

Shafqat, Safraz
Wellington Unit Limited

Shah, Anish
Infinitus Enterprise Limited

Shah, Anuj Somchand
P.I.E. Pharma Limited
Star Pharmaceuticals Limited

Shah, Jalpa
Durja Pharma Limited

Shah, Khilan Mahendra
Avacare Limited

Shah, Minal
Chela Animal Health Limited

Shah, Nishant
Durja Pharma Limited

Shah, Rahul Mahendra
Avacare Limited

Shah, Rajiv Bharat Kumar
Chela Animal Health Limited

Shah, Sh, Dr
Shah-British Enterprises Ltd

Shah, Sunil Rajen
Exonate Limited

Shahid, Waqas
Smart Instruments UK Limited

Shahzad, Sohail
UK Healthcare Pharma Limited

Shalon, Tidhar
Renew Medical UK Limited

Shand, Bryan Kay
Phytovation Limited

Shandell, Jason
Amphastar UK Ltd
International Medication Systems (U.K.)

Shank, Ms Amei W
Indivior UK Limited

Sharif, Ayesha Mehreen
AS Pharma Consultancy Limited

Sharif, Lubna
Mayfair & Hayes Pharmaceuticals Ltd

Sharif, Zahoor Ahmed
ZVF Pharma Ltd

Sharma, Ajay
AA Zentivus Ltd

Sharma, Jitendra Mahavirprasad
Bell,Sons & Co.(Druggists) Ltd

Sharma, Pushpinder
Linosa Limited

Sharma, Rohit Nitin
Acme UK Inc Limited

Sharma, Srikant
Fermenta Biotech (UK) Limited

Sharma, Sudesh
Linosa Limited

Sharov, Dmitrii
Pharm Recon Ltd

Shattock, Robin John, Professor
Vaccine Manufacturing and Innovation Centre UK

Shaukat, Khalid
Well & Well Pharma UK Ltd

Shaw, Colin Anthony
Biteback Products Ltd

Shaw, Fiona Victoria
Biteback Products Ltd

Shaw, Helen Margaret, Dr
Proveca Limited

Shaw, Ian William
Gley Skincare Limited

Shaw, John McCallum Marshall
Biocon Pharma UK Limited

Shaw, Kathleen Margaret
Biteback Products Ltd

Shaw, Lance Antony
CBDHealthcare Ltd

Shawki El Morsy Yousef, Mohamed, Dr
Bioceutics UK Ltd

Sheehan, Joseph
Kenmare Medical Limited

Sheehy, Douglas Thomas
Aimmune Therapeutics UK Ltd

Sheikh, MD Arif, Dr
Avix Pharmaceuticals Limited

Sheil, Meredith Louise
Medical Ethics UK Limited

Shelatkar, Rohit
Vitabiotics Limited

Shelton, Michael Henry
Aim-Straight Limited

Shemesh Idelson, Efrat
Zomi Ltd

Shepherd, Barry Roy
Braun International Limited
Europa-Technia Limited

Shepherd, Robert John
Stablepharma Limited

Shepherd, Tracey Marie
Europa-Technia Limited

Sheridan, William Patrick, Dr
Biocryst UK Limited

Sherman, Craig
Hope Pharmaceuticals, Ltd.

Sherman, Hope
Hope Pharmaceuticals, Ltd.

Shetty, Akshay Anand
Combe International Limited

Sheward, Martin
World Medicine Ophthalmics Ltd

Shihn, Sundip Singh
BtechLaboratories (UK) Ltd.
Furoid Ltd
Invitrohair Ltd

Shirahata, Kentaro
Auralis Limited
Viropharma Limited

Shiraishi, Koichi
Kowa Pharmaceutical Europe Co Ltd

Shiraki, Shigeru
Medics Kingdom Limited

Shirvani, Ayoub, Dr
Sina Pharm Limited

Shittu, Ade Yinka
Y Consultancy Ltd

Shodunke, Olubukola Taofik
Koasta Limited

Shomali, Bashar Basel Yacoub
Hikmacure Limited

Short, Cormac
Celadon Pharma Ltd

Short, Steven, Dr
Beacon Green Limited

Shoukat, Faisal
Oxford Pharmaceuticals Limited

Shukla, Chetan Vinodrai
Hexpress Healthcare Limited

Shur, Jagdeep Singh, Dr
Evopharm Limited
Nanopharm Limited

Shur, Kiran
Evopharm Limited

Sicklen, Clare
Janssen-Cilag Limited

Silcock, Kate
Kaizen Ceramics Ltd

Silcox, Nigel Patrick
2020 Organics Limited

Simard, Regis Jean-Pierre
Glaxo Operations UK Limited

Simkin, Richard
Indivior UK Limited

Simpson, John Andrew
Skyrocket Phytopharma (UK) Ltd

Sinclair, Christopher James, Dr
Emergent Countermeasures International

Sinclair, Leon
Medi-Cure Bio Ergonomics Ltd

Singh Heer, Jasbinder
JGPSK Limited

Singh, Amy
Zink Tattoo Care Limited

Singh, Lalasa Alina
Universal Business Services UK Ltd

Singh, Ranjan
Lukas Lab Limited

Singh, Ricky
Aramiss Technology Limited

Singh, Somendra
Universal Business Services UK Ltd

Sinnott, Richard Patrick
Skin Defence Limited

Sitlani, Vijay Indroo
Seven Seas Limited

Skelham, Karen Susan
Cambridge Sensors Ltd

Skinner, Clare
Vivonics Preclinical Limited

Skinner, Matthew
Vivonics Preclinical Limited

Slack, Anthony William
Recassa Limited

Slater, Michael Robert
Merrimack Pharmaceuticals U.K. Ltd

Slator, Thomas
Y4U Limited

Small, David Raymond
Seborgo Limited

Smallman, Hugh
Protiaso Ltd

Smart, Andrew John
Severn Biotech Limited

Smejkal, Christopher, Dr
Medisante Limited

Smith, Adam, Hon
Microbiome Technologies Ltd

Smith, Andrew
Hichrom Limited

Smith, Anthony Hugh
Life Technologies BPD UK Ltd
Thermo Fisher Scientific Life Holdings

Smith, Cindy
Elixir Pure UK Limited

Smith, Donald
1nhaler Ltd

Smith, Graham Robert
Emerald Kalama Chemical Ltd

Smith, Henry Barnabas
London Surgical Limited

Smith, Jeremy Llewellyn
Nanomed Ltd

Smith, Jimmy Ray
PCCA (UK) Holdings Limited
PCCA Limited

Smith, John Hartley
Nutrition Group PLC

Smith, Michael Patrick
Zogenix Europe Limited

Smith, Nathan James
Millpledge Limited

Smith, Nicole
Seadbincold Ltd

Smith, Paul James, Professor
Biostatus Ltd

Smith, Renford
Afro Hair and Beauty International

Smith, Rosemarie
Shanmonrie Services Limited

Smith, Ross
Medicann Pharma (UK) Ltd

Smith, Sandra Kaye
Equalbrief Limited

Smith, Stephen Rushworth
Allergy Therapeutics PLC

Smoley, David Marcus
Diba Industries Limited

Smoukov, Stoyan, Dr
Letdrop Ltd

Sneddon, Samuel Redcliffe
TTS Manufacturing Limited
Transdermal Technology & Systems (TTS)

Soares, Bernardo
Janssen-Cilag Limited

Soderlund, Karin
Getinge UK Limited

Soerensen, Marinus
New Nordic Limited

Sokolov, Dmitry
PTGO Sover UK Limited

Solomon, Charmian
Chatfield Pharmaceuticals Ltd
Chelsea Drug & Chemical Co Ltd
D.D.S.A.Pharmaceuticals Ltd
Wallis Laboratory (Sales) Ltd

Solomon, David Louis Charles, Dr
Chatfield Pharmaceuticals Ltd
Chelsea Drug & Chemical Co Ltd
D.D.S.A.Pharmaceuticals Ltd
Wallis Laboratory (Sales) Ltd

Soma, Mitesh
Bioceuticals Group Ltd
Marine Labs Limited

Somaiya, Dhirendra
Aid Pharma Limited

Sommer, Andreas Olaf
Weleda (U.K.) Limited

Soriot, Pascal Claude Roland
Astrazeneca PLC

Sorota, Richard
Ranir Limited

Southern, Paul Martin
Stride-Davies Pharma Limited

Sparks, Lester David
PCCA (UK) Holdings Limited
PCCA Limited

Sparrow, Michael John Frederick
Resolution Chemicals Limited
Resolution Generics Limited

Spavold, Stanley William Leo
Algal Omega 3 Ltd

Speirs, Andrew William
Cupid Peptide Co Ltd

Speirs, Peter Alexander
Hikma Pharmaceuticals International
Hikma UK Limited

Spendler, Jonny
Nacur Healthcare Ltd

Spillner, Ralph Enno
Aptuit (Oxford) Limited

Spinney, Russell Bevier
Terumo BCT Ltd.

Spooner, Christopher Paul
IS Pharmaceuticals Limited
Sinclair Pharmaceuticals Ltd

Spuza, Michael, Dr
Bioneb PVT Limited

Lauras, Bruno Marie Pierre
E.R.Squibb & Sons Limited

Rishworth, Joanne Elizabeth
E.R.Squibb & Sons Limited

Squire, David Nicholas
Fulhold Pharma Limited

St Ledger, Simon
Rapid Nutrition PLC

Stackawitz, Jeremy Alexander
Alba Bioscience Limited

Stahel, Rolf
Ampha Limited

Stahl, Maria Delourdes
Tetraphase UK Limited

Stallibrass, Michael James Dahl
HAV Vaccines Limited

Stamato, Carmelo
Cross Healthcare Limited
S.C.A.C. Limited

Stead Deegan, Chloe
Cool Gell Limited

Stead Deegan, Hannah
Cool Gell Limited

Stead, Martin
Cool Gell Limited

Stead, Richard George
Qures Healthcare Limited
Workstead Limited

Steele, James Andrew
Skinlikes Limited

Steele, Sheila Joyce
Jim & Sheila Ltd.

Stefani, Michelangelo
Hologic Ltd.

Stefanov, Vasil
Bulgarian Healthy Products Ltd

Steffen, Robert Tobias
Oxford Supramolecular Biotechnology

Stemmer, Michael
Hygitech Limited

Stenning, Paul David
Balmy Fox Ltd

Stenqvist, Henrik
Swedish Orphan Biovitrum Ltd

Stephen, Shontell Sparvelyn
Sparsanctuary Limited

Stephens, Kevin Marc
Agroceutical Products Ltd
Bioextractions Wales Limited

Stephens, Kevin
Almac Pharma Services Limited

Stephenson, Lynn
Living Skin Care Limited

Stephenson, Michael
Sic Services Ltd

Stephenson, Paul
Living Skin Care Limited

Stephenson, Philip Glenn
Flavour-Tech UK Limited

Stern, Charles
Parkacre Enterprises Limited

Stern, John
Parkacre Enterprises Limited

Sterritt, Carl Andrew
Pharmakrysto Ltd

Stevens-Smith, Garry Lee
Unyte Pharma Ltd

Stevenson, Alison
Innov8tor Limited

Stier, Frank
Indivior UK Limited

Stockdale, Kevin Anthony
Eco Animal Health Ltd.

Stockdale, Paul Leslie
Oxford Biodynamics PLC

Stockham, Ben Michael Paul
Pfylori Limited
Vitra Pharmaceuticals Ltd

Stockham, Dorothea Janice
Pfertec Limited
Vitra Pharmaceuticals Ltd

Stockham, Michael Arthur
Pfertec Limited
Pfylori Limited
Vitra Pharmaceuticals Ltd

Stocks, Benjamin Denys William
Porvair PLC

Stoller, Joanne
Home Health Limited

Stoloff, Gregory Alan
Infirst Healthcare Limited

Stolzenberg, Lawrence
Resolution Chemicals Limited

Stone, Anthony
Swift Dent Engineering Services Ltd

Stone, Jane
Swift Dent Engineering Services Ltd

Stonris, Radjabu Mbumbu
Gesco Cosmetics Limited

Strauss, John
Biologix Laboratories Limited

Street-Docherty, Mark Andrew
Delta Diagnostics (UK) Ltd

Baxter, Gwendoline Harriette
H.E. Stringer (Perfumery) Ltd

Baxter, Stephen David
H.E. Stringer (Perfumery) Ltd

Stringer, Nicholas
Sussex Biologicals Ltd

Strobeck, Mark
Egalet Limited

Strzelecki, Josephine Mary
Biomed Supplies Limited

Stuteley, Sean Andrew
Coating Systems (International) Ltd

Styring, Leah Jane
Millpledge Limited

Subramani, Jagadish
Vivalabs Europe Limited

Sugano, Naoaki
Taisho Pharmaceutical (Europe) Ltd

Suissa, Zvi
Cancer Genetics Ltd

Sukumaran, Sheena
Langdales Limited
Sutherland Health Limited

Sule, Sampson
Pine Technologies Limited

Sully, Jordan Marc
Natural Dermatology Ltd

Sully, Robert James
Advanz Pharma (UK) Limited

Sultan, Ibraar Mahmood
Xeal Pharma Ltd

Summan, Dev Raj
Summan International Limited

Summan, Kc
Summan International Limited

Summan, Madhu Bala
Summan International Limited

Sumser Lupson, Karen Yvonne, Dr
Brewtaal Ltd

Suryanarayan, Geeta
RG and Co Limited

Swabey, Susan Margaret
Plus Orthopedics (UK) Limited

Sweeney, Paul Joseph
LDN Pharma Limited

Sweet, Andrew Timothy, Dr
Indigo Diagnostics Limited

Sweet, Ruth Margaret, Dr
Indigo Diagnostics Limited

Swift, Benjamin
GBBC Ltd

Swift, Nigel
AAH Pharmaceuticals Limited

Syed, Rob Shiper
Virgo Trade UK Limited

Syed, Waseem Ahmed
Vision Laboratories Limited

Symonds, Stephen Daniel
Envigo RMS (UK) Limited

Szekeres, Adrian
Plantgenic Ltd

Szymanski, Christopher
Biomedical Nutrition Ltd

Tagarao, Mylene
Fairywire Ltd

Tagg, Michael James
Quantum Pharmaceutical Limited

Taheripak, Gholamreza
Genomix Ltd

Taheripak, Mohammad
Genomix Ltd

Tahiyeu, Raushan
World Medicine Limited

Tahripak, Mehdi
Genomix Ltd

Tailor, Jayesh Dulabh
BVM Medical Limited

Tailor, Jayshree Jayesh
BVM Medical Limited

Tailor, Rakesh Chhaganlal
Contura Holdings Limited
Contura Limited

Takenoshita, Takashi
Livbio Limited

Talal Elmarghni Omran, Jrid
Thexo Pharmacial Limited

Talbot, Richard Ian
Millpledge Limited

Talsma, Claudia
Rosalique Skincare Limited
Salcura Limited

Tamiola, Kamil
Peptone Ltd

Tanabe, Sohei, Dr
Kowa Pharmaceutical Europe Co Ltd

Tankel, Simon Thomas Harry
Ark Technologies Ltd

Tarnakin, Oleksiy, Dr
Anna-Med (UK) Ltd

Tarnakina, Tetyana
Anna-Med (UK) Ltd

Tarras-Wahlberg, Bo Anders Caspersson
Baxter Healthcare Limited
Claris LifeSciences (UK) Ltd

Taslaq, Samer, Dr
Northumbria Pharma Ltd

Tasse, Daniel
Indivior PLC

Tate, Mary Joan
Alinter Limited
Kew Health and Beauty Limited
Neo Laboratories Limited
Norma Chemicals Limited
Savoy Laboratories (International)
Wallace Manufacturing Chemists Ltd
Wallace Pharma Limited

Tate, Simon Robert Geoffrey
Alinter Limited
Kew Health and Beauty Limited
Neo Laboratories Limited
Norma Chemicals Limited
Savoy Laboratories (International)
Wallace Manufacturing Chemists Ltd
Wallace Pharma Limited

Tate, Simon
Norma Chemicals (U K) Ltd

Tate, Susan Clare
Tate Pharma Ltd

Tavares Veloso, Bianca
Brazilian Kimberlite Clay Ltd

Tawiah, Evelyn
Shekinah Health Consultancy Ltd

Taylor, Amanda Jane
Traditional Pure Potions Ltd

Taylor, Danny
Soft Coughs Ltd

Taylor, Howard
Rosemont Pharmaceuticals Ltd

Taylor, Liam Mark
BBI Solutions OEM Limited

Taylor, Matthew
Silver Shell Limited

Taylor, Robert Peter
Vitabiotics Limited
Vitalogic Limited

Taylor, Sheena
Silver Shell Limited

Taylor, Simone Elizabeth
Manx Healthcare Limited
Manx Pharma Ltd

Taylor, Vincent
Enchanted Brave Limited

Tayub, Romin
Jela Pharm Limited

Teasdale, Roger Peter
Nuvision Biotherapies Limited

Tedham, Martin John
Wasdell Manufacturing Limited

Teisen, Elizabeth Anne
Teisen Products Limited

Teisen, Peter Henrik
Teisen Products Limited

Teisen, Sven Christian
Teisen Products Limited

Tejani, Amirali Sharif
LPC Medical (UK) Limited

Tejani, Karim Sharif Dharamshi
LPC Medical (UK) Limited
Rusco Limited

Tejani, Nazirali Sharif Dharamshi
LPC Medical (UK) Limited

Tejani, Salim Sharif Dharamshi
LPC Medical (UK) Limited
Rusco Limited

Telford, Nathan Lee
Cool Gell Limited

Tell, Werner
Tell Products, Limited

Temperley, Mary Clementine
Make Skincare Ltd.

Templeton, Alan
E J Templeton Limited

Templeton, Colin
E J Templeton Limited

Templeton, Elizabeth Janet
E J Templeton Limited

Templeton, John Barrie
E J Templeton Limited

Templeton, Sheena
E J Templeton Limited

Temucin, Ebru Can
Merck Sharp & Dohme Limited

Ter Hovakimyan, Aleksandr
SS Products International Ltd

Thacker, Ashwin
Rena Specials Limited

Thacker, Raju
Rena Specials Limited

Thain, Andrew Robert
Cost Saving Solutions Limited
LMP (UK) Limited

Thain, Debbie Sheila
Cost Saving Solutions Limited

Thakkar, Dip
Nutramax Ltd

Tharratt, John
Bio-Tech Solutions Limited

Thaxter, Shaun
Indivior PLC

Thierry, Eric Yvan
Primius Lab Limited

Thomas, Janette Ann, Dr
Dermatek Limited

Thomas, Janette, Dr
Pellis Care Limited

Thompson, Ian
LDN Pharma Limited

Thomsen, Bruce
Coast Science UK Limited

Thomsen, Jillian
Nektar Therapeutics UK Limited

Thornley, Ross John
HOCL Limited

Thornton, Robert William
Talley Environmental Care Ltd

Thorpe, Andrew Julian
Albumedix Ltd

Tickner, Nicola Lesley
Courtin and Warner Limited

Tideswell, Stuart John
ZO-X Ltd

Tierney, Donal Thomas Martin
Cross Chemicals UK Limited

Ting, Inghua
Brassard Limited

Tiwari, Santosh Kumar
Organic Lifecare Ltd.

Tobin, James
Oxford Immunotec Global PLC

Toby, Martina Linda Simone
Venture Healthcare Ltd

Tonge, David Michael
Isola Manufacturing Co.(Wythenshawe)

Tonge, Peter Richard
Isola Manufacturing Co.(Wythenshawe)

Toombs, Ruth Vanessa
TCS Biosciences Limited

Smith, Stuart Christopher
The Toothsmith Limited

Topp, Adam
Humn Pharmaceuticals (UK) Ltd

Torok, Eva
Custom Pharmaceuticals Limited

Torrance, Christopher John, Dr
Exonate Limited

Tourette, John
Quantum Biomed Farms PLC

Tovey, Christopher John
GW Pharma Limited

Tran, Diep Duc
Diep Tran Consultancy Ltd

Traustadottir, Elin
Wellness Lab Ltd

Traynor, David Thomas
Winchpharma (Consumer Healthcare) Ltd

Traynor, Emma
Zink Tattoo Care Limited

Tregoning, Marianne Jane
100% Organics Limited

Treherne, Jonathan Mark, Dr
Nuvision Biotherapies Limited

Triguero, Jose Luis
CBD Pharma Ltd

Troche, Clemens Johannes
Chirotech Technology Limited
Dr Reddy's Laboratories (UK) Ltd
Dr. Reddy's Laboratories (EU) Ltd

Trost, Timothy
Chimerix UK Limited

Trott, Nicholas Mark
Scottish Bioenergy Cooperative Ventures
Tantillus Synergy Limited

Troutt, Peter
Elanco UK AH Limited

Trowbridge, John Barry
International Scientific Supplies

Tschudin, Marie-France
Novartis Pharmaceuticals UK Ltd

Tucker, Mark Rupert
TTS Manufacturing Limited
Transdermal Technology & Systems (TTS)

Tudor, Cameron John
Premax Europe Limited

Tuomey, David Spencer
QOL Therapeutics UK Limited

Turner, David John
Biofortuna Ltd

Turner, Julie Ann
Pharm-Assist (Regulatory Services)

Turner, Marc Leighton, Professor
Fortingall Advanced Therapeutics Ltd.
Fortingall Therapeutics International

Turner, Pamela Ann
Geryon Pharma Limited

Turner, Robert
Abtek (Biologicals) Limited

Turner, Stuart Charles
Abtek (Biologicals) Limited

Twist, Geoffrey John
Roche Products Limited

Twomey, Richard
Medlock Medical Limited
Molnlycke Health Care Limited

Tyler, Christopher Patric
Porvair PLC

Tyrakis, Petros
Cambridge Innovation Group Ltd

Uddin, Ashraf
GM Biopharma Ltd

Ueda, Yoshiro
Nikkiso UK Co., Ltd.

Ujiie, Shin
Eisai Manufacturing Limited

Uka, Onyekachi
Festus Olatoye & Onyekachi Uka London

Ullah, Rehan
Regent Pharmaceuticals Limited

Ume, Sonny Armstrong Marizu
Nnadi's Healthcare and Pharmaceuticals

Upadhyay, Kaushik
Piramal Critical Care Limited

Upton, David James
Church & Dwight UK Limited

Ur-Rehman, Muneeb
Emergencypharm Ltd.

O'Brien, Catherine
The Urban Homestead London Ltd

Utley, Emily Jane
TCS Biosciences Limited

Uysal, Serkan
Rotapharm Pharmaceutical Ltd
World Medicine Pharmaceutical Ltd

Vadukul, Bharat Jivan
BHR Pharmaceuticals Limited

Vaghjiani, Govind Samji
Invictus R & D Ltd
Percuro Medica Ltd

Vaghjiani, Hitesh Govind
Invictus R & D Ltd

Vaghjiani, Kamlesh Govind
Invictus R & D Ltd

Vaines, Peter Stephen
Vitabiotics Limited

Valentine, Matthew John
Therakind Limited

Van Alstyne, David Christian Daniel
Scottish Bioenergy Cooperative Ventures
Tantillus Synergy Limited

Van Alstyne, Polly Marston
Scottish Bioenergy Cooperative Ventures
Tantillus Synergy Limited

Van Boxmeer, Charles Henry
Georganics Ltd

Van Der Westhuizen, Petrus Phillippus
Alliance Medical Molecular Imaging
Alliance Medical Radiopharmacy Ltd

Van Herwijnen, Jan Paul
EVL Biologicals Ltd

Van Herwijnen, Johannes Robertus
Bio Provide 18 Ltd
Bio Provide 19 Ltd
Bio Provide 20 Ltd
Bio Provide Ltd
EVL Biologicals 23 Ltd
EVL Biologicals Ltd

Van Hoof, Johan
Vaccine Manufacturing and Innovation Centre UK

Van Hoorebeke, Olivier Gregory J
MW Encap Limited

Van Niekerk, Deon Ross
Derma Solutions Ltd

Van Niekerk, Scott David
Derma Solutions Ltd

Van Wegberg, Pascal Jean Jacques Petronelle
Custom Powders Limited

Varalwar, Sandeep
Vivimed Labs Europe Ltd

Varalwar, Sanketh
Vivimed Labs Europe Ltd

Varalwar, Santosh
Vivimed Labs Europe Ltd

Varalwar, Subhash
Vivimed Labs Europe Ltd

Varma, Satish
Fermenta Biotech (UK) Limited

Vas, Zsolt
Engelpharma UK Limited

Veale, Kimiko
Hannah V Limited

Veerramani, Radha Veirramani
Fourrts (UK) Pharmacare Ltd

Veerramani, Sekharipuram Viswanathan
Fourrts (UK) Pharmacare Ltd

Velastegui Suquillo, Edison Rodolfo
Aptitud Pharma Ltd

Venderbeken, Vesta
Rapid Nutrition PLC

Venkatesan, Gopalakrishnan
Pinewood Healthcare Limited
Wockhardt UK Limited

Vericat Vidal, Miquel
ND Pharma & Biotech Ltd

Verma, Mahesh Kumar
M V Locums Limited

Vernois, Joel Didier Claude
T-In Medical Limited

Verrall, Raymond Charles
Moroccan Natural Resources Ltd

Verstreken, Jan Valeer
Hologic Ltd.

Vieth, Christopher
Elemis Limited

Viggars, Julian
Blackley 2010 Limited

Villanueva, Leny
Retrobot Ltd

Virdi, Harminder Singh
LRC Products Limited

Vitug, Kezia Jayn
Roche Products Limited

Vladova, Anastasia
Vapour Chef Ltd

Vo, Hoa MY Thi
Diep Tran Consultancy Ltd

Vo-TA, Vinh-Thang
Calla Lily Personal Care Ltd

Vohra, Samir
Blackpool Medicines Limited

Von Alvensleben, Konstantin
Intrapharm Laboratories Ltd
Peckforton Pharmaceuticals Ltd

Von Bergen, Scot Frederick
Point International Limited

Vrhovec, David
Norton Healthcare Limited
Teva Pharma Holdings Limited
Teva Pharmaceuticals Limited
Teva UK Limited

Waddicar, Graeme Boyd
Aroma World Limited

Wadsworth, Charles Philip
Chempro Limited
D.D.D. Limited
Dendron Limited
Fleet Laboratories Limited
Van Vleck and Olivers Limited

Waeschle, Sascha Adrian
Cannerald Group Ltd

Waide, Andrew Keith
AWA Export Limited

Waite, Lorrenda
Shea By Day Ltd

Walker, Adam
Chemagain Limited

Walker, Ann
EVC Compounding Ltd

Walker, Kyle Matthew
Hyperion Biotechnology Limited

Walker, Neal
Aclaris Therapeutics International

Walker, William Ernest
Hyperion Biotechnology Limited

Wallenberg, Marcus
Astrazeneca PLC

Walsh, Brendan Stuart
UK Steriles Ltd

Walsh, Kirk
Catalent U.K. Swindon Zydis Ltd
Catalent UK Supply Chain Ltd
Columbia Laboratories (UK) Ltd
Molecular Profiles Ltd

Walsh, Patrick
Avista Holding Co., Ltd.

Walters, David Edward
Micropharm Limited

Walters, Howard
Taylor of London Limited

Walton, Andrew Scott
Oxford Immunotec Global PLC

Wang, Fangqian
Oxford Supramolecular Biotechnology

Wang, Ke
Edinburgh Nano Limited
Edinburgh Nanotechnology Ltd

Wang, Shunqi
Donglun Limited

Wang, Shuxiang
Pharma Syntech Ltd

Wang, Yichen
Yic Bio Ltd.

Wang, Yu
Donglun Limited

Want, Clare
Combe International Limited

Wanty, Philippe Maurice Henri
Limehurst Limited

Ward, Ellen
Zink Tattoo Care Limited

Ward, Simon Julian, Dr
Spear Therapeutics Limited

Wardini, Charbel
Lea Pharma Limited

Warmington, Graham Francis
Bio-Life International Limited
Medicleanse Limited
Nillergen Limited

Warneford, Brian Richard
Ecohydra Technologies Limited

Warner, Christopher Robert
Courtin and Warner Limited

Warner, David Alan
Courtin and Warner Limited

Warriner, Richard Earl
Neo Laboratories Limited
Norma Chemicals Limited
Savoy Laboratories (International)
Wallace Manufacturing Chemists Ltd

Wasman, Jane
Acorda Therapeutics Limited

Wastnage, Richard John
Qualasept Holdings Limited
Qualasept Limited

Waterfield, Richard Jeremy
Ventarc Limited

Watkins, Brett Alan
Luoda UK Limited

Watkins, Max Scott, Dr
Vita Animal Health Ltd
Vita Bee Health Ltd

Watkins, Maxwell Scott, Dr
Vita (Europe) Limited

Watson, Alan Cecil
Ithonpharma Ltd

Watson, Ann-Marie
Herman Claude Ltd

Watson, Benjamin Nicholas
Hyperdrug Pharmaceuticals Ltd

Watson, Christine Jennifer
Hyperdrug Pharmaceuticals Ltd

Watson, Emma
Ithonpharma Ltd

Watson, Geoffrey Walton
Hyperdrug Pharmaceuticals Ltd

Watson, John Geoffrey Frederick
Hyperdrug Pharmaceuticals Ltd

Watson, Julie Ann
Ithonpharma Ltd

Watson, Paul Aaron
Ithonpharma Ltd

Watson, Paul
Northumbria Pharma Ltd

Watson, Ryan
Ithonpharma Ltd

Watt, Christopher Dean
Microgenetics Limited
Pharmaxo Pharmacy Services Ltd
Qualasept Holdings Limited
Qualasept Limited

Watt, Maria Ann
Qualasept Holdings Limited

Watts, Garry
Juno Britain Ltd

Wayne, Marc
Spectrum Biomedical UK Limited

Webb, Jason
Arcadia Pharma Limited

Webb, Martin Barry
Talley Environmental Care Ltd

Webb, Sean Edwin Leonard George
Isca Biochemicals Limited

Webber, Paul James Hatton
Cellpath USA Limited

Webber, Peter James
Cellpath USA Limited

Webber, Philip Leslie John
Cellpath USA Limited

Wederman, Hans Jurgen Peter
Fulhold Pharma Limited

Wei, Xueli
Huayawei Biomedical Co Ltd

Weir, Robert James
Hunger Control Limited

Weis, Thomas
Indivior EU Limited
Indivior UK Limited

Welby, Anne
Welby Healthcare Limited

Welby, Stephen Michael
Welby Healthcare Limited

Wendel, Bruce Jeffrey
Prometic Pharma SMT Limited

Westcott, Guy James Roger
Biologix Laboratories Limited

Westley, Gavin David
Medical Export Co Ltd

Weymouth-Wilson, Alexander Charles, Dr
Dextra Laboratories Limited
NZP UK Limited

Whait, Charles
Ecohydra Technologies Limited

Whalen, James Lawrence
Bio Pure Technology Ltd

Whall, Richard David
BCM Limited
BCM Specials Limited

Wharton, Keith Thomas
Xcelonce Limited

Whatley, Paul Charles
Sarakan Limited

Wheatley, Clement Trevor
Cellpath USA Limited

Wheeler, David Colin
Ukann Limited

Whelan, Ian
Avisius Research Limited

Whitaker, Roger Philip
Snor-Ring Limited

White, Emily Catherine
Ace Interventional Medical Ltd

White, Gwenan Mair
AbbVie Australasia Holdings Ltd

White, Natalie
Dynamik Products Ltd

White, Peter John Pitt, Dr
Nova Bio-Pharma Technologies Ltd
Nova Laboratories Limited

Whitehead, Martin John
Castex Products Limited

Whitehead, Thomas James
Castex Products Limited

Whitehouse, Karen
Newmed Consultancy Limited

Whitehouse, Norman
Newmed Consultancy Limited

Whiteley, Lynne
Dalkeith Laboratories Limited

Whiteley, Richard John
Swann-Morton (Europe) Limited

Whitney, Brian John
Technical Textile Services Ltd

Whyard, Stephen
Pharma QP Solutions Ltd

Wigmore, Alexander James
Hewlett Healthcare Limited

Wikstrom, Ake Gunnar
Bard Pharmaceuticals Limited
Napp Pharmaceutical Group Ltd
Napp Pharmaceutical Holdings Ltd

Wilcox, Mark Harvey, Professor
Phico Therapeutics Limited

Wilder, Howard John
Onsite Diagnostics Limited
Wildrush Limited

Wilding, Mark Andrew
Lumibio Ltd

Wilkinson, Alan Shaun, Dr
Biopharma Stability Testing Laboratory

Wilkinson, Brian Andrew
Atlantia UK Ltd

Wilkinson, Kevin John
Captium Limited

Wilkinson, Kier Timothy
Proteintech Europe Limited

Wilkinson, Peter Robert
Parakill Limited

Williams, David Jeffreys
Oxford Biodynamics PLC

Williams, Diane
Byrom (South Wales) Limited

Williams, Gareth Arran
TCS Biosciences Limited

Williams, Kawan
Gitflex Ltd

Williams, Peter
Byrom (South Wales) Limited

Williams, Richard, Dr
Cherwell Therapeutics Ltd.

Williams, Russell David
Bell,Sons & Co.(Druggists) Ltd

Williamson, Derek Martin
Bioneb PVT Limited

Williamson, Michael
KMX Healthcare Ltd

Wills, Simon
Nutrapharm Ltd

Wilson, Anthony Leonard
Intelligent Fabric Technologies Holdings

Wilson, Duncan James
Aspen Medical Europe Limited

Wilson, Jonathan
Accord-UK Ltd

Wilson, Patrick Russell
Bach Flower Remedies Limited
Nelson & Russell Holdings Ltd

Wilson, Robert Nelson
Bach Flower Remedies Limited
Maxwellia Ltd
Nelson & Russell Holdings Ltd
Nelsons Aura Limited

Wilson, Stuart Mark, Dr
Microsens Biophage Limited

Winchester, Peter John
Alliance Medical Molecular Imaging

Winslade, Jacqueline
Therakind Limited

Winsor, Paul Jonathan
T-In Medical Limited

Witheridge, Reginald Laurence Kenneth
Thompson and Capper Limited

Wohlstadter, Nadine
Hyperion Catalysis EU Limited

Wohlstadter, Samuel
Hyperion Catalysis EU Limited

Wolfe, Vaughn
Bamford & Wolfe Ltd

Wood, Christopher, Dr
Protiaso Ltd

Wood, Philip Neil
Millpledge Limited

Woodings, Matthew Robert
Brunel Healthcare Manufacturing Ltd

Woodrow, Margaret Evelyn Anne
Aura Fragrances Limited

Woodrow, Michael Norman
Aura Fragrances Limited

Woodward, Ben Peter
Lipcote & Co Limited

Woodward, Charles Edward
Lipcote & Co Limited
Matthews & Wilson Limited

Wootres, Cathay Ann
Lewtress Natural Health Ltd

Wotton, Carrie
Thornit Canker Ltd.

Wright, Karl
Prime Test Limited

Wright, Lee
Encapsula Limited

Wright, Richard
Luxury CBD Oils Ltd

Wright, Sam
Prime Test Limited

Wrighton, David Terence
ESW Healthcare Limited

Wrighton, Joanne Patricia
ESW Healthcare Limited

Wrighton-Smith, Peter James, Dr
Oxford Immunotec Global PLC
Oxford Immunotec Limited

Wronski, Krzysztof Mariusz
Skin Cell Labs Limited

Wu, Bor-Wen
Designerx Europe Limited

Wulfert, Markus
Euro OTC Pharma UK Limited

Wurdak, Heiko
Re-Vire Limited

Aujla, Sukhdave Singh
John Wyeth & Brother Limited

Franklin, Ian Eric
John Wyeth & Brother Limited

Harnett, Denise Jean
John Wyeth & Brother Limited

Mount, Jacqueline Ann
John Wyeth & Brother Limited

Nordkamp, Hendrikus Hermannus
John Wyeth & Brother Limited

Pearson, Edwin James
John Wyeth & Brother Limited

Seller, Colin Malcolm
John Wyeth & Brother Limited

Wykeman, Nicolas Alexander Ulrich
Allergy Therapeutics (UK) Ltd
Allergy Therapeutics PLC

Wynn, Andrew Thomas
PW Green UK II Limited

Wynne, Neil
C P Pharmaceuticals Limited
Wallis Laboratory Limited
Wallis Licensing Limited

Wynter, Salem Ayesha
Root2tip Haircare Solutions Ltd

Xu, Minghui
Fine Contract Research Limited
Fine Organics Limited

Yablonka, Uri
Brainstorm Cell Therapeutics UK Ltd

Yakkati, Srujan
Reddy Quality Services Ltd

Yamaguchi, Kenichi
Taisho Pharmaceutical (Europe) Ltd

Yamamoto, Masato
Fujifilm Diosynth Biotechnologies UK

Yamoa, Akosua
NHC Limited

Yang, Shoufeng, Dr
Varydose Limited

Yaqoob, Isma
Lochview Pharm Ltd.

Yaqoob, Mohammed
Muhammad 786 Limited

Yaqoob, Muhammad, Dr
Interaction Chempharm Ltd

Yard, Jon Barrie
Getinge UK Limited

Yarrow, Heather Jennifer
Diomed Developments Limited

Yarrow, Michael Jonathan
Dermal Laboratories Limited
Diomed Developments Limited

Yarrow, Nicola Irene
Diomed Developments Limited

Yasuno, Tatsuyuki
Eisai Manufacturing Limited

Yateman, Robert William
Mentholatum Co Ltd

Ye, Wei
Vivi Yeah Limited

Yeuby Sohanna, Aquilar Cuevas
Medina Corp. Ltd

Yon Hin, Bernadette, Dr
Cambridge Sensors Ltd

Yoor, Brian
Abbott Iberian Investments Ltd
Abbott Vascular Devices (2) Ltd
Knoll UK Investments Unlimited

Young, Christopher John
Seven Seas Limited

Young, Iain Stewart Anderson
Algae Biotechnology Products Ltd

Youssef, Ahmad, Dr
Technical & General Limited

Yussouf, Saba
Mayfair Ventures Management Ltd

Yusufu, James Shwarpshaka
Dodi Enterprise Ltd

Zaat, Ralph Antonius, Dr
Kowa Pharmaceutical Europe Co Ltd

Zabier, Tabassam
Summer Healthcare Limited

Zajicek, George Thomas
Sarissa Biomedical Limited

Zakirullah, Mohammed
UK Seven Seas Pharma Limited

Zaltzman, Richard
London Surgical Limited

Zarrehparvar, Maziar
Prothea-X Limited

Zartaloudi, Kyriaki
Sandine Zartaux Holding Ltd
Swiss Pharma Dynamic Ltd

More Gordon, Harry
G.H. Zeal Limited

Coles, Joseph Tidboald
G.H. Zeal Limited

Excell, Geoffrey Robert
G.H. Zeal Limited

Zeine, Imtishal Whitney Zina
Rescued By Nature Limited

Zhang, Jack
Amphastar UK Ltd
International Medication Systems (U.K.)

Zhu, Lihua
Shanghai Neopharm Co., Ltd

Zlatkus, Lizebeth Herbst
Indivior PLC

Zobedey, Roza Imill
Amroz Pharm Limited

Zobedey, Yasmin Wessal
Pharmazy Limited

Zota, Moxesh
Zota Healthcare Limited

Zou, Meimei
Alphacells Biotechnologies Ltd

This page is intentionally left blank

Standard Industrial Classification

excluding

Manufacture of basic pharmaceutical products

and

Manufacture of pharmaceutical preparations

01110 Growing of cereals (except rice), leguminous crops and oil seeds
CBD Pharma Ltd
Quantum Biomed Farms PLC

01160 Growing of fibre crops
Quantum Biomed Farms PLC

01280 Growing of spices, aromatic, drug and pharmaceutical crops [13]
Alhaddag Phrma Ltd
Aventa International Corporation Ltd
Cannerald Group Ltd
East West Naturals Limited
Euroclinical Ltd
Jini Ltd
Kew Organic Limited
Medicaleaf Limited
Medicann Pharma (UK) Ltd
Redlight Exchange Ltd
Rutland Biodynamics Limited
Spectrum Biomedical UK Limited
Tomorrow Biotech Ltd

01290 Growing of other perennial crops
Cornish Lavender Limited
Rutland Biodynamics Limited

01300 Plant propagation
Cornish Lavender Limited

01490 Raising of other animals
Therapi Natural Products Ltd

01500 Mixed farming
Twisbee (UK) Limited

01629 Support activities for animal production (other than farm animal boarding)
Goat Nutrition Limited
Vita Animal Health Ltd

01630 Post-harvest crop activities
Oat Services Limited

08930 Extraction of salt
New Cheshire Salt Works Ltd

09100 Support activities for petroleum and natural gas mining
Unconventional E & P Services Ltd

09900 Support activities for other mining and quarrying
Key Empire Resources (UK) Ltd

10110 Processing and preserving of meat
Candles UK Ltd

10320 Manufacture of fruit and vegetable juice
Revive Us Limited

10410 Manufacture of oils and fats
Cannabidiol UK Ltd
Paradox Omega Oils Ltd

10612 Manufacture of breakfast cereals and cereals-based food
Oat Services Limited

10821 Manufacture of cocoa and chocolate confectionery
Festus Olatoye & Onyekachi Uka London
Ernest Jackson & Co. Limited

10822 Manufacture of sugar confectionery
Ernest Jackson & Co. Limited
Lofthouse of Fleetwood Limited

10831 Tea processing
Booteatox Limited
Wellness Lab Ltd
Your Noo Edge Ltd.

10832 Production of coffee and coffee substitutes
Cost Saving Solutions Limited
Think Noo Limited
Your Noo Edge Ltd.

10840 Manufacture of condiments and seasonings
Hedgarth Ltd
Klinge Chemicals Limited

10860 Manufacture of homogenized food preparations and dietetic food
Booteatox Limited
Farm Bionics Ltd
Glycanova UK Limited
Musclemantra Ltd
Samritz Healthcare Ltd

10890 Manufacture of other food products n.e.c. [29]
A Shroom with a View Ltd
Adam Project Ltd
Booteatox Limited
Cannabidiol UK Ltd
Cornish Lavender Limited
Edward Daniel Limited
Essential Nutrition Limited
Farm Bionics Ltd
Florence Health & Beauty Ltd
Green Manufacturing Partners Ltd
Heavenly Herb Co Ltd.
Hyperbiotics Corp Ltd
Hyperbiotics PLC
Kew Organic Limited
Langdales Limited
Lifeplan Products Limited
Microbiome Technologies Ltd
Musclemantra Ltd
Nano and Nature Pharma Ltd
Nutrapharm Ltd
Nutridote Ltd
Phytacol Limited
Quest Ingredients Limited
Revive Us Limited
Seven Seas Healthcare Limited
Think Noo Limited
This Product Ltd
Vitane Pharma Limited
Wellness Lab Ltd

10910 Manufacture of prepared feeds for farm animals
GM Globalhealth Ltd
Goat Nutrition Limited

10920 Manufacture of prepared pet foods
Goat Nutrition Limited

11010 Distilling, rectifying and blending of spirits
St Andrews Botanics Limited

11070 Manufacture of soft drinks; production of mineral waters and other bottled waters
Ad Hoque Ltd
Microbiome Technologies Ltd
Nutrapharm Ltd
Pharmaco Group Limited
SmithKline Beecham Limited

13910 Manufacture of knitted and crocheted fabrics
Intelligent Fabric Technologies Holdings

13923 manufacture of household textiles
United Colors of London (UK) Ltd

15120 Manufacture of luggage, handbags and the like, saddlery and harness
Nia Nova Ltd

15200 Manufacture of footwear
Nia Nova Ltd
United Colors of London (UK) Ltd

17211 Manufacture of corrugated paper and paperboard, sacks and bags
Pharmach Ltd

17220 Manufacture of household and sanitary goods and of toilet requisites
Pharmlife Industry Ltd

18121 Manufacture of printed labels
Pharmach Ltd

18129 Printing n.e.c.
Reelvision Print Limited

20120 Manufacture of dyes and pigments
Novartis Grimsby Limited
Vivimed Labs Europe Ltd

20130 Manufacture of other inorganic basic chemicals
BBI Solutions OEM Limited
Ideal Manufacturing Limited
JSN Chemicals Limited
Linosa Limited
Nektar Therapeutics UK Limited
New Cheshire Salt Works Ltd
Novartis Grimsby Limited
Vivimed Labs Europe Ltd

20140 Manufacture of other organic basic chemicals
Amarevida Limited
Biocon Pharma UK Limited
Bioextractions Wales Limited
Fine Contract Research Limited
Fine Organics Limited
Interaction Chempharm Ltd
JSN Chemicals Limited
Jasmine.Touch Ltd
Nektar Therapeutics UK Limited

20160 Manufacture of plastics in primary forms
Novartis Grimsby Limited

20200 Manufacture of pesticides and other agrochemical products
Corpus Nostrum Limited
Emerald Kalama Chemical Ltd
Fine Contract Research Limited
Fine Organics Limited
Point International Limited
Vita Animal Health Ltd

20411 Manufacture of soap and detergents [11]
CKC Aromatherapy Beauty Products Ltd
Farasha-Cosmetics Ltd
GM Globalhealth Ltd
Hutrade Ltd.
Ideal Manufacturing Limited
Kalula Cosmetics Ltd
Little Green Beehive Ltd
Ochil Skincare Co Ltd
Mimi Pisano Limited
Stockcare Limited
Zomi Ltd

20412 Manufacture of cleaning and polishing preparations
Thornton & Ross Limited

20420 Manufacture of perfumes and toilet preparations [20]
Acarrier Limited
BCM Limited
Combe International Limited
Cool Gell Limited
Dach Cosmeceutics Limited
Dermapharm Skincare Limited
Elemis Limited
Emerald Kalama Chemical Ltd
Pierre Fabre Limited
Farasha-Cosmetics Ltd
Ferndale Pharmaceuticals Ltd
HBNatura Ltd
Little Green Beehive Ltd
Pharmaco Group Limited
Phytacol Limited
Sandine Zartaux Holding Ltd
Skin Defence Limited
H.E. Stringer (Perfumery) Ltd
Swiss Pharma Dynamic Ltd
Thread and Co UK Limited

20530 Manufacture of essential oils
Emerald Kalama Chemical Ltd
Essenfuture Ltd
Keziah Ltd
Paradox Omega Oils Ltd
Quantum Biomed Farms PLC
Retrogrow Limited
Selepharm Ltd
H.E. Stringer (Perfumery) Ltd
Thread and Co UK Limited

20590 Manufacture of other chemical products n.e.c. [22]
Asterisk LifeSciences Ltd
BBI Solutions OEM Limited
Biokemix Worldwide Ltd
Cod Beck Blenders Limited
Exactmer Limited
FV Supplement Ltd
Pierre Fabre Limited
Hahydra Technologies Ltd
Hyperion Biotechnology Limited
JSN Chemicals Limited
Langeland Ltd
Letdrop Ltd
Mirroman Ltd
N.T. Laboratories Limited
ND Pharma & Biotech Ltd
Pharma Syntech Ltd
Point International Limited
SH Snakes UK Ltd.
SK Network Ltd
Smith & Nephew PLC
H.E. Stringer (Perfumery) Ltd
Vivimed Labs Europe Ltd

22190 Manufacture of other rubber products
SS Products International Ltd

22220 Manufacture of plastic packing goods
Pharmach Ltd

22290 Manufacture of other plastic products
Castex Products Limited
Curis Life Ltd

23440 Manufacture of other technical ceramic products
Porvair PLC

23990 Manufacture of other non-metallic mineral products n.e.c.
Bob Martin (UK) Limited

24200 Manufacture of tubes, pipes, hollow profiles and related fittings, of steel
Gimews Welding Limited

24530 Casting of light metals
Castex Products Limited

25210 Manufacture of central heating radiators and boilers
Teisen Products Limited

25730 Manufacture of tools
Castex Products Limited

25990 Manufacture of other fabricated metal products n.e.c.
Porvair PLC

26120 Manufacture of loaded electronic boards
Brown Exclusive (Worldwide) Ltd

26200 Manufacture of computers and peripheral equipment
Prime Test Limited

26400 Manufacture of consumer electronics
Brown Exclusive (Worldwide) Ltd

26600 Manufacture of irradiation, electromedical and electrotherapeutic equipment
Panaomics Limited
Prime Medical Equipment Ltd
Well & Well Pharma UK Ltd
Wenimed Ltd

26701 Manufacture of optical precision instruments
Medina Corp. Ltd
Porvair PLC
Prothea-X Limited

27200 Manufacture of batteries and accumulators
Orb Global Ltd

27310 Manufacture of fibre optic cables
Langeland Ltd

27520 Manufacture of non-electric domestic appliances
Fluss Limited

28290 Manufacture of other general-purpose machinery n.e.c.
Medina Corp. Ltd
World Max Power Enterprise Ltd

28990 Manufacture of other special-purpose machinery n.e.c.
Maklary Ltd
World Max Power Enterprise Ltd

29100 Manufacture of motor vehicles
Orb Global Ltd

31090 Manufacture of other furniture
Maklary Ltd
United Colors of London (UK) Ltd

32300 Manufacture of sports goods
Brown Exclusive (Worldwide) Ltd
Nutramax Ltd
Shekinah Health Consultancy Ltd

32500 Manufacture of medical and dental instruments and supplies [23]
Advanz Pharma (UK) Limited
Anna-Med (UK) Ltd
Appex Ltd
Avanzcare Limited
Bioceutics UK Ltd
Cambridge Advanced Technologies Ltd
Comed Healthcare UK Ltd
E-Breathe Ltd.
E.P.G Pharma Ltd
Fluss Limited
Genomix Ltd
Global Healthcare Innovations Ltd
Invizius Limited
Microfluidx Ltd
Morningside Pharmaceuticals Ltd
Prothea-X Limited
Samritz Healthcare Ltd
Shellmarks Limited
Smith & Nephew PLC
Solarius UK & Overseas Limited
Wenimed Ltd
World Max Power Enterprise Ltd
Zomi Ltd

32990 Other manufacturing n.e.c. [19]
Acle Urban Gardens Limited
Asaya Cosmeceuticals Limited
Brewtaal Ltd
CKC Aromatherapy Beauty Products Ltd
Elena's Nature Collection Ltd
Exactmer Limited
Hyperion Catalysis EU Limited
Jim & Sheila Ltd.
Kew Organic Limited
Bob Martin (UK) Limited
My Shea Limited
N.T. Laboratories Limited
Nia Nova Ltd
Pine Technologies Limited
SS Products International Ltd
Therapi Natural Products Ltd
Vita (Europe) Limited
Vita Animal Health Ltd
Vita Bee Health Ltd

33190 Repair of other equipment
Medina Corp. Ltd

36000 Water collection, treatment and supply
Vivi Yeah Limited

38220 Treatment and disposal of hazardous waste
Longwood Medevice Ltd

41100 Development of building projects
Cool Gell Limited

42990 Construction of other civil engineering projects n.e.c.
Candles UK Ltd

43999 Other specialised construction activities n.e.c.
Candles UK Ltd
NKK Investments Limited

45112 Sale of used cars and light motor vehicles
Ad Hoque Ltd

45190 Sale of other motor vehicles
Virtual Reaction Limited

46110 Agents selling agricultural raw materials, livestock, textile raw materials and semi-finished goods
CBD Pharma Ltd

46120 Agents involved in the sale of fuels, ores, metals and industrial chemicals
Virtual Reaction Limited

46180 Agents specialised in the sale of other particular products
Ace Interventional Medical Ltd
BVM Medical Limited
Indigo Diagnostics Limited
Sonifar Pharma Expert Limited
Sussex Biologicals Ltd
Xanadu Valley Limited

46190 Agents involved in the sale of a variety of goods
Q Health Direct Ltd
Rhino Education Ltd

46350 Wholesale of tobacco products
Vapour Chef Ltd

46380 Wholesale of other food, including fish, crustaceans and molluscs
Q Health Direct Ltd

46390 Non-specialised wholesale of food, beverages and tobacco
Life on Healthcare Ltd

46439 Wholesale of radio, television goods & electrical household appliances (other than records, tapes, CDs)
World Medicine Ophthalmics Ltd

46450 Wholesale of perfume and cosmetics [25]
Afro Hair and Beauty International
Asaya Cosmeceuticals Limited
Atlantis Research Limited
Beegood Enterprises Limited
Brazilian Kimberlite Clay Ltd
Dermaperfetca Ltd
Ether Cosmetics Ltd
Evorin Pharma Limited
Florence Health & Beauty Ltd
GBBC Ltd
Great British Bee Co Ltd
Hahydra Technologies Ltd
Hydro Fresh Ltd
Ibeautify Ltd
Muamko Uzuri Limited
Nocov Ltd
Pharmacare International Ltd
Royce Health Sciences Ltd
SK Network Ltd
SKN-RG Ltd
Sandine Zartaux Holding Ltd
Skindoc Formula Limited
Solarius UK & Overseas Limited
Swiss Pharma Dynamic Ltd
Winchpharma (Consumer Healthcare) Ltd

46460 Wholesale of pharmaceutical goods [158]

21CEC PX Pharm Ltd
A1 Pharmaceuticals Holdings Ltd
AAH Pharmaceuticals Limited
Accord Healthcare Limited
Akvion Limited
Al Razi Pharma UK Ltd
Alhaddag Phrma Ltd
Amarox Limited
Ambe Limited
Apotheke San Biagio SRL Ltd
Aptitud Pharma Ltd
Asaya Cosmeceuticals Limited
Astrazeneca PLC
Atnahs Pharma US Limited
Auramedicann Ltd
Avanzcare Limited
Aventa International Corporation Ltd
Beegood Enterprises Limited
Bioavexia Ltd
Bioceutics UK Ltd
Biocon Pharma UK Limited
Blackpool Medicines Limited
Bolton Pharmaceutical Company 100 Ltd
Boost Hair Limited
Britpharma UK Limited
Bulgarian Healthy Products Ltd
CM & D Pharma Limited
Cambridge Healthcare Supplies 2012
Cambridge Healthcare Supplies Ltd
Cannerald Group Ltd
Chela Animal Health Limited
Clinigen Group PLC
Clyde Valley Cannaceuticals Ltd
Corpus Nostrum Limited
Crescent Pharma Limited
Cutman Ltd
Cuttlefish Limited
DCMP 8E Cepac Limited
Dil More Remedies UK Ltd
Dong Hwa UK Ltd
Dr Pradeep Reddy's Laboratories (UK & EU)
Dynamic Development Laboratories Co Ltd
E.P.G Pharma Ltd
EVC Compounding Ltd
Elanco UK AH Limited
Engelpharma UK Limited
Ennogen Healthcare Ltd
Ennogen Pharma Ltd
Essential Pharma Limited
Evorin Pharma Limited
Florence Health & Beauty Ltd
Fluidx Limited
Focus Pharma Holdings Limited
Focus Pharmaceuticals Limited
GBBC Ltd
GM Biopharma Ltd
Geistlich Sons Limited
Gelu Life Limited
Genus Pharmaceuticals Limited
Geoorganics Limited
Go-Kyo Science Limited
Graviti Healthcare Limited
Great British Bee Co Ltd
Hashmats Health Ltd
Health Remit Limited

The Top UK Pharmaceutical Manufacturers

Healthbiotics Ltd
Herbal Food Life Limited
Hermes Pharmaceutical Limited
Hospira UK Limited
Huayawei Biomedical Co Ltd
Humn Pharmaceuticals (UK) Ltd
Hunger Control Limited
IPS International Corporation Ltd
Imphatec Ltd
Incline Therapeutics Europe Ltd.
Indigo Diagnostics Limited
Infohealth Limited
Insuphar Laboratories Limited
Juice Sauz Ltd
Keziah Ltd
Koasta Limited
Kohilam Limited
Langdales Limited
Laxmi BNS Holdings Limited
Leap Pharma Ltd
Leeds Industries (UK) Ltd
Leptrex Ltd.
Life on Healthcare Ltd
Lifeshield Limited
M & A Pharmachem Limited
M D M Healthcare Ltd
MDX Healthcare Ltd
Manx Healthcare Limited
Manx Pharma Ltd
Marlborough Pharmaceuticals Ltd
Martini International Ltd
Masters Pharmaceuticals Ltd
Medicaleaf Limited
Medisante Limited
Medison Pharma Limited
A. Menarini Diagnostics Ltd
Morningside Pharmaceuticals Ltd
NKCell Plus PLC
Napp Pharmaceutical Group Ltd
Napp Pharmaceutical Holdings Ltd
Noohra Limited
Nova Laboratories Limited
Nunataq Limited
Nutramax Ltd
Omega Pharma Limited
Oxbridge Pharma Limited
Oxford Supramolecular Biotechnology
P.I.E. Pharma Limited
PTGO Sever UK Limited
Pharm Recon Ltd
Pharma Maiden Ltd
Pharmacare International Ltd
Pharmacy Business Consultancy Ltd
Pharmadynamics UK Limited
Phytoceutical Limited
Piramal Critical Care Limited
Premax Europe Limited
Prime Medical Equipment Ltd
Principle Healthcare Limited
Q Health Direct Ltd
Redlight Exchange Ltd
Regent Pharmaceuticals Limited
Remedi Medical Holdings Ltd
Ria Generics Limited
Rosalique Skincare Limited
Rotapharm Limited
Royce Health Sciences Ltd
Sage Therapeutics Limited
Salcura Limited
Salutem Supplements Ltd
Sanhak Ltd
Sarepta International UK Ltd.

Shanghai Neopharm Co., Ltd
Shire Pharmaceuticals Limited
Sinduram Healthcare International Ltd
Skindoc Formula Limited
Skinska Pharmaceutica Limited
Solarius UK & Overseas Limited
Sonifar Pharma Expert Limited
Spectrum Biomedical UK Limited
Spey Limited
Spey Pharma Limited
Star Pharmaceuticals Limited
Stegram Pharmaceuticals Ltd
Synergetic Global Limited
T-In Medical Limited
Technical & General Limited
UK Biopharma Ltd
United Pharma Group Limited
Vitane Pharma Limited
Winchpharma (Consumer Healthcare) Ltd
World Medicine Limited
Zota Healthcare Limited

46499 Wholesale of household goods (other than musical instruments) n.e.c
Hunger Control Limited

46510 Wholesale of computers, computer peripheral equipment and software
Prime Test Limited

46520 Wholesale of electronic and telecommunications equipment and parts
Kohilam Limited

46690 Wholesale of other machinery and equipment
Prime Medical Equipment Ltd

46750 Wholesale of chemical products
Biokemix Worldwide Ltd
Cartell UK Limited
Evorin Pharma Limited
Huayawei Biomedical Co Ltd
Hydro Fresh Ltd
Pharmadynamics UK Limited

46760 Wholesale of other intermediate products
Winchpharma (Consumer Healthcare) Ltd

46900 Non-specialised wholesale trade [13]
Ambe Limited
Brosis Ltd
Cambridge Advanced Technologies Ltd
Essenfuture Ltd
Juice Sauz Ltd
Kohilam Limited
Langeland Ltd
Lifeplan Products Limited
Masters Pharmaceuticals Ltd
Q Health Direct Ltd
UK Animal Products Limited
Vita (Europe) Limited
Vita Bee Health Ltd

47110 Retail sale in non-specialised stores with food, beverages or tobacco predominating
Revive Us Limited

47190 Other retail sale in non-specialised stores
Maklary Ltd
Muamko Uzuri Limited
Nunataq Limited
This Product Ltd

47290 Other retail sale of food in specialised stores
Herbal Food Life Limited
Rescued By Nature Limited

47710 Retail sale of clothing in specialised stores
2tonk Limited

47730 Dispensing chemist in specialised stores [11]
Clyde Valley Cannaceuticals Ltd
Go-Kyo Science Limited
Hashmats Health Ltd
Hexpress Healthcare Limited
Hyperdrug Pharmaceuticals Ltd
Infohealth Limited
Koasta Limited
Lifeshield Limited
MDX Healthcare Ltd
One Stop 15 Limited
Vision Laboratories Limited

47749 Retail sale of medical and orthopaedic goods in specialised stores (not incl. hearing aids) n.e.c [13]
Ace Interventional Medical Ltd
Alvinsons Medical (PVT) Ltd
Appex Ltd
BVM Medical Limited
Fine Treatment Limited
Herbal Republic Ltd
Ibeautify Ltd
London Specialist Pharmacy Ltd
Oxbridge Pharma Limited
Pharmacare International Ltd
Rucals Ltd
Supamed Limited
Well & Well Pharma UK Ltd

47750 Retail sale of cosmetic and toilet articles in specialised stores [12]
Apotheke San Biagio SRL Ltd
Brazilian Kimberlite Clay Ltd
Ether Cosmetics Ltd
IPS International Corporation Ltd
Kalula Cosmetics Ltd
Man Oil Co Ltd
Ohemaa's Skincare Ltd.
Organic Pharmacy Limited
SKN-RG Ltd
Therapi Natural Products Ltd
Zink Tattoo Care Limited
Zomi Ltd

47789 Other retail sale of new goods in specialised stores (not commercial art galleries and opticians)
Cambridge Advanced Technologies Ltd
Fendall's Ltd.

47890 Retail sale via stalls and markets of other goods
Fendall's Ltd.
Great British Bee Co Ltd

47910 Retail sale via mail order houses or via Internet [13]
Biteback Products Ltd
Blackpool Medicines Limited
Brosis Ltd
FV Supplement Ltd
Fendall's Ltd.
Follifix Ltd
Gelu Life Limited
Hahydra Technologies Ltd
Lifeplan Products Limited
One Stop 15 Limited
Premax Europe Limited
Rucals Ltd
Vit Supermarket Ltd

47990 Other retail sale not in stores, stalls or markets
21CEC PX Pharm Ltd
Acle Urban Gardens Limited
Ohemaa's Skincare Ltd.

50200 Sea and coastal freight water transport
Festus Olatoye & Onyekachi Uka London

56290 Other food services
2tonk Limited
Bulgarian Healthy Products Ltd
Edward Daniel Limited
Tuscania Consulting Limited

58110 Book publishing
Y4U Limited

58141 Publishing of learned journals
Acarrier Limited

58190 Other publishing activities
Ambe Limited
Quality Products 360 Ltd

58290 Other software publishing
Commercial and Academic Services Ltd

59111 Motion picture production activities
Nunataq Limited

59120 Motion picture, video and television programme post-production activities
Key Empire Resources (UK) Ltd

59200 Sound recording and music publishing activities
Prime Test Limited

62012 Business and domestic software development
Peptone Ltd
Tithonus Ltd

62020 Information technology consultancy activities
Euroclinical Ltd

62090 Other information technology service activities
Alisha GXP QP Consultancy Ltd
Trintech Services Limited

63110 Data processing, hosting and related activities
Peptone Ltd

63120 Web portals
Quality Products 360 Ltd

64209 Activities of other holding companies n.e.c.
Unir Unlimited

64304 Activities of open-ended investment companies
Nocov Ltd

66190 Activities auxiliary to financial intermediation n.e.c.
Hedgarth Ltd

68209 Other letting and operating of own or leased real estate
Brosis Ltd

69102 Solicitors
Edward Daniel Limited

69109 Activities of patent and copyright agents; other legal activities n.e.c.
Natural Way Limited
Pharm Recon Ltd

70100 Activities of head offices
Maxwellia Ltd
Muamko Uzuri Limited
Nextpharma Technologies Holding Ltd
Quantum Pharma 2014 Limited
Smith & Nephew PLC
Unir Unlimited

70210 Public relations and communications activities
Tuscania Consulting Limited

70221 Financial management
Pacific Height Limited
Shekinah Health Consultancy Ltd

70229 Management consultancy activities other than financial management [11]
Avix Pharmaceuticals Limited
Britpharma UK Limited
Cuttlefish Limited
Dermapharm Skincare Limited
Hedgarth Ltd
Livbio Limited
MHR Pharmacy Ltd
MK Ventures Limited
Maxwellia Ltd
Nutrasulin Ltd.
Pharmacy Business Consultancy Ltd

71122 Engineering related scientific and technical consulting activities
Biotechflow Ltd
Geotek Coring Limited
Higgs Pharma Private Limited
Impact Pharma Solutions Ltd
Microfluidx Ltd

71200 Technical testing and analysis
Avisius Research Limited
Mark Aziz Limited
Mayuveda R & D Limited
Nagashree Ltd
Pari Medical Limited
Patheon UK Limited

72110 Research and experimental development on biotechnology [59]
2020 Organics Limited
AB Biotechnology Limited
Acarrier Limited
Aesica Formulation Development Ltd
Alphacells Biotechnologies Ltd
Apobec Discovery Ltd
Astrazeneca PLC
Bioavexia Ltd
Biocon Pharma UK Limited
Biofortuna Ltd
Biotechflow Ltd
Brewtaal Ltd
Cambridge Innovation Group Ltd
Cell Medica Limited
Chirotech Technology Limited
Circassia Pharmaceuticals PLC
Corcept Therapeutics UK Ltd
Dermatek Limited
Dextra Laboratories Limited
FV Supplement Ltd
Fujifilm Diosynth Biotechnologies UK
Genetis PLC
Genomix Ltd
Glycanova UK Limited
Huayawei Biomedical Co Ltd
Hyperion Biotechnology Limited
Immbio Therapeutics Limited
Imphatec Ltd
Indigo Diagnostics Limited
Insuphar Laboratories Limited
Livbio Limited
MC2 Therapeutics Limited
Medicaleaf Limited
Microsens Biophage Limited
ND Pharma & Biotech Ltd
NZP UK Limited
Nanomed Ltd
Nuradec Ltd
Oat Services Limited
Oncoparp Ltd
Panaomics Limited
Pegasus Equine Diagnostics Ltd
Pellis Care Limited
Pentail Enzymes Limited
Peptone Ltd
Phico Therapeutics Limited
Prometic Pharma SMT Limited
Qiagen Manchester Limited
Rotapharm Limited
Stem Cell Technology Ltd
Telix Life Sciences (UK) Ltd
Universal Cell Therapeutics Ltd.
Vernalis (R & D) Limited

Vernalis Development Limited
World Medicine Limited
World Medicine Ophthalmics Ltd
Yic Bio Ltd.
Zota Healthcare Limited
iCell Therapeutics Ltd

72190 Other research and experimental development on natural sciences and engineering [52]
Acorda Therapeutics Limited
Advanced Retention Therapeutics & Research
Ardilla Technologies UK Ltd
Atlantis Research Limited
Bespak Europe Limited
Bioextractions Wales Limited
Bionet Research Limited
Biostatus Ltd
Biotherics Limited
Boost Hair Limited
CM & D Pharma Limited
Calla Lily Personal Care Ltd
Catalent MTI Pharma Solutions Ltd
Corpus Nostrum Limited
Dodi Enterprise Ltd
E-Breathe Ltd.
Ectomedica Limited
Focus Pharma Holdings Limited
Focus Pharmaceuticals Limited
Four Pharmaceuticals Limited
Hologic Ltd.
Hyperion Catalysis EU Limited
IQ5 Consultancy Limited
Invictus R & D Ltd
Key Organics Limited
Letdrop Ltd
Life Molecular Imaging Limited
MC2 Therapeutics Limited
Medicol Limited
Mirroman Ltd
NHC Limited
Natural Way Limited
Nektar Therapeutics UK Limited
Nimasol Limited
Nutrapharm Ltd
Oncoparp Ltd
Orb Global Ltd
P & S Nano Limited
Panaomics Limited
Proveca Limited
Rosalique Skincare Limited
Salcura Limited
Siga Pharmaceuticals (Europe) Ltd
SmithKline Beecham Limited
Sonifar Pharma Expert Limited
Spear Therapeutics Limited
Supamed Limited
Trintech Services Limited
Unir Unlimited
Unyte Pharma Ltd
Yic Bio Ltd.
iCell Therapeutics Ltd

74100 Specialised design activities
RG and Co Limited

74901 Environmental consulting activities
Biotechflow Ltd
CBD Pharma Ltd

74909 Other professional, scientific and technical activities n.e.c. [35]
ADC Healthcare Limited
Auden McKenzie (Pharma Division) Ltd
Avix Pharmaceuticals Limited
Blackrock Pharmaceuticals Ltd
Clickhealth Limited
Dodi Enterprise Ltd
EHB Limited
Ectomedica Limited
Envigo RMS (UK) Limited
FPL - Formulating Partnership Ltd
Hologic Ltd.
Hunger Control Limited
Hutrade Ltd.
Hydro Fresh Ltd
IQ5 Consultancy Limited
Immbio Therapeutics Limited
Koasta Limited
Leptrex Ltd.
Longwood Medevice Ltd
Lux Viridis Services Ltd
Maxwellia Ltd
Medicann Pharma (UK) Ltd
Natural Way Limited
Nutrasulin Ltd.
Oncoparp Ltd
Oxford Immunotec Limited
Pegasus Equine Diagnostics Ltd
Penn Pharma Group Limited
Pharma QP Solutions Ltd
Quay Pharmaceuticals Limited
Shabelle Ltd
Smart Formula Limited
Speakers at The Limits Ltd.
Synergy Pharma Consultancy Ltd
Virtual Reaction Limited

74990 Non-trading company
Aurum Pharmaceuticals Limited
Xanadu Valley Limited

75000 Veterinary activities
Boehringer Ingelheim Animal Health UK
Clickhealth Limited
Dechra Limited
G.A.S. Vets (UK) Limited
Hyperdrug Pharmaceuticals Ltd
Intervet UK Production Limited
N.T. Laboratories Limited
Pegasus Equine Diagnostics Ltd
Schering-Plough Limited

77390 Renting and leasing of other machinery, equipment and tangible goods n.e.c.
Pharm Recon Ltd

77400 Leasing of intellectual property and similar products, except copyright works
Insuphar Laboratories Limited
Rotapharm Limited
Spey Limited
Spey Pharma Limited
World Medicine Limited
World Medicine Ophthalmics Ltd

80300 Investigation activities
Mirroman Ltd

81210 General cleaning of buildings
Comfort Ventures Limited

82110 Combined office administrative service activities
Advanz Pharma (UK) Limited

82920 Packaging activities
GMP Manufacturing Ltd
Parkacre Enterprises Limited

82990 Other business support service activities n.e.c. [10]
Adam Project Ltd
Biostatus Ltd
Biotherics Limited
R & R Black Brilliant Ventures PLC
Britpharma UK Limited
IQ5 Consultancy Limited
Patheon UK Limited
Shellmarks Limited
Transdermal Technology & Systems (TTS)
ZO-X Ltd

84120 Regulation of health care, education, cultural and other social services, not incl. social security
Bodeli Consultants Limited

85100 Pre-primary education
NKK Investments Limited

85590 Other education n.e.c.
Shekinah Health Consultancy Ltd

85600 Educational support services
Herman Claude Ltd

86101 Hospital activities
S.L.Cassidy Limited
Clarornell Consulting and Trading Ltd
EN RUS Group Limited

86102 Medical nursing home activities
Alvinsons Medical (PVT) Ltd

86210 General medical practice activities [15]
Adam Project Ltd
Almisbar Limited
Alvinsons Medical (PVT) Ltd
Ayurmedics Clinic Limited
Mark Aziz Limited
Cotswold Health Limited
Dr Pradeep Reddy's Laboratories (UK & EU)
Medicol Limited
Noohra Limited
Nutridote Ltd
Pari Medical Limited
Pharmlife Industry Ltd
Tawil Co Limited
Triumph Pharma Ltd
UK Biopharma Ltd

86220 Specialists medical practice activities [17]
Almisbar Limited
Anna-Med (UK) Ltd
Ayurmedics Clinic Limited
Britanica Medicines & Medical Equipment
Cambridge Innovation Group Ltd
Clarornell Consulting and Trading Ltd
Clyde Valley Cannaceuticals Ltd
Ibeautify Ltd
MHR Pharmacy Ltd
Myoproducts Limited
NKK Investments Limited
Pharmacy Business Consultancy Ltd
Private Trichology Clinic Ltd
RG and Co Limited
Supamed Limited
Tithonus Ltd
United Pharma Group Limited

86900 Other human health activities [35]
ADC Healthcare Limited
Ace Direct Ltd
Avisius Research Limited
Ayurmedics Clinic Limited
Blackpool Medicines Limited
Brewtaal Ltd
Calla Lily Personal Care Ltd
Cell Medica Limited
Clickhealth Limited
Dodi Enterprise Ltd
Drugsdirect Global Ltd
East West Naturals Limited
Engelpharma UK Limited
Herbal Food Life Limited
Herman Claude Ltd
Hyperbiotics Corp Ltd
Hyperbiotics PLC
Hyperion Biotechnology Limited
Infinitus Enterprise Limited
LDN Pharma Limited
Marigold Projects Jamaica Ltd
Miltenyi Biotec Limited
NHC Limited
NKCell Plus PLC
Nutridote Ltd
Penlan Healthcare Limited
Pharmadynamics UK Limited
Pneumoflex E.U. Limited
Qiagen Manchester Limited
Quality Products 360 Ltd
Rescued By Nature Limited
Slo Drinks Limited
Tithonus Ltd
UK Biopharma Ltd
ZO-X Ltd

87900 Other residential care activities n.e.c.
Herman Claude Ltd
KVK Limited

88990 Other social work activities without accommodation n.e.c.
Comfort Ventures Limited

90010 Performing arts
Key Empire Resources (UK) Ltd

90030 Artistic creation
Dana's Creations Ltd
ZO-X Ltd

93130 Fitness facilities
2tonk Limited

94120 Activities of professional membership organisations
Lea Pharma Limited
Noohra Limited

96020 Hairdressing and other beauty treatment
Afro Hair and Beauty International
Hadley Rose Limited
Jasmine.Touch Ltd
Kalula Cosmetics Ltd
Rescued By Nature Limited
Sparsanctuary Limited
Thread and Co UK Limited

96040 Physical well-being activities
Afro Hair and Beauty International
Blends for Massage Limited
Dana's Creations Ltd
Engelpharma UK Limited

96090 Other service activities n.e.c.
Hutrade Ltd.

98100 Undifferentiated goods-producing activities of private households for own use
Retrogrow Limited

99999 Dormant company
Bionet Research Limited
Millbrook (NI) Limited
Noorik Biopharmaceuticals Ltd
Teva Research Laboratories (NI) Ltd
Zink Tattoo Care Limited

Printed in 8pt Nimbus Sans L

Designed by URW++ Design and Development GmbH

Dellam Publishing Limited

2 Heath Drive, Sutton, Surrey, SM2 5RP

Fax: 020 8770 7478   email: enquiries@dellam.com

SAN: 0177881   EAN/GLN: 5030670177882

www.ingramcontent.com/pod-product-compliance
Lightning Source LLC
Chambersburg PA
CBHW081108080526
44587CB00021B/3505